SAT
POWER
VOCAB

Random House, Inc.
New York

www.PrincetonReview.com

The Princeton Review, Inc.
111 Speen Street, Suite 550
Framingham, MA 01701
E-mail: editorialsupport@review.com

ISBN: 978-0-804-12456-0

Editor: Alyssa Wolff
Production Editor: Lori Fromowitz
Production Coordinator: Deborah A. Silvestrini

Manufactured in the United States of America.

10 9 8 7 6 5 4 3 2 1

CONTENTS

CHAPTER 1

ORIENTATION

POWERING UP YOUR SAT VOCAB

The best way to build a solid, sophisticated vocabulary is to read voraciously.

Careful reading not only brings you into contact with new words, but also forces you to use your head to figure out what those new words mean. If you read widely enough, you will find that your vocabulary will build itself. New words are contagious if you give yourself enough exposure to them. Reading any good book is better for your vocabulary than watching television. Reading well-written magazines and newspapers can help, too.

THE DANGERS OF RELYING ON CONTEXT ALONE

The natural way to learn words is to see how other people use them—that is, to see or hear the word in context. While context may tell you how to use the word, relying on context is not without pitfalls.

First, when you encounter a new word, you can't be certain how to pronounce it unless you hear it spoken by someone whose pronunciation is authoritative. You also can't be certain the word is being used correctly. Even skillful writers and speakers occasionally misuse language. A writer or speaker may even misuse a word intentionally, perhaps for dramatic or comic effect.

Even more important, most words have many different meanings or shades of meanings. Sometimes the difference between one meaning and another can be tiny; sometimes it can be enormous. Even if you deduce the meaning from the context, you have no way of knowing whether the meaning you've deduced will apply in other cases.

Finally, context can be misleading. Below is an example of what we mean. It's a dialogue we find ourselves having over and over again with our students. The dialogue concerns the meaning of the word *formidable*, although you can substitute just about any medium-difficult word.

> Us: Do you know what *formidable* means?
> STUDENT: Sure, of course.
> Us: Good. Define it.
> STUDENT: Okay. A *formidable* opponent is someone...
> Us: Sorry to cut you off. We want the definition of *formidable*, not an example of how to use it in a sentence. Can you please define the word *formidable* for us?
> STUDENT: Sure. Ummm, let's see... (The student is still thinking of the phrase *formidable opponent*.) *Formidable* means *good* or *skillful*. Maybe *big*, *aggressive*. What about *tremendous*?
> Us: Nice try, but it means *frightening*.
> STUDENT: Really? I didn't know that. I thought it meant something else.
> Us: Well, it also means *awe-inspiring*.

WHAT'S THE POINT?

The point is that context can be misleading. Have you ever played the game Mad Libs™? In it, one player is given a text from which a number of words are missing, and the other player is asked to supply those missing words without looking at the text. The results are often funny.

Something similar—and much less funny—can happen when you rely exclusively on context to supply you with the meanings of new words. You may hit upon a meaning that seems to fit the context only to discover later that your guess was far wide of the mark.

To keep this from happening, use a dictionary.

YOU DON'T UNDERSTAND A MEANING UNLESS YOU CAN DEFINE IT IN YOUR OWN WORDS

To understand a word completely, to make a word yours, you should try to define it in your own words. Don't settle for the dictionary definition. For that matter, don't settle for our definition.

Make up your own definition. You'll understand the meaning better. What's more, you'll be more likely to remember it.

THE BEST METHOD TO MEMORIZE WORDS IS THE METHOD THAT WORKS BEST FOR YOU

Over the years, we have discovered that our students seem to have more success with some methods of learning new words than with others. We'll describe these methods in a moment. Then, at the end of this chapter, we'll outline an effective general regimen for learning new words permanently and for incorporating them into your life.

As you work through this book, you'll undoubtedly find that you need to tailor your approach to the way you think and learn best. You may discover that for a particular word one method works best, and that for another word another method works best. That's fine.

We'll show you the methods we have found to be the most successful for our students. Use the one or ones that suit *you* best.

➢ Basic Method #1: Tricks and Mnemonics

A mnemonic is a device or trick that helps you remember something specific. Grade schoolers are sometimes taught to remember the spelling of *arithmetic* by using the following mnemonic: *A Rat In The House Might Eat Tom's Ice Cream*. The first letter in each word in this silly sentence stands for the letters in *arithmetic*. Remember the sentence and you remember how to spell the word.

Mnemonics can appeal to our ears, too. How about the history mnemonic: *In fourteen hundred ninety-two, Columbus sailed the ocean blue...*? Or the spelling mnemonic: *"i" before "e" except after "c," and in words that say "a," as in "neighbor" and "weigh"*?

You Already Know How to Use Mnemonics
Whether you realize it or not, you use mnemonics all the time. When you make up a little game to remember your locker combination or a friend's birthday, you're using a mnemonic.

How Do Mnemonics Work?
All mnemonics work in the same way—by forcing you to associate what you're trying to remember with something that you already know, or with something that is easier to memorize. Patterns and rhymes are easy to memorize, which explains why so many mnemonics use them.

Incidentally, it may also explain why rhyming became a part of poetry. The earliest poets and balladeers didn't write down their compositions because many didn't know how to write. Instead, they kept the poems in their heads. Among other things, the rhymes at the ends of the lines made the poems easier to remember.

➤ Basic Method #2: Seeing Is Remembering
Letting a new word suggest a vivid mental image to you is a powerful and effective way to remember that word. Mental images are really mnemonics, too. They help you remember. The emphasis here is on suggestive mental pictures rather than on tricky abbreviations or coincidences of spelling.

Let's take the word *abridge*, for example, which means to shorten, or condense.

What image pops into your mind when you think of the word *abridge*? That's easy: a bridge. Now you need to picture something happening on or to that bridge that will help you remember the meaning of the word *abridge*. Your goal is to create such a vivid and memorable image in your mind that the next time you encounter *abridge* in your reading, you'll instantly remember what it means.

To be useful, your image must have something to do with the meaning of the word rather than merely with the way it sounds or looks. If you merely think of a bridge when you see *abridge*, you won't help yourself remember what you want to remember.

What you need is an image that suggests shortening or condensing: A dinosaur taking a big bite out of the middle of a bridge? Carpenters sawing it? The image you choose is up to you.

How About Another Example?

Another useful word on this book's master list is *gregarious*, which means sociable, enjoying the company of others. What image springs to mind? Really think now.

Can't think of an image? Be creative. A party animal is *gregarious*. How about imagining a party animal named Greg Arious. Don't stop with his name. You need a picture. So give Greg a funny hat, a noisemaker, and some polka-dot dancing shoes. Or put a lampshade on his head. Think of something that will make you think of sociability the next time you see Greg's name in a book or a magazine you read. The more real you make Greg Arious seem in your imagination, the less trouble you'll have remembering the meaning of *gregarious*.

The Crazier the Mental Image, the Better

When it comes to mental images, crazy is better than normal. Normal is bland. Normal is boring. If you could easily remember boring things, you wouldn't have any trouble learning new words.

Crazy is dramatic. Crazy leaps out at you. You remember crazy. And remember this: Anything goes when you're learning new words.

Memory Aids Have to Be Personal

Memory aids work best when you have to struggle a little to come up with them.

If you come up with your own memory aid, if it really means something to you, it will likely become a permanent part of your memory.

What If You Can't Come Up with a Mnemonic?

One of our students once told us that he had tried and tried to come up with an image for the word *proselytize*, but he hadn't been able to think of one.

We asked him what the word meant. He said, "To try to convert someone to a religion or a point of view." We just smiled and looked at him.

Suddenly, he started laughing. He had tried so hard to devise a mnemonic that he had memorized the word without realizing it.

➤ Basic Method #3: Etymological Clues

Although the English language contains hundreds of thousands of words, you will discover that many groups of words are related in meaning because they developed from a common root. When you recognize that a group of words shares a similar root, you will more easily remember the entire group.

For example, take the word *mnemonic*. You know now, if you hadn't already, that a *mnemonic* is a device that helps you remember something. We're going to show you two other words that are related to this word.

mnemonic: device to help you remember something
amnesty: a general pardon for offenses against a government
        (an official "forgetting")
amnesia: loss of memory

Pretty neat, eh? How about words from another common root:

chronological: in order according to time
syn**chron**ize: to put on the same timetable
ana**chron**ism: something out of place in time or history
chronic: continuing over a long time
chronicle: chronological record of events
chronometer: device to measure time

Sometimes it is easier to learn a whole cluster of related words than to come up with mnemonics for them individually.

The Advantages of Etymology

The principal virtues of using etymology to remember a definition are that the etymology actually relates to the word's meaning (as opposed to the image approach) and that the same etymology may be shared by lots of words. Another advantage of etymology is that it may get you interested in words. Etymology gets you involved in a story—the story of a word through centuries of history.

The Dangers of Etymology

Many vocabulary books claim that etymology helps you decipher the meanings of words. That's true sometimes, but etymology can also lead you astray.

The etymology of a word will tell you something about the word, but it will rarely give you the definition. And it's easy to be mistaken about the etymology of a word.

For example, on a certain SAT, many clever students got a question wrong because they thought that the word *verdant* was etymologically related to words like *verify, verdict, verisimilitude,* and *veritable. Verdant* must have something to do with the concept of truth or reality, they reasoned.

Clever, but wrong. *Verdant* comes from a different family of words. It comes from the same old root as does the French word *vert,* which means green. If those same clever students had recognized that connection, they might have realized that *verdant* means green with vegetation, as in *a verdant forest.*

- Similarly, a lot of words that begin with *ped* have something to do with foot: *pedestrian, pedal, pedestal, pedometer, impede, expedite.* A *pediatrician,* however, is *not* a foot doctor. A *pediatrician* is a doctor for children. A *podiatrist* is a foot doctor. (The word *pediatrician* is, however, related to the word meaning a strict teacher of children: *pedagogue.*)

Etymology is a powerful tool to remember words that you already know, but it can't always successfully determine the meanings of words you don't know.

➤ Basic Method #4: Writing on Your Brain

Many people find that they can learn new information more readily if they write it down. The physical act of writing seems to plant the information more firmly. Perhaps the explanation is that by writing you are bringing another sense into play (you've seen the word, you've said and heard the word, and now you're *feeling* the word).

You may find it useful to spend some time writing down phrases or sentences incorporating each new word. This is a good way to practice and strengthen your spelling as well.

You'll probably have more luck if you don't merely write down the word and its definition over and over again. If you've hit upon a good mnemonic or mental image to help you remember it, or you liked the etymology, write it down. You can even draw a picture or a diagram.

➤ Basic Method #5: Putting It All Together with Flash Cards and a Notebook

A flash card is a simple piece of paper or cardboard with a word on one side and a definition on the other. You may have used flash cards when you were first learning to read, or when you were first tackling a foreign language. Used in the proper spirit, flash cards can turn learning into a game.

Most of our students find it useful to make flash cards out of index cards. They write a vocabulary word on one side and the definition on the other. (You should also indicate the pronunciation if you aren't sure you'll remember it.) Then they can quiz one another or practice independently during spare moments.

Here's a basic flash card, front and back:

Front

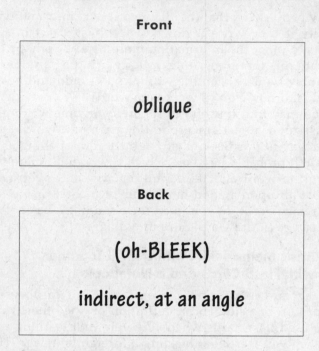

oblique

Back

(oh-BLEEK)

indirect, at an angle

You'll learn even more if you use your imagination to make the backs of your flash cards a bit more elaborate. For example, you might decorate the back of this card with a diagram of *oblique* lines—that is, lines that are neither parallel nor perpendicular to each other:

Back

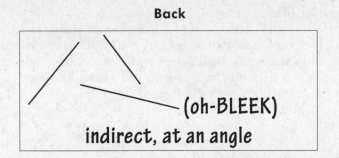

(oh-BLEEK)
indirect, at an angle

Your diagram now gives you a mental image that can help you remember the word. You'll probably think of your own mental image, one that means something to you. You could even use the word itself to create a picture that conveys the meaning of the word and that will stick in your mind to help you remember it.

Here's one possibility. We've divided the word into two parts and written them on two different lines that—surprise!—are at an *oblique* angle to each other:

Back

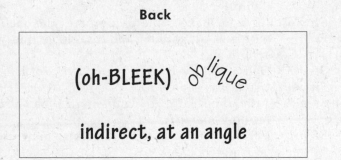

(oh-BLEEK) oblique

indirect, at an angle

Practicing with flash cards can be fun. Parents and siblings sometimes lend a hand and discover that they learn new words, too. And every time you look at the back of the card, you'll be reminded of the mnemonic, trick, or mental image you've devised to keep the word firmly in your memory.

Never an Idle Moment

Many of our students even tuck a few of their flash cards into a pocket when they head out the door in the morning. They can then work on them in spare moments—while riding on a bus or while listening to the radio. The more often you flash through your flash cards, the faster you'll build your vocabulary.

Make sure you keep track of which words you remember, and which ones you are struggling with so you can spend more time on the latter.

OVERVIEW: A MEMORIZATION GAME PLAN

Here, pulling it all together, is our step-by-step approach to memorizing new words permanently:

Step 1: Try to deduce the word's meaning from context.

Step 2: Look it up!

Step 3: Note the spelling.

Step 4: Say the word out loud.

Step 5: Read the main definition. Scan the secondary definitions.

Step 6: (If you have time) Compare the definition with the definitions and usages of the word's synonyms.

Step 7: Define the word using your own words.

Step 8: Use it in a sentence.

Step 9: Attach the word to a mnemonic, mental image, or other memory aid.

Step 10: Fill out a flash card and make a new entry in your notebook.

Step 11: Use the new word every chance you get.

Let's take a look at each of these steps.

Step 1: TRY TO DEDUCE THE WORD'S MEANING FROM CONTEXT

Context will often lead you astray, but doing a bit of detective work is a good way to sharpen your mind and hone your reading comprehension skills. And who knows? You might even guess the right meaning.

Step 2: LOOK IT UP!

Most people try to skip this step. Don't you dare! You won't know whether you're correct about the meaning of a new word until you've made sure by looking it up.

No one can learn new words without a dictionary. If you don't have one, get one now. Even good dictionaries aren't terribly expensive.

Step 3: NOTE THE SPELLING

Look at the spelling. Close your eyes and try to reconstruct the spelling. If you have trouble visualizing, test yourself by writing out the spelling on scrap paper and checking it against the dictionary.

Also, compare the spelling variations with other spelling variations you know. This is a nice trick that helps you recognize words that you think you don't know.

For example, *sober* is an adjective; the noun form is *sobriety*. Okay, with that as a clue, the noun *propriety* relates to what adjective? *Proper. Propriety* means what is socially proper or acceptable.

Here's another example: Do you know what *incisive* means? Give up? Well, you know what *decisive* means, don't you? *Decisive* relates to what word you know? *Decision*, of course. Now, what noun do you think *incisive* relates to? *Incision. Incisive* means *sharp* or *cutting*, as in an *incisive remark*, or an *incisive observation*.

Step 4: SAY THE WORD OUT LOUD

Say the word...*out loud*. Hearing the word will bring another sense into play and help you remember the word. And as we noted earlier, you don't want to make a fool of yourself by mispronouncing words.

Our Pronunciation Key

We've never liked the pronunciation keys most dictionaries use. Our key is based on consistent phonetic sounds, so you don't have to memorize it. Still, it would be a good idea to take a few minutes now and familiarize yourself with the table below. Be sure to note how the *e* and *i* are used.

The letter(s)	is (are) pronounced like the letter(s)	in the word(s)
a	a	bat, can
ah	o	con, bond
aw	aw	paw, straw
ay	a	skate, rake
e	e	stem, hem
ee	ea	steam, clean
i	i	rim, chin, hint
ing	ing	sing, ring
oh	o	row, tow
oo	oo	room, boom
ow	ow	cow, brow
oy	oy	boy, toy
u, uh	u	run, bun
y (ye, eye)	i	climb, time
ch	ch	chair, chin
f	f, ph	film, phony
g	g	go, goon
j	j	join, jungle
k	c	cool, cat
s	s	solid, wisp
sh	sh	shoe, wish
z	z	zoo, razor
zh	s	measure
uh	a	apologize

All other consonants are pronounced as you would expect. Capitalized letters are accented.

Step 5: READ THE MAIN DEFINITION; SCAN THE SECONDARY DEFINITIONS

Most dictionaries list the definitions in order of importance. That does not mean, of course, that the first definition is the one you are looking for. Read all the definitions; each will add to your understanding of the word.

Step 6: COMPARE THE DEFINITION WITH THE DEFINITIONS AND USAGES OF THE WORD'S SYNONYMS

As we showed you with the earlier examples, this step takes a little extra time. Believe us when we say that it is time well spent. Again, seeing how a word is similar to or different from synonyms or related words enhances your understanding of all of them.

Step 7: DEFINE THE WORD USING YOUR OWN WORDS

We said it before, and we'll say it again: You don't truly know what a word means unless you can define it yourself in your own way.

Step 8: USE IT IN A SENTENCE

Now that you know what the word means and what it doesn't mean, use it. Make up a sentence.

It helps to use the word in a sentence that includes a person or thing or event that you know and that creates a concrete feeling or image. For example, the sentence *They are gregarious* is not as good as *Greg, Gertrude,* and *Gretchen* are *gregarious.*

Step 9: ATTACH THE WORD TO A MNEMONIC, MENTAL IMAGE, OR OTHER MEMORY AID

With all that you've done with the word in the previous steps, you may already have memorized it. The only way to be sure, however, is to fix the word with a mnemonic.

Step 10: FILL OUT A FLASH CARD

The paperwork is very important, particularly if you're trying to learn a lot of new words in a short period of time.

Step 11: USE THE NEW WORD EVERY CHANCE YOU GET

Dare to be repetitious. If you don't keep new knowledge in shape, you won't keep it at all.

TWO FINAL WORDS OF ADVICE: BE SUSPICIOUS

You already know some of the words in the book. You may know quite a few of them. Naturally, you don't need to drill yourself on words you already know and use.

But be careful. Before skipping a word, make certain you really do know what it means. Some of the most embarrassing vocabulary mistakes occur when a person confidently uses familiar words incorrectly.

GET TO WORK

Now on to the words. Remember that you'll retain more (and have more fun) if you tackle this book a little at a time.

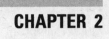

CHAPTER 2

THE
WORDS

A

ABASE (uh BAYS) *v* to humiliate; to lower in esteem or dignity; to humble
- After soaping all the windows in the old widow's mansion on Halloween, the eighth graders *abased* themselves and said that they were sorry (after the policeman told them he would arrest them if they didn't).
- I *abased* myself before the principal because I figured I had to in order to keep from being expelled.

ABASH (uh BASH) *v* to make ashamed; to embarrass
- Meredith felt *abashed* by her inability to remember her lines in the school chorus of "Old McDonald Had a Farm."

To do something without shame or embarrassment is to do it *unabashedly*.
- Karl handed in a term paper that he had *unabashedly* copied from Wikipedia.

ABATE (uh BAYT) *v* to subside; to reduce
- George spilled a cup of hot coffee on his leg. It hurt quite a bit. Then, gradually, the agony *abated*.
- Bad weather *abates* when good weather begins to return. A rainstorm that does not let up continues *unabated*.

A tax *abatement* is a reduction in taxes. Businesses are sometimes given tax *abatements* in return for building factories in places where there is a particular need for jobs.

ABDICATE (AB duh kayt) *v* to step down from a position of power or responsibility
- When King Edward VIII of England decided he would rather be married to Wallis Warfield Simpson, an American divorcée, than be king of England, he turned in his crown and *abdicated*.

Even people who aren't monarchs can *abdicate* their duties and responsibilities.
- Abby *abdicated* her responsibilities as a vice president by dumping in the garbage the reports she was supposed to present to the board of directors and flying to the Bahamas.

ABERRATION (ab uh RAY shun) *n* something not typical; a deviation from the standard
- Søren's bad behavior was an *aberration*. So was Harry's good behavior. That is, Søren's was usually good, and Harry's was usually bad.

- The chef at this restaurant is dreadful; the wonderful meal we just had was an *aberration*.
- A snowstorm in June is an *aberration*; snow doesn't normally fall in June.

An *aberration* is an *aberrant* (uh BER unt) occurrence.

- Søren's behavior was *aberrant*. The summer snowstorm was *aberrant*.

ABET (uh BET) *v* to support or encourage someone, especially someone who has done something wrong

- *Abetting* a criminal by giving her a place to hide from the police is itself a criminal act.
- In their efforts to steal millions from their clients, the dishonest bankers were *abetted* by the greed of the clients themselves.

ABEYANCE (uh BAY uns) *n* suspension; temporary cessation

- Sally wanted to bite Mr. Anderson, but her father held her in *abeyance* by grabbing her suspenders and looping them over the doorknob.
- Joe's poverty kept his addiction to video games in *abeyance*.

ABHOR (ab HOR) *v* to hate very, very much; to detest

- Emanuel *abhorred* having to wake up before dawn.

To *abhor* something is to view it with horror. Hating a person is almost friendly in comparison with *abhorring* him or her.

To *abhor* raw chicken livers is to have an *abhorrence* of them or to find them *abhorrent*.

ABJECT (AB jekt) *adj* hopeless; extremely sad and servile; defeated

- While most people would quickly recover from a stumble on stage, Mia felt *abject* humiliation.

An *abject* person is one who is crushed and without hope. A slave would be *abject*, in all likelihood.

Perhaps 90 percent of the time, when you encounter this word it will be followed by the word *poverty*. *Abject poverty* is hopeless, desperate poverty. The phrase "abject poverty" tends to be overused.

ABJURE (ab JOOR) *v* to repudiate; to take back; to refrain from

- Under pressure from his teacher, Joe *abjured* his habit of napping in class and promised to keep his eyes open for the rest of the semester.

- Jerry *abjured* chocolate for several days after eating an entire Mississippi mud cake and breaking out in hives.
- For her New Year's resolution, Ellen decided to *abjure* from abjuring from anything that she enjoyed.

ABNEGATE (AB nuh gayt) *v* to deny oneself things; to reject; to renounce
- Ascetics practice *self-abnegation* because they believe it will bring them closer to spiritual purity.

Self-abnegation is giving up oneself, usually for some higher cause.

ABOMINATION (uh bahm uh NAY shun) *n* something despised or abhorred; extreme loathing
- The lobby of the hotel was an *abomination*; there was garbage rotting in the elevator, and there were rats running on the furniture.
- Barret shuddered with *abomination* at the thought of eating Henry's fatty, salty, oily cooking.

To *abominate* something is to hate it, hate it, hate it.
- Judy *abominated* the sort of hotels that have garbage rotting in their elevators and rats running on their furniture.

ABORIGINAL (ab uh RIJ nul) *adj* native; dating back to the very beginning
- The Aborigines of Australia are the earliest known human inhabitants of the continent. They are that country's *aboriginal* inhabitants.
- While working on a new subway tunnel, the construction workers found some fragments of pottery that may have belonged to the city's *aboriginal* residents.

If you see the word "original" inside this word, then you have a built-in and easy mnemonic device!

ABORTIVE (uh BOR tiv) *adj* unsuccessful
- Marie and Elizabeth made an *abortive* effort to bake a birthday cake; that is, their effort did not result in a birthday cake.
- Fred's attempt to climb the mountain was *abortive*; he injured himself when he was halfway up.

To *abort* something is to end it before it is completed. An *aborted* pregnancy, called an *abortion,* is one that ends before the baby is born. An *abortion* in this sense doesn't have to be the result of a controversial medical procedure.

ABOUND (uh BOWND) *v* to be very numerous
- Trout *abound* in this river; there are so many of them that you can catch them with your hands.

To *abound* is to be abundant. *Abounding* and abundant mean the same thing.
- Susan's *abounding* love for Harry will never falter unless she meets someone nicer or Harry moves away.

ABRIDGE (uh BRIJ) *v* to shorten; to condense
- The thoughtful editor *abridged* the massive book by removing the boring parts.

An *abridged* dictionary is one that has been shortened to keep it from crushing desks and people's laps.

An *abridgment* is a shortened or condensed work.

ABROGATE (AB ruh gayt) *v* to abolish or repeal formally; to set aside; to nullify
- The commander of the ship had the power to *abrogate* certain laws in the event of an emergency.

When you see this word, you will often see the word "treaty" nearby. To *abrogate* a treaty is to repeal it. You can also *abrogate* a law, an agreement, or a ruling.

ABSOLUTE (AB suh loot) *adj* total; unlimited
An *absolute* ruler is one who is ruled by no one else. An *absolute* mess is a total mess. An *absolute* rule is one that has no exceptions and that you must follow, no two ways about it.

Absolute is also a noun. It means something that is total, unlimited, or perfect. Death, for living things, is an *absolute*. There just isn't any way around it.

ABSOLVE (ab ZOLV) *v* to forgive or free from blame; to free from sin; to free from an obligation
- The priest *absolved* the sinner who had come to church to confess.
- Tom's admission of guilt *absolved* Mary, who had originally been accused of the crime.

It is also possible to *absolve* someone of a responsibility.
- Jake *absolved* Ciara of her obligation to go to the prom with him; he told her it was all right if she went with the captain of the football team instead.

The act of *absolving* is called *absolution* (ab suh LOO shun).

Match each word in the first column with its definition in the second column. Check your answers in the back of the book.

1. abash		a.	step down from power
2. abate		b.	hopeless
3. abdicate		c.	unsuccessful
4. aberration		d.	forgive
5. abhor		e.	total
6. abject		f.	subside
7. abnegate		g.	detest
8. abortive		h.	shorten
9. abridge		i.	deviation
10. absolute		j.	embarrass
11. absolve		k.	renounce

ABSTINENT (AB stuh nunt) *adj* abstaining; voluntarily not doing something, especially something pleasant that is bad for you or has a bad reputation

- Beulah used to be a chain-smoker; now she's *abstinent* (it was just too hard to get those chains lit).

- Cynthia, who was dieting, tried to be *abstinent*, but when she saw the chocolate cake she realized that she would probably have to eat the entire thing.

A person who *abstains* from something is an *abstainer* and engages in *abstinence*.

ABSTRACT (AB strakt) *adj* theoretical; impersonal

- He liked oysters in the *abstract*, but when he actually tried one he became nauseated.

To like something in the *abstract* is to like the idea of it.

- Bruno doesn't like *abstract* art; he thinks that a painting should resemble something real, not a lot of splattered paint.

ABSTRUSE (ab STROOS) *adj* hard to understand

- The professor's article, on the meaning of meaning, was *abstruse*. Michael couldn't even pronounce the words in it.

Nuclear physics is a subject that is too *abstruse* for most people.

ABYSMAL (uh BIZ mul) *adj* extremely hopeless or wretched; bottomless
An *abyss* (uh BIS) is a bottomless pit, or something so deep that it seems bottomless. *Abysmal* despair is despair so deep that no hope seems possible.
- The nation's debt crisis was *abysmal;* there seemed to be no possible solution.

Abysmal is often used somewhat sloppily to mean very bad. You might hear a losing baseball team's performance referred to as *abysmal*. This isn't strictly correct, but many people do it.

ACCEDE (ak SEED) *v* to give in; to yield; to agree
- Mary *acceded* to my demand that she give back my driver's license and stop pretending to be me.

- My mother wanted me to spend the holidays at home with my family instead of on the beach with my roommates, and a quick check of my bank balance convinced me that I had no choice but to *accede* to her desire.

ACCENTUATE (ak SEN choo wayt) *v* to emphasize; to accent; to highlight
- Mr. Jones *accentuated* the positive by pointing out that his pants fit better after he lost his wallet.

- Dacia's pointed shoes *accentuated* the length and slenderness of her feet.

QUICK QUIZ   #2

Match each word in the first column with its definition in the second column. Check your answers in the back of the book.

1. abase	a. support
2. abet	b. native
3. abeyance	c. suspension
4. abjure	d. very numerous
5. abomination	e. abolish
6. aboriginal	f. give in
7. abound ·	g. something despised
8. abrogate	h. humiliate
9. accede	i. repudiate
10. accentuate	j. emphasize

ACCESS (AK sess) *n* the right or ability to approach, enter, or use
- Cynthia was one of a few people to have *access* to the president; she could get in to see him when she wanted to.
- I wanted to read my boss's written evaluation of my performance, but employees don't have *access* to those files.
- When the Joker finally gained *access* to Batman's secret Batcave, he redecorated the entire hideaway in more festive pastel colors.

Access is sometimes used as a verb nowadays. To *access* a computer file is to open it so that you can work with it. If you have *access* to someone or something, that person or thing is *accessible* to you. To say that a book is *inaccessible* is to say that it is hard to understand. In other words, it's hard to get into.

ACCLAIM (uh KLAYM) *v* to praise publicly and enthusiastically
- The author's new book was *acclaimed* by all the important reviewers, and it quickly became a bestseller.
- When the Congress or any other group of people approves a proposal by means of a voice vote, the proposal is said to have been approved by *acclamation*.

Acclaim is also a noun, as is *acclamation* (AK luh MAY shun).
- The author's new book was met with universal *acclaim*. The reviewers' response to the book was one of *acclamation*.

ACCOLADE (AK uh layd) *n* an award; an honor
This word is generally used in the plural.
- The first break-dancing troupe to perform in Carnegie Hall, the Teflon Toughs, received *accolades* from the critics as well as from the fans.

ACCORD (uh KAWRD) *v* to agree; to be in harmony; to grant or bestow
- Sprawling on the couch and watching TV all day *accords* with my theory that intense laziness is good for the heart.

ACCOST (uh KAWST) *v* to approach and speak to someone aggressively
- Amanda karate-chopped the stranger who *accosted* her in the street and was embarrassed to find he was an old, blind man.

ACCOUTERMENTS (uh KOO tur munts) *n* personal clothing, accessories, or equipment; trappings
- Alex is a light traveler; he had crammed all his *accouterments* into a single shopping bag.
- Louanne had so many silly *accouterments* in her expensive new kitchen that there wasn't really much room for Louanne.

ACCRUE (uh KROO) *v* to accumulate over time
- My savings account pays interest, but the interest *accrues* at such a slow pace that I almost feel poorer than I did when I opened it.
- Over the years, Emily's unpaid parking fines had *accrued* to the point at which they exceeded the value of her car.

ACERBIC (uh SUR bik) *adj* sour; severe; like acid in temper, mood, or tone
- Barry sat silently as his friends read the teacher's *acerbic* comments on his paper.

Acerb and *acerbic* are synonyms. *Acerbity* is the state of being *acerbic*.

ACQUIESCE (ak wee ES) *v* to comply passively; to accept; to assent; to agree
- The pirates asked Pete to walk the plank; he took one look at their swords and then *acquiesced*.

To *acquiesce* is to do something without objection—to do it *quietly*. As the similarity of their spellings indicates, the words *acquiesce* and *quiet* are closely related. They are both based on Latin words meaning rest or be quiet.

Acquiesce is sometimes used sloppily as a simple synonym for *agree* in situations in which it isn't really appropriate. For example, it isn't really possible to *acquiesce* noisily, enthusiastically, or eagerly. Don't forget the *quiet* in the middle.

To *acquiesce* is to exhibit *acquiescence*.

ACQUISITIVE (uh KWIZ uh tiv) *adj* seeking or tending to acquire; greedy
- Children are naturally *acquisitive*; when they see something, they want it, and when they want something, they take it.
- The auctioneer tried to make the grandfather clock sound interesting and valuable, but no one in the room was in an *acquisitive* mood, and the clock went unsold.
- Johnny's natural *acquisitiveness* made it impossible for him to leave the junkyard empty-handed.

ACQUIT (uh KWIT) *v* to find not guilty; to behave or conduct oneself
- The reputed racketeer had been *acquitted* of a wide variety of federal crimes.

An act of *acquitting* is called an *acquittal*.
- The prosecutors were surprised and saddened by the jury's verdict of *acquittal*.

Acquit can also have a somewhat different meaning. To *acquit* one-self in performing some duty is to do a decent job, usually under adverse conditions.

- The apprentice carpenter had very little experience, but on his first job he worked hard; he *acquitted* himself like a pro.

- The members of the lacrosse team had spent the previous week goofing around instead of practicing, but they *acquitted* them-selves in the game, easily defeating their opponents.

ACRID (AK rid) *adj* harshly pungent; bitter
- The cheese we had at the party had an *acrid* taste; it was harsh and unpleasant.

- Long after the fire had been put out, we could feel the *acrid* sting of smoke in our nostrils.

Acrid is used most often with tastes and smells, but it can be used more broadly to describe anything that is offensive in a similar way. A comment that stings like acid could be called *acrid.* So could a harsh personality.

ACRIMONIOUS (ak ruh MOH nee us) *adj* full of spite; bitter; nasty
- George and Elizabeth's discussion turned *acrimonious* when Elizabeth introduced the subject of George's perennial, incor-rigible stupidity.

- Relations between the competing candidates were so *acrimoni-ous* that each refused to acknowledge the presence of the other.

ACRONYM (AK ruh nim) *n* a word made up of the initials of other words
- Radar is an *acronym.* The letters that form it stand for Radio Detecting And Ranging. Radar is also a palindrome, that is, a word or expression that reads the same way from right to left as it does from left to right.

ACUMEN (AK yoo mun) *n* keenness of judgment; mental sharpness
- A woman who knows how to turn one dollar into a million overnight might be said to have a lot of business *acumen.*

- Ernie's lack of *acumen* led him to invest all his money in a company that had already gone out of business.

QUICK QUIZ #3

Match each word in the first column with its definition in the second column. Check your answers in the back of the book.

1. abstinent	a. hard to understand
2. abstract	b. voluntarily avoiding
3. abstruse	c. wretched
4. abysmal	d. bitter
5. accolade	e. comply
6. accost	f. harsh
7. acerbic	g. mental sharpness
8. acquiesce	h. theoretical
9. acrid	i. award
10. acrimonious	j. approach someone aggressively
11. acumen	k. sour

ACUTE (uh KYOOT) *adj* sharp; shrewd

If your eyesight is *acute,* you can see things that other people can't. You have visual *acuity* (uh KYOO uh tee). An *acute* mind is a quick, intelligent one. You have mental *acuity.* An *acute* pain is a sharp pain.

Acute means sharp only in a figurative sense. A knife, which is sharp enough to *cut,* is never said to be *acute.*

Acute is a word doctors throw around quite a bit. An *acute* disease is one that reaches its greatest intensity very quickly and then goes away. What could a disease be if it isn't *acute?* See *chronic.*

ADAGE (AD ij) *n* a traditional saying; a proverb

- There is at least a kernel of truth in the *adage* "adages usually contain at least a kernel of truth."

- The politician promised to make bold new proposals in his campaign speech, but all he did was spout stale *adages.*

- The coach had decorated the locker room with inspirational *adages,* hoping that the sayings would instill a hunger for victory in his players.

ADAMANT (AD uh munt) *adj* stubborn; unyielding; completely inflexible
- Candice was *adamant:* She would never go out with Paul again.

A very hard substance, like a diamond, is also *adamant. Adamantine* (ad uh MAN teen) and *adamant* are synonyms. *Adamancy* is being *adamant.*

ADDRESS (uh DRES) *v* to speak to; to direct one's attention to
To *address* a convention is to give a speech to the convention. To *address* a problem is to face it and set about solving it.
- Ernie *addressed* the problem of *addressing* the convention by sitting down and writing his speech.

ADDUCE (uh DOOS) *v* to bring forward as an example or as proof; to cite
- Tabitha *adduced* so many reasons for doubting Tom's claims that soon even Tom began to doubt his claims.
- In support of his client's weak case, the lawyer *adduced* a few weak precedents from English common law.

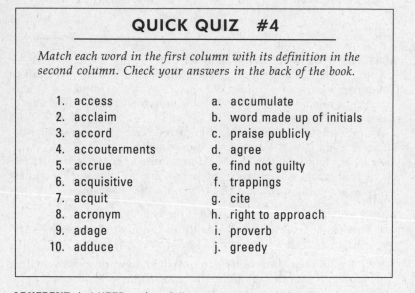

QUICK QUIZ #4

Match each word in the first column with its definition in the second column. Check your answers in the back of the book.

1. access	a. accumulate
2. acclaim	b. word made up of initials
3. accord	c. praise publicly
4. accouterments	d. agree
5. accrue	e. find not guilty
6. acquisitive	f. trappings
7. acquit	g. cite
8. acronym	h. right to approach
9. adage	i. proverb
10. adduce	j. greedy

ADHERENT (ad HEER unt) *n* follower; supporter; believer
- The king's *adherents* threw a big birthday party for him, just to show how much they liked him.

To *adhere* to something is to stick to it. *Adherents* are people who *adhere* to, or stick to, something or someone. Following someone or something, especially rules or laws, is *adherence.*

A religion could be said to have *adherents,* assuming there are people who believe in it. Governments, causes, ideas, people, philosophies, and many other things can have *adherents,* too.

ADJOURN (uh JURN) *v* to suspend until another time
In precise usage, *adjourn* implies that whatever is being *adjourned* will at some point be resumed.

To *adjourn* a meeting is to bring it to an end for now, with the suggestion that another meeting will take place at a later time.

When Congress *adjourns* at the end of a year, it doesn't shut itself down permanently; it puts its business on hold until the next session.

Thus, the baseball season *adjourns* each fall, while a single baseball game merely ends—unless it is delayed by rain or darkness.

ADJUNCT (AJ unkt) *n* something added to or connected with something else; an assistant
- Cooking is just an *adjunct* to Michael's real hobby, which is eating.
- The enthusiastic publisher released a set of audiotapes as an *adjunct* to its popular series of books.

An *adjunct* professor is one who lacks a permanent position on the faculty.

AD-LIB (AD lib) *v* to improvise; to speak or act spontaneously
- Teddy hadn't known that he would be asked to speak after dinner, so when he was called to the microphone, he had to *ad-lib.*
- The director complained that the lazy star hadn't memorized his lines; instead of following the script, he *ad-libbed* in nearly every scene.

ADMONISH (ad MAHN ish) *v* to scold gently; to warn
- The boys' father *admonished* them not to eat the pie he had just baked. When they did so anyway, he *admonished* them.

In the first sentence *admonish* means warn; in the second it means scold gently. Consider yourself *admonished* not to misuse this word.

The noun is *admonition* (ad muh NISH un) and the adjective is *admonitory* (ad MAHN i tor ee).

ADROIT (uh DROYT) *adj* skillful; dexterous; clever; shrewd; socially at ease
- Julio was an *adroit* salesperson: His highly skilled pitch, backed up by extensive product knowledge, nearly always resulted in a sale.

Adroit comes from the French word for right (as in the direction), and refers to an old superstition that right-handedness is superior. It's a synonym of *dexterous* (which comes from the Latin for right) and an antonym of *gauche* and *maladroit*.

- My brilliant accountant *adroitly* whipped my taxes into shape, then made a *gauche* remark about my ignorance of financial matters.

ADULATION (aj uh LAY shun) *n* wild or excessive admiration; flattery
- The boss thrived on the *adulation* of his scheming secretary.
- The rock star grew to abhor the *adulation* of his fans.

The verb is *adulate* (AJ uh layt).

QUICK QUIZ #5

Match each word in the first column with its definition in the second column. Check your answers in the back of the book. Note that "skillful" is the answer for two questions.

1. acute		a.	sharp
2. adulation		b.	follower
3. adamant		c.	socially awkward
4. address		d.	scold gently
5. adherent		e.	speak to
6. admonish		f.	skillful (2)
7. adroit		g.	unyielding
8. dexterous		h.	wild admiration
9. gauche			

ADULTERATE (uh DUL tuh rayt) *v* to contaminate; to make impure
- We discovered that the town's drinking water had radioactive waste in it; we discovered, in other words, that it had been *adulterated*.

Vegetarians do not like their foods *adulterated* with animal fats. *Unadulterated* means pure. *Unadulterated* joy is joy untainted by sadness.

ADVENT (AD vent) *n* arrival; coming; beginning
- The roar of gasoline-powered leaf-blowing machines signaled the *advent* of autumn.
- The rich industrialist responded to the *advent* of his estate's first income tax levy by hiring a new team of accountants.

For Christians, *Advent* is a season that begins four Sundays before Christmas. The word in that sense refers to the impending arrival of Jesus Christ. For some Christians, the word refers primarily to the second coming of Christ. In secular speech, *advent* can be used to refer to the arrival or beginning of anything.

ADVENTITIOUS (ad vent TISH us) *adj* accidental; connected to but nonetheless unrelated; irrelevant
- Arthur's skills as a businessman are *adventitious* to his position at the company; the boss hired him because he wanted a regular golf partner.

ADVERSE (ad VURS) *adj* unfavorable; antagonistic
- We had to play our soccer match under *adverse* conditions: It was snowing, and only three members of our team had bothered to show up.

Airplanes often don't fly in *adverse* weather. An airplane that took off in bad weather and reached its destination safely would be said to have overcome *adversity*. *Adversity* means misfortune or unfavorable circumstances. To do something "in the face of *adversity*" is to undertake a task despite obstacles. Some people are at their best in *adversity* because they rise to the occasion.

A word often confused with *adverse* is *averse* (uh VURS). The two are related but they don't mean quite the same thing. A person who is *averse* to doing something is a person who doesn't want to do it. To be *averse* to something is to be opposed to doing it—to have an *aversion* to doing it.

ADVOCATE (AD vuh kut) *n* a person who argues in favor of a position
- Lulu believes in eliminating tariffs and import restrictions; she is an *advocate* of free trade.
- The proposed law was a good one, but it didn't pass because it had no *advocate*; no senator stepped forward to speak in its favor.

Advocate (AD vuh kayt) can also be a verb.
- The representative of the paint company *advocated* cleaning the deck before painting it, but we were in a hurry so we painted right over the dirt.

Advocacy (AD vuh kuh see) is support of or agreement with a position.

AESTHETIC (es THET ik) *adj* having to do with artistic beauty; artistic
- Our art professor had a highly developed *aesthetic* sense; he found things to admire in paintings that, to us, looked like garbage.

Someone who admires beautiful things greatly can be called an *aesthete* (ES theet). *Aesthetics* is the study of beauty or principles of beauty.

AFFABLE (AF uh bul) *adj* easy to talk to; friendly
- Susan was an *affable* girl; she could strike up a pleasant conversation with almost anyone.
- The Jeffersons' dog was big but *affable*; it liked to lick little children on the face.

The noun is *affability*.

AFFECTATION (af ek TAY shun) *n* unnatural or artificial behavior, usually intended to impress
- Becky's English accent is an *affectation*. She spent only a week in England, and that was several years ago.
- Elizabeth had somehow acquired the absurd *affectation* of pretending that she didn't know how to turn on a television set.

A person with an *affectation* is said to be *affected*.

To *affect* a characteristic or habit is to adopt it consciously, usually in the hope of impressing other people.
- Edward *affected* to be more of an artist than he really was. Everyone hated him for it.

AFFIDAVIT (af uh DAY vit) *n* a sworn written statement made before an official
- Deanna was too ill to appear at the trial, so the judge accepted her *affidavit* in place of oral testimony.

AFFILIATE (uh FIL ee ayt) *v* to become closely associated with
- The testing company is not *affiliated* with the prestigious university, but by using a similar return address it implies a close connection.
- In an attempt to establish herself as an independent voice, the candidate chose not to *affiliate* herself with any political party.

If you are *affiliated* with something, you are an *affiliate* (uh FIL ee ut) and you have an *affiliation* (uh fil ee AY shun).
- The local television station is an *affiliate* of the major network; it carries the network's programs in addition to its own.
- Wesley had a lifelong *affiliation* with the YMCA; he was a member all his life.

AFFINITY (uh FIN uh tee) *n* sympathy; attraction; kinship; similarity
- Ducks have an *affinity* for water; that is, they like to be in it.

- Children have an *affinity* for trouble; that is, they often find themselves in it.

- Magnets and iron have an *affinity* for each other; that is, each is attracted to the other.

Affinity also means similarity or resemblance. There is an *affinity* between snow and sleet.

AFFLICTION (uh FLIK shun) *n* misery; illness; great suffering; a source of misery, illness, or great suffering

- Athlete's foot is an *affliction* that brings great pain and itchiness to its sufferers.

- Martha's eczema was an *affliction* to her; it never gave her a moment's peace from the itching.

- Working in the ghetto brought the young doctor into contact with many *afflictions*, few of which had medical cures.

AFFLUENT (AF loo unt) *adj* rich; prosperous
A person can be *affluent*; all it takes is money. A country can be *affluent*, too, if it's full of *affluent* people.
    Affluence means the same thing as wealth or prosperity.

AFFORD (uh FAWRD) *v* to give; to supply; to confer upon

- The holiday season *afforded* much happiness to the children, who loved opening presents.

- The poorly organized rummage sale *afforded* a great deal of attention but little profit to the charitable organization.

- Marilyn's busy schedule *afforded* little time for leisure.

QUICK QUIZ   #6

Match each word in the first column with its definition in the second column. Check your answers in the back of the book.

1.	adulterate	a.	opposed to
2.	adverse	b.	friendly
3.	averse	c.	rich
4.	aesthetic	d.	unnatural behavior
5.	affable	e.	artistic
6.	affectation	f.	contaminate
7.	affinity	g.	sympathy
8.	affluent	h.	unfavorable
9.	agenda	i.	program

QUICK QUIZ   #7

Match each word in the first column with its definition in the second column. Check your answers in the back of the book.

1.	adjourn	a.	person arguing for a position
2.	adjunct	b.	accidental
3.	ad-lib	c.	become closely associated
4.	advent	d.	arrival
5.	adventitious	e.	misery
6.	advocate	f.	suspend
7.	affidavit	g.	sworn written statement
8.	affiliate	h.	give
9.	affliction	i.	improvise
10.	afford	j.	something added

AFFRONT (uh FRUNT) *n* insult; a deliberate act of disrespect
- Jim's dreadful score on the back nine was an *affront* to the ancient game of golf.
- Amanda thought she was paying Liz a compliment when she said that she liked her new hair color, but Liz took it as an *affront* because she was upset about the greenish spots the hair stylist couldn't cover.

Affront can also be a verb.
- Laura *affronted* me by continually sticking out her tongue as I addressed the class.

Rude and disrespectful behavior can be described as *effrontery* (i FRUN tuh ree).

AFTERMATH (AF tur math) *n* consequence; events following some occurrence or calamity
This word comes from Middle English words meaning "after mowing;" the *aftermath* was the new grass that grew in a field after the field had been mowed. In current usage, this precise original meaning is extended metaphorically.
- Sickness and poverty are often the *aftermath* of war.
- In the *aftermath* of their defeat at the state championship, the members of the football team fought endlessly with one another and ceased to function as a team.

AGENDA (uh JEN duh) *n* program; the things to be done
- What's on the *agenda* for the board meeting? A little gossip, then lunch.

A politician is often said to have an *agenda*. The politician's *agenda* consists of the things he or she wishes to accomplish.

An *agenda,* such as that for a meeting, is often written down, but it doesn't have to be. A person who has sneaky ambitions or plans is often said to have a secret or hidden *agenda*.

AGGRANDIZE (uh GRAN dyze) *v* to exaggerate; to cause to appear greater; to increase (something) in power, reputation, wealth, etc.
- Michele couldn't describe the achievements of her company without *aggrandizing* them. That was too bad, because the company's achievements were substantial enough to stand on their own, without exaggeration.

To be *self-aggrandizing* is to aggressively increase one's position, power, reputation, or wealth, always with a distinctly negative connotation.
- Harry doesn't really need thirty bathrooms; building that big house was merely an act of *self-aggrandizement.*

AGGREGATE (AG ruh gut) *n* sum total; a collection of separate things mixed together
- Chili is an *aggregate* of meat and beans.

Aggregate (AG ruh gayt) can also be a verb or an adjective. You would make chili by *aggregating* meat and beans. Chili is an *aggregate* (AG ruh gut) food.

Similar and related words include *congregate, segregate,* and *integrate*. To *aggregate* is to bring together; to *congregate* is to get together; to *segregate* is to keep apart (or separate); to *integrate* is to unite.

AGGRIEVE (uh GREEV) *v* to mistreat; to do grievous injury to; to distress
- The ugly behavior of the juvenile delinquent *aggrieved* his poor parents, who couldn't imagine what they had done wrong.

To be *aggrieved* is to have a *grievance*.
- The jury awarded ten million dollars to the *aggrieved* former employees of the convicted embezzler.

AGHAST (uh GAST) *adj* terrified; shocked
- Even the veterans were *aghast* when they saw the extent of the carnage on the battlefield.

- The children thought their parents would be thrilled to have breakfast in bed, but both parents were *aghast* when they woke up to find their blankets soaked with orange juice and coffee.

AGNOSTIC (ag NAHS tik) *n* one who believes that the existence of a god can be neither proven nor disproven
An *atheist* is someone who does not believe in a god. An *agnostic*, on the other hand, isn't sure. He doesn't believe, but he doesn't *not* believe, either.
The noun is *agnosticism* (ag NAHS tih siz um).
- An *atheist* himself, Jon concluded from Jorge's spiritual skepticism that they shared similar beliefs. In reality, Jorge's reluctance to affirm or discredit a god's existence reflects his *agnosticism*.

AGRARIAN (uh GRAR ee un) *adj* relating to land; relating to the management or farming of land
Agrarian usually has to do with farming. Think of agriculture.
- Politics in this country often pit the rural, *agrarian* interests against the urban interests.

ALACRITY (uh LAK ri tee) *n* cheerful eagerness or readiness to respond
- David could hardly wait for his parents to leave; he carried their luggage out to the car with great *alacrity*.

ALCHEMY (AL kuh mee) *n* a seemingly magical process of transformation
In the Middle Ages, *alchemists* were people who sought ways to turn base metals into gold, attempted to create elixirs that would cure diseases or keep people alive forever, and engaged in similarly futile pseudo-scientific quests. *Alchemy* today refers to any process of transformation that is metaphorically similar.
- Through the *alchemy* of hairspray and makeup, Amelia transformed herself from a hag into a princess.

ALIENATE (AY lee uh nayt) *v* to estrange; to cause to feel unwelcome or unloved; to make hostile
An *alien* is a foreigner or stranger, whether from another planet or not. To *alienate* someone is to make that person feel like an alien.
- The brusque teacher *alienated* his students by mocking them when they made mistakes.

To be *alienated* is to be in a state of *alienation* (ay lee uh NAY shun).
- Sharon found it nearly impossible to make friends; as a result, her freshman year in college was characterized primarily by feelings of *alienation*.

ALLEGE (uh LEJ) *v* to assert without proof
- If I say, "Cedrick *alleges* that I stole his hat," I am saying two things:

    1. Cedrick says I stole his hat.
    2. I say I didn't do it.

To *allege* something is to assert it without proving it. Such an assertion is called an *allegation* (al uh GAY shun).

The adjective is *alleged* (uh LEJD). If the police accuse someone of having committed a crime, newspapers will usually refer to that person as an *alleged* criminal.
- The police have *alleged* that he or she committed the crime, but a jury hasn't made a decision yet.

ALLEGIANCE (uh LEE juns) *n* loyalty
To pledge *allegiance* to the flag is to promise to be loyal to it.
- Nolan's *allegiance* to his employer ended when a competing company offered him a job at twice his salary.
- The *allegiance* of the palace guard shifted to the rebel leader as soon as it became clear that the king had been overthrown.

ALLEGORY (AL uh gawr ee) *n* a story in which the characters are symbols with moral or spiritual meanings
- Instead of lecturing the children directly about the importance of straightening up their rooms, Mrs. Smith told them an *allegory* in which a little boy named Good was given all the candy in the world after making his bed, while a messy little girl named Bad had nothing to eat but turnips and broccoli.

ALLEVIATE (uh LEE vee ayt) *v* to relieve, usually temporarily or incompletely; to make bearable; to lessen
- Visiting the charming pet cemetery *alleviated* the woman's grief over the death of her canary.
- Aspirin *alleviates* headache pain. When your headache comes back, take some more aspirin.

ALLOCATE (AL uh kayt) *v* to distribute; to assign; to allot
- The event had been a big failure, and David, Aaliyah, and Jan spent several hours attempting to *allocate* the blame. In the end, they decided it had all been Jan's fault.
- The office manager had *allocated* just seven paper clips for our entire department.

ALLOT (uh LAHT) *v* to apportion, allocate, or assign
- The principal *allotted* students to classrooms by writing their names on pieces of paper and throwing the paper into the air.
- The president *allotted* several ambassadorships to men and women who had contributed heavily to his campaign.

A group of things that have been *allotted* is referred to as an *allotment*.
- George didn't like his natural *allotment* of physical features, so he had them altered by a plastic surgeon.

ALLOY (AL oy) *n* a combination of two or more things, usually metals
- Brass is an *alloy* of copper and zinc. That is, you make brass by combining copper and zinc.

Alloy (uh LOY) is often used as a verb. To *alloy* two things is to mix them together. There is usually an implication that the mixture is less than the sum of the parts. That is, there is often something undesirable or debased about an *alloy* (as opposed to a pure substance).

Unalloyed means undiluted or pure. *Unalloyed* dislike is dislike undiminished by any positive feelings; *unalloyed* love is love undiminished by any negative feelings.

QUICK QUIZ   #8

Match each word in the first column with its definition in the second column. Check your answers in the back of the book.

1.	aggregate	a.	get together
2.	congregate	b.	unite
3.	segregate	c.	someone unconvinced about
4.	integrate		the existence of a god
5.	agnostic	d.	relieve
6.	agrarian	e.	keep apart
7.	alacrity	f.	combination of metals
8.	allege	g.	sum total
9.	alleviate	h.	distribute
10.	allocate	i.	assert
11.	alloy	j.	cheerful eagerness
		k.	relating to land

QUICK QUIZ   #9

*Match each word in the first column with its definition in the
second column. Check your answers in the back of the book.*

1.	affront	a.	consequence
2.	aftermath	b.	mistreat
3.	aggrandize	c.	estrange
4.	aggrieve	d.	apportion
5.	aghast	e.	terrified
6.	alchemy	f.	seemingly magical transformation
7.	alienate		
8.	allegiance	g.	loyalty
9.	allegory	h.	symbolic story
10.	allot	i.	exaggerate
		j.	insult

ALLUSION (uh LOO zhun) *n* an indirect reference (often to a literary
work); a hint
To *allude* to something is to refer to it indirectly.
- When Ralph said, "I sometimes wonder whether to be or not to
be," he was *alluding* to a famous line in *Hamlet*. If Ralph had said,
"As Hamlet said, 'To be or not to be, that is the question,'" his
statement would have been a direct reference, not an *allusion*.

An *allusion* is an *allusion* only if the source isn't identified directly.
Anything else is a reference or a quotation.
- If Andrea says, "I enjoyed your birthday party," she isn't
alluding to the birthday party; she's mentioning it. But if she
says, "I like your choice of party music," she is *alluding* to the
party.

ALOOF (uh LOOF) *adj* uninvolved; standing off; keeping one's distance
- Al, on the roof, felt very *aloof*.

To stand *aloof* from a touch-football game is to stand on the sidelines
and not take part.
  Cats are often said to be *aloof* because they usually mind their
own business and don't crave the affection of people.

ALTERCATION (awl tur KAY shun) *n* a heated fight, argument, or quarrel
- Newlyweds Mary and Bill were fighting about the proper way to gargle mouthwash, and the sound of their *altercation* woke up several other guests in the hotel.
- Dr. Mason's lecture was so controversial and inflammatory that it led to an *altercation* among the members of the audience.

ALTRUISM (AL troo iz um) *n* selflessness; generosity; devotion to the interests of others
- The private foundation depended on the *altruism* of the extremely rich old man. When he decided to start spending his money on his new twenty-year-old girlfriend, the foundation went out of business.

To be *altruistic* is to help others without expectation of personal gain. Giving money to charity is an act of *altruism*. The *altruist* does it just to be nice, although he'll probably also remember to take a tax deduction.

An *altruistic* act is also an act of *philanthropy,* which means almost the same thing.

AMASS (uh MAS) *v* to pile up; to accumulate; to collect for one's own use
- By living frugally for fifty years, Jed *amassed* a large fortune.
- Billy collected bottle caps so assiduously that, before his parents realized what was happening, he had *amassed* the largest collection in the world.
- By the end of the week, the protest groups had *amassed* enough signatures on their petitions to be assured of recognition at the convention.

AMBIENCE (AM bee uns) *n* atmosphere; mood; feeling
- By decorating their house with plastic beach balls and Popsicle™ sticks, the Cramers created a playful *ambience* that delighted young children.

A restaurant's *ambience* is the look, mood, and feel of the place. People sometimes say that a restaurant has "an atmosphere of *ambience*." To do so is redundant—*atmosphere* and *ambience* mean the same thing.

Ambience is a French word that can also be pronounced "ahm BYAHNS." The adjective *ambient* (AM bee unt) means surrounding or circulating.

AMBIGUOUS (am BIG yoo us) *adj* unclear in meaning; confusing; capable of being interpreted in different ways
- We listened to the weather report, but the forecast was *ambiguous;* we couldn't tell whether the day was going to be rainy or sunny.
- The poem we read in English class was *ambiguous;* no one had any idea what the poet was trying to say.

The noun is *ambiguity* (am bih GYOO uh tee).

AMBIVALENT (am BIV uh lunt) *adj* undecided; having opposed feelings simultaneously
- Susan felt *ambivalent* about Alec as a boyfriend. Her frequent desire to break up with him reflected this *ambivalence.*

QUICK QUIZ #10

Match each word in the first column with its definition in the second column. Check your answers in the back of the book.

1. allusion		a.	atmosphere
2. aloof		b.	standoffish
3. altruism		c.	confusing
4. ambience		d.	generosity
5. ambiguous		e.	indirect reference
6. ambivalent		f.	undecided

AMELIORATE (uh MEEL yuh rayt) *v* to make better or more tolerable
- The mood of the prisoners was *ameliorated* when the warden gave them extra free time outside.
- My great-uncle's gift of several million dollars considerably *ameliorated* my financial condition.

AMENABLE (uh MEE nuh bul) *adj* obedient; willing to give in to the wishes of another; agreeable
- I suggested that Brad pay for my lunch as well as for his own; to my surprise, he was *amenable.*
- The plumber was *amenable* to my paying my bill with jelly beans, which was lucky, because I had more jelly beans than money.

AMENITY (uh MEN i tee) *n* pleasantness; attractive or comfortable feature
- The *amenities* at the local club include a swimming pool, a golf course, and a tennis court.

If an older guest at your house asks you where the *amenities* are, he or she is probably asking for directions to the bathroom.

Those little bars of soap and bottles of shampoo found in hotel rooms are known in the hotel business as *amenities*. They are meant to increase your comfort. People like them because people like almost anything that is free (although, of course, the cost of providing such *amenities* is simply added to the price of hotel rooms).

AMIABLE (AY mee uh bul) *adj* friendly; agreeable
- Our *amiable* guide made us feel right at home in what would otherwise have been a cold and forbidding museum.
- The drama critic was so *amiable* in person that even the subjects of negative reviews found it impossible not to like her.

Amicable is a similar and related word. Two not very *amiable* people might nonetheless make an *amicable* agreement. *Amicable* means politely friendly, or not hostile. Two countries might trade *amicably* with each other even while technically remaining enemies.
- Julio and Clarissa had a surprisingly *amicable* divorce and remained good friends even after paying their lawyers' fees.

AMID (uh MID) *prep* in the middle of
- *Amid* the noise and bright lights of the Fourth of July celebration, tired old Taki slept like a log.
- When the store detective found her, the lost little girl was sitting *amid* a group of teddy bears in a window display.

The English say, "Amidst," instead of *amid*, but you shouldn't. Unless, that is, you are in England. You can, however, say, "In the midst."

AMNESTY (AM nuh stee) *n* an official pardon for a group of people who have violated a law or policy
Amnesty comes from the same root as *amnesia*, the condition that causes characters in movies to forget everything except how to speak English and drive their cars.

An *amnesty* is an official forgetting. When a state government declares a tax *amnesty*, it is saying that if people pay the taxes they owe, the government will officially "forget" that they broke the law by not paying them in the first place.

The word *amnesty* always refers to a pardon given to a group or class of people. A pardon granted to a single person is simply a pardon.

AMORAL (ay MOR ul) *adj* lacking a sense of right and wrong; neither good nor bad, neither moral nor immoral; without moral feelings
- Very young children are *amoral;* when they cry, they aren't being bad or good—they're merely doing what they have to do.

A *moral* person does right; an *immoral* person does wrong; an *amoral* person simply does.

AMOROUS (AM ur us) *adj* feeling loving, especially in a sexual sense; in love; relating to love
- The *amorous* couple made quite a scene at the movie. The movie they were watching, *Love Story,* was pretty *amorous* itself. It was about an *amorous* couple, one of whom died.

AMORPHOUS (uh MOR fus) *adj* shapeless; without a regular or stable shape; bloblike
- Ed's teacher said that his term paper was *amorphous;* it was as shapeless and disorganized as a cloud.
- The sleepy little town was engulfed by an *amorphous* blob of glowing protoplasm—a higher intelligence from outer space.

To say that something has an *"amorphous* shape" is a contradiction. How can a shape be shapeless?

ANACHRONISM (uh NAK ruh niz um) *n* something out of place in time or history; an incongruity
- In this day of impersonal hospitals, a doctor who remembers your name seems like an *anachronism.*

ANALOGY (uh NAL uh jee) *n* a comparison of one thing to another; similarity
- To say having an allergy feels like being bitten by an alligator would be to make or draw an *analogy* between an allergy and an alligator bite.

Analogy usually refers to similarities between things that are not otherwise very similar. If you don't think an allergy is at all like an alligator bite, you might say, "That *analogy* doesn't hold up." To say that there is no *analogy* between an allergy and an alligator bite is to say that they are not *analogous* (uh NAL uh gus).

Something similar in a particular respect to something else is its *analog* (AN uh lawg), sometimes spelled *analogue.*

QUICK QUIZ #11

Match each word in the first column with its definition in the second column. Check your answers in the back of the book.

1.	ameliorate	a.	pleasantness
2.	amenable	b.	comparison
3.	amenity	c.	obedient
4.	amiable	d.	without moral feeling
5.	amicable	e.	feeling loving
6.	amnesty	f.	make better
7.	amoral	g.	shapeless
8.	amorous	h.	politely friendly
9.	amorphous	i.	official pardon
10.	anachronism	j.	friendly
11.	analogy	k.	incongruity

ANARCHY (AN ur kee) *n* absence of government or control; lawlessness; disorder

- The country fell into a state of *anarchy* after the rebels kidnapped the president and locked the legislature inside the Capitol.

The word doesn't have to be used in its strict political meaning. You could say that there was *anarchy* in the kindergarten when the teacher stepped out of the door for a moment. You could say it, and you would probably be right.

The words *anarchy* and *monarchy* are closely related. *Anarchy* means no leader; *monarchy,* a government headed by a king or queen, means one leader.

ANATHEMA (uh NATH uh muh) *n* something or someone loathed or detested

- Algebra is *anathema* to Dex; every time he sees an equation, he becomes sick to his stomach.

- The parents became *anathema* to the greedy children as soon as the children realized they had been left out of the will.

- The women in fur coats were *anathema* to the members of the animal-rights group.

ANCILLARY (AN suh ler ee) *adj* subordinate; providing assistance
- Although George earned his living as a high-powered Wall Street investment banker, selling peanuts at weekend Little League games provided an *ancillary* source of income.

An *ancillary* employee is one who helps another. Servants are sometimes referred to as *ancillaries* (AN suh ler eez).

ANECDOTE (AN ik doht) *n* a short account of a humorous or revealing incident
- The old lady kept the motorcycle gang thoroughly amused with *anecdote* after *anecdote* about her cute little dog.
- Alvare told an *anecdote* about the time Jessica got her big toe stuck in a bowling ball.
- The vice president set the crowd at ease with an *anecdote* about his childhood desire to become a vice president.

To say that the evidence of life on other planets is merely *anecdotal* is to say that we haven't captured any aliens, but simply heard a lot of stories from people who claimed to have been kidnapped by flying saucers.

ANGST (ahnkst) *n* anxiety; fear; dread
This is the German word for *anxiety*. A closely related word is *anguish*. In English, it is a voguish word that is usually meant to convey a deeper, more down-to-the-bone type of dread than can be described with mere English words.
- The thought of his impending examinations, for which he had not yet begun to study, filled Herman with *angst*, making it impossible for him to study.

ANGUISH (ANG gwish) *n* agonizing physical or mental pain
- Theresa had been a nurse in the emergency room for twenty years, but she had never gotten used to the *anguish* of accident victims.

ANIMOSITY (an uh MAHS uh tee) *n* resentment; hostility; ill will
- The rivals for the state championship felt great *animosity* toward each other. Whenever they ran into each other, they snarled.

A person whose look could kill is a person whose *animosity* is evident.

ANNEX (uh NEKS) *v* to add or attach
- Old McDonald increased the size of his farm by *annexing* an adjoining field.

A small connecting structure added to a building is often called an *annex* (AN eks).

- The *annex* of the elementary school had a small gymnasium.

ANNUITY (uh NOO uh tee) *n* an annual allowance or income; the annual interest payment on an investment; any regular allowance or income

- The company's pension fund provides an *annuity* for its retired employees; each receives regular payments from the fund.

- None of Herbert's books had been bestsellers, but all of them were still in print, and taken together their royalties amounted to a substantial *annuity*.

- The widow would have been destitute if her husband had not bought an insurance policy that provided a modest *annuity* for the rest of her life.

ANOMALY (uh NAHM uh lee) *n* an aberration; an irregularity; a deviation
- A snowy winter day is not an *anomaly*, but a snowy July day is.

- A house without a roof is an *anomaly*—a cold, wet *anomaly*.

A roofless house could be said to be *anomalous*. Something that is *anomalous* is something that is not normal or regular.

ANTECEDENT (an tuh SEED unt) *n* someone or something that went before; something that provides a model for something that came after it
- Your parents and grandparents could be said to be your *antecedents*; they came before you.

- The horse-drawn wagon is an *antecedent* of the modern automobile.

Antecedent can also be used as an adjective. The oil lamp was *antecedent* to the light bulb.

In grammar, the *antecedent* of a pronoun is the person, place, or thing to which it refers. In the previous sentence, the *antecedent* of *it* is *antecedent*. In the sentence "Bill and Harry were walking together, and then he hit him," it is impossible to determine what the *antecedents* of the pronouns (*he* and *him*) are.

Antecedent is related to a word that is similar in meaning: *precedent*.

ANTEDATE (AN ti dayt) *v* to be older than; to have come before
The root "ante" means before or in front of. To *antedate* is to be dated before something else.
- The Jacksons' house *antedates* the Declaration of Independence; it was built in 1774.

- Mrs. Simpson's birth *antedates* that of her daughter by twenty-four years.

ANTERIOR (an TIR ee ur) *adj* situated in front
- The children enjoy sitting dumbly and staring at the *anterior* surface of the television set.
- Your chest is situated on the *anterior* portion of your body. (The anterior end of a snake is its head.)

The opposite of *anterior* is *posterior*. You are sitting on the *posterior* end of your body.

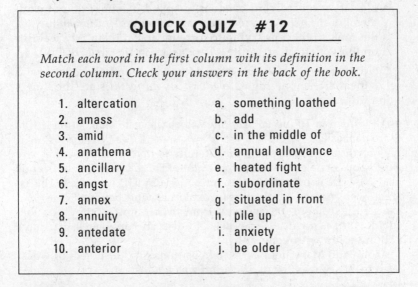

QUICK QUIZ #12

Match each word in the first column with its definition in the second column. Check your answers in the back of the book.

1. altercation		a.	something loathed
2. amass		b.	add
3. amid		c.	in the middle of
4. anathema		d.	annual allowance
5. ancillary		e.	heated fight
6. angst		f.	subordinate
7. annex		g.	situated in front
8. annuity		h.	pile up
9. antedate		i.	anxiety
10. anterior		j.	be older

ANTHOLOGY (an THAHL uh jee) *n* a collection, especially of literary works
To *anthologize* (an THAHL uh jyze) a group of literary works or other objects is to collect them into an *anthology*.
- The *Norton Anthology of English Literature* is a collection of important works by English writers.
- The chief executive officer of the big company thought so highly of himself that he privately published an *anthology* of his sayings.
- Mr. Bailey, a terrible hypochondriac, was a walking *anthology* of symptoms.

ANTHROPOMORPHIC (an thruh puh MAWR fik) *adj* ascribing human characteristics to nonhuman animals or objects

This word is derived from the Greek word *anthropos*, which means man or human, and the Greek word *morphos*, which means shape or form.

To be *anthropomorphic* is to see a human shape (either literally or metaphorically) in things that are not human. To speak of the hands of a clock, or to say that a car has a mind of its own, is to be *anthropomorphic*. To be *anthropomorphic* is to engage in *anthropomorphism*.

ANTIPATHY (an TIP uh thee) *n* firm dislike; a dislike

- I feel *antipathy* toward bananas wrapped in ham. I do not want them for dinner. I also feel a certain amount of *antipathy* toward the cook who keeps trying to force me to eat them. My feelings on these matters are quite *antipathetic* (an tip uh THET ik).

I could also say that ham-wrapped bananas and the cooks who serve them are among my *antipathies*. My *antipathies* are the things I don't like.

ANTIPODAL (an TIP ud ul) *adj* situated on opposite sides of the Earth; exactly opposite

The north and south poles are literally *antipodal*; that is, they are exactly opposite each other on the globe. There is a group of islands near New Zealand called the Antipodes (an TIP uh deez). The islands were named by European explorers who believed they had traveled just about as far away from their home as they possibly could. *Antipodal* can also be used to describe opposites that have nothing to do with geography.

- John and Mary held *antipodal* positions on the subject of working. Mary was for it, and John was against it.

The noun is *antipodes* (an TIP uh deez).

ANTIQUITY (an TIK wuh tee) *n* ancientness; ancient times

- The slow speed at which Lawrence was driving was not surprising, considering the *antiquity* of his car.

- Tamasha loved studying ancient history so much that she didn't really pay much attention to the present; when she wasn't reading old volumes in the library, she walked around in a daze, her head spinning with dreams of *antiquity*.

Overpriced chairs and other furniture from the olden days are called *antiques*. Objects or ideas that are too old-fashioned to be of use anymore are said to be *antiquated* (AN tuh kway tud). (Don't throw them out, though; sell them to an antiques dealer.)

ANTITHESIS (an TITH uh sis) *n* the direct opposite
- Erin is the *antithesis* of Aaron: Erin is bright and beautiful; Aaron is dull and plain.

APARTHEID (uh PAHRT hyte) *n* the former policy of racial segregation and oppression in the Republic of South Africa
The word *apartheid* is related to the word *apart*. Under *apartheid* in South Africa, blacks were kept apart from whites and denied all rights.

The word *apartheid* is sometimes applied to less radical forms of racial injustice and to other kinds of separation. Critics have sometimes accused American public schools of practicing educational *apartheid* by providing substandard schooling for nonwhites.

QUICK QUIZ #13

Match each word in the first column with its definition in the second column. Check your answers in the back of the book.

1.	anarchy	a.	resentment
2.	monarchy	b.	racial oppression
3.	anecdote	c.	firm dislike
4.	anguish	d.	irregularity
5.	animosity	e.	what went before
6.	anomaly	f.	agonizing pain
7.	antecedent	g.	amusing account
8.	antipathy	h.	government by king or queen
9.	antithesis	i.	lawlessness
10.	apartheid	j.	direct opposite

APATHY (AP uh thee) *n* lack of interest; lack of feeling
- The members of the student council accused the senior class of *apathy* because none of the seniors had bothered to sign up for the big fundraiser.

The word *apathetic* is the adjective form of *apathy*.
- Jill didn't care one bit about current events; she was entirely *apathetic*.

APERTURE (AP ur chur) *n* an opening
- Macon's underpants were plainly visible through the *aperture* that suddenly appeared along the rear seam of his uniform.

The opening inside a camera's lens is called its *aperture*. A photographer controls the amount of light that strikes the film by adjusting the size of the *aperture*.

APEX (AY peks) *n* highest point
A mountain's summit is also its *apex*.
- Jerry's score of 162, though poor by most standards, was the *apex* of his achievement in bowling; it was the best score he earned in thirty years.
- Mary Anne was at the *apex* of her career; she was the president of her own software company, and everyone in her industry looked up to her.

APHORISM (AF uh riz um) *n* a brief, often witty saying; a proverb
- Benjamin Franklin was fond of *aphorisms*. He was frequently *aphoristic*.
- Chef Hussain is particularly fond of Woolf's *aphorism*, "One cannot think well, love well, or sleep well, if one has not dined well."

APOCALYPSE (uh PAHK uh lips) *n* a prophetic revelation, especially one concerning the end of the world
In strict usage, *apocalypse* refers to specific Christian writings, but most people use it more generally in connection with predictions of things like nuclear war, the destruction of the ozone layer, and the spread of fast-food restaurants to every corner of the universe. To make such predictions, or to be deeply pessimistic, is to be *apocalyptic* (uh pahk uh LIP tik).

APOCRYPHAL (uh PAHK ruh ful) *adj* of dubious authenticity; fictitious; spurious
- Brandi's blog discredited the *apocryphal* report of Martians in Congress.

An *apocryphal* story is one whose truth is not proven or whose falsehood is strongly suspected. Like *apocalypse*, this word has a religious origin. The *Apocrypha* are a number of "extra" books of the Old Testament that Protestants and Jews don't include in their Bibles because they don't think they're authentic.

APOGEE (AP uh jee) *n* the most distant point in the orbit of the moon or of an artificial satellite

Apogee is derived from Greek words meaning away from the Earth. The apogee of the moon's orbit is the point at which the moon is farthest from the Earth. The word can also be used figuratively, in which case it usually means pretty much the same thing as *apex*.

- Though Mary Anne was at the *apogee* of her career, she didn't feel that her life was a success since she no longer seemed to be learning new skills.

The opposite of *apogee* is *perigee* (PER uh jee), which is derived from Greek words meaning near the Earth.

- At *perigee*, the satellite was faintly visible on the Earth to anyone with a good pair of binoculars.

In careful usage, moons and other objects orbiting planets other than the Earth do not have *apogees* and *perigees*.

APOPLEXY (AP uh plek see) *n* stroke (that is, numbness and paralysis resulting from the sudden loss of blood flow to the brain)

This word turns up repeatedly in old novels. Nowadays, its use is mostly figurative. If I say that I gave my boss *apoplexy* when I told him that I was going to take the rest of the day off, I mean that he became so angry that he seemed to be in danger of exploding. To suffer from *apoplexy*, whether literally or figuratively, is to be *apoplectic* (ap uh PLEK tik).

- The principal was *apoplectic* when he discovered that the tenth graders had torn up all the answer sheets for the previous day's SAT; he was so angry that his face turned bright red.

APOSTASY (uh PAHS tuh see) *n* abandonment or rejection of faith or loyalty

- The congregation was appalled by the *apostasy* of its former priest, who had left the church in order to found a new religion based on winning number combinations in the state lottery.

- The president was hurt by the *apostasy* of his closest advisers, most of whom had decided to cooperate with the special prosecutor by testifying against him.

A person who commits *apostasy* is called an *apostate* (uh PAHS tayt).

- In the cathedral of English literature, Professor Hanratty was an *apostate*; he thought that Shakespeare was nothing more than an untalented old hack.

APOTHEOSIS (uh pahth ee OH sis) *n* elevation to divine status; the perfect example of something
- Some people think that the Corvette is the *apotheosis* of American car making. They think it's the ideal.
- Geoffrey is unbearable to be with. He thinks he's the *apotheosis* of masculinity.

APPALLING (uh PAWL ing) *adj* causing horror or consternation
- Austin's table manners were *appalling*; he chewed with his mouth wide open, and he picked his teeth with the tip of his knife while he ate.

The word *appall* comes from a French word meaning to make pale. To be *appalled* is to be so horrified that one loses the color in one's cheeks.

QUICK QUIZ   #14

Match each word in the first column with its definition in the second column. Check your answers in the back of the book.

1. anthology	a. causing horror
2. anthropomorphic	b. opening
3. antipodal	c. exactly opposite
4. antiquity	d. abandonment of faith
5. aperture	e. ascribing human characteristics to nonhumans
6. apex	
7. apogee	f. highest point
8. apoplexy	g. stroke
9. apostasy	h. ancientness
10. appalling	i. literary collection
	j. most distant point of orbit

APPARITION (ap uh RISH un) *n* a ghost or ghostly object
- Barb said that she had seen an *apparition* and that she was pretty sure that it had been the ghost of President Grant, but it turned out to be nothing more than a sheet flapping on the clothesline.
- The bubbling oasis on the horizon was merely an *apparition*; there was nothing there but more burning sand.

APPEASE (uh PEEZ) *v* to soothe; to pacify by giving in to
- Jaleel *appeased* his angry mother by promising to make his bed every morning without fail until the end of time.
- The trembling farmer handed over all his grain, but still the emperor was not *appeased*.

The noun is *appeasement*.

APPELLATION (ap uh LAY shun) *n* a name
- Percival had a highly singular *appellation*; that is, he had an unusual name.

APPENDAGE (uh PEN dij) *n* something added on to something else; a supplement
To *append* is to add something on to something else. Your *appendix* (uh PEN diks), if you still have one, is a small, apparently useless organ attached (or *appended*) to your intestine. You have no more than one *appendix*, but you have several *appendages*, including your arms and legs. Your arms and legs are *appended* to the trunk of your body.
- Beth's husband never seemed to be more than an arm's length away from her. He seemed less like a spouse than like an *appendage*.
- Billy created a model of a spider with two extra *appendages*; the spider had ten legs instead of eight.

APPORTION (uh PAWR shun) *v* to distribute proportionally; to divide into portions
- There was nothing to eat except one hot dog, so Mr. Lucas carefully *apportioned* it among the eight famished campers.
- Because the property had been *apportioned* equally among Mr. Smith's nine children, none had enough land on which to build a house.
- The grant money was *apportioned* in such a way that the wealthy schools received a great deal while the poor ones received almost nothing.

APPOSITE (AP uh zut) *adj* distinctly suitable; pertinent
- The appearance of the mayor at the dedication ceremony was accidental but *apposite*; his great-grandfather had donated the land on which the statue had been erected.
- At the end of the discussion, the moderator made an *apposite* remark that seemed to bring the entire disagreement to a happy conclusion.

APPRAISE (uh PRAYZ) *v* to estimate the value or quality of; to judge
- When we had the beautiful old ring *appraised* by a jeweler, we were surprised to learn that the large diamond in its center was actually made of glass.

- The general coldly *appraised* the behavior of his officers and found it to be wanting.

An act of *appraising* is called an *appraisal* (uh PRAY zul).
- It is a good idea to seek an independent *appraisal* of an old painting before bidding many millions of dollars for it in an auction.

APPRECIATE (uh PREE shee ayt) *v* to increase in value
- The Browns bought their house twenty years ago for a hundred thousand dollars, but it has *appreciated* considerably since then; today it's worth almost two million dollars.

- Harry bought Joe's collection of old chewing-tobacco tins as an investment. His hope was that the tins would *appreciate* over the next few years, enabling him to turn a profit by selling them to someone else.

The opposite of *appreciate* is *depreciate*. When a car loses value over time, we say it has *depreciated*.

APPREHENSIVE (ap ruh HEN siv) *adj* worried; anxious
- The *apprehensive* child clung to his father's leg as the two of them walked into the main circus tent to watch the lion tamer.

- Rhea was *apprehensive* about the exam, because she had forgotten to go to class for several months. As it turned out, her *apprehensions* were justified. She couldn't answer a single question on the test.

A *misapprehension* is a misunderstanding.
- Rhea had no *misapprehensions* about her lack of preparation; she knew perfectly well she would fail horribly.

QUICK QUIZ #15

*Match each word in the first column with its definition in the
second column. Check your answers in the back of the book.*

1. apathy	a. of dubious authenticity
2. aphorism	b. misunderstanding
3. apocalypse	c. increase in value
4. apocryphal	d. lack of interest
5. apotheosis	e. soothe
6. appease	f. prophetic revelation
7. appreciate	g. decrease in value
8. depreciate	h. the perfect example
9. apprehensive	i. witty saying
10. misapprehension	j. worried

APPRISE (uh PRYZE) *v* to give notice to; to inform
Be careful not to confuse this word with *appraise*. They don't mean
the same thing, even though there's only one letter's difference
between them.

- The policeman *apprised* the suspect of his right to remain
  silent, but the suspect was so intoxicated that he didn't seem
  to notice.

- The president's advisers had fully *apprised* him of the worsen-
  ing situation in the Middle East, and now he was ready to act.

APPROBATION (ap ruh BAY shun) *n* approval; praise
- The crowd expressed its *approbation* of the team's performance
  by gleefully covering the field with toilet paper.

- The ambassador's actions met with the *approbation* of his
  commander in chief.

Approbation is a fancy word for *approval,* to which it is closely
related. *Disapprobation* is disapproval.

APPROPRIATE (uh PROH pree ayt) *v* to take without permission; to set
aside for a particular use
- Nick *appropriated* my lunch; he grabbed it out of my hands and
  ate it. So I *appropriated* Ed's.

- The deer and raccoons *appropriated* the vegetables in our garden
  last summer. This year we'll build a better fence.

Don't confuse the pronunciation of the verb *to appropriate* with the pronunciation of the adjective *appropriate* (uh PROH pree it). When Congress decides to buy some new submarines, it *appropriates* money for them. That is, it sets some money aside. The money thus set aside is called an *appropriation*.

When an elected official takes money that was supposed to be spent on submarines and spends it on a Rolls-Royce and a few mink coats, he is said to have *misappropriated* the money.

When the government decides to build a highway through your backyard, it *expropriates* your property for this purpose. That is, it uses its official authority to take possession of your property.

APPURTENANCE (uh PURT nuns) *n* something extra; an appendage; an accessory
- The salary wasn't much, but the *appurtenances* were terrific; as superintendent of the luxury apartment building, Joe got to live in a beautiful apartment and had free access to the tennis courts and swimming pool.

APROPOS (ap ruh POH) *adj* appropriate; coming at the right time
This word is close in meaning to *appropriate* (uh PROH pree ut), to which it is closely related.
- Susan's loving toast at the wedding dinner was *apropos*; the clown suit she wore while making it was not.
- The professor's speech was about endangered species, and the luncheon menu was perversely *apropos*: Bengal-tiger burgers and ostrich-egg omelets.

The opposite of apropos is *malapropos*.
See our listing for *malapropism*.

APT (apt) *adj* appropriate; having a tendency to; likely
- The headmaster's harsh remarks about the importance of honesty were *apt*; the entire senior class had just been caught cheating on an exam.
- Charlie is so skinny that he is *apt* to begin shivering the moment he steps out of the swimming pool.
- If Ellen insults me again, I'm *apt* to leave the room.

Apt, apropos, and *apposite* have similar meanings.

QUICK QUIZ #16

Match each word in the first column with its definition in the second column. Check your answers in the back of the book. Note that "something extra" is the answer for two questions.

1. apparition	a. something extra (2)
2. appellation	b. give notice to
3. appendage	c. ghost
4. apportion	d. likely
5. appraise	e. distribute proportionally
6. apprise	f. appropriate
7. appurtenance	g. name
8. apropos	h. estimate the value of
9. apposite	i. distinctly suitable
10. apt	

APTITUDE (AP tuh tood) *n* capacity for learning; natural ability
- Some rare students have a marked *aptitude* for taking the SAT. They earn high scores without any prep.

- I tried to repair my car, but as I sat on the floor of my garage, surrounded by mysterious parts, I realized that I had no *aptitude* for automobile repair.

The opposite of *aptitude* is *ineptitude*.

ARBITER (AHR buh tur) *n* one who decides; a judge
- An *arbiter* of fashion determines what other people will wear by wearing it herself.

An *arbiter arbitrates,* or weighs opposing viewpoints and makes decisions. The words *arbiter* and *arbitrator* mean the same thing. An *arbiter* presides over an *arbitration,* which is a formal meeting to settle a dispute.

ARBITRARY (AHR buh trer ee) *adj* random; capricious
- The grades Mr. Simone gave his English students appeared to be *arbitrary;* they didn't seem related the work the students had done in class.

- The old judge was *arbitrary* in sentencing criminals; there was no sensible pattern to the sentences he handed down.

ARCADE (ahr KAYD) *n* a passageway defined by a series of arches; a covered passageway with shops on either side; an area filled with coin-operated games

In the most precise usage, an *arcade* is an area flanked by arches in the same way that a colonnade is an area flanked by columns. In fact, an *arcade* can be a colonnade, if the arches are supported by columns.

- The new building consisted of a number of small *arcades* radiating like the spokes of a wheel from a large plaza containing a fountain.

- The penny *arcade* was misnamed since none of the games there cost less than a quarter.

ARCANE (ahr KAYN) *adj* mysterious; known only to a select few

- The rites of the secret cult were *arcane;* no one outside the cult knew what they were.

- The *arcane* formula for the cocktail was scrawled on a faded scrap of paper.

- We could make out only a little of the *arcane* inscription on the old trunk.

ARCHAIC (ahr KAY ik) *adj* extremely old; ancient; outdated

- The tribe's traditions are *archaic.* They have been in force for thousands of years.

Archaic civilizations are ones that disappeared a long time ago. An *archaic* meaning of a word is one that isn't used anymore.

QUICK QUIZ #17

Match each word in the first column with its definition in the second column. Check your answers in the back of the book.

1.	approbation	a.	misuse public money
2.	appropriate	b.	extremely old
3.	misappropriate	c.	take without permission
4.	expropriate	d.	weigh opposing views
5.	aptitude	e.	mysterious
6.	arbiter	f.	approval
7.	arbitrate	g.	random
8.	arbitrary	h.	take property officially
9.	arcane	i.	judge
10.	archaic	j.	natural ability

ARCHETYPE (AHR kuh type) *n* an original model or pattern

An *archetype* is similar to a *prototype*. A *prototype* is a first, tentative model that is made but that will be improved in later versions. Henry Ford built a *prototype* of his Model T in his basement. His mother kicked him out, so he had no choice but to start a motor car company.

An *archetype* is usually something that precedes something else.
- Plato is the *archetype* of all philosophers.

An *archetype* is *archetypal* or *archetypical*.

ARCHIPELAGO (ahr kuh PEL uh goh) *n* a large group of islands
- Sumatra, Borneo, and the Philippines are among the numerous island nations that constitute the Malay *Archipelago*.

- The disgruntled taxpayer declared himself king of an uninhabited *archipelago* in the South Pacific, but his new country disappeared twice each day at high tide.

- The children lay on their backs in the field and gazed up with wonder at the shimmering *archipelago* of the Milky Way.

ARCHIVES (ahr KYVZE) *n* a place where historical documents or materials are stored; the documents or materials themselves
In careful usage, this word is always plural.
- The historical society's *archives* were a mess; boxes of valuable documents had simply been dumped on the floor, and none of the society's records were in chronological order.

- The curator was so protective of the university's *archives* that he hovered behind the researcher and moaned every time he turned a page in one of the ancient volumes.

Archive can also be a verb. To *archive* computer data is to transfer them (in careful usage, data is plural) onto disks or tapes and store them in a safe spot.

A person who *archives* things in *archives* is called an *archivist* (AHR kuh vust). Things that have to do with *archives* are said to be *archival* (ahr KYE vul). This word has other uses as well. In the world of photocopying, for example, a copy that doesn't deteriorate over time is said to be *archival*.
- A Xerox™ copy is *archival*; a copy made on heat-sensitive paper by a facsimile machine is not.

ARDENT (AHR dunt) *adj* passionate; enthusiastic
- Larry's *ardent* wooing finally got on Cynthia's nerves, and she told him to get lost.

- Blanche happily made cakes from morning to night. She was an *ardent* baker.

To be *ardent* is to have *ardor*.
- The young lovers were oblivious to everything except their *ardor* for each other.

ARDUOUS (AHR joo us) *adj* hard; difficult
- Climbing the mountain was *arduous*. We were so exhausted when we got to the top that we forgot to enjoy the view.
- The *arduous* car trip was made even more difficult by the fact that all four tires went flat, one after another.

ARID (AR id) *adj* very dry; lacking life, interest, or imagination
- When the loggers had finished, what had once been a lush forest was now an *arid* wasteland.
- The professor was not known for having a sense of humor. His philosophical writings were so *arid* that a reader could almost hear the pages crackle as he turned them.

ARISTOCRATIC (uh ris tuh KRAT ik) *adj* of noble birth; snobbish
- Prince Charles is *aristocratic*. He is a member of the British *aristocracy*.
- Polo, which Prince Charles enjoys, is often said to be an *aristocratic* sport because it is typically played by privileged people.

It is possible to be an *aristocrat* (uh RIS tuh krat) without being rich, although *aristocrats* tend to be quite wealthy. There is nothing you can do to become an *aristocrat*, short of being born into a family of them.

People who act as though they think they are better than everyone else are often said to be *aristocratic*. A person with an "*aristocratic* bearing" is a person who keeps his or her nose in the air and looks down on everyone else.

ARMAMENT (AHR muh munt) *n* implements of war; the process of arming for war
This word is often used in the plural: *armaments*. The word *arms* can be used to mean weapons. To *arm* a gun is to load it and ready it for fire.
- In the sorry history of the relationship between the two nations, argument led inexorably to *armament*.
- Sarah had dreams of being a distinguished professor of mathematics, but midway through graduate school she decided that she just didn't have the intellectual *armament*, so she became a waitress instead.

- The megalomaniacal leader spent so much on *armaments* that there was little left to spend on food, and his superbly equipped soldiers had to beg in order to eat.

ARMISTICE (AHR muh stus) *n* truce
- *Armistice* Day (the original name of Veterans Day) commemorated the end of the First World War.
- The warring commanders negotiated a brief *armistice* so that dead and wounded soldiers could be removed from the battlefield.

ARRAIGN (uh RAYN) *v* to bring to court to answer an indictment; to accuse
- The suspect was indicted on Monday, *arraigned* on Tuesday, tried on Wednesday, and sentenced on Thursday.
- The editorial in the student newspaper *arraigned* the administration for permitting the vandals to escape prosecution.

An act of *arraigning* is called an *arraignment*.
- At his *arraignment* in federal court, Harry entered a plea of not guilty to the charges that had been brought against him.

ARRANT (AR unt) *adj* utter; unmitigated; bad
This word is often followed by either nonsense or fool. *Arrant* nonsense is complete, total, no-doubt-about-it nonsense. An *arrant* fool is an absolute fool.

Arrant should not be confused with *errant* (ER unt), which means wandering or straying or in error. An *errant* fool is a fool who doesn't know where he's going.

ARREARS (uh RIRZ) *n* the state of being in debt; unpaid debts
- Amanda was several months in *arrears* with the rent on her apartment, and her landlord threatened to evict her.
- After Jason settled his *arrears* at the club, the committee voted to restore his membership.

ARSENAL (AHRS nul) *n* a collection of armaments; a facility for storing or producing armament; a supply of anything useful
- The nation's nuclear *arsenal* is large enough to destroy the world several times over.
- For obvious reasons, smoking was not permitted inside the *arsenal*.
- Jeremy had an *arsenal* of power tools that he used in staging remodeling assaults against his house.

QUICK QUIZ #18

Match each word in the first column with its definition in the second column. Check your answers in the back of the book.

1.	arcade	a.	where documents are stored
2.	archipelago	b.	utter
3.	archives	c.	implements of war
4.	arid	d.	unpaid debts
5.	armament	e.	accuse
6.	armistice	f.	group of islands
7.	arraign	g.	very dry
8.	arrant	h.	truce
9.	arrears	i.	arched passageway
10.	arsenal	j.	supply of something useful

ARTFUL (AHRT ful) *adj* crafty; wily; sly
- After dinner, the *artful* counselor told the campers that there was a madman loose in the woods, thus causing them to lie quietly in the tent.

The *Artful* Dodger is a sly con man in Charles Dickens's *Oliver Twist*.

Someone who is *artless*, on the other hand, is simple and honest. Young children are charmingly *artless*.

ARTICULATE (ahr TIK yuh layt) *v* to pronounce clearly; to express clearly
- Sissy had a lisp and could not *articulate* the s sound; she called herself Thithy.

- Saeed had no trouble *articulating* his needs; he had typed up a long list of toys that he wanted for Christmas, and he handed it to Santa Claus.

Articulate (ahr TIK yuh lut) can also be an adjective. An *articulate* person is one who is good at *articulating*.

ARTIFICE (AHRT uh fus) *n* a clever trick; cunning
- The Trojan Horse was an *artifice* designed to get the soldiers inside the walls.

- Mrs. Baker had to resort to *artifice* to get her children to take their medicine: She told them that it tasted like chocolate syrup.

Artifice and *artificial* are related words.

ARTISAN (AHRT uh zun) *n* a person skilled in a craft
- The little bowl—which the Andersons' dog knocked off the table and broke into a million pieces—had been meticulously handmade by a charming old *artisan* who had used a glazing technique passed down for generations.

ASCENDANCY (uh SEN dun see) *n* supremacy; domination
- Handheld gadgets have been in *ascendancy* for the past few years.
- The *ascendancy* of the new regime had been a great boon for the economy of the tiny tropical kingdom.

When something is in *ascendancy*, it is *ascendant*.

ASCERTAIN (as ur TAYN) *v* to determine with certainty; to find out definitely
- With a quick flick of his tongue, Wendell *ascertained* that the pie that had just landed on his face was indeed lemon meringue.
- The police tried to trace the phone call, but they were unable to *ascertain* the exact location of the caller.
- Larry believed his wife was seeing another man; the private detective *ascertained* that that was the case.

ASCETIC (uh SET ik) *adj* hermitlike; practicing self-denial
- The college student's apartment, which contained no furniture except a single tattered mattress, was uncomfortably *ascetic*.
- In his effort to save money, Roy led an *ascetic* existence: He never went out, he never ate anything but soup, and he never had any fun.

Ascetic can also be a noun. A person who leads an *ascetic* existence is an *ascetic*. An *ascetic* is someone who practices *asceticism*.

A similar-sounding word with a very different meaning is *aesthetic* (es THET ik). Don't be confused.

ASCRIBE (uh SKRYBE) *v* to credit to or assign; to attribute
- Mary was a bit of a nut; she *ascribed* powerful healing properties to the gravel in her driveway.
- When the scholar *ascribed* the unsigned limerick to Shakespeare, his colleagues did not believe him.

ASKANCE (uh SKANS) *adv* with suspicion or disapproval
- When Herman said that he had repaired the car by pouring apple cider into its gas tank, Jerry looked at him *askance*.

- The substitute teacher looked *askance* at her students when they insisted that it was the school's policy to award an A to any student who asked for one.

ASPERSION (uh SPUR zhun) *n* a slanderous or damning remark
To cast *aspersions* is to utter highly critical or derogatory remarks. To call someone a cold-blooded murderer is to cast an *aspersion* on that person's character.
- The local candidate had no legitimate criticisms to make of his opponent's record, so he resorted to *aspersions*.

ASSAIL (uh SAYL) *v* to attack vigorously
- With a series of bitter editorials, the newspaper *assailed* the group's efforts to provide free cosmetic surgery for wealthy people with double chins.
- We hid behind the big maple tree and *assailed* passing cars with salvos of snowballs.

An attacker is sometimes called an *assailant* (uh SAY lunt), especially by police officers on television shows.

ASSERT (uh SURT) *v* to claim strongly; to affirm
- The defendant continued to *assert* that he was innocent, despite the fact that the police had found a clear videotape of the crime, recovered a revolver with his fingerprints on it, and found all the stolen money in the trunk of his car.
- When Buzz *asserted* that the UFO was a hoax, the little green creature pulled out out a ray-gun and incinerated him.

To *assert* yourself is to express yourself boldly.
- Mildred always lost arguments because she was always too timid to *assert* herself.

ASSESS (uh SES) *v* to evaluate; to estimate; to appraise
- When seven thugs carrying baseball bats began walking across the street toward her car, Dolores quickly *assessed* the situation and drove away at about one hundred miles per hour.
- *Assessing* the damage caused by the storm was difficult because the storm had washed away all the roads, making it nearly impossible to enter the area.
- After *assessing* his chances in the election—only his parents would promise to vote for him—the candidate dropped out of the race.

To *reassess* is to rethink or reevaluate something.

ASSIDUOUS (uh SIJ oo us) *adj* hardworking; busy; quite diligent
- The workmen were *assiduous* in their effort to get nothing done; instead of working, they drank coffee all day long.
- Wendell was the only *assiduous* student in the entire math class; all the other students tried to copy their homework from him.

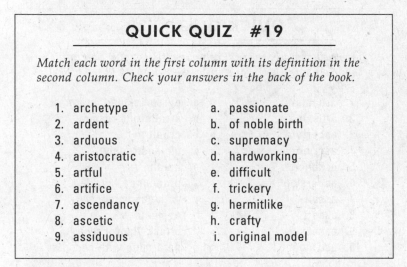

Match each word in the first column with its definition in the second column. Check your answers in the back of the book.

1. archetype	a. passionate
2. ardent	b. of noble birth
3. arduous	c. supremacy
4. aristocratic	d. hardworking
5. artful	e. difficult
6. artifice	f. trickery
7. ascendancy	g. hermitlike
8. ascetic	h. crafty
9. assiduous	i. original model

ASSIMILATE (uh SIM uh layt) *v* to take in; to absorb; to learn thoroughly
To *assimilate* an idea is to take it in as thoroughly as if you had eaten it. (Your body *assimilates* nutrients from the food you eat.) To *assimilate* knowledge is to absorb it, to let it soak in. People can be *assimilated*, too.
- Margaret didn't have any friends when she first went to the new school, but she was gradually *assimilated*—she became part of the new community. When she was chosen for the cheerleading squad, her *assimilation* was complete.

ASSUAGE (uh SWAYJ) *v* to soothe; to pacify; to ease the pain of; to relieve
- Beth was extremely angry, but I *assuaged* her by promising to leave the house and never return.
- The thunderstorm made the baby cry, but I *assuaged* her fears by singing her a lullaby.

ASTRINGENT (uh STRIN junt) *adj* harsh; severe; withering
- Edmund's *astringent* review enumerated so many dreadful flaws in the new book that the book quickly disappeared from the best-seller list.

- The coach's remarks to the team after losing the game were *astringent* but apparently effective: The team won the next three games in a row.

Astringent is related to *stringent*, which means strict. The noun is *astringency*.

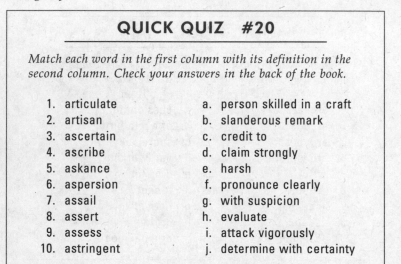

QUICK QUIZ #20

Match each word in the first column with its definition in the second column. Check your answers in the back of the book.

1. articulate		a.	person skilled in a craft
2. artisan		b.	slanderous remark
3. ascertain		c.	credit to
4. ascribe		d.	claim strongly
5. askance		e.	harsh
6. aspersion		f.	pronounce clearly
7. assail		g.	with suspicion
8. assert		h.	evaluate
9. assess		i.	attack vigorously
10. astringent		j.	determine with certainty

ASTUTE (uh STOOT) *adj* shrewd; keen in judgment
- Morris was an *astute* judge of character; he was very good at seeing what people were really like despite what they pretended to be.
- Yael, who notices everything important and many things that other people don't see, is an *astute* observer.

ASYLUM (uh SYE lum) *n* a mental hospital or similar institution; refuge; a place of safety
- After Dr. Jones incorrectly diagnosed her nail-biting as the symptom of a severe mental illness, Stella was confined in a lunatic *asylum* for thirty-seven years.
- "The woods are my *asylum*," Marjorie said. "I go there to escape the insanity of the world."
- The United States granted *asylum* to the political dissidents from a foreign country, thus permitting them to remain in the United States and not forcing them to return to their native country, where they certainly would have been imprisoned.

ATHEIST (AY thee ist) *n* one who does not believe in the existence of any god or divine being
- Hadley had always imagined a big religious wedding, but Emma, a life-long *atheist*, preferred a Vegas elopement.

The noun form is *atheism*. *Atheism* is often confused with *agnosticism*, but the two are not the same.

ATONE (uh TOHN) *v* to make amends
The verb *atone* is followed by the preposition "for." To *atone* for your sins is to do something that makes up for the fact that you committed them in the first place.
- The pianist *atoned* for his past failures by winning every award at the international competition.

The noun is *atonement*.
- The thief donated his ill-gotten cash to the orphanage as an *atonement* for stealing from the bank.

ATROPHY (A truh fee) *v* to wither away; to decline from disuse
- The weightlifter's right arm was much thinner and less bulgy than his left; it had *atrophied* severely during the six weeks it had been in a cast.
- The students' interest in algebra had *atrophied* to the point at which they could scarcely keep their eyes open in class.

The opposite of *atrophy* is *hypertrophy* (hye PUR truh fee).
- Weightlifting makes a muscle grow, or experience *hypertrophy*.

ATTEST (uh TEST) *v* to give proof of; to declare to be true or correct; to give testimony
- Helen's skillful guitar playing *attested* to the endless hours she had spent practicing.

To *attest* to something is to *testify* or bear witness.
- At the parole hearing, the police officer *attested* to Henry's eagerness to rob more banks, and the judge sent Henry back to prison for at least another year.

ATTRIBUTE (uh TRIB yoot) *v* to credit to or assign; to ascribe
- Sally attributed her success as a student to the fact that she always watched television while doing her homework. She said that watching *Scooby-Doo* made it easier to concentrate on her arithmetic. Sally's parents were not convinced by this *attribution* (a truh BYOO shun).
- The scientist, who was always making excuses, *attributed* the failure of his experiment to the fact that it had been raining that day in Phoenix, Arizona.

Attribute (A truh byoot) can also be a noun, in which case it means a characteristic or a distinctive feature.

- Great big arms and legs are among the *attributes* of many professional football players.

ATTRITION (uh TRISH un) *n* gradual wearing away, weakening, or loss; a natural or expected decrease in numbers or size

- Mr. Gregory did not have the heart to fire his workers even though his company was losing millions each year. He altruistically preferred to lose workers through *attrition* when they moved away, retired, or decided to change jobs.

AUDACITY (aw DAS uh tee) *n* boldness; reckless daring; impertinence

- Edgar's soaring leap off the top of the building was an act of great *audacity*.

- Ivan had the *audacity* to tell that nice old lady to shut up.

A person with *audacity* is said to be *audacious*.

- Bert made the *audacious* decision to climb Mt. Everest in bowling shoes.

AUGMENT (awg MENT) *v* to make bigger; to add to; to increase

- The army *augmented* its attack by sending in a few thousand more soldiers.

To *augment* a record collection is to add more records to it.

- Adding another example to this definition would *augment* it.

The act of *augmenting* is called *augmentation*.

AUGUR (AW gur) *v* to serve as an omen or be a sign; to predict or foretell

- The many mistakes made by the dancers during dress rehearsal did not *augur* well for their performance later that night.

- The eleven touchdowns and four field goals scored in the first quarter *augured* victory for the high school football team.

The act of *auguring* is called *augury* (AW guh ree).

- Elizabeth believed that most of the market consultants had no solid basis for their predictions and that financial *augury* as practiced by them was mere hocus-pocus.

AUGUST (aw GUST) *adj* inspiring admiration or awe

- The prince's funeral was dignified and *august*; the wagon with his coffin was drawn by a dozen black horses, and the road on which they walked was covered with rose petals.

- The queen's *august* manner and regal bearing caused everyone in the room to fall silent the moment she entered.

AUSPICES (AW spuh sez) *n* protection; support; sponsorship
You will find *auspice* in the dictionary, but this word is almost always used in the plural, and it is usually preceded by the words "under the."
- The fund-raising event was conducted under the *auspices* of the local volunteer organization, whose members sold tickets, parked cars, and cleaned up afterward.

AUSPICIOUS (aw SPISH us) *adj* favorable; promising; pointing to a good result
- A clear sky in the morning is an *auspicious* sign on the day of a picnic.
- The first quarter of the football game was not *auspicious;* the home team was outscored by thirty points.

AUSTERE (aw STEER) *adj* unadorned; stern; forbidding; without excess
- The Smiths' house was *austere;* there was no furniture in it, and there was nothing hanging on the walls.
- Quentin, with his *austere* personality, didn't make many friends. Most people were too intimidated by him to introduce themselves and say hello.

The noun *austerity* (aw STER uh tee) is generally used to mean roughly the same thing as poverty. To live in *austerity* is to live without comforts.

AUTOCRATIC (aw tuh KRAT ik) *adj* ruling with absolute authority; extremely bossy
- The ruthless dictator's *autocratic* reign ended when the rebels blew up his palace with plastic explosives.
- A two-year-old can be very *autocratic*—he wants what he wants when he wants it.
- No one at our office liked the *autocratic* manager. He always insisted on having his own way, and he never let anyone make a decision without consulting him.

An *autocrat* is an absolute ruler. *Autocracy* (aw TAHK ruh see), a system of government headed by an *autocrat,* is not democratic—the people don't get a say.

QUICK QUIZ #21

Match each word in the first column with its definition in the second column. Check your answers in the back of the book.

1.	assimilate	a.	shrewd
2.	assuage	b.	boldness
3.	astute	c.	favorable
4.	attrition	d.	make bigger
5.	audacity	e.	soothe
6.	augment	f.	extremely bossy
7.	auspicious	g.	absorb
8.	austere	h.	unadorned
9.	autocratic	i.	gradual wearing away

AUTONOMOUS (aw TAHN uh mus) *adj* acting independently
- The West Coast office of the law firm was quite *autonomous*; it never asked the East Coast office for permission before it did anything.

An *autonomous* nation is one that is independent—it governs itself. It is said to have *autonomy*.

To act *autonomously* is to act on your own authority. If something happens *autonomously*, it happens all by itself.

AUXILIARY (awg ZIL yuh ree) *adj* secondary; additional; giving assistance or aid
- When Sam's car broke down, he had to switch to an *auxiliary* power source; that is, he had to get out and push.

- The spouses of the firefighters established an *auxiliary* organization whose purpose was to raise money for the fire department.

AVAIL (uh VAYL) *v* to help; to be of use; to serve
- My preparation did not *avail* me on the test; the examination covered a chapter other than the one that I had studied. I could also say that my preparation *availed* me nothing, or that it was of no *avail*. In the second example, I would be using *avail* as a noun.

To be *availing* is to be helpful or of use. To be *unavailing* is to be unhelpful or of no use.
- The rescue workers tried to revive the drowning victim, but their efforts were *unavailing*, and the doctor pronounced him dead.

AVANT-GARDE (ah vahnt GAHRD) *n* the vanguard; members of a group, especially of a literary or artistic one, who are at the cutting edge of their field

- When his Off-off-off-off-Broadway play moved to Broadway, Harold was thrust against his will from the *avant-garde* to the establishment.

This word can also be an adjective.

- The *avant-garde* literary magazine was filled with empty pages to convey the futility of literary expression.

AVARICE (AV ur is) *n* greed; excessive love of riches

- The rich man's *avarice* was annoying to everyone who wanted to lay hands on some of his money.

Avarice is the opposite of generosity or philanthropy.

To be *avaricious* is to love wealth above all else and not to share it with other people.

AVERSION (uh VUR zhun) *n* a strong feeling of dislike

- Many children have a powerful *aversion* to vegetables. In fact, many of them believe that broccoli is poisonous.

- I knew that it would be in my best financial interest to make friends with the generous, gullible millionaire, but I could not overcome my initial *aversion* to his habit of sucking his thumb in public.

To have an *aversion* to something is to be *averse* (uh VURS) to it.

- I am *averse* to the idea of letting children sit in front of the television like zombies from morning to night.

Many people confuse *averse* with *adverse* (AD vurs), but they are not the same word. *Adverse* means unfavorable. A field-hockey game played on a muddy field in pouring rain would be a field-hockey game played under *adverse* conditions. The noun is *adversity*.

AVERT (uh VURT) *v* to turn away; to prevent

- Devi *averted* her eyes and pretended not to see Doug slip on the ice so he wouldn't be embarrassed.

- The company temporarily *averted* disaster by stealing several million dollars from the employees' pension fund.

AVID (AV id) *adj* eager; enthusiastic

- Eloise is an *avid* bridge player; she would rather play bridge than eat.

To be *avid* about playing bridge is to play bridge with *avidity* (uh VID uh tee).

QUICK QUIZ #22

Match each word in the first column with its definition in the second column. Check your answers in the back of the book.

1.	asylum	a.	refuge
2.	atone	b.	strong feeling of dislike
3.	atrophy	c.	give proof of
4.	attest	d.	turn away
5.	attribute	e.	make amends
6.	augur	f.	credit to
7.	august	g.	help
8.	auspices	h.	wither away
9.	auxiliary	i.	inspiring awe
10.	avail	j.	vanguard
11.	avant-garde	k.	secondary
12.	aversion	l.	eager
13.	avert	m.	protection
14.	avid	n.	serve as an omen

AVOW (uh VOW) *v* to claim; to declare boldly; to admit
- At the age of twenty-five, Louis finally *avowed* that he couldn't stand his mother's apple pie.

To *avow* something is to declare or admit something that most people are reluctant to declare or admit.
- Mr. Smith *avowed* on television that he had never paid any income tax. Shortly after this *avowal*, he received a lengthy letter from the Internal Revenue Service.

An *avowed* criminal is one who admits he is a criminal. To *disavow* is to deny or repudiate someone else's claim.
- The mayor *disavowed* the allegation that he had embezzled campaign contributions.

AVUNCULAR (uh VUNG kyuh lur) *adj* like an uncle, especially a nice uncle
What's an uncle like? Kind, helpful, generous, understanding, and so on, in an uncle-y sort of way. This is a fun word to use, although it's usually hard to find occasions to use it.
- Professor Zia often gave us *avuncular* advice; he took a real interest in our education and helped us with other problems that weren't related to multi-dimensional calculus.

AWRY (uh RYE) *adj* off course; twisted to one side
- The hunter's bullet went *awry*. Instead of hitting the bear, it hit his truck.
- When we couldn't find a restaurant, our dinner plans went *awry*.
- The old man's hat was *awry*; it had dipped in front of his left eye.

AXIOM (AK see um) *n* a self-evident rule or truth; a widely accepted saying
"Everything that is living dies" is an *axiom*.

An *axiom* in geometry is a rule that doesn't have to be proved because its truth is accepted as obvious, self-evident, or unprovable.

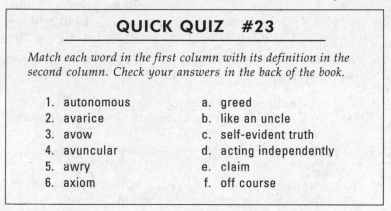

QUICK QUIZ #23

Match each word in the first column with its definition in the second column. Check your answers in the back of the book.

1.	autonomous	a.	greed
2.	avarice	b.	like an uncle
3.	avow	c.	self-evident truth
4.	avuncular	d.	acting independently
5.	awry	e.	claim
6.	axiom	f.	off course

B

BACCHANAL (BAK uh nuL) *n* a party animal; a drunken reveler; a drunken revelry or orgy
Bacchus (BAK us) was the Greek god of wine and fertility. To be a bacchanal is to act like *Bacchus*. People often use *bacchanal* as a word for the sort of social gathering that Bacchus would have enjoyed.
- The fraternity was shut down by the university after a three-day *bacchanal* that left a dozen students in the infirmary.

A good word for such a party would be *bacchanalia* (bak uh NAY lee uh).

BALEFUL (BAYL ful) *adj* menacing; threatening

Almost every time you see this word, it will be followed by the word "glance." A *baleful* glance is a look that could kill. Other things can be *baleful*, too.

- The students responded to the professor's feeble joke by sitting in *baleful* silence.

BALK (bawk) *v* to abruptly refuse (to do something); to stop short

- Susan had said she would be happy to help out with the charity event, but she *balked* at the idea of sitting on a flagpole for a month.

- Vernon *balked* when the instructor told him to do a belly-flop from the high diving board; he did not want to do it.

In baseball, a *balk* occurs when a pitcher begins the pitching motion, but then interrupts it to do something else, such as attempt to throw out a runner leading off from first base. In baseball, a *balk* is illegal.

BALLYHOO (BAL ee hoo) *n* sensational advertising or promotion; uproar

This is an informal word of unknown though distinctly American origin.

- Behind the *ballyhoo* created by the fifty-million-dollar promotional campaign, there was nothing but a crummy movie that no one really wanted to see.

- The public relations director could think of no legitimate case to make for her client, so she resorted to *ballyhoo*.

- The candidate tried to give his speech, but his words could not be heard above the *ballyhoo* on the convention floor.

BALM (bawm) *n* something that heals or soothes

- After Ted had suffered through the endless concert by the New York Philharmonic Orchestra, the sound of the Guns N' Roses album played at full volume on his iPod was a *balm* to his ears.

Balmy (BAW mee) weather is mild, pleasant, wonderful weather. In slang usage, a *balmy* person is someone who is eccentric or foolish.

BANAL (buh NAL) *adj* unoriginal; ordinary

- The dinner conversation was so *banal* that Amanda fell asleep in her dessert dish.

A *banal* statement is a boring, trite, and uncreative statement. It is a *banality*.

- What made Yu fall asleep was the *banality* of the dinner conversation.

This word can also be pronounced "BANE ul."

BANDY (BAN dee) *v* to toss back and forth; to exchange
- Isadora sat on the hillside all day, eating M&Ms and watching the wind *bandy* the leaves on the trees.
- The enemies *bandied* insults for a few minutes, then jumped on each other and began to fight.

BANE (bayn) *n* poison; torment; cause of harm
Bane means poison (wolfbane is a kind of poisonous plant), but the word is usually used figuratively. To say that someone is the *bane* of your existence is to say that that person poisons your enjoyment of life.
Baneful means harmful.

BANTER (BAN tur) *n* an exchange of good-humored or mildly teasing remarks
- The handsome young teacher fell into easy *banter* with his students, who were not much younger than he.
- Phoebe was interested in the news, but she hated the phony *banter* of the correspondents.

Banter can also be a verb. To *banter* with someone is to converse using *banter*.

BAROQUE (buh ROHK) *adj* extravagantly ornate; flamboyant in style
In the study of art, architecture, and music, *baroque*, or *Baroque*, refers to a highly exuberant and ornate style that flourished in Europe during the seventeenth and early eighteenth centuries. Except when used in this historical sense, the word now is almost always pejorative.
- Devin's writing style was a little *baroque* for my taste; he used so many fancy adjectives and adverbs that it was hard to tell what he was trying to say.

BARRAGE (buh RAHZH) *n* a concentrated outpouring of artillery fire, or of anything else
- To keep the enemy soldiers from advancing up the mountain, the commander directed a steady *barrage* against the slope just above them.
- Rhoda's new paintings—which consisted of bacon fat dribbled on the bottoms of old skillets—were met by a *barrage* of negative reviews.

Barrage can also be a verb.
- At the impromptu press conference, eager reporters *barraged* the Pentagon spokesman with questions.

BASTION (BAS chun) *n* stronghold; fortress; fortified place
- Mrs. Garnett's classroom is a *bastion* of banality; that is, it's a place where originality seldom, if ever, makes its way inside.
- The robbers terrorized the village for several weeks, and then escaped to their *bastion* high in the treacherous mountains.

BAUBLE (BAW bul) *n* a gaudy trinket; a small, inexpensive ornament
- The children thought they had discovered buried treasure, but the old chest turned out to contain nothing but cheap costume jewelry and other *baubles*.
- Sally tried to buy Harry's affection by showering him with *baubles*, but Harry held out for diamonds.

QUICK QUIZ #24

Match each word in the first column with its definition in the second column. Check your answers in the back of the book.

1.	bacchanal	a.	extravagantly ornate
2.	baleful	b.	menacing
3.	balk	c.	toss back and forth
4.	ballyhoo	d.	sensational advertising
5.	balm	e.	outpouring of artillery fire
6.	bandy	f.	exchange of teasing remarks
7.	banter	g.	party animal
8.	baroque	h.	gaudy trinket
9.	barrage	i.	abruptly refuse
10.	bauble	j.	something that heals

BEDLAM (BED lum) *n* noisy uproar and chaos; a place characterized by noisy uproar and chaos
In medieval London, there was a lunatic asylum called St. Mary of Bethlehem, popularly known as *Bedlam*. If a teacher says that there is *bedlam* in her classroom, she means that her students are acting like lunatics.
- A few seconds after Enron announced that it was going out of business, there was *bedlam* on the floor of the New York Stock Exchange.

BEGET (bih GET) *v* to give birth to; to create; to lead to; to cause
- Those who lie should be creative and have good memories, since one lie often *begets* another lie, which *begets* another.

BEGRUDGE (bi GRUJ) *v* to envy another's possession or enjoyment of something; to be reluctant to give, or to give grudgingly
- The famous author *begrudged* his daughter her success as a writer; he couldn't believe that she made the best-seller's list.

BEHEST (bi HEST) *n* command; order
- The president was impeached after the panel discovered that the illegal acts had been committed at his *behest*.
- At my *behest*, my son cleaned up his room.

BELABOR (bi LAY bur) *v* to go over repeatedly or to an absurd extent
- For more than an hour, the boring speaker *belabored* his point about the challenge of foreign competition.
- Mr. Irving spent the entire period *belaboring* the obvious; he made the same dumb observation over and over again.

BELEAGUER (bih LEE gur) *v* to surround; to besiege; to harass
- No one could leave the *beleaguered* city; the attacking army had closed off all the exits.
- Oscar felt *beleaguered* at work. He was months behind in his assignments, and he had little hope of catching up.
- The *beleaguered* executive seldom emerged from the his office as he struggled to deal with the growing scandal.

BELIE (bih LYF) *v* to give a false impression of; to contradict
- Melvin's smile *belied* the grief he was feeling; despite his happy expression he was terribly sad inside.
- The messy appearance of the banquet table *belied* the huge effort that had gone into setting it up.

A word that is sometimes confused with *belie* is *betray*. To rework the first example above: Melvin was smiling, but a small tear in one eye *betrayed* the grief he was feeling.

BELITTLE (bih LIT ul) *v* to make to seem little; to put someone down
- We worked hard to put out the fire, but the fire chief *belittled* our efforts by saying he wished he had brought some marsh-mallows.

The word *belittling* is the adjective form of *belittle*.
- The chairman's *belittling* comments made everyone feel small.

QUICK QUIZ #25

Match each word in the first column with its definition in the second column. Check your answers in the back of the book.

1.	banal	a.	make to seem little
2.	bane	b.	unoriginal
3.	bastion	c.	go over repeatedly
4.	beget	d.	stronghold
5.	belabor	e.	poison
6.	beleaguer	f.	give a false impression
7.	belie	g.	surround
8.	belittle	h.	give birth to

BELLIGERENT (buh LIJ ur unt) *adj* combative; quarrelsome; waging war
- Al was so *belligerent* that the party had the feel of a boxing match.

A bully is *belligerent*. To be *belligerent* is to push other people around, to be noisy and argumentative, to threaten other people, and generally to make a nuisance of oneself.

Opposing armies in a war are referred to as *belligerents*. Sometimes one *belligerent* in a conflict is more *belligerent* than the other.

BEMOAN (bi MOHN) *v* to mourn about; to lament
- West *bemoaned* the D he had received on his chemistry exam, but he didn't study any harder for future tests.
- Rather than *bemoaning* the cruelty and injustice of their fate, the hostages quietly dug a tunnel under the prison wall and escaped.

BEMUSED (bih MYOOZD) *adj* confused; bewildered
- The two stood *bemused* in the middle of the parking lot at Disneyland, trying to remember where they had parked their car.
- Ralph was *bemused* when all lights and appliances in his house began switching on and off for no apparent reason.

To *muse* is to think about or ponder things. To be *bemused*, then, is to have been thinking about things to the point of confusion.

People often use the word *bemused* when they really mean *amused*, but *bemusement* is no laughing matter. *Bemused* means confused.

BENEDICTION (ben uh DIK shun) *n* a blessing; an utterance of good wishes

In certain church services, a *benediction* is a particular kind of blessing. In secular usage, the word has a more general meaning.

- Jack and Jill were married without their parents' *benediction*; in fact, their parents had no idea that Jack and Jill had married.

The opposite of *benediction* is *malediction* (mal uh DIK shun), which means curse or slander.

- Despite the near-universal *malediction* of the critics, the sequel to *Gone with the Wind* became a huge bestseller.

BENEFACTOR (BEN uh fak tur) *n* one who provides help, especially in the form of a gift or donation

To give benefits is to be a *benefactor*. To receive benefits is to be a *beneficiary*. People very, very often confuse these two words. It would be to their benefit to keep them straight.

If your next-door neighbor rewrites his life insurance policy so that you will receive all his millions when he dies, then you become the *beneficiary* of the policy. If your neighbor dies, he is your *benefactor*.

A *malefactor* (MAL uh fak tur) is a person who does bad things.

- Batman and Robin made life hell for *malefactors* in Gotham City.

Remember Maleficent, Sleeping Beauty's evil nemesis? Her name is a variation of this idea.

BENEVOLENT (beh NEV uh lunt) *adj* generous; kind; doing good deeds

Giving money to the poor is a *benevolent* act. To be *benevolent* is to bestow benefits. The United Way, like any charity, is a *benevolent* organization.

Malevolent (muh LEV uh lunt) means evil, or wishing to do harm.

BENIGHTED (bi NYTE ud) *adj* ignorant; unenlightened

To be *benighted* is to be intellectually in the dark—to be lost in intellectual nighttime.

- Not one of Mr. Emerson's *benighted* students could say with certainty in which century the Second World War had occurred.

BENIGN (bih NYNE) *adj* gentle; not harmful; kind; mild

- Karla has a *benign* personality; she is not at all unpleasant to be with.
- The threat of revolution turned out to be *benign*; nothing much came of it.
- Charlie was worried that he had cancer, but the lump on his leg turned out to be *benign*.

The difference between a *benign* person and a *benevolent* (see separate entry) one is that the *benevolent* one is actively kind and generous, while the *benign* one is more passive. *Benevolence* is usually active generosity or kindness, while *benignancy* tends to mean simply not causing harm.

The opposite of a *benign* tumor is a *malignant* one. This is a tumor that can kill you. A *malignant* personality is one you wish a surgeon would remove. *Malignant* means nasty, evil, full of ill will. The word *malignant* also conveys a sense that evil is spreading, as with a cancer. An adjective that means the same thing is *malign*.

As a verb, *malign* has a different meaning. To *malign* someone is to say unfairly bad things about that person, to injure that person by telling evil lies about him or her. *Slander* and *malign* are synonyms.

QUICK QUIZ   #26

Match each word in the first column with its definition in the second column. Check your answers in the back of the book.

1. belligerent		a.	intending harm
2. bemused		b.	donor
3. benefactor		c.	not harmful
4. beneficiary		d.	deadly
5. benevolent		e.	confused
6. benign		f.	generous
7. malignant		g.	combative
8. malign		h.	injure with lies
9. malevolent		i.	one who receives benefits
10. malefactor		j.	evildoer

BEQUEST (bih KWEST) *n* something left to someone in a will
If your next-door neighbor leaves you all his millions in a will, the money is a *bequest* from him to you. It is not polite to request a *bequest*. Just keep smiling and hope for the best.

To leave something to someone in a will is to *bequeath* it. A *bequest* is something that has been *bequeathed*.

BEREAVED (buh REEVD) *adj* deprived or left desolate, especially through death
- The new widow was still *bereaved* when we saw her. Every time anyone mentioned her dead husband's name, she burst into tears.

- The children were *bereaved* by the death of their pet. Then they got a new pet.

Bereft (buh REFT) means the same thing as *bereaved*.

BESET (bih SET) *v* to harass; to surround
- The bereaved widow was *beset* by grief.

- Problems *beset* the expedition almost from the beginning, and the mountain climbers soon returned to their base camp.

- The little town was *beset* by robberies, but the police could do nothing.

BESTOW (bi STOH) *v* to present as a gift; to confer
This word is usually used with "on" or "upon."
- Mary Agnes had *bestowed* upon all her children a powerful hatred for vegetables of any kind.

- Life had *bestowed* much good fortune on Lester; in his mind, however, that did not make up for the fact that he had never won more than a few dollars in the lottery.

BILIOUS (BIL yus) *adj* ill-tempered; cranky
Bilious is derived from bile, a greenish-yellow liquid excreted by the liver. In the Middle Ages, bile was one of several "humors" that were thought to govern human emotion. In those days, anger and crankiness were held to be the result of an excess of bile. *Bilious* today can be used in a specific medical sense to refer to excretions of the liver or to particular medical conditions involving those same secretions, but it is usually used in a figurative sense that dates back to medieval beliefs about humors. To be *bilious* is to be in a grumpy, angry mood.
- The new dean's *bilious* remarks about members of the faculty quickly made her one of the least popular figures on campus.

- The speaker was taken aback by the *biliousness* of the audience; every question from the floor had had a nasty tone, and none of his jokes had gotten any laughs.

- Norbert's wardrobe was distinctly *bilious*; almost every garment he owned was either yellow or green.

BIVOUAC (BIV wak) *n* a temporary encampment, especially of soldiers.
- The tents and campfires of the soldiers' *bivouac* could be seen from the top of a nearby mountain, and the enemy commander launched a devastating barrage.

Bivouac can also be a verb, and it can be used to refer to people other than soldiers.

- Prevented by darkness from returning to their base camp, the climbers were forced to *bivouac* halfway up the sheer rock wall.

BLANCH (blanch) *v* to turn pale; to cause to turn pale

- Margaret *blanched* when Jacob told her their vacation house was haunted.

- The hot, dry summer had left the leaves on the trees looking *blanched* and dry.

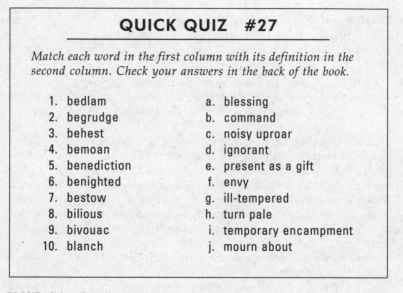

QUICK QUIZ #27

Match each word in the first column with its definition in the second column. Check your answers in the back of the book.

1.	bedlam	a.	blessing
2.	begrudge	b.	command
3.	behest	c.	noisy uproar
4.	bemoan	d.	ignorant
5.	benediction	e.	present as a gift
6.	benighted	f.	envy
7.	bestow	g.	ill-tempered
8.	bilious	h.	turn pale
9.	bivouac	i.	temporary encampment
10.	blanch	j.	mourn about

BLAND (bland) *adj* mild; tasteless; dull; unlively

- George ate only *bland* foods because he believed that anything with too much flavor in it would make him tense and excitable.

- After the censors had finished with it, the formerly X-rated movie was so *bland* and unexciting that no one went to see it.

- Harriet's new boyfriend was *bland* in the extreme, but that was probably a good thing since her previous one was a circus performer.

BLANDISHMENT (BLAND ish munt) *n* flattery
This word is often plural.

- Angela was impervious to the *blandishments* of her employees; no matter how much they flattered her, she refused to give them raises.

BLASPHEMY (BLAS fuh mee) *n* irreverence; an insult to something held sacred; profanity

In the strictest sense, to commit *blasphemy* is to say nasty, insulting things about God. The word is used more broadly, though, to cover a wide range of nasty, insulting comments.

To *blaspheme* (blas FEEM) is to use swear words or say deeply irreverent things. A person who says such things is *blasphemous*.

BLATANT (BLAYT unt) *adj* unpleasantly or offensively noisy; glaring

- David was *blatantly* critical of our efforts; that is, he was noisy and obnoxious in making his criticisms.

Blatant is often confused with *flagrant*, since both words mean glaring. *Blatant* indicates that something was not concealed very well, whereas *flagrant* indicates that something was intentional. A *blatant* act is usually also a *flagrant* one, but a *flagrant* act isn't necessarily *blatant*. You might want to refer to the listing for *flagrant*.

QUICK QUIZ #28

Match each word in the first column with its definition in the second column. Check your answers in the back of the book.

1. bequest
2. bequeath
3. bereaved
4. beset
5. blasphemy
6. blatant

a. left desolate
b. something left in a will
c. harass
d. offensively noisy
e. leaving in a will
f. irreverence

BLIGHT (blyte) *n* a disease in plants; anything that injures or destroys

- An early frost proved a *blight* to the citrus crops last year, so we had no orange juice for breakfast.

BLISS (blis) *n* perfect contentment; extreme joy

- After spending his vacation in a crowded hotel with throngs of noisy conventioneers, Peter found that returning to work was *bliss*.

- Paul and Mary naively expected that every moment of their married life would be *bliss*; rapidly, however, they discovered that they were no different from anyone else.

Anything that promotes feelings of *bliss* can be said to be *blissful*. A *blissful* vacation would be one that made you feel serenely and supremely content.

BLITHE (blythe) *adj* carefree; cheerful
- The *blithe* birds in the garden were making so much noise that Jamilla began to think about the shotgun in the attic.
- The children were playing *blithely* next to the hazardous-waste dump. While they played, they were *blithely* unaware that they were doing something dangerous.

To be *blithely* ignorant is to be happily unaware.

BLUSTER (BLUS tur) *v* to roar; to be loud; to be tumultuous
- The cold winter wind *blustered* all day long, rattling the windows and chilling everyone to the bone.

A day during which the wind *blusters* would be a *blustery* (BLUS tur ee) day.
- The golfers happily blamed all their bad shots on the *blustery* weather.

Bluster can also be a noun.
- Sadie was so used to her mother's angry shouting that she was able to tune out the *bluster* and get along with her work.

BOMBAST (BAHM bast) *n* pompous or pretentious speech or writing
- If you stripped away the *bombast* from the candidate's campaign speeches, you would find nothing but misconceptions and lies.
- The magazine writer resorted to *bombast* whenever his deadline was looming; thoughtful opinions required time and reflection, but he could become pompous almost as rapidly as he could type.

The adjective is *bombastic* (bahm BAS tik).

BON VIVANT (BON vee VAHN) *n* a person who enjoys good food, good drink, and luxurious living
This is a French expression.
- Jacques played the *bon vivant* when he was with his friends, but when he was alone he was a drudge and a workaholic.

BONA FIDE (BOH nuh FYDE) *adj* sincere; done or made in good faith; authentic; genuine
- The signature on the painting appeared to be *bona fide*; it really did seem to be Van Gogh's.

BOON (boon) *n* a blessing; a benefit
- Construction of the nuclear-waste incinerator was a *boon* for the impoverished town; the fees the town earned enabled it to repair its schools and rebuild its roads.
- The company car that came with Sam's new job turned out not to be the *boon* it had first appeared to be; Sam quickly realized that he was expected to spend almost all his time in it, driving from one appointment to another.

BOOR (boor) *n* a rude or churlish person
A *boor* is not necessarily a *bore*. Don't confuse these two words.
- The *boor* at the next table kept climbing up on his chair and shouting at the waitress.

To be a *boor* is to be *boorish* (BOOR ish).
- "Don't be *boorish*," Sue admonished Charles at the prom after he had insulted the chaperone and eaten his dinner with his fingers.

BOOTY (BOO tee) *n* goods taken from an enemy in war; plunder; stolen or confiscated goods
- The principal's desk was filled with *booty*, including squirt guns, chewing gum, slingshots, and candy.
- The gear of the returning soldiers was so loaded down with *booty* that the commanding officer had to issue weight restrictions.

QUICK QUIZ   #29

Match each word in the first column with its definition in the second column. Check your answers in the back of the book.

1.	bland	a.	pompous speech
2.	blandishment	b.	luxurious liver
3.	bliss	c.	mild
4.	bluster	d.	plunder
5.	bombast	e.	flattery
6.	bon vivant	f.	rude person
7.	bona fide	g.	perfect contentment
8.	boon	h.	sincere
9.	boor	i.	roar
10.	booty	j.	blessing

BOTCH (bahch) *v* to bungle; to ruin through poor or clumsy effort
- Melvin *botched* his science project by pouring soda into his ant farm.

- The carpenter had *botched* his repair of our old porch, and the whole thing came crashing down when Aunt Sylvia stepped on it.

BOURGEOIS (boor ZHWAH) *adj* middle class, usually in a pejorative sense; boringly conventional

The original *bourgeoisie* (boor zhwaw ZEE) were simply people who lived in cities, an innovation at the time. They weren't farmers and they weren't nobles. They were members of a new class—the middle class. Now the word is used mostly in making fun of or sneering at people who seem to think about nothing but their possessions and other comforts and about conforming with other people who share those concerns.

A hip young city dweller might reject life in the suburbs as being too *bourgeois*. A person whose dream is to have a swimming pool in his backyard might be called *bourgeois* by someone who thinks there are more important things in life. Golf is often referred to as a *bourgeois* sport.

BOVINE (BOH vyne) *adj* cow related; cowlike
- Cows are *bovine*, obviously. Eating grass is a *bovine* concern.

There are a number of similar words based on other animals:
    canine (KAY nyne): dogs
    equine (EE kwyne): horses
    feline (FEE lyne): cats
    piscine (PYE seen): fish
    porcine (POR syne): pigs
    ursine (UR syne): bears

BRACING (BRAY sing) *adj* invigorating
- Before breakfast every morning, Lulu enjoyed a *bracing* swim in the Arctic Ocean.

- Andrew found the intellectual vigor of his students to be positively *bracing*.

- A *bracing* wind was blowing across the bay, causing Sally's sailboat to move so swiftly that she had difficulty controlling it.

BRANDISH (BRAN dish) *v* to wave or display threateningly
- *Brandishing* a knife, the robber told the frightened storekeeper to hand over all the money in the cash register.

- I returned to the garage *brandishing* a flyswatter, but the swarming insects were undeterred, and they continued to go about their business.

BRAVADO (bruh VAH doh) *n* a false show or ostentatious show of bravery or defiance
- The commander's speech was the product not of bravery but of *bravado*; as soon as the soldiers left the room, he collapsed in tears.
- With almost unbelievable *bravado*, the defendant stood before the judge and told her that he had no idea how his fingerprints had gotten on the murder weapon.

BRAWN (brawn) *n* big muscles; great strength
- All the other boys in the class thought it extremely unfair that Sean had both brains and *brawn*.
- The old engine didn't have the *brawn* to propel the tractor up the side of the steep hill.

To be *brawny* (BRAW nee) is to be muscular.
- The members of the football team were so *brawny* that each one needed two seats on the airplane in order to sit comfortably.

BRAZEN (BRAY zun) *adj* impudent; bold
Brazen comes from a word meaning brass. To be *brazen* is to be as bold as brass. (*Brazen* can also be used to refer to things that really are made of brass, or that have characteristics similar to those of brass. For example, the sound of a trumpet might be said to be *brazen*.)
- The students' *brazen* response to their teacher's request was to stand up and walk out of the classroom.
- The infantry made a *brazen* charge into the heart of the enemy position.

BREACH (breech) *n* a violation; a gap or break
Breach is closely related to break, a word with which it shares much meaning.
- Most of the senators weren't particularly bothered by the fact that one of their colleagues had been taking bribes, but they viewed his getting caught as an indefensible *breach* of acceptable behavior.
- At first, the water trickled slowly through the *breach* in the dam, but it gradually gathered force, and soon both the dam and the town below it had been washed away.

BREVITY (BREV i tee) *n* briefness
- The audience was deeply grateful for the *brevity* of the after-dinner speaker's remarks.
- The reader of this book may be grateful for the *brevity* of this example.

Brevity is related to the word *abbreviate*.

BRINK (bringk) *n* edge
- The mother became very nervous when she saw her toddler dancing along the *brink* of the cliff.
- The sputtering engine sent the airliner on a steep downward course that brought it to the *brink* of disaster; then the pilot woke up and pulled back on the throttle.

Brinkmanship (often also *brinksmanship*) is a political term describing an effort by one country or official to gain an advantage over another by appearing willing to push a dangerous situation to the *brink*, such as by resorting to nuclear weapons. To engage in *brinkmanship* is to appear willing to risk the destruction of the world rather than to lose a particular conflict.

BRISTLE (BRIS ul) *v* to stiffen with anger; to act in a way suggestive of an animal whose hair is standing on end; to appear in some way similar to hair standing on end
Bristles are short, stiff hairs. A *bristle* brush is a brush made out of short, stiff hairs from the backs of pigs or other animals. When a pig *bristles*, it makes the short, stiff hairs on its back stand up. When a person *bristles*, he or she acts in a way that is reminiscent of a *bristling* pig.
- Arnie is the sensitive type; he *bristled* when I told him his story-telling was merely okay.
- The lightning bolt was so close it made my hair *bristle*.
- The captured vessel *bristled* with antennae, strongly suggesting that it was a spy ship, as the government contended, and not a fishing boat, as the government continued to claim.

BROACH (brohch) *v* to open up a subject for discussion, often a delicate subject
- Henrietta was proud of her new dress, so no one knew how to *broach* the subject with her of how silly grandmothers look in leather.

BROMIDE (BROH myde) *n* a dull, obvious, overfamiliar saying; a cliché
Bromide also refers to certain compounds containing the element
bromine (BROH meen). Potassium *bromide* is a substance that was
once used as a sedative. A *bromide* is a statement that is so boring
and obvious that it threatens to sedate the listener.

- Mr. Patel seemed to speak exclusively in *bromides*. When you
  hand him his change, he says, "A penny saved is a penny
  earned." When he asks for help, he says, "Many hands make
  light work."

BROUHAHA (BROO hah hah) *n* uproar; hubbub

- The *brouhaha* arising from the party downstairs kept the children awake for hours.

BRUSQUE (brusk) *adj* abrupt in manner; blunt

- The critic's review of the new play was short and *brusque*; he
  wrote, "It stinks."
- Samantha felt that the waiter had been *brusque* when he told
  her to put on shoes before entering the restaurant, so she spoke
  to the manager and had the waiter fired.

BUCOLIC (byoo KAHL ik) *adj* charmingly rural; rustic; countrylike

- The changing of the autumn leaves, old stone walls, distant
  views, and horses grazing in green meadows are examples of
  bucolic splendor.
- The *bucolic* scene didn't do much for the city child, who preferred screaming fire engines and honking horns to the sounds
  of a babbling brook.

BUFFOON (buh FOON) *n* a joker, especially one who is coarse or acts
like an ass

- Maria seems to go out only with *buffoons*; her last boyfriend
  entertained us at Thanksgiving by standing on the table and
  reciting dirty limericks.
- Orville put on women's clothing and pretended to be Pippi
  Longstocking; he figured that someone at the wedding reception had to play the *buffoon* and that he might as well be the
  one.

BULWARK (BUL wurk) *n* a wall used as a defensive fortification; anything
used as the main defense against anything else

- The civilians used bulldozers to create an earthen *bulwark*
  around their town, but the attacking soldiers used larger bulldozers to destroy it.

- As a *bulwark* against Billy, I turned off my phone, but he foiled me by coming over to my house and talking to me in person.
- The Bill of Rights is the *bulwark* of American liberty.

The *bulwarks* of a ship are the parts of the ship's sides that extend above the main deck.

BUREAUCRACY (byoo RAHK ruh see) *n* a system of government administration consisting of numerous bureaus or offices, especially one run according to inflexible and inefficient rules; any large administrative system characterized by inefficiency, lots of rules, and red tape
- The Department of Motor Vehicles is a *bureaucracy*. The forms you have to fill out all request unnecessary information. After you finally get everything all filled out and handed in, you don't hear another word from the department for many months.

The people who work in a *bureaucracy* are called *bureaucrats*. These people and the inefficient procedures they follow might be called *bureaucratic*. Administrative systems outside the government can be *bureaucratic,* too. A high school principal who requires teachers and students to fill out forms for everything might be called *bureaucratic*.

BURGEON (BUR jun) *v* to expand; to flourish
- The *burgeoning* weeds in our yard soon overwhelmed the grass.

BURLESQUE (bur LESK) *n* a ludicrous, mocking, lewd imitation
- Vaudeville actors frequently performed *burlesque* works on the stage.

Burlesque, parody, lampoon, and *caricature* share similar meanings.

BYZANTINE (BIZ un teen) *adj* extremely intricate or complicated in structure; having to do with the Byzantine Empire.
The *Byzantine* Empire consisted of remnants of the Roman Empire bordering on the Mediterranean Sea, and it lasted from roughly the middle of the fifth century until the middle of the fifteenth century. Its principal city was Constantinople, which is now Istanbul, Turkey. *Byzantine* architecture was (and is) characterized by domes, spires, minarets, round arches, and elaborate mosaics. When used in this precise historical sense, the word is always capitalized; when used in its figurative meaning, it often is not.
- Angela couldn't follow the book's *byzantine* plot, so she read the first and last chapters and tried to guess what happened in the middle parts.

- The emperor's bodyguards uncovered a *byzantine* scheme in which his minister of defense had planned to kill him by infusing his cologne with poison.

This word is pronounced and mispronounced in many ways. Our pronunciation is the preferred one.

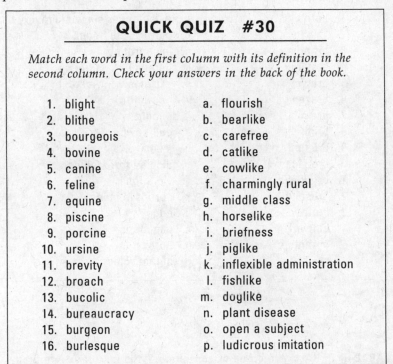

QUICK QUIZ   #30

Match each word in the first column with its definition in the second column. Check your answers in the back of the book.

1.	blight	a.	flourish
2.	blithe	b.	bearlike
3.	bourgeois	c.	carefree
4.	bovine	d.	catlike
5.	canine	e.	cowlike
6.	feline	f.	charmingly rural
7.	equine	g.	middle class
8.	piscine	h.	horselike
9.	porcine	i.	briefness
10.	ursine	j.	piglike
11.	brevity	k.	inflexible administration
12.	broach	l.	fishlike
13.	bucolic	m.	doglike
14.	bureaucracy	n.	plant disease
15.	burgeon	o.	open a subject
16.	burlesque	p.	ludicrous imitation

C

CABAL (kuh BAL) *n* a group of conspirators; the acts of such a group; a clique

- The despised new dictator had been a part of the *cabal* that for years had plotted the overthrow of the kindly old king.

- The high-level *cabal* against the company's president accelerated rapidly and resulted in her ouster.

- Winifred wanted to be popular and go to parties on weekends, but she was never able to penetrate the *cabal* that controlled the limited supply of fun at her high school.

CACHE (kash) *n* a hiding place; the things hidden in a secret place
This word comes from a French word meaning to hide.

- The taxi driver kept his cash in a *cache* behind his tape-player. Unfortunately, a robber who had merely intended to steal the tape-player discovered the *cache* and also stole the cash.

- The bandits had a *cache* of weapons near their hideout in the mountains.

CACOPHONY (kuh KAHF uh nee) *n* harsh-sounding mixture of words, voices, or sounds
- The parade's two marching bands played simultaneously; the resulting *cacophony* drove many spectators to tears.

A *cacophony* isn't just a lot of noise—it's a lot of noise that doesn't sound good together. A steam whistle blowing isn't a *cacophony*. But a high school orchestra that had never rehearsed together might very well produce a *cacophony*. The roar of engines, horns, and sirens arising from a busy city street would be a *cacophony*. A lot of people all shouting at once would produce a *cacophony*.

Euphony is the opposite of *cacophony*. *Euphony* is pleasing sound.

CADENCE (KAYD uns) *n* rhythm; the rise and fall of sounds
- We wished the tone of Irwin's words would have a more pleasing *cadence*, but he spoke in a dull monotone.

CAJOLE (kuh JOHL) *v* to persuade someone to do something he or she doesn't want to do
- I didn't want to give the speech, but Enrique *cajoled* me into doing it by telling me what a good speaker I am. As it turned out, he simply hadn't been able to find anyone else.

CALAMITY (kuh LAM uh tee) *n* a disaster
- Trouble always seemed to follow Martha Jane Canary. That's why she was known as *Calamity* Jane.
- During the first few months we lived in our house, we suffered one *calamity* after another: First the furnace exploded; then the washing machine stopped working; then the roof began to leak.
- Misfortune quickly turned into *calamity* when the burning car set off the hydrogen bomb.

CALLOUS (KAL us) *adj* insensitive; emotionally hardened
- The *callous* biology teacher gave a B to the whining student, even though he swore that such a low grade would keep him out of medical school.
- Living in Arizona for ten years has made Sally so *callous* that she isn't even moved by the most beautiful sunset over the Grand Canyon.

A *callus* (KAL us) is a patch of thickened or roughened skin. A *callous* person is someone who has a metaphorical *callus* covering his or her emotions.

CALLOW (KAL oh) *adj* immature
- The patient was alarmed by the *callowness* of the medical staff. The doctors looked too young to have graduated from high school, much less from medical school.

To be *callow* is to be youthfully naive, inexperienced, and unsophisticated.

CALUMNY (KAL um nee) *n* slander; a maliciously false statement
- The candidate resorted to *calumny* whenever he couldn't think of anything merely mean to say about his opponent.
- When Mr. McCoy could no longer withstand the *calumnies* of his accusers, he told them the truth: The thief was actually his brother.

To utter *calumnies* about someone is to *calumniate* (kuh LUM nee ayt) that person.
- The newspaper editorial writer had already *calumniated* everyone in town, so he started again from the top of the list.

CANDOR (KAN dur) *n* truthfulness; sincere honesty
- My best friend exhibited *candor* when he told me that for many years now he has believed me to be a jerk.
- Teddy appreciated Ross's *candor;* Teddy was glad to know that Ross thought Teddy's sideburns looked stupid.

To show *candor* is to be *candid*. What is *candid* about *candid* photos? The photos are *candid* because they are truthful in showing what people do. *Candid* does *not* mean concealed or hidden, even though the camera on the old television show *Candid Camera* was concealed. To be *candid* is to speak frankly.

CANON (KAN un) *n* a rule or law, especially a religious one; a body of rules or laws; an official set of holy books; an authoritative list; the set of works by an author that are accepted as authentic
- Timothy tried to live in accordance with the *canons* of fairness, honesty, and responsibility that his parents laid down for their children.
- Brigadoon is part of Shakespeare's *canon*.

Canon also has some specific meanings and usages within the Roman Catholic church.

CANT (kant) *n* insincere or hypocritical speech
- The political candidate resorted to *cant* whenever he was asked about any of the substantial issues of the campaign.

CANVASS (KAN vus) *v* to seek votes or opinions; to conduct a survey
This is not the same word as canvas, the rough cotton cloth that circus tents, among other things, used to be made of.

- In the last few days before the election, the campaign volunteers spread out to *canvass* in key districts.

- The polling organization *canvassed* consumers to find out which brand of drain cleaner made them feel most optimistic about the global economy.

Canvass can also be a noun. A *canvass* is an act of *canvassing*.

- After an exhaustive *canvass* of consumers, the polling organization discovered that Sludge-X made consumers feel most optimistic about the global economy.

CAPACIOUS (kuh PAY shus) *adj* spacious; roomy; commodious
Something that is *capacious* has a large capacity.

- Holly had a *capacious* mouth into which she poured the contents of a family-sized box of Milk Duds™.

- The Stones' house was *capacious* but not particularly gracious; it felt and looked like the inside of a barn.

- Arnold's memory for insults was *capacious*; he could remember every nasty thing that anyone had ever said about him.

CAPITAL (KAP ut ul) *n* the town or city that is the seat of government; money, equipment, and property owned by a business; wealth used in creating more wealth

- Austin is the official *capital* of Texas; it is also the self-proclaimed live music *capital* of the world.

- Ivan inherited his family's business, but then, through foolish management, exhausted its *capital* and drove it into bankruptcy.

- Orson wanted to buy a professional football team, but he was unable to come up with the necessary *capital*; in fact, he was able to raise only $400.

- The Sterns didn't have much money, so they invested human *capital*; they built it themselves.

Don't confuse this word with **capitol**, which is the building legislatures meet in.

CAPITALISM (KAP uh tuh liz um) *n* an economic system in which businesses are owned by private citizens (not by the government) and in which the resulting products and services are sold with relatively little government control
The American economy is *capitalist*. If you wanted to start a company to sell signed photographs of yourself, you could. You, and

not the government, would decide how much you would charge for the pictures. Your success or failure would depend on how many people decided to buy your pictures.

QUICK QUIZ #32

Match each word in the first column with its definition in the second column. Check your answers in the back of the book.

1.	cabal	a.	slander
2.	cache	b.	rule or law
3.	calamity	c.	hiding place
4.	callous	d.	seek votes or opinions
5.	calumny	e.	seat of government
6.	canon	f.	hypocritical speech
7.	cant	g.	roomy
8.	canvass	h.	group of conspirators
9.	capacious	i.	insensitive
10.	capital	j.	disaster

CAPITULATE (kuh PICH uh layt) *v* to surrender; to give up or give in
- On the twentieth day of the strike, the workers *capitulated* and went back to work without a new contract.
- So few students paid attention to Mr. Hernandez that he had to *recapitulate* his major points at the end of the class.

To *recapitulate* is not to *capitulate* again. To *recapitulate* is to summarize.

CAPRICIOUS (kuh PRISH us) *adj* unpredictable; likely to change at any moment
- Arjun was *capricious*. One minute he said his favorite car was a Volkswagen; the next minute he said it was a Toyota.
- The weather is often said to be *capricious*. One minute it's snowing; the next minute it's 120 degrees in the shade.

A *caprice* (kuh PREES) is a whim.
- Kendra attempted a quadruple somersault off the ten-meter diving board as a *caprice*. It was a painful *caprice*.

CAPTIVATE (KAP tuh vayt) *v* to fascinate; to enchant; to enrapture
- The magician *captivated* the children by making their parents disappear in a big ball of blue smoke.

SAT POWER VOCAB

- Frank wasn't *captivating* when Melinda came to call on him; he was wearing Ninja Turtle pajamas, and he hadn't brushed his teeth.

CARCINOGENIC (kahr sin uh JEN ik) *adj* causing cancer
- The tobacco industry has long denied that cigarette smoke is *carcinogenic*.

An agent that causes cancer is a *carcinogen* (kahr SIN uh jun).
- The water flowing out of the chemical factory's waste pipe was black, bubbling, and undoubtedly loaded with *carcinogens*.

CARDINAL (KAHRD nul) *adj* most important; chief
- The *cardinal* rule at our school is simple: No chewing gum in the building.
- The "*cardinal* virtues" are said to be fortitude, justice, prudence, and temperance.

CAREEN (kuh REEN) *v* to swerve; to move rapidly without control; to lean to one side
- The drunk driver's automobile bounced off several lampposts as it *careened* along the waterfront, eventually running off the end of the pier and plunging into the harbor.
- The ship *careened* heavily in the storm, causing all of the cargo in its hold to shift to one side.

CARICATURE (KAR uh kuh chur) *n* a portrait or description that is purposely distorted or exaggerated, often to prove some point about its subject
- Khoa sat for a *caricature* at the end of the marathon, but wasn't pleased with the result: The portrait exaggerated his already dominant acne.

Editorial cartoonists often draw *caricatures*. Big noses, enormous glasses, floppy ears, and other distortions are common in such drawings. A politician who has been convicted of bribery might be depicted in a prison uniform or with a ball and chain around his ankle. If the politician has big ears to begin with, the ears might be drawn vastly bigger.

A *caricature* uses exaggeration to bring out the hidden character of its subject.

The word can also be used as a verb. To *caricature* someone is to create such a distorted portrait.

CARTOGRAPHY (kahr TAHG ruh fee) *n* the art of making maps and charts
- The United States Department of State employs a large *cartography* department because the boundaries of the world's countries are constantly changing and maps must constantly be updated and redrawn.

A person who makes maps or charts is called a *cartographer* (kahr TAHG ruh fur).

CASCADE (kas KAYD) *n* a waterfall; anything resembling a waterfall
- Water from the burst main created a *cascade* that flowed over the embankment and into our living room.
- When the young star of the movie stubbed his toe while putting on his ostrich-skin cowboy boots, his fans responded with a *cascade* of get-well cards.

Cascade can also be a verb.
- Silver dollars *cascaded* from the slot machine when Christine said the magic word that she had learned in *SAT Power Vocab*.

CASTIGATE (KAS tuh gayt) *v* to criticize severely; to chastise
- Jose's mother-in-law *castigated* him for forgetting to pick her up at the airport.

CATACLYSM (KAT uh kliz um) *n* a violent upheaval; an earthquake; a horrible flood
- The government's attempts at economic reform initiated a *cataclysm* that left the country's structure in ruins.
- The earthquake's epicenter was in midtown Manhattan, but the effects of the *cataclysm* could be felt as far away as Chicago.
- Suddenly, the sky opened, and the clouds unleashed a *cataclysm* that nearly washed away the town.

The adjective form of this word is *cataclysmic* (kat a KLIZ mik).
- Early on Tuesday morning, fans were still celebrating the team's *cataclysmic* 105–7 defeat of the Tigers.

CATALYST (KAT uh list) *n* in chemistry, something that changes the rate of a chemical reaction without itself being changed; anyone or anything that makes something happen without being directly involved in it
- When the mad scientist dropped a few grains of the *catalyst* into his test tube, the bubbling liquid began to boil furiously.

This word is often used outside the laboratory as well. The launching of *Sputnik* by the Russians provided the *catalyst* for the creation of the modern American space program.

- The tragic hijacking provided the *catalyst* for Congress's new anti-terrorist legislation.

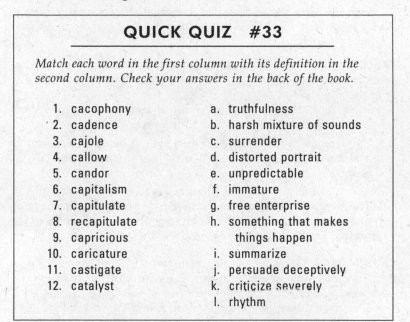

QUICK QUIZ   #33

Match each word in the first column with its definition in the second column. Check your answers in the back of the book.

1. cacophony
2. cadence
3. cajole
4. callow
5. candor
6. capitalism
7. capitulate
8. recapitulate
9. capricious
10. caricature
11. castigate
12. catalyst

a. truthfulness
b. harsh mixture of sounds
c. surrender
d. distorted portrait
e. unpredictable
f. immature
g. free enterprise
h. something that makes things happen
i. summarize
j. persuade deceptively
k. criticize severely
l. rhythm

CATEGORICAL (kat uh GOR uh kul) *adj* unconditional; absolute
A *categorical* denial is one without exceptions—it covers every *category*.

- Crooked politicians often make *categorical* denials of various charges against them. Then they go to jail.

- I *categorically* refuse to do anything whatsoever at any time, in any place, with anyone.

CATHARSIS (kuh THAR sis) *n* purification that brings emotional relief or renewal
To someone with psychological problems, talking to a psychiatrist can lead to a *catharsis*. A *catharsis* is a sometimes traumatic event after which one feels better.

A *catharsis* is *cathartic*. Some people find emotional movies *cathartic*—watching one often allows them to release buried feelings. *Cathartic* can also be a noun.

CATHOLIC (KATH lik) *adj* universal; embracing everything
- Da Vinci was a *catholic* genius who excelled at everything he did.

Parochial means narrow-minded, so *parochial* and *catholic* are almost opposites.

   Catholic with a small *c* means universal. *Catholic* with a large C means *Roman Catholic* or pertaining to an ancient, undivided Christian church.

CAUCUS (KAW kus) *n* a meeting of the members of a political party or political faction; a political group whose members have common interests or goals
- In some states, delegates to political conventions are elected; in other states, they are selected in *caucuses*.

- The women in the state legislature joined together in an informal *caucus* in order to increase their influence on equal pay issues.

This word can also be a verb. To *caucus* is to hold a *caucus*.
- The members of the *caucus caucused* for several days in the hope of agreeing on a new method for selecting new members of the *caucus*. They couldn't agree, so they disbanded.

CAUSTIC (KAW stik) *adj* like acid; corrosive
Paint remover is a *caustic* substance; if you spill it on your skin, your skin will burn.
- The *caustic* detergent ate right through Henry's laundry.

- The teacher's *caustic* criticism of Sally's term paper left her in tears.

Caustic can be used figuratively as well. A *caustic* comment is one that is so nasty or insulting that it seems to sting or burn the person to whom it is directed.

CAVALIER (kav uh LIR) *adj* arrogant; haughty; carefree; casual
- The vain actor was so *cavalier* that he either didn't notice or didn't care that he had broken Loretta's heart.

- Mrs. Perkins felt that her daughter and son-in-law were somewhat *cavalier* about their housework; she objected, for example, to the fact that they seldom did any laundry, preferring to root around in the laundry hamper for something clean enough to wear again.

CAVIL (KAV ul) *v* to quibble; to raise trivial objections
- Writing the organization's new by-laws would have been much simpler if it hadn't been the chairman's habit to *cavil* about every point raised.

- The lawyer believed that he was raising important objections, but the judge felt that he was merely *caviling*, and she told him to shut up.

Cavil can also be a noun.
- The critic raised a few *cavils* about the author's writing style, but on the whole the review was favorable.

QUICK QUIZ #34

Match each word in the first column with its definition in the second column. Check your answers in the back of the book.

1.	captivate	a.	violent upheaval
2.	carcinogenic	b.	swerve
3.	cardinal	c.	political meeting
4.	careen	d.	waterfall
5.	cartography	e.	fascinate
6.	cascade	f.	quibble
7.	cataclysm	g.	most important
8.	caucus	h.	art of making maps
9.	cavalier	i.	arrogant
10.	cavil	j.	causing cancer

CELIBACY (SEL uh buh see) *n* abstinence from sex

People who practice *celibacy* don't practice sex. *Celibacy* is one of the requirements for Catholic priesthood.

To practice *celibacy* is to be *celibate*. You will look a very long time in Hollywood before you find a *celibate* celebrity.

CENSURE (SEN shur) *v* to condemn severely for doing something bad
- The Senate sometimes *censures* senators for breaking laws or engaging in behavior unbecoming to an elected official.

Censure can also be a noun.
- The clumsy physician feared the *censure* of his fellow doctors, so he stopped treating anything more complicated than the common cold.

A Senate that made a habit of *censuring* senators might be said to be *censorious*. To be *censorious* is to be highly critical—to do a lot of *censuring*.

CEREBRAL (suh REE brul) *adj* brainy; intellectually refined
Your *cerebrum* is the biggest part of your brain. To be *cerebral* is to do and care about things that really smart people do and care about.
   A *cerebral* discussion is one that is filled with big words and concerns abstruse matters that ordinary people can't understand.
   • Sebastian was too *cerebral* to be a baseball announcer; he kept talking about the existentialism of the outfield.

This word can also be pronounced "SER uh brul."

CHAFF (chaf) *n* worthless stuff
In agricultural usage, *chaff* is the husk left over after grain has been threshed. Outside of a wheat farm, *chaff* is any worthless stuff, especially any worthless stuff left over after valuable stuff has been separated out or removed.
   • Any car in which young children regularly ride gradually fills up with crumbs, cereal, gum wrappers, bits of paper, and other *chaff*.
   • The mountain of crumpled paper on which Harry lay snoring was the *chaff* he had produced in his effort to write a term paper.

CHAGRIN (shuh GRIN) *n* humiliation; embarrassed disappointment
   • Much to my *chagrin*, I began to giggle during the eulogy at the funeral.
   • Doug was filled with *chagrin* when he lost the race because he had put his shoes on the wrong feet.

The word *chagrin* is sometimes used incorrectly to mean surprise. There is, however, a definite note of shame in *chagrin*.
   To be *chagrined* is to feel humiliated or mortified.

CHAMELEON (kuh MEEL yun) *n* a highly changeable person
In the reptile world, a *chameleon* is a lizard that can change its color to match its surroundings. In the human world, a *chameleon* is a person who changes his or her opinions or emotions to reflect those of the people around him or her.
   • Rita was a social *chameleon*; when she was with her swimming-team friends, she made fun of the students on the yearbook staff, and when she was with her yearbook friends, she made fun of the students on the swimming team.

CHAMPION (CHAM pee un) *v* to defend; to support
   • During his campaign, the governor had *championed* a lot of causes that he promptly forgot about once he was elected.

CHANNEL (CHAN ul) *v* to direct; to cause to follow a certain path
- When the dean asked Eddie to explain how he had managed to earn three Ds and a C minus during the previous semester, Eddie said, "Well, you know what can happen when you *channel* all your efforts into one course."
- Young people arrested for painting graffiti on subway cars were placed in a rehabilitation program that attempted to *channel* their artistic abilities into socially acceptable pursuits, such as painting the interiors of subway-station bathrooms.

CHARISMA (kuh RIZ muh) *n* a magical-seeming ability to attract followers or inspire loyalty
- The glamorous presidential candidate had a lot of *charisma*; voters didn't seem to support him so much as be entranced by him.
- The evangelist's undeniable *charisma* enabled him to bring in millions and millions of dollars in donations to his television show.

To have *charisma* is to be *charismatic*.

QUICK QUIZ #35

Match each word in the first column with its definition in the second column. Check your answers in the back of the book.

1.	categorical	a.	unconditional
2.	catharsis	b.	relieving purification
3.	catholic	c.	abstinence from sex
4.	caustic	d.	brainy
5.	celibacy	e.	humiliation
6.	censure	f.	magical attractiveness
7.	cerebral	g.	corrosive
8.	chagrin	h.	condemn severely
9.	charisma	i.	universal

CHARLATAN (SHAR luh tun) *n* fraud; quack; con man
- Buck was selling what he claimed was a cure for cancer, but he was just a *charlatan* (the pills were jelly beans).
- The flea market usually attracts a lot of *charlatans* who sell phony products that don't do what they claim they will.

CHASM (KAZ um) *n* a deep, gaping hole; a gorge
- Mark was so stupid that his girlfriend wondered whether there wasn't a *chasm* where his brain should be.

- The bad guys were gaining, so the hero grabbed the heroine and swung across the *chasm* on a slender vine.

CHASTE (chayst) *adj* pure and unadorned; abstaining from sex
- The novel's author had a *chaste* but powerful writing style; he used few adjectives and even fewer big words, but he nonetheless succeeded in creating a vivid and stirring portrait of a fascinating world.

- Felix enjoyed *Cinderella*, but he found the movie a bit *chaste* for his liking.

To be *chaste* is to be in a state of *chastity* (CHAS tuh tee).
- Rick chose to live a life of *chastity* by becoming a monk.

CHASTISE (chas TYZE) *v* to inflict punishment on; to discipline
- Mother *chastised* us for firing our bottle rockets too close to the house.

- *Chastising* the dog for sleeping on the beds never seemed to do any good; the minute we turned our backs, he'd curl up next to the pillows.

CHERUB (CHER ub) *n* a cute chubby-cheeked child; a kind of angel
- The bank robber had the face of a *cherub* and the arrest record of a hardened criminal.

To look or act like a *cherub* is to be *cherubic* (chuh ROO bik). Religiously speaking, a *cherub* is an angel of the sort you see depicted on valentines and Christmas cards: a small child, with wings and no clothes. In careful usage, the correct plural is *cherubim* (CHER oo bim), but most people just say *cherubs*.

CHICANERY (shi KAY nuh ree) *n* trickery; deceitfulness; artifice, especially legal or political
- Political news would be dull were it not for the *chicanery* of our elected officials.

CHIMERA (kye MEER uh) *n* an illusion; a foolish fancy
- Jie's dream of becoming a movie star was just a *chimera*.

- Could you take a picture of a *chimera* with a camera? No, of course not. It wouldn't show up on the film.

Be careful not to mispronounce this word. Its apparent similarity to *chimney* is just a *chimera*.

CHOLERIC (KAHL ur ik) *adj* hot-tempered; quick to anger
- The *choleric* watchdog would sink his teeth into anyone who came within biting distance of his doghouse.
- When the grumpy old man was in one of his *choleric* moods, the children refused to go near him.
- The *choleric* administrator kept all the secretaries in a state of terror.

CHORTLE (CHAWR tul) *v* to chuckle with glee
A *chortle* is a cross between a chuckle and a snort. The word was coined by Lewis Carroll in *Through the Looking Glass.*
- The toddler *chortled* as he arranged his gleaming Christmas presents on the living-room couch.
- The children were supposed to be asleep, but I could tell that they were reading their new joke book because I could hear them *chortling* through the door.

Chortle can also be a noun.
- Professor Smith meant his lecture to be serious, but the class responded only with *chortles*.

CHRONIC (KRAHN ik) *adj* constant; lasting a long time; inveterate
- DJ's *chronic* back pains often kept him from football practice, but the post-game internal bleeding lasted only a day.

Someone who always comes in last could be called a *chronic* loser.
Chronic is usually associated with something negative or undesirable: *chronic* illness, *chronic* failure, *chronic* depression. You would be much less likely to encounter a reference to *chronic* success or *chronic* happiness, unless the writer or speaker was being ironic.

A *chronic* disease is one that lingers for a long time, doesn't go away, or keeps coming back. The opposite of a *chronic* disease is an *acute* disease. An *acute* disease is one that comes and goes very quickly. It may be severe, but it doesn't last forever.

CHRONICLE (KRAHN uh kul) *n* a record of events in order of time; a history
- Sally's diary provided her mother with a detailed *chronicle* of her daughter's extracurricular activities.

Chronicle can also be used as a verb.
- The reporter *chronicled* all the events of the revolution.

Chronology and *chronicle* are nearly synonyms: Both provide a *chronological* list of events.
Chronological means in order of time.

QUICK QUIZ #36

Match each word in the first column with its definition in the second column. Check your answers in the back of the book.

1.	charlatan	a.	in order of occurrence
2.	chasm	b.	constant
3.	chastise	c.	hot-tempered
4.	chicanery	d.	punish
5.	chimera	e.	account of past times
6.	choleric	f.	list in time order
7.	chronic	g.	illusion
8.	chronological	h.	fraud
9.	chronology	i.	gaping hole
10.	chronicle	j.	trickery

CHURL (churl) *n* a rude person; a boor
- Too much wine made Rex act like a *churl*; he thumped his forefinger on the waiter's chest and demanded to speak to the manager.

To be a *churl* is to be *churlish*. The state of being *churlish* is known as *churlishness*.
- Rex's *churlish* behavior toward the waiter made him unwelcome at the restaurant.

- Everyone was appalled by Rex's *churlishness*.

CHUTZPAH (HUT spuh) *n* brazenness; audacity
This slang word comes from Yiddish.
- The bank manager had so much *chutzpah* that during a recent robbery, he asked the stick-up men to sign a receipt for the money they were taking. And they did it!

CIPHER (SYE fer) *n* zero; a nobody; a code; the solution to a code
- The big red *cipher* at the top of his paper told Harold that he hadn't done a good job on his algebra exam.

- Michael was a *cipher*; after he had transferred to a new school, no one could remember what he looked like.

- Heather loved codes, and she quickly figured out the simple *cipher* that the older girls had used to write one another secret messages about boys.

To *decipher* (di SYE fer) a coded message is to decode it. To *encipher* (en SYE fer) a message is to put it into code.

- Boris's emotions were hard to *decipher*; the expression on his face never gave one a clue as to what he was feeling or thinking.

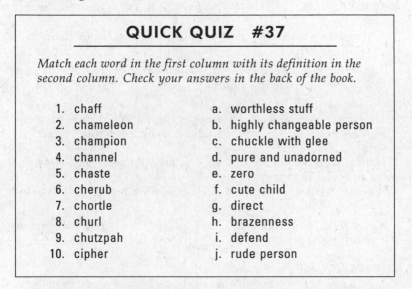

QUICK QUIZ   #37

Match each word in the first column with its definition in the second column. Check your answers in the back of the book.

1.	chaff	a.	worthless stuff
2.	chameleon	b.	highly changeable person
3.	champion	c.	chuckle with glee
4.	channel	d.	pure and unadorned
5.	chaste	e.	zero
6.	cherub	f.	cute child
7.	chortle	g.	direct
8.	churl	h.	brazenness
9.	chutzpah	i.	defend
10.	cipher	j.	rude person

CIRCUITOUS (sur KYOO uh tus) *adj* roundabout; not following a direct path

- The *circuitous* bus route between the two cities went here, there, and everywhere, and it took an extremely long time to get anywhere.

- The salesman's route was *circuitous*—it wound aimlessly through many small towns.

A *circuitous* argument is one that rambles around for quite a while before making its point.

A *circuitous* argument is very similar to a *circular* argument, which is one that ends up where it begins or attempts to prove something without offering any new information. To say, "Straight means not curved, and curved means not straight," is to give a circular, or tautological, definition of the word *straight*.

CIRCUMLOCUTION (sur kum loh KYOO shun) *n* an indirect expression; use of wordy or evasive language

- The lawyer's *circumlocution* left everyone in the courtroom wondering what had been said.

- The indicted executive evaded the reporters' questions by resorting to *circumlocution*.

To use a lot of big, vague words and to speak in a disorganized way is to be *circumlocutory*.

CIRCUMNAVIGATE (sur kum NAV uh gayt) *v* to sail or travel all the way around
- Magellan's crew was the first to *circumnavigate* the globe.
- *Circumnavigating* their block took the little boys most of the morning because they stopped in nearly every yard to play with their new action figures.

The word can also be used figuratively.
- Jefferson skillfully *circumnavigated* the subject of his retirement; in his hour-long speech, he talked about everything but it.

CIRCUMSCRIBE (SUR kum skrybe) *v* to draw a line around; to set the limits; to define; to restrict
- The Constitution clearly *circumscribes* the restrictions that can be placed on our personal freedoms.
- A barbed-wire fence and armed guards *circumscribed* the movement of the prisoners.

CIRCUMSPECT (SUR kum spekt) *adj* cautious
- As a public speaker, Nick was extremely *circumspect;* he always took great care not to say the wrong thing or give offense.
- The *circumspect* general did everything he could not to put his soldiers at unnecessary risk.

The word *circumspect* comes from Greek roots meaning around and look (as do the words *circle* and *inspect*). To be *circumspect* is to look around carefully before doing something.

CIRCUMVENT (sur kum VENT) *v* to frustrate as though by surrounding
- Our hopes for an early end of the meeting were *circumvented* by the chairperson's refusal to deal with the items on the agenda.
- The angry school board *circumvented* the students' effort to install televisions in every classroom.

CITADEL (SIT uh dul) *n* a fortress defending a city; a stronghold; a bulwark
- From the *citadel* on top of the hill, the king's soldiers could fire down on the troops attacking the city.
- The president viewed the university as a *citadel* of learning, as a fortress against the forces of ignorance.

CIVIL (SIV ul) *adj* polite; civilized; courteous
- Our dinner guests conducted themselves *civilly* when we told them we weren't going to serve them dinner after all. They didn't bang their cups on the table or throw their plates to the floor.

The word *civil* also has other meanings. *Civil* rights are rights established by law. *Civil* service is government service. Consult your dictionary for the numerous shades of meaning.

CLANDESTINE (klan DES tin) *adj* concealed or secret, usually for an evil or subversive purpose
- The meetings held by the terrorists were not as *clandestine* as they imagined; their meeting room had been bugged by the CIA.
- Unable to persuade Congress to back the cause, the White House conducted a *clandestine* fund-raising campaign to raise money for the revolutionary faction.

CLASSIC (KLAS ik) *adj* top-notch; of the highest quality; serving as a standard or model
- The baseball game was a *classic* contest; it was one of the finest games I have ever seen.
- Little Rudolph is a *classic* example of what happens when parents give a child anything he wants; he is a whining, wheedling, annoying little brat.

This word can also be a noun.
- The *Adventures of Huckleberry Finn* is an American *classic*; many readers view it as the Great American Novel.

The adjective *classical* is closely related but usually distinct in meaning. *Classical* literature is the literature of ancient Greece and Rome. Ancient Greek and Latin are *classical* languages. *Classical* history is the history of ancient Greece and Rome. The neoclassical period in American architecture was a period in which American builders were heavily influenced by the architecture of ancient Greece and Rome. (The Parthenon is a *classic* example of *classical* architecture.) In music, *classical* refers to European music of the second half of the eighteenth century. Mozart is an example of a *classical* composer.

When people in an academic setting refer to "the *classics*," they are almost always referring to the literature and languages of ancient Greece and Rome. A *classics* major is a student who concentrates in that literature and those languages.

CLEAVE (kleev) *v* to cling; to split

This fascinating word can be its own opposite. When one thing *cleaves* to another, they stick together closely. But when you split them apart, you can also be said to be *cleaving* them (as with a *cleaver*).

- When a child is frightened, it *cleaves* to its parent, and no one is able to cleave them.

- The streamlined front of the automobile is designed to *cleave* the air, reducing wind resistance.

- The explorers had powerful machetes, but the jungle was so dense that they were unable to *cleave* a path through it.

Something that has been split is *cleft* (kleft).

CLEMENCY (KLEM un see) *n* mercy; forgiveness; mildness
- The governor committed an act of *clemency* when he released all the convicts from the state penitentiary.

Mild weather is called *clement* weather; bad weather is called *inclement*.
- You should wear a coat and carry an umbrella in *inclement* weather.

CLICHÉ (klee SHAY) *n* an overused saying or idea
- The expression "you can't judge a book by its cover" is a *cliché;* it's been used so many times, that freshness has been worn away.

Clichés are usually true. That's why they've been repeated often enough to become overused. But they are boring. A writer who uses a lot of *clichés*—referring to a foreign country as "a land of contrasts," describing spring as "a time of renewal," saying that a snowfall is "a blanket of white"—is not interesting to read, because there is nothing new about these observations.

CLIMATIC (kly MAT ik) *adj* having to do with the climate
- The buildup of carbon dioxide in the atmosphere appears to be causing pronounced *climatic* changes all over the world.

Do not confuse this word with *climactic* (kly MAK tik), which means coming to or having to do with a climax.

CLIQUE (kleek) *n* an exclusive group bound together by some shared quality or interest
- The high school newspaper staff was a real *clique;* they all hung out together and wouldn't talk to anyone else. It was hard to have fun at that school if you weren't a member of the right *clique.* The cheerleaders were *cliquish* as well.

QUICK QUIZ #38

Match each word in the first column with its definition in the second column. Check your answers in the back of the book.

1.	circuitous	a.	cautious
2.	circumlocution	b.	draw a line around
3.	circumscribe	c.	mercy
4.	circumspect	d.	polite
5.	circumvent	e.	roundabout
6.	civil	f.	frustrate
7.	clique	g.	overused saying
8.	clemency	h.	indirect expression
9.	inclement	i.	exclusive group
10.	cliché	j.	bad, as in weather

CLOISTER (KLOY stur) *n* a covered walk, with columns on one side, that runs along the perimeter of a courtyard, especially in a convent or monastery; a convent or monastery; a tranquil, secluded place

In its first two meanings, this word is of interest primarily to people who are interested in convents and monasteries. More generally the word is used in connection with places that suggest the tranquil seclusion of a convent or monastery.

- Virginia viewed her office as a *cloister* to which she could withdraw from the chaos of the production line.

- The little clearing in the woods was Billy's *cloister*; he went there to meditate and recharge his mental batteries.

To *cloister* someone or something is to put him, her, or it in seclusion.

- After his hectic week, David *cloistered* himself on the golf course for the entire three-day weekend.

CLONE (klohn) *n* an exact duplicate; an organism genetically identical to another

- The new store was a *clone* of the old one; even the sales clerks looked the same.

- Margaret's daughter Eloise looked so much like her that Eloise seemed less like her child than like her *clone*.

This word can also be a verb. To *clone* something is to make an exact duplicate of it.

- Isaac spent his life trying to find a way to *clone* himself, because he believed that the world would be a better, more interesting place if it were filled with Isaacs.

CLOUT (klowt) *n* a blow; influence
- When Winnona kept jumping higher and higher on the bed despite her father's warnings, her collision with the ceiling gave her a *clout* on the head that made her see stars.
- Jim has a lot of *clout* at the bank, perhaps because his father is the president.

CLOY (kloy) *v* to cause to feel too full, especially when indulging in something overly sweet; to become wearisome through excess
- After a few bites, the delicious dessert began to *cloy*, and Leo thought that he was going to be sick.
- The new perfume was *cloying*; it smelled good at first, but soon the fragrance began to seem almost suffocating.

QUICK QUIZ   #39

Match each word in the first column with its definition in the second column. Check your answers in the back of the book.

1.	circumnavigate	a.	having to do with the climate
2.	citadel	b.	blow
3.	clandestine	c.	cling
4.	classic	d.	sail all the way around
5.	cleave	e.	covered walk
6.	climatic	f.	secret
7.	cloister	g.	fortress defending a city
8.	clone	h.	exact duplicate
9.	clout	i.	top-notch
10.	cloy	j.	cause to feel too full

COALESCE (koh uh LES) *v* to come together as one; to fuse; to unite
- When the dough *coalesced* into a big blob, we began to wonder whether the cookies would be edible.
- The people in our neighborhood *coalesced* into a powerful force for change in the community.

A *coalition* is a group of people that has come together for some purpose, often a political one.

- The Southern *coalition* in Congress is the group of representatives from Southern states who often vote the same way.

Coal miners and cola bottlers might *coalesce* into a *coalition* for the purpose of persuading coal mine owners to provide cola machines in coal mines.

CODDLE (KAHD ul) *v* to baby

- Old Mrs. Smythe had dozens of cats, and she *coddled* them all by feeding them fresh cream, liver, and chocolate pudding.

- Mr. Katz *coddled* his new employees because he didn't want them to quit as a group on the day before Christmas, as his previous employees had done.

COERCE (koh URS) *v* to force someone to do or not to do something

- Darth Vader tried flattery, Darth Vader tried gifts, Darth Vader even tried to *coerce*, but Darth Vader was never able to make Han Solo reveal the hidden rebel base.

The noun is *coercion* (koh UR shun).

COGENT (KOH junt) *adj* powerfully convincing

- Shaft was *cogent* in explaining why he needed the confidential files, so we gave them to him.

- The lawyer's argument on his client's behalf was not *cogent*, so the jury convicted his client. The jury was persuaded by the *cogency* of the prosecuting attorney's argument.

Cogent reasons are extremely persuasive ones.

COGITATE (KAHJ uh tayt) *v* to ponder; to meditate; to think carefully about

- When the professor had a particularly difficult problem to solve, he would climb a tree with a bag of jellybeans and *cogitate* until he had a solution.

- Jerry claimed that he was *cogitating*, but most people I know don't snore when they *cogitate*.

An act of *cogitating* is called *cogitation* (kahj uh TAY shun).

- *Cogitation* was apparently painful to Rebecca; whenever she thought carefully about something, her eyes squinted, her hands shook, and she broke into a sweat.

COGNITIVE (KAHG nu tiv) *adj* dealing with how we know the world around us through our senses; mental
Scientists study the *cognitive* apparatus of human beings to pattern how computers should gather information about the world.

Cognition is knowing.

COGNIZANT (KAHG nu zunt) *adj* aware; conscious
To be *cognizant* of your responsibilities is to know what your responsibilities are.

- Al was *cognizant* of the dangers of sword swallowing, but he tried it anyway and hurt himself quite badly.

COHERENT (koh HEER unt) *adj* holding together; making sense

- After puzzling over Grace's disorganized Holy Roman Empire essay for almost an hour, Ms. Fabricius needed only twenty minutes to read Arjun's *coherent* paper on the Defenestration of Prague.

A *coherent* wad of cotton balls is one that holds together.

A *coherent* explanation is an explanation that makes sense; the explanation holds together.

To hold together is to *cohere*.

COHORT (KOH hawrt) *n* a group
In ancient Rome, a *cohort* was a military division of several hundred soldiers. In careful modern usage, *cohort* often retains a shade of this original meaning.

- The IRS office was surrounded by a *cohort* of disgruntled tax-payers demanding the head of the lead agent.

Cohort is increasingly used to mean companion or accomplice, but many careful speakers and writers would consider this to be careless usage. An example: The armed robber and his *cohort* were both sentenced to hundreds of years in prison.

COLLOQUIAL (kul OH kwee ul) *adj* conversational; informal in language
A writer with a *colloquial* style is a writer who uses ordinary words and whose writing seems as informal as common speech.

"The way I figure it" is a *colloquial* expression, or a *colloquialism*; People often say it but it isn't used in formal prose.

A *colloquy* (KAHL uh kwee) is a conversation or conference.

COLLUSION (kuh LOO zhun) *n* conspiracy; secret cooperation

- The increase in oil prices was the result of *collusion* by the oil-producing nations.

- There was *collusion* among the owners of the baseball teams; they agreed secretly not to sign any expensive free agents.

If the baseball owners were in *collusion*, then you could say that they had *colluded*. To *collude* is to conspire.

COMMEMORATE (kuh MEM uh rayt) *v* to honor the memory of; to serve as a memorial to

- The big statue in the village square *commemorates* the founding of the town 250 years ago.

- The members of the senior class painted a mural on the cafeteria wall to *commemorate* their graduation.

An act of *commemorating* is a *commemoration* (kuh MEM uh RAY shun).

- The *commemoration* ceremony for the new building lasted so long that the weary participants forgot what they were supposed to be *commemorating*.

COMMENSURATE (kuh MEN sur it) *adj* equal; proportionate

- Ryan's salary is *commensurate* with his ability; like his ability, his salary is small.

- The number of touchdowns scored by the team and the number of its victories were *commensurate* (both zero).

COMMISERATE (kuh MIZ uh rayt) *v* to express sorrow or sympathy for; to sympathize with; to pity

To *commiserate* with someone is to "share the misery" of that person.

- My grandmother *commiserated* with me when I told her about the terrible day I had had at school.

- In the aftermath of the flood, the mayor was quick to *commiserate* but slow to offer any aid.

- The other members of the tennis team *commiserated* with their captain after his humiliating loss in the finals of the tournament.

Commiseration (kuh miz uh RAY shun) is an act of *commiserating*.

- The new widow was weary of the *commiseration* of her friends and eager to get on with her life. This is one of many words starting with "com" or "con" that mean "with" somebody or something. Watch out for others throughout this section. Can you find some that don't share this meaning?

COMMODIOUS (kuh MOH dee us) *adj* spacious; roomy; capacious

- The rooms in the old hotel were so *commodious* that Sheila nearly got lost on her way to the bathroom.

- The millionaire's house was *commodious* but not particularly attractive; the big rooms were filled with ugly furniture.

COMPATIBLE (kum PAT uh bul) *adj* harmonious; capable of functioning, working, or living together in harmony; consistent

- My college roommate and I were completely *compatible*; we both liked to leave the lights and television on when we slept, and we both smoked cigars.

- Urban's new computer was not *compatible* with his old printer; when he hooked the two of them together, they both exploded.

The opposite of *compatible* is *incompatible*.

- Ken and Gina got divorced because they had decided, after thirty-five years of marriage and seven children, that they were simply *incompatible*.

The noun is *compatibility*.

COMPELLING (kum PEL ing) *adj* forceful; causing to yield

- A *compelling* argument for buying a security system is one that makes you go out and buy a security system.

- The recruiter's speech was so *compelling* that nearly everyone in the auditorium enlisted in the Army when it was over.

To *compel* someone to do something is to force him or her to do it.

- Our consciences *compelled* us to turn over the money we had found to the authorities.

The noun is *compulsion*, which also means an irresistible impulse to do something irrational.

COMPENDIUM (kum PEN dee um) *n* a summary; an abridgment

- A yearbook often contains a *compendium* of the offenses, achievements, and future plans of the members of the senior class.

COMPETENT (KAHM puh tunt) *adj* capable; qualified

- The plumber Melody hired to fix her leaky pipes was not *competent*; when the plumber had finished, the pipes were leakier than they had been before.

- Peter is a *competent* student but not an exceptional one; he earns average grades and he never makes observations that cause his teachers to gasp with wonder.

- I didn't feel *competent* to rebuild my car's engine, so I let a trained mechanic do the job.

Not to be *competent* is to be *incompetent*. An *incompetent* person is one who lacks *competence* (KAHM puh tuns).

QUICK QUIZ #40

Match each word in the first column with its definition in the second column. Check your answers in the back of the book.

1. coalesce		a.	perceptive
2. coalition		b.	unite
3. coerce		c.	conversational
4. cogent		d.	force someone to do
5. cognitive			something
6. cognizant		e.	proportionate
7. coherent		f.	making sense
8. colloquial		g.	group with a purpose
9. collusion		h.	powerfully convincing
10. commensurate		i.	summary
11. compelling		j.	forceful
12. compendium		k.	conspiracy
		l.	dealing with how we know our environment

COMPILE (kum PYLE) *v* to gather together; to gather together into a book
- At the end of a long career, the company president *compiled* his thoughts about business in a booklet that was distributed to all the company's employees.
- In a dozen years in the big leagues, the pitcher *compiled* a record of victories that placed him in contention for a spot in the Hall of Fame.

The result of an act of *compiling* is a *compilation* (KAHM puh lay shun).
- At the end of the semester, the second-grade teacher sent each child home with a *compilation* of his or her classroom work.

COMPLACENT (kum PLAY sunt) *adj* self-satisfied; overly pleased with oneself; contented to a fault
- The *complacent* camper paid no attention to the poison ivy around his campsite, and ended up going to the hospital.
- The football team won so many games that it became *complacent*, and the worst team in the league won the game.

To fall into *complacency* is to become comfortably uncaring about the world around you.

- The president of the student council was appalled by the *complacency* of his classmates; not one of the seniors seemed to care about the theme.

Don't confuse *complacent* with *complaisant* (kum PLAY zunt), which means eager to please.

COMPLEMENT (KAHM pluh munt) *v* to complete or fill up; to be the perfect counterpart
This word is often confused with *compliment*, which means to praise. It's easy to tell them apart. *Complement* is spelled like *complete*.
- The flower arrangement *complemented* the table decorations.

Complement can also be a noun.
- Fish-flavored ice cream was a perfect *complement* to the seafood dinner.

COMPLICITY (kum PLIS uh tee) *n* participation in wrongdoing; the act of being an accomplice
- There was *complicity* between the bank robber and the dishonest teller. The teller neglected to turn on the alarm, and the robber rewarded him by sharing the loot.
- *Complicity* among the students made it impossible to find out which of them had pulled the fire alarm.

COMPLY (kum PLY) *v* to act or be in accordance (with)
- The doctor *complied* with my wishes and told me that I had to stay in bed all day eating ice cream and watching TV.
- The company's most successful salesman refused to *comply* with a rule requiring all men to wear neckties, so the company changed the rule.

To *comply* with something is to be in *compliance* (kum PLY uns) with it.
- The Internal Revenue Service doesn't have the resources to audit every tax return; for the most part, it depends on the voluntary *compliance* of taxpayers.

QUICK QUIZ #41

Match each word in the first column with its definition in the second column. Check your answers in the back of the book.

1.	coddle	a.	spacious
2.	cogitate	b.	honor the memory of
3.	cohort	c.	harmonious
4.	commemorate	d.	ponder
5.	commiserate	e.	capable
6.	commodious	f.	baby
7.	compatible	g.	gather together
8.	competent	h.	group
9.	compile	i.	act in accordance
10.	comply	j.	express sorrow for

COMPOSED (kum POHZD) *adj* calm; tranquil

- The defendant was eerily *composed* when the judge read the jury's guilty verdict; he almost seemed to welcome his conviction.

- Billy's mother somehow managed to remain *composed* in the ticket line at Disneyland, despite the fact that Billy was clinging to her leg and crying at the top of his lungs.

To be *composed* is to have *composure* (kum POH zhur).

- The judges were most impressed by the young dancer's *composure*; despite the pressure of the nationally televised recital, she remained calm and finished her routine without making a single error.

COMPREHENSIVE (kahm pruh HEN siv) *adj* covering or including everything

- The insurance policy was *comprehensive*; it covered all possible losses.

- Maria's knowledge of English is *comprehensive*; she even understands what *comprehensive* means.

A *comprehensive* examination is one that covers everything in the course or in a particular field of knowledge.

COMPRISE (kum PRYZE) *v* to consist of

- A football team *comprises* eleven players on offense and eleven players on defense.

- A company *comprises* employees.

This word is often misused. Be careful. Players do *not* "comprise" a football team, and employees do *not* "comprise" a company. Nor can a football team be said to be "*comprised* of" players, or a company to be "*comprised* of" employees. These are common mistakes. Instead, you can say that players *constitute* or *compose* a team, and that employees *constitute* or *compose* a company.

You can also say that a team *consists* of players or a company *consists* of employees.

COMPROMISE (KAHM pruh myze) *n* a settlement of differences in which each side gives up something

- Bill and Phil couldn't settle their argument about the composition of the moon, so they agreed to a *compromise*; on evenly numbered days they would believe that it was made of green cheese, and on oddly numbered days they would believe that it was made of soap.

This word can also be a verb. To *compromise* is to make a *compromise*.

- Even after a year of negotiations, the leaders of the two warring countries refused to *compromise*; each wished to be viewed as the victor in their dispute.

To *compromise* can also mean to abandon or give up. To *compromise* one's principles is to do something in violation of one's principles.

- Sally chose detention for violating her high school's dress code rather than *compromise* her belief in freedom of expression.

COMPUNCTION (kum PUNK shun) *n* remorse; a feeling of uneasiness at doing something wrong

- Ms. Riley had no *compunction* about overeating if she thought that her meal was low in fat.

- The bank robber was absolutely without *compunction*; he filled his satchel with cash as calmly as if he had been filling it with groceries.

CONCAVE (kahn KAYV) *adj* curved inward, like the inside of a circle or a sphere

If you cut a volleyball in half, the inside surface of each half would be *concave*. The outside surface of each half would be *convex* (kahn VEKS). It's easy to keep these two words straight. A *concave* surface goes in, the way a cave does. A *convex* surface goes out, in a way that will vex you if you don't remember the part about the cave.

- A big optical telescope is likely to have both a *concave* reflective surface and a number of *convex* lenses.

CONCEDE (kun SEED) *v* to acknowledge as true or right; to grant or yield

- The candidate *conceded* the election shortly before midnight, after it had become abundantly clear that his opponent was going to win by a landslide.
- Jerry refused to *concede* defeat, even though his football team was losing 63–14.

To *concede* is to make a *concession* (kun SESH un).

- Despite his *concession* that he didn't know what he was talking about, Harry continued to argue his point as strongly as before.

CONCENTRIC (kun SEN trik) *adj* having the same center

- The inner and outer edges of a doughnut are *concentric* circles. So are the rings on an archery target.

CONCERT (KAHN surt) *n* combined action; agreement

- By acting in *concert*, the three boys were able to lift the rock that none of them had been able to lift while acting alone.

A *concerted* (kun SUR tud) effort is one made by individuals acting in *concert*.

CONCILIATORY (kun SIL ee uh tor ee) *adj* making peace; attempting to resolve a dispute through goodwill
To be *conciliatory* is to kiss and make up.

- Come on—be *conciliatory*!
- The formerly warring countries were *conciliatory* at the treaty conference.
- After dinner at the all-you-can-eat pancake house, the divorced couple began to feel *conciliatory*, so they flew to Las Vegas and were remarried.

When peace has been made, we say that the warring parties have come to a *reconciliation* (rek un sil ee AY shun). To *reconcile* (REK un syle) is to bring two things into agreement.

- The accountant managed to *reconcile* the company books with the cash on hand only with great creativity.

CONCISE (kun SYSE) *adj* brief and to the point; succinct
- The scientist's explanation was *concise;* it was brief and it helped us understand the difficult concept.

To be *concise* is to say much with few words. A *concise* speaker is one who speaks *concisely* or with *concision.*

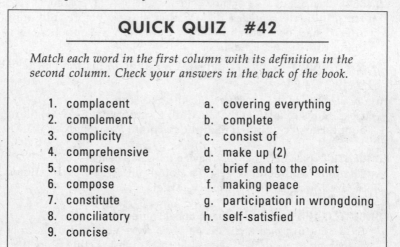

QUICK QUIZ   #42

Match each word in the first column with its definition in the second column. Check your answers in the back of the book.

1. complacent	a. covering everything
2. complement	b. complete
3. complicity	c. consist of
4. comprehensive	d. make up (2)
5. comprise	e. brief and to the point
6. compose	f. making peace
7. constitute	g. participation in wrongdoing
8. conciliatory	h. self-satisfied
9. concise	

CONCOCT (kun KAHKT) *v* to create by mixing ingredients; to devise
- Using only the entirely unexciting groceries she found in the refrigerator, the master chef *concocted* a fabulous seven-course meal that left her guests shaking their heads.
- Because so many of the streets were flooded from the rains, Sylvia had to *concoct* an elaborate plan to drive to the super-market and back.

A *concoction* (kun KAHK shun) is something that has been *concocted.*
- After proudly announcing that they had made dessert, the children brought in an unsettling *concoction* that appeared to contain nothing edible.

CONCOMITANT (kun KAHM uh tunt) *adj* following from; accompanying; going along with
- Derek Jeter's success on the baseball field, and the *concomitant* increase in the size of his bank account, made him the envy of all professional baseball players.
- Along with his large cash donation, the philanthropist made a *concomitant* promise to support the new library with smaller gifts in the coming years.

CONCORD (KAHN kord) *n* harmony; agreement

Nations that live in *concord* are nations that live together in peace.

- The war between the neighboring tribes ended thirty years of *concord*.

- The faculty meeting was marked by *concord;* no one yelled at anyone else.

Discord is the opposite of *concord*. A faculty meeting where everyone yelled at one another would be a faculty meeting marked by *discord*. It would be a *discordant* meeting.

An *accord* is a formal agreement, usually reached after a dispute.

CONCURRENT (kun KUR unt) *adj* happening at the same time; parallel

- The criminal was sentenced to two *concurrent* fifteen-year sentences; the sentences will run at the same time, and he will be out of jail in fifteen years.

- High prices, falling demand, and poor weather were three *concurrent* trends that made life especially difficult for corn farmers last month.

To *concur* means to agree.

- The assistant wanted to keep his job, so he always *concurred* with his boss.

CONDESCEND (KAHN duh send) *v* to stoop to someone else's level, usually in an offensive way; to patronize

- I was surprised that the president of the company had *condescended* to talk with me, a mere temporary employee.

Many grown-ups make the mistake of *condescending* to young children, who usually prefer to be treated as equals, or at least as rational beings.

CONDONE (kun DOHN) *v* to overlook; to permit to happen

To *condone* what someone does is to look the other way while it happens or to permit it to happen by not doing anything about it.

- The principal *condoned* the hoods' smoking in the bathroom; he simply ignored it.

CONDUCIVE (kun DOO siv) *adj* promoting

- The chairs in the library are *conducive* to sleep. If you sit in them to study, you will fall asleep.

- The foul weather was not *conducive* to our having a picnic.

CONFEDERATE (kun FED ur ut) *n* an ally; an accomplice

- The rebels had few *confederates* in the countryside; as a result, they were never able to field much of an army.

- It took the police several months to track down the embezzler's *confederates*, but they were eventually able to arrest most of them.

A group of *confederates* is a *confederation* (kun fed ur AY shun). The *Confederacy* (kun FED ur uh see), formally known as the *Confederate* States of America, was the *confederation* of eleven southern states that seceded from the United States of America between 1860 and 1861, precipitating the Civil War.

Confederate, pronounced "kun FED uh rayt," is a verb.

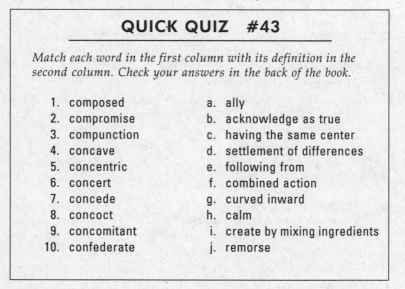

QUICK QUIZ   #43

Match each word in the first column with its definition in the second column. Check your answers in the back of the book.

1.	composed	a.	ally
2.	compromise	b.	acknowledge as true
3.	compunction	c.	having the same center
4.	concave	d.	settlement of differences
5.	concentric	e.	following from
6.	concert	f.	combined action
7.	concede	g.	curved inward
8.	concoct	h.	calm
9.	concomitant	i.	create by mixing ingredients
10.	confederate	j.	remorse

CONFER (kun FER) *v* to exchange ideas; to consult with; to bestow
- The referees *conferred* briefly before ruling that the pass had been incomplete and that no touchdown had been scored.
- I told the salesman that I needed to *confer* with my wife by telephone before signing a formal agreement to buy the old ocean liner.
- The administration decided to *confer* an honorary degree upon the old millionaire because it hoped doing so would cause him to leave a large donation to the university in his will.

A *conference* (KAHN fer uns) is a meeting at which people *confer*.

CONFIDANT (KAHN fu dahnt) *n* a person with whom secrets or private thoughts are shared
- A *confidant* is a person in whom one can confide (kun FYDE).

- Sally's brother was also her *confidant*; when she had a problem that she felt she could discuss with no one else, she called him.

A female *confidant* is a *confidante*, but the pronunciation remains the same.

CONFIGURATION (kun fig yuh RAY shun) *n* arrangement
- The *configuration* of the seats was such that no one in the audience had a clear view of the stage.
- My wife and I loved the exterior of the house, but we hated the *configuration* of the rooms.
- By slightly altering the *configuration* of chips on the motherboard of his laptop computer, Zach was able to turn it into a combination death ray and time machine.

To *configure* is to arrange.

CONFLAGRATION (kahn fluh GRAY shun) *n* a large fire
- The smoldering rags in the dumpster ignited the drums of explosive chemicals, and the small fire rapidly became a *conflagration* that enveloped the entire block.

CONFLUENCE (KAHN floo uns) *n* a flowing together, especially of rivers; the place where they begin to flow together
- The *confluence* of the Missouri and Mississippi rivers is at St. Louis; that's the place where they join together.
- There is a remarkable *confluence* in our thoughts: We think the same way about almost everything.
- A *confluence* of many factors (no ice, bad food, terrible music) made it inevitable that the party would be a flop.

CONFOUND (kun FOUND) *v* to bewilder; to amaze; to throw into confusion
- The team's inability to score *confounded* the coach, who had expected an easy victory.
- Allen's failure to understand his computer continues to *confound* his efforts to become computer-literate.

CONGEAL (kun JEEL) *v* to solidify; to jell
- The bacon grease *congealed* into a smooth white mass when we put the skillet in the freezer.
- It took several years for my ideas about invisibility to *congeal* to the point at which I could begin manufacturing and marketing vanishing pills.

CONGENIAL (kun JEEN yul) *adj* agreeably suitable; pleasant
- The little cabin in the woods was *congenial* to the writer; he was able to get a lot of writing done there.
- The new restaurant has a *congenial* atmosphere. We enjoy just sitting there playing with the ice in our water glasses.

When people get along together at a restaurant and don't throw food at one another, they are being *congenial*.

Genial and *congenial* share similar meanings. *Genial* means pleasing, kind, sympathetic, or helpful. You can be pleased by a *genial* manner or by a *genial* climate.

CONGENITAL (kun JEN uh tul) *adj* describing a trait or condition acquired between conception and birth; innate

A *congenital* birth defect is one that is present at birth but was not caused by one's genes.

The word is also used more loosely to describe any (usually bad) trait or behavior that is so firmly fixed it seems to be a part of a person's nature.

A *congenital* liar is a natural liar, a person who can't help but lie.

QUICK QUIZ   #44

Match each word in the first column with its definition in the second column. Check your answers in the back of the book.

1.	concord	a.	agreeably suitable
2.	discord	b.	innate
3.	concurrent	c.	harmony
4.	condescend	d.	flowing together
5.	condone	e.	promoting
6.	conducive	f.	stoop or patronize
7.	confluence	g.	overlook
8.	congenial	h.	happening at the same time
9.	congenital	i.	disharmony

CONGREGATE (KAHN grih gayt) *v* to come together
- Protestors were granted permission to *congregate* peacefully on the plaza.

The noun form is *congregation* and can refer to the membership of a house of worship.
- About half the *congregation* attended the sunrise service.

Aggregate also has to do with coming together. Can you think of additional words with the same root?

CONJECTURE (kun JEK chur) *v* to guess; to deduce or infer on slight evidence
- If forced to *conjecture,* I would say the volcano will erupt in twenty-four hours.

Conjecture can also be a noun.
- The divorce lawyer for Mr. Davis argued that the putative cause of the lipstick on his collar was mere *conjecture.*

A *conjecture* is *conjectural.*

CONJUGAL (KAHN juh gul) *adj* having to do with marriage
- After twenty-eight years of *conjugal* bliss, May divorced Ben when Ben suddenly confessed that he never liked the way she flossed her teeth.

CONJURE (KAHN jur) *v* to summon or bring into being as if by magic
- The chef *conjured* (or *conjured* up) a fabulous gourmet meal using nothing more than the meager ingredients in Lucy's kitchen.
- The wizard *conjured* (or *conjured* up) an evil spirit by mumbling some magic words and throwing a little powdered eye of newt into the fire.

CONNIVE (kuh NYVE) *v* to conspire; to aid or encourage a wrong by feigning ignorance of it
- An investigation revealed that virtually the entire police department had been *conniving* with the neighborhood drug dealers, giving them immunity in exchange for a cut of the profits.

The noun is *connivance* (kuh NYVE uns).

CONSERVATORY (kun SER vuh tawr ee) *n* a greenhouse, usually one attached to another structure; a music or drama school
- On sunny mornings, Mrs. Klein liked to have breakfast in the *conservatory,* surrounded by her orchids and miniature palm trees.
- After college, Hugo spent six years studying the violin at a Viennese *conservatory.*

QUICK QUIZ #45

Match each word in the first column with its definition in the second column. Check your answers in the back of the book.

1.	confer	a.	solidify
2.	confidant	b.	having to do with marriage
3.	configuration	c.	greenhouse
4.	conflagration	d.	arrangement
5.	confluence	e.	large fire
6.	confound	f.	person with whom secrets
7.	congeal		are shared
8.	conjugal	g.	conspire
9.	connive	h.	exchange ideas
10.	conservatory	i.	bewilder
		j.	flowing together

CONNOISSEUR (kahn uh SUR) *n* an expert, particularly in matters of art or taste

- The artist's work was popular, but *connoisseurs* rejected it as amateurish.

- Frank was a *connoisseur* of bad movies. He had seen them all and knew which ones were genuinely dreadful and which ones were merely poorly made.

- The meal was exquisite enough to impress a *connoisseur*.

- I like sculpture, but I'm no *connoisseur;* I probably can't describe to you why one statue is better than another.

CONSECRATE (KAHN suh krayt) *v* to make or declare sacred

- The Veterans Day speaker said that the battlefield had been *consecrated* by the blood of the soldiers who had died there.

- The priest *consecrated* the building by sprinkling holy water on it.

- The college chaplain delivered a sermon at the *consecration* (kahn suh KRAY shun) ceremony for the new chapel.

The opposite of *consecrate* is *desecrate* (DES uh krayt), which means to treat irreverently. The vandals *desecrated* the cemetery by knocking down all the tombstones.

Desecrate can also be applied to areas outside religion.
- Their act of vandalism was a *desecration*.
- Doodling in a book *desecrates* the book, even if the book isn't a Bible.
- The graffiti on the front door of the school is a *desecration*.

CONSENSUS (kun SEN sus) *n* unanimity or general agreement
When there is a *consensus,* everybody feels the same way.

Contrary to how the word is often used, *consensus* implies more than just a rough agreement or a majority opinion. Election results don't reflect a *consensus* unless everyone or nearly everyone votes for the same candidate.

CONSIGN (kun SYNE) *v* to hand over; to assign; to entrust; to banish
- Upon her retirement, Dinah *consigned* to her co-workers the contents of her desk.
- Two decades after Frank's death, most critics *consigned* his novels to the literary trash heap.

The noun form, *consignment* (kun SYNE munt), refers to that which is handed over.
- The bookstore owner was waiting anxiously for the publisher to send her a new *consignment* of books; with no books to sell, she had little to do at work all day.

CONSOLIDATE (kun SAHL uh dayt) *v* to combine or bring together; to solidify; to strengthen
- The new chairman tried to *consolidate* the company's disparate operations into a single unit that would be easier to manage.
- I *consolidated* the money in my many bank accounts by withdrawing it from all of them and putting it in a box that I kept under my bed.
- The baseball team *consolidated* its hold on first place by winning all of its remaining games.

CONSONANT (KAHN suh nunt) *adj* harmonious; in agreement
- Our desires were *consonant* with theirs; we all wanted the same thing.
- The decision to construct a new gymnasium was *consonant* with the superintendent's belief in physical education.

The opposite of *consonant* is *dissonant* (DIS uh nunt), which means inharmonious. *Dissonant* voices are voices that don't sound good together.

QUICK QUIZ #46

Match each word in the first column with its definition in the second column. Check your answers in the back of the book.

1. congregate	a. incompatible
2. conjecture	b. harmonious
3. conjure	c. make sacred
4. connoisseur	d. unanimity
5. consecrate	e. summon as if by magic
6. desecrate	f. treat irreverently
7. consensus	g. artistic expert
8. consonant	h. guess
9. dissonant	i. get together

CONSPICUOUS (kun SPIK yoo us) *adj* easily seen; impossible to miss
- There was a *conspicuous* absence of good food at the terrible party, and many of the guests went out to a restaurant afterward.
- The former president made a *conspicuous* display of his gleaming wristwatch; he had just signed a promotional contract with the watch's manufacturer.
- *Conspicuous* consumption is a variety of showing off that consists of making a public display of buying and using a lot of expensive stuff.

The opposite of *conspicuous* is *inconspicuous*.

CONSTITUENCY (kun STICH oo un see) *n* the group of voters represented by a politician; a group of supporters for anything
- The ninety-year-old candidate did most of his campaigning on college campuses, even though his natural *constituency* was the town's large population of senior citizens.
- The company's president failed to build a *constituency* on the board to support his plan to raise his salary by 300 percent.

A *constituency* is made up of *constituents* (kun STICH oo unts).
- The senator never forgot who had elected him; he spent most of his time in Washington doing favors for his *constituents*.

CONTEMPT (kun TEMPT) *n* disdain; disgrace

- The lawyer's *contempt* for the judge was clear; when she said "Your honor," she had both thumbs in her ears and was twiddling her fingers at him.
- I have nothing but *contempt* for people who say one thing and do another.
- The dishonest storekeeper was held in *contempt* by the townspeople, virtually all of whom began shopping somewhere else.

You will often find this word used in a legal context in the phrase *contempt* of court. Someone is typically charged with *contempt* of court for being disrespectful of the judge or rules of legal procedure.

CONSTRUE (kun STROO) *v* to interpret

- Preston *construed* his contract as giving him the right to do anything he wanted.
- The law had always been *construed* as permitting the behavior for which Katya had been arrested.
- The meaning of the poem, as I *construed* it, had to do with the love of a man for his dog.

To *misconstrue* is to misinterpret.

- Tommy *misconstrued* Pamela's smile, but he certainly did not *misconstrue* the slap she gave him.

CONSUMMATE (kun SUM it) *adj* perfect; complete; supremely skillful

- A *consummate* pianist is an extremely good one. Nothing is lacking in the way he or she plays.

Consummate (KAHN suh mayt) is also a verb. Notice the different pronunciation. To *consummate* something is to finish it or make it complete. Signing a contract would *consummate* an agreement.

CONTENTIOUS (kun TEN shus) *adj* argumentative; quarrelsome

- Liz figured that her *contentious* style would make her a perfect litigator; after law school, however, the would-be trial attorney discovered that passing the bar requires more than a will to argue.

A person looking for a fight is *contentious.*

Two people having a fight are *contentious.*

To be *contentious* in a discussion is to make a lot of noisy objections.

A *contender* is a fighter. To *contend* is to fight or argue for something. Someone who breaks the law may have to *contend* with the law.

CONTIGUOUS (kun TIG yoo us) *adj* side by side; adjoining

Two countries that share a border are *contiguous;* so are two events that happened one right after the other.

If two countries are *contiguous,* the territory they cover is continuous. That is, it spreads or continues across both countries without any interruption.

CONTINGENT (kun TIN junt) *adj* dependent; possible

- Our agreement to buy their house is *contingent* upon the sellers' finding another house to move into. That is, they won't sell their house to us unless they can find another house to buy.

- My happiness is *contingent* on yours; if you're unhappy, I'm unhappy.

- The Bowdens were prepared for any *contingency.* Their front hall closet contained a first-aid kit, a fire extinguisher, a life raft, a parachute, and a pack of sled dogs.

A *contingency* is a possibility or something that may happen but is at least as likely not to happen.

- Several *contingencies* stand between us and the successful completion of our business proposal; several things could happen to screw it up.

CONTINUUM (kun TIN yoo um) *n* a continuous whole without clear division into parts

- The spectrum of visible light is a *continuum* in which each color blends into its neighbors.

- Einstein's theory of relativity holds that space and time are not distinct dimensions but inseparable aspects of a *continuum.*

CONTRABAND (KAHN truh band) *n* smuggled goods

- The military police looked for *contraband* in the luggage of the returning soldiers, and they found plenty of it, including captured enemy weapons and illegal drugs.

- The head of the dormitory classified all candy as *contraband,* then went from room to room confiscating it, so that he could eat it himself.

CONTRETEMPS (KAHN truh tahn) *n* an embarrassing occurrence; a mishap

- Newell lost his job over a little *contretemps* involving an office party, the photocopier, and his rear end.

CONTUMELY (kun TOO muh lee) *n* rudeness; insolence; arrogance
- In the opinion of the teacher, the student's sticking out his tongue during the Pledge of Allegiance was unforgivable *contumely*.

To be guilty of *contumely* is to be *contumelious* (kahn too MEE lee us).
- The *contumelious* prisoners stuck out their tongues at their jailers.

QUICK QUIZ #47

Match each word in the first column with its definition in the second column. Check your answers in the back of the book.

1.	consign	a.	combine
2.	consolidate	b.	embarrassing occurrence
3.	conspicuous	c.	continuous whole
4.	consternation	d.	hand over
5.	constituency	e.	group of voters
6.	contempt	f.	smuggled goods
7.	continuum	g.	disdain
8.	contraband	h.	sudden confusion
9.	contretemps	i.	rudeness
10.	contumely	j.	easily seen

CONTRITE (kun TRYTE) *adj* admitting guilt; especially feeling remorseful
To be *contrite* is to admit whatever terrible thing you did.
- Mira was *contrite* about her mistake, so we forgave her.

A criminal who won't confess his crime is not *contrite*.
Saying that you're sorry is an act of *contrition* (kun TRISH un).

CONTRIVED (kun TRYVED) *adj* artificial; labored
- Sam's acting was *contrived:* No one in the audience believed his character or enjoyed his performance.
- The artist was widely admired for his originality, but his paintings seemed *contrived* to me.
- No one laughed at Mark's *contrived* attempt at humor.

A *contrivance* is a mechanical device, usually something rigged up.

CONUNDRUM (kuh NUN drum) *n* a puzzle or problem without a solution
- What to do about the dirty dishes piling up in the sink was a *conundrum* that the four roommates could not even begin to solve.
- English grammar was a *conundrum* to Marcia; she just couldn't figure out how to put two words together.

CONVENE (kun VEEN) *v* to gather together; to assemble; to meet
- For their annual meeting, the members of the physicians' organization *convened* on the first tee of the seaside golf course.
- Mr. Jenkins *convened* the workers in the cafeteria to tell them they had all been fired.

A *convention* is an event at which people *convene* for the purpose of exchanging information, learning new skills, eating rich food, and going shopping.

CONVENTIONAL (kun VEN shun nul) *adj* common; customary; unexceptional
- The architect's *conventional* designs didn't win him awards for originality.

Tipping the waiter in a restaurant is a *conventional* courtesy. *Conventional* wisdom is what everyone thinks.
- The bland politician maintained his popularity by never straying far from the *conventional* wisdom about any topic.

CONVERSANT (kun VUR sunt) *adj* familiar; experienced
- After just two days on the job, Gloria was not yet *conversant* with the many rules laid down by her new employer.
- Several weeks' worth of watching the sports channel had made Omar *conversant* with the rules of football, even though he had never played the game himself.

CONVERSE (KAHN vurs) *n* the opposite
- Freddy followed not the rule but its *converse*; that is, he did the opposite of what he was supposed to do.

CONVEY (kun VAY) *v* to transport; to conduct; to communicate
- The train *conveyed* us across the border in the middle of the night.
- The red pipes *convey* the hot water, and the blue ones convey the cold.
- The look on my mother's face is impossible for me to *convey*; her expression is indescribable.

A *conveyance* (kun VAY uns) is an act of transporting or a means of transporting, especially a vehicle. A bus is a public *conveyance*.

CONVICTION (kun VIK shun) *n* strong belief; a determination of guilt
- It is Terence's *conviction* that the Earth is the center of the universe, but Terence's conviction is wrong.
- Ever since his *conviction* for first-degree murder, Lester had been spending quite a bit of time in jail.

CONVIVIAL (kun VIV ee ul) *adj* fond of partying; festive
A *convivial* gathering is one in which the people present enjoy eating, drinking, and being together.
To be *convivial* is to be an eager but generally well-behaved party animal.
A *convivial* person is the opposite of an antisocial person.

CONVOLUTION (kahn vuh LOO shun) *n* a twist or turn; the act of twisting or turning
- I couldn't follow all the *convolutions* in the plot of the murder mystery; every character seemed to have a dozen identities, and every occurrence turned out to be something other than what it had appeared to be at first.
- Locked within the *convolutions* of a DNA molecule is the secret of life.

A *convoluted* plot is a plot that has lots of twists and turns. A *convoluted* argument is one that is so complex that it is difficult to follow, just as a twisted path would be hard to follow. If you have a simple story to tell, don't *convolute* (kahn vuh LOOT) it by making it more complicated than it needs to be.

COPIOUS (KOH pee us) *adj* abundant; plentiful
- The champagne at the wedding reception was *copious* but not very good.
- Matt had a *copious* supply of nails in his workshop. Everywhere you stepped, it seemed, there was a pile of nails.
- Phil ate *copiously* at the banquet and went home feeling quite sick.

QUICK QUIZ #48

Match each word in the first column with its definition in the second column. Check your answers in the back of the book.

1.	construe	a.	admitting guilt
2.	consummate	b.	interpret
3.	contentious	c.	perfect
4.	contiguous	d.	labored
5.	contingent	e.	dependent
6.	contrite	f.	abundant
7.	contrived	g.	adjoining
8.	conventional	h.	argumentative
9.	convivial	i.	festive
10.	copious	j.	common

CORDIAL (KAWR jul) *adj* gracious; warm; sincere
- We received a *cordial* welcome from our host, who was clearly delighted that my wife and I had come to spend several months with him.
- The police officer was *cordial*; he smiled and shook my hand before he led me off to jail.

To be *cordial* is to do things *cordially* or with *cordiality* (kawr jee AL uh tee).

COROLLARY (KOR uh ler ee) *n* something that follows; a natural consequence
In mathematics, a *corollary* is a law that can be deduced without further proof from a law that has already been proven.
- Bloodshed and death are *corollaries* of any declaration of war.
- Higher prices were a *corollary* of the two companies' agreement not to compete.

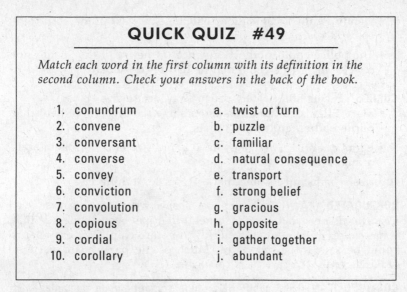

QUICK QUIZ #49

Match each word in the first column with its definition in the second column. Check your answers in the back of the book.

1. conundrum
2. convene
3. conversant
4. converse
5. convey
6. conviction
7. convolution
8. copious
9. cordial
10. corollary

a. twist or turn
b. puzzle
c. familiar
d. natural consequence
e. transport
f. strong belief
g. gracious
h. opposite
i. gather together
j. abundant

CORPOREAL (kawr PAWR ee ul) *adj* material; tangible; having substance, like the body

- Steve was mildly crazy; he believed that at night his thoughts became *corporeal* and wandered around his house eating potato chips and doing laundry.

This word is often confused with *corporal* (KAWR puh rul), which means having to do with the body. Beating a criminal is *corporal* punishment. Someone who has a lot of body fat is *corpulent* (KAWR pyuh lunt). A body of people is called a *corps* (kohr), like the army *corps*.

CORRELATION (kawr uh LAY shun) *n* a mutual relation between two or more things

- The *correlation* between cigarette smoking and lung cancer has been established to the satisfaction of everyone except the manufacturers of cigarettes.

- There is a strong *correlation* between the quality of a football team and the number of games that it wins in a season. That is, the quality of a football team and its number of victories are strongly *correlated*.

CORROBORATE (kuh ROB uh rayt) *v* to confirm; to back up with evidence

- I knew my statement was correct when my colleague *corroborated* it.

- Henny Penny's contention that the sky was falling could not be *corroborated*. That is, no one was able to find any fallen sky.

- The police could find no evidence of theft and thus could not *corroborate* Greg's claim that he had been robbed.

CORROSIVE (kuh ROH siv) *adj* eating away; destructive

- Mary Ellen's chutney contained some *corrosive* ingredient that burned a hole in Jeremy's plate.

- Large quantities of money have a *corrosive* effect on the morals of many people.

A *corrosive* substance is one that *corrodes* something else.

CORRUGATED (KAWR uh gay tud) *adj* shaped with folds or waves
Corrugated sheet metal is sheet metal that has been shaped so that it has ridges and valleys, like a ridged potato chip. Corduroy pants could be said to be *corrugated*. Much of the paperboard used in making cardboard cartons is *corrugated*.

COSMOPOLITAN (kahz muh PAHL uh tun) *adj* at home in many places or situations; internationally sophisticated

- Marcello's interests were *cosmopolitan*—he liked Greek wine, German beer, Dutch cheese, Japanese cars, and French fries.

- A truly *cosmopolitan* traveler never feels like a foreigner anywhere on Earth.

- New York is a *cosmopolitan* city; you can hear nearly every language spoken there.

COTERIE (KOH tuh ree) *n* a group of close associates; a circle (of friends or associates)

- The visiting poet-in-residence quickly developed a large *coterie* of student admirers, all of whom hoped that the visitor would be able to help them find publishers for their poems.

- In Mary's opinion, if you weren't a part of her *coterie*, then you weren't anybody at all.

COUNTENANCE (KOWN tuh nuns) *n* face; facial expression, especially an encouraging one

- His father's confident *countenance* gave Lou the courage to persevere.

- Ed's harsh words belied his *countenance*, which was kind and encouraging.

Countenance can also be a verb. To *countenance* something is to condone it or tolerate it.

- Dad *countenanced* our backyard rock fights even though he didn't really approve of them.

COUP (koo) *n* a brilliant victory or accomplishment; the violent overthrow of a government by a small internal group
- Winning a gold medal at the Olympics was a real *coup* for the fifty-year-old man.
- The student council's great *coup* was persuading Foo Fighters to play at our prom.
- In the attempted *coup* in the Philippines, some army officers tried to take over the government.

The full name for this type of *coup* is *coup d'état* (koo day TAH). A *coup de grace* (koo duh GRAHS) is a final blow or concluding event.

COVENANT (KUV uh nunt) *n* a solemn agreement; a contract; a pledge
- The warring tribes made a *covenant* not to fight each other anymore.
- We signed a *covenant* never to drive Masha's father's car without permission again.

COVERT (KOV urt) *adj* secret; hidden
To be *covert* is to be covered.
   Covert activities are secret activities.
   A *covert* military operation is one the public knows nothing about.
   The opposite of *covert* is *overt*. *Overt* (OH vurt) means open or unconcealed.

COVET (KUV it) *v* to wish for enviously
- To *covet* thy neighbor's wife is to want thy neighbor's wife for thyself.
- Any position at MTV is a highly *coveted* job.

To be *covetous* is to be envious.

COWER (KOW ur) *v* to shrink away or huddle up in fear
- The sound of her boss's footsteps in the hallway made Leah *cower* behind her desk like a wounded animal.
- When Tyson turned on the lights, he found the children *cowering* behind the couch; the movie on TV had scared the wits out of them.
- In the morning, the children found their new puppy *cowering* in the corner of his box, afraid of his new environment.

CRASS (kras) *adj* extremely unrefined; gross; stupid
- Sending a get-well card to the man who had just died was a pretty *crass* gesture, in the opinion of his widow.
- The seventh-grade mixer was spoiled by the *crassness* of the seventh-grade boys, who shouted rude remarks at the girls and then ran off to hide in the restroom.

CRAVEN (KRAY vun) *adj* cowardly
- The *craven* soldier turned his back on his wounded comrade and ran for the safety of the trenches.
- The second-grade bully was full of bluster when the kindergartners were on the playground, but he became quite *craven* when the third graders came out for their recess.

CREDULOUS (KREJ uh lus) *adj* eager to believe; gullible
- The *credulous* housewife believed that she had won a million dollars through an email scam.

- Judy was so *credulous* that she simply nodded happily when Kirven told her he could teach her how to fly. Judy's *credulity* (kri DYOOL uh tee) was limitless.

Credulous should not be confused with *credible*. To be *credible* is to be believable. Almost anything, however *incredible*, is *credible* to a *credulous* person.

- Larry's implausible story of heroism was not *credible*. Still, *credulous* old Louis believed it.

A story that cannot be believed is *incredible*. If you don't believe that story someone just told you, you are *incredulous*. If something is *credible*, it may gain *credence* (KREED uns), which means belief or intellectual acceptance.

- No one could prove Frank's theory, but his standing at the university helped it gain *credence*.

Another similar word is *creditable,* which means worthy of credit or praise.

- Our record in raising money was very *creditable;* we raised several thousand dollars every year.

CRESCENDO (kruh SHEN doh) *n* a gradual increase in the volume of a sound; a gradual increase in the intensity of anything

- The concert ended with a stirring *crescendo* that began with a single note from a single violin and built up to a thunderous roar from every instrument in the orchestra.

- The fund-raising campaign built slowly to a *crescendo* of giving that pushed the total well beyond the original goal.

CRESTFALLEN (KREST fawl un) *adj* dejected; dispirited
Your *crest* (krest) is the highest point of your body—your head. When your *crest* falls—when your head is drooping—you are dejected or dispirited. You are *crestfallen.*

- The big red F on her science paper left Zoe *crestfallen*, until she realized that the F stood for "Fantastic."

- I was *crestfallen* when I opened my Christmas presents; all I got were underwear and socks.

QUICK QUIZ #51

Match each word in the first column with its definition in the second column. Check your answers in the back of the book.

1.	corporeal	a.	destructive
2.	correlation	b.	cowardly
3.	corrosive	c.	mutual relation
4.	corrugated	d.	gradual increase in volume
5.	coterie	e.	tangible
6.	cower	f.	dejected
7.	crass	g.	extremely unrefined
8.	craven	h.	group of close associates
9.	crescendo	i.	shaped with folds
10.	crestfallen	j.	huddle in fear

CREVICE (KREV us) *n* a narrow split, crack, or fissure
- The winning lottery ticket I had found on the sidewalk fell into a *crevice* between the two buildings, and I never saw it again.

A large *crevice* in a glacier on the Earth's surface is usually called a *crevasse* (kruh VAS). The tiny crack in a rock face from which a mountain climber hangs by his fingernails is a *crevice*; the deep crack in a glacier into which a mountain climber falls, never to be seen again, is a *crevasse*.

CRINGE (krinj) *v* to shrink back with fear; to cower; to be servile or suck up in a horrible way,
- Alison *cringed* when the doctor came striding toward her with a long hypodermic needle in his hand.

- The *cringing* jester eventually began to annoy the king, who told the jester to stop fawning.

CRITERION (krye TEER ee un) *n* standard; basis for judgment
- When Norm judges a meal, he has only one *criterion*: Is it edible?

- In choosing among the linemen, the most important *criterion* was quickness.

The plural of *criterion* is *criteria*. You can't have *one criteria*; you can only have one *criterion*. If you have two or more, you have *criteria*. There is no such thing as *criterions* and no such thing as *a criteria*.

CRITIQUE (kruh TEEK) *n* a critical review
- The reviewer's brutal *critique* of my latest book made me reluctant ever to pick up a pen again.
- Lloyd liked to help out around the kitchen by offering concise *critiques* of nearly every move his wife made.

Critique can also be used as a verb.
- The art teacher *critiqued* the students' projects in front of the entire class, making some of the students feel utterly miserable.

Critique is neutral—it doesn't necessarily have a negative connotation, though it is related to several words that typically do. A *critic* is one who expresses an opinion, often unfavorable, which is also called being *critical*.

CRUX (kruks) *n* the central point; the essence
The *crux* of an argument is the crucial part of it. *Crux* and crucial are related words. Often when you see this word, it will be followed by "of the matter." The *crux* of the matter is the heart of the matter.
- Building a lot of atom bombs and dropping them on the capital was the *crux* of the renegade general's plan to topple the existing government.

CRYPTIC (KRIP tik) *adj* mysterious; mystifying
- Elaine's remarks were *cryptic*; Jerry was baffled by what she said.

A *cryptic* statement is one in which something important remains hidden.
- The ghost made *cryptic* comments about the *crypt* from which he had just emerged; that is, no one could figure out what the ghost meant.

CUISINE (kwi ZEEN) *n* a style of cooking
Cuisine is the French word for kitchen and cooking. A restaurant advertising French *cuisine* is a restaurant that serves food prepared in a French style. A restaurant advertising Italian *cuisine* is slightly absurd, since *cuisine* is French not Italian, but this usage is common and everyone understands it.

CULINARY (KYOO luh ner ee) *adj* relating to cooking or the kitchen
A cooking school is sometimes called a *culinary* institute.
- Allison pursued her *culinary* interests by attending the *culinary* institute. Her first meal, which was burned beyond recognition, was a *culinary* disaster.

CULL (kul) *v* to pick out from among many; to select; to collect
- The farmer *culled* the best raspberries from his new crop and sold them for twenty-five cents apiece.
- The poet *culled* a few of his favorite poems from among his collected works and had them printed in a special edition.
- On the first day of school, the veteran teacher *culled* the trouble-makers from her classroom and had them assigned to other teachers.

CULMINATE (KUL muh nayt) *v* to climax; to reach full effect
- Connie's years of practice *culminated* in a great victory at the international juggling championship.
- The masquerade ball was the *culmination* of our fund-raising efforts.

QUICK QUIZ #52

Match each word in the first column with its definition in the second column. Check your answers in the back of the book.

1. credulous		a.	related to cooking
2. credible		b.	believable
3. incredible		c.	believability
4. incredulous		d.	worthy of praise
5. credence		e.	eager to believe
6. creditable		f.	unbelieving
7. criterion		g.	unbelievable
8. cryptic		h.	climax
9. culinary		i.	standard
10. culminate		j.	mysterious

CULPABLE (KUL puh bul) *adj* deserving blame; guilty
- The accountant's failure to spot the errors made him *culpable* in the tax-fraud case.
- We all felt *culpable* when the homeless old man died in the doorway of our apartment building.

A person who is *culpable* (a *culprit*) is one who can be blamed for doing something.

To decide that a person is not *culpable* after all is to *exculpate* (EK skul payt) that person.

- Lou's confession didn't *exculpate* Bob, because one of the things that Lou confessed was that Bob had helped him do it.

The opposite of *exculpate* is *inculpate*. To *inculpate* is to accuse someone of something.

CURB (kurb) *v* to restrain or control

- The best way I've found to *curb* my appetite is to eat a couple of pints of coffee ice cream; once I've done that, I'm not hungry anymore.

- The scout leader did his best to *curb* the young scouts' natural tendency to beat up one another.

A *curb* is something that *curbs*. The *curb* on a street is a barrier that *curbs* cars from driving onto the sidewalk.

CURMUDGEON (kur MUJ un) *n* a difficult, bad-tempered person

- Old age had turned kindly old Mr. Green into a *curmudgeon*; he never seemed to see anything that didn't displease him, and he always had something nasty to say to the people who came to visit.

The words "old" and *curmudgeon* often appear together. Sometimes *curmudgeon* is used affectionately, as when we refer to an elderly person who is humorously grumpy from the aches and pains of life. A *curmudgeon* can be said to be *curmudgeonly*.

CURSORY (KUR suh ree) *adj* hasty; superficial

- To give a book a *cursory* reading is to skim it quickly without comprehending much.

- The *cursor* on Dave's computer made a *cursory* sweep across the data as he scrolled down the page.

To make a *cursory* attempt at learning French is to memorize a couple of easy words and then give up.

Match each word in the first column with its definition in the second column. Check your answers in the back of the book.

1.	crevice	a.	restrain
2.	cringe	b.	pick out from among many
3.	critique	c.	critical review
4.	crux	d.	style of cooking
5.	cuisine	e.	shrink back with fear
6.	cull	f.	central point
7.	curb	g.	narrow split
8.	curmudgeon	h.	quick and unthorough
9.	cursory	i.	difficult, bad-tempered person

CURTAIL (kur TAYL) *v* to shorten; to cut short
- The vet *curtailed* his effort to cut the cat's tail with the lawn mower. That is, he stopped trying.

To *curtail* a tale is to cut it short.

CYNIC (SIN ik) *n* one who deeply distrusts human nature; one who believes humans are motivated only by selfishness
- When the pop star gave a million dollars to the museum, *cynics* said he was merely trying to buy himself a reputation as a cultured person.

To be *cynical* is to be extremely suspicious of the motivations of other people.

Cynicism is general grumpiness and pessimism about human nature.

QUICK QUIZ #54

Match each word in the first column with its definition in the second column. Check your answers in the back of the book.

1.	culpable	a.	free from guilt
2.	exculpate	b.	shorten
3.	cursory	c.	one who distrusts humanity
4.	curtail	d.	hasty
5.	cynic	e.	guilty

D

DAUNT (dawnt) *v* to make fearful; to intimidate
- The steepness of the mountain *daunted* the team of amateur climbers, because they hadn't realized what they were in for.
- The size of the players on the visiting team was *daunting;* the players on the home team began to perspire nervously.

To be *dauntless* or *undaunted* is to be fearless or unintimidated.
- The rescue crew was *undaunted* by the flames and ran into the burning house to look for survivors. The entire crew was *dauntless* in its effort to save the people inside.

DEARTH (durth) *n* lack; scarcity
- There is no *dearth* of comedy at a convention of clowns.
- When there is a *dearth* of food, many people may starve.
- There was a *dearth* of gaiety at the boring Christmas party.

DEBACLE (di BAHK ul) *n* violent breakdown; sudden overthrow; overwhelming defeat
- A political debate would become a *debacle* if the candidates began screaming and throwing dinner rolls at each other.

This word can also be pronounced "day BAHK ul."

DEBASE (di BAYS) *v* to lower in quality or value; to degrade
- To deprive a single person of his or her constitutional rights *debases* the liberty of us all.
- The high school teacher's reputation as a great educator was *debased* when it was discovered that his students' test scores dropped by five points after they utilized his test-taking strategies.

The noun is *debasement*. See our listing for abase.

DEBAUCHERY (di BAW chuh ree) *n* wild living; excessive intemperance
- *Debauchery* can be expensive; fortunately for Jeff, his wallet matched his appetite for extravagant pleasures. He died a poor, albeit happy, man.

To *debauch* is to seduce or corrupt. Someone who is *debauched* has been seduced or corrupted.

DEBILITATE (di BIL uh tayt) *v* to weaken; to cripple
- The football player's career was ended by a *debilitating* injury to his knee.

To become *debilitated* is to suffer a *debility*, which is the opposite of an ability.

- A surgeon who becomes *debilitated* is one who has lost the ability to operate on the *debilities* of other people.

DEBUNK (di BUNK) *v* to expose the nonsense of

- The reporter's careful exposé *debunked* the company's claim that it had not been dumping radioactive waste into the Hudson River.

- Paul's reputation as a philanthropist was a towering lie just waiting to be *debunked*.

Bunk, by the way, is nonsense or meaningless talk.

DECADENT (DEK uh dunt) *adj* decaying or decayed, especially in terms of morals

A person who engages in *decadent* behavior is a person whose morals have decayed or fallen into ruin.

- Carousing in local bars instead of going to class is *decadent*.

Decadent behavior is often an affectation of bored young people. The noun is *decadence*.

DECIMATE (DES uh mayt) *v* to kill or destroy a large part of

To *decimate* an army is to come close to wiping it out.

- When locusts attack a crop, they sometimes *decimate* it, leaving very little that's fit for human consumption.

- You might say in jest that your family had *decimated* its turkey dinner on Thanksgiving, leaving nothing but a few crumbs and a pile of bones.

The noun is *decimation*.

DECOROUS (DEK ur us) *adj* proper; in good taste; orderly

Decorous behavior is good, polite, orderly behavior.

To be *decorous* is to be sober and tasteful.

- The New Year's Eve crowd was relatively *decorous* until midnight, when they went wild.

To behave *decorously* is to behave with *decorum* (di KOR um).

DECREE (di KREE) *n* an official order, usually having the force of law

- The crazy king's latest *decree* forbade the wearing of hats and the eating of asparagus.

This word can also be a verb. To *decree* something is to declare it formally and officially.

- In a last-ditch attempt to win favor among wealthy voters, the president *decreed* that thenceforth only poor people would have to pay taxes.

DECRY (di KRY) *v* to put down; to denounce

- The newspaper editorial *decried* efforts by the police chief to root out corruption in the police department, saying that the chief was himself corrupt and could not be trusted.

- The environmental organization quickly issued a report *decrying* the large mining company's plan to reduce the entire mountain to rubble in its search for uranium.

DEDUCE (di DOOS) *v* to conclude from the evidence; to infer

To *deduce* something is to conclude it without being told it directly.

- From the footprints on the ground, Clarice *deduced* that the criminal had feet.

- Daffy *deduced* from the shape of its bill that the duck was really a chicken. That the duck was really a chicken was Daffy's *deduction*.

DEEM (deem) *v* to judge; to consider

- Mother *deemed* it unwise to lure the bear into the house by smearing honey on the front steps.

- My paper was *deemed* to be inadequate by my teacher, and he gave it a failing grade.

- After taking but a single bite, Angus *deemed* the meal to be delectable.

DEFAME (di FAYM) *v* to libel or slander; to ruin the good name of

To *defame* someone is to make accusations that harm the person's reputation.

- The local businessman accused the newspaper of *defaming* him by publishing an article that said his company was poorly managed.

To *defame* is to take away fame, to take away a good name.

To suffer such a loss of reputation is to suffer *defamation*.

- The businessman who believed he had been *defamed* by the newspaper sued the paper's publisher for *defamation*.

Match each word in the first column with its definition in the second column. Check your answers in the back of the book.

1.	daunt	a.	conclude from evidence
2.	dearth	b.	lack
3.	debacle	c.	kill a large part of
4.	debauchery	d.	libel or slander
5.	debilitate	e.	make fearful
6.	decadent	f.	decaying or decayed
7.	decimate	g.	proper
8.	decorous	h.	weaken
9.	deduce	i.	violent breakdown
10.	defame	j.	wild living

DEFERENCE (DEF ur uns) *n* submission to another's will; respect; courtesy
To show *deference* to another is to place that person's wishes ahead of your own.

- Dean showed *deference* to his grandfather: He let the old man have first dibs on the birthday cake.

- Danny stopped texting at the dinner table in *deference* to the wishes of his mother.

To show *deference* to another is to *defer* to that person.
- Joe was supposed to go first, but he *deferred* to Steve, who had been waiting longer.

To show *deference* is also to be *deferential* (def uh REN shul).
- Joe was being *deferential* when he allowed Steve to go first.

DEFICIT (DEF uh sit) *n* a shortage, especially of money
- The national *deficit* is the amount by which the nation's revenues fall short of its expenditures.

- Frank had forgotten to eat lunch; he made up the *deficit* at dinner by eating seconds of everything.

- Unexpectedly large legal fees left the company with a *deficit* in its operating budget.

Deficit is related to the words *deficiency* and *defect*.

DEFILE (di FYLE) *v* to make filthy or foul; to desecrate
- The snowy field was so beautiful that I hated to *defile* it by driving across it.
- In the night, vandals *defiled* the painting behind the altar by covering it with spray paint.

DEFINITIVE (di FIN uh tiv) *adj* conclusive; providing the last word
- Walter wrote the *definitive* biography of Keats; nothing more could have been added by another book.
- The army completely wiped out the invaders; its victory was *definitive*.
- No one could find anything to object to in Cindy's *definitive* explanation of how the meteorite had gotten into the bathtub.

DEFT (deft) *adj* skillful
- The store detective was so *deft* in his capture of the shoplifter that none of the customers was aware of what was going on.
- In one *deft* move, the shortstop scooped the ball out of the dirt and flipped it to the second baseman.

DEFUNCT (di FUNKT) *adj* no longer in effect; no longer in existence
- Most of the businesses in the oldest section of downtown were now *defunct*; the new specialty stores on the other side of the river had put them out of business.
- My already limited interest in cutting the grass was just about *defunct* by the time the grass was actually ready to cut, so I never got around to doing it.
- The long spell of extremely hot weather left my entire garden *defunct*.

Defunct is related to the word function.

DEGENERATE (di JEN uh rayt) *v* to break down; to deteriorate
- The discussion quickly *degenerated* into an argument.
- Over the years, the nice old neighborhood had *degenerated* into a terrible slum.
- The fans' behavior *degenerated* as the game went on.

A person whose behavior has *degenerated* can be referred to as a *degenerate* (di JEN ur it).
- The mood of the party was spoiled when a drunken *degenerate* wandered in from off the street.

Degenerate (di JEN ur it) can also be an adjective, meaning *degenerated*.
- The slum neighborhood was *degenerate*.
- The fans' *degenerate* behavior prompted the police to make several arrests.

DEGRADE (di GRAYD) *v* to lower in dignity or status; to corrupt; to deteriorate
- Being made to perform menial duties at the behest of overbearing male senior partners clearly *degrades* the law firm's female associates.
- The former bank president felt *degraded* to work as a teller, but he was unable to find any other job. The former bank president felt that working as a teller was *degrading*.
- The secret potion had *degraded* over the years to the point at which it was no longer capable of turning a person into a frog.

Degradation (deg ruh DAY shun) is the act of *degrading* or the state of being *degraded*.

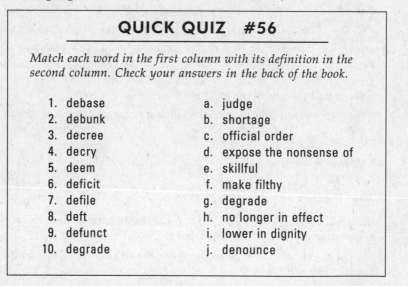

QUICK QUIZ #56

Match each word in the first column with its definition in the second column. Check your answers in the back of the book.

1.	debase	a.	judge
2.	debunk	b.	shortage
3.	decree	c.	official order
4.	decry	d.	expose the nonsense of
5.	deem	e.	skillful
6.	deficit	f.	make filthy
7.	defile	g.	degrade
8.	deft	h.	no longer in effect
9.	defunct	i.	lower in dignity
10.	degrade	j.	denounce

DEIGN (dayn) *v* to condescend; to think it in accordance with one's dignity (to do something)
- When I asked the prince whether he would be willing to lend me five bucks for the rest of the day, he did not *deign* to make a reply.

DEITY (DEE uh tee) *n* a god or goddess
- Members of the ancient tribe believed that the big spruce tree in the middle of the forest was an angry *deity* that punished them by ruining crops and bringing bad weather.
- Many of Elvis's fans view him as a *deity*; a few even believe that listening to his records can cure cancer.

To treat someone or something as a *deity* is to *deify* (DEE uh fy) it.
- Sasha *deified* money; the "almighty dollar" was her god.

DEJECTED (di JEK tid) *adj* depressed; disheartened
- Barney was *dejected* when he heard that Fred had gone to the lodge without him, but he cheered up later when Betty made him some brownies.
- The members of the losing field-hockey team looked *dejected*; their heads were bowed, and they were dragging their sticks.

To be *dejected* is to be in a state of *dejection* (di JEK shun). Rejection often causes *dejection*.

DELECTABLE (di LEK tuh bul) *adj* delightful; delicious
- Vince's success as a writer was made all the more *delectable* to him by the failure of his closest rival.
- The Christmas turkey looked *delectable* from a distance, but it was so dry and leathery that it was nearly impossible to eat.

DELETERIOUS (del uh TIR ee us) *adj* harmful
- Smoking cigarettes is *deleterious* to your health.
- Is watching a lot of TV really *deleterious*? Of course not.

DELINEATE (di LIN ee ayt) *v* to describe accurately; to draw in outline
- After Jack had *delineated* his plan, we had no doubt about what he intended to do.
- Sharon's peculiar feelings about her pet gorilla were *delineated* in the newspaper article about her.
- The portrait artist *delineated* Sarah's features, then filled in the shading.

The noun is *delineation*.

DELINQUENT (di LING kwent) *adj* neglecting a duty or law; late in payment
- The *delinquent* father failed to show up for visits with his children from his first marriage.
- The city's motor vehicle bureau decided to impound the cars of drivers who had been *delinquent* in paying their traffic tickets.

- The telephone company charges a late fee for customers who are *delinquent* in paying their bills.

Delinquent can also be a noun. A person who fails to pay his or her taxes is a tax *delinquent* and is subject to prosecution. A juvenile *delinquent* is a young person who habitually breaks the law.

DELUDE (dye LOOD) *v* to deceive
- The con man *deluded* us into thinking that he would make us rich. Instead, he tricked us into giving him several hundred dollars.
- The *deluded* mental patient believed that he was a chicken sandwich.
- Lori is so persuasive that she was able to *delude* Leslie into thinking she was a countess.

To be *deluded* is to suffer from a *delusion*.
- That he was a great poet was the *delusion* of the English teacher, who could scarcely write two complete sentences in a row.
- Todd, the well-known jerk, suffered from the *delusion* that he was a genuinely nice man.

DELUGE (DEL yooj) *n* a flood; an inundation
A *deluge* is a flood, but the word is often used figuratively.
- The $1 million reward for the lost poodle brought in a *deluge* of hot leads. The distraught owner was *deluged* by phone calls all week.

DELVE (delv) *v* to search or study intensively
Delve originally meant to dig, and you occasionally find the word still used in this way. A miner might be said to *delve* the Earth for ore, for example. In its modern meaning, *delve* means to dig metaphorically. To *delve* into a subject is to dig deeply into it—not with a shovel, but with your mind.
- Janice was afraid to *delve* into her childhood memories because she was afraid of what she might remember.

DEMAGOGUE (DEM uh gahg) *n* a leader who uses prejudice to get more power
A *demagogue* is a leader, but not in a good sense of the word. He manipulates the public to support his aims, but he is little different from a dictator. A *demagogue* is often a despot.

This word can also be spelled *demagog*. The methods a *demagogue* uses are *demagoguery* (DEM uh gahg uh ree) or *demagogy* (DEM uh gahg ee).

DEMEANOR (di MEE nur) *n* behavior; manner
- You could tell by Barclay's *demeanor* that he was a jerk; he picked his nose two nostrils at a time, and he snorted loudly whenever he heard or saw something that he didn't like.
- The substitute teacher was thrilled by the *demeanor* of the children until she realized that they had glued her coffee mug to her table.

Don't confuse this word with the verb to *demean*, or the adjective *demeaning*. To *demean* something is to lower its dignity or stature.

DEMISE (di MYZE) *n* death
- Aunt Isabel was grief-stricken about the *demise* of her favorite rose-bush; that plant was the only friend she had ever had.
- Ever since the legislature had passed an income tax, Senator Jones had been working to bring about its *demise*.
- Oscar's arrest for possession of cocaine led quickly to the *demise* of his law practice.

DEMOGRAPHY (di MAHG ruh fee) *n* the statistical study of characteristics of populations
Democracy is rule by the people. A graph is a written record or picture describing something. *Demography* is the study of characteristics shared by groups of people. When a magazine announces that 75 percent of its readers drink Scotch and that 53 percent of them earn more than $100,000 per year, it is referring to the results of a *demographic* (dem uh GRAF ik) study. The characteristics measured in such a study are referred to as the *demographics* of the group being studied. A person who studies *demographics* is a *demographer* (di MAHG ruh fur).
- Computers have made it possible for companies to learn quite a bit about the *demographics* of their customers, such as how old they are, how much money they make, how many children they have, and what other products they buy.

DEMUR (di MUR) *v* to object; to take exception
- Diego *demurred* when I suggested that he eat the entire plate of "seriously spicy" chicken wings at Fred's Diner.

Don't confuse this word with *demure* on the next page.

QUICK QUIZ #57

Match each word in the first column with its definition in the second column. Check your answers in the back of the book.

1.	deign	a.	delightful
2.	deity	b.	death
3.	dejected	c.	god or goddess
4.	delectable	d.	take exception
5.	delinquent	e.	study of population
6.	delve		characteristics
7.	demeanor	f.	depressed
8.	demise	g.	search intensively
9.	demography	h.	behavior
10.	demur	i.	condescend
		j.	neglecting a duty

DEMURE (di MYOOR) *adj* shy; reserved; sedate
Don't confuse this word with *demur*.
- Jenna was a *demure* child; she sat quietly next to her mother with her hands folded in her lap.

DENIZEN (DEN i zun) *n* inhabitant
To be a *denizen* of a country is to live there. A citizen of a country is usually also a *denizen*.

To be a *denizen* of a restaurant is to go there often—so often that people begin to wonder whether you live there.

Fish are sometimes referred to as *"denizens* of the deep." Don't refer to them this way yourself; the expression is a cliché.

DENOMINATION (di nahm uh NAY shun) *n* a classification; a category name
Religious *denominations* are religious groups consisting of a number of related congregations. Episcopalians and Methodists represent two distinct Christian *denominations*.

Denomination is often used in connection with currency. When a bank robber demands bills in small *denominations*, he or she is demanding bills with low face values: ones, fives, and tens.

DENOTE (di NOHT) *v* to signify; to indicate; to mark
- Blue stains in the sink *denote* acidic water in the pipes.
- The doll's name—Baby Wet 'n' Mess—*denotes* exactly what it does.

DENOUNCE (di NOWNS) *v* to condemn
- The president publicly *denounced*, but privately celebrated, the illegal activities of the director of the Central Intelligence Agency.
- In order to avoid being sent to jail, the political prisoner *denounced* the cause in which he believed.

An act of *denouncing* is a *denunciation* (di nun see AY shun).

DEPICT (di PIKT) *v* to portray, especially in a picture; to describe
If you think you see the same root as in picture, you're right. To *depict* is to draw a picture in someone's mind.
- The enormous mural *depicts* various incidents from the Bible.
- The candidate's brochures accurately *depicted* his opponent as a swindler and a charlatan, but his television commercials were distorted.

The noun form of the word is *depiction*.
- The author's *depiction* (di PIK shun) of New York was not believable to anyone who has ever been to the city; for one thing, she described the Empire State Building as being seven stories tall.

DEPLETE (di PLEET) *v* to decrease the supply of; to exhaust; to use up
- After three years of careless spending, the young heir had *depleted* his inheritance to the point at which he was nearly in danger of having to work for a living. He regretted this *depletion*.
- Irresponsible harvesting has seriously *depleted* the nation's stock of old-growth trees.
- Illness has *depleted* Simone's strength to the point at which she could barely stand without assistance.

Replete means full. The noun is *repletion*.
- Ozzy's stomach was *replete* after consuming eleven pints of chocolate-chip ice cream.

DEPLORE (di PLAWR) *v* to regret; to condemn; to lament
- *Deploring* waste is one thing; actually learning to be less wasteful is another.
- Maria claimed to *deplore* the commercialization of Christmas, but she did spend several thousand dollars on Christmas presents for each of her children.

DEPLOY (di PLOY) *v* to station soldiers or armaments strategically; to arrange strategically
- The Soviet soldiers were *deployed* along the border of Afghanistan, ready to attack.
- The United States has nuclear missiles *deployed* all over Europe.
- At the banquet, the hostess *deployed* her army of waiters around the garden, hoping that none of the guests would have to wait more than a few seconds to receive a full glass of champagne.

DEPOSE (di POHZ) *v* to remove from office or position of power
- The disgruntled generals *deposed* the king, then took him out to the courtyard and shot him.

DEPRAVITY (di PRAV uh tee) *n* extreme wickedness or corruption
- Mrs. Prudinkle wondered whether the *depravity* of her class of eight-year-olds was the result of their watching Saturday morning television.

To exhibit *depravity* is to be *depraved* (di PRAYVD).

DEPRECATE (DEP ruh kayt) *v* to express disapproval of
- To *deprecate* a colleague's work is to risk making yourself unwelcome in your colleague's office.

"This stinks!" is a *deprecating* remark.
- The critic's *deprecating* comments about my new novel put me in a bad mood for an entire month.
- To be *self-deprecating* is to belittle one's own efforts, often in the hope that someone else will say, "No, you're wonderful!"

DEPREDATE (DEP ruh dayt) *v* to prey upon; to plunder
A *predator* is someone who preys on others. To *depredate* is to take what belongs to others, by violence if necessary.
- The greedy broker *depredated* his elderly clients, stealing many millions of dollars before he was finally caught and sent to jail.

An act or instance of *depredating* is a *depredation* (dep ruh DAY shun) or predation (pri DAY shun).
- Despite the frequent *depredations* of the enemy soldiers, the villagers rebuilt their homes and went on with their lives.

QUICK QUIZ   #58

Match each word in the first column with its definition in the second column. Check your answers in the back of the book.

1.	demure	a.	decrease the supply of
2.	denomination	b.	condemn
3.	denote	c.	arrange strategically
4.	denounce	d.	classification
5.	depict	e.	prey upon
6.	deplete	f.	portray
7.	deplore	g.	signify
8.	deploy	h.	remove from office
9.	depose	i.	shy
10.	depredate	j.	lament

DERIDE (di RYDE) *v* to ridicule; to laugh at contemptuously

- Gerald *derided* Diana's driving ability after their hair-raising trip down the twisting mountain road.

- Sportswriters *derided* Columbia's football team, which hadn't won a game in three years.

- The boss *derided* his secretary mercilessly, so she quit her job. She was someone who could not accept *derision* (di RIZH un).

QUICK QUIZ #59

Match each word in the first column with its definition in the second column. Check your answers in the back of the book.

1. deference		a.	deteriorate
2. definitive		b.	ridicule
3. degenerate		c.	describe accurately
4. deleterious		d.	respect
5. delineate		e.	conclusive
6. delude		f.	express disapproval of
7. deluge		g.	harmful
8. demagogue		h.	inhabitant
9. denizen		i.	deceive
10. depravity		j.	flood
11. deprecate		k.	extreme wickedness
12. deride		l.	rabble-rousing leader

DERELICT (DER uh likt) *adj* neglectful; delinquent; deserted
- The crack-addicted mother was *derelict* in her duty to her children; they were running around on the city streets in filthy clothes.
- Navigation was made difficult by the rotting hulls of the *derelict* ships that were scattered around the bay.

Derelict can also be a noun.
- The only car in sight was a rusty *derelict* that had been stripped to its chassis by vandals.

DEROGATORY (dih RAHG uh tor ee) *adj* disapproving; degrading
Derogatory remarks are negative remarks expressing disapproval. They are nastier than merely critical remarks.
- Stephen could never seem to think of anything nice to say about anyone; virtually all of his comments were *derogatory*.

DESICCATE (DES uh kayt) *v* to dry out
- The hot wind *desiccated* the few grapes remaining on the vine; after a day or two, they looked like raisins.
- After a week without water, the *desiccated* plant fell over and died.

Plums become prunes through a process of *desiccation*.

DESIST (di ZIST) *v* to stop doing (something)
- For several hours, I *desisted* from eating any of the pumpkin pie, but then I weakened and ate three pieces.
- The judge issued a cease-and-*desist* order that forbade Mr. Jones to paint obscene words on the garage door of his neighbor's house.

DESPONDENT (dih SPAHN dunt) *adj* extremely depressed; full of despair
- The cook became *despondent* when the wedding cake fell on the floor fifteen minutes before the reception.
- After the death of his wife, the man was *despondent* for many months.
- The team fell into *despondency* after losing the state championship game by a single point.

DESPOT (DES puht) *n* an absolute ruler; an autocrat
- Stephen was a *despot*; workers who disagreed with him were fired.
- The island kingdom was ruled by a ruthless *despot* who executed suspected rebels at noon each day in the village square.

To act like a *despot* is to be *despotic* (di SPAH tik).
- There was cheering in the street when the country's *despotic* government was overthrown.

DESTITUTE (DES tuh toot) *adj* extremely poor; utterly lacking
Destitute people are people without money or possessions, or with very little money and very few possessions.

To be left *destitute* is to be left without money or property. The word can also be used figuratively. A teacher might accuse her students of being *destitute* of brains, or intellectually *destitute*.

DESULTORY (DES ul tor ee) *adj* without a plan or purpose; disconnected; random
- Aadi made a few *desultory* attempts to start a garden, but nothing came of them.
- In his *desultory* address, Rizal skipped from one topic to another and never came to the point.
- The discussion at our meeting was *desultory*; no one's comments seemed to bear any relation to anyone else's.

DEVOUT (di VOWT) *adj* deeply religious; fervent
- Mary was such a *devout* Catholic that she decided to become a nun and spend the rest of her life in a convent.
- Bill is a *devout* procrastinator; he never does anything today that he can put off until tomorrow—or, better yet, the day after that.

Devout is related to *devoted*. Someone who is *devoted* to something is a *devotee*.

DEXTROUS (DEX trus) *adj* skillful; adroit
Dextrous often, but not always, connotes physical ability. Like *adroit*, it comes from the Latin word for right (as in the direction), because right-handed people were once considered physically and mentally superior.
- Though not imposing in stature, Rashid was the most *dextrous* basketball player on the court; he often beat taller competitors with his nimble management of the ball.
- Ilya was determined not to sell the restaurant on eBay; even the most *dextrous* negotiator could not sway him.

You may also see this word spelled *dexterous*. *Dexterity* is the noun form. For an antonym, see *gauche*.

DIALECTICAL (dye uh LEK ti kul) *adj* relating to discussions; relating to the rules and methods of reasoning; approaching truth in the middle of opposing extremes
The game of Twenty Questions is *dialectical,* in that the participants attempt to narrow down a chosen object by asking a series of ever more specific questions.
   The noun is *dialectic.*

DIATRIBE (DYE uh trybe) *n* a bitter, abusive denunciation
- Arnold's review of Norman Mailer's new book rapidly turned into a *diatribe* against Mailer's writing.
- The essay was more of a *diatribe* than a critique; you could almost hear the sputtering of the author as you read it.

DICHOTOMY (dye KAHT uh mee) *n* division into two parts, especially contradictory ones
- There has always been a *dichotomy* between what Harry says and what he does; he says one thing and does the other.
- Linda could never resolve the *dichotomy* between her desire to help other people and her desire to make lots and lots of money, so she decided just to make lots and lots of money.

DICTUM (DIK tum) *n* an authoritative saying; an adage; a maxim; a proverb
"No pain, no gain" is a hackneyed *dictum* of sadistic coaches everywhere.

DIDACTIC (dye DAK tik) *adj* intended to teach; morally instructive; pedantic
- Luther's seemingly amusing talk had a *didactic* purpose; he was trying to show his listeners the difference between right and wrong.
- The priest's conversation was always *didactic*. He never said anything that wasn't intended to teach a lesson.
- The new novel is painfully *didactic;* the author's aim is always to instruct and never to entertain.

DIFFIDENT (DIF i dunt) *adj* timid; lacking in self-confidence
Diffident and *confident* are opposites.
- The *diffident* student never made a single comment in class.
- Sebastian's stammer made him *diffident* in conversation and shy in groups of strangers.
- Carla's *diffidence* led many participants to believe she hadn't been present at the meeting, even though she had.

DIFFUSE (di FYOOZ) *v* to cause to spread out; to cause to disperse; to disseminate
- The tear gas *diffused* across the campus; students as far away as the library reported that their eyes were stinging.

If something is spread out, it is *diffuse* (di FYOOS).
- Resistance to the proposition was so *diffuse* that the opposition movement was never able to develop any momentum.

The noun is *diffusion*.

DIGRESS (dye GRES) *v* to stray from the main subject
Speaking metaphorically, to *digress* is to leave the main highway in order to travel aimlessly on back roads. When a speaker *digresses*, he departs from the main topic and tells a story only distantly related to it.

Such a story is called a *digression*. Sometimes a writer's or speaker's *digressions* are more interesting than his or her main points.
- After a lengthy *digression*, the lecturer returned to his speech and brought it to a conclusion.

DILAPIDATED (di LAP uh day tid) *adj* broken-down; fallen into ruin
This word comes from a Latin word meaning to pelt with stones.

- A *dilapidated* house is one that is in such a state of ruin that it appears to have been attacked or pelted with stones.

- Our car was so *dilapidated* that you could see the pavement whizzing past through the big holes in the rusty floor.

DILATE (dye LAYT) *v* to make larger; to become larger; to speak or write at length

- Before examining my eyes, the doctor gave me some eyedrops that *dilated* my pupils.

- The pores in the skin *dilate* in hot weather to cool the skin.

- The evening speaker *dilated* on his subject for so long that most of the people in the audience fell asleep.

The noun is *dilation*.

DILEMMA (di LEM uh) *n* a situation in which one must choose between two equally attractive choices; any problem or predicament
Dilemma comes from Greek words meaning double proposition. In careful usage, the word retains this sense and is used only when the choice is between two things. In less formal usage, though, the word is used to mean any problem or predicament. If you are stuck on the "horns of a dilemma," you are having trouble choosing between two equally attractive choices.

- Freddy wanted both a new car and a new boat, but had only enough money to buy one of them; he solved his *dilemma* by buying the car and charging the boat.

Dilemma is a close synonym of quandary.

DILETTANTE (DIL uh tahnt) *n* someone with superficial knowledge of the arts; an amateur; a dabbler
To be a *dilettante* is to dabble in something rather than doing it in a serious way.

- Reginald said he was an artist, but he was merely a *dilettante*; he didn't know a pencil from a paintbrush.

- Antonella dismissed the members of the ladies' sculpture club as nothing more than a bunch of *dilettantes*.

QUICK QUIZ   #60

Match each word in the first column with its definition in the second column. Check your answers in the back of the book.

1.	derogatory	a.	without purpose
2.	desiccate	b.	extremely depressed
3.	despondent	c.	amateur
4.	despot	d.	stray from the main subject
5.	destitute	e.	extremely poor
6.	desultory	f.	timid
7.	dextrous	g.	dry out
8.	dialectical	h.	disapproving
9.	dictum	i.	absolute ruler
10.	didactic	j.	intended to teach
11.	diffident	k.	relating to discussions
12.	digress	l.	authoritative saying
13.	dilettante	m.	skillful

DIMINUTION (di muh NOO shun) *n* the act or process of diminishing; reduction

- The process was so gradual that Basil didn't notice the *diminution* of his eyesight; it seemed to him that he had simply woken up blind one morning.

- The *diminution* of the value of savings means that I am not as wealthy as I used to be.

Diminutive (di MIN yoo tiv) means very small.

- The giant's wife was surprisingly *diminutive*; when she stood beside her husband, she looked like his child.

QUICK QUIZ #61

Match each word in the first column with its definition in the second column. Check your answers in the back of the book.

1.	derelict	a.	division into two parts
2.	desist	b.	cause to spread out
3.	devout	c.	stop doing
4.	diatribe	d.	reduction
5.	dichotomy	e.	predicament
6.	diffuse	f.	deeply religious
7.	dilapidated	g.	make larger
8.	dilate	h.	broken-down
9.	dilemma	i.	neglectful
10.	diminution	j.	bitter denunciation

DIRE (DYE ur) *adj* disastrous; desperate
- The tornado struck the center of town, with *dire* results; nearly every building was flattened.
- The family's situation was quite *dire*; they had no clothes, no food, and no shelter.

DIRGE (durj) *n* a funeral song
A *dirge* is a mournful song played at your funeral with the intention of making everyone who knew you feel terribly sad.
- Johann's new composition was so *dirge-like* that it sounded like it ought to be played at a funeral.

DISAFFECT (dis uh FEKT) *v* to cause to lose affection; to estrange; to alienate
- With years of nitpicking, pestering, and faultfinding, Amanda *disaffected* her children.
- My students' nasty comments did not *disaffect* me; I gave them all A's anyway, to show them that I loved them.

Disaffection (dis uh FEK shun) is the loss of affection—easy to remember. To be *disaffected* is to be no longer content or no longer loyal.
- The assassination attempt was made by a *disaffected* civil servant who felt that the government had ruined his life.

DISARRAY (dis uh RAY) *n* disorder; confusion

An *array* is an orderly arrangement of objects or people. *Disarray* is the breakdown of that order.

- My children played in my office for several hours yesterday, and they left the place in *disarray*, with papers and supplies scattered everywhere.

- The entire company had been in *disarray* ever since federal officers had arrested most of the vice presidents.

Disarray can also be a verb. To *disarray* something is to throw it into disarray.

- The intermittent artillery bombardment *disarrayed* the soldiers, making it impossible for them to organize a counterattack.

DISCERN (dih SURN) *v* to have insight; to see things clearly; to discriminate; to differentiate

To *discern* something is to perceive it clearly. A writer whose work demonstrates *discernment* is a writer who is a keen observer.

- The ill-mannered people at Tisha's party proved that she had little *discernment* when it came to choosing friends.

DISCLAIM (dis KLAYM) *v* to deny any claim to; to renounce

- The mayor publicly *disclaimed* any personal interest in his brother's concrete company, even though he was a major stockholder.

A *disclaimer* (dis KLAY mur) is an act or statement that *disclaims*. An advertisement that makes a bold claim in large type ("Cures cancer!") will often also make a meek *disclaimer* in tiny type ("Except in living things") in order to keep it from violating truth-in-advertising laws.

DISCOMFIT (dis KUM fit) *v* to frustrate; to confuse

- Sheila was *discomfited* by her secretary's apparent inability to type, write a grammatical sentence, answer the telephone, or recite the alphabet; in fact, she began to think that he might not be fully qualified for the job.

To *discomfit* is not the same as to *discomfort* (dis KUM furt), which means to make uncomfortable or to make uneasy, although the two words are used more or less interchangeably by many, many people.

DISCONCERT (dis kun SERT) *v* to upset; to ruffle; to perturb

- Professor Jones used to *disconcert* his students by scrunching up his face and plugging his ears when one of them would begin to say something.

- The jet's engine was making a *disconcerting* sound that reminded me of the sound of an old boot bouncing around inside a clothes dryer; I was worried that we were going to crash.
- The boos of the audience did not *disconcert* Bob; he droned on with his endless, boring speech regardless.

If you think of a concert as an event in which musicians play together, it makes sense that *disconcert* means to cause to come apart.

DISCOURSE (DIS kawrs) *n* spoken or written expression in words; conversation

- The level of *discourse* inside the dining hall was surprisingly high; the students were discussing not drugs or sex but philosophy.
- The company's imposing president was not one for *discourse*; when he opened his mouth, it was to issue a command.
- There is no more *discourse* in American society; there is only television.

See our listing for discursive.

DISCREET (dih SKREET) *adj* prudent; judiciously reserved
To make *discreet* inquiries is to ask around without letting the whole world know you're doing it.

- The psychiatrist was very *discreet;* no matter how much we pestered him, he wouldn't gossip about the problems of his famous patients.

He had *discretion* (di SKRESH un).

To be *indiscreet* is to be imprudent and especially to say or do things you shouldn't.

- It was *indiscreet* of Laura to tell Salima how much she hated Bailey's new hairstyle, because Salima always tells Bailey everything.
- When Laura told Salima, she committed an *indiscretion*.

DISCRETE (dih SKREET) *adj* unconnected; separate; distinct
Do not confuse *discrete* with *discreet*.

- The twins were identical but their personalities were *discrete*.
- The drop in the stock market was not the result of any single force but of many *discrete* trends.

When things are all jumbled up together, they are said to be *indiscrete*, which means not separated or sorted.

DISCREPANCY (dis KREP un see) *n* difference; inconsistency

- There was a slight *discrepancy* between the amount of money that was supposed to be in the account and the amount of money that actually was; gradually the accountant concluded that Logan had stolen seven million dollars.

The adjective is *discrepant* (dis KREP unt).

DISCURSIVE (dis KUR siv) *adj* rambling from one topic to another, usually aimlessly

- Betty is an extremely *discursive* writer; she can't write about one thing without being reminded of another, and she can't write about that without being reminded of something else altogether.

- My mother's letter was long and *discursive*; if she had a point, she never got to it.

QUICK QUIZ #62

Match each word in the first column with its definition in the second column. Check your answers in the back of the book.

1.	dire	a.	renounce
2.	dirge	b.	cause to lose affection
3.	disaffect	c.	perturb
4.	disarray	d.	frustrate
5.	disclaim	e.	disorder
6.	discomfit	f.	difference
7.	disconcert	g.	funeral song
8.	discourse	h.	aimlessly rambling
9.	discrepancy	i.	conversation
10.	discursive	j.	disastrous

DISCRIMINATE (dih SKRIM uh nayt) *v* to notice or point out the difference between two or more things; to discern; to differentiate

A person with a refined aesthetic sense is able to *discriminate* subtle differences where a less observant person would see nothing. Such a person is *discriminating*. This kind of *discrimination* is a good thing. To *discriminate* unfairly, though, is to dwell on differences that shouldn't make a difference. It is unfair—and illegal—to *discriminate* between black people and white people in selling a house. Such a practice is not *discriminating* (which is good), but *discriminatory* (which is wrong).

Indiscriminate means not *discriminating;* in other words, random or haphazard.

DISDAIN (dis DAYN) *n* arrogant scorn; contempt
- Bertram viewed the hot dog with *disdain,* believing that to eat such a disgusting food was beneath him.
- The millionaire looked upon the poor workers with evident *disdain.*

Disdain can also be a verb. The millionaire in the previous example could be said to have *disdained* those workers.
To be filled with *disdain* is to be *disdainful.*

DISGRUNTLE (dis GRUN tul) *v* to make sulky and dissatisfied; to discontent
- Eileen had such a nasty disposition that she tended to *disgruntle* anyone who worked for her.

The adjective *disgruntled* means discontented or dissatisfied.
- The children were *disgruntled* by the lumps of coal in their Christmas stockings.
- The rotten eggs on Alice's doorstep were placed there by a *disgruntled* former employee.

DISINFORMATION (dis in fer MAY shun) *n* false information purposely disseminated, usually by a government, for the purpose of creating a false impression
- The CIA conducted a *disinformation* campaign in which it tried to persuade the people of Cuba that Fidel Castro was really a woman.
- The government hoped to weaken the revolutionary movement by leaking *disinformation* about it to the local press.

DISINTERESTED (dis IN truh stid) *adj* not taking sides; unbiased
Disinterested should *not* be used to mean *uninterested.* If you don't care about knowing something, you are *uninterested,* not *disinterested.*
- A referee should be *disinterested.* He or she should not be rooting for one of the competing teams.

A *disinterested* observer is one who has no personal stake in or attachment to what is being observed.
- Meredith claimed that the accident had been Louie's fault, but several *disinterested* witnesses said that Meredith had actually bashed into his car after jumping the median and driving in the wrong lane for several miles.

SAT POWER VOCAB

DISMAL (DIZ mul) *adj* dreary; causing gloom; causing dread
- The weather has been *dismal* ever since our vacation began; a cold wind has been blowing, and it has rained almost every day.
- The new television show received *dismal* ratings and was canceled before its third episode had aired.
- The view from the top of the hill was *dismal*; every house in the valley had been destroyed by the flood.

DISMAY (dis MAY) *v* to fill with dread; to discourage greatly; to perturb
- The carnage in the field *dismayed* the soldiers, and they stood frozen in their steps.
- Peter *dismayed* his children by criticizing nearly everything they did and never finding anything nice to say about their schoolwork.
- The new police officer has a *dismaying* tendency to help himself to the money in the cash registers of the stores on his beat.

As a noun, *dismay* means dread, anxiety, or sudden disappointment.

DISPARAGE (dih SPAR ij) *v* to belittle; to say uncomplimentary things about, usually in a somewhat indirect way
- The mayor *disparaged* our efforts to beautify the town square when he said that the flower bed we had planted looked somewhat worse than the bed of weeds it had replaced.
- My guidance counselor *disparaged* my high school record by telling me that not everybody belongs in college.

QUICK QUIZ #63

Match each word in the first column with its definition in the second column. Check your answers in the back of the book.

1.	discern	a.	have insight
2.	discreet	b.	belittle
3.	discrete	c.	not separated
4.	indiscrete	d.	not taking sides
5.	discriminate	e.	arrogant scorn
6.	disdain	f.	prudent
7.	disinterested	g.	unconnected
8.	disparage	h.	differentiate

DISPARATE (DIS pur it) *adj* different; incompatible; unequal

- Our interests were *disparate:* Cathy liked to play with dolls, and I liked to throw her dolls out the window.

- The *disparate* interest groups were united only by their intense dislike of the candidate.

- The novel was difficult to read because the plot consisted of dozens of *disparate* threads that never came together.

The noun form of *disparate* is *disparity* (dih SPAR i tee). *Disparity* means inequality. The opposite of *disparity* is *parity*.

DISPASSIONATE (dis PASH uh nut) *adj* unaffected by passion; impartial; calm

Impassioned (im PASH und) means passionate, emotional, all worked up. To be *dispassionate* is to be cool and objective, to not let judgment be affected by emotions.

- The prosecutor's *dispassionate* enumeration of the defendant's terrible crimes had a far more devastating effect on the jury than a passionate, highly emotional speech would have had. The judge had no interest in either side of the dispute; she was a dispassionate observer.

- Larry's *dispassionate* manner often fooled people into thinking he did not care.

Impassive (im PAS iv) is a related word that means revealing no emotions, or expressionless.

DISPERSE (dis PURS) *v* to scatter; to spread widely; to disseminate

- The crowd *dispersed* after the chief of police announced that he would order his officers to open fire if everyone didn't go home.

- Engineers from the oil company tried to use chemical solvents to *disperse* the oil slick formed when the tanker ran aground on the reef and split in two.

- When the seed pod of a milkweed plant dries and breaks apart, the wind *disperses* the seeds inside, and new milkweed plants sprout all over the countryside.

An act of *dispersing* is called *dispersion* (dis PUR zhun).

- The fluffy part of a milkweed seed facilitates its *dispersion* by the wind.

DISPIRIT (dis PIR ut) *v* to discourage; to dishearten; to lose spirit
- The coach tried not to let the team's one thousandth consecutive defeat *dispirit* him, but somehow he couldn't help but feel discouraged.
- The campers looked tired and *dispirited*; it had rained all night, and their sleeping bags had all washed away.

DISPOSITION (dis puh ZISH un) *n* characteristic attitude; state of mind; inclination; arrangement
- Mary Lou had always had a sweet *disposition*; even when she was a baby, she smiled almost constantly and never complained.
- My natural *disposition* is to play golf all the time and not care about anything or anyone else. I am *disposed* (dis POHZD) to play golf all the time.
- The seemingly random *disposition* of buildings on the campus su ggested that no one had given much thought to how the ...us ought to be laid out.

... is an attitude or state of mind beforehand.
... metal music of the warm-up band, the Snakeheads,
... ably *predispose* the audience to enjoy the Barry

... pruh PAWR shuh nut) *adj* out of proportion; too

... of the candy was *disproportionate*; she gave her-
... ...an she gave me.
... ...er seemed to be devoting a *disproportionate* amount of
... ...tention to my brother, so I sat down in the middle of the
k... ...hen floor and began to scream my head off.

The opposite of *disproportionate* is *proportionate*.

DISQUIET (dis KWYE ut) *v* to make uneasy
- The movie's graphic depiction of childbirth *disquieted* the children, who had been expecting a story about a stork.
- The silence in the boss's office was *disquieting*; everyone was afraid that it was the calm before the storm.

Disquiet can also be used as a noun meaning unease or nervousness.

QUICK QUIZ   #64

Match each word in the first column with its definition in the second column. Check your answers in the back of the book.

1. disgruntle
2. disinformation
3. dismal
4. dismay
5. dispassionate
6. disperse
7. dispirit
8. disposition
9. disproportionate
10. disquiet

a. scatter
b. impartial
c. dreary
d. discourage
e. false information purposely disseminated
f. characteristic attitude
g. out of proportion
h. make sulky
i. fill with dread
j. make uneasy

DISSEMBLE (di SEM bul) *v* to conceal the real nature of; to act or speak falsely in order to deceive
- Anne successfully *dissembled* her hatred for Beth; in fact, Beth viewed Anne as her best friend.

- When asked by young children about Santa Claus, parents are allowed to *dissemble*.

To *dissemble* is not the same thing as to *disassemble*, which means to take apart.

DISSEMINATE (dih SEM uh nayt) *v* to spread the seeds of something; to scatter; to make widely known
News is *disseminated* through many media: internet, radio, television, newspapers, magazines, and gossips.

DISSENT (di SENT) *v* to disagree; to withhold approval
- The chief justice *dissented* from the opinion signed by the other justices; in fact, he thought their opinion was crazy.

- Jim and Bob say I'm a jerk; I *dissent*.

A person who *dissents* is a *dissenter*.
- The meeting had lasted so long that when I moved that it be adjourned, there were no *dissenters*.

Dissent can also be a noun.

- The *dissent* of a single board member was enough to overturn any proposal; every board member had absolute veto power.

Dissent is related to the words consent and assent (which mean agreement).

DISSERVICE (di SUR vus) *n* a harmful action; an ill turn
- Inez did a *disservice* to her parents by informing the police that they were growing marijuana in their garden.
- The reviewer did a grave *disservice* to the author by inaccurately describing what his book was about.

DISSIDENT (DIS uh dunt) *n* a person who disagrees or dissents
- The old Soviet regime usually responded to *dissidents* by imprisoning them.
- The plan to build a nuclear power plant in town was put on hold by a group of *dissidents* who lay down in the road in front of the bulldozers.

Dissident can also be an adjective. A *dissident* writer is a writer who is a *dissident*.

DISSIPATE (DIS uh payt) *v* to thin out, drift away, or dissolve; to cause to thin out, drift away, or dissolve; to waste or squander
- The smoke *dissipated* as soon as we opened the windows.
- Ilya's anger *dissipated* as the day wore on, and he gradually forgot what had upset him.
- The police *dissipated* the riotous crowd by spraying the demonstrators with fire hoses and firing rubber bullets over their heads.
- Alex won the weekly lottery but *dissipated* the entire winnings in one abandoned, fun-filled weekend.

We can also say that a person is *dissipated*, by which we mean that he indulges in wild living. Alex is *dissipated*.

DISSOLUTION (dis uh LOO shun) *n* the breaking up or dissolving of something into parts; disintegration
- Nothing could prevent the *dissolution* of the Jesse Ventura Fan Club after he retired to seek a political career.

A person who is *dissolute* has lived life in the fast lane too long. *Dissolute* and *dissipated* are synonyms in this sense.

DISSUADE (di SWAYD) *v* to persuade not to
Dissuade is the opposite of *persuade*.
- The 100 degree heat and the 100 percent relative humidity did not *dissuade* me from playing tennis all afternoon.

Dissuasion (di SWAY zhun) is the opposite of persuasion.
- Gentle *dissuasion* is usually more effective than hitting a person over the head with a two-by-four.

DISTEND (di STEND) *v* to swell; to extend a great deal
- The tire *distended* alarmingly as the forgetful gas station attendant kept pumping more and more air into it.

- A *distended* belly is one symptom of malnutrition.

A swelling is a *distension*.

DISTINCT (di STINKT) *adj* separate; different; clear and unmistakable
- The professor was able to identify eleven *distinct* species of ants in the corner of his backyard.

- The twins were identical, but the personality of each was *distinct* from that of the other.

To make a *distinction* (di STINK shun) between two things is to notice what makes each of them *distinct* from the other. A *distinction* can also be a distinguishing characteristic.
- Alan, Alex, and Albert had the *distinction* of being the only triplets in the entire school system.

The opposite of *distinct* is *indistinct*.

DISTINGUISH (di STING gwish) *v* to tell apart; to cause to stand out
- The rodent expert's eyesight was so acute that he was able to *distinguish* between a shrew and a vole at more than a thousand paces.

- I studied and studied but I was never able to *distinguish* between *discrete* and *discreet*.

- His face had no *distinguishing* characteristics; there was nothing about his features that stuck in your memory.

- Lou's uneventful career as a dogcatcher was not *distinguished* by adventure or excitement.

DIURNAL (dye UR nul) *adj* occurring every day; occurring during the daytime
Diurnal is the opposite of *nocturnal*. A *nocturnal* animal is one that is active primarily during the night; a *diurnal* animal is one that is active primarily during the day.
- The rising of the sun is a *diurnal* occurrence; it happens every day.

DIVINE (di VYNE) *v* to intuit; to prophesy

- I used all of my best mind-reading skills, but I could not *divine* what Lester was thinking.

- The law firm made a great deal of money helping its clients *divine* the meaning of obscure federal regulations.

The act of *divining* is called *divination*.

DIVULGE (di VULJ) *v* to reveal, especially to reveal something that has been a secret

- The secret agent had to promise not to *divulge* the contents of the government files, but the information in the files was so fascinating that he told everyone he knew.

- We begged and pleaded, but we couldn't persuade Lester to *divulge* the secret of his chocolate-chip cookies.

DOCILE (DAHS ul) *adj* easily taught; obedient; easy to handle

- The *docile* students quietly memorized all the lessons their teacher told them.

- The baby raccoons appeared *docile* at first, but they were almost impossible to control.

- Mia's *docility* (dah SIL i tee) fooled the professor into believing that she was incapable of thinking for herself.

DOCTRINAIRE (dahk truh NAYR) *adj* inflexibly committed to a doctrine or theory without regard to its practicality; dogmatic

A *doctrinaire* supporter of manned space flights to Pluto would be someone who supported such space flights even though it might be shown that such lengthy journeys could never be undertaken.

A *doctrinaire* opponent of fluoridation of water would be someone whose opposition could not be shaken by proof that fluoride is good for teeth and not bad for anything else.

A person with *doctrinaire* views can be called a *doctrinaire*.

DOCUMENT (DOK yuh ment) *v* to support with evidence, especially written evidence

- The first *documented* use of the invention occurred in 1978, according to the encyclopedia.

- Arnold *documented* his record-breaking car trip around the world by taking a photograph of himself and his car every hundred miles.

- The scientist made a lot of headlines by announcing that he had been taken aboard a flying saucer, but he was unable to *document* his claim, and his colleagues didn't believe him.

QUICK QUIZ #65

Match each word in the first column with its definition in the second column. Check your answers in the back of the book.

1.	dissemble	a.	disagree
2.	dissent	b.	support with evidence
3.	disservice	c.	conceal the real nature of
4.	dissident	d.	reveal
5.	dissuade	e.	person who disagrees
6.	distinct	f.	intuit
7.	diurnal	g.	persuade not to
8.	divine	h.	occurring every day
9.	divulge	i.	harmful action
10.	document	j.	separate

DOGMATIC (dawg MAT ik) *adj* arrogantly assertive of unproven ideas; stubbornly claiming that something (often a system of beliefs) is beyond dispute

A *dogma* is a belief. A *dogmatic* person, however, is stubbornly convinced of his beliefs.

- Marty is *dogmatic* on the subject of the creation of the world; he sneers at anyone whose views are not identical to his.

- The philosophy professor became increasingly *dogmatic* as he grew older and became more firmly convinced of his strange theories.

The opinions or ideas *dogmatically* asserted by a *dogmatic* person are known collectively as *dogma*.

DOLDRUMS (DOHL drumz) *n* low spirits; a state of inactivity

This word is plural in form, but it takes a singular verb. In addition, it is almost always preceded by the. To sailors, the *doldrums* is an ocean area near the equator where there is little wind. A sailing ship in the *doldrums* is likely to be moving slowly or not moving at all.

To the rest of us, the *doldrums* is a state of mind comparable to that frustratingly calm weather near the equator.

- Meredith has been in the *doldrums* ever since her pet bees flew away; she mopes around the house and never wants to do anything.

DOLEFUL (DOHL ful) *adj* sorrowful; filled with grief

- A long, *doleful* procession followed the horse-drawn hearse as it wound slowly through the village.

- Aunt Gladys said she loved the pencil holder that her niece had made her for Christmas, but the *doleful* expression on her face told a different story.

An essentially interchangeable word is *dolorous* (DOHL ur us).

DOLT (dohlt) *n* a stupid person; a dunce

- "*Dolts* and idiots," said Mrs. Wier when her husband asked her to describe her new students.

- The farmer's *doltish* (DOHL tish) son rode the cows and milked the horses.

DOMESTIC (duh MES tik) *adj* having to do with the household or family; not foreign

A home that enjoys *domestic* tranquillity is a happy home.

A maid is sometimes referred to as a *domestic* engineer or simply as a *domestic*.

To be *domestic* is to enjoy being at home or to be skillful at doing things around the house.

Domestic wine is wine from this country, as opposed to wine imported from, say, France.

The *domestic* steel industry is the steel industry in this country.

A country that enjoys *domestic* tranquillity is a happy country on the homefront.

QUICK QUIZ #66

Match each word in the first column with its definition in the second column. Check your answers in the back of the book.

1. disparate	a.	committed to a theory
2. disseminate	b.	thin out
3. dissipate	c.	of the household
4. dissolution	d.	firmly held system of ideas
5. distend	e.	easily taught
6. distinguish	f.	arrogantly assertive
7. docile	g.	swell
8. doctrinaire	h.	tell apart
9. dogmatic	i.	incompatible
10. dogma	j.	spread seeds
11. domestic	k.	disintegration

DORMANT (DOR munt) *adj* inactive; as though asleep; asleep
Dormant, like *dormitory,* comes from a root meaning sleep.
- Mt. Vesuvius erupted violently and then fell *dormant* for several hundred years.

Many plants remain *dormant* through the winter; that is, they stop growing until spring.
- Frank's interest in playing the piano was *dormant* and, quite possibly, dead.
- The snow fell silently over the *dormant* village, which became snarled in traffic jams the following morning.

The noun is *dormancy.*

DOTAGE (DOH tij) *n* senility; foolish affection
To *dote* (doht) on something is to be foolishly or excessively affectionate toward it. For some reason, old people are thought to be especially prone to doing this. That's why *dotage* almost always applies to old people.
- My grandmother is in her *dotage*; she spends all day in bed watching soap operas and combing the hair on an old doll she had as a little girl.

A senile person is sometimes called a *dotard* (DOH turd).

DOUBLE ENTENDRE (DUH bul awn TAWN druh) *n* a word or phrase having a double meaning, especially when the second meaning is risqué
- The class president's speech was filled with *double entendres* that only the students understood; the teachers were left to scratch their heads as the students were doubled over with laughter.

DOUR (door) *adj* forbidding; severe; gloomy
- The Latin teacher was a *dour* old man who never had a kind word for anyone, even in Latin.
- The police officer *dourly* insisted on giving me a traffic ticket, even though I promised to repair my rear headlight.

This word can also be pronounced "dowr."

DOWNCAST (DOWN kast) *adj* directed downward; dejected
- The children's *downcast* faces indicated that they were sad that Santa Claus had brought them nothing for Christmas.
- The entire audience seemed *downcast* by the end of the depressing movie.
- My six-week struggle with the flu had left me feeling *downcast* and weak.

DOWNPLAY (DOWN play) *v* to minimize; to represent as being insignificant

- The doctor had tried hard to *downplay* the risks involved in the operation, but Harry knew that having his kidney replaced was not minor surgery.

- The parents tried to *downplay* Christmas because their daughter was very young and they didn't want her to become so excited that she wouldn't be able to sleep.

- Superman *downplayed* his role in rescuing the children, but everyone knew what he had done.

DRACONIAN (dray KOH nee un) *adj* harsh; severe; cruel
This word is often capitalized. It is derived from the name of Draco, an Athenian official who created a notoriously harsh code of laws. Because of this history, the word is most often used to describe laws, rules, punishments, and so forth.

- The judge was known for handing down *draconian* sentences; he had once sentenced a shoplifter to life in prison without parole.

- Mrs. Jefferson is a *draconian* grader; her favorite grade is D, and she has never given an A in her entire life.

DROLL (drohl) *adj* humorous; amusing in an odd, often understated, way
This word is slightly stilted, and it is not a perfect substitute for funny in every situation. *The Three Stooges*, for example, are not *droll*.

- The children entertained the dinner guests with a *droll* rendition of their parents' style of arguing.

- The speaker's attempts to be *droll* were met with a chilly silence from the audience.

DROSS (drahs) *n* worthless stuff, especially worthless stuff arising from the production of valuable stuff
In metal smelting, the *dross* is the crud floating on top of the metal once it is molten. Outside of this precise technical meaning, the word is used figuratively to describe any comparably worthless stuff.

- Hilary's new novel contains three or four good paragraphs; the rest is *dross*.

- The living room was filled with the *dross* of Christmas: mounds of wrapping paper and ribbon, empty boxes, and toys that no one would ever play with.

DUBIOUS (DOO bee us) *adj* full of doubt; uncertain
- I was fairly certain that I would be able to fly if I could merely flap my arms hard enough, but Mary was *dubious;* she said I'd better flap my legs as well.

- We were *dubious* about the team's chance of success and, as it turned out, our *dubiety* (doo BYE uh tee) was justified: The team lost.

Dubious and *doubtful* don't mean exactly the same thing. A *dubious* person is a person who has doubts. A *doubtful* outcome is an outcome that isn't certain to occur.
- Sam's chances of getting the job were *doubtful* because the employer was *dubious* of his claim that he had been president of the United States while in high school.

Something beyond doubt is *indubitable.* A dogmatic person believes his opinions are *indubitable.*

DUPLICITY (doo PLIS uh tee) *n* the act of being two-faced; double-dealing; deception
- Dave, in his *duplicity,* told us he wasn't going to rob the bank and then went right out and robbed it.

- Liars engage in *duplicity* all the time; they say one thing and do another.

- The *duplicitous* salesman sold the red sports car to someone else even though he had promised to sell it to us.

DURESS (doo RES) *n* coercion; compulsion by force or threat
This word is often preceded by under.
- Mrs. Maloney was under *duress* when she bought her son a candy bar; the nasty little boy was screaming and crying.

- The court determined that the old man had been under *duress* when he signed his new will, in which he left all his money to his lawyer; in fact, the court determined that the lawyer had held a gun to the old man's head while he signed it.

QUICK QUIZ #67

Match each word in the first column with its definition in the second column. Check your answers in the back of the book.

1. dormant   a. uncertainty
2. dubiety   b. double-dealing
3. duplicity   c. inactive

QUICK QUIZ #68

Match each word in the first column with its definition in the second column. Check your answers in the back of the book.

1. doldrums
2. doleful
3. dolt
4. dotage
5. double entendre
6. dour
7. downcast
8. downplay
9. draconian
10. droll
11. dross
12. duress

a. forbidding
b. humorous
c. senility
d. double meaning
e. stupid person
f. harsh
g. worthless stuff
h. coercion
i. minimize
j. sorrowful
k. low spirits
l. dejected

E

EBB (eb) *v* to diminish; to recede
Ebb comes from an old word meaning low tide, and it is still used in this way. When a tide *ebbs*, it pulls back or goes down. Other things can *ebb*, too.

- My interest *ebbed* quickly when my date began to describe the joys of stamp collecting.

- The team's enthusiasm for the game *ebbed* as the other team ran up the score.

The opposite of *ebb* is flood or flow.

- On a typical trading day, the Dow Jones Industrial Average *ebbs* and flows in a seemingly haphazard way.

EBULLIENT (ih BUL yunt) *adj* boiling; bubbling with excitement; exuberant
A boiling liquid can be called *ebullient*. More often, though, this word describes excited or enthusiastic people.

The roaring crowd in a full stadium before the World Series might be said to be *ebullient*.

A person overflowing with enthusiasm might be said to be *ebullient*.

- Cammie was *ebullient* when her fairy godmother said she could use one of her three wishes to wish for three more wishes.

Someone or something that is *ebullient* is characterized by *ebullience*.

ECCENTRIC (ek SEN trik) *adj* not conventional; a little kooky; irregular

- The *eccentric* inventor spent all his waking hours fiddling with what he said was a time machine, but it was actually just an old telephone booth.

- Fred's political views are *eccentric:* He believes that we should have kings instead of presidents and that the government should raise money by holding bake sales.

- The rocket followed an *eccentric* course; first it veered in one direction, then it veered in another, then it crashed.

An *eccentric* person is a person who has *eccentricities* (ek sen TRIS uh teez).

ECCLESIASTICAL (i klee zee AS ti kul) *adj* having to do with the church

- The priest had few *ecclesiastical* duties because he had neither a church nor a congregation.

- The large steeple rising from the roof gave the new house an oddly *ecclesiastical* feel.

ECLECTIC (ih KLEK tik) *adj* choosing the best from many sources; drawn from many sources

- Adolfo's taste in art was *eclectic*. He liked the Old Masters, the Impressionists, and Walt Disney.

- The *eclectic* menu included dishes from many different countries.

- George's *eclectic* reading made him well rounded.

ECLIPSE (i KLIPS) *v* to block the light of; to overshadow; to reduce the significance of; to surpass

In an *eclipse* of the moon, the sun, Earth, and moon are arranged in such a way that the Earth prevents the light of the sun from falling on the moon. In an *eclipse* of the sun, the moon passes directly between the Earth and the sun, preventing the light of the sun from falling on the Earth. In the first instance, the Earth is said to *eclipse* the moon; in the second instance, the moon is said to *eclipse* the sun.

This word can also be used figuratively.

- Lois's fame *eclipsed* that of her brother, Louis, who made fewer movies and was a worse actor.

- The spelling team's glorious victory in the state spelling championship was *eclipsed* by the arrest of their captain on charges of possessing cocaine.

ECOSYSTEM (EK oh sis tum) *n* a community of organisms and the physical environment in which they live

Ecology is the science of the relationships between organisms and their environment. The adjective is *ecological* (EK uh lahj i kul).

- The big muddy swamp is a complex *ecosystem* in which the fate of each species is inextricably linked with the fate of many others.

EDICT (EE dikt) *n* an official decree

- The new king celebrated his rise to power by issuing hundreds of *edicts* governing everything from curbside parking to the wearing of hats.

- By presidential *edict*, all government offices were closed for the holiday.

EDIFICE (ED uh fis) *n* a big, imposing building

- Mr. and Mrs. Stevens had originally intended to build a comfortable little cottage in which to spend their golden years, but one thing led to another and they ended up building a sprawling *edifice* that dwarfed all other structures in the area.

An architect who designs massive or grandiose buildings is sometimes said to have an "edifice complex." Get it?

EDIFY (ED uh fye) *v* to enlighten; to instruct, especially in moral or religious matters

- We found the pastor's sermon on the importance of not eating beans to be most *edifying*.

- The teacher's goal was to *edify* her students, not to force a handful of facts down their throats.

- We would have felt lost at the art show had not the excellent and informative programs been provided for our *edification*.

EFFACE (ih FAYS) *v* to erase; to rub away the features of

- The inscription on the tombstone had been *effaced* by centuries of weather.

- The vandals *effaced* the delicate carving by rubbing it with sandpaper.

- We tried to *efface* the dirty words that had been written on the front of our house, but nothing would remove them.

To be *self-effacing* is to be modest.
- John is *self-effacing:* When he won an Olympic gold medal, all he said was, "Aw, shucks. I'm just a regular fella."

EFFECTUAL (i FEK choo ul) *adj* effective; adequate
- Polly is an *effectual* teacher, but she is not a masterful one; her students come away from her class with a solid understanding of the subject but with little else.

- Even with all her years of experience, Mrs. Jones had not yet hit on an *effectual* method of getting her children to go to bed.

Something that is not *effectual* is *ineffectual* (IN i fek choo ul).
- The plumber tried several techniques for stopping a leak, all of them *ineffectual*.

EFFICACY (EF i kuh see) *n* effectiveness
- Federal law requires manufacturers to demonstrate both the safety and the *efficacy* of new drugs. The manufacturers must prove that the new drugs are *efficacious* (ef i KAY shus).

EFFIGY (EF uh jee) *n* a likeness of someone, especially one used in expressing hatred for the person of whom it is a likeness
- The company's founder had been dead for many years, but the employees still passed under his gaze because his *effigy* had been carved in the side of the building.

- The members of the senior class hanged the principal in *effigy;* they made a dummy out of some old burlap bags and strung it up in the tree beside the parking lot.

This word is often heard in the clichéd phrase burned an *effigy*, as in, "The chief of staff was so unpopular that White House staffers openly burned an *effigy* of him at the holiday party."

EFFUSION (ih FYOO zhun) *n* a pouring forth
- When the child was rescued from the well, there was an intense *effusion* of emotion from the crowd that had gathered around the hole.

- The madman's writings consisted of a steady *effusion* of nonsense.

To be *effusive* is to be highly emotional.
- Anna's *effusive* thanks for our silly little present made us feel somewhat embarrassed, so we decided to move to a different lunch table.

EGALITARIAN (ih gal uh TAYR ee un) *adj* believing in the social and economic equality of all people
- People often lose interest in *egalitarian* measures when such measures interfere with their own interests.

Egalitarian can also be used as a noun to characterize a person.
An *egalitarian* advocates *egalitarianism*.

EGOCENTRIC (ee goh SEN trik) *adj* selfish; believing that one is the center of everything
- Nevitt was so *egocentric* that he could never give anyone else credit for doing anything.
- *Egocentric* Lou never read the newspaper unless there was something in it about him.
- It never occurred to the *egocentric* musician that his audiences might like to hear someone else's songs every once in a while.
- An *egoist* is an *egocentric* person. He believes the entire universe exists for his benefit.

An *egotist* is another type of *egocentric*. An *egotist* is an *egoist* who tells everyone how wonderful he is.

EGREGIOUS (i GREE jus) *adj* extremely bad; flagrant
Save this word for things that are worse than bad.
- The mother's *egregious* neglect was responsible for her child's accidental cross-country ride on the freight train.
- Erik's manners were *egregious;* he ate his mashed potatoes with his fingers and slurped the peas right off his plate.

QUICK QUIZ   #69

Match each word in the first column with its definition in the second column. Check your answers in the back of the book.

1.	ebullient	a.	pouring forth
2.	eccentric	b.	self-obsessed person
3.	eclectic	c.	extremely bad
4.	edify	d.	not conventional
5.	efface	e.	drawn from many sources
6.	effusion	f.	bubbling with excitement
7.	egalitarian	g.	erase
8.	egocentric	h.	selfish
9.	egotist	i.	enlighten
10.	egregious	j.	believing in social equality

QUICK QUIZ #70

Match each word in the first column with its definition in the second column. Check your answers in the back of the book.

1. ebb	a. official decree
2. ecclesiastical	b. feeling of great joy
3. eclipse	c. having to do with the church
4. ecosystem	d. big, imposing building
5. edict	e. likeness of someone
6. edifice	f. surpass
7. effectual	g. effective
8. efficacy	h. effectiveness
9. effigy	i. diminish
10. elation	j. organisms and their environment

ELECTORATE (i LEK tuh rut) *n* the body of people entitled to vote in an election; the voters

- In order to be elected, a candidate usually has to make a lot of wild, irresponsible promises to the *electorate*.

- The losing candidate attributed her loss not to any fault in herself but to the fickleness of the *electorate*.

The adjective is *electoral* (i LEK tuh rul).

ELEGY (EL uh jee) *n* a mournful poem or other piece of writing; a mournful piece of music

- Most critics agreed that Stan's best poem was an *elegy* he wrote following the death of his pet pigeon.

- My new book is an *elegy* to the good old days—the days before everything became so terrible.

An *elegy* is *elegiac* (el i JYE uk).

- The little article in the newspaper about Frank's retirement had an *elegiac* tone that Frank found disconcerting.

ELICIT (ih LIS it) *v* to bring out; to call forth

- The interviewer skillfully *elicited* our true feelings by asking us questions that got to the heart of the matter.

- The defendant tried to *elicit* the sympathy of the jury by appearing at the trial in a wheelchair, but the jury convicted him anyway.

Don't confuse this word with *illicit*.

ELITE (i LEET) *n* the best or most select group
- Alison is a member of bowling's *elite*; she bowls like a champion with both her right hand and her left.
- As captain of the football team, Bobby was part of the high school's *elite*, and he never let you forget it.

This word can also be an adjective.
- The presidential palace was defended by an *elite* corps of soldiers known to be loyal to the president.

To be an *elitist* (i LEET ust) is to be a snob; to be *elitist* is to be snobby.

ELLIPTICAL (ih LIP ti kul) *adj* oval; missing a word or words; obscure
This word has several meanings. Consult a dictionary if you are uncertain.
- The orbit of the Earth is not perfectly round; it is *elliptical*.

An egg may have an *elliptical* shape.

An *elliptical* statement is one that is hard or impossible to understand, either because something is missing from it or because the speaker or writer is trying to be hard to understand.
- The announcement from the State Department was purposely *elliptical*—the government didn't really want reporters to know what was going on.

ELOCUTION (el uh KYOO shun) *n* the art of public speaking
- The mayor was long on *elocution* but short on execution; he was better at making promises than at carrying them out.
- Professor Jefferson might have become president of the university if he had had even rudimentary skills of *elocution*.
- In *elocution* class, Father Ficks learned not to yell "SHADUPP!" when he heard whispering in the congregation.

A *locution* (loh KYOO shun) is a particular word or phrase. Someone who speaks well is *eloquent* (EL uh kwent).

ELUSIVE (ih LOO siv) *adj* hard to pin down; evasive
To be *elusive* is to *elude,* which means to avoid, evade, or escape.
- The answer to the problem was *elusive*; every time the mathematician thought he was close, he discovered another error. (Or, one could say that the answer to the problem *eluded* the mathematician.)

- The *elusive* criminal was next to impossible for the police to catch. (The criminal *eluded* the police.)
- The team played hard, but victory was *elusive* and they suffered another defeat. (Victory *eluded* the hard-playing team.)

EMACIATE (i MAY shee ayt) *v* to make extremely thin through starvation or illness
- A dozen years in a foreign prison had *emaciated* poor old George, who had once weighed more than three hundred pounds but now weighed less than ninety.

The act of *emaciating* is called *emaciation* (i may shee AY shun).
- The saddest thing to see in the refugee camp was the *emaciation* of the children, some of whom had not had a real meal in many weeks.

EMANATE (EM uh nayt) *v* to come forth; to issue
- Contradictory orders *emanated* from many offices in the government building, leaving the distinct impression that no one was in charge.
- The dreadful sound *emanating* from the house up the street turned out to be not that of a cat being strangled but that of a violin being played by someone who didn't know how to play it.

Something that emanates is an *emanation* (em uh NAY shun).
- The mystic claimed to be receiving mental *emanations* from the ghost of Alexander's long-dead aunt.

EMANCIPATE (i MAN suh payt) *v* to liberate; to free from bondage or restraint
- Refrigerators, microwave ovens, and automatic dishwashers have *emancipated* modern homemakers from much of the drudgery of meal preparation and cleanup.
- My personal computer has *emancipated* me from my office; I am now able to work out of my home.

The noun is *emancipation* (i man suh PAY shun).
- President Lincoln announced that he had *emancipated* the slaves in his *Emancipation* Proclamation.

EMBARGO (em BAHR goh) *n* a government order suspending foreign trade; a government order suspending the movement of freight-carrying ships in and out of the country's ports
- For many years, there has been an *embargo* in the United States on cigars produced in Cuba.

- Jerry imposed a household *embargo* on rented movies; for the next six months, he said, no rented movies would be allowed in the house.

For a near synonym, see our second definition of sanction.

EMBELLISH (im BEL ish) *v* to adorn; to beautify by adding ornaments; to add fanciful or fictitious details to

A *belle* is a beautiful young woman. To *embellish* is to make beautiful or to adorn. Note that the word can have negative connotations, as when a person adds false facts to a story.

- Cynthia *embellished* her plain white wedding gown by gluing zirconium crystals to it.

- Hugh could never leave well enough alone; when he told a story, he liked to *embellish* it with facts that he had made up.

- Edward was guilty of *embellishing* his résumé by adding a college degree that he had not earned and a great deal of job experience that he had not had.

EMBODY (em BAH dee) *v* to personify; to give physical form to

- Kindly old Mr. Benson perfectly *embodied* the loving philosophy that he taught.

- The members of the club were a bunch of scoundrels who came nowhere near *embodying* the principles upon which their club had been founded.

The noun is *embodiment*.

QUICK QUIZ   #71

Match each word in the first column with its definition in the second column. Check your answers in the back of the book.

1. electorate	a. art of public speaking
2. elegy	b. body of voters
3. elite	c. government order
4. elocution	suspending trade
5. emaciate	d. adorn
6. emanate	e. personify
7. emancipate	f. mournful poem
8. embargo	g. liberate
9. embellish	h. most select group
10. embody	i. make extremely thin
	j. come forth

EMBROIL (im BROYL) *v* to involve in conflict; to throw into disorder
- For the last twenty years, Mr. and Mrs. Brown have been *embroiled* in a legal battle with the city over the camels in their backyard.
- Fighting and shouting *embroiled* the classroom, leading the teacher to walk out of the room.

An *imbroglio* (im BROHL yoh) is a confused, difficult, or embarrassing situation.

EMBRYONIC (em bree AHN ik) *adj* undeveloped; rudimentary
An *embryo* (EM bree oh) is any unborn animal or unformed plant that is in the earliest stages of development. *Embryonic* can be used to describe such an undeveloped organism, but it also has a broader meaning.
- The plans for the new building are pretty *embryonic* at this point; they consist of a single sketch on the back of a cocktail napkin.
- Our fund-raising campaign has passed the *embryonic* stage, but it still hasn't officially gotten under way.

EMIGRATE (EM uh grayt) *v* to leave a country permanently; to expatriate
- Pierre *emigrated* from France because he had grown tired of speaking French. Pierre became an *émigré* (EM uh gray).
- The Soviet dissidents were persecuted by the secret police, so they sought permission to *emigrate.*

At the heart of this word is the word *migrate*, which means to move from one place or country to another. *Emigrate* adds to migrate the sense of moving *out of* some place in particular.
On the other end of every *emigration* is an *immigration* (think of this as "in-migration"). See *immigration.*
- When Solange *emigrated* from France, she *immigrated* to the United States.

EMINENT (EM uh nunt) *adj* well-known and respected; standing out from all others in quality or accomplishment; outstanding
- The visiting poet was so *eminent* that our English teacher asked the poet for his autograph. Our English teacher thought the poet was *preeminent* in his field.
- The entire audience fell silent when the *eminent* musician walked onto the stage and picked up his banjo and bongo drums.

Don't confuse this word with *imminent.*

EMISSARY (EM uh ser ee) *n* a messenger or representative sent to represent another

To *emit* is to send out. An *emission* is something sent out. An *emissary* is a person sent out as a messenger or representative.

- The king was unable to attend the wedding, but he sent an *emissary*—his brother.
- The surrender of the defeated country was negotiated by *emissaries* from the two warring sides.
- The company's president couldn't stand to fire an employee two days before his pension would have taken effect, so he sent an *emissary* to do it instead.

EMPATHY (EM puh thee) *n* identification with the feelings or thoughts of another

- Shannon felt a great deal of *empathy* for Bill's suffering; she knew just how he felt.

To feel *empathy* is to *empathize* (EM puh thyze), or to be *empathic* (em PATH ik).

- Samuel's tendency to *empathize* with creeps may arise from the fact that Samuel himself is a creep.

This word is sometimes confused with *sympathy*, which is compassion or shared feeling, and *apathy* (AP uh thee), which means indifference or lack of feeling. *Empathy* goes a bit further than sympathy; both words mean that you understand someone's pain or sorrow, but *empathy* indicates that you also feel the pain yourself.

EMPIRICAL (em PIR uh kul) *adj* relying on experience or observation; not merely theoretical

- The apple-dropping experiment gave the scientists *empirical* evidence that gravity exists.
- Nicky's idea about the moon being made of pizza dough was not *empirical*.
- We proved the pie's deliciousness *empirically*, by eating it.

EMPOWER (im POW ur) *v* to give power or authority to; to enable
- The city council *empowered* the dog catcher to do whatever he wanted to with the dogs he caught.
- In several states, legislatures have *empowered* notaries to perform marriages.
- The sheriff formed a posse and *empowered* it to arrest the fugitive.

EMULATE (EM yuh layt) *v* to strive to equal or excel, usually through imitation
- To *emulate* someone is to try to be just as good as, or better than, him or her.
- The American company *emulated* its successful Japanese competitor but never quite managed to do as well.
- Little Joey imitated his athletic older brother in the hope of one day *emulating* his success.
- I got ahead by *emulating* those who had succeeded before me.

ENCROACH (en KROHCH) *v* to make gradual or stealthy inroads into; to trespass
- As the city grew, it *encroached* on the countryside surrounding it.
- With an *encroaching* sense of dread, I slowly pushed open the blood-spattered door.
- My neighbor *encroached* on my yard by building his new stockade fence a few feet on my side of the property line.

ENDEAR (in DEER) *v* to make dear; to make beloved
- Merv *endeared* himself to Oprah by sending her a big box of chocolates on her birthday.
- I did not *endear* myself to my teacher when I put thumbtacks on the seat of her chair.
- Edgar has the *endearing* (in DEER ing) habit of giving hundred-dollar bills to people he meets.

An *endearment* (in DEER munt) is an expression of affection.
- "My little pumpkin" is the *endearment* Arnold Schwarzenegger's mother uses for her little boy.

ENDEMIC (en DEM ik) *adj* native; restricted to a particular region or era; indigenous
- You won't find that kind of tree in California; it's *endemic* to our part of the country.
- That peculiar strain of influenza was *endemic* to a small community in South Carolina; there were no cases anywhere else.
- The writer Tom Wolfe coined the term "Me Decade" to describe the egocentricity *endemic* in the 1970s.

ENERVATE (EN ur vayt) *v* to reduce the strength or energy of, especially to do so gradually
- Sander felt *enervated* by his long ordeal and couldn't make himself get out of bed.
- Clinging to a flagpole for a month without food or water *enervated* me, and one day I fell asleep and ended up on the ground.
- Life itself seemed to *enervate* the old man. He grew weaker and paler with every breath he drew.

ENFRANCHISE (en FRAN chyze) *v* to grant the privileges of citizenship, especially the right to vote
- In the United States, citizens become *enfranchised* on their eighteenth birthdays. American women were not *enfranchised* until the adoption of the Nineteenth Amendment in 1920, which gave them the right to vote.

To *disfranchise* (or *disenfranchise*) someone is to take away the privileges of citizenship or to take away the right to vote.
- One of the goals of the reform candidate was to *disfranchise* the bodies at the cemetery, which had somehow managed to vote for the crooked mayor.

ENGAGING (in GAY jing) *adj* charming; pleasing; attractive
- Susan was an *engaging* dinner companion; she was lively, funny, and utterly charming.
- The book I was reading wasn't terribly *engaging*; in fact, it was one of those books that is hard to pick up.

ENGENDER (en JEN dur) *v* to bring into existence; to create; to cause
- My winning lottery ticket *engendered* a great deal of envy among my co-workers; they all wished that they had won.
- Smiles *engender* smiles.
- The bitter lieutenant *engendered* discontent among his troops.

ENIGMA (uh NIG muh) *n* a mystery
- Ben is an *enigma*; he never does any homework but he always gets good grades.
- The wizard spoke in riddles and *enigmas*, and no one could understand what he was saying.

An *enigma* is *enigmatic* (en ig MAT ik).
- Ben's good grades were *enigmatic*. So was the wizard's speech.

ENMITY (EN muh tee) *n* deep hatred; animosity; ill will
Enmity is what enemies feel toward each other. If this word reminds you of the word enemy, you have a built-in mnemonic.
- The *enmity* between George and Ed was so strong that the two of them could not be in a room together.
- There was long-standing *enmity* between students at the college and residents of the town.

ENORMITY (i NOR muh tee) *n* extreme evil; a hideous offense; immensity
- Hitler's soldiers stormed through the village, committing one *enormity* after another.

"Hugeness" or "great size" is not the main meaning of *enormity*. When you want to talk about the gigantic size of something, use *immensity* instead.

ENNUI (AHN wee) *n* boredom; listless lack of interest
Ennui is the French word for boredom. Studying French vocabulary words fills some people with *ennui*.
- The children were excited to open their Christmas presents, but within a few hours an air of *ennui* had settled on the house, and the children were sprawled on the living room floor, wishing vaguely that they had something interesting to do.

- The playwright's only real talent was for engendering *ennui* in the audiences of his plays.

ENSUE (in SOO) *v* to follow immediately afterward; to result
- Janet called Debbie a liar, and a screaming fight *ensued*.

- I tried to talk my professor into changing my D into an A, but nothing *ensued* from our conversation.

EPHEMERAL (i FEM ur al) *adj* lasting a very short time
Ephemeral comes from the Greek and means lasting a single day. The word is usually used more loosely to mean lasting a short time.

Youth and flowers are both *ephemeral*. They're gone before you know it.

Some friendships are *ephemeral*.
- The tread on those used tires will probably turn out to be *ephemeral*.

QUICK QUIZ   #73

Match each word in the first column with its definition in the second column. Check your answers in the back of the book.

1.	emulate	a.	cause to exist
2.	encroach	b.	mystery
3.	endemic	c.	remove voting rights
4.	enervate	d.	reduce the strength of
5.	enfranchise	e.	native
6.	disfranchise	f.	grant voting rights
7.	engender	g.	strive to equal
8.	enigma	h.	lasting a very short time
9.	enormity	i.	extreme evil
10.	ephemeral	j.	trespass

Match each word in the first column with its definition in the second column. Check your answers in the back of the book.

1. embroil
2. embryonic
3. emissary
4. empathy
5. empower
6. endear
7. engaging
8. enmity
9. ennui
10. ensue

a. charming
b. messenger or representative
c. make dear
d. involve in conflict
e. identification with feelings
f. boredom
g. undeveloped
h. give authority
i. follow immediately afterward
j. deep hatred

ENTAIL (in TAYL) *v* to have as a necessary consequence; to involve
- Painting turned out to *entail* a lot more work than I had originally thought; I discovered that you can't simply take a gallon of paint and heave it against the side of your house.

- Peter was glad to have the prize money, but winning it had *entailed* so much work that he wasn't sure the whole thing had been worth it.

- Mr. Eanes hired me so quickly that I hadn't really had a chance to find out what the job would *entail*.

ENTITY (EN tuh tee) *n* something that exists; a distinct thing
- The air force officer found an *entity* in the cockpit of the crashed spacecraft, but he had no idea what it was.

- The identity card had been issued by a bureaucratic *entity* called the Office of Identification.

- Mark set up his new company as a separate *entity*; it had no connection with his old company.

The opposite of an *entity* is a *nonentity*.

ENTREAT (in TREET) *v* to ask earnestly; to beg; to plead
- The frog *entreated* the wizard to turn him back into a prince, but the wizard said that he would have to remain a frog a little bit longer.

- My nephew *entreated* me for money for most of a year, and in the end I gave him a few hundred dollars.

An instance of *entreating* is called an *entreaty* (in TREE tee).

- My mother was deaf to my *entreaties*; she made me attend my cousin's wedding even though I repeatedly begged her not to.

ENTREPRENEUR (ahn truh pruh NOOR) *n* an independent business person; one who starts, runs, and assumes the risk of operating an independent business enterprise

- Owen left his job at Apple to become an *entrepreneur*; he started his own computer company to make specialized computers for bookies.

- A majority of beginning business school students say they would like to become *entrepreneurs*, but most of them end up taking high-paying jobs with consulting firms or investment banks.

An *entrepreneur* is *entrepreneurial* (ahn truh pruh NOOR ee ul).

- Hector started his own jewelry business, but he had so little *entrepreneurial* ability that he soon was bankrupt.

ENUMERATE (i NOO muh rayt) *v* to name one by one; to list

- When I asked Beverly what she didn't like about me, she *enumerated* so many flaws that I eventually had to ask her to stop.

- After the doctor from the public health department had *enumerated* all the dreadful sounding diseases that were rampant in the water park, I decided I didn't want to visit it after all.

Things too numerous to be listed one by one are *innumerable* (i NOO muh ruh bul).

ENVISION (in VIZH un) *v* to imagine; to foresee

- Perry's teachers *envisioned* great things for him, so they were a little surprised when he decided to become a professional gambler.

This word is different from, but means pretty much exactly the same thing, as *envisage* (en VIZ ij). The two can be used interchangeably, although envisage is perhaps a bit more stilted.

EPICURE (EP i kyoor) *n* a person with refined taste in wine and food
Epicurus was a Greek philosopher of the fourth century BC who believed that pleasure (rather than, say, truth or beauty) was the highest good. The philosophical system he devised is known as *Epicureanism*. A teeny shadow of *Epicurus* is retained in our word *epicure*, since an *epicure* is someone who takes an almost philosophical sort of pleasure from fine food and drink.

- Ann dreaded the thought of cooking for William, who was a well-known *epicure* and would undoubtedly be hard to please.

The adjective is *epicurean* (ep i KYOOR ee un).

EPIGRAM (EP uh gram) *n* a brief and usually witty or satirical saying
People often find it difficult to remember the difference between an *epigram* and an:
  epigraph: an apt quotation placed at the beginning of a book or essay
  epitaph: a commemorative inscription on a grave
  epithet: a term used to characterize the nature of something; sometimes a disparaging term used to describe a person.
An *epigram* is *epigrammatic* (ep uh gruh MAT ik).

EPILOGUE (EP uh log) *n* an afterword; a short concluding chapter of a book; a short speech at the end of a play
In the theater, an *epilogue* is a short speech, sometimes in verse, that is spoken directly to the audience at the end of a play. In classical drama, the character who makes this concluding speech is called *Epilogue*. Likewise, a *prologue* (PROH log) is a short speech, sometimes in verse, that is spoken directly to the audience at the beginning of a play. A *prologue* sets up the play, an *epilogue* sums it up. *Epilogue* is also (and more commonly) used outside the theater.

- In a brief *epilogue*, the author described what had happened to all the book's main characters in the months since the story had taken place.

EPITOME (i PIT uh mee) *n* a brief summary that captures the meaning of the whole; the perfect example of something; a paradigm

- The first paragraph of the new novel is an *epitome* of the entire book; you can read it and understand what the author is trying to get across. It *epitomizes* the entire work.

- Luke's freshman year was the *epitome* of a college experience; he made friends, joined a fraternity, and ate too much pizza.

- Eating corn dogs and drinking root beer is the *epitome* of the good life, as far as Wilson is concerned.

EPOCH (EP uk) *n* an era; a distinctive period of time
Don't confuse *epoch* with *epic*, which is a long poem or story.
- The coach's retirement ended a glorious *epoch* in the history of the university's football team.

The adjective is *epochal* (EP uh kul). An *epochal* event is an extremely important one—the sort of significant event that might define an epoch.
- The British Open ended with an *epochal* confrontation between Jack Nicklaus and Tom Watson, the two best golfers in the world at that time.

EQUANIMITY (ek wuh NIM uh tee) *n* composure; calm
- The entire apartment building was crumbling, but Rachel faced the disaster with *equanimity*. She ducked out of the way of a falling beam and continued searching for an exit.
- John's mother looked at the broken glass on the floor with *equanimity*; at least he didn't hurt himself when he knocked over the vase.

EQUESTRIAN (i KWES tree un) *adj* having to do with horseback riding
Equus, a famous play by Peter Shaffer, portrays a troubled stable boy and his relationship with horses. *Equine* (EE kwyne) means horselike or relating to horses.
- I've never enjoyed the *equestrian* events in the Olympics because I think people look silly sitting on the backs of horses.
- Billy was very small but he had no *equestrian* skills, so he didn't make much of a jockey.

Equestrian can also be used as a noun meaning one who rides on horseback.

QUICK QUIZ #75

Match each word in the first column with its definition in the second column. Check your answers in the back of the book.

1.	entail	a.	having to do with horseback riding
2.	entity	b.	era
3.	entreat	c.	independent businessperson
4.	entrepreneur	d.	imagine
5.	enumerate	e.	something that exists
6.	envision	f.	person with refined taste
7.	epicure	g.	plead
8.	epilogue	h.	afterword
9.	epoch	i.	have as a necessary consequence
10.	equestrian	j.	name one by one

EQUITABLE (EK wuh tuh bul) *adj* fair

- King Solomon's decision was certainly *equitable*; each mother would receive half the child.

- The pirates distributed the loot *equitably* among themselves, so that each pirate received the same share as every other pirate.

- The divorce settlement was quite *equitable*. Sheila got the right half of the house, and Tom got the left half.

Equity is fairness; *inequity* is unfairness. *Iniquity* and *inequity* both mean unfair, but *iniquity* implies wickedness as well. By the way, *equity* has a meaning in business.

EQUIVOCAL (ih KWIV uh kul) *adj* ambiguous; intentionally confusing; capable of being interpreted in more than one way

Ambiguous means unclear. To be *equivocal* is to be intentionally ambiguous.

- Joe's response was *equivocal*; we couldn't tell whether he meant yes or no, which is precisely what Joe wanted.

- Dr. Festen's *equivocal* diagnosis made us think that he had no idea what Mrs. Johnson had.

To be *equivocal* is to *equivocate*. To *equivocate* is to mislead by saying confusing or ambiguous things.

- When we asked Harold whether that was his car that was parked in the middle of the hardware store, he *equivocated* and asked, "In which aisle?"

ERUDITE (ER yoo dyte) *adj* scholarly; deeply learned

- The professor said such *erudite* things that none of us had the slightest idea of what he was saying.

- The *erudite* biologist was viewed by many of his colleagues as a likely winner of the Nobel Prize.

To be *erudite* is to possess *erudition* (er yoo DISH un), or extensive knowledge.

- Mr. Fernicola's vast library was an indication of his *erudition*.

QUICK QUIZ #76

Match each word in the first column with its definition in the second column. Check your answers in the back of the book.

1. epigram	a.	brief summary
2. epigraph	b.	fair
3. epitaph	c.	composure
4. epithet	d.	intentionally confusing
5. epitome	e.	apt quotation
6. equanimity	f.	say confusing things
7. equitable	g.	inscription on a grave
8. equivocal	h.	scholarly
9. equivocate	i.	brief, witty saying
10. erudite	j.	characterizing term

ESOTERIC (es uh TER ik) *adj* hard to understand; understood by only a select few; peculiar

- Chicken wrestling and underwater yodeling were just two of Earl's *esoteric* hobbies.

- The author's books were so *esoteric* that even his mother didn't buy any of them.

ESPOUSE (eh SPOWZ) *v* to support; to advocate

- The Mormons used to *espouse* bigamy, or marriage to more than one woman.

- Alex *espoused* so many causes that he sometimes had trouble remembering which side he was on.
- The candidate for governor *espoused* a program in which all taxes would be abolished and all the state's revenues would be supplied by income from bingo and horse racing.

ESTIMABLE (ES tuh muh bul) *adj* worthy of admiration; capable of being estimated
- The prosecutor was an *estimable* opponent, but Perry Mason always won his cases.
- He swallowed a hundred goldfish, ate a hundred hot dogs in an hour, and drank a dozen beers, among other *estimable* achievements.
- The distance to the green was not *estimable* from where the golfers stood because they could not see the flag.

Something that cannot be *estimated* is *inestimable* (in ES tuh muh bul).
- The precise age of the dead man was *inestimable* because the corpse had thoroughly decomposed.

ESTRANGE (i STRAYNJ) *v* to make unfriendly or hostile; to cause to feel removed from
- Tereza's *estranged* husband had been making unkind comments about her ever since the couple had separated.
- Isaac had expected to enjoy his twenty-fifth reunion, but once there he found that he felt oddly *estranged* from his old university; he just didn't feel that he was a part of it anymore.

ETHEREAL (ih THIR ee ul) *adj* heavenly; as light and insubstantial as a gas or ether
- The *ethereal* music we heard turned out to be not angels plucking on their harps but the wind blowing through the slats of the metal awning.
- The *ethereal* mist on the hillside was delicate and beautiful.

ETHICS (ETH iks) *n* moral standards governing behavior
- Irene didn't think much of the *ethics* of most politicians; she figured they were all taking bribes.
- The dentist's habit of stealing the gold dentalwork of his patients was widely considered to be a gross violation of dental *ethics*.

To have good ethics is to be *ethical* (ETH i kul). Stealing gold dentalwork is not *ethical* behavior. It is *unethical* (un ETH i kul) behavior.

EULOGY (YOO luh jee) *n* a spoken or written tribute to a person, especially a person who has just died

- The *eulogy* Michael delivered at his father's funeral was so moving that it brought tears to the eyes of everyone present.

- Mildred was made distinctly uncomfortable by Merle's *eulogy*; she didn't appreciate Merle pointing out her late father's flaws.

To give a *eulogy* about someone is to *eulogize* (YOO luh jyze) that person. Don't confuse this word with *elegy*, which means a mournful song or poem. For a close synonym to *eulogy*, see our entry for panegyric.

EUPHEMISM (YOO fuh miz um) *n* a pleasant or inoffensive expression used in place of an unpleasant or offensive one

- Aunt Angie, who couldn't bring herself to say the word *death*, said that Uncle George had taken the big bus uptown. "Taking the big bus uptown" was her *euphemism* for dying.

- The sex-education instructor wasn't very effective. She was so embarrassed by the subject that she could only bring herself to speak *euphemistically* about it.

EVANESCENT (ev uh NES unt) *adj* fleeting; vanishing; happening for only the briefest period

- Meteors are *evanescent*: They last so briefly that it is hard to tell whether one has actually appeared.

EXACERBATE (ig ZAS ur bayt) *v* to make worse

- Dipping Austin in lye *exacerbated* his skin condition.

- The widow's grief was *exacerbated* by the minister's momentary inability to remember her dead husband's name.

- The fender-bender was *exacerbated* when two more cars plowed into the back of Margaret's car.

EXACTING (ig ZAK ting) *adj* extremely demanding; difficult; requiring great skill or care

- The *exacting* math teacher subtracted points if you didn't show every step of your work.

- The surgeon's *exacting* task was to reconnect the patient's severed eyelid.

EXALT (ig ZAWLT) *v* to raise high; to glorify

- The manager decided to *exalt* the lowly batboy by asking him to throw the first pitch in the opening game of the World Series.

The adjective *exalted* is used frequently. Being queen of England is an *exalted* occupation.

- Diamante felt *exalted* when he woke up to discover that his great-uncle had left him $100 million.
- Cleaning out a septic tank is not an *exalted* task.

Be careful not to confuse this word with *exult,* listed later.

EVINCE (i VINS) *v* to demonstrate convincingly; to prove
- Oscar's acceptance speech at the awards ceremony *evinced* an almost unbearable degree of smugness and self-regard.
- The soldiers *evinced* great courage, but their mission was hopeless, and they were rapidly defeated.

EVOKE (i VOHK) *v* to summon forth; to draw forth; to awaken; to produce or suggest
- The car trip with our children *evoked* many memories of similar car trips I had taken with my own parents when I was a child.
- Professor Herman tried repeatedly but was unable to *evoke* any but the most meager response from his students.
- Paula's Christmas photographs *evoked* both the magic and the crassness of the holiday.

The act of *evoking* is called *evocation* (e voh KAY shun). A visit to the house in which one grew up often leads to the *evocation* of old memories. Something that *evokes* something else is said to be *evocative* (i VAHK uh tiv).
- The old novel was highly *evocative* of its era; when you read it, you felt as though you had been transported a hundred years into the past.

Don't confuse this word with *invoke*, which is listed separately.

EXASPERATE (ig ZAS puh rayt) *v* to annoy thoroughly; to make very angry; to try the patience of
- The child's insistence on hopping backward on one foot *exasperated* his mother, who was in a hurry.
- The algebra class's refusal to answer any questions was extremely *exasperating* to the substitute teacher.

EXCISE (ek SYZE) *v* to remove by cutting, or as if by cutting
- Tevy's editor at the publishing house *excised* all of the obscene parts from his novel, leaving it just eleven pages long.
- The surgeon used a little pair of snippers to *excise* Alice's extra fingers.

The noun form of the word is *excision*.

- The *excision* (ek SIZH un) of Dirk's lungs left him extremely short of breath.

EXEMPLIFY (ig ZEM pluh fye) *v* to illustrate by example; to serve as a good example

- Fred participated in every class discussion and typed all of his papers. His teacher thought Fred *exemplified* the model student; Fred's classmates thought he was sycophantic.

An *exemplar* (ig ZEM plahr) is an ideal model or a paradigm. *Exemplary* (ig ZEM plur ee) means outstanding or worthy of imitation.

EXEMPT (ig ZEMPT) *adj* excused; not subject to

- Certain kinds of nonprofit organizations are *exempt* from taxation.

- David was *exempt* from jury duty because he was self-employed.

Exempt can also be a verb. To *exempt* something or someone is to make it exempt.

- Doug's flat feet and legal blindness *exempted* him from military service.

Exemption (ig ZEMP shun) is the state of being *exempt*. An *exemption* is an act of *exempting*.

EXHAUSTIVE (ig ZAWS tiv) *adj* thorough; rigorous; complete; painstaking

- Before you use a parachute, you should examine it *exhaustively* for defects. Once you jump, your decision is irrevocable.

EXHORT (ig ZORT) *v* to urge strongly; to give a serious warning to

- The coach used his bullhorn to *exhort* us to try harder.

- The fearful forest ranger *exhorted* us not to go into the cave, but we did so anyway and became lost in the center of the Earth.

The adjective is *hortatory* (HOR tuh tor ee).

QUICK QUIZ #77

Match each word in the first column with its definition in the second column. Check your answers in the back of the book.

1.	esoteric	a.	peculiar
2.	espouse	b.	make worse
3.	ethereal	c.	extremely demanding
4.	euphemism	d.	raise high
5.	evanescent	e.	inoffensive substitute term
6.	exacerbate	f.	urge strongly
7.	exacting	g.	annoy thoroughly
8.	exalt	h.	heavenly
9.	exasperate	i.	advocate
10.	exemplify	j.	fleeting
11.	exhaustive	k.	illustrate by example
12.	exhort	l.	thorough

EXHUME (ig ZOOM) *v* to unbury; to dig out of the ground

- Grave robbers once *exhumed* freshly buried bodies in order to sell them to physicians and medical students.

- Researchers *exhumed* the body of President Garfield to determine whether or not he had been poisoned to death.

- While working in his garden, Wallace *exhumed* an old chest filled with gold coins and other treasure.

See our listing for posthumous, a related word.

EXIGENCY (EK si jen see) *n* an emergency; an urgency

- An academic *exigency:* You haven't opened a book all term and the final is tomorrow morning.

Exigent means urgent.

EXISTENTIAL (eg zis TEN shul) *adj* having to do with existence; having to do with the body of thought called existentialism, which basically holds that human beings are responsible for their own actions but is otherwise too complicated to summarize in a single sentence

This word is overused but under-understood by virtually all of the people who use it. Unless you have a very good reason for throwing it around, you should probably avoid it.

EXODUS (EK suh dus) *n* a mass departure or journey away
Exodus is the second book of the Bible. It contains an account of the
Exodus, the flight of Moses and the Israelites from Egypt. When the
word refers to either the book of the Bible or the flight of Moses, it
is capitalized. When the word refers to any other mass departure,
it is not.

- Theodore's boring slide show provoked an immediate *exodus*
  from the auditorium.

- City planners were at a loss to explain the recent *exodus* of small
  businesses from the heart of the city.

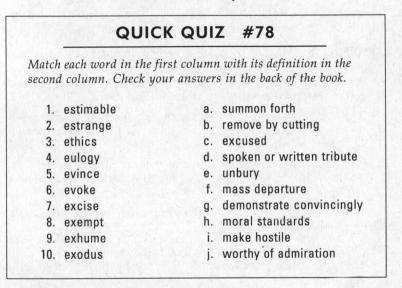

QUICK QUIZ   #78

*Match each word in the first column with its definition in the
second column. Check your answers in the back of the book.*

1.	estimable	a.	summon forth
2.	estrange	b.	remove by cutting
3.	ethics	c.	excused
4.	eulogy	d.	spoken or written tribute
5.	evince	e.	unbury
6.	evoke	f.	mass departure
7.	excise	g.	demonstrate convincingly
8.	exempt	h.	moral standards
9.	exhume	i.	make hostile
10.	exodus	j.	worthy of admiration

EXONERATE (ig ZAHN uh rayt) *v* to free completely from blame; to
exculpate

- The defendant, who had always claimed he wasn't guilty,
  expected to be *exonerated* by the testimony of his best friend.

- Our dog was *exonerated* when we discovered that it was in fact
  the cat that had eaten all the doughnuts.

EXORBITANT (ig ZAWR buh tunt) *adj* excessively costly; excessive
This word literally means out of orbit. Prices are *exorbitant* when
they get sky-high.

- Meals at the new restaurant were *exorbitant*; a garden salad cost
  seventy-five dollars.

- The better business bureau cited the discount electronic store
  for putting an *exorbitant* mark-up on portable tape recorders.

- The author was *exorbitant* in his use of big words; nearly every page in the book sent me to the dictionary.

EXPATRIATE (eks PAY tree ayt) *v* to throw (someone) out of his or her native land; to move away from one's native land; to emigrate
- The rebels were *expatriated* by the nervous general, who feared that they would cause trouble if they were allowed to remain in the country.

- Hugo was fed up with his native country, so he *expatriated* to America. In doing so, Hugo became an *expatriate* (eks PAY tree ut).

To *repatriate* (ree PAY tree ayt) is to return to one's native citizenship; that is, to become a *repatriate* (ree PAY tree it).

EXPEDIENT (ik SPEE dee unt) *adj* providing an immediate advantage; serving one's immediate self-interest; practical
- Since the basement had nearly filled with water, the plumber felt it would be *expedient* to clear out the drain.

- The candidate's position in favor of higher pay for teachers was an *expedient* one adopted for the national teachers' convention but abandoned shortly afterward.

Expedient can also be used as a noun for something *expedient.*
- The car repairman did not have his tool kit handy, so he used chewing gum as an *expedient* to patch a hole.

The noun *expedience* or *expediency* is practicality or being especially suited to a particular goal.

EXPEDITE (EK spi dyte) *v* to speed up or ease the progress of
- The post office *expedited* mail delivery by hiring more letter carriers.

- The lawyer *expedited* the progress of our case through the courts by bribing a few judges.

- Our wait for a table was *expedited* by a waiter who mistook Angela for a movie star.

EXPIATE (EK spee ayt) *v* to make amends for; to atone for
- The convicted murderer attempted to *expiate* his crime by making pot holders for the family of his victim.

The act of *expiating* is *expiation* (ek spee AY shun).
- Wendell performed many hours of community service in *expiation* of what he believed to be his sins as a corporate lawyer.

EXPLICATE (EK spli kayt) *v* to make a detailed explanation of the meaning of

- The professor's attempt to *explicate* the ancient text left his students more confused than they had been before the class began.

The act of *explicating* is *explication* (ek spli KAY shun).

- *Explication* of difficult poems was one of the principal activities in the English class.

Something that cannot be explained is *inexplicable*.

EXPLICIT (ik SPLIS it) *adj* clearly and directly expressed

- The sexually *explicit* movie received an X rating.

- The machine's instructions were *explicit*—they told us exactly what to do.

- No one *explicitly* asked us to set the barn on fire, but we got the impression that that was what we were supposed to do.

Implicit means indirectly expressed or implied.

- Gerry's dissatisfaction with our work was *implicit* in his expression, although he never criticized us directly.

EXPOSITION (ek spuh ZISH un) *n* explanation; a large public exhibition

- The master plumber's *exposition* of modern plumbing technique was so riveting that many of the young apprentice plumbers in the audience forgot to take notes.

- Charlie was overwhelmed by the new fishing equipment he saw displayed and demonstrated at the international fishing *exposition*.

To *expound* is to give an *exposition*. The adjective is *expository* (ek SPAHZ i tawr ee).

EXPUNGE (ik SPUNJ) *v* to erase; to eliminate any trace of

- Vernon's conviction for shoplifting was *expunged* from his criminal record when lightning struck the police computer.

- The blow to Wyman's head *expunged* his memory of who he was and where he had come from.

- It took Zelda five years and several lawsuits to *expunge* the unfavorable rating from her credit report.

EXQUISITE (EKS kwi zit) *adj* extraordinarily fine or beautiful; intense

- While we had cocktails on the porch, we watched an *exquisite* sunset that filled the entire sky with vivid oranges and reds.

- The weather was *exquisite*; the sun was shining and the breeze was cool.

- Pouring the urn of hot coffee down the front of his shirt left Chester in *exquisite* agony.

EXTANT (EK stunt) *adj* still in existence
- Paul rounded up all *extant* copies of his embarrassing first novel and had them destroyed.

- So many copies of the lithograph were *extant* that none of them had much value.

EXTOL (ik STOHL) *v* to praise highly; to laud
- The millionaire *extolled* the citizen who returned his gold watch but the only reward was a heartfelt handshake.

EXTORT (ik STAWRT) *v* to obtain through force, threat, or illicit means
The root "tort" means to twist. To *extort* is to twist someone's arm to get something.
- Josie *extorted* an A from her teacher by threatening to reveal publicly that he gave all the athletes As on their final exams.

The act of *extorting* is *extortion* (ik STAWR shun).
- Joe's conviction for *extortion* was viewed as an impressive qualification by the mobsters for whom he now worked.

See our listing for tortuous.

EXTRANEOUS (ik STRAY nee us) *adj* unnecessary; irrelevant; extra
- Extra ice cream would never be *extraneous,* unless everyone had already eaten so much that no one wanted any more.

- The book's feeble plot was buried in a lot of *extraneous* material about a talking dog.

- The salad contained several *extraneous* ingredients, including hair, sand, and a single dead fly.

To be *extraneous* is to be *extra* and always with the sense of being unnecessary.

EXTRAPOLATE (ik STRAP uh layt) *v* to project or deduce from something known; to infer
- George's estimates were *extrapolated* from last year's data; he simply took all the old numbers and doubled them.

- Emeril came up with a probable recipe by *extrapolating* from the taste of the cookies he had eaten at the store.

- By *extrapolating* from a handful of pottery fragments, the archaeologists formed a possible picture of the ancient civilization.

To *extrapolate,* a scientist uses the facts he has to project to facts outside; to *interpolate* (in TUR puh layt), he tries to fill the gaps within his data.

EXTREMITY (ik STREM uh tee) *n* the outermost point or edge; the greatest degree; grave danger; a limb or appendage of the body
- The explorers traveled to the *extremity* of the glacier then fell off.
- Even in the *extremity* of his despair, he never lost his love for tennis.
- Ruth was at her best in *extremity*; great danger awakened all her best instincts.
- During extremely cold weather, blood leaves the *extremities* to retain heat in the vital organs.

EXTRICATE (EK struh kayt) *v* to free from difficulty
- It took two and a half days to *extricate* the little girl from the abandoned well into which she had fallen.
- Yoshi had to pretend to be sick to *extricate* himself from the blind date with the ventriloquist who brought her puppet on the date with her.
- Monica had no trouble driving her car into the ditch, but she needed a tow truck to *extricate* it.

Something that is permanently stuck is *inextricable* (in EKS tri kuh bul).

EXTROVERT (EKS truh vurt) *n* an open, outgoing person; a person whose attention is focused on others rather than on himself or herself
- Maria was quite an *extrovert*; she walked boldly into the roomful of strange adults and struck up many friendly conversations.
- Damian was an *extrovert* in the sense that he was always more interested in other people's business than in his own.

An *introvert* (IN truh vurt) is a person whose attention is directed inward and who is concerned with little outside himself or herself.
- Ryan was an *introvert*; he spent virtually all his time in his room, writing in his diary and talking to himself. An *introvert* is usually introspective.

EXUBERANT (ig ZOO buh runt) *adj* highly joyous or enthusiastic; over-flowing; lavish

- The children's *exuberant* welcome brought tears of joy to the eyes of the grumpy visitor.
- Quentin was nearly a hundred years old, but he was still in *exuberant* health; he walked twelve miles every morning and lifted weights every evening.
- The flowers in Mary's garden were *exuberantly* (ig ZOO buh runt lee) colorful; her yard contained more bright colors than a box of crayons.

Exuberance (ig ZOO buh runs) is the state of being *exuberant*.

- The *exuberance* of her young students was like a tonic to the jaded old teacher.

EXULT (ig ZULT) *v* to rejoice; to celebrate

- The women's team *exulted* in its victory over the men's team at the badminton finals. They were *exultant*.

QUICK QUIZ #79

Match each word in the first column with its definition in the second column. Check your answers in the back of the book.

1. exigency	a. free from blame
2. existential	b. clearly expressed
3. exonerate	c. indirectly expressed
4. expatriate	d. having to do with existence
5. expedient	e. outgoing person
6. expedite	f. speed up
7. explicit	g. infer
8. implicit	h. free from difficulty
9. extol	i. immediately advantageous
10. extraneous	j. unnecessary
11. extrapolate	k. inwardly directed person
12. extricate	l. throw out of native land
13. extrovert	m. emergency
14. introvert	n. rejoice
15. exult	o. praise highly

F

FABRICATION (FAB ruh kay shun) *n* a lie; something made up
- My story about being the prince of Wales was a *fabrication*. I'm really the king of Denmark.
- The suspected murderer's alibi turned out to be an elaborate *fabrication*; in other words, he was lying when he said that he hadn't killed the victim.

To create a *fabrication* is to *fabricate*.

FACADE (fuh SAHD) *n* the front of a building; the false front of a building; the false front or misleading appearance of anything
- The building's *facade* was covered with so many intricate carvings that visitors often had trouble finding the front door.
- What appeared to be a bank at the end of the street was really a plywood *facade* that had been erected as a set for the motion picture.
- Gretchen's kindness is just a *facade*; she is really a hostile, scheming bully.

FACET (FAS it) *n* any of the flat, polished surfaces of a cut gem; aspect
- Karen loved to admire the tiny reflections of her face in the *facets* of the diamonds in her engagement ring.
- The two most important *facets* of Dan's personality were niceness and meanness.

Anything that has many *facets* can be said to be *multifaceted* (mul tee FAS it ud).
- Lonnie is a *multifaceted* performer; she can tell jokes, sing songs, juggle bowling pins, and dance.

FACETIOUS (fuh SEE shus) *adj* humorous; not serious; clumsily humorous
- David was sent to the principal's office for making a *facetious* remark about the intelligence of the French teacher.
- Our proposal about shipping our town's garbage to the moon was *facetious*, but the first selectman took it seriously.

FACILE (FAS il) *adj* fluent; skillful in a superficial way; easy
To say that a writer's style is *facile* is to say both that it is skillful and that it would be better if the writer exerted himself or herself more. The word *facile* almost always contains this sense of superficiality.
- Paolo's poems were *facile* rather than truly accomplished; if you read them closely, you soon realized they were filled with clichés.
- The CEO of the company was a *facile* speaker. He could speak engagingly on almost any topic with very little preparation. He spoke with great *facility*.

FACTION (FAK shun) *n* a group, usually a small part of a larger group, united around some cause; disagreement within an organization
- At the Republican National Convention, the candidate's *faction* spent much of its time shouting at the other candidate's *faction*.
- The faculty was relatively happy, but there was a *faction* that called for higher pay.
- When the controversial topic of the fund drive came up, the committee descended into bitterness and *faction*. It was a *factious* topic.

FALLACY (FAL uh see) *n* a false notion or belief; a misconception
- Peter clung to the *fallacy* that he was a brilliant writer, despite the fact that everything he had ever written had been rejected by every publisher to whom he had sent it.

- That electricity is a liquid was but one of the many *fallacies* spread by the incompetent science teacher.

The adjective is *fallacious* (fuh LAY shus).

FARCICAL (FARS i kul) *adj* absurd; ludicrous
- The serious play quickly turned *farcical* when the leading man's belt broke and his pants fell to his ankles.
- The formerly secret documents detailed the CIA's *farcical* attempt to discredit the dictator by sprinkling his shoes with a powder that was supposed to make his beard fall out.

Farcical means like a *farce*, which is a mockery or a ridiculous satire.

FASTIDIOUS (fa STID ee us) *adj* meticulous; demanding; finicky
- Mrs. O'Hara was a *fastidious* housekeeper; she cleaned up our crumbs almost before they hit the floor.
- Jeb was so *fastidious* in his work habits that he needed neither a wastebasket nor an eraser.
- The *fastidious* secretary was nearly driven mad by her boss, who used the floor as a file cabinet and his desk as a pantry.

FATALIST (FAYT uh list) *n* someone who believes that future events are already determined and that humans are powerless to change them
- The old man was a *fatalist* about his illness, believing there was no sense in worrying about something he could not control.
- Carmine was such a *fatalist* that he never wore a seat belt; he said that if he were meant to die in a car accident, there was nothing he could do to prevent it.

Fatalist is closely related to the word *fate*. A *fatalist* is someone who believes that *fate* determines everything.
    To be a *fatalist* is to be *fatalistic*.

FATHOM (FATH um) *v* to understand; to penetrate the meaning of
At sea, a *fathom* is a measure of depth equal to six feet. *Fathoming*, at sea, is measuring the depth of the water, usually by dropping a weighted line over the side of a boat. On land, to *fathom* is to do the rough figurative equivalent of measuring the depth of water.
- I sat through the entire physics lecture, but I couldn't even begin to *fathom* what the professor was talking about.
- Arthur hid his emotions behind a blank expression that was impossible to *fathom*.

FATUOUS (FACH oo us) *adj* foolish; silly; idiotic
- Pauline is so pretty that her suitors are often driven to *fatuous* acts of devotion. They are *infatuated* with her.

FAUNA (FAW nuh) *n* animals
- We saw little evidence of *fauna* on our walk through the woods. We did, however, see plenty of *flora,* or plants.

The phrase *flora* and *fauna* means plants and animals. The terms are used particularly in describing what lives in a particular region or environment.

Arctic *fauna* are very different from tropical *fauna.*
- In Jim's yard, the *flora* consists mostly of weeds.

It's easy to remember which of these words means what. Just replace *flora* and *fauna* with *flowers* and *fawns.*

FAUX (foh) *adj* false

Faux marble is wood painted to look like marble. A *faux* pas (foh pah) literally means false step, but is used to mean an embarrassing social mistake.
- Susannah's necklace is made of *faux* pearls, as the mugger found out when he got to the pawn shop.
- At the royal banquet, Derik committed the minor *faux* pas of eating salad with the wrong fork.

FAWN (fawn) *v* to exhibit affection; to seek favor through flattery; to kiss up to someone
- The old women *fawned* over the new baby, pinching its cheeks and making little gurgling sounds.
- The king could not see through the *fawning* of his court; he thought all the counts and dukes really liked him.

FECUND (FEE kund) *adj* fertile; productive
- The *fecund* mother rabbit gave birth to hundreds and hundreds of little rabbits.
- The child's imagination was so *fecund* that dozens of stories hopped out of him like a bunch of baby rabbits.
- Our compost heap became increasingly *fecund* as it decomposed.

The state of being *fecund* is *fecundity* (fi KUN di tee).
This word can also be pronounced "FEK und."

QUICK QUIZ #81

Match each word in the first column with its definition in the second column. Check your answers in the back of the book.

1. fabrication	a. plants
2. facetious	b. fertile
3. facile	c. absurd
4. faction	d. one who believes in fate
5. farcical	e. humorous
6. fastidious	f. animals
7. fatalist	g. superficially skillful
8. fatuous	h. group with a cause
9. fauna	i. lie
10. flora	j. meticulous
11. fecund	k. foolish

FEIGN (fayn) *v* to make a false representation of; to pretend
- Ike *feigned* illness at work in order to spend the day at the circus.
- The children *feigned* sleep in the hope of catching a glimpse of Santa Claus.
- Agony of the sort that Frances exhibited cannot be *feigned*; she had obviously been genuinely hurt.

A *feigning* motion, gesture, or action is a *feint* (faynt), which can also be used as a verb.
- The boxer *feinted* with his right hand and then knocked out his distracted opponent with his left.

FELICITY (fuh LIS uh tee) *n* happiness; skillfulness, especially at expressing things; adeptness
- Love was not all *felicity* for Judy and Steve; they argued all the time. In fact their relationship was characterized by *infelicity*.
- Shakespeare wrote with great *felicity*. His works are filled with *felicitous* expressions.

FERVOR (FUR vur) *n* great warmth or earnestness; ardor; zeal
- Avid baseball fans frequently display their *fervor* for the game by throwing food at bad players.

FESTER (FES tur) *v* to generate pus; to decay
- Mr. Baker had allowed the wound on his arm to *fester* for so long that it now required surgery.
- For many years, resentment had *festered* beneath the surface of the apparently happy organization.

FETISH (FET ish) *n* an object of obsessive reverence, attention, or interest
- Jeff had made a *fetish* of his garage; he even waxed the concrete floor.
- Clown shoes were Harriet's *fetish*; whenever she saw a pair, she had to buy it.

Though many people associate the word *fetish* with an object of sexual desire (and that is one definition), the original meaning is actually a religious one. A *fetish* was an object that was worshipped because it was believed to have magical powers or because it was believed to be the incarnation of a particular spirit, similar to an idol.

FETTER (FET ur) *v* to restrain; to hamper
- In his pursuit of an Olympic gold medal, the runner was *fettered* by multiple injuries.

To be *unfettered* is to be unrestrained or free of hindrances.
- After the dictator was deposed, a novelist produced a fictional account of the dictatorship that was *unfettered* by the strict rules of censorship.

A *fetter* is literally a chain (attached to the foot) that is used to restrain a criminal or, for that matter, an innocent person. A figurative *fetter* can be anything that hampers or restrains someone.
- The housewife's young children were the *fetters* that prevented her from pursuing a second Master's degree.

FIASCO (fee AS koh) *n* a complete failure or disaster; an incredible screwup
- The tag sale was a *fiasco*; it poured down rain all morning, and nobody showed up.
- The birthday party turned into a *fiasco* when the candles on the cake exploded.

FIAT (FYE ut) *n* an arbitrary decree or order
- The value of the country's currency was set not by the market but by executive *fiat*.

- The president of the company ruled by *fiat*; there was no such thing as a discussion of policy, and disagreements were not allowed.

This word can also be pronounced "FEE ut."

FICKLE (FIK ul) *adj* likely to change for no good reason
- Cats are *fickle*: One day they love you; the next day they hiss at you.

- The weather had been *fickle* all day; one moment the sun was shining, the next it was pouring down rain.

- The Taylors were so *fickle* that their architect finally told them he would quit the job if they made any more changes in the plans for their new house.

QUICK QUIZ #82

Match each word in the first column with its definition in the second column. Check your answers in the back of the book.

1.	facade	a.	object of obsessive reverence
2.	facet	b.	exhibit affection
3.	fallacy	c.	complete failure
4.	fathom	d.	make a false representation of
5.	faux	e.	front of a building
6.	fawn	f.	decay
7.	feign	g.	arbitrary decree
8.	fester	h.	misconception
9.	fetish	i.	penetrate the meaning of
10.	fiasco	j.	likely to change for no good reason
11.	fiat	k.	aspect
12.	fickle	l.	false

FIDELITY (fuh DEL uh tee) *n* faithfulness; loyalty
- The motto of the United States Marine Corps is *semper fidelis,* which is Latin for always loyal.

A *high-fidelity* record player is one that is very faithful in reproducing the original sound of whatever was recorded.
- The crusader's life was marked by *fidelity* to the cause of justice.
- The soldiers couldn't shoot straight, but their *fidelity* to the cause of freedom was never in question.

Infidelity means faithlessness or disloyalty. Marital *infidelity* is another way of saying adultery. Early phonograph records were marked by *infidelity* to the original.

FIGMENT (FIG munt) *n* something made up or invented; a fabrication
- The three-year-old told his mother there were skeletons under his bed, but they turned out to be just a *figment* of his overactive imagination.
- These French-speaking hummingbirds inside my head—are they real, or are they a *figment*?

FIGURATIVE (FIG yur uh tiv) *adj* based on figures of speech; expressing something in terms usually used for something else; metaphorical
- When the mayor said that the housing market had sprouted wings, he was speaking *figuratively*. The housing market hadn't really sprouted wings; it had merely risen so rapidly that it had almost seemed to fly.

To say that the autumn hillside was a blaze of color is to use the word *blaze* in a *figurative* sense. The hillside wasn't really on fire, but the colors of the leaves made it appear (somewhat) as though it were.

A *figurative* meaning of a word is one that is not *literal*. A *literal* statement is one in which every word means exactly what it says. If the housing market had *literally* sprouted wings, genuine wings would somehow have popped out of it.

People very, very often confuse these words, using one when they really mean the other.
- Desmond could *literally* eat money if he chewed up and swallowed a dollar bill. Desmond's car eats money only *figuratively*, in the sense that it is very expensive to operate.

FINESSE (fi NES) *n* skillful maneuvering; subtlety; craftiness
- The doctor sewed up the wound with *finesse,* making stitches so small one could scarcely see them.
- The boxer moved with such *finesse* that his opponent never knew what hit him.

FISCAL (FIS kul) *adj* pertaining to financial matters; monetary
- Having no sense of *fiscal* responsibility, he was happy to waste his salary on a life-size plastic flamingo with diamond eyes.
- A *fiscal* year is any twelve-month period established for accounting purposes.
- Scrooge Enterprises begins its *fiscal* year on December 25 to make sure that no one takes Christmas Day off.

FLAGRANT (FLAY grunt) *adj* glaringly bad; notorious; scandalous
An example of a *flagrant* theft would be stealing a car from the parking lot of a police station. A *flagrant* spelling error is a very noticeable one. See the listing for *blatant*, as these two words are often confused.

FLAUNT (flawnt) *v* to show off; to display ostentatiously
- The brand-new millionaire annoyed all his friends by driving around his old neighborhood to *flaunt* his new Rolls-Royce.
- Colleen *flaunted* her engagement ring, shoving it in the face of almost anyone who came near her.

This word is very often confused with *flout*.

FLEDGLING (FLEJ ling) *adj* inexperienced or immature
- A *fledgling* bird is one still too young to fly; once its wing feathers have grown in, it is said to be *fledged*.
- Lucy was still a *fledgling* caterer when her deviled eggs gave the whole party food poisoning.

Full-fledged means complete, full-grown.
- Now that Lucy is a *full-fledged* gourmet chef, her deviled eggs poison only a couple of people annually.

FLIPPANT (FLIP unt) *adj* frivolously disrespectful; saucy; pert; flip
- I like to make *flippant* remarks in church to see how many old ladies will turn around and glare at me.

The act or state of being *flippant* is *flippancy* (FLIP un see).
- The *flippancy* of the second graders was almost more than the substitute teacher could stand.

Flip is another form of the word that is in common usage.

FLORID (FLAWR id) *adj* ruddy; flushed; red-faced
- Ike's *florid* complexion is the result of drinking a keg of beer and eating ten pounds of lard every day.

Florid is related to floral and florist, so it also means excessively flowery, overdramatic, or ornate.

- My brother is still making fun of that *florid* love poem Ted sent me.

FLOUT (flowt) *v* to disregard something out of disrespect
- A driver *flouts* the traffic laws by driving through red lights and knocking down pedestrians.

To *flaunt* success is to make certain everyone knows that you are successful. To *flout* success is to be contemptuous of success or to act as though it means nothing at all.

FODDER (FAHD ur) *n* coarse food for livestock; raw material
- The cattle for some reason don't like their new *fodder*, which is made of ground-up fish bones and cabbage.
- Estelle was less embarrassed than usual when her father acted stupidly in public because his behavior was *fodder* for her new stand-up comedy routine.

Fodder and *food* are derived from the same root.

FOIBLE (FOY bul) *n* a minor character flaw
- Patti's *foibles* included a tendency to prefer dogs to people.
- The delegates to the state convention ignored the candidates' positions on the major issues and concentrated on their *foibles*.

FOLLY (FAHL ee) *n* foolishness; insanity; imprudence
- You don't seem to understand what *folly* it would be to design a paper raincoat.
- The policeman tried to convince Buddy of the *folly* of running away from home; he explained to him that his bed at home was more comfortable than a sidewalk, and that his mother's cooking was better than no cooking at all.

Folly and *fool* are derived from the same root.

FOMENT (foh MENT) *v* to stir up; to instigate
- The bad news from abroad *fomented* pessimism among professional investors.
- The radicals spread several rumors in an effort to *foment* rebellion among the peasants.

QUICK QUIZ #83

Match each word in the first column with its definition in the second column. Check your answers in the back of the book.

1.	felicity	a.	loyalty
2.	fervor	b.	stir up
3.	fetter	c.	restrain
4.	fidelity	d.	meaning exactly what it says
5.	figurative	e.	minor character flaw
6.	literal	f.	show off
7.	finesse	g.	based on figures of speech
8.	flagrant	h.	to disregard contemptuously
9.	flaunt	i.	skillful maneuvering
10.	flout	j.	happiness
11.	foible	k.	glaringly bad
12.	foment	l.	zeal

FORAY (FAWR ay) *n* a quick raid or attack; an initial venture
- The minute Shelly left for the party, her younger sisters made a *foray* on her makeup; they ended up smearing her lipstick all over their faces.
- My *foray* into the world of advertising convinced me that my soul is much too sensitive for such a sleazy business.
- The young soldier's ill-fated *foray* into the woods ended with his capture by an enemy patrol.

FORBEAR (for BAYR) *v* to refrain from; to abstain
- Stephen told me I could become a millionaire if I joined him in his business, but his lack of integrity makes me nervous so I decided to *forbear*.
- George *forbore* to punch me in the nose, even though I told him that I thought he was a sniveling idiot.

The noun is *forbearance*.

A *forebear* (FOR bayr)—sometimes also spelled *forbear*—is an ancestor.

FOREGO (for GOH) *v* to do without; to forbear
- We had some of the chocolate cake, some of the chocolate mousse, and some of the chocolate cream pie, but we were worried about our weight so we decided to *forego* the chocolate-covered potato chips. That is, we *forewent* them.

Can also be spelled *forgo*.

FOREBODE (fawr BOHD) *v* to be an omen of; to predict; to foretell
- The baby's purple face, quivering chin, and clenched fists *forebode* a temper tantrum.

Sometimes *forebode* means to predict or prophesy (PRAHF uh sye).
- Bea *forebodes* tragedy every time she gazes into her crystal ball, unless the person paying for her fortune-telling wants only the good news.

A *foreboding* is the feeling that something awful is about to happen.
- When Rafi saw the killer shark leap toward him with a gun under one fin and a knife under the other, he had a *foreboding* that something not particularly pleasant was about to happen to him.

To *bode* and *forebode* are synonyms.

FORECLOSE (fawr KLOHZ) *v* to deprive a mortgagor of his or her right to redeem a property; to shut out or exclude
- If you don't make the mortgage payments on your house, the bank may *foreclose* on the loan, take possession of the house, and sell it in order to raise the money you owe.

- Even though he never made a single payment on his house, Tom still can't understand why the bank *foreclosed* on the mortgage.

- When Tom developed an allergy to it, he was *foreclosed* from eating his favorite food, corn on the cob.

An act of *foreclosing* is a *foreclosure* (fawr KLOH zhur).

QUICK QUIZ   #84

Match each word in the first column with its definition in the second column. Check your answers in the back of the book.

1.	figment	a.	foolishness
2.	fiscal	b.	inexperienced
3.	fledgling	c.	something made up
4.	flippant	d.	raw material
5.	florid	e.	quick raid
6.	fodder	f.	monetary
7.	folly	g.	flushed
8.	foray	h.	be an omen of
9.	forebode	i.	frivolously disrespectful
10.	foreclose	j.	shut out

FORENSIC (fuh REN sik) *adj* related to or used in courts of law
- Before seeking an indictment, the prosecutor needed a report from the *forensic* laboratory, which he felt certain would show that the dead man had been strangled with his belt.

Forensics can also be the study or practice of debate.
- Because she likes to argue, Brooke assumed she would be the star of the *forensics* team; however, she soon found that the competition involved much more than shouting.

FORESTALL (fawr STAWL) *v* to thwart, prevent, or hinder something from happening; to head off
- To *forestall* embarrassing questions about her haircut, Ann decided to wear a bag over her head until the hair grew in.

- Let's *forestall* a depressing January by not spending any money on Christmas presents this year.

FORSAKE (for SAYK) *v* to abandon; to renounce; to relinquish
- We urged Buddy to *forsake* his life with the alien beings and return to his job at the drugstore.

- All the guru's followers had *forsaken* him, so he became a real estate developer and turned his temple into an apartment building.

FORSWEAR (fawr SWAYR) *v* to retract, renounce, or recant; to take back
- The thief had previously testified that he had been in Florida during the theft, but a stern glance from the judge quickly made him *forswear* that testimony.
- For my New Year's resolution, I decided to *forswear* both tobacco and alcohol; then I lit a cigar and opened a bottle of champagne to celebrate the new me.
- *Forswear* your gluttonous ways! Go on a diet!

FORTE (FOR tay) *n* a person's strong point, special talent, or specialty
- Lulu doesn't have a *forte*; she doesn't do anything particularly well.
- Uncle Joe likes to knit, but his real *forte* is needlepoint.

FORTHRIGHT (FAWRTH ryte) *adj* frank; outspoken; going straight to the point
- When the minister asked Lucy whether or not she would take Clay as her lawfully wedded husband, she answered with a *forthright*, "No!"
- I know I asked for your honest opinion on my dress, but I didn't expect you to be that *forthright*.

FORTUITOUS (for TOO uh tus) *adj* accidental; occurring by chance
- The program's outcome was not the result of any plan but was entirely *fortuitous*.
- The object was so perfectly formed that its creation could not have been *fortuitous*.

Fortuitous is often misused to mean lucky or serendipitous. Don't make that same mistake. It means merely accidental.

FOSTER (FAWS tur) *v* to encourage; to promote the development of
- Growing up next door to a circus *fostered* my love of elephants.
- By refusing to be pressured into burning its "controversial" books, the library will *foster* new ideas instead of smothering them.
- The wolves who raised me lovingly *fostered* my ability to run on my hands and knees.

FOUNDER (FOWN dur) *v* to fail; to collapse; to sink
- The candidate's campaign for the presidency *foundered* when it was revealed that he had once been married to a drug addict.
- Zeke successfully struggled through the first part of the course but *foundered* when the final examination was given.

• The ship *foundered* shortly after it hit the iceberg.

Be careful not to confuse this word with *flounder,* which means to move clumsily or in confusion.

• Our field hockey team *floundered* helplessly around the field while the opposing team scored goal after goal.

• The witness began to *flounder* as the attorney fired question after question.

If you want to remember the difference between the two words, think that when a person *flounders,* he is flopping around like a flounder.

FRAGMENTARY (FRAG mun tar ee) *adj* incomplete; disconnected; made up of fragments

• Since the coup leaders refuse to allow the press into the country, our information is still *fragmentary* at this point.

• She has only a *fragmentary* knowledge of our national anthem; she can sing the first, fifth, and eleventh lines, and that's all.

To *fragment* (frag MENT) is to break into pieces. Note carefully the pronunciation of this verb.

Fragmented means split up or divided. *Fragmentary* and *fragmented* are not quite synonyms.

FRATERNAL (fruh TUR nul) *adj* like brothers

• The *fraternal* feelings of the group were strengthened by monthly fishing trips.

• A *fraternity* is an organization of men who have bound themselves together in a relationship analogous to that of real brothers.

FRENETIC (fruh NET ik) *adj* frantic; frenzied

• There was a lot of *frenetic* activity in the office, but nothing ever seemed to get accomplished.

• The bird's *frenetic* attempt to free itself from the thorn bush only made the situation worse.

FRUGAL (FROO gul) *adj* economical; penny-pinching

• Laura was so *frugal* that she even tried to bargain with the checkout girl at the discount store.

• We were as *frugal* as we could be, but we still ended up several thousand dollars in debt.

• Hannah's *frugality* annoyed her husband, who loved spending money on tech gadgets.

FRUITFUL (FROOT ful) *adj* productive; producing good or abundant results; successful

- The collaboration between the songwriter and the lyricist proved so *fruitful* that last year they won a Tony for Best Musical.

- Our brainstorming session was *fruitful*; we figured out how to achieve world peace and came up with a way to convert old socks into clean energy.

Fruitless (FROOT lus) means unproductive, pointless, or unrewarding. A cherry tree without any cherries is *fruitless* in both the literal and the figurative sense of the word. A *fruitless* search turns up nothing.

To reach *fruition* (froo ISH un) is to accomplish or fulfill what has been sought or striven for.

- The *fruition* of all Diana's dreams arrived when Charles asked her to be his wife.

FUEL (fyool) *v* to stimulate; to ignite; to kindle, as if providing with fuel

- Her older sister's sarcasm only *fueled* Wendy's desire to live several thousand miles away.

- Juan *fueled* Juana's suspicions by telling her out of the blue that he was not planning a surprise party for her.

- The taunts of the opposing quarterback backfired by *fueling* our team's quest for victory.

FULMINATE (FUL muh nayt) *v* to denounce vigorously; to protest vehemently against something

- In every sermon, the bishop *fulminates* against the evils of miniskirts, saying that they are the sort of skirt that the devil would wear.

- The old man never actually went after any of his numerous enemies; he just sat in his room *fulminating*.

- The principal's *fulminations* (ful muh NAY shuns) had no effect on the naughty sophomores; they went right on smoking cigarettes and blowing their smoke in his face.

Fulmination is a close synonym to diatribe.

FURTIVE (FUR tiv) *adj* secretive; sly
- Cal wiggled his ears while the countess was talking to him in a *furtive* attempt to catch our attention.
- The burglars were *furtive*, but not *furtive* enough; the alert policeman grabbed them as they carried the TV through the Rubenstein's back door.

FUTILE (FYOOT ul) *adj* useless; hopeless
- A D+ average and no extracurricular interests to speak of meant that applying to Harvard was *futile*, but Lucinda hoped against hope.

Something *futile* is a *futility* (fyoo TIL uh tee).
- Lucinda doesn't know what a *futility* it is.

QUICK QUIZ #86

Match each word in the first column with its definition in the second column. Check your answers in the back of the book.

1.	forbear	a.	economical
2.	forebear	b.	ancestor
3.	forgo	c.	move in confusion
4.	forsake	d.	do without
5.	fortuitous	e.	refrain from
6.	founder	f.	sink
7.	flounder	g.	secretive
8.	frenetic	h.	accidental
9.	frugal	i.	abandon
10.	furtive	j.	frantic

G

GAFFE (gaf) *n* a social blunder; an embarrassing mistake; a faux pas
- In some cultures, burping after you eat is considered a sign that you liked the meal. In our culture, it's considered a *gaffe*.
- You commit a *gaffe* when you ask a man if he's wearing a toupee.
- Michael Kinsley defines a politician's *gaffe* as "when one inadvertently tells the truth."

GALVANIZE (GAL vuh nyze) *v* to startle into sudden activity; to revitalize
- The student council president hoped his speech would *galvanize* the student body into rebelling against standardized tests. But his speech was not as *galvanic* (gal VAHN ik) as he would have liked, and his listeners continued to doze in their seats.
- Dullsville was a sleepy little town until its residents were *galvanized* by the discovery that they all knew how to whistle really well.

To *galvanize* something is literally to cover it in zinc, which protects it and makes it stronger. But its figurative definition is much more common in everyday speech.

GAMBIT (GAM but) *n* a scheme to gain an advantage; a ploy
- Bobby's opening *gambit* at the chess tournament allowed him to take control of the game from the beginning.
- Meg's *gambit* to get a new car consisted of telling her father that everyone else in her class had a new car.
- My young son said he wanted a drink of water, but I knew that his request was merely a *gambit* to stay up later.

GAMUT (GAM ut) *n* the full range (of something)
- The baby's emotions run the *gamut* from all-out shrieking to contented cooing.
- Charlotte's professor said that her essay covered the *gamut* of literary mistakes, from bad spelling to outright plagiarism.

GARNER (GAHR nur) *v* to gather; to acquire; to earn
- Steve continues to garner varsity letters, a fact that will no doubt *garner* him a reputation as a great athlete.
- Mary's articles about toxic waste *garnered* her a Pulitzer Prize.

GARRULOUS (GAR uh lus) *adj* talkative; chatty
- Gabriella is gregarious and *garrulous;* she loves to hang out with the gang and gab.

GASTRONOMY (gas TRAHN uh mee) *n* the art of eating well
- The restaurant's new French chef is so well versed in *gastronomy* that she can make a pile of hay taste good. In fact, I believe that hay is what she served us for dinner last night.
- I have never eaten a better meal. It is a *gastronomic* (gas truh NAHM ik) miracle.

GAUCHE (gohsh) *adj* unskillful; awkward; maladroit

Remember *dextrous*? Well, *gauche* is pretty much the exact opposite. It is the French word for left—the connection is that left-handed people were once thought to be clumsy (this was clearly before the invention of left-handed scissors) and perverse, even evil. These days, *gauche* tends to describe social, rather than physical, ineptness.
- Smadar had a poor sense of comic timing, and her *gauche* attempts to mock her left-handed friends soon left her with none.

GENERIC (je NER ik) *adj* general; common; not protected by trademark
- The machinery Pedro used to make his great discovery was entirely *generic*; anyone with access to a hardware store could have done what he did.

- The year after he graduated from college, Paul moved to New York and wrote a *generic* first novel in which a young man graduates from college, moves to New York, and writes his first novel.

- Instead of buying expensive name-brand cigarettes, Rachel buys a *generic* brand and thus ruins her health at far less expense.

GENESIS (JEN uh sis) *n* origin; creation; beginning
Genesis is the name of the first book of the Bible. It concerns the *genesis* of the world, and in it Adam and Eve realize that it is never wise to listen to the advice of serpents.
- It's hard to believe that the Boeing 747 has its *genesis* in the flimsy contraption built by the Wright brothers.

GENOCIDE (JEN uh syde) *n* the extermination of a national, racial, or religious group
- Hitler's policy of *genocide* made him one of the most hated men in history.

When a word ends with the suffix "cide," it generally has to do with some form of murder. *Homicide* (HAHM uh syde) means murder; *matricide* (MA truh syde) means mother-murder; *patricide* (PA truh syde) means father-murder; *suicide* (SOO uh syde) means self-murder. An *insecticide* (in SEK tuh syde) is a substance that "murders" insects.

GERMANE (jur MAYN) *adj* applicable; pertinent; relevant
- "Whether or not your mother and I give you too small an allowance," said Cleo's father sternly, "is not *germane* to my suggestion that you clean up your room more often."

- One of the many *germane* points he raised during his speech was that someone is going to have to pay for all these improvements.

- Claiming that Arnold's comments were not *germane* to the discussion at hand, the president of the company told him to sit down and shut up.

QUICK QUIZ #87

Match each word in the first column with its definition in the second column. Check your answers in the back of the book.

1.	gaffe	a.	full range
2.	galvanize	b.	gather
3.	gambit	c.	startle into sudden activity
4.	gamut	d.	art of eating well
5.	garner	e.	social blunder
6.	gastronomy	f.	extermination of a national, racial, or religious group
7.	generic	g.	origin
8.	genesis	h.	scheme to gain an advantage
9.	genocide	i.	common
10.	germane	j.	applicable

GENRE (ZHAHN ruh) *n* a type or category, especially of art or writing
The novel is one literary *genre.* Poetry is another.
- Daoyen displayed a great talent for a particular *genre:* the bawdy limerick.

GENTEEL (jen TEEL) *adj* refined; polite; aristocratic; affecting refinement
- The ladies at the ball were too *genteel* to accept our invitation to the wrestling match.

A person who is *genteel* has *gentility.*

GESTICULATE (jes TIK yuh layt) *v* to make gestures, especially when speaking or in place of speaking
- Massimo *gesticulated* wildly on the other side of the theater in an attempt to get our attention.
- The after-dinner speaker *gesticulated* in such a strange way that the audience paid more attention to his hands than to his words.

A person who *gesticulates* makes *gesticulations.*

GHASTLY (GAST lee) *adj* shockingly horrible; frightful; ghostlike
- The most *ghastly* crime ever recorded in these parts was committed by One-Eye Sam, and it was too horrifying to describe.
- You have a rather *ghastly* color all of a sudden. Have you just spotted One-Eye Sam?

GLUT (glut) *n* surplus; an overabundance
- The international oil shortage turned into an international oil *glut* with surprising speed.
- We had a *glut* of contributions but a dearth, or scarcity, of volunteers; it seemed that people would rather give their money than their time.

GRANDILOQUENT (gran DIL uh kwunt) *adj* pompous; using a lot of big, fancy words in an attempt to sound impressive
- The governor's speech was *grandiloquent* rather than eloquent; there were some six-dollar words and some impressive phrases, but he really had nothing to say.
- The new minister's *grandiloquence* got him in trouble with deacons, who wanted him to be more restrained in his sermons.

GRANDIOSE (GRAN dee ohs) *adj* absurdly exaggerated
- The scientist's *grandiose* plan was to build a huge shopping center on the surface of the moon.
- Their house was genuinely impressive, although there were a few *grandiose* touches: a fireplace the size of a garage, a kitchen with four ovens, and a computerized media center in every room.

To be *grandiose* is to be characterized by *grandiosity* (gran dee AHS uh tee).

GRATIS (GRAT us) *adj* free of charge
- Since Gary drove his car through Whitney's plateglass living room window, he provided her with a new one, *gratis*.
- I tried to pay for the little mint on my pillow, but the chambermaid explained that it was *gratis*.
- When the waiter told Herbert that the drink was *gratis*, Herbert started to shout. He said, "I didn't order any damned *gratis*. I want some brandy, and I want it now!"

If something *gratis* is freely given, then it makes sense that a *gratuity* is an amount that is paid by choice, and that *gratuitous* violence in a movie is violence that is unwarranted, or not essential to the plot. *Gratis* can also be pronounced "GRAY tus."

GRATUITOUS (gruh TOO uh tus) *adj* given freely (said of something bad); unjustified; unprovoked; uncalled for
- The scathing review of the movie contained several *gratuitous* remarks about the sex life of the director.
- Their attack against us was *gratuitous*; we had never done anything to offend them.

SAT POWER VOCAB

Gratuitous is often misunderstood because it is confused with *gratuity*. A *gratuity* is a tip, like the one you leave in a restaurant. A *gratuity* is a nice thing. *Gratuitous*, however, is not nice. Don't confuse these words.

GRAVITY (GRAV uh tee) *n* seriousness
- The anchorman's nervous giggling was entirely inappropriate, given the *gravity* of the situation.
- No one realized the *gravity* of Myron's drug addiction until it was much too late to help him.

Gravity is the force that makes apples fall down instead of up, and the word also carries a different sort of weightiness.

At the heart of the word *gravity* is the word *grave*, which means serious.

GREGARIOUS (gruh GAR ee us) *adj* sociable; enjoying the company of others
- Dirk was too *gregarious* to enjoy the fifteen years he spent in solitary confinement.
- Kyle wasn't very *gregarious;* she went to the party, but she spent most of her time hiding in a closet.

In biology, *gregarious* is used to describe animals that live in groups. Bees, which live together in large colonies, are said to be *gregarious* insects.

GRIEVOUS (GREE vus) *adj* tragic; agonizing; severe
- When Sarah found out that Thomas didn't have her money, she threatened to do him *grievous* harm.
- The memory of all the times I've yelled at my children is *grievous* to me.

GRIMACE (GRIM is) *v* to make an ugly, disapproving facial expression
- Don't *grimace*, Daniel, or your face will freeze that way!
- Tom couldn't help *grimacing* when he heard that the Pettibones were coming over for supper; he had hated the Pettibones ever since they had borrowed his riding lawn mower and ridden it into the lake.

This word can also be used as a noun. The expression on the face of a person who is *grimacing* is called a *grimace.*
- The *grimace* on the face of the judge when Lila played her violin did not bode well for her chances in the competition.

GUILE (gyle) *n* cunning; duplicity; artfulness
- José used *guile*, not intelligence, to win the spelling bee; he cheated.
- Stuart was shocked by the *guile* of the automobile mechanic, who had poked a hole in his radiator and then told him that it had sprung a leak.

To be *guileless* is to be innocent or naive. *Guileless* and *artless* are synonyms.

The word *beguile* also means to deceive, but in a charming and not always bad way.
- Clarence found Mary's beauty so *beguiling* that he did anything she asked of him.

GUISE (gyze) *n* appearance; semblance
- Every night the emperor enters the princess's room in the *guise* of a nightingale, and every night the princess opens her window and shoos him out.

A *guise* can also mean a false appearance or a pretense.
- How was I supposed to know that I couldn't trust Hortense? She had the *guise* of an angel!

QUICK QUIZ   #88

Match each word in the first column with its definition in the second column. Check your answers in the back of the book.

1. futile	a.	chatty
2. garrulous	b.	surplus
3. gauche	c.	cunning
4. genre	d.	unjustified
5. genteel	e.	seriousness
6. gesticulate	f.	make gestures
7. glut	g.	hopeless
8. grandiloquent	h.	refined
9. grandiose	i.	sociable
10. gratuitous	j.	pompous
11. gravity	k.	absurdly exaggerated
12. gregarious	l.	type of art
13. guile	m.	awkward

QUICK QUIZ #89

Match each word in the first column with its definition in the second column. Check your answers in the back of the book.

1. ghastly
2. gratis
3. grievous
4. grimace
5. guise

a. free of charge
b. shockingly horrible
c. make an ugly face
d. tragic
e. appearance

H

HABITUATE (huh BICH oo wayt) *v* to train; to accustom to a situation
- Putting a clock in a puppy's bed is supposed to help *habituate* it to its new home, but most puppies become homesick anyway.
- The best way to *habituate* yourself to daily exercise is to work out first thing in the morning.

If you are a frequent visitor to a place, you may be said to be a *habitué* (huh BICH oo way) of that place.
- Alice is a *habitué* of both the bar at the end of her street and the gutter in front of it.

HACKNEYED (HAK need) *adj* overused; trite; stale
- Michael's book was full of clichés and *hackneyed* phrases.
- The intelligent design issue had been discussed so much as to become *hackneyed*.

"As cold as ice" is a *hackneyed* expression.

HALCYON (HAL see un) *adj* peaceful; carefree; serene
- Why does everyone talk about the *halcyon* days of youth? Most of the kids I know don't exactly live serene, carefree lives.
- These *halcyon* skies are a good harbinger of a pleasant vacation.

HAPLESS (HAP lis) *adj* unlucky
- Joe's *hapless* search for fun led him from one disappointment to another.
- Alex led a *hapless* existence that made all his friends' lives seem fortunate by comparison.

HARASS (HAR us) *v* to attack repeatedly; to torment or pester
- The unruly students so *harassed* their uncoordinated physical education teacher that she finally went crazy and quit.
- Warren's female employees are victims of sexual *harassment* (HAR us munt). If people outside his company ever find out about Warren's record of sexual *harassment*, he'll never be able to get another job. Good!

HARBINGER (HAR bin jur) *n* a forerunner; a signal of
Warm weather is the *harbinger* of spring.
- A cloud of bad breath and body odor, which preceded him by several yards everywhere he went, was Harold's *harbinger*.

HARP (harp) *v* to repeat tediously; to go on and on about something
- "Will you quit *harping* on my hair?" Tim shouted at his mother. "I don't have to get it cut if I don't want to!"

Don't confuse *harp* with *carp* (carp). *Carping* is complaining excessively or finding unreasonable fault with something. If you were to complain that someone had been *harping* on something when they actually hadn't been, you would be *carping*.

HARRY (HAR ee) *v* to harass; to annoy
- The soldiers vowed to *harry* their opponents until they finally surrendered the town.

The adjective is *harried*.
- No wonder that mother has a *harried* look. She's been taking care of six children all day.

HEDONISM (HEED uh niz um) *n* the pursuit of pleasure as a way of life
A *hedonist* practices *hedonism* twenty-four hours a day.
- Yoshi's life of *hedonism* came to an end when his lottery winnings ran out; his massaging armchair and wide-screen TV were repossessed, he had to eat macaroni and cheese instead of champagne and lobster, and he could no longer pay to have models fan him with palm fronds and feed him grapes.

HEGEMONY (hi JEM uh nee) *n* leadership, especially of one nation over another
- America once held an unchallenged nuclear *hegemony*.
- Japan and Germany vie for *hegemony* in the foreign-car market.

HEINOUS (HAY nus) *adj* shockingly evil; abominable; atrocious
- Bruno is a *heinous* villain; his crimes are so horrible that people burst into tears at the mere sound of his name.

- Gertrude's treatment of her cat was *heinous*; she fed him dry food for nearly every meal, and she never gave him any chicken livers.

HERALD (HER uld) *n* a royal proclaimer; a harbinger
- The queen sent a *herald* to proclaim victory.
- A robin is sometimes viewed as a *herald* of spring; its song announces that winter has finally ended.

Herald can also be a verb. To *herald* something is to be a *herald* of it, to proclaim news of it, to announce it, to proclaim it.
- The members of the football team *heralded* their victory through the town by honking their car horns continuously while driving slowly up and down the streets for several hours.

HERESY (HER uh see) *n* any belief that is strongly opposed to established beliefs
Galileo was tried for the *heresy* of suggesting that the sun did not revolve around Earth. He was almost convicted of being a *heretic* (HER uh tik), but he recanted his *heretical* (huh RET i kul) view.

HERMETIC (hur MET ik) *adj* impervious to external influence; airtight
- The president led a *hermetic* existence in the White House, as his advisers attempted to seal him off from the outside world.
- The old men felt vulnerable and unwanted outside the *hermetic* security of their club.
- The poisonous substance was sealed *hermetically* inside a glass cylinder.

HEYDAY (HAY day) *n* golden age; prime
- In his *heyday*, Vernon was a world-class athlete; today he's just Vernon.
- The *heyday* of the British Navy ended a long, long time ago.

HIATUS (hye AY tus) *n* a break or interruption, often from work
- Spencer looked forward to spring break as a welcome *hiatus* from the rigors of campus parties.

HIERARCHY (HYE uh rahr kee) *n* an organization based on rank or degree; pecking order
- Kendra was very low in the State Department *hierarchy*. In fact, her phone number wasn't even listed in the State Department directory.

- There appeared to be no *hierarchy* in the newly discovered tribe; there were no leaders and, for that matter, no followers.

The adjective is *hierarchical* (hye uh RAHRK i kul).

HISTRIONIC (his tree AHN ik) *adj* overly dramatic; theatrical
- Adele's *histrionic* request for a raise embarrassed everyone in the office. She gesticulated wildly, jumped up and down, pulled out handfuls of hair, threw herself to the ground, and groaned in agony.

- The chairman's *histrionic* presentation persuaded no one.

- The young actor's *histrionics* made everyone in the audience squirm.

Histrionic behavior is referred to as *histrionics*.

HOARY (HOHR ee) *adj* gray or white with age; ancient; stale
- The dog's *hoary* muzzle and clouded eyes betrayed her advanced age.

- The college's philosophy department was a bit on the *hoary* side; the average age of those professors must have been at least seventy-five.

- Don't you think that joke's getting a little *hoary*? You must have told it twenty times at this party alone.

HOMAGE (AHM ij) *n* reverence; respect
- Every year, thousands of tourists travel to Graceland to pay *homage* to Elvis Presley; thousands more stay home and pay *homage* to him in their local supermarkets and pizza parlors, where they catch glimpses of him ducking into the men's room or peering through the windows.

- Sanford erected the new office building in *homage* to himself; he had a statue of himself installed in the lobby, and he commissioned a big sign proclaiming the building's name: the Sanford Building.

HOMILY (HAHM uh lee) *n* a sermon
- The football coach often began practice with a lengthy *homily* on the virtues of clean living.

HOMOGENEOUS (hoh muh JEE nee us) *adj* uniform; made entirely of one thing
- The kindergarten class was extremely *homogeneous*: All the children had blond hair, blue eyes, red shoes, and the same last name.

Homogenized (huh MAHJ uh nyzed) milk is milk in which the cream, which usually floats on top, has been permanently mixed with the rest of the milk. (Skim milk is milk from which the layer of cream has been skimmed off.) When milk is *homogenized*, it becomes a *homogeneous* substance—that is, it's the same throughout, or uniform.

To be *heterogeneous* (het ur uh JEE nee us) is to be mixed or varied.

- On Halloween the children amassed a *heterogeneous* collection of candy, chewing gum, popcorn, and cookies.

The nouns are *homogeneity* (hoh muh juh NEE uh tee) and *heterogeneity* (het uh roh juh NEE uh tee), respectively.

HUBRIS (HYOO bris) *n* arrogance; excessive pride
- If you're ever assigned to write an essay about why the hero of a play comes to a tragic end, it's a safe bet to say that it was *hubris* that brought about his downfall.

- Steven has a serious case of *hubris*; he's always claiming to be the handsomest man on the beach when he's really a ninety-seven-pound weakling.

HUSBANDRY (HUZ bun dree) *n* thrifty management of resources; livestock farming
Husbandry is the practice of conserving money or resources. To *husband* is to economize.
- Everyone *husbanded* oil and electricity during the energy crisis of the 1970s.

HYPERBOLE (hye PUR buh lee) *n* an exaggeration used as a figure of speech; exaggeration
- When Joe said, "I'm so hungry I could eat a horse," he was using *hyperbole* to convey the extent of his hunger.

- The candidate was guilty of *hyperbole*; all the facts in his speech were exaggerated.

HYPOCRISY (hi PAHK ruh see) *n* insincerity; two-facedness
- The candidate's most obvious qualification for office was his *hypocrisy*; he gave speeches in praise of "family values" even though his own family was in a shambles.

- Oki despises *hypocrisy* so much that she sometimes goes too far in the other direction. When Julia asked whether Oki liked her new dress, Oki replied, "No. I think it's ugly."

A person who practices *hypocrisy* is a *hypocrite* (HIP uh krit). A *hypocrite* is a person who says one thing and does another. A *hypocrite* is *hypocritical* (hip uh KRIT i kul). It's *hypocritical* to praise someone for her honesty and then call her a liar behind her back.

HYPOTHETICAL (hye puh THET uh kul) *adj* uncertain; unproven
- There were several *hypothetical* explanations for the strange phenomenon, but no one could say for certain what had caused it.

A *hypothetical* explanation is a *hypothesis* (hye PAHTH uh sis), the plural of which is *hypotheses* (hye PAHTH uh seez).

QUICK QUIZ   #90

Match each word in the first column with its definition in the second column. Check your answers in the back of the book. Note that "attack repeatedly" is the answer for two questions.

1. habituate	a.	arrogance
2. halcyon	b.	peaceful
3. harass	c.	royal proclaimer
4. harbinger	d.	insincerity
5. harp	e.	gray or white with age
6. harry	f.	attack repeatedly (2)
7. heinous	g.	reverence
8. herald	h.	repeat tediously
9. hoary	i.	accustom to a situation
10. homage	j.	shockingly evil
11. hubris	k.	precursor
12. hypocrisy		

QUICK QUIZ   #91

Match each word in the first column with its definition in the second column. Check your answers in the back of the book.

1. hackneyed		a.	leadership
2. hapless		b.	uniform
3. harbinger		c.	airtight
4. hedonism		d.	forerunner
5. hegemony		e.	pecking order
6. heresy		f.	overused; trite
7. hermetic		g.	exaggeration
8. heyday		h.	golden age
9. hiatus		i.	varied
10. hierarchy		j.	unlucky
11. histrionic		k.	uncertain; unproven
12. homily		l.	overly dramatic
13. homogeneous		m.	break
14. heterogeneous		n.	sermon
15. husbandry		o.	thrifty management of resources
16. hyperbole		p.	lifelong pursuit of pleasure
17. hypothetical		q.	strongly contrary belief

I

ICONOCLAST (eye KAHN uh klast) *n* one who attacks popular beliefs or institutions

Iconoclast comes from Greek words meaning image breaker. The original *iconoclasts* were opponents of the use of *icons*, or sacred images, in certain Christian churches. Today the word is used to refer to someone who attacks popular figures and ideas—a person to whom "nothing is sacred."

- The popular columnist was an inveterate *iconoclast*, avidly attacking public figures no matter what their party affiliations.

- To study and go to class is to be an *iconoclast* on that particular campus, which has a reputation for being the biggest party school in the country.

- Herbert's *iconoclastic* (eye kahn uh KLAS tik) views were not popular with the older members of the board.

IDEOLOGY (eye dee AHL uh jee) *n* a system of social or political ideas
Conservatism and liberalism are competing *ideologies.*

- The candidate never managed to communicate his *ideology* to the voters, so few people were able to grasp what he stood for.

- The senator's tax proposal had more to do with *ideology* than with common sense; his plan, though consistent with his principles, was clearly impractical.

A dogmatic person attached to an *ideology* is an *ideologue* (EYE dee uh lawg). An *ideologue* is doctrinaire.
Ideology is sometimes pronounced "ID ee ahl uh jee."

IDIOM (ID ee um) *n* an expression whose meaning is different from the literal meaning of the words; a language or dialect used by a group of people
It's sometimes hard for foreigners to grasp all the *idioms* we use in English. They have special trouble with expressions like "letting the cat out of the bag." To let the cat out of the bag is to give away a secret, not to let a cat out of a bag. The expression is an *idiom*, not a literal statement of fact. Other languages have *idioms*, too. In French, "my little cabbage" is a term of endearment. This word can also be used to refer to a language, dialect, or even jargon spoken by a group of people.

- Jerry didn't get along very well with the people in the computer department because he didn't understand their *idiom*.

Idiomatic is an adjective that describes an *idiom*.

- This rule of grammar may seem peculiar to everyone else in the country because it is only *idiomatic* to the people living in that small region.

IDIOSYNCRASY (id ee oh SINK ruh see) *n* a peculiarity; an eccentricity

- Eating green beans drenched in ketchup for breakfast was one of Jordana's *idiosyncrasies.*

- The doctor's interest was aroused by an *idiosyncrasy* in Bill's skull: There seemed to be a coin slot in the back of his head.

A person who has an *idiosyncrasy* is said to be *idiosyncratic* (id ee oh sin KRAT ik).

- Tara's driving was somewhat *idiosyncratic*; she sometimes seemed to prefer the sidewalk to the street.

IDYLLIC (eye DIL ik) *adj* charming in a rustic way; naturally peaceful

- They built their house on an *idyllic* spot. There was a babbling brook in back and an unbroken view of wooded hills in front.

- Our vacation in the country was *idyllic*; we went for long walks down winding dirt roads and didn't watch television all week.

An *idyllic* time or place could also be called an *idyll* (EYE dul).

IGNOMINY (IG nuh min ee) *n* deep disgrace
- After the big scandal, the formerly high-flying investment banker fell into a life of shame and *ignominy*.
- The *ignominy* of losing the spelling bee was too much for Arnold, who decided to give up spelling altogether.

Something that is deeply disgraceful is *ignominious* (ig nuh MIN ee us).
- Lola's plagiarizing of Nabokov's work was an *ignominious* act that got her suspended from school for two days.

ILLICIT (i LIS it) *adj* illegal; not permitted
Criminals engage in *illicit* activities.
Don't confuse this word with *elicit*, listed previously.
- The police interviewed hundreds of witnesses, trying to *elicit* clues that might help them stop an *illicit* business.

IMBUE (im BYOO) *v* to inspire; to permeate or tinge
- Was it the young poet's brilliant writing or his dashing appearance that *imbued* the girls with such a love of poetry?
- Henrietta soaked her white dress in a bathtub of tea to *imbue* it with a subtle tan color.

The word *infuse* is a close synonym.

IMMIGRATE (IM i grayt) *v* to move permanently to a new country
It's easy to confuse this word with *emigrate*. To avoid this, just remember that *emigrate* means exit, and *immigrate* means come *in*.
- Edwin *immigrated* to Canada, thinking the move would give his two-year-old daughter a better shot at attending the University of Toronto preschool.

The noun form of the word is *immigration*.

IMMINENT (IM uh nunt) *adj* just about to happen
- The pink glow in the east made it clear that sunrise was *imminent*.
- Patrice had a strange feeling that disaster was *imminent*, then the jumbo jet crashed into her garage.

Don't confuse this word with *eminent*, listed previously.

IMMUTABLE (i MYOO tuh bul) *adj* unchangeable
- Jerry's mother had only one *immutable* rule: no dancing on the dinner table.
- The statue of the former principal looked down on the students with an *immutable* scowl.

Something that is changeable is said to be *mutable*.

- The *mutable* shoreline shifted continually as the tides moved sand first in one direction and then in another.

- Sonrisa's moods were *mutable;* one minute she was kind and gentle; the next minute she was screaming with anger.

Both *immutable* and *mutable* are based on a Latin root meaning change. So are *mutation* and *mutant*.

IMPARTIAL (im PAHR shul) *adj* fair; not favoring one side or the other; unbiased

- Jurors are supposed to be *impartial* rather than *partial*; they aren't supposed to make up their minds until they've heard all the evidence.

- Beverly tried to be an *impartial* judge at the beauty contest, but in the end she couldn't help selecting her own daughter to be the new Honeybee Queen.

The noun is *impartiality* (im pahr shee AL uh tee).

IMPASSE (IM pas) *n* a deadlock; a situation from which there is no escape

- After arguing all day, the jury was forced to admit they had reached an *impasse*; they had examined and reexamined the evidence, but they still could not reach a unanimous verdict.

- We seem to have reached an *impasse*. You want to spend the money on a pair of hockey skates for yourself, while I want to donate it to charity.

IMPEACH (im PEECH) *v* to accuse or indict; to challenge; to call into question

- Congress is still trying to decide whether to *impeach* the president for spilling fingerpaint in the Oval Office.

To *impeach* a political figure is not to throw the person out of office; it is to accuse him or her of an offense for which he or she will be thrown out of office if found guilty. President Clinton was *impeached*, but he was not convicted. Had President Nixon been *impeached*, he would have been tried by the Senate. If found guilty, he would have been given the boot. Instead, realizing the jig was up, he resigned.

Impeach also has a meaning that has nothing to do with removing political figures from office.

- It's not fair to *impeach* my morals just because I use swear words every once in a while.

To be *unimpeachable* is to be above suspicion or impossible to discredit.

- If the president proves to be a man of *unimpeachable* honor, he will not be impeached.

IMPECCABLE (im PEK uh bul) *adj* flawless; entirely without sin
- The children's behavior was *impeccable*; they didn't pour dye into the swimming pool.
- Hal's clothes were always *impeccable*; even the wrinkles were perfectly creased.

By the way, *peccable* means liable to sin. And while we're at it, a *peccadillo* is a minor sin.

IMPECUNIOUS (im pi KYOO nee us) *adj* without money; penniless
- Can you lend me five million dollars? I find myself momentarily *impecunious*.
- When his dream of making a fortune selling talking T-shirts evaporated, Arthur was left *impecunious*.

The word *pecuniary* (pi KYOO nee er ee) means relating to money. To *peculate* (PEK yuh layt) is to embezzle or steal money.

IMPEDE (im PEED) *v* to obstruct or interfere with; to delay
- The faster I try to pick up the house, the more the cat *impedes* me; he sees me scurrying around, and, thinking I want to play, he runs up and winds himself around my ankles.
- The fact that the little boy is missing all his front teeth *impedes* his speaking clearly.

Something that *impedes* is an *impediment* (im PED uh munt).
- Irene's inability to learn foreign languages was a definite *impediment* to her mastery of French literature.

IMPENDING (im PEND ing) *adj* approaching; imminent; looming
- Jim's *impending* fiftieth birthday filled him with gloom; he was starting to feel old.
- The scowl on her husband's face alerted Claire to an *impending* argument.
- The reporter didn't seem to notice his rapidly *impending* deadline; he poked around in his office as if he had all the time in the world.

The verb is *impend*.

IMPENETRABLE (im PEN uh truh bul) *adj* incapable of being penetrated; impervious; incomprehensible

- The fortress on the top of the hill was *impenetrable* to the poorly armed soldiers; although they tried for days, they were unable to break through its thick stone walls.

- For obvious reasons, knights in the Middle Ages hoped that their armor would be *impenetrable*.

- This essay is utterly *impenetrable*. There isn't one word in it that makes sense to me.

- I was unable to guess what Bob was thinking; as usual, his expression was *impenetrable*.

Impenetrable is a close synonym to impregnable.

IMPERATIVE (im PER uh tiv) *adj* completely necessary; vitally important

- The children couldn't quite accept the idea that cleaning up the playroom was *imperative*; they said they didn't mind wading through the toys strewn on the floor, even if they did occasionally fall down and hurt themselves.

This word can also be used as a noun, in which case it means a command, order, or requirement. A doctor has a moral *imperative* to help sick people instead of playing golf—unless, of course, it's his day off, or the people aren't very sick.

IMPERIAL (im PEER ee ul) *adj* like an emperor or an empire

Imperial, *emperor*, and *empire* are all derived from the same root. England's *imperial* days are over, now that the British Empire has broken apart.

- The palace was decorated with *imperial* splendor.

- George's *imperial* manner was inappropriate since he was nothing more exalted than the local dogcatcher.

A similar word is *imperious* (im PEER ee us), which means bossy and, usually, arrogant.

- The director's *imperious* style rubbed everyone the wrong way; he always seemed to be giving orders, and he never listened to what anyone said.

IMPETUOUS (im PECH oo wus) *adj* rash; overimpulsive; headlong

- Jeremy is so *impetuous* that he ran out and bought an engagement ring for a girl who smiled at him in the subway.

- Olive's decision to drive her car into the lake to see whether it would float was an *impetuous* one that she regretted as soon as water began to seep into the passenger compartment.

QUICK QUIZ #92

Match each word in the first column with its definition in the second column. Check your answers in the back of the book.

1.	idiom	a.	accuse
2.	imbue	b.	approaching
3.	impasse	c.	nonliteral expression
4.	impeach	d.	obstruct
5.	impecunious	e.	without money
6.	impede	f.	inspire
7.	impending	g.	rash
8.	impenetrable	h.	completely necessary
9.	imperative	i.	deadlock
10.	impetuous	j.	impervious

QUICK QUIZ #93

Match each word in the first column with its definition in the second column. Check your answers in the back of the book.

1.	iconoclast	a.	peculiarity
2.	ideology	b.	naturally peaceful
3.	idiosyncrasy	c.	like an emperor
4.	idyllic	d.	flawless
5.	ignominy	e.	attacker of popular beliefs
6.	illicit	f.	just about to happen
7.	imminent	g.	fair
8.	immutable	h.	system of social ideas
9.	impartial	i.	bossy
10.	impeccable	j.	deep disgrace
11.	imperial	k.	unchangeable
12.	imperious	l.	illegal

IMPERVIOUS (im PUR vee us) *adj* not allowing anything to pass through; impenetrable

- A raincoat, if it is any good, is *impervious* to water. It is made of an *impervious* material.

- David was *impervious* to criticism—he did what he wanted to do no matter what anyone said.

IMPETUOUS (im PECH oo wus) *adj* impulsive; extremely impatient

- *Impetuous* Dick always seemed to be running off to buy a new car, even if he had just bought one the month before.

- Samantha was so *impetuous* that she never took more than a few seconds to make up her mind.

IMPLEMENT (IM pluh munt) *v* to carry out

- Leo developed a plan for shortening the grass in his yard, but he was unable to *implement* it because he didn't have a lawn mower.

- The government was better at creating new laws than it was at *implementing* them.

IMPLICATION (im pluh KAY shun) *n* something implied or suggested; ramification

- When you said I looked healthy, was that really meant as an *implication* that I've put on weight?

- A 100 percent cut in our school budget would have troubling *implications*; I simply don't think the children would receive a good education if they didn't have teachers, books, or a school.

Intimation is a close synonym for *implication*. To imply something is to suggest it.

- When Peter's girlfriend said, "My, you certainly know how to drive a car fast, don't you?" in a trembling voice, she was *implying* that Peter was going too fast.

To *imply* something is not at all the same thing as to *infer* (in FUR) it, even though many people use these two words interchangeably. To *infer* is to figure out what is being *implied*. The act of *inferring* is an *inferrence* (IN fur ens).

- Peter was so proud of his driving that he did not infer the meaning of his girlfriend's *implication*.

IMPORTUNE (im pawr TOON) *v* to urge with annoying persistence; to trouble

- "I hate to *importune* you once again," said the woman next door, "but may I please borrow some sugar, eggs, milk, flour, butter, jam, and soup?"

The word *importuning* can also be used as a noun.

- The ceaseless *importuning* of her children finally drove Sophie over the brink; she stuffed the entire brood in the car and left them with her mother-in-law.

To *importune* or be characterized by *importuning* is to be *importunate* (im PAWR chuh nit).

- Leslie's *importunate* boyfriend called her day and night to ask her if she still loves him; after the hundredth such phone call, she understandably decided that she did not.

IMPOTENT (IM puh tunt) *adj* powerless; helpless; unable to perform
Impotent means not *potent*—not powerful.

- Joe and Olga made a few *impotent* efforts to turn aside the steamroller, but it squished their vegetable garden anyway.

- We felt *impotent* in the face of their overpowering opposition to our plan.

Omnipotent (ahm NIP uh tunt) means all powerful. After winning a dozen games in a row, the football team began to feel *omnipotent*.

IMPOVERISH (im PAH vrish) *v* to reduce to poverty; to make destitute

- Mr. DeZinno spent every penny he had on lottery tickets, none of which was a winner; he *impoverished* himself in his effort to become rich.

- The ravages of the tornado *impoverished* many families in our town and placed a heavy strain on our local government's already limited resources.

Impoverishment (im PAHV rish munt) is poverty or the act of reducing to poverty.

- The Great Depression led to the *impoverishment* of many formerly well-off families in America.

IMPREGNABLE (im PREG nuh bul) *adj* unconquerable; able to withstand attack; impenetrable

- Again and again, the army unsuccessfully attacked the fortress, only to conclude that it was *impregnable*.

- There's no point in trying to change Mr. Roberts's attitude about hairstyles; you will find that his belief in a link between long hair and communism is utterly *impregnable*.

- Thanks to repeated applications of Turtle Wax, my car's finish is *impregnable*; the rain and snow bounce right off it.

IMPRESARIO (im pruh SAHR ee oh) *n* a person who manages public entertainments (especially operas, but other events as well)
- Monsieur Clovis, the *impresario* of the Little Rock Operetta House, is as temperamental as some of his singers; if he doesn't get his way, he holds his breath until he turns blue.
- Val calls himself an *impresario,* but he is really just a lazy guy who likes to hang around rock concerts making a nuisance of himself.

IMPROMPTU (im PRAHMP too) *adj* done without preparation, on the spur of the moment
- When Dimitri's mother-in-law dropped in without warning, he prepared her an *impromptu* meal of the foods he had on hand—coffee and tomato sauce.
- The actress did her best to pretend her award acceptance speech was *impromptu,* but everyone could see the notes tucked into her dress.

IMPROVISE (IM pruh vyze) *v* to perform without preparation; to make do with whatever materials are available
- Forced to land on a deserted island, the shipwrecked sailors *improvised* a shelter out of driftwood and sand.
- When the choir soloist forgot the last verse of the hymn, she hastily *improvised* a version of her own.

Improvisation (im prahv uh ZAY shun) is the act or an instance of *improvising.*
- The forgetful choir soloist fortunately had a knack for *improvisation.*

IMPUGN (im PYOON) *v* to attack, especially to attack the truth or integrity of something
- The critic *impugned* the originality of Jacob's novel, claiming that long stretches of it had been lifted from the work of someone else.
- Fred said I was *impugning* his honesty when I called him a dirty liar, but I told him he had no honesty to *impugn.* This just seemed to make him angrier.

IMPUNITY (im PYOO nuh tee) *n* freedom from punishment or harm
- Babies can mash food into their hair with *impunity;* no one gets angry at them because babies aren't expected to be polite.

INADVERTENT (in ad VUR tunt) *adj* unintentional; heedless; not planned
- Paula's snub of Lauren was entirely *inadvertent*; she hadn't meant to turn up her nose and treat Lauren as though she were a piece of furniture.
- Isabelle's *inadvertent* laughter during the sad part of the movie was a great embarrassment to her date.
- While ironing a shirt, Steven *inadvertently* scorched one sleeve; it was really the collar that he had meant to scorch.

INALIENABLE (in AY lee un uh bul) *adj* sacred; incapable of being transferred, lost, or taken away
- In my household, we believe that people are born with an *inalienable* right to have desserts after meals.
- According to the religion Jack founded, all left-handed people have an *inalienable* right to spend eternity in paradise; needless to say, Jack is left-handed.

INANE (i NAYN) *adj* silly; senseless
- Their plan to make an indoor swimming pool by flooding their basement was *inane*.
- Mel made a few *inane* comments about the importance of chewing only on the left side of one's mouth, and then he passed out beneath the table.

Something that is *inane* is an *inanity* (i NAN i tee).

INAUGURATE (in AW gyuh rayt) *v* to begin officially; to induct formally into office
- The mayor *inaugurated* the new no-smoking policy and then celebrated by lighting up a big cigar.
- The team's loss *inaugurated* an era of defeat that lasted for several years.

To *inaugurate* a U.S. president is to make him take the oath of office and then give him the keys to the White House.

QUICK QUIZ #94

*Match each word in the first column with its definition in the
second column. Check your answers in the back of the book.*

1. implication
2. importune
3. impoverish
4. impregnable
5. impresario
6. impromptu
7. improvise
8. impunity
9. inadvertent
10. inalienable

a. unintentional
b. urge with annoying
    persistence
c. person who manages public
    entertainments
d. something suggested
e. freedom from punishment
f. unconquerable
g. done on the spur of the
    moment
h. unassailable
i. reduce to poverty
j. perform without preparation

QUICK QUIZ #95

*Match each word in the first column with its definition in the
second column. Check your answers in the back of the book.*

1. impervious
2. impetuous
3. implement
4. impotent
5. impugn
6. inane
7. inaugurate

a. begin officially
b. carry out
c. powerless
d. impenetrable
e. silly
f. attack the truth of
g. impulsive

INCANDESCENT (in kun DES unt) *adj* brilliant; giving off heat or light
An *incandescent* light bulb is one containing a wire or filament that
gives off light when it is heated. An *incandescent* person is one who
gives off light or energy in a figurative sense.
*   Jan's ideas were so *incandescent* that simply being near her
    made you feel as though you understood the subject for the
    first time.

INCANTATION (in kan TAY shun) *n* a chant; the repetition of statements or phrases in a way reminiscent of a chant
- Much to our delight, the wizard's *incantation* eventually caused the small stone to turn into a sleek black BMW.
- The students quickly became deaf to the principal's *incantations* about the importance of school spirit.

INCARNATION (in kahr NAY shun) *n* embodiment
- Nina is the *incarnation* of virtue; she has never done anything wrong since she was born.
- Nina's brother Ian, however, is so evil that some people consider him the devil *incarnate* (in KAHR nit). That is, they consider him to be the embodiment of the devil, or the devil in human form.

If you believe in *reincarnation* (ree in kahr NAY shun), you believe that after your body dies, your soul will return to Earth in another body, perhaps that of a housefly. In such a case, you would be said to have been *reincarnated* (ree in KAHR nay tud), regrettably, as a housefly.

INCENDIARY (in SEN dee er ee) *adj* used for setting property on fire; tending to arouse passion or anger; inflammatory
- Although the inspector from the arson squad found a scorched *incendiary* device in the gutted basement of the burned-down house, the neighbors insisted that the fire was accidental.
- The lyrics of the heavy-metal star's songs are so *incendiary* that his fans routinely trash the auditorium during his performances.
- On July 3, the newspaper published an *incendiary* editorial urging readers to celebrate the nation's birthday by setting flags on fire.

To *incense* (in SENS) is to anger.

INCENSE (in SENS) *v* to make very angry
- Jeremy was *incensed* when I told him that even though he was stupid and loathsome, he would always be my best friend.
- My comment about the lovely painting of a tree *incensed* the artist, who said it was actually a portrait of his mother.

INCESSANT (in SES unt) *adj* unceasing
- I will go deaf and lose my mind if your children don't stop the *incessant* bickering.

- The noise from the city street was *incessant;* there always seemed to be a fire engine or a police car screaming by.

A *cessation* is a ceasing.

INCIPIENT (in SIP ee unt) *adj* beginning; emerging
- Sitting in class, Henrietta detected an *incipient* tingle of boredom that told her she would soon be asleep.
- Support for the plan was *incipient,* and the planners hoped it would soon grow and spread.

The *inception* of something is its start or formal beginning.

INCISIVE (in SYE siv) *adj* cutting right to the heart of the matter
When a surgeon cuts into you, he or she makes an *incision.* To be *incisive* is to be as sharp as a scalpel in a figurative sense.
- After hours of debate, Louis offered a few *incisive* comments that made it immediately clear to everyone how dumb the original idea had been.
- Lloyd's essays were always *incisive;* he never wasted any words, and his reasoning was sharp and persuasive.

INCLINATION (in kluh NAY shun) *n* tendency; preference; liking
- My natural *inclination* at the end of a tiring morning is to take a long nap rather than a brisk walk, even though I know that the walk would be more likely than the nap to make me feel better. It could also be said that I have a *disinclination* (dis in kluh NAY shun) to take walks.
- Nudists have an *inclination* to ridicule people who wear clothes, while people who wear clothes have the same *inclination* toward nudists.

To have an *inclination* to do something is to be inclined (in KLYND) to do it.
- I am *inclined* to postpone my study of vocabulary in order to take a nap right now.

If you picture someone physically leaning, or *inclining,* toward something, you have a built-in memory device for this word.

INCONGRUOUS (in KAHN groo us) *adj* not harmonious; not consistent; not appropriate; not fitting in
- The ultramodern kitchen seemed *incongruous* in the restored eighteenth-century farmhouse. It was an *incongruity* (in kun GROO uh tee).
- Bill's membership in the motorcycle gang was *incongruous* with his mild personality and his career as a management consultant.

INCORRIGIBLE (in KOR uh juh bul) *adj* incapable of being reformed
- The convict was an *incorrigible* criminal; as soon as he got out of prison, he said, he was going to rob another doughnut store.
- Bill is *incorrigible*—he eats three bags of potato chips every day even though he knows that eating two would be better for him.
- The ever-cheerful Annie is an *incorrigible* optimist.

Think of *incorrigible* as incorrectable. The word *corrigible* is rarely seen or used these days.

INCREMENT (IN cruh munt) *n* an increase; one in a series of increases
- Bernard received a small *increment* in his salary each year, even though he did less and less work with every day that passed.
- This year's fund-raising total represented an *increment* of 1 percent over last year's. This year's total represented an *incremental* change from last year's.
- Doug built up his savings account *incrementally*, one dollar at a time.

INCULCATE (in KUL kayt) *v* to instill or implant by repeated suggestions or admonitions
- It took ten years, but at last we've managed to *inculcate* in our daughter the habit of shaking hands.
- The preacher who believes that stern sermons will *inculcate* morals in his congregation frequently finds that people stop coming to church at all.

INCUMBENT (in KUM bunt) *adj* currently holding an office; obligatory
- The *incumbent* dog warden would love to surrender his job to someone else, but no one else is running for the job.
- An *incumbent* senator usually has a distinct advantage over any opponent because being in office makes it easier for him or her to raise the millions of dollars needed to finance a modern political campaign.

Incumbent can also be a noun. In a political race, the *incumbent* is the candidate who already holds the office. When *incumbent* means obligatory, it is usually followed by upon.
- It is *incumbent* upon me, as Lord High Suzerain of the Universe, to look out for the welfare of all life forms.

INDICT (in DYTE) *v* to charge with a crime; to accuse of wrongdoing
- After a five-day water fight, the entire freshman dorm was *indicted* on a charge of damaging property.

- The mob boss had been *indicted* many times, but he had never been convicted because his high-priced lawyers had always been able to talk circles around the district attorney.

An act of *indicting* is an *indictment*.
- The broken fishbowl and missing fish were a clear *indictment* of the cat.

INDIFFERENT (in DIF ur unt) *adj* not caring one way or the other; apathetic; mediocre
- Pedro was *indifferent* about politics; he didn't care who was elected to office so long as no one passed a law against Monday Night Football.

- We planted a big garden but the results were *indifferent;* only about half of the flowers came up.

- The painter did an *indifferent* job, but it was good enough for Susan, who was *indifferent* about painting.

The noun is *indifference*.
- Henry's *indifference* was extremely annoying to Melissa, who loved to argue but found it difficult to do so with people who had no opinions.

QUICK QUIZ #96

Match each word in the first column with its definition in the second column. Check your answers in the back of the book.

1.	incandescent	a.	increase
2.	incantation	b.	make very angry
3.	incense	c.	beginning
4.	incessant	d.	chant
5.	incipient	e.	not harmonious
6.	incisive	f.	incapable of being reformed
7.	incongruous	g.	not caring; mediocre
8.	incorrigible	h.	cutting right to the heart
9.	increment	i.	unceasing
10.	indifferent	j.	brilliant

INDIGENOUS (in DIJ uh nus) *adj* native; originating in that area
- Fast-food restaurants are *indigenous* to America, where they were invented.
- The grocer said the corn had been locally grown, but it didn't appear to be *indigenous*.
- The botanist said that the small cactus was *indigenous* but that the large one had been introduced to the region by Spanish explorers.

INDIGENT (IN di junt) *adj* poor
- The *indigent* family had little to eat, nothing to spend, and virtually nothing to wear.
- Rusty had once been a lawyer but now was *indigent*; he spent most of his time sleeping on a bench in the park.

Don't confuse this word with *indigenous*, listed earlier.

INDIGNANT (in DIG nunt) *adj* angry, especially as a result of something unjust or unworthy; insulted
- Ted became *indignant* when the policewoman accused him of stealing the nuclear weapon.
- Isabel was *indignant* when we told her all the nasty things that Blake had said about her over the public address system.

INDOLENT (IN duh lunt) *adj* lazy
- The *indolent* teenagers slept late, moped around, and never looked for summer jobs.

Indolence is the noun.
- Inheriting a lot of money enabled Rodney to do what he loved most: pursue a life of *indolence*.

INDUCE (in DOOS) *v* to persuade; to influence; to cause
- "Could I *induce* you to read one more chapter?" the little boy asked his father at bedtime; the father was so astonished that his little boy understood such a big, important-sounding word that he quickly complied with the request.

Something that persuades is an *inducement*.
- The dusty, neglected-looking mannequins in the store window were hardly an *inducement* to shop there.

INDULGENT (in DUL junt) *adj* lenient; yielding to desire
- The nice mom was *indulgent* of her children, letting them have all the candy, cookies, and ice cream that they wanted, even for breakfast.

- Our *indulgent* teacher never punished us for not turning in our homework. She didn't want us to turn into ascetic grinds.

Someone who is *self-indulgent* yields to his or her every desire.

INEFFABLE (in EF uh bul) *adj* incapable of being expressed or described
- The simple beauty of nature is often so *ineffable* that it brings tears to our eyes.

The word *effable*—expressible—is rarely used.

INELUCTABLE (in uh LUK tuh bul) *adj* inescapable; incapable of being resisted or avoided
- The overmatched opposing football team could not halt our *ineluctable* progress down the field, and we easily scored a touchdown.
- If you keep waving that sword around in this crowded room, I'm afraid a tragedy will be *ineluctable*.
- With slow but *ineluctable* progress, a wave of molasses crept across the room, silently engulfing the guests at the cocktail party.

INEPT (in EPT) *adj* clumsy; incompetent; gauche
- Joshua is an *inept* dancer; he is as likely to stomp on his partner's foot as he is to step on it.
- Julia's *inept* attempt at humor drew only groans from the audience.

To be *inept* is to be characterized by *ineptitude,* which is the opposite of aptitude.
- The woodworking class's *ineptitude* was broad and deep; there was little that they were able to do and nothing that they were able to do well.

The opposite of *inept* is *adept* (uh DEPT). *Adept* and *adroit* are synonyms.

INERADICABLE (in uh RAD uh kuh bul) *adj* incapable of being removed or destroyed or eradicated
- The subway officials did their best to scrub the graffiti off the trains, but the paint the vandals had used proved to be *ineradicable*; not even cleaning fluid would remove it.
- Tim wore saddle shoes and yellow socks on the first day of high school, garnering himself an *ineradicable* reputation as a nerd.

QUICK QUIZ #97

Match each word in the first column with its definition in the second column. Check your answers in the back of the book.

1.	incarnation	a.	hostile invasion
2.	incendiary	b.	instill
3.	inclination	c.	used for setting property on fire
4.	inculcate		
5.	incumbent	d.	currently holding office
6.	incursion	e.	charge with a crime
7.	indict	f.	tendency
8.	induce	g.	embodiment
9.	ineluctable	h.	persuade
10.	ineradicable	i.	incapable of being removed
		j.	inescapable

INERT (in URT) *adj* inactive; sluggish; not reacting chemically

- The baseball team seemed strangely *inert;* it was as though they had lost the will to play.

- Having colds made the children *inert* and reluctant to get out of bed.

- Helium is an *inert* gas: It doesn't burn, it doesn't explode, and it doesn't kill you if you inhale it.

To be *inert* is to be characterized by *inertia.* As it is most commonly used, *inertia* means lack of get-up-and-go, or an inability or unwillingness to move.

In physics, *inertia* refers to an object's tendency to continue doing what it's doing (either moving or staying still) unless it's acted on by something else.

INEXORABLE (in EK sur uh bul) *adj* relentless; inevitable; unavoidable

- The *inexorable* waves pounded the shore, as they have always pounded it and as they always will pound it.

- Eliot drove his father's car slowly but *inexorably* through the grocery store, wrecking aisle after aisle despite the manager's anguished pleading.

- *Inexorable* death finds everyone sooner or later.

INFAMOUS (IN fuh mus) *adj* shamefully wicked; having an extremely bad reputation; disgraceful
Be careful with the pronunciation of this word.

To be *infamous* is to be *famous* for being evil or bad. An *infamous* cheater is one whose cheating is well known.

- Deep within the prison was the *infamous* torture chamber, where hooded guards tickled their prisoners with feathers until they confessed.

Infamy is the state of being *infamous*.

- The former Nazi lived the rest of his life in *infamy* after the court convicted him of war crimes and atrocities.

- President Roosevelt said that the date of the Japanese attack on Pearl Harbor would "live in *infamy*."

INFATUATED (in FACH oo ay tid) *adj* foolish; foolishly passionate or attracted; made foolish; foolishly in love
To be *infatuated* is to be *fatuous* or foolish.

- I was so *infatuated* with Polly that I drooled and gurgled whenever she was near.

- The *infatuated* candidate thought so highly of himself that he had the walls of his house covered with his campaign posters.

- My ride in Boris's racing car *infatuated* me; I knew immediately that I would have to have a racing car, too.

QUICK QUIZ   #98

Match each word in the first column with its definition in the second column. Check your answers in the back of the book.

1. indigenous	a. native
2. indigent	b. inactive
3. indignant	c. lazy
4. indolent	d. foolish
5. indulgent	e. shamefully wicked
6. ineffable	f. poor
7. inept	g. relentless
8. inert	h. angry
9. inexorable	i. clumsy
10. infamous	j. lenient
11. infatuated	k. inexpressible

INFER (in FUR) *v* to conclude; to deduce
- Raizel said she loved the brownies, but I *inferred* from the size of the piece left on her plate that she had actually despised them.
- She hadn't heard the score, but the silence in the locker room led her to *infer* that we had lost.

Infer is often confused with *imply*. To *imply* something is to hint at it, suggest it, or state it indirectly. To *infer* something is to figure out what it is without being told directly.

An *inference* is a deduction or conclusion.

INFINITESIMAL (in fin uh TES uh mul) *adj* very, very, very small; infinitely small

Infinitesimal does not mean huge, as some people incorrectly believe.
- An *infinitesimal* bug of some kind crawled into Heather's ear and bit her in a place she couldn't scratch.
- Our chances of winning were *infinitesimal,* but we played our hearts out anyway.

INFLAMMATORY (in FLAM uh tawr ee) *adj* fiery; tending to arouse passion or anger; incendiary
- Maxine's *inflammatory* speech about animal rights made her listeners so angry that they ran out of the building and began ripping the fur coats off passersby.

Inflammatory should not be confused with *inflammable* (in FLAM uh bul) or *flammable,* both of which mean capable of literally bursting into flames. An angry speech is *inflammatory,* but fortunately it is not inflammable. (In careful usage, *inflammable* is preferred; flammable was coined to prevent people from thinking that things labeled inflammable were incapable of catching on fire.)

The verb is *inflame.*

INFLUX (IN fluks) *n* inflow; arrival of large numbers of people or things; inundation
- The *influx* of ugly clothes in the stores this fall can only mean that fashion designers have lost their minds once again.
- Heavy spring rains brought an *influx* of mud to people's basements.

Be careful not to confuse *influx* with in *flux.* In *flux* means in a state of change.

INFRACTION (in FRAK shun) *n* violation; infringement; the breaking of a law

To *fracture* is to break. An *infraction* is breaking a rule or law.

- "I'm warning you, Prudence," said the headmistress. "Even the slightest *infraction* of school rules will get you expelled."

- Driving seventy miles an hour in a thirty-mile-an-hour zone is what Fred would call a minor *infraction* of the traffic laws, but the policeman did not agree, and Fred's license was suspended for a year.

INFRASTRUCTURE (IN fruh struk chur) *n* the basic framework of a system; foundation

- The country's political *infrastructure* was so corrupt that most of the citizens welcomed the coup.

- When people talk about "the nation's crumbling *infrastructure*," they are usually referring to deteriorating highways, crumbling bridges, poorly maintained public buildings, and other neglected public resources.

INFRINGE (in FRINJ) *v* to violate; to encroach or trespass

- The court ruled that the ugly color of Zeke's neighbor's house did not *infringe* on any of Zeke's legal rights as a property owner.

- Whenever Patrick comes into her room, Liz always shouts, "Mom! He's *infringing* on my personal space!"

An act of *infringing* is an *infringement*.

- It is a clear *infringement* of copyright to photocopy the entire text of a book and sell copies to other people.

INFUSE (in FYOOZ) *v* to introduce into; to instill; to imbue

- Everyone in the wedding party was nervous until the subtle harmonies of the string quartet *infused* them with a sense of tranquillity; of course, they had also drunk quite a bit of champagne.

- The couple's redecoration job somehow managed to *infuse* the whole house with garishness; before, only the kitchen had been garish.

An act of *infusing* or something that *infuses* is an *infusion*.

- Whenever I have a cough, my grandmother steeps an *infusion* of herbs that cures me right away.

INGENUOUS (in JEN yoo us) *adj* frank; without deception; simple; artless; charmingly naive

- A young child is *ingenuous*. He doesn't know much about the ways of the world, and certainly not enough to deceive anyone.

- An *ingenue* (AHN ji noo) is a somewhat naive young woman, especially a movie actress or character.

Disingenuous means crafty or artful.

- The movie producer was being *disingenuous* when he said, "I don't care about making money on this movie. I just want every man, woman, and child in the country to see it."

INGRATIATE (in GRAY shee ayt) *v* to work to make yourself liked

- Putting tacks on people's chairs isn't exactly the best way to *ingratiate* yourself with them.

- Licking the hands of the people he met did not *ingratiate* Rashid with most of the guests at the cocktail party, although he did make a favorable impression on the poodle.

The act of *ingratiating* is *ingratiation* (in gray shee AY shun).

- Bella's attempts at *ingratiation* were unsuccessful; her teacher could tell she was being insincere when she told him how nice he looked.

- "That's the loveliest, most flattering dress I've ever seen you wear, Miss Ford," the class goody-goody told the teacher *ingratiatingly*.

INHERENT (in HAIR unt) *adj* part of the essential nature of something; intrinsic

Wetness is an *inherent* quality of water. (You could also say that wetness is *inherent* in water.)

- There is an *inherent* strength in steel that cardboard lacks.

- The man's *inherent* fatness, jolliness, and beardedness made it easy for him to play the part of Santa Claus.

INIMICAL (i NIM i kul) *adj* unfavorable; harmful; detrimental; hostile

- All that makeup you wear is *inimical* to a clear complexion; it smothers your pores and prevents your skin from breathing.

- The reviews of his exhibition were so *inimical* that Charles never sculpted again.

INIMITABLE (i NIM i tuh bul) *adj* impossible to imitate; incomparable; matchless; the best
- Dressed in a lampshade and a few pieces of tinsel, Frances managed to carry off the evening in her usual *inimitable* style.
- Fred's dancing style is so *inimitable* that anyone who follows his act looks like a drunk elephant by comparison.

INJUNCTION (in JUNGK shun) *n* a command or order, especially a court order
- Wendy's neighbors got a court *injunction* prohibiting her from playing her radio.
- Herbert, lighting up, disobeyed his doctor's *injunction* to stop smoking.

INNATE (i NAYT) *adj* existing since birth; inborn; inherent
- Joseph's kindness was *innate*; it was part of his natural character.
- Bill has an apparently *innate* ability to throw a football. You just can't teach someone to throw a ball as well as he can.
- There's nothing *innate* about good manners; all children have to be taught to say "Please" and "Thank you."

INNOCUOUS (i NAHK yoo us) *adj* harmless; banal
Innocuous is closely related, in both origin and meaning, to *innocent*.
- The speaker's voice was loud, but his words were *innocuous*; there was nothing to get excited about.
- Meredith took offense at Bruce's *innocuous* comment about the saltiness of her soup.

INNUENDO (in yoo EN doh) *n* an insinuation; a sly hint
- I resent your *innuendo* that I'm not capable of finishing what I start.
- Oscar tried to hint that he wanted a new fishing pole for his birthday, but Maxine didn't pick up on the *innuendo*, and she gave him a bowling ball instead.

The plural is *innuendos*.
- Although his opponent never actually said Senator Hill cheated on his wife, the public *innuendos* were enough to ruin Hill's chances for reelection.

INORDINATE (in OR duh nit) *adj* excessive; unreasonable
- The math teacher paid an *inordinate* amount of attention to grammar rather than algebra.
- The limousine was *inordinately* large, even for a limousine; there was room for more than a dozen passengers.

- Romeo's love for Juliet was perhaps a bit *inordinate,* given the outcome of their relationship.

INQUISITION (in kwi ZISH un) *n* ruthless questioning; an official investigation characterized by cruelty
- I keep telling you that I got home late because I missed the bus! What is this, some kind of *inquisition*?
- During the Spanish Inquisition, people were substantially better off if they were not found to be heretics. The Spanish *inquisitors* weren't fond of heresy.

An *inquisitive* (in KWI zuh tiv) person is a person who has a lot of questions. This word does not connote cruelty or ruthlessness. When a five-year-old asks where babies come from, he is being *inquisitive*; he is not behaving like an *inquisitor*.

INSATIABLE (in SAY shuh bul) *adj* hard or impossible to satisfy; greedy; avaricious
- Peter had an *insatiable* appetite for chocolate macadamia ice cream; he could never get enough. Not even a gallon of chocolate macadamia was enough to *sate* (sayt) or *satiate* (SAY shee ayt) his craving.
- Peter's addiction never reached *satiety* (suh TYE uh tee or SAY she uh tee).

QUICK QUIZ #99

Match each word in the first column with its definition in the second column. Check your answers in the back of the book.

1.	inflammatory	a.	basic framework of a system
2.	influx	b.	violate
3.	infraction	c.	tending to arouse passion or anger
4.	infrastructure		
5.	infringe	d.	violation
6.	infuse	e.	insinuation
7.	ingratiate	f.	harmful
8.	inimical	g.	inflow
9.	inimitable	h.	work to make yourself liked
10.	innuendo	i.	introduce into
		j.	impossible to imitate

INSIDIOUS (in SID ee us) *adj* treacherous; sneaky
* Winter was *insidious;* it crept in under the doors and through cracks in the windows.
* Cancer, which can spread rapidly from a small cluster of cells, is an *insidious* disease.

INSINUATE (in SIN yoo ayt) *v* to hint; to creep in
* When I told her that I hadn't done any laundry in a month, Valerie *insinuated* that I was a slob.
* He didn't ask us outright to leave; he merely *insinuated,* through his tone and his gestures, that it was time for us to go.
* Jessica *insinuated* her way into the conversation by moving her chair closer and closer to where we were sitting.

To *insinuate* is to make an *insinuation.*

INSIPID (in SIP id) *adj* dull; bland; banal
* Barney's jokes were so *insipid* that no one in the room managed to force out so much as a chuckle.
* We were bored to death at the party; it was full of *insipid* people making *insipid* conversation.
* The thin soup was so *insipid* that all the spices in the world could not have made it interesting.

INSOLENT (IN suh lunt) *adj* arrogant; insulting
- The ill-mannered four-year-old was so *insolent* that his parents had a hard time finding a babysitter.
- The *insolent* sales clerk clearly didn't like answering customers' questions.

INSOUCIANT (in SOO see unt) *adj* nonchalant; lighthearted; carefree
- Sebastian delighted in observing the *insouciant* play of children, but he didn't want any children of his own.
- She is so charmingly *insouciant*, with her constant tap dancing and her little snatches of song, that no one can stand to be in the same room with her. Her *insouciance* (in SOO see uns) drives people crazy.
- "I don't care whether you marry me or not," Mike said *insouciantly*. "I've decided to join the circus anyway."

INSTIGATE (IN stuh gayt) *v* to provoke; to stir up
- The strike was *instigated* by the ambitious union president, who wanted to get his name into the news.
- The CIA tried unsuccessfully to *instigate* rebellion in the tiny country by distributing pamphlets that, as it turned out, were printed in the wrong language.

INSUFFERABLE (in SUF ur uh bul) *adj* unbearable; intolerable
- The smell of cigar smoke in this room is absolutely *insufferable*; I'm afraid I'll suffocate if I remain here for another minute.
- Gretchen's husband is an *insufferable* boor; he chews with his mouth open and wipes his nose on the tablecloth.

INSULAR (IN suh lur) *adj* like an island; isolated
The Latin word for island is *insula*. From it we get the words *peninsula* ("almost an island"), *insulate* (*insulation* makes a house an island of heat), and *insular*, among others.
- The *insular* little community had very little contact with the world around it.

Something that is *insular* has *insularity*.
- The *insularity* of the little community was so complete that it was impossible to buy a big-city newspaper there.

INSUPERABLE (in SOO pur uh bul) *adj* unable to be overcome; insurmountable; overwhelming
- There are a number of *insuperable* obstacles in my way, beginning with that mile-high boulder directly in my path.

- Against seemingly *insuperable* odds, the neighborhood touch-football team made it all the way to the Super Bowl.
- Henry believes that no task is *insuperable*; the key to success, he says, is to break the task into manageable steps.

INSURGENT (in SUR junt) *n* a rebel; someone who revolts against a government
- The heavily armed *insurgents* rushed into the presidential palace, but they paused to taste the fresh blueberry pie on the dinner table and were captured by the president's bodyguards.

This word can also be an adjective. A rebellion is an *insurgent* activity.

Insurgency is another word for rebellion; so is *insurrection*.

INSURRECTION (in sur EK shun) *n* an act of open rebellion against authority; a revolt
- When their mother denied them TV privileges for a week, the Eisenman twins organized an *insurrection* in which they stormed the den, dragged the TV into their bedroom, and barred the door.

INTEGRAL (IN tuh grul) *adj* essential
- A solid offense was an *integral* part of our football team; so was a strong defense.
- Dave was *integral* to the organization; it could never have gotten along without him.

INTEGRATE (IN tuh grayt) *v* to combine two or more things into a whole
This word is related to *segregate, aggregate,* and *congregate,* all of which describe joining or separating. It has the same root as *integer,* which means a whole number.
- Marisol's class *integrated* history and language so that students learned Roman history and Latin at the same time.

The noun form is *integration,* which often refers to the end of racial segregation.

INTERIM (IN tur im) *n* meantime; an intervening time; a temporary arrangement
- Miss Streisand will not be able to give singing lessons until her laryngitis is better. In the *interim*, Miss Midler will give lessons instead.

This word can also be an adjective.

- The *interim* professor had an easier time with the unruly students than did his predecessor because he carried a large club to class with him every day.

INTERLOPER (in tur LOH pur) *n* intruder; trespasser; unwanted person

- I love deer in the wild, but when they get into my backyard I can't help thinking of them as *interlopers*.

- The year-round residents of the resort town viewed summertime visitors as *interlopers* who contributed nothing to the town except traffic jams and trash.

INTERLUDE (IN tur lood) *n* an intervening episode; an intermission; a pause

- Wasn't that a pleasant *interlude*? I just love getting away from my office and shooting the rapids for an hour or two.

- "Clara's *Interlude*" is a musical piece written by—who else?—Clara.

- Miss Prince's School for Young Ladies is so genteel that during games they call halftime "the *interlude*."

See our listing for prelude.

INTERMINABLE (in TUR muh nuh bul) *adj* seemingly unending; tediously long

To *terminate* is to end, as in the movie *Terminator*. *Interminable* means unending.

- The meeting was supposed to be short, but Ted's *interminable* lists of statistics dragged it out for three hours.

- Winter must seem *interminable* in Moscow; the weather usually starts getting cold in September and doesn't warm up until April.

INTERMITTENT (in tur MIT unt) *adj* occasional; repeatedly starting and stopping; recurrent
- The *intermittent* hooting of an owl outside my window made it hard for me to sleep last night; every time I would begin to drop off, the owl would start up again.
- *Intermittent* rain showers throughout the day kept the lawn too wet for croquet.
- Alan's three-year-old is only *intermittently* polite to grown-ups; sometimes he answers the questions they ask him, and sometimes he throws blocks at them.

INTERSPERSE (in tur SPURS) *v* to place at intervals; to scatter among
- When I plant a row of tomatoes, I always *intersperse* a few marigold plants because even a scattering of marigolds helps to keep pests away.
- The wildly unpredictable company had had periods of enormous profitability *interspersed* with periods of near-bankruptcy.
- The place mats are made of straw *interspersed* with ribbon.

INTERVENE (in tur VEEN) *v* to come between opposing groups; to mediate; to take place; to occur between times

- Barry and his sister might have argued all day if their mother hadn't *intervened*; she stepped between them and told them she would knock their heads together if they didn't stop bickering.
- Don't hesitate to *intervene* if you see a cat creeping toward a bird; the cat is up to no good, and the bird will thank you for butting in.
- Al and Mike were having a pretty good time in their sailboat until the hurricane *intervened*.
- So much had happened to Debbie in the *intervening* years that she felt a little nervous on her way to her twenty-fifth high school reunion.

INTIMATE (IN tuh mayt) *v* to hint or imply

- Rosie said she was fine, but her slumped, defeated-looking posture *intimated* otherwise.
- Are you *intimating* that I'm not strong enough to lift these measly little barbells?

INTRACTABLE (in TRAK tuh bul) *adj* uncontrollable; stubborn; disobedient

- The *intractable* child was a torment to his nursery school teacher.
- Lavanya was *intractable* in her opposition to pay increases for the library employees; she swore she would never vote to give them a raise.
- The disease was *intractable*. None of the dozens of medicines the doctor tried had the slightest effect on it.

The opposite of *intractable* is *tractable*.

INTRANSIGENT (in TRAN suh junt) *adj* uncompromising; stubborn

- Vijay was an *intransigent* hard-liner, and he didn't care how many people he offended with his views.
- The jury was unanimous except for one *intransigent* member, who didn't believe that anyone should ever be forced to go to jail.

The noun is *intransigence*.

INTRICATE (IN truh kit) *adj* complicated; sophisticated; having many parts or facets

- It's always a mistake to put off assembling *intricate* toys until Christmas Eve.
- The details of the agreement were so *intricate* that it took four lawyers an entire year to work them out.
- The *intricately* carved prism cast a beautiful rainbow across the ceiling.

The noun is *intricacy* (IN truh kuh see).

INTRIGUE (IN treeg) *n* a secret scheme; a crafty plot

- When the king learned of the duke's *intrigue* against him, he had the duke thrown into the dungeon.
- Monica loves *intrigue*; she's never happier than when she's reading a long, complicated spy story.

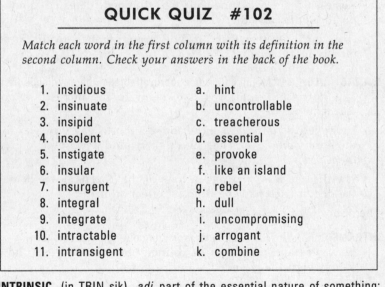

QUICK QUIZ #102

Match each word in the first column with its definition in the second column. Check your answers in the back of the book.

1. insidious	a. hint
2. insinuate	b. uncontrollable
3. insipid	c. treacherous
4. insolent	d. essential
5. instigate	e. provoke
6. insular	f. like an island
7. insurgent	g. rebel
8. integral	h. dull
9. integrate	i. uncompromising
10. intractable	j. arrogant
11. intransigent	k. combine

INTRINSIC (in TRIN sik) *adj* part of the essential nature of something; inherent

- Larry's *intrinsic* boldness was always getting him into trouble.
- There was an *intrinsic* problem with Owen's alibi: It was a lie.

The opposite of *intrinsic* is *extrinsic*.

INTROSPECTIVE (in truh SPEC tiv) *adj* tending to think about oneself; examining one's feelings
- The *introspective* six-year-old never had much to say to other people but always seemed to be turning something over in her mind.
- Randy's *introspective* examination of his motives led him to conclude that he must have been at fault in the breakup of his marriage.

See *extrovert,* listed previously.

INUNDATE (IN un dayt) *v* to flood; to cover completely with water; to overwhelm
- The tidal wave *inundated* the tiny island kingdom. Fortunately, no one died from the deluge.
- The mother was *inundated* with telegrams and gifts after she gave birth to octuplets.

INVECTIVE (in VEK tiv) *n* insulting or abusive speech
- The critic's searing review was filled with bitterness and *invective.*
- Herman wasn't much of an orator, but he was brilliant at *invective.*

INVETERATE (in VET ur it) *adj* habitual; firm in habit; deeply rooted
- Eric was such an *inveterate* liar on the golf course that when he finally made a hole-in-one, he marked it on his score card as a zero.
- Larry's practice of spitting into the fireplace became *inveterate* despite his wife's protestations.

INVIDIOUS (in VID ee us) *adj* causing envy or resentment; offensively harmful
- Under the guise of paying them a compliment, Stephanie made an *invidious* comparison between the two girls, causing them to feel jealous of each other instead of flattered.
- The racist candidate brought the crowd's simmering hatred to a boil with an *invidious* speech in which he referred to whites as "the master race."

INVIOLATE (in VYE uh lit) *adj* free from injury; pure
- The tiny church remained *inviolate* throughout the entire war; although bombs dropped all around it, not a stone in its facade was harmed.

- Her morals are *inviolate* even after four years in college; in fact, she was a senior before she even saw a keg of beer.

A related word is *inviolable* (in VYE uh luh bul), which means unassailable or incapable of being violated.

- There's no such thing as an *inviolable* chain e-mail; sooner or later, someone always breaks the chain.

INVOKE (in VOHK) *v* to entreat or pray for; to call on as in prayer; to declare to be in effect

- Oops! I just spilled cake mix all over my mother's new kitchen carpet. I'd better go *invoke* her forgiveness.

- This drought has lasted for so long that I'm just about ready to *invoke* the Rain God.

- The legislature passed a law restricting the size of the state's deficit, but it then neglected to *invoke* it when the deficit soared above the limit.

The noun is *invocation* (in vuh KAY shun).

IRASCIBLE (i RAS uh bul) *adj* easily angered or provoked; irritable
A grouch is *irascible*.

- The CEO was so *irascible,* his employees were afraid to talk to him for fear he might hurl paperweights at them.

IRIDESCENT (ir i DES unt) *adj* displaying glowing, changing colors
This word is related to *iris,* the colored part of your eye.

- It's strange to think that plain old gasoline can create such a lovely *iridescent* sheen on the water's surface.

- An appraiser judges the quality of an opal by its color and *iridescence* (ir i DES uns) more than by its size.

QUICK QUIZ #103

Match each word in the first column with its definition in the second column. Check your answers in the back of the book.

1.	intermittent	a.	secret scheme
2.	intersperse	b.	displaying glowing, changing colors
3.	intervene		
4.	intimate	c.	pray for
5.	intricate	d.	complicated
6.	intrigue	e.	hint
7.	invidious	f.	come between opposing groups
8.	inviolate		
9.	invoke	g.	occasional
10.	iridescent	h.	causing resentment
		i.	place at intervals
		j.	free from injury

IRONIC (eye RAHN ik) *adj* meaning the opposite of what you seem to say; using words to mean something other than what they seem to mean Don't use the alternate form, *ironical*.

- Eddie was being *ironic* when he said he loved Peter like a brother; in truth, he hated him.

- Credulous George never realized that the speaker was being *ironic* as he discussed a plan to put a nuclear-missile silo in every backyard in America.

IRREVOCABLE (i REV uh kuh bul) *adj* irreversible
To *revoke* (ri VOHK) is to take back. Something *irrevocable* cannot be taken back.

- My decision not to wear a Tarzan costume and ride on a float in the Macy's Thanksgiving Day Parade is *irrevocable*; there is absolutely nothing you could do or say to make me change my mind.

- After his friend pointed out that the tattoo was spelled incorrectly, Tom realized that his decision to get a tattoo was *irrevocable*.

Something that can be reversed is *revocable* (REV uh kuh bul).

ITINERANT (eye TIN ur unt) *adj* moving from place to place

- The life of a traveling salesman is an *itinerant* one.

- The *itinerant* junk dealer passes through our neighborhood every month or so, pulling his wagon of odds and ends.

- The international banker's *itinerant* lifestyle began to seem less glamorous to him after his first child was born.

A closely related word is *itinerary*, which is the planned route or schedule of a trip.

- The tour guide handed each traveler an *itinerary* of the tour bus route so they would know what to expect throughout the day.

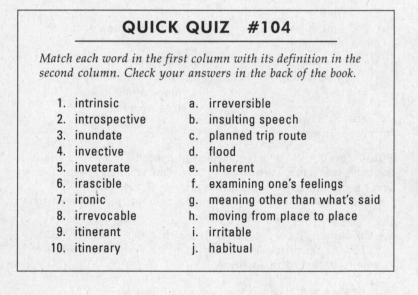

QUICK QUIZ #104

Match each word in the first column with its definition in the second column. Check your answers in the back of the book.

1.	intrinsic	a.	irreversible
2.	introspective	b.	insulting speech
3.	inundate	c.	planned trip route
4.	invective	d.	flood
5.	inveterate	e.	inherent
6.	irascible	f.	examining one's feelings
7.	ironic	g.	meaning other than what's said
8.	irrevocable	h.	moving from place to place
9.	itinerant	i.	irritable
10.	itinerary	j.	habitual

J

JARGON (JAHR gun) *n* the specialized language or vocabulary of a particular job or trade; meaningless or pretentious language; a local dialect or idiom or vernacular

- This contract is full of legal *jargon*; there are so many "heretofores" and "whereinafters" that I can't figure out where I'm supposed to sign it.

- Ever since she went into therapy, Liz has been talking about "healingness" and "connectedness" and spouting so much other self-help *jargon* that it's sometimes hard to listen to her.

- If you pad a term paper with big words and convoluted phrases, your professor may say you've been writing in *jargon*.
- When he visited a tiny island off the coast of France, Phil commented, "I've studied French for twenty years, but I'll be damned if I can make out a word of the *jargon* on this island."

JAUNT (jawnt) *n* a short pleasure trip
- My uncle never stays home for long; he's always taking off on *jaunts* to hot new vacation spots.

Jaunt can also be used as a verb.
- If my uncle keeps *jaunting* off to all these hot new vacation spots, he'll spend all the money I'm hoping to inherit from him.

Jaunty (JAWN tee) means lighthearted, sprightly, or dapper.
- The happy young girl walked down the street with a *jaunty* step.

JINGOISM (JING goh iz um) *n* belligerent, chauvinistic patriotism; warmongering
- The president's aggressive foreign policy betrays the *jingoism* that hides below his genial surface.
- The skinheads marched down the street, chanting, "Foreigners Go Home!" and other *jingoistic* (jing goh IS tik) slogans.

JOCULAR (JAHK yuh lur) *adj* humorous; jolly; fond of joking
- Even her husband's *jocular* mood doesn't cheer up Angela on her birthday.
- Annabelle's *jocular* nature was evident in the grin that was almost always on her face.

The meaning of *jocund* (JAHK und) is similar to that of *jocular*, but it is not exactly the same. *Jocund* means cheerful, merry, or pleasant rather than overtly funny.

Jocose (joh KOHS) is another word with a similar meaning; it is slightly stronger than *jocular*. (The root of *jocose* derives from the Latin for "joke," while the root of *jocular* derives from the Latin for "little joke.") A *jocose* man might be considered funnier than a *jocular* man, but both would give a party a *jocund* atmosphere.

JUBILATION (JOO buh LAY shun) *n* exultant joy
- In an excess of *jubilation* at the good news, Rebecca flung her arms around a total stranger.
- The *jubilation* of the crowd was palpable when the mayor announced that the rich old lady had given the town seven million dollars toward the construction of a new zoo.

To be filled with *jubilation* is to be *jubilant* (JOO buh lunt). New Year's Eve parties are supposed to be *jubilant*.

A *jubilant* celebration, especially one connected with an important anniversary, is a *jubilee* (joo buh LEE).

JUDICIOUS (joo DISH us) *adj* exercising sound judgment
- The judge was far from *judicious;* he told the jury that he thought the defendant looked guilty and said that anyone who would wear a red bow tie into a courtroom deserved to be sent to jail.
- The firefighters made *judicious* use of flame-retardant foam on the brush fire before it spread to nearby homes.
- The mother of twin boys *judiciously* used an electron microscope and a laser to divide the ice cream into equal parts.

The word *judicial* is obviously closely related, but there is a critically important difference in meaning between it and *judicious*. A judge is *judicial* simply by virtue of being a judge; *judicial* means having to do with judges, judgment, or justice. But a judge is *judicious* only if he or she exercises sound judgment.

JUNTA (HOON tuh) *n* a small group ruling a country after a coup d'état
- After the rebels had executed the king, they installed a *junta* of former generals to lead the country until elections could be held.
- The first thing the *junta* did after seizing power was to mandate ice cream at breakfast.
- The president's principal advisers were so secretive and so protective of their access to the president that reporters began referring to them as the *junta*.

JUXTAPOSE (JUK stuh pohz) *v* to place side by side
- Comedy and tragedy were *juxtaposed* in the play, which was alternately funny and sad.
- *Juxtaposing* the genuine painting and the counterfeit made it much easier to tell which was which.

The noun is *juxtaposition* (juk stuh puh ZISH un).

K

KARMA (KAHR muh) *n* good or bad emanations from someone or something

In Hindu or Buddhist belief, *karma* has to do with the idea that a person's actions in life determine his or her fate in a future existence.

- "If you keep on messing up your rooms," the babysitter warned the children, "it will be your *karma* to come back to Earth as a pig."

In popular usage, *karma* is roughly the same thing as vibes.

- "This house has an evil *karma*," the same babysitter told her charges. "Children who don't go to bed on time end up with a mysterious curse on their heads."

KINETIC (ki NET ik) *adj* having to do with motion; lively; active

Kinetic energy is energy associated with motion. A speeding bullet has a lot of *kinetic* energy.

Kinetic art is art with things in it that move. A mobile is an example of *kinetic* art.

A *kinetic* personality is a lively, active, and moving personality.

QUICK QUIZ   #105

Match each word in the first column with its definition in the second column. Check your answers in the back of the book.

1. jargon	a. humorous
2. jaunt	b. specialized language
3. jingoism	c. good or bad emanations
4. jocular	d. belligerent patriotism
5. jubilation	e. small ruling group
6. junction	f. exultant joy
7. junta	g. short pleasure trip
8. karma	h. convergence

L

LABYRINTH (LAB uh rinth) *n* a maze; something like a maze
- Each of the fifty floors in the office building was a *labyrinth* of dark corridors and narrow passageways.
- The bill took many months to pass through the *labyrinth* of congressional approval.

A *labyrinth* is *labyrinthine* (lab uh RINTH in, lab uh RINTH ine, or lab uh RINTH een) or mazelike.
- Before beginning construction on the new house, the contractor had to weave his way through the *labyrinthine* bureaucracy in order to obtain a building permit.

LACONIC (luh KAHN ik) *adj* using few words, especially to the point of seeming rude
- The manager's *laconic* dismissal letter left the fired employees feeling angry and hurt.
- When she went backstage, June discovered why the popular rock musician was so *laconic* in public: His voice was high and squeaky.

LAMENT (luh MENT) *v* to mourn
- From the balcony of the bullet-pocked hotel, the foreign correspondents could hear hundreds of women and children *lamented* the fallen soldiers.
- As the snowstorm gained in intensity, Stan *lamented* his decision that morning to dress in shorts and a T-shirt.

Lamentable (LAM en tuh bul) or (luh MEN tuh bul) means regrettable.

LAMPOON (lam POON) *v* to satirize; to mock; to parody
- The irreverent students mercilessly *lampooned* their Latin teacher's lisp in a skit at the school talent show.
- *The Harvard Lampoon,* the nation's oldest humor magazine, has *lampooned* just about everything there is to *lampoon.*

LANGUISH (LANG gwish) *v* to become weak, listless, or depressed
- The formerly eager and vigorous accountant *languished* in his tedious job at the international conglomerate.
- The longer Jill remained unemployed, the more she *languished* and the less likely it became that she would find another job.

To *languish* is to be *languid*.
- The child seemed so *languid* that his father thought he was sick and called the doctor. It turned out that the little boy had simply had an overdose of television.

LARCENY (LAHR suh nee) *n* theft; robbery
- Bill's ten previous convictions for *larceny* made the judge unwilling to suspend his latest jail sentence.
- Helping yourself to a few cookies is not exactly *larceny*, but just try explaining that to Aunt Edna, who believes that if people want to eat in her house they should bring their own food.

The strict legal definition of *larceny* is theft without breaking in, or without the use of force. Grand *larceny* is major theft. To be *larcenous* (LAHR suh nus) is to be the sort of person who commits *larceny*.
- Amy and Tim felt almost irresistibly *larcenous* as they walked through their rich aunt's house admiring paintings and antiques that they hoped to inherit someday; it was all they could do to keep from backing their car up to the front door and making off with a few pieces of furniture.

LARGESS (lahr JES) *n* generous giving of gifts (or the gifts themselves); generosity; philanthropy
- Sam was marginally literate at best. Only the *largess* of his uncle got Sam into the Ivy League school.

Largess can also be spelled *largesse*.

LASCIVIOUS (luh SIV ee us) *adj* lustful; obscene; lewd
- Clarence's *lascivious* comments made his female associates extremely uncomfortable.

LATENT (LAYT unt) *adj* present but not visible or apparent; potential
- At four, Maria was a *latent* shopaholic; she learned to read by browsing the descriptions in clothing catalogs.

LAUD (lawd) *v* to praise; to applaud; to extol; to celebrate
- The bank manager *lauded* the hero who trapped the escaping robber. The local newspaper published a *laudatory* editorial on this intrepid individual.

Laudatory means praising.

Giving several million dollars to charity is a *laudable* act of philanthropy. *Laudable* means praiseworthy.

LAVISH (LAV ish) *v* to spend freely or bestow generously; to squander
- My father *lavishes* so many birthday presents on his relatives that they panic when it's time for them to give him something in return.
- City Hall has *lavished* money on the street-cleaning program, but our streets are dirtier than ever.

Lavish is also an adjective.
- Don't you think Miss Woodstone is a little too *lavish* with her praise? She slathers so much positive reinforcement on her students that they can't take her seriously at all.

LAYMAN (LAY mun) *n* a nonprofessional; a person who is not a member of the clergy
- The surgeon tried to describe the procedure in terms a *layman* could understand, but he used so much medical jargon that I had no idea what he was talking about.
- Shakira considered herself an excellent painter, but she was distinctly a *layman*; she couldn't make much headway on any canvas that didn't have numbers printed on it.

Laymen are known collectively as the *laity* (LAY i tee).
- The new minister tried hard to involve the *laity* in his services; unfortunately, the last time a *layman* preached a sermon, he spent most of the time talking about his new boat. Perhaps that's just the risk you run when you use a lay preacher.

LEGACY (LEG uh see) *n* something handed down from the past; a bequest
- The *legacy* of the corrupt administration was chaos, bankruptcy, and despair.
- A shoebox full of baseball cards was the dead man's only *legacy*.
- To be a *legacy* at a college sorority is to be the daughter of a former sorority member.

LETHARGY (LETH ur jee) *n* sluggishness; laziness; drowsiness; indifference
- After a busy week of sports, homework, and work, the student relished the *lethargy* of Saturday morning.
- The *lethargy* of the staff caused what should have been a quick errand to expand into a full day's work.

To be filled with *lethargy* is to be *lethargic*.
- The *lethargic* (luh THAR jik) teenagers took all summer to paint the Hendersons' garage.

LEVITY (LEV uh tee) *n* lightness; frivolity; unseriousness

To *levitate* something is to make it so light that it floats up into the air. *Levity* comes from the same root and has to do with a different kind of lightness.

- The speaker's *levity* was not appreciated by the convention of funeral directors, who felt that a convention of funeral directors was no place to tell jokes.

- The judge's attempt to inject some *levity* into the dreary court proceedings (by setting off a few firecrackers in the jury box) was entirely successful.

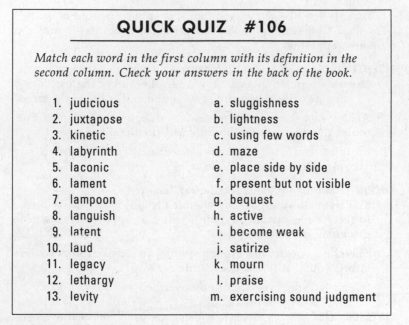

QUICK QUIZ #106

Match each word in the first column with its definition in the second column. Check your answers in the back of the book.

1. judicious	a. sluggishness
2. juxtapose	b. lightness
3. kinetic	c. using few words
4. labyrinth	d. maze
5. laconic	e. place side by side
6. lament	f. present but not visible
7. lampoon	g. bequest
8. languish	h. active
9. latent	i. become weak
10. laud	j. satirize
11. legacy	k. mourn
12. lethargy	l. praise
13. levity	m. exercising sound judgment

LIAISON (LEE uh zahn) *n* connection; association; alliance; secret love affair

- In her new job as *liaison* between the supervisor and the staff, Anna has to field complaints from both sides.

- The condor breeders worked in *liaison* with zoo officials to set up a breeding program in the wild.

- You mean you didn't know that the conductor and the first violinist have been having an affair? Believe me, that *liaison* has been going on for years.

LIBEL (LYE bul) *n* a written or published falsehood that injures the reputation of, or defames, someone
- The executive said that the newspaper had committed *libel* when it called him a stinking, no-good, corrupt, incompetent, overpaid, lying, worthless moron. He claimed that the newspaper had *libeled* him, and that its description of him had been *libelous*. At the trial, the jury disagreed, saying that the newspaper's description of the executive had been substantially accurate.

Don't confuse this word with *liable*, which has an entirely different meaning.

Slander is just like *libel* except that it is spoken instead of written. To *slander* someone is to say something untrue that injures that person's reputation.

LICENTIOUS (lye SEN shus) *adj* lascivious; lewd; promiscuous; amoral
- Barney's reputation as a *licentious* rake makes the mothers of teenage girls lock their doors when he walks down the street.
- Ashley said the hot new novel was deliciously *licentious*, but I found the sex scenes to be dull and predictable.

The act or state of being *licentious* is *licentiousness*. The Puritans saw *licentiousness* almost everywhere.

LIMPID (LIM pid) *adj* transparent; clear; lucid
- The river flowing past the chemical plant isn't exactly *limpid*; in fact, it's as opaque as paint, which is apparently one of its principal ingredients.
- Theodora's poetry has a *limpid* quality that makes other writers' efforts sound stiff and overformal.
- In bad writing, eyes are often described as "*limpid* pools."

LISTLESS (LIST lis) *adj* sluggish; without energy or enthusiasm
- You've been acting *listless* today. Are you sure you're feeling well?
- The children had been dragged to so many museums that by the time they reached the dinosaur exhibit, their response was disappointingly *listless*.
- Harry's *listless* prose style constantly threatens to put his readers soundly to sleep.
- The lettuce looked so *listless* by the time I got around to making a salad that I threw it out and served tomatoes instead.

The noun is *listlessness*.

LITANY (LIT un ee) *n* recital or list; tedious recounting
- Ruth's *litany* of complaints about her marriage to Tom is longer than most children's letters to Santa.
- She's so defensive that if she suspects even a hint of criticism, she launches into a *litany* of her accomplishments.

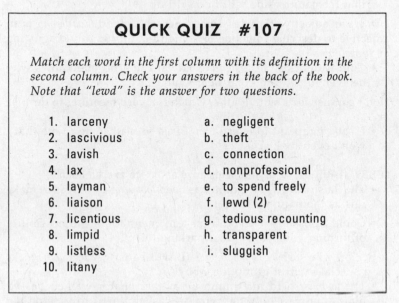

QUICK QUIZ #107

Match each word in the first column with its definition in the second column. Check your answers in the back of the book. Note that "lewd" is the answer for two questions.

1.	larceny	a.	negligent
2.	lascivious	b.	theft
3.	lavish	c.	connection
4.	lax	d.	nonprofessional
5.	layman	e.	to spend freely
6.	liaison	f.	lewd (2)
7.	licentious	g.	tedious recounting
8.	limpid	h.	transparent
9.	listless	i.	sluggish
10.	litany		

LITIGATE (LIT uh gayt) *v* to try in court; to engage in legal proceedings
- His lawyer thought a lawsuit would be fruitless, but the client wanted to *litigate*. He was feeling *litigious* (li TIJ us); that is, he was feeling in a mood to go to court.
- When the company was unable to recover its money outside of court, its only option was to *litigate*.

To *litigate* is to engage in *litigation*; a court hearing is an example of *litigation*.

LIVID (LIV id) *adj* discolored; black and blue; enraged
- Proof of George's clumsiness could be seen in his *livid* shins; he bumped into so many things as he walked that his lower legs were deeply bruised.
- When Christopher heard that his dog had chewed up his priceless stamp collection, he became *livid*, and he nearly threw the poor dog through the window.

People often use *livid* to mean pale, which is almost the opposite of what the word really means. When you see a ghost, your face does not become *livid*; it becomes *pallid*.

LOATH (lohth) *adj* extremely unwilling; reluctant
- Edward was *loath* to stir out of his house on the freezing cold morning, even though he had signed up to take part in the Polar Bear Club's annual swim.
- I am *loath* to pull my finger out of the dike, because I am afraid that the countryside will flood if I do.

Loath is an adjective that describes a person's mood. *Loathsome* is an adjective to describe someone or something thoroughly disgusting or repellent.
- Cold water is so *loathsome* to Edward that no one knows why he even joined the Polar Bear Club.

Don't confuse *loath* with loathe, which is a verb meaning to despise or hate.
- I *loathe* eggplant in every form. It is so loathsome to me that I won't even look at it.

LOBBY (LAHB ee) *v* to urge legislative action; to exert influence
- The Raisin Growers' Union has been *lobbying* Congress to make raisins the national fruit.
- Could I possibly *lobby* you for a moment about the possibility of turning your yard into a parking lot?

A person who *lobbies* is a *lobbyist* (LAHB ee ist). A *lobbyist* works for a special interest group, or lobby.
- The *lobbyist* held his thumb up as the senator walked passed him to indicate how the senator was supposed to vote on the bill that was then before the Senate.

LOQUACIOUS (loh KWAY shus) *adj* talking a lot or too much
- The child was surprisingly *loquacious* for one so small.
- Mary is so *loquacious* that Belinda can sometimes put down the telephone receiver and run a load of laundry while Mary is talking.

A *loquacious* person is one who is characterized by *loquaciousness* or *loquacity* (loh KWAS uh tee).
- The English teacher's *loquacity* in class left little time for any of the students to speak, which was fine with most of them.

LOUT (lowt) *n* boor; oaf; clod
- The visiting professor had been expecting to teach a graduate seminar, but instead he found himself stuck with a class of freshman *louts* who scarcely knew how to write their own names.

- That stupid *lout* has no idea how to dance. I think he broke my foot when he stepped on it.

To be a *lout* or act like a *lout* is to be *loutish*.
- Jake's *loutish* table manners disgust everyone except his seven-year-old nephew, who also prefers to chew with his mouth open.

LUCID (LOO sid) *adj* clear; easy to understand
- The professor's explanation of the theory of relativity was so astonishingly *lucid* that even I could understand it.
- Hubert's remarks were few but *lucid:* He explained the complicated issue with just a handful of well-chosen words.
- The extremely old man was *lucid* right up until the moment he died; his body had given out but his mind was still going strong.

To *elucidate* something is to make it clear, to explain it.

LUDICROUS (LOO di krus) *adj* ridiculous; absurd
- It was *ludicrous* for me to have expected my three puppies to behave themselves while I was out; every pair of shoes I own has become a chew toy.
- Wear glass slippers to a ball? Why, the idea is *ludicrous*! One false dance step and they would shatter.

LUGUBRIOUS (loo GOO bree us) *adj* exaggeratedly mournful
To be mournful is to be sad and sorrowful. To be *lugubrious* is to make a big show of being sad and sorrowful.
- Harry's *lugubrious* eulogy at the funeral of his dog eventually made everyone start giggling.
- The valedictorian suddenly turned *lugubrious* and began sobbing and tearing her hair at the thought of graduating from high school.

LUMINOUS (LOO muh nus) *adj* giving off light; glowing; bright
- The moon was a *luminous* disk in the cloudy nighttime sky.
- The snow on the ground appeared eerily *luminous* at night—it seemed to glow.
- The dial on my watch is *luminous*; it casts a green glow in the dark.

LYRICAL (LIR i kul) *adj* melodious; songlike; poetic

Lyrics are the words to a song, but *lyrical* can be used to apply to other things.

- Even the sound of traffic is *lyrical* to the true city lover.

- Albert is almost *lyrical* on the subject of baked turnips, which he prefers to all other foods.

- The Jeffersons' *lyrical* description of the two-week vacation in Scotland made the Washingtons want to pack their bags and take off on a Scottish vacation of their own.

QUICK QUIZ #108

Match each word in the first column with its definition in the second column. Check your answers in the back of the book.

1.	libel	a.	giving off light
2.	slander	b.	try in court
3.	litigate	c.	exaggeratedly mournful
4.	loquacious	d.	easy to understand
5.	lucid	e.	written injurious falsehood
6.	lugubrious	f.	spoken injurious falsehood
7.	luminous	g.	talking a lot

QUICK QUIZ #109

Match each word in the first column with its definition in the second column. Check your answers in the back of the book. Note that "lewd" is the answer for two questions.

1.	livid	a.	extremely unwilling
2.	loath	b.	ridiculous
3.	lobby	c.	black and blue
4.	lout	d.	oaf
5.	ludicrous	e.	melodious
6.	lyrical	f.	urge legislative action

M

MACHINATION (mak uh NAY shun) *n* scheming activity for an evil purpose
This word is almost always used in the plural—*machinations*—in which form it means the same thing.

- The ruthless *machinations* of the mobsters left a trail of blood and bodies.

- The *machinations* of the conspirators were aimed at nothing less than the overthrow of the government.

This word is often used incorrectly to mean something like "machinelike activity." It should not be used in this way.

MAGNANIMOUS (mag NAN uh mus) *adj* forgiving; unresentful; noble in spirit; generous

- The boxer was *magnanimous* in defeat, telling the sports reporters that his opponent had simply been too talented for him to beat.

- Mrs. Jones *magnanimously* offered the little boy a cookie when he came over to confess that he had accidentally broken her window while playing baseball.

MAGNATE (MAG nayt) *n* a rich, powerful, or very successful business-person

- John D. Rockefeller was a *magnate* who was never too cheap to give a shoeshine boy a dime for his troubles.

MALAISE (ma LAYZ) *n* a feeling of depression, uneasiness, or queasiness

- *Malaise* descended on the calculus class when the teacher announced a quiz.

MALAPROPISM (MAL uh prahp iz um) *n* humorous misuse of a word that sounds similar to the word intended but has a ludicrously different meaning
In Richard Sheridan's 1775 play, *The Rivals*, a character named Mrs. Malaprop calls someone "the pineapple of politeness" instead of "the pinnacle of politeness." In Mrs. Malaprop's honor, similar verbal boo-boos are known as *malapropisms*. Another master of the *malapropism* was Emily Litella, a character played by Gilda Radner on the television show *Saturday Night Live*, who thought it was ridiculous for people to complain that there was "too much violins" on television. Incidentally, Sheridan derived Mrs. Malaprop's name from *malapropos*, a French import that means not apropos or not appropriate. See our listing for apropos.

MALFEASANCE (mal FEE zuns) *n* an illegal act, especially by a public official
- President Ford officially pardoned former president Nixon before the latter could be convicted of any *malfeasance*.

MALIGNANT (muh LIG nuhnt) *adj* causing harm
Many words that start with *mal-* connote evil or harm, just as words that begin with *ben-* generally have good connotations. *Malignant* and *benign* are often used to describe tumors or physical conditions that are either life-threatening or not.
- Lina has had recurring tumors since the operation; we're just glad that none of them have proved *malignant*.

MALINGER (muh LING ger) *v* to pretend to be sick to avoid doing work
- Indolent Leon always *malingered* when it was his turn to clean up the house.
- Arthur is artful, and he always manages to *malinger* before a big exam.

MALLEABLE (MAL ee uh bul) *adj* easy to shape or bend
- Modeling clay is very *malleable*. So is Stuart. We can make him do whatever we want him to do.

MANDATE (MAN dayt) *n* a command or authorization to do something; the will of the voters as expressed by the results of an election
- Our *mandate* from the executive committee was to find the answer to the problem as quickly as possible.
- The newly elected president felt that the landslide vote had given him a *mandate* to do whatever he wanted to do.

Mandate can also be a verb. To *mandate* something is to command or require it.

A closely related word is *mandatory*, which means required or obligatory.

MANIA (MAY nee uh) *n* crazed, excessive excitement; insanity; delusion
- At Christmas time, a temporary *mania* descended on our house as Mother spent hour after hour stirring pots on the stove, Father raced around town delivering presents, and we children worked ourselves into a fever of excitement about what we hoped to receive from Santa Claus.
- Molly's *mania* for cleanliness makes the house uncomfortable—especially since she replaced the bedsheets with plastic drop-cloths.

- The *mania* of the Roman emperor Caligula displayed itself in ways that are too unpleasant to talk about.

A person with a *mania* is said to be a *maniac* (MAY nee ak).
- Molly, the woman with the *mania* for cleanliness, could also be said to be a maniac for cleanliness, or to be a cleanliness *maniac*.

A *maniac* is often said to be *maniacal* (muh NYE uh kul). A *maniacal* football coach might order his players to sleep with footballs under their pillows, so that they would dream only of football.

A person with a *mania* can also be said to be *manic* (MAN ik). A *manic-depressive* is a person who alternates between periods of excessive excitement and deep depression. A *manic* tennis player is one who rushes frantically around the court as though her shoes were on fire.

MANIFEST (MAN uh fest) *adj* visible; evident
- Daryl's anger at us was *manifest:* You could see it in his expression and hear it in his voice.
- There is *manifest* danger in riding a pogo stick along the edge of a cliff.

Manifest can also be a verb, in which case it means to show, to make visible, or to make evident.
- Lee has been sick for a very long time, but it was only recently that he began to *manifest* symptoms.
- Rebecca *manifested* alarm when we told her that the end of her ponytail had been dipped into the bucket of paint.

A visible sign of something is called a *manifestation* of it. A lack of comfort and luxury is the most obvious *manifestation* of poverty.

MANIFESTO (man uh FES toh) *n* a public declaration of beliefs or principles, usually political ones
The *Communist Manifesto* was a document that spelled out Karl Marx's vision of a Communist world.
- Jim's article about the election was less a piece of reporting than a *manifesto* of his political views.

MARGINAL (MAHR juh nul) *adj* related to or located at the margin or border; at the lower limit of quality; insignificant
- The *marginal* notes in Sue's high school Shakespeare books are really embarrassing to her now, especially the spot in *Romeo and Juliet* where she wrote, "How profound!"
- Mrs. Hoadly manages to eke out a *marginal* existence selling the eggs her three chickens lay.

- Sam satisfied the *marginal* requirements for the job, but he certainly didn't bring anything more in the way of talent or initiative.
- The difference in quality between these two hand towels is only *marginal*.

A person who just manages to qualify for something may be said to qualify for it only *marginally*.
- Arnie was *marginally* better off after he received a ten-dollar-per-week raise.

MARSHAL (MAHR shul) *v* to arrange in order; to gather together for the purpose of doing something
- The statistician *marshaled* his facts numerous times before making his presentation.
- The general *marshaled* his troops in anticipation of making an attack on the enemy fortress.
- We *marshaled* half a dozen local groups in opposition to the city council's plan to bulldoze our neighborhood.

MARTIAL (MAHR shul) *adj* warlike; having to do with combat
Martial is often confused with *marital* (MAR ih tul), which means having to do with marriage. Marriages are sometimes *martial,* but don't confuse these words.
    Karate and judo are often referred to as *martial* arts.
- The parade of soldiers was *martial* in tone; the soldiers carried rifles and were followed by a formation of tanks.
- The school principal declared *martial* law when food riots erupted in the cafeteria.

MARTYR (MAHR tur) *n* someone who gives up his or her life in pursuit of a cause, especially a religious one; one who suffers for a cause; one who makes a show of suffering in order to arouse sympathy
Many of the saints were also *martyrs;* they were executed, often gruesomely, for refusing to renounce their religious beliefs.
- Jacob is a *martyr* to his job; he would stay at his desk twenty-four hours a day if his wife and the janitor would let him.
- Eloise played the *martyr* during hay-fever season, trudging wearily from room to room with a jumbo box of Kleenex™ in each hand.

MATERIALISTIC (muh tir ee ul IS tik) *adj* preoccupied with material things; greedy for possessions

- All young children are innocently *materialistic*; when they see something that looks interesting, they don't see why they shouldn't have it.

- The *materialistic* bride-to-be registered for wedding presents at every store in town, including the discount pharmacy.

- People are always going on and on about today's *materialistic* society, but the craving to own more stuff has probably been with us since prehistoric times.

MATRICULATE (muh TRIK yuh layt) *v* to enroll, especially at a college

- Benny told everyone he was going to Harvard, but he actually *matriculated* to the local junior college.

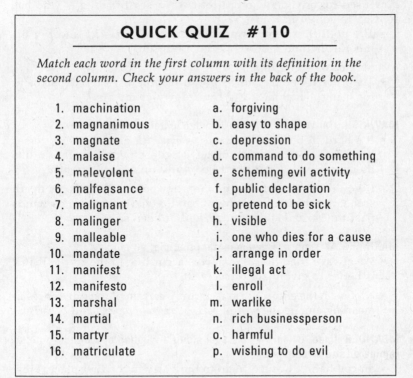

QUICK QUIZ #110

Match each word in the first column with its definition in the second column. Check your answers in the back of the book.

1.	machination	a.	forgiving
2.	magnanimous	b.	easy to shape
3.	magnate	c.	depression
4.	malaise	d.	command to do something
5.	malevolent	e.	scheming evil activity
6.	malfeasance	f.	public declaration
7.	malignant	g.	pretend to be sick
8.	malinger	h.	visible
9.	malleable	i.	one who dies for a cause
10.	mandate	j.	arrange in order
11.	manifest	k.	illegal act
12.	manifesto	l.	enroll
13.	marshal	m.	warlike
14.	martial	n.	rich businessperson
15.	martyr	o.	harmful
16.	matriculate	p.	wishing to do evil

MAUDLIN (MAWD lin) *adj* silly and overly sentimental
- The high school reunion grew more and more *maudlin* as the participants shared more and more memories.
- Magdalen had a *maudlin* concern for the worms in her yard; she would bang a gong before walking in the grass in order to give them a chance to get out of her way.

MAVERICK (MAV ur ik) *n* a nonconformist; a rebel
The word *maverick* originated in the Old West. It is derived from the name of Samuel A. Maverick, a Texas banker who once accepted a herd of cattle in payment of a debt. Maverick was a banker, not a rancher. He failed to confine or brand his calves, which habitually wandered into his neighbors' pastures. Local ranchers got in the habit of referring to any unbranded calf as a *maverick*. The word is now used for anyone who has refused to be "branded"—who has refused to conform.
- The political scientist was an intellectual *maverick;* most of his theories had no followers except himself.

Maverick can also be an adjective.
- The *maverick* police officer got in trouble with the department for using illegal means to track down criminals.

MAWKISH (MAW kish) *adj* overly sentimental; maudlin
- It's hard to believe that Trudy's *mawkish* greeting card verses have made her so much money; I guess people really do like their greeting cards to be filled with mushy sentiments.
- I would have liked that movie a lot better if the dog's death scene, in which a long line of candle-bearing mourners winds past the shrouded doghouse, hadn't been so *mawkish*.

MAXIM (MAK sim) *n* a fundamental principle; an old saying
- We always tried to live our lives according to the *maxim* that it is better to give than to receive.
- No one in the entire world is entirely certain of the differences in meaning among the words *maxim, adage, proverb,* and *aphorism*.

MEANDER (mee AN dur) *v* to travel along a winding or indirect route; to ramble or stray from the topic
- Since I hadn't wanted to go to the party in the first place, I just *meandered* through the neighborhood, walking up one street and down another, until I was pretty sure everyone had gone home.
- The river *meanders* across the landscape in a series of gentle curves.

- Professor Jones delivered a *meandering* lecture that touched on several hundred distinct topics, including Tina's hairstyle, the disappearance of the dinosaurs, Latin grammar, and quantum mechanics.

MEDIATE (MEE dee ayt) *v* to help settle differences
- The United Nations representative tried to *mediate* between the warring countries, but the soldiers just kept shooting at one another.
- Joe carried messages back and forth between the divorcing husband and wife in the hope of *mediating* their differences.

To *mediate* is to engage in *mediation*. When two opposing groups, such as a trade union and the management of a company, try to settle their differences through *mediation*, they call in a *mediator* to listen to their cases and to make an equitable decision.

MEDIUM (MEE dee um) *n* the means by which something is conveyed or accomplished; a substance through which something is transferred or conveyed; the materials used by an artist
- We are trying to decide whether print or television will be a better *medium* for this advertisement.
- Coaxial cable is the *medium* by which cable television programming is distributed to viewers.
- Phil is an unusual artist; his preferred *medium* is sand mixed with corn syrup.

The plural of *medium* is *media*. When people talk about the *media*, they're usually talking about the communications *media*: television, newspapers, radio, and magazines.
- The *media* instantly seized on the trial's lurid details.

In careful usage, *media* takes a plural verb, even when the word is being used in a collective sense as the rough equivalent of *press*.
- The *media* have a responsibility to report the facts fairly and without favor.

MELANCHOLY (MEL un kahl ee) *adj* gloomy; depressed and weary
- Thomas always walks around with as *melancholy* an expression as he can manage, because he thinks that a gloomy appearance will make him seem mysterious and interesting to girls.
- The *melancholy* music in the restaurant basically killed what was left of my appetite; the songs made me feel so sad I didn't want to eat.

Melancholy is also a noun.
- The spider webs and dead leaves festooning the wedding cake brought a touch of *melancholy* to the celebration.

The alternative adjective *melancholic* (MEL un kahl ik) and noun *melancholia* (mel un KOH lee uh) are occasionally heard.

MELEE (MAY lay) *n* a brawl; a confused fight or struggle; a violent free-for-all; tumultuous confusion
- A *melee* broke out on the football field as our defeated players vented their frustrations by sticking their tongues out at the other team's cheerleaders.
- In all the *melee* of shoppers trying to get through the front door of the department store, I got separated from my friend.

MELLIFLUOUS (muh LIF loo us) *adj* sweetly flowing
Mellifluous comes from Greek words meaning, roughly, "honey flowing." We use the word almost exclusively to describe voices, music, or sounds that flow sweetly, like honey.
- Melanie's clarinet playing was *mellifluous;* the notes flowed smoothly and beautifully.

MENAGERIE (muh NAJ uh ree) *n* a collection of animals
In olden times, kings kept royal *menageries* of exotic animals. These were the first zoos.
- The Petersons have quite a *menagerie* at their house now that both the cat and the dog have had babies.
- Doug referred to his office as "the *menagerie*" because his co-workers acted like animals.

QUICK QUIZ #111

Match each word in the first column with its definition in the second column. Check your answers in the back of the book.

1. malapropism
2. mania
3. marginal
4. materialistic
5. mawkish
6. meander
7. medium
8. melancholy
9. melee
10. menagerie

a. travel along a winding route
b. humorous misuse of a word
c. the means by which something is conveyed
d. preoccupied with material things
e. crazed excitement
f. gloomy
g. insignificant
h. overly sentimental
i. collection of animals
j. brawl

MENDACIOUS (men DAY shus) *adj* lying; dishonest

Thieves are naturally *mendacious*. If you ask them what they are doing, they will automatically answer, "Nothing."

- The jury saw through the *mendacious* witness and convicted the defendant.

To be *mendacious* is to engage in *mendacity,* or lying. I have no flaws, except occasional *mendacity*. Don't confuse this word with *mendicant,* listed below.

MENDICANT (MEN di kunt) *n* a beggar

- The presence of thousands of *mendicants* in every urban area is a sad commentary on our national priorities.

MENTOR (MEN tur) *n* a teacher, tutor, counselor, or coach; especially in business, an experienced person who shows an inexperienced person the ropes

Mentor is too big a word to apply to just any teacher. A student might have many teachers but only one *mentor*—the person who taught him what was really important.

- Chris's *mentor* in the pole vault was a former track star who used to hang out by the gym and give the students pointers.

- Young men and women in business often talk about the importance of having a *mentor*—usually an older person at the same company who takes an interest in them and helps them get ahead by showing them the ropes.

MERCENARY (MUR suh ner ee) *n* a hired soldier; someone who will do anything for money

If an army can't find enough volunteers or draftees, it will sometimes hire *mercenaries*. The magazine *Soldier of Fortune* is aimed at *mercenaries* and would-be *mercenaries;* it even runs classified advertisements by soldiers looking for someone to fight.

You don't have to be a soldier to be a *mercenary*. Someone who does something strictly for the money is often called a *mercenary*.

- Our business contains a few dedicated workers and many, many *mercenaries,* who want to make a quick buck and then get out.

- Larry's motives in writing the screenplay for the trashy movie were strictly *mercenary*—he needed the money.

Mercenary can also be used as an adjective.

MERCURIAL (mur KYOOR ee ul) *adj* emotionally unpredictable; rapidly changing in mood

A person with a *mercurial* personality is one who changes rapidly and unpredictably between one mood and another.

- *Mercurial* Helen was crying one minute, laughing the next.

METAMORPHOSIS (met uh MOR fuh sis) *n* a magical change in form; a striking or sudden change

- When the magician passed his wand over Eileen's head, she underwent a bizarre *metamorphosis:* She turned into a hamster.
- Damon's *metamorphosis* from college student to Hollywood superstar was so sudden that it seemed a bit unreal.

To undergo a *metamorphosis* is to *metamorphose.*

QUICK QUIZ #112

Match each word in the first column with its definition in the second column. Check your answers in the back of the book.

1. maudlin
2. maverick
3. maxim
4. mediate
5. mellifluous
6. mendacious
7. mendicant
8. mentor
9. mercenary
10. mercurial
11. metamorphosis

a. teacher
b. fundamental principle
c. lying
d. help settle differences
e. sweetly flowing
f. nonconformist
g. emotionally unpredictable
h. magical change in form
i. overly sentimental
j. hired soldier
k. beggar

METICULOUS (muh TIK yuh lus) *adj* precise and careful about details; fussy

- Patrick is *meticulous* about keeping his desk clean; he comes in early every morning to polish his paper clips.
- The doctor paid *meticulous* attention to his patients; he made careful notes of even tiny changes in their illnesses.
- Putting together a dollhouse is too *meticulous* a job for a three-year-old child; there are too many small parts and too many details that have to be attended to.

MICROCOSM (MYE kruh kahz um) *n* the world in miniature

The *cosmos* is the heavens, *cosmopolitan* means worldly, and a *microcosm* is a miniature version of the world. All three words are related.

- Our community, which holds so many different communities, institutions, businesses, and types of people, is a *microcosm* of the larger world.

The opposite of *microcosm* is a *macrocosm* (MAK ruh kahz um). A *macrocosm* is a large-scale representation of something, or the universe at large.

MILIEU (mil YOO) *n* environment; surroundings

- A caring and involved community is the proper *milieu* for raising a family.

- The farmer on vacation in the big city felt out of his *milieu*.

MILLENNIUM (mi LEN ee um) *n* a period of 1,000 years; a thousandth anniversary

- Purists say that the new *millennium* began in 2001, but the fear of widespread computer problems actually made 2000 the more important new year.

- In the first *millennium* after the birth of Christ, humankind made great progress—but pre-sweetened cereals didn't appear until close to the end of the second *millennium*.

The adjective is *millennial* (mi LEN ee ul).

MINUSCULE (MIN uh skyool) *adj* very tiny

Be careful with the spelling of this word. People tend to spell it "miniscule." Think of *minus*.

- Hank's salary was *minuscule,* but the benefits were pretty good: He got to sit next to the refrigerator and eat all day long.

Minute (mye NOOT) is a synonym for *minuscule*. The small details of something are the *minutiae* (mi NOO shi ee).

MIRE (myre) *n* marshy, mucky ground

- Walking through the *mire* in stiletto heels is not a good idea; your shoes are liable to become stuck in the muck.

- So many cars had driven in and out of the field that the grass had turned to *mire*.

Mire can also be used as a verb whose sense can be either literal or figurative.

- The horses were so *mired* in the pasture that they couldn't go another step.

- I'd love to join you tonight, but I'm afraid I'm *mired* in a sewing project and can't get away.

A *quagmire* is a swamp or marsh or, figuratively, a complicated predicament.

- They say that twenty people sank into the *quagmire* behind Abel's Woods and their bodies were never found.

- Because she was afraid that everyone would hate her if she told the truth, Louise entangled herself in a *quagmire* of lies and half-truths, and everybody hated her.

MISANTHROPIC (mis un THRAHP ik) *adj* hating mankind

A *misogynist* (mis AH juh nist) hates women. A *misanthropic* person doesn't make distinctions; he or she hates everyone. The opposite of a *misanthrope* (MIS un throhp) is a *philanthropist* (fuh LAN thruh pist).

Curiously, there is no word for someone who hates men only.

MITIGATE (MIT uh gayt) *v* to moderate the effect of something

- The sense of imminent disaster was *mitigated* by the guide's calm behavior and easy smile.

- The effects of the disease were *mitigated* by the experimental drug treatment.

- Nothing Joel said could *mitigate* the enormity of forgetting his mother-in-law's birthday.

Unmitigated means absolute, unmoderated, not made less intense or severe.

MODE (mohd) *n* method of doing; type; manner; fashion

- Lannie's *mode* of economizing is to spend lots of money on top-quality items that she thinks will last longer than cheap ones.

- When a big tree fell across the highway, Draco shifted his Jeep™ into four-wheel *mode* and took off across country.

- I'm not interested in dressing in the latest *mode*; a barrel and a pair of flipflops are fashionable enough for me.

MODULATE (MAHJ uh layt) *v* to reduce or regulate; to lessen the intensity of

- Please *modulate* your voice, dear! A well-bred young lady doesn't scream obscenities at the top of her lungs.

- Milhouse *modulated* his sales pitch when he realized that the hard sell wasn't getting him anywhere.

MOLLIFY (MAHL uh fye) *v* to soften; to soothe; to pacify
- Lucy *mollified* the angry police officer by kissing his hand.
- My father was not *mollified* by my promise never to crash his car into a brick wall again.
- The baby-sitter was unable to *mollify* the cranky child, who cried all night.

MOMENTUM (muh MEN tum) *n* force of movement; speed; impetus
- The locomotive's *momentum* carried it through the tunnel and into the railroad terminal.
- She starts out small, with just a little whimpering. Then her bad mood picks up *momentum*, and in no time at all she's lying on the floor kicking and screaming.
- Even when they're both being driven at the same speed, a big car is harder to stop than a small one because the big car has more *momentum*.

MONOLITHIC (mah nuh LITH ik) *adj* massive, solid, uniform, and unyielding
A *monolith* is a huge stone shaft or column. Many other things can be said to be *monolithic*.
A huge corporation is often said to be *monolithic*, especially if it is enormous and powerful and all its parts are dedicated to the same purpose.
If the opposition to a plan were said to be *monolithic*, it would probably consist of a large group of people who all felt the same way.

MORATORIUM (mawr uh TAWR ee um) *n* a suspension of activity; a period of delay
- The president of the beleaguered company declared a *moratorium* on the purchase of office supplies, hoping that the money saved by not buying paper clips might help to keep the company in business a little bit longer.
- The two countries agreed to a *moratorium* on the production of new nuclear weapons while their leaders struggled to work out the terms of a permanent ban.

MORES (MAWR ayz) *n* customary moral standards
- According to the *mores* of that country, women who wear revealing clothing are lewd and licentious.
This noun is always plural.

MORIBUND (MOR uh bund) *adj* dying

- The steel industry in this country was *moribund* a few years ago, but now it seems to be reviving somewhat.

- The senator's political ideas were *moribund;* no one thinks that way anymore.

A dying creature could be said to be *moribund,* too, although this word is usually used in connection with things that die only figuratively.

MOROSE (muh ROHS) *adj* gloomy; sullen

- Louise was always so *morose* about everything that she was never any fun to be with.

- New Yorkers always seemed *morose* to the writer who lived in the country; he thought they seemed beaten down by the city.

MORTIFY (MOR tuh fye) *adj* to humiliate

- I was *mortified* when my father asked my girlfriend whether she thought I was a dumb, pathetic wimp.

- We had a *mortifying* experience at the opera; when Stanley's cell phone rang, the entire orchestra stopped playing and stared at him for several minutes.

MOTIF (moh TEEF) *n* a recurring theme or idea

- The central *motif* in Barry's first novel seems to be that guys named Barry are too sensitive for other people to appreciate fully.

- Andrea's new apartment is okay-looking, but it would be more impressive if owls weren't the main decorative *motif.*

MOTLEY (MAHT lee) *adj* extremely varied or diverse; heterogeneous; multicolored

- Louise's friends are a *motley* group of artists, bankers, and sanitation engineers.

- One glance at her date's *motley* tuxedo convinced Cathy that she didn't want to go to the prom after all; the jacket looked more like a quilt than like a piece of formal clothing.

MUNDANE (mun DAYN) *adj* ordinary; pretty boring; not heavenly and eternal

- My day was filled with *mundane* chores: I mowed the lawn, did the laundry, and fed the dog.

- Dee's job was so *mundane* she sometimes had trouble remembering whether she was at work or asleep.

- The monk's thoughts were far removed from *mundane* concerns; he was contemplating all the fun he was going to have in heaven.

MUNICIPAL (myoo NIS uh pul) *adj* pertaining to a city (or town) and its government
- All the *municipal* swimming pools closed after Labor Day because the city didn't have the staff to keep them open any longer.
- The town plans to build a *municipal* birdhouse to keep its pigeons off the streets.

A *municipality* (myoo nis uh PAL uh tee) is a distinct city or town, and usually one that has its own government. The government of such a city or town is often referred to as a *municipal* government.

MUNIFICENT (myoo NIF uh sunt) *adj* very generous; lavish
- The *munificent* millionaire gave lots of money to any charity that came to him with a request.
- Mrs. Bigelow was a *munificent* hostess; there was so much wonderful food and wine at her dinner parties that the guests had to rest between courses. She was known for her *munificence*.

MUSE (myooz) *v* to ponder; to meditate
- "I wonder whether I'll win the flower-arranging prize," Melanie *mused*, staring pensively at her vaseful of roses and licorice sticks.
- Fred meant to get some work done, but instead he sat at his desk *musing* all afternoon, and then it was time to go home.

Muse can also be a noun. In Greek mythology, the nine Muses were patron goddesses of the arts. In modern usage, a *muse* is anyone who inspires an artist's creativity.
- "Beatrice, you are my *muse*. You inspire all my best poetry," John said to his pet guinea pig.

To be *bemused* is to be preoccupied or engrossed.
- Charlie was too *bemused* to notice that wine from a spilled goblet was dripping into his lap.

MUSTER (MUS tur) *v* to assemble for battle or inspection; to summon up
- The camp counselor *mustered* the girls in her cabin for bunk inspection. She really had to *muster* up all her courage to do it, because the girls were so rowdy they never did what she told them.

"To pass muster" is an idiomatic expression that means to be found to be acceptable.

- Luckily, the cabin passed *muster*; the camp director never noticed the dust under the beds.

MYOPIA (mye OH pee uh) *adj* nearsightedness; lack of foresight

Myopia is the fancy medical name for the inability to see clearly at a distance. It's also a word used in connection with people who lack other kinds of visual acuity.

- The president suffered from economic *myopia*; he was unable to see the consequences of his fiscal policies.

- The workers' dissatisfaction was inflamed by management's *myopia* on the subject of wages.

To suffer *myopia* is to be *myopic* (mye AHP ik). Some people who wear glasses are *myopic*. So are the people who can't see the consequences of their actions.

MYRIAD (MIR ee ud) *n* a huge number

- A country sky on a clear night is filled with a *myriad* of stars.

- There are a *myriad* of reasons why I don't like school.

This word can also be used as an adjective. *Myriad* stars is a lot of stars. The teenager was weighted down by the *myriad* anxieties of adolescence.

MYSTIC (MIS tik) *adj* otherworldly; mysterious; enigmatic

- The swirling fog and the looming stalactites gave the cave a *mystic* aura, and we felt as though we'd stumbled into Arthurian times.

A word essentially identical in meaning is *mystical* (MIS ti kul).

- The faint, far-off trilling of the recorder gave the music a *mystical* quality.

Mystic can also be a noun. A *mystic* is a person who has, or seems to have, contact with other worlds.

- Michaela the *Mystic* stared into her clouded crystal ball and remarked, "Time to get out the Windex™."

Mysticism (MIS tuh siz um) is the practice or spiritual discipline of trying to reach or understand God through deep meditation.

QUICK QUIZ #113

Match each word in the first column with its definition in the second column. Check your answers in the back of the book.

1. microcosm
2. milieu
3. minuscule
4. misanthropic
5. mitigate
6. mollify
7. monolithic
8. moribund
9. morose
10. mortify
11. mundane
12. munificent
13. myopia
14. myriad

a. a huge number
b. moderate the effect of
c. massive and unyielding
d. humiliate
e. ordinary
f. soften
g. nearsightedness
h. very tiny
i. gloomy
j. environment
k. very generous
l. dying
m. world in miniature
n. hating mankind

QUICK QUIZ #114

Match each word in the first column with its definition in the second column. Check your answers in the back of the book.

1. meticulous
2. millennium
3. mire
4. mode
5. modulate
6. momentum
7. moratorium
8. mores
9. motif
10. motley
11. municipal
12. muse
13. muster
14. mystic

a. method of doing
b. reduce or regulate
c. extremely varied
d. force of movement
e. period of one thousand years
f. recurring theme
g. precise and careful about details
h. otherworldly
i. customary moral standards
j. marshy, mucky ground
k. assemble for battle
l. ponder
m. suspension of activity
n. pertaining to a city or town

N

NARCISSISM (NAHR si siz um) *n* excessive love of one's body or oneself

- In Greek mythology, Narcissus was a boy who fell in love with his own reflection. To engage in *narcissism* is to be like Narcissus.

- Throwing a kiss to your reflection in the mirror is an act of *narcissism*—so is filling your living room with all your bowling trophies or telling everyone how smart and good-looking you are. You are a *narcissist* (NAHR suh sist).

Someone who suffers from *narcissism* is said to be *narcissistic* (nahr si SIS tik).

- The selfish students were bound up in *narcissistic* concerns and gave no thought to other people.

NEBULOUS (NEB yuh lus) *adj* vague; hazy; indistinct
- Oscar's views are so *nebulous* that no one can figure out what he thinks about anything.
- The community's boundaries are somewhat *nebulous;* where they are depends on whom you ask.
- Molly's expensive new hairdo was a sort of *nebulous* mass of wisps, waves, and hair spray.

A *nebula* (NEB yuh luh) is an interstellar cloud, the plural of which is *nebulae* (NEB yuh lee).

NEFARIOUS (ni FAR ee us) *adj* evil; flagrantly wicked
- The radicals' *nefarious* plot was to destroy New York by filling the reservoirs with strawberry Jell-O™.
- The convicted murderer had committed a myriad of *nefarious* acts.

NEMESIS (NEM uh sis) *n* unconquerable opponent or rival; one who seeks just compensation or revenge to right a wrong
- In Greek mythology, *Nemesis* was the goddess of divine retribution. If you were due for a punishment, she made sure you got it.
- Nacho-flavored tortilla chips are the dieter's *nemesis;* one bite, and you don't stop eating till the bag is gone.
- Betsy finally met her *nemesis*, in the form of a teacher who wouldn't accept any excuses.

NEOLOGISM (nee OL uh jiz um) *n* a new word or phrase; a new usage of a word
Pedants don't like *neologisms.* They like the words we already have. But at one time every word was a *neologism.* Someone somewhere had to be the first to use it.

NEOPHYTE (NEE uh fyte) *n* beginner; novice
- The student librarian was such a *neophyte* that she reshelved all the books upside down.
- I'm not being fussy. I just don't like the idea of having my cranium sawn open by a *neophyte* surgeon!

The prefix "neo" means new, recent, or revived. A *neologism* (nee AH luh jiz um), for example, is a new word or an old word used in a new way. A *neonate* (NEE oh nayt) is a newborn. *Neoprene* (NEE uh preen) is a new kind of synthetic rubber—or at least it was new when it was invented. (It's the stuff that wet suits are made of.)

NEPOTISM (NEP uh tiz um) *n* showing favoritism to friends or family in business or politics
- Clarence had no business acumen, so he was counting on *nepotism* when he married the boss's daughter.

NIHILISM (NYE uh liz um) *n* the belief that there are no values or morals in the universe
- A *nihilist* does not believe in any objective standards of right or wrong.

NIRVANA (nur VAH nuh) *n* a blissful, painless, worry-free state
According to Buddhist theology, you reach *nirvana* once you have purged your soul of hatred, passion, and self-delusion. Once you have reached *nirvana*, you will no longer have to undergo the cycle of reincarnation.

In common English usage, the word's meaning is looser, and *nirvana* often refers to a mental state rather than a physical one.
- Though many thought the band's sound was annoying, listening to it sent me to a state of pure *nirvana*.
- *Nirvana* for Judy consisted of a hot bubble bath and a hot fudge sundae at the end of a long day.

NOISOME (NOY sum) *adj* offensive or disgusting; stinking; noxious
- When I opened the refrigerator after returning from vacation, such a *noisome* odor leaped out at me that I bolted from the apartment.
- The *noisome* brown liquid seeping out of the floor of my bathroom certainly isn't water. At any rate, it doesn't taste like water.

NOMADIC (noh MAD ik) *adj* wandering from place to place; without a permanent home
A *nomad* (NOH mad) is one of a group of wandering people who move from place to place in search of food and water for themselves and for their animals. The Bedouins, members of various Arab tribes that wander the deserts of North Africa and elsewhere, are nomads. To be *nomadic* is to be like a nomad.
- Lila spent her senior year living in a tent with a *nomadic* tribe of sheep herders.
- Ever since he graduated from college, my brother has been living a *nomadic* life; his only home is his car, and he moves it every day.

NOMENCLATURE (NOH mun klay chur) *n* a set or system of names; a designation; a terminology
- I'd become a botanist in a minute, except that I'd never be able to memorize all that botanic *nomenclature.*

In the Bible, Adam invented *nomenclature* when he gave all the animals names. You could call him the world's first *nomenclator* (NOH mun klay tur). A *nomenclator* is a giver of names.

NOMINAL (NOM uh nul) *adj* in name only; insignificant; A-OK (during rocket launches)
- Bert was the *nominal* chair of the committee, but Sue was the one who ran things.
- The cost was *nominal* in comparison with the enormous value of what you received.
- "All systems are *nominal,*" said the NASA engineer as the space shuttle successfully headed into orbit.

NONCHALANT (non shuh LAHNT) *adj* indifferent; coolly unconcerned; blasé
- Omar was acting awfully *nonchalant* for someone who had just been invited to dinner at the White House; he was yawning and using a corner of the invitation to clean his nails.
- "I don't care that my car was stolen," Blanca said in a *nonchalant* voice. "Daddy will buy me a new one."
- Unconcerned with all the worry his disappearance had caused, the cat sat down and *nonchalantly* began to wash his face.

The noun is *nonchalance.*

NOSTALGIA (nahs TAL juh) *n* sentimental longing for the past; homesickness
- A wave of *nostalgia* overcame me when the old Biggie Smalls song came on the radio; hearing it took me right back to 1997.
- Some people who don't remember what the decade was really like feel a misplaced *nostalgia* for the 1950s.

To be filled with *nostalgia* is to be *nostalgic.*
- As we talked about the fun we'd had together in junior high school, we all began to feel a little *nostalgic.*

NOTORIOUS (noh TOR ee us) *adj* famous for something bad
A well-known actor is famous; a well-known criminal is *notorious.*
- No one wanted to play poker with Jeremy because he was a *notorious* cheater.
- Rana's practical jokes were *notorious;* people always kept their distance when she came into the room.

To be *notorious* is to have *notoriety* (noh tuh RYE uh tee).
- Jesse's *notoriety* as a bank robber made it difficult for him to find a job in banking.

NOVEL (NAHV ul) *adj* new; original
- Ray had a *novel* approach to homework: He did the work before the teacher assigned it.

NOXIOUS (NAHK shus) *adj* harmful; offensive
- Smoking is a *noxious* habit in every sense.
- Poison ivy is a *noxious* weed.
- The mothers' committee believed that rock 'n' roll music exerted a *noxious* influence on their children.

NUANCE (NOO ahns) *n* a subtle difference or distinction
- The artist's best work explored the *nuance* between darkness and deep shadow.
- Harry was incapable of *nuance*; everything for him was either black or white.

In certain Chinese dialects, the difference between one word and its opposite is sometimes nothing more than a *nuance* of inflection.

NULLIFY (NUL uh fye) *v* to repeal; to cancel; to void
Null means empty or ineffective. In math a *null* set is a set without numbers. To *nullify* means to make empty or ineffective.
- A moment after the ceremony, the bride asked a lawyer to *nullify* the prenuptial contract she had signed the day before; she no longer felt that $50,000 a month in alimony would be enough.
- It's hard to believe that Saudi Arabia still hasn't *nullified* the law that prohibits women to drive.

To annul is to cancel or make void a marriage or a law.

QUICK QUIZ   #115

Match each word in the first column with its definition in the second column. Check your answers in the back of the book.

1.	narcissism	a.	excessive love of self
2.	nebulous	b.	in name only
3.	nefarious	c.	harmful
4.	neologism	d.	original
5.	nepotism	e.	evil
6.	nihilism	f.	subtle difference
7.	nominal	g.	famous for something bad
8.	nostalgia	h.	vague
9.	notorious	i.	longing for the past
10.	novel	j.	favoritism
11.	noxious	k.	belief in the absence of all
12.	nuance		values and morals
		l.	new word

QUICK QUIZ   #116

Match each word in the first column with its definition in the second column. Check your answers in the back of the book.

1.	nebulous	a.	wandering from place to
2.	nemesis		place
3.	neophyte	b.	vague
4.	nirvana	c.	blissful, worry-free state
5.	noisome	d.	system of names
6.	nomadic	e.	downfall
7.	nomenclature	f.	repeal
8.	nonchalant	g.	indifferent
9.	nullify	h.	beginner
		i.	offensive or disgusting

O

OBDURATE (AHB duh rit) *adj* stubborn and insensitive

Obdurate contains one of the same roots as *durable* and *endurance;* each word conveys a different sense of hardness.

- The committee's *obdurate* refusal to listen to our plan was heart-breaking to us since we had spent ten years coming up with it.

- The child begged and begged to have the bubble-gum machine installed in his bedroom, but his parents were *obdurate* in their insistence that it should go in the kitchen.

OBEISANCE (oh BAY suns) *n* a bow or curtsy; deep reverence

- When the substitute teacher walked into the room, the entire class rose to its feet in mocking *obeisance* to her.

- "You'll have to show me *obeisance* once I'm elected queen of the prom," Diana proclaimed to her servile roommates, who promised that they would.

OBFUSCATE (AHB fuh skayt) *v* to darken; to confuse; to make confusing

- The spokesman's attempt to explain what the president had meant merely *obfuscated* the issue further. People had hoped the spokesman would elucidate the issue.

- Too much gin had *obfuscated* the old man's senses.

- The professor's inept lecture gradually *obfuscated* a subject that had been crystal clear to us before.

To *obfuscate* something is to engage in *obfuscation.*

- Lester called himself a used-car salesman, but his real job was *obfuscation:* He sold cars by confusing his customers.

OBJECTIVE (ahb JEK tiv) *adj* unbiased; unprejudiced

- It's hard for me to be *objective* about her musical talent because she's my daughter.

- Although the judges at the automobile show were supposed to make *objective* decisions, they displayed a definite bias against cars with tacky hood ornaments.

The opposite of *objective* is *subjective.*

Someone who is *objective* is said to have *objectivity* (ahb jek TIV uh tee).

Objective can also be a noun, in which case it means goal, destination, or aim.

- My life's one *objective* is to see that my father never embarrasses me in public again.

OBLIQUE (oh BLEEK) *adj* indirect; at an angle

In geometry, lines are said to be *oblique* if they are neither parallel nor perpendicular to one another. The word has a related meaning outside of mathematics. An *oblique* statement is one that does not directly address the topic at hand, that approaches it as if from an angle.

An allusion could be said to be an *oblique* reference.

An *oblique* argument is one that does not directly confront its true subject.

To insult someone *obliquely* is to do so indirectly.

- Essence sprinkled her student council speech with *oblique* references to the principal's new toupee; the principal is so dense that he never figured out what was going on, but the rest of us were rolling on the floor.

OBLIVION (uh BLIV ee un) *n* total forgetfulness; the state of being forgotten

- A few of the young actors would find fame, but most were headed for *oblivion*.

- After tossing and turning with anxiety for most of the night, Marisol finally found the *oblivion* of sleep.

To be *oblivious* is to be forgetful or unaware.

- Old age had made the retired professor *oblivious* of all his old theories.

- The workmen stomped in and out of the room, but the happy child, playing on the floor, was *oblivious* of all distraction.

It is also acceptable to say "*oblivious* to" rather than "*oblivious* of."

OBSCURE (ub SKYOOR) *adj* unknown; hard to understand; dark

- The comedy nightclub was filled with *obscure* comedians who stole one another's jokes and seldom got any laughs.

- The artist was so *obscure* that even his parents had trouble remembering his name.

- The noted scholar's dissertation was terribly *obscure*; it had to be translated from English into English before anyone could make head or tail of it.

- Some contemporary poets apparently believe that the only way to be great is to be *obscure.*

- The details of the forest grew *obscure* as night fell.

The state of being *obscure* in any of its senses is called *obscurity.*

OBSEQUIOUS (ub SEE kwee us) *adj* fawning; subservient; sucking up to
- Ann's assistant was so *obsequious* that she could never tell what he really thought about anything.
- My *obsequious* friend seemed to live only to make me happy and never wanted to do anything if I said I didn't want to do it.

OBTRUSIVE (ub TROO siv) *adj* interfering; meddlesome; having a tendency to butt in
- I like to walk up and down the halls of my dorm checking up on my friends' grades after midterms. People call me *obtrusive*, but I think of myself as caring and interested.
- The taste of anchovies would be *obtrusive* in a birthday cake; it would get in the way of the flavor of the cake.

The verb is *obtrude*, which is related to the verb *intrude*.

OBTUSE (ahb TOOS) *adj* insensitive; blockheaded
- Karen was so *obtuse* that she didn't realize for several days that Caleb had asked her to marry him.
- The *obtuse* student couldn't seem to grasp the difference between addition and subtraction.

OBVIATE (AHB vee ayt) *v* to make unnecessary; to avert
- Their move to Florida *obviated* the need for heavy winter clothes.
- My worries about what to do after graduation were *obviated* by my failing three of my final exams.
- Robert *obviated* his arrest for tax evasion by handing a blank check to the IRS examiner and telling him to fill in any amount he liked.

OCCULT (uh KULT) *adj* supernatural; magic; mystical
- I don't mind having a roommate who's interested in *occult* rituals, but I draw the line at her burning chicken feathers under my bed.
- There's a store on Maple Street called Witch-O-Rama; it sells crystal balls, love potions, and other *occult* supplies.

Occult can also be a noun.
- Marie has been interested in the *occult* ever since her stepmother turned her butler into a gerbil.

Occult can also be pronounced "AH kult."

ODIOUS (OH dee us) *adj* hateful; evil; vile
- Don won the election by stooping to some of the most *odious* tricks in the history of politics.

Odium (OH dee um) is hatred, deep contempt, or disgrace.

ODYSSEY (AHD uh see) *n* a long, difficult journey, usually marked by many changes of fortune

In Homer's epic poem *The Odyssey*, Odysseus spends ten years struggling to return to his home in Ithaca, and when he finally arrives, only his dog recognizes him. In modern usage, an *odyssey* is any long and difficult journey.
- Any adolescent making the *odyssey* into adulthood should have a room of his own, preferably one that's not part of his parents' house.
- My quick trip up to the corner hardware store to buy a new shower head turned into a day-long *odyssey* that took me to every plumbing-supply store in the metropolitan area.

OFFICIOUS (uh FISH us) *adj* annoyingly eager to help or advise
- The *officious* officer could never resist sticking his nose into other people's business.
- The *officious* salesperson refused to leave us alone, so we finally left without buying anything.

OLFACTORY (ahl FAK tur ee) *adj* pertaining to the sense of smell
- That stew's appeal is primarily *olfactory*; it smells great, but it doesn't have much taste.
- I have a sensitive *olfactory* nerve. I can't be around cigarettes, onions, or people with bad breath.

For a related word, see our entry for *gustatory*. It's much like *olfactory*, but for the sense of taste.

OLIGARCHY (AHL uh gahr kee) *n* government by only a very few people
- They've set up a virtual *oligarchy* in that country; three men are making all the decisions for twenty million people.
- Whenever Rick's parents tell him that they're in charge of the family, he tells them that he can't survive under an *oligarchy*.

An *oligarch* (AHL uh gahrk) is one of the few ruling leaders.

OMINOUS (AHM uh nus) *adj* threatening; menacing; portending doom
- The sky looks *ominous* this afternoon; there are black clouds in the west, and I think it is going to rain.

- Mrs. Lewis's voice sounded *ominous* when she told the class that it was time for a little test.

This word is related to *omen*.

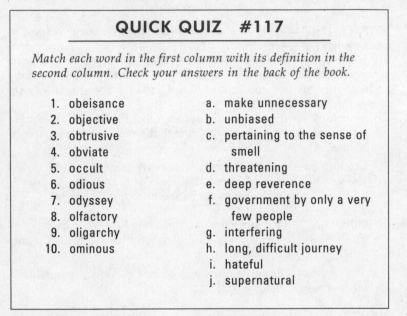

QUICK QUIZ #117

Match each word in the first column with its definition in the second column. Check your answers in the back of the book.

1. obeisance
2. objective
3. obtrusive
4. obviate
5. occult
6. odious
7. odyssey
8. olfactory
9. oligarchy
10. ominous

a. make unnecessary
b. unbiased
c. pertaining to the sense of smell
d. threatening
e. deep reverence
f. government by only a very few people
g. interfering
h. long, difficult journey
i. hateful
j. supernatural

OMNISCIENT (ahm NISH unt) *adj* all-knowing; having infinite wisdom
Omni- is a prefix meaning all. To be *omnipotent* (ahm NIP uh tunt) is to be all-powerful. An *omnivorous* (ahm NIV ur us) animal eats all kinds of food, including meat and plants. Something *omnipresent* (AHM ni prez unt) seems to be everywhere. In March, mud is *omnipresent*. "Sci" is a word root meaning knowledge or knowing. *Prescient* (PRESH unt) means knowing beforehand; *nescient* (NESH unt) means not knowing, or ignorant.

- When Lucy was a small child, she thought her parents were *omniscient*. Now that she's a teenager, she realizes they don't know anything at all.

- The novel's narrator has an *omniscient* point of view, so his words often clue the reader in to things the characters in the story don't know.

ONEROUS (AHN ur us) *adj* burdensome; oppressive
- We were given the *onerous* task of cleaning up the fairgrounds after the carnival.

- The job had long hours, but the work wasn't *onerous;* Bill spent most of his time sitting with his feet on the desk.

This word can be pronounced "OH nur us."

OPAQUE (oh PAYK) *adj* impossible to see through; impossible to understand
- The windows in the movie star's house were made not of glass but of some *opaque* material intended to keep his fans from spying on him.
- We tried to figure out what Horace was thinking, but his expression was *opaque:* It revealed nothing.
- Jerry's mind, assuming he had one, was *opaque.*
- The statement was *opaque;* no one could make anything of it.

The noun form of *opaque* is *opacity* (oh PAS uh tee).

OPPROBRIOUS (uh PROH bree us) *adj* damning; extremely critical; disgraceful
- The principal gave an *opprobrious* lecture about apathy, saying that the students' uncaring attitude was ruining the school.

Opprobrium (uh PROH bree um) is reproach, scorn, or disgrace.
- Penny brought *opprobrium* on herself by robbing the First National Bank and spray painting naughty words on its marble walls.

OPULENT (AHP yuh lunt) *adj* luxurious
- Everything in the *opulent* palace was made of gold—except the toilet-paper holder, which was made of platinum.
- The investment banker had grown so accustomed to an *opulent* lifestyle that he had trouble adjusting to the federal penitentiary.

Opulence is often ostentatious.

ORDINANCE (AWR duh nuns) *n* law; regulation; decree
- I'm sorry, but you'll have to put your bathing suit back on; the town passed an *ordinance* against nude swimming at this beach.
- According to a hundred-year-old local *ordinance,* two or more people standing on a street corner constitutes a riot.

Don't confuse ordinance with *ordnance* (AWRD nuns). *Ordnance* is military weapons or artillery.

ORTHODOX (OR thuh dahks) *adj* conventional; adhering to established principles or doctrines, especially in religion; by the book
- The doctor's treatment for Lou's cold was entirely *orthodox:* plenty of liquids, aspirin, and rest.

- Austin's views were *orthodox*; there was nothing shocking about any of them.

The body of what is *orthodox* is called *orthodoxy*.
- The teacher's lectures were characterized by strict adherence to *orthodoxy*.

To be unconventional is to be *unorthodox*.
- "Swiss cheese" is an *unorthodox* explanation for the composition of the moon.

OSCILLATE (AHS uh layt) *v* to swing back and forth; to pulsate; to waver or vacillate between beliefs or ideas
- We watched the hypnotist's pendulum *oscillate* before our eyes, and soon we became sleepy.
- Mrs. Johnson can't make up her mind how to raise her children; she *oscillates* between strictness and laxity depending on what kind of mood she's in.

OSMOSIS (ahs MOH sis) *n* gradual or subtle absorption
In science, *osmosis* is the diffusion of a fluid through a membrane. It is *osmosis* that controls the flow of liquids in and out of cells. In general usage, *osmosis* is a figurative instance of absorption.
- I learned my job by *osmosis*; I absorbed the knowledge I needed from the people working around me.

OSTENSIBLE (ah STEN suh bul) *adj* apparent (but misleading); professed
- Blake's *ostensible* mission was to repair a broken telephone, but his real goal was to eavesdrop on the boss's conversation.
- Trevor's *ostensible* kindness to squirrels belied his deep hatred of them.

OSTENTATIOUS (ahs ten TAY shus) *adj* excessively conspicuous; showing off
- The designer's use of expensive materials was *ostentatious*; every piece of furniture was covered with silk or velvet, and every piece of hardware was made of silver or gold.
- The donor was *ostentatious* in making his gift to the hospital. He held a big press conference to announce it and then walked through the wards to give patients an opportunity to thank him personally.
- The young lawyer had *ostentatiously* hung his Harvard diploma on the door to his office.

To be *ostentatious* is to engage in *ostentation*.

- Lamar wore solid-gold shoes to the party; I was shocked by his *ostentation*.

QUICK QUIZ #118

Match each word in the first column with its definition in the second column. Check your answers in the back of the book.

1.	obdurate	a.	forgetfulness
2.	obfuscate	b.	hard to understand
3.	oblique	c.	stubborn
4.	oblivion	d.	insensitive
5.	obscure	e.	burdensome
6.	obsequious	f.	luxurious
7.	obtuse	g.	indirect
8.	officious	h.	misleadingly apparent
9.	onerous	i.	showing off
10.	opaque	j.	impossible to see through
11.	opulent	k.	confuse
12.	orthodox	l.	fawning
13.	ostensible	m.	conventional
14.	ostentatious	n.	annoyingly helpful

OSTRACIZE (AHS truh syze) *v* to shun; to shut out or exclude a person from a group

- After she'd tattled to the counselor about her bed being short-sheeted, Tracee was *ostracized* by the other girls in the cabin; they wouldn't speak to her, and they wouldn't let her join in any of their games.

- That poor old man has been *ostracized* by our town for long enough; I'm going to visit him today.

The act of *ostracizing* is called *ostracism* (AHS truh siz um).

- Carl's letter to the editor advocating a cut in the school budget led to his *ostracism* by the educational committee.

OUST (owst) *v* to eject; to expel; to banish
- Robbie was *ousted* from the Cub Scouts for forgetting his Cub Scout manual thirty-seven times.
- If the patrons at O'Reilly's get rowdy, the bartender *ousts* them with a simple foot-to-behind maneuver.

An instance of *ousting* is called an *ouster* (OW stur).
- After the president's *ouster* by an angry mob, the vice president moved into his office and lit one of his cigars.

OVERRIDE (OH vur ryde) *v* to overrule; to prevail over
- The legislature threatened to *override* the governor's veto of the bill creating the state's first income tax.
- My mother *overrode* my decision to move into my girlfriend's house.
- Greed *overrode* common sense yesterday as thousands of frenzied people drove through a major blizzard to catch the post-holiday sales.

OVERTURE (OH vur chur) *n* opening move; preliminary offer
In music, an *overture* is a composition that introduces a larger work, often by weaving together bits and pieces of what is to come. (Most people think it's okay to talk through the *overture*, even though it's not.) Outside of music, the word has a related but distinct meaning.
- The zoo bought a new male gorilla named Izzy to mate with Sukey, its female gorilla, but Sukey flatly rejected Izzy's romantic *overtures*, and no new gorillas were born.
- At contract time, management's *overture* to the union was instantly rejected, since the workers had decided to hold out for significantly higher wages.

OXYMORON (ahk see MAWR ahn) *n* a figure of speech in which two contradictory words or phrases are used together
"My girlfriend's sweet cruelty" is an example of an *oxymoron*. Other examples of *oxymorons* are "jumbo shrimp," "fresh-squeezed juice from concentrate," and "live recording."

QUICK QUIZ #119

Match each word in the first column with its definition in the second column. Check your answers in the back of the book.

1.	omniscient	a.	exclude from a group
2.	opprobrious	b.	swing back and forth
3.	ordinance	c.	eject
4.	oscillate	d.	damning
5.	osmosis	e.	gradual or subtle absorption
6.	ostracize	f.	law
7.	oust	g.	figure of speech linking two
8.	override	h.	all-knowing
9.	overture	i.	opening move
10.	oxymoron	j.	prevail over
		k.	contradictory words or phrases

P

PACIFY (PAS uh fye) *v* to calm someone down; to placate

A parent gives a baby a *pacifier* to *pacify* him or her. A *pacifist* is someone who does not believe in war.

PAINSTAKING (PAYN stay king) *adj* extremely careful; taking pains

Painstaking = pains-taking = taking pains.

- The jeweler was *painstaking* in his effort not to ruin the $50 million diamond necklace.

PALATABLE (PAL uh tuh bul) *adj* pleasant to the taste; agreeable to the feelings

- You can certainly drink hot chocolate with lobster soufflé if you want to, but champagne might be a more *palatable* alternative.

- Rather than telling Frank that his essay was worthless, Hilary told him that his essay was not quite representative of his talents; by diluting her criticism she made it more *palatable* to Frank.

The word *palate* (PAL ut) refers both to the roof of the mouth and, more commonly, to the sense of taste. A gourmet is said to have a finely developed *palate*; someone who finds even the most exotic foods boring is said to have a jaundiced *palate*.

PALLIATE (PAL ee ayt) *v* to relieve or alleviate something without getting rid of the problem; to assuage; to mitigate
- You take aspirin in the hope that it will *palliate* your headache.

Aspirin is a *palliative* (PAL yuh tiv).

PALLOR (PAL ur) *n* paleness; whiteness
- Regina's ghostly *pallor* can only mean one thing: she just caught sight of her blind date for the evening.

- The pediatrician was concerned by the child's *pallor* but could find no other symptoms of illness.

In the nineteenth century, a *pallid* (PAL ud) look was fashionable among European and American women. To maintain an attractive *pallor*, women kept out of the sun and sometimes took drugs to lighten their complexions.

PALPABLE (PAL puh bul) *adj* capable of being touched; obvious; tangible
- The tumor was *palpable;* the doctor could feel it with his finger.

- Harry's disappointment at being rejected by every college in America was *palpable;* it was so obvious that you could almost reach out and touch it.

- There was *palpable* danger in flying the kite in a thunderstorm.

The opposite of *palpable* is *impalpable*.

PALTRY (PAWL tree) *adj* insignificant; worthless
- The lawyer's efforts on our behalf were *paltry;* they didn't add up to anything.

- The *paltry* fee he paid us was scarcely large enough to cover our expenses.

PANACEA (pan uh SEE uh) *n* something that cures everything
- The administration seemed to believe that a tax cut would be a *panacea* for the country's economic ills.

- Granny believed that her "rheumatiz medicine" was a *panacea.* No matter what you were sick with, that was what she prescribed.

PANDEMIC (pan DEM ik) *adj* prevalent throughout a large area
- The Black Plague was virtually *pandemic* throughout Europe during the fourteenth century.

- Cheating was *pandemic* on the campus of the military academy; cadets were carrying more crib sheets than books.

This word can also be a noun. A *pandemic* is an *epidemic* (ep i DEM ik) on a larger scale.

- The shortage of vaccine turned the winter flu epidemic into a *pandemic*.

Like the Latin "omni," the Greek prefix "pan" means all. A *panacea* (pan uh SEE uh) is a cure for all ills. A *panoramic* (pah uh RAM ik) view is one that seems to surround you. The Pan-American Games are open to contestants from throughout the Western Hemisphere.

A closely related word is *endemic* (en DEM ik), which means peculiar to a particular place or people.

PANEGYRIC (pan i JIR ik) *n* elaborate praise; eulogy
- As the Soviet official's brief introductory speech turned into a three-hour *panegyric* on the accomplishments of Lenin, the members of the audience began to snooze in their seats.

- Dan has been in advertising for too long; he can't say he likes something without escalating into *panegyric*.

- "All these *panegyrics* are embarrassing me," lied the actress at the dinner in her honor.

PARABLE (PAR uh bul) *n* religious allegory; fable; morality tale
- The story of the tortoise and the hare is a *parable* about the importance of persistent effort.

- Early religious lessons were often given in the form of *parables* because the stories made the lessons easier to understand.

PARADIGM (PAR uh dime) *n* a model or example
- Mr. Hufstader is the best teacher in the whole world; his classroom should be the *paradigm* for all classrooms.

- In selecting her wardrobe, messy Ana apparently used a scarecrow as her *paradigm*.

A *paradigm* is *paradigmatic* (par uh dig MAT ik).
- Virtually all the cars the company produced were based on a single, *paradigmatic* design.

PARADOX (PAR uh dahks) *n* a true statement or phenomenon that nonetheless seems to contradict itself; an untrue statement or phenomenon that nonetheless seems logical
- Mr. Cooper is a political *paradox*; he's a staunch Republican who votes only for Democrats.

- One of Xeno's *paradoxes* seems to prove the impossibility of an arrow's ever reaching its target: If the arrow first moves half the distance to the target, then half the remaining distance, then half the remaining distance, and so on, it can never arrive.

A *paradox* is *paradoxical*.
- Pasquale's dislike of ice cream was *paradoxical* considering that he worked as an ice-cream taster.

PARAGON (PAR uh gahn) *n* a model or pattern of excellence
- Irene is a such a *paragon* of virtue that none of her classmates can stand her; they call her a goody-goody.

- The new manual is unusual in the computer world in that it is a *paragon* of clear writing; after reading it, you understand exactly how the software works.

- Mario named his fledgling restaurant *Paragon* Pizza, hoping that the name would make people think his pizzas were better than they actually were.

PARALLEL (PAR uh lel) *adj* similar; comparable
- Before they learn to cooperate, young children often engage in what psychologists call *parallel* play; rather than playing one game together, they play separate games side by side.

- Bill and Martha have *parallel* interests in the yard; Bill's favorite activity is mowing, and Martha's is pruning.

Parallel can also be a noun, in which case it refers to something identical or similar in essential respects. Pessimistic economists sometimes say that there are many disturbing *parallels* between today's economy and the Great Depression of the thirties.

Parallel can also be a verb. To say that two murder cases *parallel* each other is to say that they are similar in many ways.

PARANOIA (par uh NOY uh) *n* a mental illness in which the sufferer believes people are out to get him; unreasonable anxiety
- Margaret's *paranoia* has increased to the point where she won't even set foot out of the house because she is afraid that the people walking by are foreign agents on a mission to assassinate her.

- Worrying that one is going to die someday is not *paranoia*; it's just worrying, since one really is going to die someday.

A person with *paranoia* is said to be *paranoid* (PAR uh noyd). The word has a precise clinical meaning, but it is often used loosely or figuratively.
- Harry told Sally that she was *paranoid* to believe her dinner guests hated her cooking; in fact, her guests enjoyed her lasagna.

PARANORMAL (par uh NOR mul) *adj* having to do with an event or events that can't be explained scientifically; supernatural

- Numerous *paranormal* events have occurred in that house since the Austins bought it; last night, an umbrella opened itself and began flying around the room, and just this morning the dining-room table turned into a little man with a long gray beard.

Extrasensory perception, clairvoyance, and the ability to bend spoons with one's thoughts are said to be examples of *paranormal* phenomena.

Paranormal is often a polite synonym for phony.

PAROCHIAL (puh ROH kee ul) *adj* narrow or confined in point of view; provincial

- The townspeople's concerns were entirely *parochial;* they worried only about what happened in their town and not about the larger world around it.

- The journalist's *parochial* point of view prevented him from becoming a nationally known figure.

A lot of people think a *parochial* school is a religious school. Traditionally, a *parochial* school is just the school of the parish or neighborhood. In other contexts *parochial* has negative connotations.

PARODY (PAR uh dee) *n* a satirical imitation

- At the talent show the girls sang a terrible *parody* of a Beatles song called "I Want to Hold Your Foot."

Some *parodies* are unintentional and not very funny.

- The unhappy student accused Mr. Benson of being not a teacher but a *parody* of one.

Parody can also be a verb. To *parody* something is to make a *parody* of it. A *parody* is *parodic* (puh ROD ik).

PAROXYSM (PAR uk siz um) *n* a sudden, violent outburst; a severe attack

- Sheldon flew into a *paroxysm* of rage and threw books across the room after finding that his apartment has been burglarized.

- Forty years of cigarette smoking had made John prone to agonizing *paroxysms* of coughing.

PARSIMONIOUS (pahr suh MOH nee us) *adj* stingy
- The widow was so *parsimonious* that she hung used teabags out to dry on her clothesline so that she would be able to use them again.
- We tried to be *parsimonious,* but without success. After just a few days at the resort we realized we had spent all the money we had set aside for our entire month-long vacation.

To be *parsimonious* is to practice *parsimony*.

PARTISAN (PAHR tuh zun) *n* one who supports a particular person, cause, or idea
- Henry's plan to give himself the award had no *partisan* except himself.
- I am the *partisan* of any candidate who promises not to make promises.
- The mountain village was attacked by *partisans* of the rebel chieftain.

Partisan can also be used as an adjective meaning biased, as in *partisan* politics. An issue that everyone agrees on regardless of the party he or she belongs to is a *nonpartisan* issue. *Bipartisan* means supported by two (bi) parties.
- Both the Republican and Democratic senators voted to give themselves a raise. The motion had *bipartisan* support.

PARTITION (pahr TISH un) *n* division; dividing wall
- The teacher's *partition* of the class into "smarties" and "dumbies" may not have been educationally sound.
- In the temporary office there were plywood *partitions* rather than real walls between the work areas.

Partition can also be a verb. To *partition* something is to divide it by creating *partitions*.
- After the Second World War, Germany was *partitioned* into two distinct countries, East Germany and West Germany.
- Ann and David used a wall of bookcases to *partition* off a study from one corner of their living room.

QUICK QUIZ #120

Match each word in the first column with its definition in the second column. Check your answers in the back of the book.

1.	pacify	a.	obvious
2.	painstaking	b.	model
3.	palliate	c.	supporter of a cause
4.	palpable	d.	narrow in point of view
5.	paltry	e.	contradictory truth
6.	panacea	f.	stingy
7.	paradigm	g.	calm someone down
8.	paradox	h.	cure for everything
9.	parochial	i.	insignificant
10.	parody	j.	extremely careful
11.	parsimonious	k.	satirical imitation
12.	partisan	l.	alleviate

QUICK QUIZ #121

Match each word in the first column with its definition in the second column. Check your answers in the back of the book.

1.	palatable	a.	model of excellence
2.	pallor	b.	pleasant to the taste
3.	pandemic	c.	supernatural
4.	panegyric	d.	prevalent throughout a large area
5.	parable	e.	morality tale
6.	paragon	f.	sudden, violent outburst
7.	parallel	g.	paleness
8.	paranoia	h.	unreasonable anxiety
9.	paranormal	i.	similar
10.	paroxysm	j.	elaborate praise

PASTORAL (PAS tur ul) *adj* rural; rustic; peaceful and calm, like the country
* When I'm in the city, I long for the *pastoral* life, but the second I get into the country, I almost die of boredom.
* Lyme disease has made people a little less intrigued with living in *pastoral* splendor than they used to be.
* Bruce is writing the *pastoral* movement of his symphony now. The harps will symbolize the gentle patter of rain pattering down on the fields and spoiling everyone's vacation.

Halcyon is a synonym for *pastoral*, but *pastoral* has more of a country association.

PATENT (PAYT unt) *adj* obvious
* To say that the Earth is flat is a *patent* absurdity since the world is obviously spherical.
* It was *patently* foolish of Lee to think that he could sail across the Pacific Ocean in a washtub.

PATERNAL (puh TUR nul) *adj* fatherly; fatherlike
* Rich is *paternal* toward his niece.

Maternal (muh TUR nul) means motherly or momlike.

PATHOLOGY (puh THAHL uh jee) *n* the science of diseases
Pathology is the science or study of diseases, but not necessarily in the medical sense. *Pathological* means relating to *pathology*, but it also means arising from a disease. So if we say Brad is an inveterate, incorrigible, *pathological* (path uh LAHJ uh kul) liar, we are saying that Brad's lying is a sickness.

PATHOS (PAY thahs) *n* that which makes people feel pity or sorrow
* Laura's dog gets such a look of *pathos* whenever he wants to go for a walk that it's hard for Laura to turn him down.
* There was an unwitting *pathos* in the way the elderly shop-keeper had tried to spruce up his window display with crude decorations cut from construction paper.

Don't confuse *pathos* with *bathos* (BAY thahs). *Bathos* is trite, insincere, sentimental *pathos*.
* Terry said the new novel was deeply moving, but I found it to be filled with *bathos*, and I didn't shed a tear.

PATINA (PAT uh nuh) *n* surface discoloration caused by age and oxidation
* Antiques dealers don't refer to the tarnish on old silver as tarnish; they call it *patina*, and say that it adds value to the silver.

- The Statue of Liberty's distinctive green color is due to its *patina*; the statue is made of copper, not cheese.

- Long use and exposure to sunlight give old furniture a *patina* that is impossible to reproduce in modern imitations; the color of a new piece never looks quite as rich and dark as the color of an old one.

PATRIARCH (PAY tree ahrk) *n* the male head of a family or tribe

- The *patriarch* of the Murphy family, Jacob V. Murphy, made millions selling cobra fillets and established the Murphy family's empire in the snake meat business.

The adjective is *patriarchal* (pay tree AHRK ul).

- In the *patriarchal* country of Spambulia, the ruling monarch can never be a woman, though the current king is such a numbskull that his sister runs things behind the scenes.

A female head of a family is a *matriarch*, and such a family would be described as *matriarchal*.

- Spambulia is considering becoming a *matriarchy* (MAY tree ahr kee).

PATRICIAN (puh TRISH un) *n* a person of noble birth; an aristocrat

- Mr. Perno was a *patrician*, and he was never truly happy unless his place at the dinner table was set with at least half a dozen forks.

Patrician can also be an adjective. Polo is a *patrician* sport.

- The noisy crowd on the luxury ocean liner was *patrician* in dress but not in behavior; they were wearing tuxedos but throwing deck chairs into the ocean.

PATRIMONY (PAT ruh moh nee) *n* an inheritance, especially from a father; a legacy

- This thorny patch of ground isn't much, but it's my *patrimony*; it's all that my father left to me in his will.

- If Bob keeps spending at this rate, he will have exhausted his entire *patrimony* by the end of the year.

Patronage is a related word that means support (particularly financial support). *Patronage* is given by a patron.

PATRONIZE (PAY truh nyze) *v* to treat as an inferior; to condescend to

- Our guide at the art gallery was extremely *patronizing*, treating us as though we wouldn't be able to distinguish a painting from a piece of sidewalk without her help.

- We felt *patronized* by the waiter at the fancy restaurant; he ignored all our efforts to attract his attention and then pretended not to understand our accents.

Patronize also means to frequent or be a regular customer of. To *patronize* a restaurant is to eat there often, not to treat it as an inferior.

PAUCITY (PAW suh tee) *n* scarcity
- There was a *paucity* of fresh vegetables at the supermarket, so we had to buy frozen ones.
- The plan was defeated by a *paucity* of support.
- There is no *paucity* of water in the ocean.

PECCADILLO (pek uh DIL oh) *n* a minor offense
- The smiling defendant acted as though first-degree murder were a mere *peccadillo* rather than a hideous crime.
- The reporters sometimes seemed more interested in the candidates' sexual *peccadillos* than in their inane programs and proposals.

PECULIAR (puh KYOOL yur) *adj* unusual; bizarre; individual; belonging to a particular region
- There's a *peculiar* smell in this room. Are you wearing perfume made from floor wax and old socks?
- The *peculiar* look in his eye just before he opened the door was what tipped me off to the surprise party awaiting me inside.
- That method of cooking shrimp is *peculiar* to this region; it isn't done anywhere else.
- Marlene's way of pronouncing "orange" is *peculiar* to a tiny region in Upstate New York.

PEDANTIC (puh DAN tik) *adj* boringly scholarly or academic
- The discussion quickly turned *pedantic* as each participant tried to sound more learned than all the others.
- The professor's interpretation of the poem was *pedantic* and empty of genuine feeling.

A *pedantic* person is called a *pedant* (PED unt). A *pedant* is fond of *pedantry* (PED un tree).

PEDESTRIAN (puh DES tree un) *adj* unimaginative; banal
A *pedestrian* is someone walking, but to be *pedestrian* is to be something else altogether.
- Mary Anne said the young artist's work was brilliant, but I found it to be *pedestrian;* I've seen better paintings in kindergarten classrooms.
- The menu was *pedestrian;* I had encountered each of the dishes dozens of times before.

PEJORATIVE (pi JOR uh tiv) *adj* negative; disparaging
"Hi, stupid" is a *pejorative* greeting. "Loudmouth" is a nickname with a *pejorative* connotation.
- Abe's description of the college as "a pretty good school" was unintentionally *pejorative.*

PENCHANT (PEN chunt) *n* a strong taste or liking for something; a predilection
- Dogs have a *penchant* for chasing cats and mail carriers.

PENITENT (PEN uh tunt) *adj* sorry; repentant; contrite
- Julie was *penitent* when Kanye explained how much pain she had caused him.
- The two boys tried to sound *penitent* at the police station, but they weren't really sorry that they had herded the sheep into Mr. Ingersoll's house. They were *impenitent.*

PENSIVE (PEN siv) *adj* thoughtful and sad
- Norton became suddenly *pensive* when Jack mentioned his dead father.

QUICK QUIZ #122

Match each word in the first column with its definition in the second column. Check your answers in the back of the book.

1.	patent	a.	male head of a family
2.	paternal	b.	minor offense
3.	pathology	c.	unimaginative
4.	patriarch	d.	thoughtful and sad
5.	patrician	e.	boringly scholarly
6.	patronize	f.	science of diseases
7.	paucity	g.	treat as an inferior
8.	peccadillo	h.	negative
9.	pedantic	i.	obvious
10.	pedestrian	j.	aristocrat
11.	pejorative	k.	scarcity
12.	penchant	l.	fatherly
13.	penitent	m.	sorry
14.	pensive	n.	strong liking

PEREGRINATION (per uh gruh NAY shun) *n* wandering; traveling; expedition

- The baby made a wavering *peregrination* around the room in search of all the raisins she had dropped during her previous wavering peregrination.

- Matthew's *peregrinations* across Europe have given him a vaguely continental accent and a walletful of unusable currency.

PEREMPTORY (puh REMP tuh ree) *adj* final; categorical; dictatorial
Someone who is *peremptory* says or does something without giving anyone a chance to dispute it.

- Asher's father *peremptorily* banished him to his room.

PERENNIAL (puh REN ee ul) *adj* continual; happening again and again or year after year

- Mr. Lorenzo is a *perennial* favorite of students at the high school because he always gives everyone an A.

- Milton was a *perennial* candidate for governor; every four years he printed up another batch of his BINGO AND HORSE RACING bumper stickers.

Flowers called *perennials* are flowers that bloom year after year without being replanted.

Biennial (bye EN ee ul) and *centennial* (sen TEN ee ul) are related words. *Biennial* means happening once every two years (*biannual* means happening twice a year). *Centennial* means happening once every century.

PERFIDY (PUR fuh dee) *n* treachery
- It was the criminals' natural *perfidy* that finally did them in, as each one became an informant on the other.
- I was appalled at Al's *perfidy*. He had sworn to me that he was my best friend, but then he asked my girlfriend to the prom.

To engage in *perfidy* is to be *perfidious* (pur FID ee us).

PERFUNCTORY (pur FUNGK tuh ree) *adj* unenthusiastic; careless
- John made a couple of *perfunctory* attempts at answering the questions on the test, but then he put down his pencil and his head and slept until the end of the period.
- Sandra's lawn mowing was *perfunctory* at best: She skipped all the difficult parts and didn't rake up any of the clippings.

PERIPATETIC (per uh peh TET ik) *adj* wandering; traveling continually; itinerant
- Groupies are a *peripatetic* bunch, traveling from concert to concert to follow their favorite rock stars.

PERIPHERY (puh RIF uh ree) *n* the outside edge of something
- José never got involved in any of our activities; he was always at the *periphery*.
- The professional finger painter enjoyed his position at the *periphery* of the art world.

To be at the *periphery* is to be *peripheral* (puh RIF uh rul). A *peripheral* interest is a secondary or side interest.

Your *peripheral* vision is your ability to see to the right and left while looking straight ahead.

PERJURY (PUR jur ee) *n* lying under oath
- The defendant was acquitted of bribery but convicted of *perjury* because he had lied on the witness stand during his trial.

To commit *perjury* is to *perjure* oneself.
- The former cabinet official *perjured* himself when he said that he had not committed *perjury* during his trial for bribery.

PERMEATE (PUR mee ayt) *v* to spread or seep through; to penetrate
- A horrible smell quickly *permeated* the room after Jock lit a cigarette.
- Corruption had *permeated* the company; every single one of its executives belonged in jail.

Something that can be *permeated* is said to be *permeable*. A *permeable* raincoat is one that lets water seep through.

PERNICIOUS (pur NISH us) *adj* deadly; extremely evil
- The drug dealers conducted their *pernicious* business on every street corner in the city.
- Lung cancer is a *pernicious* disease.

PERPETRATOR (PUR pi tray tur) *n* the one who committed the act
- Police officers sometimes refer to the *perpetrator* of a crime simply as the "perp."
- When Miss Walsh found glue on her chair, she speedily apprehended the *perpetrator* and sent him to the principal.
- The restaurant critic so disliked his meal at Pierre's restaurant that he referred to Pierre not as the meal's chef but as its *perpetrator*.

PERPETUATE (pur PECH oo ayt) *v* to make something perpetual; to keep from perishing
- By calling his secretary Fluffy, Quentin helped *perpetuate* the stereotype of office personnel as unskilled employees.
- The new forestry bill contained conservation measures intended to help *perpetuate* the nation's timber resources.

QUICK QUIZ   #123

Match each word in the first column with its definition in the second column. Check your answers in the back of the book.

1.	partition	a.	keep from perishing
2.	pastoral	b.	division
3.	pathos	c.	rural
4.	patina	d.	the one who committed the act
5.	patrimony	e.	stubborn
6.	peculiar	f.	surface discoloration
7.	peregrination	g.	wandering
8.	perpetrator	h.	that which makes people feel pity or sorrow
9.	perpetuate	i.	unusual
10.	perverse	j.	inheritance

PERQUISITE (PUR kwuh zit) *n* a privilege that goes along with a job; a "perk"
- Free access to a photocopier is a *perquisite* of most office jobs.
- The big corporate lawyer's *perquisites* included a chauffeured limousine, a luxurious apartment in the city, and all the chocolate ice cream he could eat.

A *perquisite* should not be confused with a *prerequisite* (pree REK wuh zit), which is a necessity.
- Health and happiness are two *prerequisites* of a good life.
- A college degree is a *prerequisite* for many high-paying jobs.

PERTINENT (PUR tuh nunt) *adj* relevant; dealing with the matter at hand
- The suspect said that he was just borrowing the jewelry for a costume ball. The cop said he did not think that was *pertinent*.

By the way, *impertinent* means disrespectful.

PERTURB (pur TURB) *v* to disturb greatly
- Ivan's mother was *perturbed* by his aberrant behavior at the dinner table. Ivan's father was not bothered. Nothing bothered Ivan, Sr. He was *imperturbable*.

PERUSE (puh ROOZ) *v* to read carefully

This word is misused more often than it is used correctly. To *peruse* something is not to skim it or read it quickly. To *peruse* something is to study it or read it with great care.

- The lawyer *perused* the contract for many hours, looking for a loophole that would enable his client to back out of the deal.

To *peruse* something is to engage in *perusal*.

- My *perusal* of the ancient texts brought me no closer to my goal of discovering the meaning of life.

QUICK QUIZ   #124

Match each word in the first column with its definition in the second column. Check your answers in the back of the book.

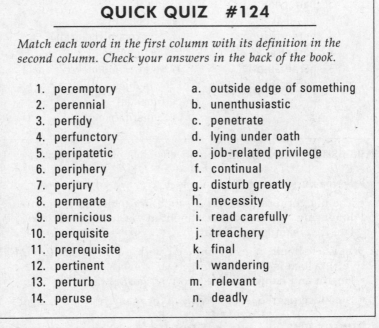

1.	peremptory	a.	outside edge of something
2.	perennial	b.	unenthusiastic
3.	perfidy	c.	penetrate
4.	perfunctory	d.	lying under oath
5.	peripatetic	e.	job-related privilege
6.	periphery	f.	continual
7.	perjury	g.	disturb greatly
8.	permeate	h.	necessity
9.	pernicious	i.	read carefully
10.	perquisite	j.	treachery
11.	prerequisite	k.	final
12.	pertinent	l.	wandering
13.	perturb	m.	relevant
14.	peruse	n.	deadly

PERVADE (pur VAYD) *v* to spread throughout

- A terrible smell *pervaded* the apartment building after the sewer main exploded.
- On examination day, the classroom was *pervaded* by a sense of imminent doom.

Something that *pervades* is *pervasive*.

- There was a *pervasive* feeling of despair on Wall Street on the day the Dow-Jones industrial average fell more than 500 points.
- There was a *pervasive* odor of mold in the house, and we soon discovered why: The basement was filled with the stuff.

PERVERSE (pur VURS) *adj* contrary; stubborn
- It is *perverse* of Steve to insist on having the window seat, since looking down from great heights makes him airsick.
- Ralph takes a *perverse* pleasure in making his garden the ugliest on the block; it pleases him to know that he deeply annoys his neighbors.

PETULANT (PECH uh lunt) *adj* rude; cranky; ill-tempered
- Gloria became *petulant* when we suggested that she leave her pet cheetah at home when she came to spend the weekend; she said that we had insulted her cheetah and that an insult to her cheetah was an insult to her.
- The *petulant* waiter slammed down our water glasses and spilled a tureen of soup onto Roger's kilt.

To be *petulant* is to engage in *petulance,* or rudeness.

PHANTASM (FAN taz um) *n* apparition; ghost; phantom
- The fountain that seemed to be gurgling on the horizon turned out to be a *phantasm*; after hours and hours of driving, Meredith was still surrounded by nothing but sand.
- Though Aaron seems confident, fear and insecurity hover in his background like *phantasms* ready to haunt him again at any moment.

PHILANTHROPY (fi LAN thruh pee) *n* love of mankind, especially by doing good deeds
- His gift of one billion dollars to the local orphanage was the finest act of *philanthropy* I've ever seen.

A charity is a *philanthropic* (fi lun THRAH pik) institution. An altruist is someone who cares about other people. A *philanthropist* (fi LAN thruh pist) is actively doing things to help, usually by giving time or money.

PHILISTINE (FIL i steen) *n* a smugly ignorant person with no appreciation of intellectual or artistic matters
- The novelist dismissed his critics as *philistines,* saying they wouldn't recognize a good book if it crawled up and bit them on the nose; the critics, in reply, dismissed the novelist as a *philistine* who wouldn't recognize a good book if it crawled up and rolled itself into his typewriter.

Philistine can also be an adjective. To be *philistine* is to act like a *philistine.*

PHLEGMATIC (fleg MAT ik) *adj* calm or indifferent; not easily roused to excitement

Phlegmatic derives from *phlegm* (flem). According to medieval lore, *phlegm* was one of the four "bodily humors" and caused sluggishness. Nowadays, *phlegm* means mucus, but a *phlegmatic* person is not someone with a runny nose.

- It must be true that opposites attract; Debbie becomes upset at the slightest provocation, while Webbie is so *phlegmatic* that nothing seems to bother him at all.

- Vinnie tried to be *phlegmatic* about his eleven last-place finishes on field day, but as soon as he got home, he broke down and cried like a baby.

For a synonym, see our entry for stolid.

PILGRIMAGE (PIL grum ij) *n* religious or spiritual journey; excursion; peregrination

A *pilgrim* is someone who takes a long journey from home for a religious or spiritual reason. A *pilgrim* makes a *pilgrimage*.

- Every year, thousands of tone-deaf people make a *pilgrimage* to the shrine of St. Piano, hoping that musical ability will be restored to them.

- Someday I'm going to make a *pilgrimage* back to the most important spots of my childhood, beginning with the McDonald's™ across the street from my old house.

PIOUS (PYE us) *adj* reverent or devout; outwardly (and sometimes falsely) reverent or devout; hypocritical

This is a sometimes confusing word with meanings that are very nearly opposite each other.

A *pious* Presbyterian is one who goes to church every Sunday and says his prayers every night before bed. *Pious* in this sense means something like religiously dutiful.

Pious can also be used to describe behavior or feelings that aren't religious at all but are quite hypocritical.

- The adulterous minister's sermon on marital fidelity was filled with *pious* disregard for his own sins.

The state of being *pious* is *piety* (PYE uh tee). The opposite of *pious* is *impious* (IM pee us).

PIVOTAL (PIV uh tul) *adj* crucial

Pivotal is the adjective form of the verb to *pivot*. To *pivot* is to turn on a single point or shaft. A basketball player *pivots* when he turns while leaving one foot planted in the same place on the floor.

A *pivotal* comment is a comment that turns a discussion. It is an important comment.

A *pivotal* member of a committee is a crucial or important member of a committee.

- Sofia's contribution was *pivotal;* without it, we would have failed.

PLACATE (PLAY kayt) *v* to pacify; to appease; to soothe

- The tribe *placated* the angry volcano by tossing a few teenagers into the raging crater.

- The beleaguered general tried to *placate* his fierce attacker by sending him a pleasant flower arrangement. His implacable enemy decided to attack anyway.

PLACEBO (pluh SEE boh) *n* a fake medication; a fake medication used as a control in tests of the effectiveness of drugs

- Half the subjects in the experiment received the real drug; half were given *placebos.* Of the subjects given *placebos,* 50 percent reported a definite improvement, 30 percent reported a complete cure, and 20 percent said, "Oh, I bet you just gave us a placebo."

- Mrs. Walters is a total hypochondriac; her doctor prescribes several *placebos* a week just to keep her from calling him so often.

PLAINTIVE (PLAYN tiv) *adj* expressing sadness or sorrow

- The lead singer's *plaintive* love song expressed his sorrow at being abandoned by his girlfriend for the lead guitarist.

- The chilly autumn weather made the little bird's song seem *plaintive.*

You could also say that there was *plaintiveness* in that bird's song.
Don't confuse *plaintive* with *plaintiff.* A *plaintiff* is a person who takes someone to court—who makes a legal complaint.

PLATITUDE (PLAT uh tood) *n* a dull or trite remark; a cliché

- The principal thinks he is a great orator, but his loud, boring speech was full of *platitudes.*

- Instead of giving us any real insight into the situation, the lecturer threw *platitudes* at us for the entire period. It was a *platitudinous* speech.

PLATONIC (pluh TAHN ik) *adj* nonsexual; purely spiritual

Platonic love is love that never gets physical. It is supposed to be free from desire and possessiveness, which is why you hardly ever see it in real life. The word is derived from the name of the Greek philosopher Plato, who believed, among other things, that physical objects are just the impermanent representations of unchanging ideas.

- "Let's keep our relationship *platonic* for a while," Ken told his would-be girlfriend. "After all, we only met five minutes ago, and it won't be dark for several hours."

- Ravi and Gina's marriage is entirely *platonic*; they live in separate cities, and they seldom even speak to each other.

PLAUSIBLE (PLAW zuh bul) *adj* believable; convincing

- "You're going to have to come up with a more *plausible* alibi," Doris told her drunken husband sternly after he told her he had been working late and then fell face forward into the living room.

- Irene's excuse is hardly *plausible*; how could a parakeet chew up someone's homework?

To be not *plausible* is to be *implausible*.

- The theory that tiny little men move the pictures around inside the television is interesting but *implausible*; for one thing, you never see anyone putting food in a TV.

To be *plausible* is to have plausibility. To be *implausible* is to have implausibility.

PLEBEIAN (pluh BEE un) *adj* common; vulgar; low-class
Plebeian is the opposite of *aristocratic*.

- Sarah refused to eat frozen dinners, saying they were too *plebeian* for her discriminating palate.

PLETHORA (PLETH ur uh) *n* an excess

- We ate a *plethora* of candy on Halloween and a *plethora* of turkey on Thanksgiving.

- Letting the air force use our backyard as a bombing range created a *plethora* of problems.

PLIABLE (PLY uh bul) *adj* flexible; easy to bend; easy to convince, persuade, or mold

- If you work the modeling clay until it is *pliable*, you will find that it is easier to mold into shapes.

- The tennis coach preferred working with very young children, because he found them to be more *pliable* than older players, who had often become set in their ways.

- Sharon was so *pliable* that she would instantly change her mind whenever anyone disagreed with her.

To be *pliable* is to have *pliability* (ply uh BIL i tee).
- William's heavy vinyl gloves lost their *pliability* in the cold weather, and he found it difficult to move his fingers.

PLIGHT (plyte) *n* a dangerous, distressing, or unpleasant situation
- Whenever the heroine finds herself in a seemingly hopeless *plight* in an old-fashioned movie—whether it's being tied to railroad tracks or hanging on to a cliff edge—it's pretty certain she'll be rescued soon.
- "What a *plight* you're in," Claudia observed as she watched her sister cowering in a corner surrounded by rabid dogs.
- Moved by the *plight* of the hostages, the rich man assembled an army of mercenaries to rescue them.

PLUNDER (PLUN dur) *v* to loot; to ransack
- Mrs. Ort told her son to stop *plundering* the refrigerator before he ate up all the food that she had prepared for her guests.
- The victorious soldiers *plundered* the town until there was nothing left to steal.

Plunder can also be a noun.
- The pirates' ship was loaded with *plunder*, all of which had been stolen from merchant vessels.

PLURALISM (PLOOR uh liz um) *n* a condition of society in which distinct groups exist and function together yet retain their own identities
- *Pluralism* is the only hope for American society; our country is made up of too many different kinds of people for a single culture to prevail.
- Anne's reading habits reflected a healthy *pluralism*; she read all the classics, but she also enjoyed murder mysteries and historical novels.

To be characterized by *pluralism* is to be *pluralistic* (ploor uh LIS tik).
- The members of a *pluralistic* society must accommodate themselves to a broad range of cultural peculiarities.

POIGNANT (POYN yunt) *adj* painfully emotional; extremely moving; sharp or astute
The words *poignant* and *pointed* are very closely related, and they share much of the same range of meaning.
A *poignant* scene is one that is so emotional or moving that it is almost painful to watch.
- All the reporters stopped taking notes as they watched the old woman's *poignant* reunion with her daughter, whom she hadn't seen in forty-five years.

Poignant can also mean pointed in the sense of sharp or astute. A *poignant* comment might be one that shows great insight. To be *poignant* is to have *poignancy*.

QUICK QUIZ #125

Match each word in the first column with its definition in the second column. Check your answers in the back of the book.

1.	phantasm	a.	fake medication
2.	phlegmatic	b.	nonsexual
3.	pilgrimage	c.	coexistence of distinct
4.	placebo		groups
5.	platonic	d.	religious journey
6.	plausible	e.	calm or indifferent
7.	pliable	f.	flexible
8.	plight	g.	believable
9.	plunder	h.	dangerous situation
10.	pluralism	i.	apparition
		j.	ransack

QUICK QUIZ #126

Match each word in the first column with its definition in the second column. Check your answers in the back of the book.

1.	pervade	a.	painfully emotional
2.	petulant	b.	spread throughout
3.	philanthropy	c.	pacify
4.	philistine	d.	smugly ignorant person
5.	pious	e.	excess
6.	pivotal	f.	expressing sadness
7.	placate	g.	reverent
8.	plaintive	h.	trite remark
9.	platitude	i.	rude
10.	plebeian	j.	crucial
11.	plethora	k.	love for mankind
12.	poignant	l.	low class

POLARIZE (POH luh ryze) *v* to break up into opposing factions or groupings

- The issue of what kind of sand to put in the sandbox *polarized* the nursery school class; some students would accept nothing but wet, while others wanted only dry.
- The increasingly acrimonious debate between the two candidates *polarized* the political party.

POLEMIC (puh LEM ik) *n* a powerful argument often made to attack or refute a controversial issue

- The book was a convincing *polemic* that revealed the fraud at the heart of the large corporation.
- Instead of the traditional Groundhog Day address, the state senator delivered a *polemic* against the sales tax.

A *polemic* is *polemical*.

PONDEROUS (PAHN dur us) *adj* so large as to be clumsy; massive; dull

- The wedding cake was a *ponderous* blob of icing and jelly beans.
- The chairman, as usual, gave a *ponderous* speech that left half his listeners snoring in their plates.

PONTIFICATE (pahn TIF uh kayt) *v* to speak pompously or dogmatically

- Whenever my next-door neighbor begins *pontificating* about zoning laws, I quietly tiptoe back inside; I am tired of being lectured by that pompous ass.
- Mr. Burgess doesn't so much speak as *pontificate*; he makes even "hello" sound like a proclamation from on high.

The act of *pontificating* is *pontification* (pahn tif uh KAY shun).

POROUS (PAWR us) *adj* filled with many tiny holes; permeable; absorbent

- You just can't build a *porous* boat and expect it to float.
- If my socks were not made of a *porous* material, my feet would be soaking wet with perspiration.
- They're advertising a paper towel so *porous* that one sheet can soak up a whole sinkful of water.

To be *porous* is to have *porousness* or *porosity* (paw RAHS uh tee).

- *Porosity* is not a desirable quality in an umbrella.

PORTENT (POR tent) *n* an omen; a sign of something coming in the future

- The distant rumbling we heard this morning was a *portent* of the thunderstorm that hit our area this afternoon.

- Stock market investors looked for *portents* in their complicated charts and graphs; they hoped that the market's past behavior would give them clues as to what would happen in the future.

Portentous (por TENT uhs) is the adjective form of *portent*, meaning ominous or filled with *portent*. But it is very often used to mean pompous, or self-consciously serious or ominous sounding. It can also mean amazing or prodigious.

A *portentous* speech is not one that you would enjoy listening to.

A *portentous* announcement might be one that tried to create an inappropriate sense of alarm in those listening to it.

Portentous can also mean amazing or astonishing. A *portentous* sunset might be a remarkably glorious one rather than an ominous or menacing one.

POSTERITY (pahs TER uh tee) *n* future generations; descendants; heirs
- Richard necessarily paints for *posterity*; nobody alive has any interest in his pictures.

- There's no point in protecting the world's oil reserves for posterity if we don't also leave *posterity* any air to breathe.

- Samantha is saving her diaries for *posterity*; she hopes that her daughters and granddaughters will enjoy them.

POSTHUMOUS (PAHS chuh mus) *adj* occurring after one's death; published after the death of the author
- The *posthumous* publication of Hemingway novels has become a minor literary industry, even though Hemingway clearly had good reasons for keeping the novels unpublished.

POSTULATE (PAHS chuh lut) *n* something accepted as true without proof; an axiom
A *postulate* is taken to be true because it is convenient to do so.
- We might be able to prove a *postulate* if we had the time, but not now. A theorem is something that is proven using *postulates*.

Postulate (PAHS chuh layt) can be used as a verb, too.
- Sherlock Holmes rarely *postulated* things, waiting for evidence before he made up his mind.

POSTURE (PAHS chur) *v* to act or speak artificially or affectedly
- Jessica is always *posturing* about the plight of farm workers, even though she has never set foot on a farm in her life.

- The creative writing workshop quickly disintegrated into an orgy of *posturing* by the self-important student poets, all of whom were trying to prove that they were tortured geniuses.

PRAGMATIC (prag MAT ik) *adj* practical; down-to-earth; based on experience rather than theory

A *pragmatic* person is one who deals with things as they are rather than as they might be or should be.

- Erecting a gigantic dome of gold over our house would have been the ideal solution to fix the leak in our roof, but the small size of our bank account forced us to be *pragmatic;* we patched the hole with a dab of tar instead.

Pragmatism (PRAG muh tiz um) is the belief or philosophy that the value or truth of something can be measured by its practical consequences.

PRATTLE (PRAT ul) *v* to chatter on and on; to babble childishly

- Billie Jean *prattles* ceaselessly about the only things that interest her: makeup, shopping, and her weight.

This word can also be a noun.

- A baby's *prattle* is utterly adorable unless you have to listen to it all day long.

PRECARIOUS (pri KAR ee us) *adj* dangerously insecure or unsteady

- The boulder was balanced in a *precarious* position over the lip of the cliff, and it threatened to fall at any moment onto the heads of the heedless skiers below.

- Juliet is earning a *precarious* living as a strolling knife-sharpener; her position would be considerably less *precarious* if more people were interested in having their knives sharpened by someone strolling down the street.

PRECEDENT (PRES uh dunt) *n* an earlier example or model of something

Precedent is a noun form of the verb to *precede,* or go before. To set a *precedent* is to do something that sets an example for what may follow.

- Last year's million-dollar prom set a *precedent* that the current student council hopes will not be followed in the future. That is, the student council hopes that future proms won't cost a million dollars.

To be *unprecedented* is to have no *precedent,* to be something entirely new.

- Urvashi's consumption of 500 hot dogs was *unprecedented;* no one had ever eaten so many hot dogs before.

PRECEPT (PREE sept) *n* a rule to live by; a principle establishing a certain kind of action or behavior; a maxim

- "Love thy neighbor" is a *precept* we have sometimes found difficult to follow; our neighbor is a noisy oaf who painted his house electric blue and who throws his empty beer cans into our yard.

PRECIPITATE (pri SIP uh tayt) *v* to cause to happen abruptly

- A panic among investors *precipitated* last Monday's crisis in the stock market.

- The police were afraid that arresting the angry protestors might *precipitate* a riot.

Precipitate (pri SIP uh tit) can also be an adjective, meaning unwisely hasty or rash. A *precipitate* decision is one made without enough thought beforehand.

- The guidance counselor, we thought, was *precipitate* when he had the tenth grader committed to a mental hospital for saying that homework was boring.

PRECIPITOUS (pri SIP uh tus) *adj* steep

Precipitous means like a precipice, or cliff. This word and *precipitate* are closely related, as you probably guessed. But they don't mean the same thing, even though *precipitous* is often used loosely to mean the same thing as *precipitate*.

A mountain can be *precipitous*, meaning either that it is steep or that it comprises lots of steep cliffs.

Precipitous can also be used to signify things that are only figuratively steep. For example, you could say that someone had stumbled down a *precipitous* slope into drug addiction.

QUICK QUIZ #127

Match each word in the first column with its definition in the second column. Check your answers in the back of the book.

1. polarize	a.	massive and clumsy
2. polemic	b.	rule to live by
3. ponderous	c.	practical
4. portent	d.	powerful refutation
5. portentous	e.	steep
6. postulate	f.	cause to happen abruptly
7. pragmatic	g.	cause opposing positions
8. precedent	h.	ominous
9. precept	i.	earlier example
10. precipitate	j.	omen
11. precipitous	k.	axiom

PRECLUDE (pri KLOOD) *v* to prevent something from ever happening
- Ann feared that her abysmal academic career might *preclude* her becoming a brain surgeon.

PRECOCIOUS (pri KOH shus) *adj* unusually mature; uncommonly gifted
- The *precocious* child could tie her shoes five minutes after she was born and tap dance before she was a month old.
- Beethoven's father was so proud of his son's *precocious* musical genius that he used to wake the boy up in the middle of the night and make him play the piano for guests.

To be *precocious* is to exhibit *precociousness* or *precocity* (pri KAHS uh tee).
- Mr. and Mrs. Sherman were alarmed by the *precocity* of their son; at age fourteen, he was busy planning for his retirement.

PRECURSOR (pri KUR sur) *n* forerunner; something that goes before and anticipates or paves the way for whatever it is that follows
- The arrival of a million-dollar check in the mail might be the *precursor* of a brand-new car.
- A sore throat is often the *precursor* of a cold.
- Hard work on the practice field might be the *precursor* of success on the playing field.

PREDECESSOR (PRED uh ses ur) *n* someone or something that precedes in time

- "My *predecessor* left this office rather messy," Mr. Griggs apologized as he led his associates past a pile of dusty boxes.

- His *predecessor* had been so beloved by the nation that the new president resigned himself to being viewed as inferior.

- The new model of the minivan is a wonderful vehicle, but its *predecessor* was riddled with engineering flaws.

Just as a *predecessor* comes before, a *successor* (suk SES ur) comes after.

- People who hadn't liked the old minivan were pleased by its *successor* because the manufacturer had eliminated most of the engineering flaws that had plagued the earlier vehicle.

PREDICAMENT (pri DIK uh munt) *n* a dangerous or unpleasant situation; a dilemma

- Lisa's kitten is always having to be rescued from one *predicament* or another; yesterday, she got stuck inside a hollow log, and the day before, Lisa closed her in the automatic garage door.

- "Now, let's see. How will I escape from this *predicament*?" asked Monty as he stared at the tiger charging toward him.

PREDILECTION (pred uh LEK shun) *n* a natural preference for something

- The impatient judge had a *predilection* for well-prepared lawyers who said what they meant and didn't waste his time.

- Joe's *predilection* for saturated fats has added roughly a foot to his waistline in the past twenty years.

PREDISPOSE (pree di SPOHZ) *v* to make susceptible; to put in a frame of mind for; to incline toward

- The fact that Selma grew up in the desert probably *predisposed* her to working with cactuses.

- Since the little boy was used to moving, he arrived in the new neighborhood already *predisposed* to make new friends.

To be *predisposed* is to have a *predisposition* (pree dis puh ZI shun).

- Mr. Bigelow had a strong *predisposition* against eating lunch, but when he saw the sumptuous banquet laid out in the conference room, he pushed his way to the head of the line and made a pig of himself.

PREDOMINANT (pri DAHM uh nunt) *adj* most important; dominant; having power over others

- The *predominant* quality of Luther's painting is its boring grayness; he calls it "Fog at Dusk."
- Miranda's speech ranged over many topics, but its *predominant* subject was the need for more vending machines in the student lounge.
- The admiral's audience was composed *predominantly* of penguins; there were a few polar bears here and there, but for the most part it was penguins, penguins, penguins.

To be *predominant* is to *predominate* (pri DAHM uh nayt).

- Deep discounts *predominated* the week before Christmas as retailers tried frantically to boost sales at the end of a disappointing holiday season.

QUICK QUIZ #128

Match each word in the first column with its definition in the second column. Check your answers in the back of the book.

1. pontificate
2. porous
3. posterity
4. posthumous
5. posture
6. prattle
7. precarious
8. precocious
9. predecessor
10. predicament

a. occurring after one's death
b. future generations
c. unusually mature
d. filled with many tiny holes
e. dangerously insecure
f. chatter on and on
g. speak pompously
h. dangerous situation
i. speak artificially
j. something that precedes in time

PREEMINENT (pree EM uh nunt) *adj* better than anyone else; outstanding; supreme

- The nation's *preeminent* harpsichordist would be the best harpsichordist in the nation.
- The Nobel Prize-winning physicist was *preeminent* in his field, but he was still a lousy teacher.

See our listing for *eminent*.

PREEMPT (pree EMPT) *v* to seize something by prior right
When television show A *preempts* television show B, television show A is shown at the time usually reserved for television show B. The word *preempt* implies that television show A is more important than television show B and thus has a greater right to the time slot.
A *preemptive* action is one that is undertaken in order to prevent some other action from being undertaken.

- When the air force launched a *preemptive* strike against the missile base, the air force was attacking the missiles in order to prevent the missiles from attacking the air force.

PREGNANT (PREG nunt) *adj* highly significant; overflowing
Biologically speaking, to be *pregnant* is to carry a developing fetus in one's uterus; outside of this precise usage, the word has a more general, figurative meaning.

- There was a *pregnant* pause in the room as the elves considered the alarming implications of Santa's announcement that from now on all toys would be bought from Toys "R" Us™.

- India's message to her boyfriend contained only one sentence, yet that one sentence was *pregnant* with meaning ("I am pregnant").

PRELUDE (PREL yood) *n* introduction; something that precedes something else

- As a *prelude* to her recital, Mrs. Oliver lectured for about an hour on some of the finer points of the composition she was about to sing.

- Stretching exercises should be a *prelude* to any long bout of exercise; stretching muscles before exerting them helps protect them from injury.

PREMEDITATED (pri MED i tayt ud) *adj* planned beforehand; prearranged; plotted
To *meditate* is to think long and hard about something. To *premeditate* is to think or plan something carefully before doing it. *Premeditated* murder is considered worse than just killing someone on the spur of the moment because deliberate violence is viewed as being more heinous than spontaneous fury.

- Tomas's seemingly fortuitous rise to the presidency had actually been carefully *premeditated*; for twenty years, he had been quietly sucking up to anyone in the company whom he felt could advance his career.

PREMISE (PREM is) *n* an assumption; the basis for a conclusion
- In deciding to eat all the ice cream in the freezer, my *premise* was that if I didn't do it, you would.
- Based on the *premise* that two wrongs don't make a right, I forgave him for insulting me rather than calling him a nasty name.

PREPONDERANCE (pri PAHN dur uns) *n* superiority in weight, number, size, extent, influence, etc.; majority; predominance
- Looking around the well-dressed crowd at the ball, Richard was surprised to notice a *preponderance* of women wearing baseball caps.
- The *preponderance* of onions in the stew made us suspect that our host had been trying to save money when he made it because onions were its least expensive ingredient.

PREPOSSESS (pree puh ZES) *v* to preoccupy; to influence beforehand or prejudice; to make a good impression on beforehand
This word has several common meanings. Be careful.
When a person is *prepossessed* by an idea, he or she can't get it out of his or her mind.
- My dream of producing energy from old chewing-gum wrappers *prepossessed* me, and I lost my job, my home, my wife, and my children.
- Experience had *prepossessed* Larry's mother not to believe him when he said that someone else had broken the window; Larry had broken it every other time, so she assumed that he had broken it this time.
- The new girl in the class was extremely *prepossessing*. The minute she walked into the room, her classmates rushed over to introduce themselves.

Unprepossessing means unimpressive, but the word is only mildly negative.
- The quaint farmhouse had an *unprepossessing* exterior, but a beautiful interior. Who would have imagined?

PREROGATIVE (pri RAHG uh tiv) *n* a right or privilege connected exclusively with a position, a person, a class, a nation, or some other group or classification
- Giving traffic tickets to people he didn't like was one of the *prerogatives* of Junior's job as a policeman.

- Sentencing people to death is a *prerogative* of many kings and queens.

- Big mansions and fancy cars are among the *prerogatives* of wealth.

PRESAGE (PRES ij) *v* to portend; to foreshadow; to forecast or predict
- Patty's sullen looks *presage* yet another family battle.

- They say a bad dress rehearsal *presages* a good performance, but I have found that often a bad dress rehearsal is followed by an equally bad show.

- The meteorologist's record at *presaging* the weather was not impressive; he was correct only about half the time.

PRESENTIMENT (pri ZEN tuh munt) *n* the feeling that something (especially something bad) is about to happen
- My *presentiment* that I was about to be fired turned out to be incorrect; my boss had asked to see me only because he wanted to tell me that he had given me a raise.

- "I knew the boat would sink," Aunt Louise said triumphantly. "I just had a *presentiment* about it when I saw that leaky bottom."

PRESUMABLY (pri ZOO muh blee) *adv* probably; the assumption is that; doubtless
- *Presumably* Elsie would have worn her glasses if she had known that her driver's test was today.

- The gardener said he would come a little early next week, *presumably* to rake up all the dead leaves before mowing.

PRESUPPOSE (pree suh POHZ) *v* to assume beforehand; to take for granted in advance; to require as a prior condition
- We mustn't *presuppose* that the new headmaster hates girls just because he's always been in charge of boys' schools before; after all that time spent living with boys, it may actually be boys whom he hates.

- A high score does not *presuppose* good play by either team; sometimes sloppy teams run up a big score through carelessness.

- Because his father is a famous actor, Phil often encounters the *presupposition* that he can act, too.

QUICK QUIZ #129

Match each word in the first column with its definition in the second column. Check your answers in the back of the book.

1.	predispose	a.	majority
2.	predominant	b.	portend
3.	pregnant	c.	most important
4.	prelude	d.	feeling that something is about to happen
5.	premeditated		
6.	preponderance	e.	introduction
7.	presage	f.	make susceptible
8.	presentiment	g.	planned beforehand
9.	presumably	h.	highly significant
10.	presuppose	i.	assume beforehand
		j.	probably

PREVAIL (pri VAYL) *v* to triumph; to overcome rivals; (with *on*, *upon*, or *with*) to persuade

When justice *prevails,* it means that good defeats evil.

- The prosecutor *prevailed* in the murder trial; the defendant was found guilty.

- My mother *prevailed* on me to make my bed. She told me she would punish me if I didn't, so I did.

The adjective *prevailing* means most frequent or predominant. The *prevailing* opinion on a topic is the one that most people hold. If the *prevailing* winds are out of the north, then the wind is out of the north most of the time. A *prevailing* theory is the one most widely held at the time. It is *prevalent* (PREV uh lunt).

PRIMAL (PRYE mul) *adj* first; original; of the greatest importance

- All of us can trace our ancestry back to one-celled creatures swimming about in a sort of *primal* soup of water, amino acids, gunk, and who knows what else.

- The throbbing music engendered a sort of *primal* excitement in the crowd, causing people to bang their chests and jump up and down on their seats.

- *Primal* among a puppy's needs is access to expensive shoes that it can chew.

PRISTINE (PRIS teen) *adj* original; unspoiled; pure

An antique in *pristine* condition is one that hasn't been tampered with over the years. It's still in its original condition.

A *pristine* mountain stream is a stream that hasn't been polluted.

PRIVATION (prye VAY shun) *n* lack of comforts or necessities; poverty

- Oh, come on, Karen! Not having an indoor swimming pool isn't exactly a *privation*, you know!

- In wartime, most people readily accustom themselves to a level of *privation* that they would never accept under ordinary circumstances.

- For Owen, the fact that he never had to make his bed more than made up for the numerous *privations* of life in a pup tent.

Deprivation (DEP ruh vay shun) is the state of being deprived of things, especially things important to one's well-being.

PROCLAIM (proh KLAYM) *v* to announce; declare; make known

- "I hereby *proclaim* that today is Hot Dog Day," announced the befuddled governor on the first day of Hot Dog Week.

- The blossoms on the cherry trees *proclaimed* spring from every branch.

Ordinary people don't usually *proclaim* things, unless they're trying to throw their weight around.

- The king *proclaimed* that taxes would be raised throughout the realm. Mr. Bendel reported the king's *proclamation* (prahk luh MAY shun) to his family.

PROCURE (pruh KYOOR) *v* to obtain or acquire by special means

- It took a lot of effort and know-how to *procure* Oreos™ at the health spa, but Stuart bribed the chief chef.

- Our efforts to *procure* a thousand cases of champagne in time for the party ended in failure; we were able to find only nine hundred.

- The bookstore manager said that the bestseller was sold out, and that additional copies were not *procurable* (pruh KYOOR uhb ul).

A *procurement* is something that has been procured.

- The practical joker seemed listless and depressed while he waited for the novelty company to ship his next *procurement* of exploding cigars.

PRODIGAL (PRAHD uh gul) *adj* wastefully extravagant
- The chef was *prodigal* with his employer's money, spending thousands of dollars on ingredients for what was supposed to be a simple meal.
- The young artist was *prodigal* with his talents: He wasted time and energy on greeting cards that might have been devoted to serious paintings.
- The *prodigal* gambler soon found that he couldn't afford even a two-dollar bet.

To be *prodigal* is to be characterized by *prodigality*.

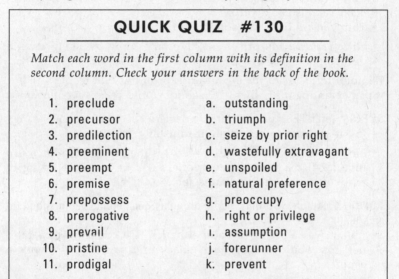

QUICK QUIZ #130

Match each word in the first column with its definition in the second column. Check your answers in the back of the book.

1. preclude
2. precursor
3. predilection
4. preeminent
5. preempt
6. premise
7. prepossess
8. prerogative
9. prevail
10. pristine
11. prodigal

a. outstanding
b. triumph
c. seize by prior right
d. wastefully extravagant
e. unspoiled
f. natural preference
g. preoccupy
h. right or privilege
i. assumption
j. forerunner
k. prevent

PRODIGIOUS (pruh DIJ us) *adj* extraordinary; enormous
- To fill the Grand Canyon with Ping-Pong™ balls would be a *prodigious* undertaking; it would be both extraordinary and enormous.
- The little boy caught a *prodigious* fish—it was ten times his size and might more easily have caught him had their situations been reversed.

See also *prodigy*.

PRODIGY (PRAHD uh jee) *n* an extremely talented child; an extraordinary accomplishment or occurrence
- The three-year-old *prodigy* could play all of Beethoven and most of Brahms on his harmonica.

- Barry was a mathematical *prodigy;* he had calculated *pi* to 100 decimal places almost before he could walk.

- Josephine's tower of dominoes and Popsicle™ sticks was a *prodigy* of engineering.

PROFANE (proh FAYN) *adj* not having to do with religion; irreverent; blasphemous
Profane is the opposite of sacred. Worshiping the almighty dollar is *profane.* *Profane* can also mean disrespectful of religion. Cursing in class would also be *profane.*
Sticking out your tongue in church would be a *profane* gesture.
Profane can also be a verb.

- You *profaned* the classroom by cursing in it.

- Nick *profaned* his priceless Egyptian statue by using it as a doorstop.

The noun form of *profane* is *profanity* (proh FAN uh tee).
Spray painting the hallways at school would be an act of *profanity.*

PROFESS (pruh FES) *v* to declare; to declare falsely or pretend
- Jason *professed* to have taught himself calculus.

- No one in our town was fooled by the candidate's *professed* love for llama farmers; everyone knew he was just trying to win votes from the pro-llama faction.

PROFICIENT (pruh FISH unt) *adj* thoroughly competent; skillful; good (at something)
- Lillian was a *proficient* cabinetmaker. She could make a cabinet that would make you sit back and say, "Now, there's a cabinet."

- I fiddled around at the piano for many years but never became *proficient* at playing.

- Lucy was merely competent, but Molly was *proficient* at plucking canaries.

Proficiency is the state of being *proficient.*

PROFLIGATE (PRAHF luh git) *adj* extravagantly wasteful and, usually, wildly immoral
- The fraternity members were a *profligate* bunch; they held all-night parties on weeknights and nearly burned down their fraternity house with their shenanigans every weekend.

- The young heir was *profligate* with his fortune, spending millions on champagne and racehorses.

PROFOUND (pruh FOUND) *adj* deep (in several senses)

Profound understanding is deep understanding.

To say something *profound* is to say something deeply intelligent or discerning.

Profound respect is deep respect. *Profound* horror is deep horror. The noun form of *profound* is *profundity* (pruh FUN duh tee).

PROFUSE (pruh FYOOS) *adj* flowing; extravagant

- When we gave Marian our house, our car, and all our clothes, her gratitude was *profuse.*

- My teacher said I had done a good job, but his praise was far from *profuse.* I got the feeling he hadn't really liked my epic poem about two dinosaurs who fall in love just before they become extinct.

- The grieving widow's tears were *profuse.* She had tears in *profusion.*

PROGENY (PRAHJ uh nee) *n* offspring; descendants

- Mr. March is rich in nothing but *progeny;* he says he'd rather have a million children than a million dollars.

- The first release of the word-processing software was balky and unreliable, but its *progeny* have been quite impressive.

- A single rabbit may be the *progenitor* (proh GEN uh tur) of hundreds of offspring in his lifetime.

PROLETARIAT (proh luh TER ee ut) *n* the industrial working class

The *proletariat* is the laboring class—blue-collar workers or people who roll up their shirtsleeves to do an honest day's work.

PROLIFERATE (proh LIF uh rayt) *v* to spread or grow rapidly

- Honey bees *proliferated* when we filled our yard with flowering plants.

- Coughs and colds *proliferate* when groups of children are cooped up together during the winter.

- The police didn't know what to make of the *proliferation* of counterfeit money in the north end of town.

PROLIFIC (proh LIF ik) *adj* abundantly productive; fruitful or fertile

A *prolific* writer is a writer who writes a lot of books. A *prolific* artist is an artist who paints a lot of pictures.

- The old man had been extraordinarily *prolific;* he had thirty children and more than one hundred grandchildren.

QUICK QUIZ #131

Match each word in the first column with its definition in the second column. Check your answers in the back of the book.

1.	prodigious	a.	declare
2.	prodigy	b.	irreverent
3.	profane	c.	abundantly productive
4.	profess	d.	flowing
5.	proficient	e.	extremely talented child
6.	profligate	f.	extraordinary
7.	profound	g.	spread rapidly
8.	profuse	h.	deep
9.	proletariat	i.	thoroughly competent
10.	proliferate	j.	extravagantly wasteful
11.	prolific	k.	industrial working class

PROMULGATE (PRAHM ul gayt) *v* to proclaim; to publicly or formally declare something
- The principal *promulgated* a new dress code over the loudspeaker system: Red, green, yellow, and blue were the only permissible artificial hair colors.

PROPAGATE (PRAHP uh gayt) *v* to reproduce; to multiply; to spread or disseminate
- It shocked the nation when Tom gave up his career in professional basketball and devoted his life to *propagating* tree fungi.
- The Cold Sun Society is dedicated to *propagating* the theory that the sun is a huge iceball, and its members wear winter coats all year long to protect them from icy blasts of sunlight.

The act of *propagating* is *propagation* (prahp uh GAY shun).
- Because there are so many endangered plants nowadays, many gardeners have become interested in the *propagation* of rare seeds to keep old strains from disappearing.

PROPENSITY (pruh PEN suh tee) *n* a natural inclination or tendency; a predilection
- Jessie has a *propensity* for saying stupid things: Every time she opens her mouth, something stupid comes out.
- Edwin's *propensity* to sit around all day doing nothing came into conflict with his mother's *propensity* to kick him out of the house.

PROPITIOUS (pruh PISH us) *adj* marked by favorable signs or conditions
- Rush hour is not a *propitious* time to drive into the city.

- The early negotiations between the union and the company had been so *propitious* that no one was surprised when a new contract was announced well before the strike deadline.

PROPONENT (pruh POH nunt) *n* an advocate; a supporter of a position
Proponent and *opponent* are antonyms.
- The *proponents* of a tax increase will probably not be re-elected next fall.

PROPRIETARY (pruh PRYE uh ter ee) *adj* characteristic of an owner of property; constituting property
To take a *proprietary* interest in something is to act as though you own it.
- George felt *proprietary* about the chocolate-cookie recipe; he had invented it himself.

- The company's design for musical toilet paper is *proprietary;* the company owns it, and outsiders can't look at it for nothing.

A *proprietor* (pruh PRYE uh tur) is an owner.

PROPOUND (pruh POWND) *v* to set forth or propose; to offer for consideration
Propound, propose, and *proposition* have the same root: a Latin word meaning to set forth.
- "This evening," began the scientist, "I plan to *propound* my hypothesis that trees grow because invisible giants pull them out of the ground."

PROPRIETY (pruh PRYE uh tee) *n* properness; good manners
- The old lady viewed the little girl's failure to curtsy as a flagrant breach of *propriety.* She did not approve of or countenance such *improprieties.*

- *Propriety* prevented the young man from trashing the town in celebration of his unexpected acceptance by the college of his choice.

Propriety derives from *proper,* not *property,* and should not be confused with *proprietary.*

PROSAIC (proh ZAY ik) *adj* dull; unimaginative; like prose (as opposed to poetry)
- His description of the battle was so *prosaic* that it was hard for his listeners to believe that any of the soldiers had even been wounded, much less blown to smithereens.

- The little boy's ambitions were all *prosaic:* He said he wanted to be an accountant, an auditor, or a claims adjuster.

PROSCRIBE (proh SKRYBE) *v* to outlaw; to prohibit
- Spitting on the sidewalk and shooting at road signs were both *proscribed* activities under the new administration.
- The young doctor *proscribed* smoking in the waiting room of his office.

The act of *proscribing* is *proscription;* an individual act of *proscribing* is also a *proscription.*

PROSELYTIZE (PRAHS uh luh tyze) *v* to convert (someone) from one religion or doctrine to another; to recruit converts to a religion or doctrine
- The former Methodist had been *proselytized* by a Lutheran deacon.
- The airport terminal was filled with *proselytizers* from a dozen different sects, cults, and religions. They were attempting to *proselytize* the passengers walking through the terminal.

PROTAGONIST (proh TAG uh nist) *n* the leading character in a novel, play, or other work; a leader or champion
- Martin Luther King, Jr., was a *protagonist* in the long and continuing struggle for racial equality.
- The *protagonist* of the movie was an eleven-year-old boy who saved his hometown from destruction by eating all the doughnuts that the mad scientist had been using to fuel his nuclear reactor.
- The mad scientist was the boy's chief *antagonist.* An *antagonist* is an opponent or adversary.

PROTÉGÉ (PROH tuh zhay) *n* a person under the care of someone interested in his welfare or career
- "I would like you to meet my *protégé,* Dirk Simpson," said Miss Charlton. "I am training him to manage my estate and will leave the bulk of my fortune to him when I pass away."
- Walter is always approaching important men in the company and asking them to be his mentor. But nowadays most executives don't have time for *protégés;* they're too busy looking after their own jobs.

In careful usage, a female *protégé* is a *protégée.*
- Under the watchful eye of her mentor, the *protégée* flourished and eventually became the second female executive in the company.

PROTOCOL (PROH tuh kawl) *n* diplomatic etiquette and customs
- When she was made ambassador to France, she spent months studying French *protocol* before she felt comfortable with her new role.
- It isn't exactly *protocol*, but diplomats' children can generally behave as badly as they want and not get punished for it.

QUICK QUIZ #132

Match each word in the first column with its definition in the second column. Check your answers in the back of the book.

1. primal		a.	reproduce
2. pristine		b.	set forth
3. privation		c.	original
4. proclaim		d.	person under the care of someone
5. procure		e.	lack of comforts
6. progeny		f.	announce
7. propagate		g.	diplomatic etiquette
8. propound		h.	perfectly clean and untouched
9. protégé		i.	offspring
10. protocol		j.	obtain by special means

PROTRACT (proh TRAKT) *v* to prolong
- The trial was so *protracted* that one of the jurors died of old age.
- The commencement speaker promised not to *protract* his remarks, but then he spoke for two solid hours. It was a *protracted* speech.

PROVIDENT (PRAHV uh dunt) *adj* preparing for the future; providing for the future; frugal
- We were *provident* with our limited food supplies, knowing that the winter ahead would be long and cold.
- The *provident* father had long ago set aside money for the college education of each of his children.

To be *improvident* is to fail to provide for the future.
- It was *improvident* of the grasshopper not to store any food for the winter, unlike his acquaintance the *provident* ant.

Match each word in the first column with its definition in the second column. Check your answers in the back of the book.

1. promulgate	a. natural inclination
2. propensity	b. good manners
3. propitious	c. advocate
4. proponent	d. prohibit
5. proprietary	e. prolong
6. propriety	f. leading character
7. prosaic	g. constituting property
8. proscribe	h. frugal
9. proselytize	i. dull
10. protagonist	j. marked by favorable signs
11. protract	k. convert
12. provident	l. proclaim

PROVINCIAL (pruh VIN shul) *adj* limited in outlook to one's own small corner of the world; narrow

- The farmers were *provincial;* they had no opinions about anything but the price of corn and no interest in anything except growing more of it.
- New Yorkers have reputations for being sophisticated and cosmopolitan, but most of them are actually *provincial;* they act as though nothing of interest had ever happened west of the Hudson River.

PROVISIONAL (pruh VIZH uh nul) *adj* conditional; temporary; tentative

- Louis had been accepted as a *provisional* member of the club. He wouldn't become a permanent member until the other members had had a chance to see what he was really like.
- The old man's offer to donate $10,000 to the charity was *provisional;* he said that he would give the money only if the charity could manage to raise a matching sum.

PROVOCATION (prahv uh KAY shun) *n* the act of provoking; incitement; cause

- That stupid dog starts barking at any *provocation,* including the sound of a window washer clearing his throat.

- The police arrested the young man without *provocation*; he had been doing nothing illegal.
- Despite the bully's *provocations*, Tony refused to be drawn into a fight.

To *provoke* (pruh VOHK) is to incite someone to anger.

PROWESS (PROW is) *n* exceptional skill or strength; uncommon bravery
- Annie is famous all across the country for her *prowess* on horseback; in fact, some people say she's one of the most talented trick riders in the world.
- Although he boasts of having great *prowess* in the kitchen, Dudley knows how to make nothing but toast.

PROXIMITY (prok SIM uh tee) *n* nearness
- I can't stand being in the *proximity* of a kid's birthday party. There is just too much noise.
- In a big city, one is almost always in the *proximity* of a restaurant.

PRUDENT (PROOD unt) *adj* careful; having foresight
- Joe is a *prudent* money manager. He doesn't invest heavily in racehorses, and he puts only a small part of his savings in the office football pool. Joe is the epitome of *prudence*.

The opposite of *prudent* is *imprudent*.
- It was *imprudent* of us to pour gasoline all over the floor of our living room and then light a fire in the fireplace.

PRURIENT (PROOR ee unt) *adj* having lustful thoughts or desires; causing lust
- Since Miss Goggins was afraid that art books with naked statues in them would appeal to teenagers' *prurient* interests, she had all the art books removed from the library shelves.

To be *prurient* is to exhibit *prurience* (PROOR ee uns).
- Gael's love of exotic foods almost amounted to *prurience*; she eats them with an eagerness that can only be described as lust.

PSEUDONYM (SOO duh nim) *n* a false name; an alias
- Dr. Seuss was the *pseudonym* of Theodor Seuss Geisel.
- The philandering couple used *pseudonyms* when they checked into the hotel for the afternoon because they didn't want anyone to know what they were up to.
- "I'm going to use a *pseudonym* so as not to attract people's attention when I go out in public," announced the famous actor. "I'll call myself Rumblebumble Wart."

The prefix *"pseudo"* (SOO doh) means false. A *pseudointellectual* is someone who pretends to be interested in intellectual things.

PSYCHE (SYE kee) *n* the human soul; the mind; the spirit
- While in medical school, Nancy noticed that she was far more interested in her patients' *psyches* than in their bodies, so she decided to become a psychiatrist.
- Mel has a fragile *psyche*; when anyone criticizes him, he pouts for days and refuses to eat.

PUMMEL (PUM ul) *v* to pound or punch with the fists
- Unable to think of a clever rejoinder to her brother's taunts, Tracy decided to *pummel* him.
- You often have to *pummel* bread dough in order to knead it correctly.
- The unprepared football team suffered an embarrassing *pummeling* in the opening round of the state tournament; they lost by a score of 58–0.

PUNCTILIOUS (pungk TIL ee us) *adj* meticulously attentive to detail; scrupulously exact
- Mr. Richards's secretary drives him crazy with her *punctilious* habit of going through his correspondence and correcting grammatical errors in the letters people send to him.
- The prosecutor's *punctilious* recitation of the case against the defendant left the jury no choice but to convict.
- The new architect was hardly *punctilious*; when he drew the plans for the new skyscraper, he forgot to put in any floors.

Punctilious is a more erudite way to say anal-retentive.

PUNDIT (PUN dit) *n* an expert; an authority; a learned person
- I can never decide what the most important issues of the day are, so I let the *pundits* who write the columns on the editorial page tell me.

PUNGENT (PUN junt) *adj* sharp-tasting or sharp-smelling; acrid; caustic
- Peter's parents are such bland eaters that every time they come to dinner he purposely serves them some incredibly *pungent* dish.
- The simmering soup gave off a *pungent* aroma that stung the nostrils of the cook.
- Rachel's wit is a little too *pungent* for me; there is a tinge of cruelty in the jokes she tells about her friends.

PUNITIVE (PYOO nuh tiv) *adj* inflicting a punishment
- Zoe's father was incredibly *punitive*; once, he grounded her for breathing too loudly.
- Claude designs clothes so tight that wearing them is almost *punitive*.
- Todd was ordered to pay a one-thousand-dollar fine plus three thousand dollars in *punitive* damages for having written insulting graffiti on the Purvises' garage door.

PURBLIND (PUR blynde) *adj* dim-sighted; practically blind; lacking understanding or imagination
- Surgery is not a job for the *purblind*; last week, the myopic Dr. Jones sewed his watch inside someone's abdomen.
- "I can no longer live with such a *purblind* woman," moaned the famous tenor. "She actually finds it embarrassing when I break into song in the middle of the street."

PURITANICAL (pyoor uh TAN i kul) *adj* severe and strict about morals
In the sixteenth and seventeenth centuries, the Puritans were a group of Protestants who viewed pleasure and luxury as sinful and adhered strictly to simple and severe religious beliefs. With a capital P, *Puritanical* means having to do with the Puritans; with a lower-case p, *puritanical* has a broader meaning, and it is almost never a compliment.
- Ursula's parents are quite *puritanical*; they won't let her talk to boys and won't let her stay out past seven-thirty without a chaperon.
- Molly was so anxious not to be thought *puritanical* that she told the Hell's Angels she would love to spend the week with them in Las Vegas.

PURPORTED (pur PORT id) *adj* rumored; claimed
- The heiress is *purported* to have been kidnapped by adventurers and buried in a concrete vault beneath the busiest intersection in Times Square. No one believes this story except the psychic who was consulted by the police.

To *purport* something is to claim or allege it.

PUTATIVE (PYOO tuh tiv) *adj* commonly accepted; supposed; reputed
- The *putative* reason for placing the monument downtown is that nobody had wanted it uptown.

When you use the word *putative,* you emphasize that the reason is only supposed, not proven.

QUICK QUIZ #134

Match each word in the first column with its definition in the second column. Check your answers in the back of the book.

1. provincial
2. provisional
3. proximity
4. prudent
5. purported
6. putative

a. commonly accepted
b. nearness
c. narrow in outlook
d. rumored
e. careful
f. conditional

QUICK QUIZ #135

Match each word in the first column with its definition in the second column. Check your answers in the back of the book.

1. provocation
2. prowess
3. prurient
4. pseudonym
5. psyche
6. pummel
7. punctilious
8. pundit
9. pungent
10. punitive
11. purblind
12. puritanical

a. false name
b. having lustful thoughts or desires
c. dim-sighted
d. incitement
e. very severe about morals
f. inflicting a punishment
g. exceptional skill or strength
h. pound with fists
i. learned person
j. meticulously attentive to detail
k. human soul or mind
l. sharp-tasting

Q

QUAINT (kwaynt) *adj* pleasantly old-fashioned; picturesque
- Janet had always longed to live in a *quaint* old cottage, so when she bought her split-level ranch house she glued moss and hollyhocks all over the outside.
- In this town people have the *quaint* custom of throwing their plates at the hostess when they've finished eating.

QUALIFY (KWAHL uh fye) *v* to modify or restrict
You already know the primary meaning of *qualify*. Here's another meaning.
- Susan *qualified* her praise of Judith by saying that her kind words applied only to Judith's skillful cooking and not to her abhorrent personality. Judith was upset by Susan's *qualification*.
- The library trustees rated their fund-raiser a *qualified* success; many more people than expected had come, but virtually no money had been raised.

An *unqualified* success is a complete, unrestricted success.

QUALITATIVE (KWAHL uh tay tiv) *adj* having to do with the *quality* or *qualities* of something (as opposed to the *quantity*)
If a school achieves a *qualitative* improvement in enrollment, it means the school is being attended by better students. If the school achieves a *quantitative* improvement, it means the school is being attended by more students.
- The difference between the two restaurants was *quantitative* rather than *qualitative*. Both served the same dreadful food, but the second restaurant served more of it.

QUANDARY (KWAHN dree) *n* state of perplexity; predicament; dilemma
- Joe is in a *quandary*; tomorrow he's scheduled to marry three different women in three different towns, and he can't decide whether to try to pull it off or move to another country.
- "You place me in a *quandary*," observed the professor to his pleading student. "If I don't give you an A, you'll be expelled—even though your work deserves no higher than a D-plus." Then the professor remembered that Candy almost never came to class and decided he wasn't in much of a quandary after all.

QUASI (KWAH zee) *adv* or (KWAY zye) *adj* almost; near; resembling
This word is always used in combination with other words.

- She managed to come up with a *quasi-plausible* excuse for being out all night, so the headmistress decided to give her one more chance.
- Claire makes all her own clothes; as a result, she always looks *quasi-fashionable* instead of truly stylish.
- Our invention was a *quasi-success*; it didn't do what we wanted it to do, but it also didn't blow up.

QUAY (kee) *n* a landing on the edge of the water; wharf; pier

- The party is being held on the *quay*; that means that at least five people will get pushed into the water at some point during the evening.
- The hurricane washed away every boat moored along the *quay*, but the boats that had been pulled onto dry land before the storm were undamaged.

QUELL (kwel) *v* to put an end to; to squelch; to suppress

- Only his girlfriend could *quell* Whit's wrath at not having been chosen for the varsity team.
- A mutiny arose when the cafeteria ran out of ice cream, but the food service manager *quelled* it by offering chocolate pudding instead.

QUERULOUS (KWER uh lus) *adj* complaining; grumbling; whining
Although a *query* is a question, *querulous* does not mean questioning.

- The exasperated mother finally managed to hush her *querulous* child.
- The *querulous* voices of the students, who believed that their quizzes had been graded too harshly, could be heard all the way at the other end of the school building.

QUERY (KWIR ee) *n* a question; an inquiry

- Please save any *queries* for the end of the lecture, or the professor will lose his train of thought and start singing the national anthem.
- The manuscript was so covered with *queries* from her editor that Nancy could see that she had a major revision ahead of time.

Query is a verb as well.

- "Do you really think the Earth is round?" Doug *queried* scornfully.

QUEUE (kyoo) *n* a line or file
- The British are famous for waiting patiently in long *queues*, while the Germans are notorious for pushing to the head of the line.

This word can also be a verb.
- People were so eager for tickets that they started to *queue* up the night before the box office opened.

QUIESCENT (kwee ES unt) *adj* motionless; at rest; still
- Clear your brain of all irrelevant thoughts; let your mind become *quiescent*. Then, and only then, will you truly be ready to learn why I should take over the world.

The noun is *quiescence*.
- Theodore was bubbling over with energy as a young man, but in old age he settled into a peaceful *quiescence* (kwee ES uns).

QUINTESSENTIAL (kwin tuh SEN chul) *adj* being the most perfect example of
- Lacey is the *quintessential* volunteer; she works twenty-three hours per day on different charitable causes.

The noun is *quintessence* (kwin TES uns). When you have reduced something to its most pure and concentrated form, you have captured its *quintessence*.

QUIXOTIC (kwik SAHT ik) *adj* romantic or idealistic to a foolish or impractical degree
The word *quixotic* is derived from the name of Don Quixote, the protagonist of Miguel de Cervantes's classic seventeenth-century novel. Don Quixote had read so many romances about the golden age of chivalry that he set out to become a knight himself and have chivalrous adventures. Instead, his romantic idealism almost invariably got him into trouble. To be *quixotic* is to be as foolish or impractical as Don Quixote in pursuing an ideal.
- For many years Mr. Morris had led a *quixotic* effort to repeal the federal income tax.
- The political organization had once been a powerful force in Washington, but its membership had dwindled, and its causes had become increasingly *quixotic*.

QUIZZICAL (KWIZ i kul) *adj* teasing; mocking; questioning; inquisitive
In archaic English, to quiz someone was to make fun of him or her. Our word *quizzical* often retains vestiges of this meaning.
- Josh gave Jennifer's waistline a *quizzical* glance as she reached for her third piece of pie.

Increasingly in modern usage, *quizzical* also means questioning or inquisitive.
- The policeman's *quizzical* expression hinted that perhaps I hadn't explained very well why I had to speed on the highway.

QUOTIDIAN (kwoh TID ee un) *adj* daily; everyday; ordinary
- Having an airplane crash in your backyard isn't exactly a *quotidian* event; in fact, for most people it isn't even a weekly one.
- Marvin's diary was dull to read; it was filled almost entirely with thoroughly *quotidian* observations about meals and the weather.

QUICK QUIZ   #136

Match each word in the first column with its definition in the second column. Check your answers in the back of the book.

1. qualify	a. having to do with quantity
2. qualitative	b. foolishly romantic
3. quantitative	c. complaining
4. querulous	d. modify or restrict
5. quixotic	e. having to do with quality

QUICK QUIZ   #137

Match each word in the first column with its definition in the second column. Check your answers in the back of the book.

1. quaint	a. pleasantly old-fashioned
2. quandary	b. question
3. quasi	c. motionless
4. quay	d. being the most perfect example of
5. quell	e. put an end to
6. query	f. a landing on the edge of the water
7. queue	g. teasing
8. quiescent	h. state of perplexity
9. quintessential	i. daily
10. quizzical	j. almost
11. quotidian	k. line

R

RAMIFICATION (ram uh fuh KAY shun) *n* a consequence; a branching out

A tree could be said to *ramify*, or branch out, as it grows. A *ramification* is a consequence that grows out of something in the same way that a tree branch grows out of a tree trunk.

- The professor found a solution to the problem, but there are many *ramifications;* some experts are afraid that he has created more problems than he has solved.

RAMPANT (RAM punt) *adj* widespread; uncontrollable; prevalent; raging

- A rumor the princess is expecting triplets is running *rampant* through the village; by noon, everyone in the county will have heard it.

- Crime was *rampant* in the high school building; every locker had been broken into.

- A *rampant* horde of squealing fans swarmed the rock star.

RANCOR (RANG kur) *n* bitter, long-lasting ill will or resentment

- The mutual *rancor* felt by the two nations eventually led to war.

- Jeremy's success produced such feelings of *rancor* in Jessica, his rival, that she was never able to tolerate being in the same room with him again.

To feel *rancor* is to be *rancorous*.

- The *rancorous* public exchanges between the two competing boxers are strictly for show; outside the ring, they are the best of friends.

RAPACIOUS (ruh PAY shus) *adj* greedy; plundering; avaricious

- Wall Street investment bankers are often accused of being *rapacious*, but they claim they are performing a valuable economic function.

The noun form is *rapacity* (ruh PAS uh tee).

RAPTURE (RAP chur) *n* ecstasy; bliss; unequaled joy

- Nothing could equal the Americans' *rapture* on spotting a Burger King™ in Calcutta; they had been terrified that they were going to have to eat unfamiliar food.

- Winning an Oscar sent Dustin into a state of *rapture*. "I can't believe this is happening to me!" he exclaimed.

To be full of *rapture* is to be *rapturous* (RAP chur us).

- Omar doesn't go in for *rapturous* expressions of affection; a firm handshake and a quick punch on the shoulder is enough for him.

Rapt is an adjective meaning entranced or ecstatic.

- The children listened with *rapt* attention to the storyteller; they didn't notice the pony standing in the hallway behind them.

To be *enraptured* (en RAP churd) is to be enthralled or in a state of *rapture*.

- *Enraptured* by Danielle Steele's thrilling prose style, Frank continued reading until the library was ready to close.

RAREFIED (RAR uh fyde) *adj* esoteric; interesting to a select group only; exalted; thin

- Wendell's musical compositions are so *rarefied* that only a few people can really appreciate them.

- Your book is too *rarefied* to reach a mass audience; why don't you take out the Old French epics and throw in a few car chases or something?

- The atmosphere atop Mount Everest was so *rarefied* that the climber could hardly breathe.

The verb is *rarefy* (RAR uh fye). Note carefully the pronunciation of these words.

RATIFY (RAT uh fye) *v* to confirm; to approve something formally

- If the latest version of the disarmament treaty isn't *ratified* soon, we must prepare for the possibility of war.

- The powerless legislature had no choice but to *ratify* the edicts of the dictator.

- According to the rules of P.S. 49, the student council president cannot take office until the entire student body has *ratified* his election. That is why P.S. 49 has never had a student council president.

The noun is *ratification*.
For a synonym, see our first definition of sanction.

RATIOCINATION (rash ee oh suh NAY shun) *n* logical reasoning

- Winning the love of Wilma was clearly not a problem that could be solved by *ratiocination* alone; Fred decided to turn off his computer and ask her out.

The verb is *ratiocinate* (rash ee OHS uh nayt). Note carefully the pronunciation of these words.

RATIONALE (rash uh NAL) *n* underlying reason; basis; reasoning
- "My *rationale* is simple," the doctor explained as he rummaged around in his drawer for a larger spoon. "If one dose of medicine is good, fifty doses must be better."
- Alice's *rationale* for buying a new coat was sound; her old coat had a broken zipper.

To *rationalize* (RASH uh nuh lyze) is to give a reason, but more in the sense of offering an excuse.

RAUCOUS (RAW kus) *adj* stridently loud; harsh; rowdy
- Crows are my least favorite bird in the early morning; their *raucous* cawing wakes me, and I can't get back to sleep.
- "If you don't stop that *raucous* behavior, I'll—I'll put you in the corner!" said the new teacher in a quavering voice as the students got increasingly rowdy.
- Jed laughed *raucously* when his sister toppled off her chair.

REACTIONARY (ree AK shuh ner ee) *adj* ultraconservative; right-wing; backward-thinking
- Grandpa Gus is so *reactionary* that he doesn't think women should be allowed to vote.
- There's no point in proposing a welfare bill as long as this *reactionary* administration remains in power.

This word can also be a noun.
- I am a *reactionary* on the subject of candy; I believe that the old, established kinds are the best.

REBUFF (ri BUF) *v* to snub; to reject
- Ashley has been trying to tame the squirrels in her yard, but so far they've *rebuffed* her efforts; she hasn't even been able to get them to eat the food she leaves for them on her porch.
- Don't be surprised if Willie *rebuffs* your advances; if you want him to kiss you, you're just going to have to invest in some false teeth.

This word can also be a noun.
- I invited my parents to the Metallica concert, but I was met with a horrified *rebuff*; in fact, my parents said they would rather die than go.

REBUKE (ri BYOOK) *v* to criticize sharply

- We trembled as Mr. Solomon *rebuked* us for flipping over his car and taking off the tires.

A piece of sharp criticism is called a *rebuke*.

- When the students got caught cheating on their French test, the principal delivered a *rebuke* that made their ears twirl.

REBUT (ri BUT) *v* to contradict; to argue in opposition to; to prove to be false

- They all thought I was crazy, but none of them could *rebut* my argument.
- The defense attorney attempted to *rebut* the prosecutor's claim that the defendant's fingerprints, hair, clothing, signature, wallet, wristwatch, credit cards, and car had been found at the scene of the crime.

An act or instance of *rebutting* is called a *rebuttal*. *Rebut* and *refute* are synonyms.

RECALCITRANT (ri KAL suh trunt) *adj* stubbornly defiant of authority or control; disobedient

- The *recalcitrant* cancer continued to spread through the patient's body despite every therapy and treatment the doctors tried.
- The country was in turmoil, but the *recalcitrant* dictator refused even to listen to the pleas of the international representatives.

RECANT (ri KANT) *v* to publicly take back and deny (something previously said or believed); to openly confess error

- The chagrined scientist *recanted* his theory that mice originated on the moon; it turned out that he had simply mixed up the results of two separate experiments.
- The secret police tortured the intellectual for a week, by tickling his feet with a feather duster, until he finally *recanted*.

An act of *recanting* is called a *recantation*.

RECIDIVISM (ri SID uh viz um) *n* the act of repeating an offense

- There's not much evidence that imprisoning people reforms them; the rate of *recidivism* among released convicts is high.

A person who repeats an offense is a *recidivist* (ri SID uh vist).

- "My son is quite a *recidivist*," Mrs. Korman told her friends ruefully. "Every time I turn my back, he sneaks up to watch more TV."

QUICK QUIZ #138

Match each word in the first column with its definition in the second column. Check your answers in the back of the book.

1.	rampant	a.	confirm
2.	rapture	b.	logical reasoning
3.	rarefied	c.	ecstasy
4.	ratify	d.	ultraconservative
5.	ratiocination	e.	widespread
6.	rationale	f.	stridently loud
7.	raucous	g.	esoteric
8.	reactionary	h.	underlying reason
9.	rebuff	i.	snub
10.	recidivism	j.	act of repeating an offense

RECIPROCAL (ri SIP ruh kul) *adj* mutual; shared; interchangeable
- The Rochester Club had a *reciprocal* arrangement with the Duluth Club. Members of either club had full privileges of membership at the other.
- Their hatred was *reciprocal*; they hated each other.

To *reciprocate* is to return in kind, to interchange, or to repay.
- Our new neighbors had had us over for dinner several times, but we were unable to *reciprocate* immediately because our dining room was being remodeled.

Reciprocity (res uh PRAHS uh tee) is a *reciprocal* relation between two parties, often whereby both parties gain.

RECLAIM (ri KLAYM) *v* to make uncultivated areas of land fit for cultivation; to recover usable substances from refuse; to claim again; to demand the restoration of
- A century ago, turning a swamp into cropland was called *reclaiming* it; now it is called destroying wetlands.
- At the recycling facility, massive electromagnets are used to *reclaim* steel and iron from scrap metal.
- Anthony was able to *reclaim* his briefcase from the lost-and-found after accurately describing its contents to the clerk.

This word can also be pronounced "ree KLAYM." The noun is *reclamation* (rek luh MAY shun).

RECLUSIVE (ri KLOOS iv) *adj* hermitlike; withdrawn from society
- The crazy millionaire led a *reclusive* existence, shutting himself up in his labyrinthine mansion and never setting foot in the outside world.

- Our new neighbors were so *reclusive* that we didn't even meet them until a full year after they had moved in.

A *reclusive* person is a *recluse*.
- After his wife's death, the grieving old man turned into a *recluse* and seldom ventured out of his house.

Emily Dickinson, one of America's most creative poets, became a *recluse* (REK loos) after her father's death in 1874—she kept in contact with friends and family through cards and letters.

RECONDITE (REK un dyte) *adj* hard to understand; over one's head
- The philosopher's thesis was so *recondite* that I couldn't get past the first two sentences.

- Every now and then the professor would lift his head from his desk and deliver some *recondite* pronouncement that left us scratching our heads and trying to figure out what he meant.

- The scholarly journal was so *recondite* as to be utterly incomprehensible.

QUICK QUIZ #139

Match each word in the first column with its definition in the second column. Check your answers in the back of the book.

1.	ramification	a.	hard to understand
2.	rancor	b.	criticize sharply
3.	rapacious	c.	consequence
4.	rebuke	d.	mutual
5.	rebut	e.	hermitlike
6.	recalcitrant	f.	bitter resentment
7.	recant	g.	stubbornly defiant
8.	reciprocal	h.	publicly deny
9.	reclusive	i.	contradict
10.	recondite	j.	greedy

RECRIMINATION (ri krim uh NAY shun) *n* a bitter counteraccusation, or the act of making a bitter counteraccusation

- Melissa was full of *recrimination*. When I accused her of stealing my pen, she angrily accused me of being careless, evil, and stupid.

The word is often used in the plural.

- The courtroom echoed with the *recriminations* of the convicted defendant as he was taken off to the penitentiary.

To make a *recrimination* is to *recriminate*. The adjective is *recriminatory* (ruh KRIM uh nuh tor ee).

REDEEM (ri DEEM) *v* to buy back; to fulfill; to make up for; to rescue from sin

- When I heard that my husband had pawned my mink coat in order to buy me a birthday present, I went straight to the pawnshop and *redeemed* it with the money I had been going to spend on a birthday present for him.
- The troubled company *redeemed* its employees' shares for fifty cents on the dollar.
- I won't marry you until you *redeem* your promise to build a roof over our heads.
- Barbara will never *redeem* herself in her boss's eyes until she returns every single paper clip she "borrowed."
- Reverend Coe is obsessed with *redeeming* the souls of the people who play cards. His favorite tactic is crashing a bridge party and asking, "Who will bid for the redemption (ri DEMP shun) of your souls?"

Someone who is so evil that they cannot be rescued from sin or wrong-doing is *irredeemable* (ir uh DEEM uh bul).

REDOLENT (RED uh lunt) *adj* fragrant

- The air in autumn is *redolent* of wood smoke and fallen leaves.
- The flower arrangements on the tables were both beautiful and *redolent*.

Something that is *redolent* has *redolence*. *Redolent* also means suggestive.

- The new play was *redolent* of one I had seen many years ago.

REDRESS (ri DRES) *v* to remedy; to make amends for

- The head of the environmental group explained that by suing the chemical factory for violating clean air laws, he was using the courts to *redress* a civil wrong.

Redress, pronounced "REE dres," is a noun meaning *reparation,* compensation, or making amends for a wrong.

- "Of course, there is no *redress* for what you've suffered," the lawyer told his client, who was wearing a neck brace and pretending to limp. "Still, I think we should ask for seven and a half million dollars and see what happens."

REDUNDANT (ri DUN dunt) *adj* unnecessarily repetitive; excessive; excessively wordy

- Eric had already bought paper plates, so our purchase of paper plates was *redundant.*
- Shawn's article was *redundant*—he kept saying the same thing over and over again.

An act of being *redundant* is a *redundancy.* The title "Department of *Redundancy* Department" is *redundant.*

REFERENDUM (ref uh REN dum) *n* a public vote on a measure proposed or passed by a legislature

- At the last minute, the state legislators snuck a large pay raise for themselves into the appropriations bill, but voters got wind of the scheme and demanded a *referendum.*

Referendum and refer are closely related. In a *referendum,* a bill from the legislature is referred to the electorate for approval.

REFUTE (ri FYOOT) *v* to prove to be false; to disprove

- His expensive suit and imported shoes clearly *refuted* his claim that he was poor.
- I *refuted* Billy's mathematical proof by showing him that it depended on two and two adding up to five.

An act of *refuting* is called a *refutation.*

- The audience enjoyed the panelist's humorous *refutation* of the main speaker's theory about the possibility of building an antigravity airplane.

Something that is indubitable, something that cannot be disproven, is *irrefutable.*

- Claudia's experiments with jelly beans and pencil erasers offered *irrefutable* proof that jelly beans taste better than pencil erasers.

REFRACTORY (ri FRAK tuh ree) *adj* disobedient and hard to manage; resisting treatment

- Bobby is such a *refractory* little boy when it comes to haircuts that he has to be tied up and hoisted into the barber's chair.
- The old man viewed all children as drooling, complaining, *refractory* little monsters.

SAT POWER VOCAB

- The doctors prescribed ten antibiotics before finding one that worked on Helen's *refractory* infection.

REGIME (ri ZHEEM) *n* a governing power; a system of government; a period during which a government is in power
- According to rules issued by the new *regime*, anyone caught wearing red shoes will be arrested and thrown into the penitentiary.
- The older reporters spent much of their time reminiscing bitterly about how much better things had been during the previous *regime*, when the newspaper had been owned by a private family instead of a corporate conglomerate.

REGIMEN (REJ uh mun) *n* a regulated course
- Mrs. Stewart is having trouble following the new *regimen* her doctor gave her; she can handle the dieting and exercise, but sleeping on a bed of nails is hard for her.
- It takes most new students a long time to get used to the *regimen* at boarding school; that is why this headmaster doesn't allow children to write letters home until the beginning of the second semester.

REITERATE (ree IT uh rayt) *v* to say again; to repeat
- The candidate had *reiterated* his position so many times on the campaign trail that he sometimes even muttered it in his sleep.
- To *reiterate*, let me say once again that I am happy to have been invited to the birthday celebration of your adorable Pekingese.

An act of *reiterating* is called a *reiteration*.

RELEGATE (REL uh gayt) *v* to banish; to send away
- The most junior of the junior executives was *relegated* to a tiny, windowless office that had once been a broom closet.
- The new dad's large collection of jazz records was *relegated* to the cellar to make room for the new baby's larger collection of stuffed animals. The father objected to the *relegation* of his record collection to the cellar, but his objection did no good.

RELENTLESS (ri LENT lis) *adj* continuous; unstoppable
To *relent* is to stop or give up. *Relentless*, or *unrelenting*, means not stopping.
- The insatiable rabbit was *relentless*; it ate and ate until nothing was left in the botanical garden.
- The torrential rains were *relentless*, eventually creating a deluge.

RELINQUISH (ri LING kwish) *v* to release or let go of; to surrender; to stop doing
- The hungry dog refused to *relinquish* the enormous beef bone that he had stolen from the butcher's shop.
- The retiring president *relinquished* control of the company only with the greatest reluctance.
- Sandra was eighty-five years old before she finally *relinquished* her view of herself as a glamorous teenaged beauty.

REMISSION (ri MISH un) *n* the temporary or permanent disappearance of a disease; pardon
- Isabel's cancer has been in *remission* for several years now— long enough for most people to have trouble remembering the dark period when she was gravely ill.
- The appeals court granted Ronnie a partial *remission* of his crimes; it threw out two of his convictions, but it upheld the third.

One of the meanings of *remit* is to send back or pay; a *remission*, then, can also mean payment.
- When companies ask for prompt *remissions* of their bills, I just laugh and put the bills away in a drawer.

REMONSTRATE (ri MAHN strayt) *v* to argue against; to protest; to raise objections
- My boss *remonstrated* with me for telling all the secretaries they could take off the rest of the week.
- The manager *remonstrated,* but the umpire continued to insist that the base runner had been out at third. When the manager continued to *remonstrate,* the umpire threw him out of the game.

An act of *remonstrating* is a *remonstration.*

REMUNERATION (ri myoo nuh RAY shun) *n* payment; recompense
- "You mean you expect *remuneration* for working here?" the magazine editor asked incredulously when the young college graduate inquired as to what sort of salary she might expect to earn as an editorial assistant.
- There is a strong positive correlation between people's satisfaction with their jobs and their level of *remuneration;* the more they're paid, the better they like their work.
- The firefighter viewed the child's hug as more than adequate *remuneration* for crawling through the burning building to save her.

Remuneration may be one way to redress a crime.

RENAISSANCE (REN uh sahns) *n* a rebirth or revival

The capitalized R *Renaissance* was a great blossoming of art, literature, science, and culture in general that transformed Europe between the fourteenth and seventeenth centuries. The word is also used in connection with lesser rebirths.

- The declining neighborhood underwent a *renaissance* when a group of investors bought several crumbling tenements and turned them into attractive apartment buildings.

- The small college's football team had endured many losing seasons but underwent a dramatic *renaissance* when the new coach recruited half-a-dozen 400-pound freshmen.

Renaissance can also be spelled *renascence* (ri NAY suns).

REND (rend) *v* to tear; to rip

A *heart-rending* story is one that is so terribly sad that it tears a reader's heart in two.

- I realize you're upset about not being invited to the dance, but *rending* your clothing and tearing out your hair is getting a little too emotional, don't you think?

Something ripped or torn can be described as *rent* (rent).

RENDER (REN dur) *v* to make; to cause to be; to provide; to depict

- Steve's funny faces *rendered* his sister incoherent with laughter.

- "We can *render* some form of financial assistance, if that is what you desire," the official suggested delicately.

- Sitting all night on the bottom of the pond had *rendered* the car useless for almost anything except continuing to sit on the bottom of the pond.

- Benson decided to *render* his mother in oil after determining that watercolor wasn't a substantial enough medium for the portrait of such a sourpuss. Benson's mother was not pleased with his rendering.

RENOUNCE (ri NOWNSE) *v* to give up formally or resign; to disown; to have nothing to do with anymore

- Despite the pleadings and protestations of her parents, Deborah refused to *renounce* her love for the leader of the motorcycle gang.

- The presidential candidate *renounced* his manager after it was revealed that the zealous manager had tried to murder the candidate's opponent in the primary.

To *renounce* is to make a *renunciation* (ri nun see AY shun).

QUICK QUIZ #140

Match each word in the first column with its definition in the second column. Check your answers in the back of the book.

1.	reclaim	a.	remedy
2.	redeem	b.	disobedient
3.	redress	c.	public vote
4.	referendum	d.	make fit for cultivation
5.	refractory	e.	disappearance of a disease
6.	regime	f.	regulated course
7.	regimen	g.	payment
8.	remission	h.	buy back
9.	remuneration	i.	rip
10.	rend	j.	governing power

QUICK QUIZ #141

Match each word in the first column with its definition in the second column. Check your answers in the back of the book.

1.	recrimination	a.	surrender
2.	redolent	b.	disown
3.	redundant	c.	rebirth
4.	refute	d.	argue against
5.	reiterate	e.	fragrant
6.	relegate	f.	banish
7.	relinquish	g.	say again
8.	remonstrate	h.	bitter counteraccusation
9.	renaissance	i.	unnecessarily repetitive
10.	renounce	j.	prove to be false

REPARATION (rep uh RAY shun) *n* paying back; making amends; compensation

To make a *reparation* is to *repair* some damage that has occurred. This word is often used in the plural.

- The defeated country demanded *reparations* for the destruction it had suffered at the hands of the victorious army.

- After the accident we sought *reparation* in court, but our lawyer was not competent so we didn't win a cent.

Something that cannot be *repaired* is *irreparable* (i REP uh ruh bul).

REPARTEE (rep ur TEE) *n* a quick, witty reply; witty, spirited conversation full of quick, witty replies
- "Toilethead" is four-year-old Max's preferred *repartee* to almost any question.
- When Annette first came to college, she despaired of ever being able to keep up with the *repartee* of the clever upperclassmen, but eventually she, too, got the hang of being insufferable.

REPERCUSSION (ree pur KUSH un) *n* a consequence; an indirect effect
- One *repercussion* of the new tax law was that accountants found themselves with a lot of new business.
- The declaration of war had many *repercussions,* including a big increase in production at the bomb factory.

REPLENISH (ri PLEN ish) *v* to fill again; to resupply; to restore
- The manager of the hardware store needed to *replenish* his stock; quite a few of the shelves were empty.
- The commanding general *replenished* his army with a trainload of food and other supplies.
- After the big Thanksgiving meal, everyone felt *replenished.*

An act of *replenishing* is a *replenishment.*
- The *replenishment* of our firewood supply was our first thought after the big snowstorm.

REPLETE (ri PLEET) *adj* completely filled; abounding
- The once-polluted stream was now *replete* with fish of every description.
- The bride wore a magnificent sombrero *replete* with fuzzy dice and campaign buttons.
- Tim ate all nine courses at the wedding banquet. He was filled to the point of *repletion.*

REPLICATE (REP li kayt) *v* to reproduce exactly; to duplicate; to repeat
When you *replicate* something, you produce a perfect *replica* (REP-li kuh) of it.
- Other scientists were unable to *replicate* Harold's startling experimental results, and in short order Harold was exposed as a fraud.

- At his weekend house in the country, Arthur tried to *replicate* the cozy English cottage in which he had been raised; his first step was to replace the asphalt shingles with thatch.
- Some simple organisms *replicate* by splitting themselves in two.

REPOSE (ri POHZ) *n* rest; tranquillity; relaxation
- As Carol struggled to pack the enormous crates, her husband lolled back on the sofa in an attitude of *repose*; as a matter of fact, he was sound asleep.
- "Something attempted, something done, has earned a night's *repose*" is a favorite saying of Ruby's grandmother; it means she's tired and wants to go to bed.

REPREHENSIBLE (rep ri HEN suh bul) *adj* worthy of severe blame or censure
- He put the cat in the laundry chute, tied the dog to the chimney, and committed several other *reprehensible* acts.
- Malcolm's manners were *reprehensible:* He ate his soup by drinking it from his empty wineglass and flipped his peas into his mouth with the back of his salad fork.

REPRESS (ri PRES) *v* to hold back; to conceal from oneself; to suppress
- Stella could not *repress* her feeling of horror at the sight of her neighbor's wallpaper.
- The government's crude attempt to *repress* the rebellion in the countryside only made it easier for the rebels to attract new recruits.
- *Repressing* painful memories is often psychologically harmful; the painful memories tend to pop up again when one is least prepared to deal with them.

The act of *repressing* is *repression*.

REPRIMAND (REP ruh mand) *n* stern reproof; official rebuke
- David was relieved to see that the officer intended to give him a verbal *reprimand* instead of a speeding ticket.
- Otto received his father's *reprimand* in stony silence because he did not want to give that mean old man the satisfaction of seeing his son cry.

This word can also be a verb.
- Ned's governess threatened to *reprimand* him and his friends if they continued to throw water balloons at the neighbor's house.

REPRISAL (ri PRYE zul) *n* a military action undertaken in revenge for another; an act of taking "an eye for an eye"
- The raid on the Iranian oil-drilling platform was a *reprisal* for the Iranians' earlier attack on the American tanker.
- Fearing *reprisals,* the CIA beefed up its security after capturing the insurgent leader.

REPROACH (ri PROHCH) *v* to scold, usually in disappointment; to blame; to disgrace
- The police officer *reproached* me for leaving my car parked overnight in a no-standing zone.

Reproach can also be a noun. To look at someone with *reproach* is to look at that person critically or accusingly. To be filled with *self-reproach* can mean to be ashamed.

Impeccable behavior that's beyond fault is *irreproachable.*
- Even though Jerome did hit Mabel on the head, his motive was *irreproachable:* He had merely been trying to kill a fly perched on her hairnet.

REPROBATE (REP ruh bayt) *n* a depraved, wicked person; a degenerate
- My Uncle Bob was a well-known old *reprobate*; he spent most of his time lying drunk in the gutter and shouting obscenities at women and children passing by.
- Everyone deplored the *reprobate's* behavior while he was alive, but now that he's dead everyone wants to read his memoirs.

REPROVE (ri PROOV) *v* to criticize mildly
- Aunt May *reproved* us for eating too much, but we could tell she was actually thrilled that we had enjoyed the meal.
- My friend *reproved* me for leaving my dirty dish in the sink.

An act of *reproving* is called a *reproof.*
- The judge's decision was less a sentence than a gentle *reproof;* he put Jerry on probation and told him never to get in trouble again.

REPUDIATE (ri PYOO dee ayt) *v* to reject; to renounce; to disown; to have nothing to do with
- Hoping to receive a lighter sentence, the convicted gangster *repudiated* his former connection with the mob.

REPUGNANT (ri PUG nunt) *adj* repulsive; offensive; disgusting
- The thought of striking out on his own is absolutely *repugnant* to Allan; he would much prefer to continue living in his old room, driving his parents' car, and eating meals prepared by his mother.

- Even the tiniest lapse in etiquette was *repugnant* to Mrs. Mason; when little Angela picked her nose and wiped it on the tablecloth, Mrs. Mason nearly burst her girdle.
- Kelly's roommate, a classical music major, found Kelly's love of hip-hop totally *repugnant*.

REQUISITE (REK wuh zit) *adj* required; necessary
- Howard bought a hunting rifle and the *requisite* ammunition.
- As the *requisite* number of members was not in attendance, the chairman adjourned the meeting just after it had begun.

Requisite can also be a noun, meaning a requirement or a necessity. A hammer and a saw are among the *requisites* of the carpenter's trade.

A *prerequisite* is something required before you can get started. A high school diploma is usually a *prerequisite* to entering college.

RESIGNATION (rez ig NAY shun) *n* passive submission; acquiescence
- No one had expected that Warren would take being kicked off the team with so much *resignation*; he simply hung up his uniform and walked sadly out of the locker room.
- There was *resignation* in Alex's voice when he announced at long last that there was nothing more that he could do.

To exhibit *resignation* is to be *resigned* (ri ZYNDE). Note carefully this particular meaning of the word.
- After collecting several hundred rejection slips, Darla finally *resigned* herself to the fact that her novel would never be published.

RESOLUTE (REZ uh loot) *adj* determined; firm; unwavering
- Uncle Ted was *resolute* in his decision not to have a good time at our Christmas party; he stood alone in the corner and muttered to himself all night long.
- The other team was strong, but our players were *resolute*. They kept pushing and shoving until, in the final moments, they won the roller-derby tournament.

Someone who sticks to his New Year's *resolution* is *resolute*. *Resolute* and *resolved* are synonyms.

To be *irresolute* is to be wavering or indecisive.
- Our *irresolute* leader led us first one way and then the other way in the process of getting us thoroughly and completely lost.

QUICK QUIZ #142

Match each word in the first column with its definition in the second column. Check your answers in the back of the book.

1.	render	a.	stern reproof
2.	repartee	b.	reproduce exactly
3.	replicate	c.	quick, witty reply
4.	repose	d.	depraved, wicked person
5.	repress	e.	retaliation
6.	reprimand	f.	cause to be
7.	reprisal	g.	repulsive
8.	reprobate	h.	hold back
9.	repugnant	i.	passive submission
10.	resignation	j.	tranquillity

QUICK QUIZ #143

Match each word in the first column with its definition in the second column. Check your answers in the back of the book.

1.	reparation	a.	act of revenge
2.	repercussion	b.	determined
3.	replenish	c.	worthy of blame
4.	replete	d.	consequence
5.	reprehensible	e.	scold
6.	reprisal	f.	completely filled
7.	reproach	g.	paying back
8.	reprove	h.	necessary
9.	repudiate	i.	criticize mildly
10.	requisite	j.	fill again
11.	resolute	k.	reject

RESPITE (RES pit) *n* a period of rest or relief
- We worked without *respite* from five in the morning until five in the afternoon.
- The new mother fell asleep when her baby stopped crying, but the *respite* was brief; the baby started up again almost immediately.

RESPLENDENT (ri SPLEN dunt) *adj* brilliantly shining; radiant; dazzling
- In the morning sunlight, every drop of dew was *resplendent* with color; unfortunately, no one was awake to see it.
- Betsy's gown looked *resplendent* in the candlelight; the gown was made of nylon, and it was so shiny you could practically see your reflection in it.

RESURRECTION (rez uh REK shun) *n* return to life; revival
In Christian belief, the *Resurrection* is Jesus' return to life on the third day after his crucifixion. In general usage, the word refers to any revival.
- Polly's tablecloth has undergone quite a *resurrection*; the last time I saw it, she was using it as a dress.
- The new chairman brought about the *resurrection* of the company by firing a few dozen vice presidents and putting a lock on the office supplies.

RETICENT (RET uh sint) *adj* quiet; restrained; reluctant to speak, especially about oneself
- Luther's natural *reticence* made him an ideal speaker: His speeches never lasted more than a few minutes.
- Kaynard was *reticent* on the subject of his accomplishments; he didn't like to talk about himself.

To be *reticent* is to be characterized by *reticence*.

RETORT (ri TAWRT) *v* to make a sharp reply
- "Twinkle, twinkle, little star—what you say is what you are," Leslie *retorted* hotly when her playmate called her a doo-doo brain.
- When Laurie accused Peggy of being drunk, Peggy *retorted*, "Whoeryooshayingsdrunk?" and fell over on the sidewalk.

This word can also be a noun.
- Jeff can never think of a good *retort* when he needs one; the perfect line usually comes to him only later, usually in the middle of the night.

RETROSPECT (RE truh spekt) *n* looking backward; a review
- In *retrospect*, I was probably out of line when I yelled at my mother for telling me she liked what I was wearing and saying that she hoped I would have a nice day.

A *retrospective* (re truh SPEK tiv) is an exhibition of an artist's work from over a period of years.
- Seeing an advertisement for a *retrospective* of his films made the director feel old.

Prospect (PRAH spekt) is the opposite of *retrospect*. A *prospect* is a view—either literal or figurative—that lies before you, or in the future.
- George's heart sings at the *prospect* of being a game-show contestant; he believes that answering questions on television is the true path to enlightenment.
- The Emersons named their new house *Prospect* Point because it offered magnificent views of the surrounding countryside.

REVAMP (ree VAMP) *v* to revise; to renovate
- The struggling college's *revamped* curriculum offers such easy electives as Shakespeare's Furniture and Spelling for Spokesmodels.
- Susan is *revamping* her résumé to make it seem more impressive; she's getting rid of the part that describes her work experience, and she's adding a part that is entirely made up.

REVEL (REV ul) *v* to enjoy thoroughly; to take delight in; to carouse
- Ken is *reveling* in luxury now that he has finally come into his patrimony.
- Tammy *reveled* in every bite of the forbidden dessert; it had been so long since she had eaten chocolate cake that she wanted it to last as long as possible.

To *revel* is to engage in *revelry* (REV ul ree).
- The sounds of *revelry* arising from the party below kept the children awake until all of their parents' guests had gone. (To *revel* is not to engage in revelation; revelation is the noun form of reveal.)

A person who *revels* is a *reveler* (REV uh lur).
- Amanda thought that all her guests had gone home, but then she found one last drunken *reveler* snoring in her bedroom closet.

REVERE (ri VEER) *v* to respect highly; to honor
- Einstein was a preeminent scientist who was *revered* by everyone, even his rivals. Einstein enjoyed nearly universal *reverence* (REV uh rins).

To be *irreverent* is to be mildly disrespectful.
- Peter made jokes about his younger sister's painting. She was perturbed at his *irreverence* and began to cry.

REVILE (ri VYLE) *v* to scold abusively; to berate; to denounce
- In Dickens's *Oliver Twist*, poor Oliver is *reviled* for daring to ask for more gruel.
- The president of the sorority *reviled* the newest member for not wearing enough makeup.

REVULSION (ruh VUL shun) *n* loathing; repugnance; disgust
- The princess pulled back in *revulsion* when she realized that her kiss hadn't turned the frog into a prince after all.
- "Please don't talk about dead lizards while I'm eating," said Sally with *revulsion*.

There is no such word as *revulse* (so you don't need to know how to pronounce it).

RHAPSODIZE (RAP suh dyze) *v* to speak extremely enthusiastically; to gush
- Danielle *rhapsodized* about the little dog, saying that she had never seen a more beautiful, friendly, fabulous little dog in her entire life.
- Hugh never has a kind word to say about anything, so when he *rhapsodized* about the new restaurant we figured that we probably ought to try it.

One who *rhapsodizes* can be said to be *rhapsodic* (rap SAHD ik).
- The review of the play was far from *rhapsodic*. In fact, it was so harshly negative that the play closed the next day.

RHETORIC (RET ur ik) *n* the art of formal speaking or writing; inflated discourse
A talented public speaker might be said to be skilled in *rhetoric*.

The word is often used in a pejorative sense to describe speaking or writing that is skillfully executed but insincere or devoid of meaning.

A political candidate's speech that was long on drama and promises but short on genuine substance might be dismissed as "mere *rhetoric*."

To use *rhetoric* is to be *rhetorical* (ruh TOR ik uhl). A *rhetorical* question is one the speaker intends to answer himself or herself—that is, a question asked only for *rhetorical* effect.

RIBALD (RIB uld) *adj* indecent or vulgar; off-color
- Most of the songs on that new album have *ribald* lyrics that will give heart attacks to mothers all over the nation.

Ribald language or horsing around is called *ribaldry* (RIB uld ree).
- The freshman dormitory was characterized primarily by *ribaldry* and beer.

RIFE (ryfe) *adj* occurring frequently; widespread; common; swarming
- Fistfights were *rife* in that part of town, largely because there was an all-night bar in nearly every storefront.
- The committee's planning sessions were *rife* with backstabbing and petty quarrels.
- Below decks, this ship is *rife* with rats and other pests.

RIGOROUS (RIG ur us) *adj* strict; harsh; severe
To be *rigorous* is to act with *rigor*.
- Our exercise program was *rigorous* but effective; after just a few months, our eighteen hours of daily exercise had begun to pay off.
- The professor was popular largely because he wasn't *rigorous*; there were no tests in his course and only one paper, which was optional.

RIVET (RIV it) *v* to engross; to hold firmly
On a construction site, a *rivet* is a metal pin that is used to fasten things together, and *riveting* is the act of fastening things in this manner. Outside of a construction site, *rivet* means much the same thing, except figuratively.
- After reading the first paragraph, I was *riveted* to the murder mystery until I had finished the final one.
- Dr. Connors *riveted* the attention of his audience with a description of his method of turning himself into a lizard.

If something *rivets* in this way, it is said to be *riveting*.
- Shayla has the most *riveting* green eyes I've ever seen—or perhaps those are contact lenses.

The figurative definition of *rivet* is close to transfix.

ROBUST (roh BUST) *adj* strong and healthy; vigorous
- The ninety-year-old woman was still *robust*. Every morning she ran several miles down to the ocean and jumped in.
- The tree we planted last year isn't looking *robust*. Most of the leaves have fallen off, and the bark has begun to peel.

ROGUE (rohg) *n* a criminally dishonest person; a scoundrel
A *rogue* is someone who can't be trusted. This word is often used, however, to characterize a playfully mischievous person.
- *Huckleberry Finn* is a bit of a *rogue*; while his actions are technically criminal, he performs them with noble intentions and a humorous spirit.

ROUT (rowt) *v* to put to flight; to scatter; to cause a huge defeat
- Brighton High School's debate team *routed* the team from Pittsford, leaving the Pittsford captain sobbing among his notecards.
- *Routing* the forces of pestilence and famine turned out to be a bigger job than Mark had anticipated, so he stopped trying and went to law school instead.

This word can also be a noun.
- Last week's basketball game was a *rout*, not a contest; our team lost by a margin of more than fifty points.

RUDIMENTARY (roo duh MEN tuh ree) *adj* basic; crude; unformed or undeveloped
- The boy who had lived with wolves for fifteen years lacked even the most *rudimentary* social skills.
- The strange creature had small bumps on its torso that appeared to be *rudimentary* limbs.

RUE (roo) *v* to mourn; to regret
- I *rue* the day I walked into this place; nothing even remotely good has happened to me since then.
- The middle-aged man *rued* his misspent youth—all that time wasted studying, when he could have been meeting girls.

Rueful is the adjective form of rue.
- It's hard for Howie not to feel *rueful* when he remembers the way he fumbled the ball in the last two seconds of the game, ending his team's thirty-year winning streak.
- Whenever Olga's mother gets a *rueful* look in her eye, Olga knows she's about to make some kind of remark about how fast time passes.

RUMINATE (ROO muh nayt) *v* to contemplate; to ponder; to mull over

Ruminate comes from a Latin word meaning to chew cud.

Cows, sheep, and other cud-chewing animals are called *ruminants*. To *ruminate* is to quietly chew on or ponder your own thoughts.

- The teacher's comment about the causes of weather set me to *ruminating* about what a nice day it was and to wishing that I were outside.

An act of *ruminating* is called a *rumination*.

- Serge was a private man; he kept his *ruminations* to himself.

RUSTIC (RUS tik) *adj* rural; lacking urban comforts or sophistication; primitive

- Life in the log cabin was too *rustic* for Leah; she missed hot showers, electricity, and ice.

- We enjoyed the *rustic* scenery as we traveled through the countryside.

Rustic can be used as a noun. A *rustic* is an unsophisticated person from the country.

To *rusticate* is to spend time in the country.

QUICK QUIZ #144

Match each word in the first column with its definition in the second column. Check your answers in the back of the book.

1.	respite	a.	basic
2.	reticent	b.	contemplate
3.	revere	c.	vigorous
4.	rhetoric	d.	formal writing or speaking
5.	rigorous	e.	restrained
6.	robust	f.	rural
7.	rogue	g.	period of rest
8.	rudimentary	h.	strict
9.	ruminate	i.	honor
10.	rustic	j.	scoundrel

S

SACCHARINE (SAK uh rin) *adj* sweet; excessively or disgustingly sweet
Saccharin is a calorie-free sweetener; *saccharine* means sweet. Except for the spelling, this is one of the easiest-to-remember words there is.

Saccharine can be applied to things that are literally sweet, such as sugar, *saccharin*, fruit, and so on. It can also be applied to things that are sweet in a figurative sense, such as children, personalities, and sentiments—especially things that are *too* sweet, or sweet in a sickening way.

- We wanted to find a nice card for Uncle Mo, but the cards in the display at the drugstore all had such *saccharine* messages that we would have been too embarrassed to send any of them.

- The love story was so *saccharine* that I vowed never to see another sappy, predictable movie again.

SACRILEGE (SAK ruh lij) *n* a violation of something sacred; blasphemy

- The minister committed the *sacrilege* of delivering his sermon while wearing his golf shoes; he didn't want to be late for his tee-off time, which was just a few minutes after the scheduled end of the service.

- The members of the fundamentalist sect believed that dancing, going to movies, and watching television were *sacrileges*.

To commit a *sacrilege* is to be *sacrilegious*.
Be careful with the spelling of these words.

SACROSANCT (SAK roh sangkt) *adj* sacred; held to be inviolable
A church or temple is *sacrosanct*. So, for Christians, is belief in the divinity of Jesus. *Sacrosanct* is also used loosely, and often ironically, outside of religion.

- Mr. Peters's lunchtime trip to his neighborhood bar was *sacrosanct*; he would no sooner skip it than he would skip his mother's funeral.

SAGACIOUS (suh GAY shus) *adj* discerning; shrewd; keen in judgment; wise

- Edgar's decision to move the chickens into the barn turned out to be *sagacious*; about an hour later, the hailstorm hit.

- The announcer's *sagacious* commentary made the baseball game seem vastly more profound than we had expected it to be.

To be *sagacious* is to have *sagacity* (suh GAS uh tee). A similar word is *sage*, which means wise, possessing wisdom derived from experience or learning.

- When we were contemplating starting our own popcorn business, we received some *sage* advice from a man who had lost all his money selling candied apples.

- The professor's critique, which comprised a few *sage* comments, sent me back to my room feeling pretty stupid.

Sage can also be a noun. A wise person, especially a wise old person, is often called a *sage*.

SALIENT (SAYL yunt) *adj* sticking out; conspicuous; leaping
A *salient* characteristic is one that leaps right out at you.

- Ursula had a number of *salient* features including, primarily, her nose, which stuck out so far that she was constantly in danger of slamming it in doors and windows.

SALLY (SAL ee) *n* a sudden rushing attack; an excursion; an expedition; a repartee; a clever rejoinder

- Our cat made a lightning-fast *sally* into the TV room, then dashed out of the house with the parakeet squawking in his mouth.

- Let's take a little *sally* down Newbury Street; there are some nice, expensive shops there I've been meaning to peek into.

- Tony didn't know the answer to the professor's question, but his quick-witted *sally* made the whole class laugh, including the professor.

This word can be used as a verb as well.

- The first sentence of the mystery is, "One fine morning, Randall Quarry *sallied* forth from his Yorkshire mansion and was never seen again."

SALUTARY (SAL yuh ter ee) *adj* healthful; remedial; curative

- Lowered blood pressure is among the *salutary* effects of exercise.

- The long sea voyage was *salutary;* when Elizabeth landed she looked ten years younger than she had when she set sail.

SALUTATION (sal yoo TAY shun) *n* greeting; welcome; opening words of greeting

- "Hello, you stinking, stupid swine" is not the sort of warm, supportive *salutation* James had been expecting from his girl-friend.

- Unable to recognize the man coming toward her, Lila waved her hand in *salutation* and hoped the gesture would fool him into thinking she knew who he was.

A *salutatory* (suh LOO tuh tawr ee) is a welcoming address given to an audience. At a high school commencement, it is the speech given by the *salutatorian* (suh loo tuh TAWR ee un), the student with the second-highest grade point average in the graduating class. (The student with the highest average is the valedictorian.)

SANCTIMONIOUS (sangk tuh MOH nee us) *adj* pretending to be devout; affecting religious feeling

- The *sanctimonious* old bore pretended to be deeply offended when Lucius whispered a mild swearword after dropping the hammer on his bare foot.

- Simon is an egoist who speaks about almost nothing but caring for one's fellow man. His altruism is *sanctimonious.*

SANCTION (SANGK shun) *n* official permission or approval; endorsement; penalty; punitive measure

- Without the *sanction* of the historical commission, Cynthia was unable to paint her house purple and put a flashing neon sign over the front door.

- The babysitter wasn't sure whether it was okay for Alex to knock over Andy's block tower, so she called the boys' parents and received their *sanction* first.

Strangely, *sanction* also has a meaning that is nearly opposite to approval or permission. (*Cleave* is another word that is very nearly its own antonym.)

- "Unless your puny little nation stops selling poisoned fruit to other nations," the secretary of state threatened, "we'll impose so many *sanctions* on you that you won't know which way is up."

- For many years international *sanctions* on South Africa included the banning of its athletes from competing in the Olympics.

This word can be a verb as well.

- The manager of the apartment complex won't *sanction* your flooding the weight room to make a swimming pool.

SANGUINE (SANG gwin) *adj* cheerful; optimistic; hopeful

- Miguel was *sanguine* about his chances of winning the Nobel Peace Prize, even though, as an eighth grader, he hadn't yet done anything to deserve it.

- The ebullient checkers champion remained *sanguine* in defeat; he was so sure of himself that he viewed even catastrophe as merely a temporary setback.

Don't confuse *sanguine* (a nice word) with *sanguinary* (not a nice word). *Sanguinary* means bloodthirsty.

SARCASM (SAHR kaz um) *n* a tone used to convey irony, or the fact that the intended meaning is opposite from the written or spoken one

- Hank believes that *sarcasm* is the key to breaking the ice with girls. "Is that your real hair, or did you just join the circus?" he asked Jeanette.

To use *sarcasm* is to be *sarcastic* (sahr KAS tik).

- The mayor was enraged by the *sarcastic* tone of the newspaper's editorial about his arrest for possession of cocaine.

- "Nice outfit," Martin said *sarcastically* as he eyed his sister's faded bathrobe, fluffy slippers, and knee-high nylons.

SARDONIC (sahr DAHN ik) *adj* mocking; scornful
- Isabella's weak attempts at humor were met by nothing but a few scattered pockets of *sardonic* laughter.
- Even George's friends found him excessively *sardonic*; he couldn't discuss anything without mocking it, and there was almost nothing about which he could bring himself to say two nice words in a row.

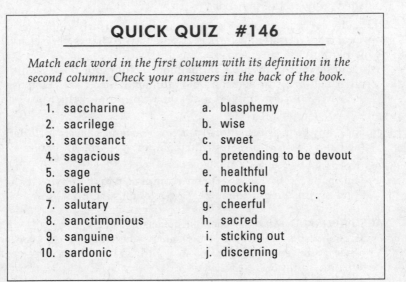

QUICK QUIZ #146

Match each word in the first column with its definition in the second column. Check your answers in the back of the book.

1. saccharine	a. blasphemy
2. sacrilege	b. wise
3. sacrosanct	c. sweet
4. sagacious	d. pretending to be devout
5. sage	e. healthful
6. salient	f. mocking
7. salutary	g. cheerful
8. sanctimonious	h. sacred
9. sanguine	i. sticking out
10. sardonic	j. discerning

SAVANT (suh VAHNT) *n* a scholar; a knowledgeable and learned person
- Bertrand is a real *savant* about architecture. You can't go on a walk without him stopping to point out every architectural point of interest he sees. That's why no one will go on walks with him anymore.
- The abbot of the monastery is a great *savant* in the fields of church history and religious art.

Perhaps because *savant* is a French word (it derives from the French savoir, to know), it tends to be used in association with more sophisticated feats of knowledge. You're be unlikely to hear someone be described as a baseball *savant*, for example. An idiot *savant* is a person who, though mentally handicapped, has an astonishing mastery of one particular subject.
- Ed is an idiot *savant*; he can't speak, read, or dress himself, but he is capable of playing intricate piano pieces after hearing them just once.

Savoir-faire (sav wahr FER) is a French phrase that has been adopted into English. It is social grace, or the knowledge of what to do and how to behave in any situation.

- Priscilla was nervous at the diplomat's party, but her instinctive *savoir-faire* kept her from making major blunders.

SCANT (skant) *adj* limited; meager; barely sufficient

- Soap and water are in *scant* supply around here. You'll be able to take a shower only once per month.

- Finding the recipe too bland, she added a *scant* tablespoonful of lemon juice to the mixture.

- Mrs. Doudy has rather *scant* knowledge of home economics. She's been teaching her students to hem things with tape and safety pins.

Scant can be a verb as well.

- Don't *scant* me on mashed potatoes—you know they're my favorite.

Scant and *scanty* (SKAN tee) have similar but not quite identical meanings. *Scant* means barely sufficient in amount, while *scanty* means barely sufficient in number, extent, or quantity.

- The beggar has scant food and *scanty* clothes.

SCHISM (SIZ um) *n* division; separation; discord or disharmony

- There's been a *schism* in the ranks of the Flat Earth Society; one faction believes that the Earth is flat because it was created that way, while the other faction believes the Earth used to be round but was rolled flat by beings from outer space.

SCINTILLATE (SIN tuh layt) *v* to sparkle, either literally or figuratively

- Stars and diamonds *scintillate*—so do witty comments, charming personalities, and anything else that can be said to sparkle.

- Stefan was a quiet drudge at home, but at a party he could be absolutely *scintillating*, tossing off witty remarks and charming everyone in the room.

- Benny's grades last term weren't *scintillating*, to put it mildly; he had four Ds and an F.

The act of *scintillating* is called *scintillation*.

SCORN (skawrn) *v* to disdain; to find someone or something contemptible

- "I *scorn* your sweaty, mindless athletics," said the president of the literary club to the captain of the football team. "I prefer spending a quiet afternoon by myself reading the works of the great poets."

- Morris *scorns* every kind of cat food except the most expensive brand.

This word can be a noun as well as a verb.

- "Your clothes are totally pathetic, Dad," said Reba, her voice dripping with *scorn*. Her father gave her a *scornful* look and said, "Do you really believe I care what a five-year-old thinks of the way I dress?"

SCRUPULOUS (SKROO pyuh lus) *adj* strict; careful; hesitant for ethical reasons

- Leela was *scrupulous* in keeping her accounts; she knew where every penny came from and where every penny went.

- We tried to be *scrupulous* about not dripping paint, but by the time the day was over there was nearly as much paint on the floor as there was on the walls.

- Philip was too *scrupulous* to make a good used-car dealer; every time he started to lie, he was overcome by ethical doubts.

A *scruple* is a qualm or moral doubt. To have no *scruples*—to be *unscrupulous*—is to have no conscience.

SCRUTINIZE (SKROOT uh nyze) *v* to examine very carefully

- I *scrutinized* the card catalog at the library but couldn't find a single book on the topic I had chosen for my term paper.

- The rocket scientists *scrutinized* thousands of pages of computer printouts, looking for a clue to why the rocket had exploded.

- My mother *scrutinized* my clothes and my appearance before I left for the evening, but even after several minutes of careful analysis she was unable to find anything to complain about.

To *scrutinize* something is to subject it to *scrutiny*.

- The clever forgery fooled the museum curator but did not withstand the *scrutiny* of the experts; after studying for several weeks, the experts pronounced the painting to be a fake.

Something that cannot be examined is *inscrutable*. *Inscrutable* means mysterious, impossible to understand.

- We had no idea what Bill was thinking, because his smile was *inscrutable*. Poker players try to be *inscrutable* to their opponents.

SEAMLESS (SEEM lus) *adj* without a seam; without anything to indicate where two things were joined together; smooth

- After lots of revision, Jennifer succeeded in reworking the two halves of her novel into a *seamless* whole.

- The most interesting thing Beth said all evening was that her new, *seamless* underpants were considerably less bulky than the kind she had formerly worn.
- His excuse is *seamless*, I have to admit; I know he's lying, but I can't find a hole in his story.

SECEDE (si SEED) *v* to withdraw from an alliance
- When the southern states *seceded* from the Union, they probably never expected to create quite as much of a ruckus as they did.
- If taxes keep rising, our state is going to *secede* from the nation and become a tax-free society financed by revenues from bingo and horse-racing.
- When Edward's mother made him clean his room, he *seceded* from his family and moved into the basement, where he could keep things as messy as he wanted.

An act of *seceding* is *secession* (suh SESH un).
- Edward's mother refused to recognize his *secession*. She made him clean up the basement, too.

QUICK QUIZ #147

Match each word in the first column with its definition in the second column. Check your answers in the back of the book.

1. sally	a.	biting irony
2. salutation	b.	scholar
3. sanction	c.	sudden rushing attack
4. sarcasm	d.	withdraw from an alliance
5. savant	e.	smooth
6. scant	f.	disdain
7. schism	g.	official permission or
8. scorn		approval
9. seamless	h.	greeting
10. secede	i.	division
	j.	limited

SECLUSION (si KLOO zhun) *n* aloneness; withdrawal from other people
- The poet spent her final years in *seclusion*, remaining alone in a darkened room and listening to "Stairway to Heaven" over and over again.
- Some people can study better with other people around, but I need total *seclusion* and an endless supply of coffee.
- The prisoner was causing so much trouble that his guards agreed it would be best to put him in *seclusion* for the time being.
- Roberta lives in a *secluded* house at the end of a dead-end street; the lots on either side of hers are empty.

The verb is *seclude* (si KLOOD).

SECT (sekt) *n* a small religious subgroup or religion; any group with a uniting theme or purpose
- Jack dropped out of college and joined a religious *sect* whose members were required to live with animals and surrender all their material possessions to the leaders of the *sect*.
- After the schism of 1949, the religious denomination split up into about fifty different *sects*, all of them with near identical beliefs and none of them speaking to the others.

Matters pertaining to *sects* are *sectarian* (sek TER ee un).
- The company was divided by *sectarian* fighting between the research and marketing departments, each of which had its own idea about what the new computer should be able to do.

To be *sectarian* is also to be single-mindedly devoted to a *sect*. *Nonsectarian* means not pertaining to any particular *sect* or group.
- Milly has grown so *sectarian* since becoming a Moonie that she can't really talk to you anymore without trying to convert you.

SECULAR (SEK yuh lur) *adj* having nothing to do with religion or spiritual concerns
- The group home had several nuns on its staff, but it was an entirely *secular* operation; it was run by the city, not the church.
- The priest's *secular* interests include German food and playing the trombone.

SEDENTARY (SED un ter ee) *adj* largely confined to sitting down; not physically active
- Writing is a *sedentary* life; just about the only exercise you get is walking to the mailbox to see whether anyone's sent you a check, and you don't even need to do that often.

- When people get older, they tend to become more *sedentary*; my octogenarian aunt even uses her car to visit her next-door neighbor.
- If you want to stay in shape with that *sedentary* job, you'll have to make sure to get lots of exercise in your spare time.

SEDITION (si DISH un) *n* treason; the incitement of public disorder or rebellion
- The political group was charged with *sedition* because it had advocated burning the capital to the ground.

SEGREGATE (SEG ruh gayt) *v* to separate
- Rico kept his prize-winning poodle, Fluffy, *segregated* from his other two dogs, which were mixed breeds.

The noun form is *segregation*, which can also refer to periods in history when people of different races were kept apart by social norms or law. In other nations, *segregation* has been called by other names: See *apartheid*.

Integrate, congregate, segregate, and *aggregate*—all words about joining and separating—share a common root.

SELF-MADE (self MAYD) *adj* having succeeded in life without help from others
- John is a *self-made* man; everything he's accomplished, he's accomplished without benefit of education or support from powerful friends. Like most *self-made* men, John can't stop talking about how much he's managed to accomplish despite his humble origins.
- Being a wildly successful *self-made* politician, Maggie had little sympathy with the idea of helping others who hadn't gotten as far as she. "I pulled myself up by my own bootstraps; why can't they?" she would say, staring out her limousine window at the wretched souls living in cardboard boxes on the streets.

Self-esteem (self i STEEM) is the opinion one has of oneself.
- Patty's *self-esteem* is so low that she can't even bring herself to say hello to people in passing because she can't imagine why they would want to talk to her.

Something is *self-evident* (self EV i dunt) if it is obvious without needing to be pointed out.
- Most Americans believe that certain rights, such as the right to speak freely, are *self-evident*.

A *self-possessed* (self puh ZEST) person is one who has good control of his or her feelings.

- The only time Valerie's *self-possession* (self puh ZESH un) ever breaks down is when someone in the audience yawns.

A *self-righteous* (self RYE chus) person is sanctimonious, smug, and intolerant of others, believing that everything he or she does is right.

- "It's a good thing some of us have proper respect for others' possessions," said Tiffany *self-righteously* after discovering that her roommate had wiped her nose on the handkerchief that Tiffany had bought.

A *self-satisfied* (self SAT is fyde) person is, obviously, satisfied—oversatisfied—with himself or herself.

- My *self-satisfied* sister announced to my mother that she had done a much better job of making her bed than I had.

A *self-starter* (self STAR tur) takes initiative and doesn't need the help of others to get going.

- Sandra is a great *self-starter*. The second the professor gives a paper assignment, she rushes out to the library and checks out all the books she'll need. I'm not a good *self-starter* at all. I prefer to sit around watching TV until the day of the deadline, then ask the professor for an extension.

SENSORY (SEN suh ree) *adj* having to do with the senses or sensation
- Babies enjoy bright colors, moving objects, pleasant sounds, and other forms of *sensory* stimulation.

Your ears, eyes, and tongue are all *sensory* organs. It is through them that your *senses* operate.

Extrasensory perception is the supposed ability of some people to perceive things without using the standard senses of sight, hearing, smell, touch, or taste.

Two similar-sounding and often confusing words are *sensual* and *sensuous*. To be *sensual* is to be devoted to gratifying one's senses through physical pleasure, especially sexual pleasure; to be *sensuous* is to delight the senses. A *sensual* person is one who eagerly indulges his or her physical desires. A *sensuous* person is one who stimulates the senses of others.

SENTENTIOUS (sen TEN shus) *adj* preachy; pompous; excessively moralizing; self-righteous
- The new headmistress made a *sententious* speech in which she urged the student body to follow her illustrious example.

- I can stand a boring lecture, but not a *sententious* one, especially when I know that the professor giving it has absolutely nothing to brag about.

SENTIENT (SEN shunt) *adj* able to perceive by the senses; conscious

Human beings are *sentient*. Rocks are not.

- While trees are not, strictly speaking, *sentient* beings, many credible people claim to have communicated with them.

SEQUESTER (si KWES tur) *v* to set or keep apart

- Since much of the rest of the city had become a battle zone, the visiting entertainers were *sequestered* in the international hotel.

- The struggling writer *sequestered* himself in his study for several months, trying to produce the Great American Novel.

- Juries are sometimes *sequestered* during trials to prevent them from talking to people or reading newspapers.

QUICK QUIZ   #148

Match each word in the first column with its definition in the second column. Check your answers in the back of the book.

1.	scintillate	a.	sparkle
2.	scrupulous	b.	having nothing to do with religion
3.	scrutinize		
4.	secular	c.	treason
5.	sedition	d.	having to do with the senses
6.	segregate	e.	set apart
7.	sensory	f.	strict
8.	sensual	g.	delighting the senses
9.	sensuous	h.	examine very carefully
10.	sentient	i.	devoted to pleasure
11.	sequester	j.	conscious
		k.	separate

SERENDIPITY (ser un DIP uh tee) *n* accidental good fortune; discovering good things without looking for them

- It was *serendipity* rather than genius that led the archaeologist to his breathtaking discovery of the ancient civilization. While walking his dog in the desert, he tripped over the top of a buried tomb.

Something that occurs through *serendipity* is *serendipitous*.

- Our arrival at the airport *serendipitously* coincided with that of the queen, and she offered us a ride to our hotel in her carriage.

SERENE (suh REEN) *adj* calm; peaceful; tranquil; untroubled
- In the lake's *serene* blue depths lie the keys my father hurled off the deck in a fit of temper a couple of days ago after learning that I had totaled his car.
- "Try to look *serene*, dear," said the pageant director to the girl playing the Virgin Mary. "Mary should not look as though she wants to punch Joseph out."

The state of being *serene* is *serenity* (suh REN uh tee).
- Kelly was a nervous wreck for an hour before the guests arrived, but as soon as the doorbell rang she turned into *serenity* itself.

SERPENTINE (SUR pun teen) *adj* snakelike in either shape or movement; winding, as a snake travels

A *serpent* (SUR punt) is a snake. To be *serpentine* is to be like a serpent.
- Dan despises interstate highways, preferring to travel on *serpentine* state roads that wind through the hills and valleys.

For a close synonym, see our entry for tortuous.

SERVILE (SUR vyle) *adj* submissive and subservient; like a servant
- Cat lovers sometimes say that dogs are too *servile* because they follow their owners everywhere and slobber all over them at every opportunity.
- The horrible boss demanded *servility* from his employees; when he said, "Jump!" he expected them to ask, "How high?"

A similar word is *slavish* (SLAY vish), which means even more subservient than *servile*. *Slavish* devotion to a cause is devotion in spite of everything. An artist's *slavish* imitator would be an imitator who imitated everything about the artist.

SHACKLE (SHAK ul) *n* a manacle; a restraint
- As soon as the bad guys left the room, the clever detective slipped out of his *shackles* by using his teeth to fashion a small key from a ballpoint pen.
- "Throw off the *shackles* of your restrictive upbringing and come skinny-dipping with me!" shouted Andy as he stripped off his clothes and jumped into the pool, but everyone else just stood quietly and stared at him.

This word can also be used as a verb.
- The circus trainer used heavy iron chains to *shackle* his bears when they weren't performing.

SHIBBOLETH (SHIB uh luth) *n* a distinctive word, pronunciation, or behavior that typifies a particular group; a slogan or catchword
- That large government programs are inherently bad is a *shibboleth* of the Republican party.

A *shibboleth* can also be a common saying that is essentially meaningless.
- The old housewife's *shibboleth* that being cold makes a person more likely to catch a cold has been discredited by modern medical experts.

SHREWD (shrood) *adj* wily; cunning; sly
- Foxes actually are every bit as *shrewd* as they're portrayed to be in folklore; hunters say foxes under pursuit are often able to trick even trained foxhounds into following a false trail.

- There was a *shrewd* look in the old shopkeeper's eye as he watched the city slickers venture into his country store and calculated the percentage by which he would be able to overcharge them for junk that none of the locals would have given a second glance.

QUICK QUIZ   #149

Match each word in the first column with its definition in the second column. Check your answers in the back of the book.

1. seclusion	a. wily
2. sect	b. snakelike
3. sedentary	c. preachy
4. self-made	d. calm
5. sententious	e. largely confined to sitting down
6. serene	
7. serpentine from others	f. having succeeded without help
8. shackle	g. small religious subgroup
9. shibboleth	h. manacle
10. shrewd	i. aloneness
	j. catchword

SINGULAR (SING gyuh lur) *adj* unique; superior; exceptional; strange
- Darren had the *singular* ability to stand on one big toe for several hours at a time.
- The man on the train had a *singular* deformity: Both of his ears were on the same side of his head.

A *singularity* is a unique occurrence. *Singularity* is also the quality of being unique.

SINISTER (SIN ih stur) *adj* evil, wicked; foreshadowing evil, trouble, or wickedness
- The house on the hill is pretty by day, but at night it casts *sinister* shadows and emits frightening moans.

SKIRMISH (SKUR mish) *n* a fight between small numbers of troops; a brief conflict
- I was expecting a couple of *skirmishes* during the Scout campout—arguments about who got to shower first, and things like that—but not this out-and-out war between the girls in the different patrols.
- Soldiers on both sides felt insulted when the CNN reporter referred to their recent battle as a *"skirmish."*
- A *skirmish* broke out at the hockey game when a player threw a punch at the opposing team's goalie.

This word can also be a verb.
- The principal *skirmished* with the students over the issue of hair length.

SKITTISH (SKIT ish) *adj* nervous; easily startled; jumpy
- The farm animals all seemed *skittish*, and no wonder—a wolf was walking back and forth outside their pen, reading a cookbook and sharpening his knife.
- "Why are you so *skittish* tonight?" the babysitter asked the young children. "Is it my pointed teeth, or is it the snake in my knapsack?"

SLAKE (slayk) *v* to quench; to satisfy; to assuage
- Soda doesn't *slake* your thirst as well as plain old water.
- Irene's thirst for companionship was *slaked* by her next-door neighbor, who spent most of every day drinking coffee with her in her kitchen.
- My hairdresser's admiration *slaked* my fear that shaving my head hadn't been the best move.

SLANDER (SLAN dur) *v* to speak badly about someone publicly; to defame; to spread malicious rumor

- Jonathan *slandered* Mr. Perriwinkle by ·telling everyone in school that the principal was a thief; Mr. Perriwinkle resented this *slander*. Since he was the principal, he expelled the *slanderous* student.

SLOTH (slawth) *n* laziness; sluggishness

You may have seen a picture of an animal called a *sloth*. It hangs upside down from tree limbs and is never in a hurry to do anything. To fall into *sloth* is to act like a *sloth*.

- Yusuke's weekends were devoted to *sloth*. He never arose before noon, and he seldom left the house before Monday morning.

To be lazy and sluggish is to be *slothful*.

- Ophelia's *slothful* husband virtually lived on the couch in the living room, and the television remote-control device was in danger of becoming grafted to his hand.

SOBRIETY (suh BRYE uh tee) *n* the state of being sober; seriousness

A *sober* person is a person who isn't drunk. A *sober* person can also be a person who is serious, solemn, or not ostentatious. *Sobriety* means both "undrunkness" and seriousness or solemnity.

- *Sobriety* was such an unfamiliar condition that the reforming alcoholic didn't recognize it at first.

Sobriety of dress is one characteristic of the hardworking Amish.

SOLACE (SAHl is) *n* consolation; comfort

- The broken-hearted country-western singer found *solace* in a bottle of bourbon; then he wrote a song about finding *solace* in a bottle of bourbon.
- The Red Sox just lost the pennant, and there is no *solace* for baseball fans in the city of Boston tonight.

This word can also be a verb.

- I've heard a lot of come-ons in my day, but "May I *solace* you?" has to be a first.

SOLICITOUS (suh LIS uh tus) *adj* eager and attentive, often to the point of hovering; anxiously caring or attentive

- Every time we turned around, we seemed to step on the foot of the *solicitous* salesman, who appeared to feel that if he left us alone for more than a few seconds, we would decide to leave the store.

- When the sick movie star sneezed, half-a-dozen *solicitous* nurses came rushing into his hospital room.

The noun is *solicitude.*

SOLIDARITY (sahl uh DAR uh tee) *n* sense of unity; a sense of sharing a common goal or attitude
- Working on New Year's Eve wasn't as depressing as Russell had been fearing; there was a sense of *solidarity* in the newsroom that was at least as enjoyable as any New Year's Eve party he had ever been to.

- To promote a sense of *solidarity* among our campers, we make them wear ugly uniforms and wake them up early; they don't have a good time, but they learn to stick together because they hate our rules so much.

- *Solidarity* was an appropriate name for the Polish labor union since it represented a decision by workers to stand up together against their government.

SOLVENT (SAHL vunt) *adj* not broke or bankrupt; able to pay one's bills
- Jerry didn't hope to become a millionaire; all he wanted to do was remain *solvent.*

To be broke is to be *insolvent.* An *insolvent* company is one that can't cover its debts.

The state of being *solvent* is called *solvency;* the state of being *insolvent* is called *insolvency.*

SOPHOMORIC (sahf uh MAWR ik) *adj* juvenile; childishly goofy
- The dean of students suspended the fraternity's privileges because its members had streaked through the library wearing togas, soaped the windows of the administration building, and engaged in other *sophomoric* antics during Parents' Weekend.

- "I expect the best man to be *sophomoric*—but not the groom. Now, give me that slingshot, and leave your poor fiancée alone!" the minister scolded Andy at his wedding rehearsal.

- The misbehaving tenth graders didn't mind being called *sophomoric;* after all, they were sophomores (SAHF uh mawrz).

SOPORIFIC (sahp uh RIF ik) *adj* sleep inducing; boring; sleepy
- The doctor calmed his hysterical patient by injecting him with some sort of *soporific* medication.

- Sam's *soporific* address was acknowledged not by applause but by a chorus of snores.

- The *soporific* creature from the bottom of the sea lay in a gigantic blob on the beach for several days and then roused itself enough to consume the panic-stricken city.

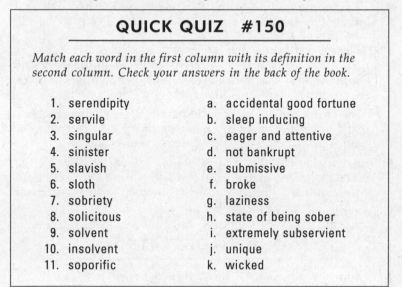

QUICK QUIZ #150

Match each word in the first column with its definition in the second column. Check your answers in the back of the book.

1.	serendipity	a.	accidental good fortune
2.	servile	b.	sleep inducing
3.	singular	c.	eager and attentive
4.	sinister	d.	not bankrupt
5.	slavish	e.	submissive
6.	sloth	f.	broke
7.	sobriety	g.	laziness
8.	solicitous	h.	state of being sober
9.	solvent	i.	extremely subservient
10.	insolvent	j.	unique
11.	soporific	k.	wicked

SORDID (SOR did) *adj* vile; filthy; squalid
- The college roommates led a *sordid* existence, surrounded by dirty laundry, rotting garbage, and filthy dishes.
- The conspirators plotted their *sordid* schemes at a series of secret meetings in an abandoned warehouse.
- The leprosy blight had turned a once-pretty neighborhood into a *sordid* outpost of despair and crime.

SOVEREIGN (SAHV run) *n* supreme ruler; monarch
- Wouldn't the people in this country be surprised to learn that their *sovereign* is not a human but a mynah bird?

Sovereign can also be used as an adjective, in which case it means principal or foremost.
- Getting those kids to school safely should be the bus driver's *sovereign* concern, but I'm afraid he's really more interested in finding a place to stop for a doughnut as soon as he has finished his route.

Sovereignty (SAHV run tee) means supremacy of authority—it's what kings exercise over their kingdoms.

- The disgruntled Californians declared *sovereignty* over some rocks in the middle of the Pacific Ocean and declared their intention of establishing a new nation.

SPATE (spayt) *n* a sudden outpouring

- Julia has received a *spate* of media coverage in the days since her new movie was released; last week, her picture was on the covers of both *Time* and *Newsweek*.

- "The recent *spate* of pickpocketing in the area makes me think that Gotham's citizens are ignoring our public awareness ad campaign," bemoaned Police Commissioner Gordon.

In British usage, a *spate* is a literal flood.

- When the *spate* had abated, the villagers were horrified to discover how hard it is to remove mud from upholstered furniture.

For a synonym, see our entry for influx.

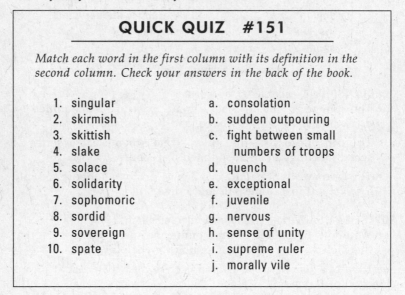

QUICK QUIZ #151

Match each word in the first column with its definition in the second column. Check your answers in the back of the book.

1. singular	a. consolation
2. skirmish	b. sudden outpouring
3. skittish	c. fight between small
4. slake	numbers of troops
5. solace	d. quench
6. solidarity	e. exceptional
7. sophomoric	f. juvenile
8. sordid	g. nervous
9. sovereign	h. sense of unity
10. spate	i. supreme ruler
	j. morally vile

SPAWN (spawn) *v* to bring forth; to produce a large number

- A best-selling book or blockbuster movie will *spawn* dozens of imitators.

SPECIOUS (SPEE shus) *adj* deceptively plausible or attractive
- The charlatan's *specious* theories about curing baldness with used tea bags charmed the studio audience but did not convince the experts, who believed that fresh tea bags were more effective.
- The river's beauty turned out to be *specious;* what had looked like churning rapids from a distance was, on closer inspection, some sort of foamy industrial waste.

To be *specious* is to be characterized by *speciousness*.

SPECTER (SPEK tur) *n* ghost; phantom
- The *specter* of old Miss Shaffer still haunts this house, making mysterious coughing noises and leaving tattered issues of *TV Guide* in unexpected spots.
- As the girls gazed at him, transfixed with horror, he gradually shriveled up and turned into a *specter* before their eyes. "I told you we shouldn't touch that switch," Suzy snapped at Muffy.

A *specter* doesn't have to be a literal ghost.
- The *specter* of the Great Depression continued to haunt the Reeses, making them reluctant to spend money on anything that seemed even remotely frivolous.

To be *spectral* (SPEK trul) is to be ghostly or *specterlike*.
- The ladies in the Library Club were hoping to give the Halloween funhouse a thoroughly *spectral* atmosphere, but their limited budget permitted them to buy only a couple of rolls of orange and black crepe paper and some candy corn.

SPECTRUM (SPEK trum) *n* a broad sequence or range of different but related things or ideas
- The entire *spectrum* of acting theories is represented in this workshop, from the notion that all you have to do to act is act to the belief that you must truly become the character in order to be convincing.
- If the *spectrum* of political beliefs were an actual line, Rob's views would occupy a point slightly left of center. He's liberal enough to irritate his parents, but too conservative to earn the total trust of his leftist friends.

SPORADIC (spuh RAD ik) *adj* stopping and starting; scattered; occurring in bursts every once in a while
- Kyle's attention to his schoolwork was *sporadic* at best; he tended to lose his concentration after a few minutes of effort.

SPURIOUS (SPYOOR ee us) *adj* false; fake
An apocryphal story is one whose truth is uncertain. A *spurious* story, however, is out-and-out false, no doubt about it.
- The political candidate attributed his loss to numerous *spurious* rumors that had hounded him throughout his campaign.

SPURN (spurn) *v* to reject disdainfully; to scorn
- The female peacock *spurned* the male's advances day after day; she took so little notice of him that he might as well have sold his tail feathers and tried to make time with the chickens.

- Preschoolers usually *spurn* their parents' attempts to serve them healthy meals; they turn up their noses at nice, wholesome fruits and vegetables and ask where the chips are.

- Elizabeth *spurned* Jeff's apologies; she could see that he wasn't sorry at all, and that he was, in fact, on the verge of laughing.

SQUALOR (SKWAHL ur) *n* filth; wretched, degraded, or repulsive living conditions
- If people live in *squalor* for too long, the ruling elite can count on an insurgency.

SQUANDER (SKWAHN dur) *v* to waste
- Jerry failed to husband his inheritance; instead, he *squandered* it on trips to Las Vegas.

STAGNATION (stag NAY shun) *n* motionlessness; inactivity
- The company grew quickly for several years; then it fell into *stagnation*.

- Many years of carelessly dumping garbage next to the river led to the gradual *stagnation* of the water because the trash covered the bottom and made an impromptu dam.

To fall into *stagnation* is to *stagnate*. To be in a state of *stagnation* is to be *stagnant*.

STALWART (STAWL wurt) *adj* sturdily built; robust; valiant; unwavering
- "Don't forget," Elbert droned to Frieda, "that those brawny, *stalwart* youths you seem to admire so much have little to recommend them, intellectually speaking."

- The chipmunk made a *stalwart* effort to defend her babies from the sallies of the cat, but it was my own efforts with a water pistol that finally drove the attacker away.

- Ernie has been a *stalwart* friend through thick and thin, even when I used to pretend not to recognize him as I passed him in the hall.

STARK (stahrk) *adj* utter; unmitigated; harsh; desolate
- *Stark* terror leaped into the babysitter's eyes when she realized that both the car and the triplets were missing.

- A lump rose in Bly's throat when she saw the view out her apartment window for the first time; the room faced a *stark*, deserted alley whose only adornment was a rusty old fire escape.

This word can also be an adverb, in which case it means utterly and absolutely.
- Billy used to answer the door *stark* naked, just to see what would happen; lots of things happened.

- If you play that song one more time, I will go *stark*, raving mad, and throw the stereo out the window.

STATIC (STAT ik) *adj* stationary; not changing or moving
- Sales of the new book soared for a few weeks then became *static*.

- The movie was supposed to be a thriller, but we found it tediously *static*; nothing seemed to happen from one scene to the next.

STAUNCH (stawnch) *adj* firmly committed; firmly in favor of; steadfast
A *staunch* Republican is someone who always votes for Republican candidates.

A *staunch* supporter of tax reform would be someone who firmly believes in tax reform.

To be *staunch* in your support of something is to be unshakable.

STEADFAST (STED fast) *adj* loyal; faithful
- *Steadfast* love is love that never wavers. To be *steadfast* in a relationship is to be faithfully committed.

To be *steadfast* is to be like a rock: unchanging, unwavering, unmoving.

STIGMATIZE (STIG muh tyze) *v* to brand with disgrace; to set a mark of disgrace upon
- Steve once went into the girls' bathroom by accident, and this mistake *stigmatized* him for the rest of his high school career.

A *stigma* is a mark of disgrace.

STINT (stint) *v* to restrict or hold back on; to be frugal
- "Please don't *stint*, ladies," wheedled the con man as he waved his jar around drunkenly. "Every penny you give me goes to support the orphanage."

- David's eyes glowed as he beheld his hot fudge sundae; the waiter certainly had not *stinted* on the hot fudge, which was flowing out of the bowl and onto the tablecloth.

The adjective is *stinting* (or *unstinting*). When *stint* is used as a noun, it means a period of time spent doing a job or special duty.
- Ed would have done a *stint* in the military, but he didn't like the thought of having to keep his sergeant's shoes polished.

STIPEND (STYE pund) *n* income; allowance; salary
- The *stipend* this university pays its teaching assistants is so low that some of them are forced to rummage for food in the dumpster behind McDonald's™.
- In addition to his commissions, the salesman received a small *stipend* to cover his travel expenses.
- An allowance is a *stipend* that a child receives from his or her parents. It is always too small.

STIPULATE (STIP yuh layt) *v* to require something as part of an agreement
- You are well advised to *stipulate* the maximum amount you will pay in any car-repair contract.

Guarantees often *stipulate* certain conditions that must be met if the guarantee is to be valid.

STOIC (STOH ik) *adj* indifferent (at least outwardly) to pleasure or pain, to joy or grief, to fortune or misfortune
- Nina was *stoic* about the death of her canary; she went about her business as though nothing sad had happened.
- We tried to be *stoic* about our defeat, but as soon as we got into the locker room, we all began to cry and bang our foreheads on our lockers.

STOLID (STAHL id) *adj* not easily roused to emotion; impassive; apathetic; phlegmatic
- Not a ripple of emotion passed across her brother's *stolid* countenance when she told him that his best friend had just asked her to marry him. "That's nice," he said, without looking away from the TV.
- Our local veterinarian no longer treats farm animals because the *stolid* expressions of cows make him feel uneasy and depressed.
- In professional football, the *stolid* performers sometimes have longer careers than the flashy superstars, who have a tendency to burn themselves out after a few years.

STOUT (stowt) *adj* plump; stocky; substantial
- Mr. Barton was built a little bit like a beach ball; he was *stout* in the middle and skinny at either end.
- Mr. Reardon never goes for a walk without carrying a *stout* stick along; he uses it to steady his balance, knock obstacles out of his path, and scare away dogs and small children.

Stout also means brave, plucky, or resolute. The "*stout-hearted* men" in the well-known song are courageous men.
- "I don't mind walking home over Haunted Hill," the little boy said *stoutly*.

STRATAGEM (STRAT uh jum) *n* a maneuver designed to outwit an enemy; a scheme; a ruse
- The Pied Piper's *stratagem* was successful; entranced by the sound of his pipe, the rats followed him out of town and never came back.
- Our *stratagem* for replacing the real newspaper with a parody issue involved kidnapping the driver of the delivery truck and taking over the delivery route ourselves.
- Jordan has devised a little *stratagem* to test whether the Easter Bunny really exists; the next time he writes him a letter, he's going to drop it in the mailbox without showing it to his parents first.

To devise *stratagems* toward a particular goal is to develop a strategy.

STRATUM (STRAT um) *n* a layer; a level
The middle class is one *stratum* of society.
The plural of *stratum* is *strata*. A hierarchy is composed of *strata*.
To *stratify* is to make into layers.
This word can also be pronounced "STRAY tum."

STRICTURE (STRIK chur) *n* a restriction; a limitation; a negative criticism
- Despite the *strictures* of apartment living, we enjoyed the eight years we spent in New York City.
- The unfavorable lease placed many *strictures* on how the building could be used.
- The poorly prepared violinist went home trembling after his concert to await the inevitable *strictures* of the reviewers.

QUICK QUIZ   #152

Match each word in the first column with its definition in the second column. Check your answers in the back of the book.

1. sordid
2. spawn
3. specious
4. sporadic
5. spurious
6. squander
7. stagnation
8. static
9. staunch
10. steadfast
11. stigmatize
12. stipulate
13. stoic
14. stratum
15. stricture

a. disgrace
b. stopping and starting
c. restriction
d. inactivity
e. require
f. indifferent to pain, pleasure
g. bring forth
h. vile
i. firmly committed (2)
j. layer
k. stationary
l. deceptively plausible
m. false
n. waste

QUICK QUIZ   #153

Match each word in the first column with its definition in the second column. Check your answers in the back of the book.

1. specious
2. specter
3. spectrum
4. spurn
5. stalwart
6. stark
7. stint
8. stipend
9. stolid
10. stout

a. stocky
b. reject
c. robust
d. restrict
e. phantom
f. desolate
g. not easily roused to emotion
h. deceptive
i. broad sequence
j. allowance

STRIFE (stryfe) *n* bitter conflict; discord; a struggle or clash
- Marital *strife* often leads to divorce.

STRINGENT (STRIN junt) *adj* strict; restrictive
- The restaurant's *stringent* dress code required male diners to wear a suit coat and tie or they had to leave.
- The IRS accountant was quite *stringent* in his interpretation of the tax code; he disallowed virtually all of Leslie's deductions.

STUPENDOUS (stoo PEN dus) *adj* remarkable; extraordinary; remarkably large or extraordinarily gigantic
- Everyone had told Chet to expect a *stupendous* view from the top of the Empire State Building, but the weather was foggy on the day he visited, and all he could see was clouds.
- A *stupendous* pile of laundry awaited Phyllis when she returned from her business trip; she had forgotten to tell her children that they should do their own wash while she was gone.
- To climb Mount Everest on a bicycle would be a *stupendous* accomplishment.

STUPOR (STOO pur) *n* a stunned condition; near-unconsciousness; apathy; inertia
- After Thanksgiving dinner, we were all too full to do anything except lie around on the floor in a *stupor* and watch the dog walk in circles in front of the fireplace.
- Polls indicated that the new anchorman was sending viewers into a *stupor* of boredom, so he was quickly replaced by a baton twirler and relegated to doing the weather report.

To be in a *stupor* is to be *stuporous* (STOO pur us). To *stupefy* (STOO puh fy) is to astonish or stun.

STYMIE (STYE mee) *v* to thwart; to get in the way of; to hinder
Stymie is a golfing term. A golfer is *stymied* when another player's ball lies on the direct path between his or her own ball and the cup. Off the golf course, one might be *stymied* by one's boss.
- In my effort to make a name for myself in the company, I was *stymied* by my boss, who always managed to take credit for all the good things I did and to blame me for his mistakes.

SUBJUGATE (SUB juh gayt) *v* to subdue and dominate; to enslave
- I bought the fancy riding lawn mower because I thought it would make my life easier, but it quickly *subjugated* me; all summer long, it seems, I did nothing but change its oil, sharpen its blades, and drive it back and forth between my house and the repair shop.

- The tyrant *subjugated* all the peasants living in the kingdom; once free, they were now forced to do his bidding.

SUBLIME (suh BLYME) *adj* awesome; extremely exalted; lofty; majestic
- After winning $70 million in the lottery and quitting our jobs as sewer workers, our happiness was *sublime*.
- Theodore was a *sublime* thinker; after pondering even a difficult problem for just a few minutes, he would invariably arrive at a concise and elegant solution.
- The soup at the restaurant was *sublime*. I've never tasted anything so good.

The noun form of *sublime* is *sublimity* (suh BLIM i tee). Don't confuse *sublime* with *subliminal* (suh BLIM uh nuhl), which means subconscious, or *sublimate*, which means to suppress one's subconscious mind.

SUBORDINATE (suh BOR duh nit) *adj* lower in importance, position, or rank; secondary
- My desire to sit on the couch and watch television all night long was *subordinate* to my desire to stand in the kitchen eating junk food all night long, so I did the latter instead of the former.

A vice president is *subordinate* to a president.

Subordinate (suh BOR duh nayt) can also be a verb. To *subordinate* something in relation to something else is to make it secondary or less important.

To be *insubordinate* (in suh BOR duh nit) is not to acknowledge the authority of a superior. An army private who says, "Bug off!" when ordered to do something by a general is guilty of being *insubordinate* or of committing an act of *insubordination*.

SUBSIDIARY (sub SID ee er ee) *adj* supplemental; additional; secondary or subordinate
- The Watsons pay their kids both a weekly allowance and a *subsidiary* sum for doing particular chores; the system worked until the children decided they would rather be broke than do chores.
- Poor Carrie doesn't seem to realize that she's stuck in a *subsidiary* position for at least the near future; Mr. Vitale will never promote her unless someone quits, and no one's going to quit with the job market the way it is.

This word can also be a noun, in which case it often refers to a small company owned by or closely associated with a larger company.
- Acme Corp's main business is manufacturing boomerangs, but it has *subsidiaries* that make everything from tennis balls to french fries.

SUBSIDIZE (SUB suh dyze) *v* to provide financial aid; to make a financial contribution
- The professor's assertion that cigarette smoking can be healthful was discredited when a reporter discovered that the tobacco industry had *subsidized* his research.
- The school lunch program is *subsidized* by the state; the school system is reimbursed by the state for a portion of what it spends on pizza and peach cobbler.

SUBSTANTIATE (sub STAN shee ayt) *v* to prove; to verify; to confirm
- Experts from the transit department were unable to *substantiate* the woman's assertion that little men from the center of the Earth had invaded the subway system and were planning to take over the world.
- The prosecutor did her best to *substantiate* the charge against the defendant, but it was an uphill job; she couldn't find a single witness willing to testify against him.
- Lawrence's entire scientific career is built on *unsubstantiated* theories; a case in point is his ten-year study of communication between rocks.

Substantial is a related word that means of significant size, worth, or importance. You could say that by *substantiating* something, you make it more *substantial*.

SUBSTANTIVE (SUB stan tiv) *adj* having substance; real; essential; solid; substantial
- The differences between the two theories were not *substantive;* in fact, the two theories said the same thing with different words.
- The gossip columnist's wild accusations were not based on anything *substantive;* her source was a convicted perjurer, and she had made up all the quotations.

SUBTERFUGE (SUB tur fyooj) *n* artifice; a trick or stratagem; a ruse
- Pearl isn't allowed to wear jeans to school, so she has gotten into the habit of leaving a pair of jeans in the bushes behind her house and changing into them in her best friend's garage. This little *subterfuge* is about to be discovered, however, because Pearl's mother is dropping in on the school unexpectedly today to bring her the lunchbox she left at home this morning.

SUBTLE (SUT ul) *adj* not obvious; able to make fine distinctions; ingenious; crafty

- The alien beings had created a shrewd replica of Mr. Jenson, but his wife did notice a few *subtle* differences, including the fact that the new Mr. Jenson had no pulse.

- Jim's *subtle* mind enables him to see past problems that confuse the rest of us.

- The burglar was *subtle;* he had come up with a plan that would enable him to steal all the money in the world without arousing the suspicions of the authorities.

Something *subtle* is a *subtlety.*

SUBVERSIVE (sub VUR siv) *adj* corrupting; overthrowing; undermining; insurgent

- The political group destroyed the Pentagon's computer files, hijacked *Air Force One,* and engaged in various other *subversive* activities.

- Madeline's efforts to teach her first-grade students to read were thwarted by that most *subversive* of inventions, the television set.

SUCCINCT (suk SINGKT) *adj* brief and to the point; concise

- Aaron's *succinct* explanation of why the moon doesn't fall out of the sky and crash into the Earth quickly satisfied even the most skeptical of the seventh graders.

- We were given so little room in which to write on the examination that we had no choice but to keep our essays *succinct.*

SUCCUMB (suh KUM) *v* to yield or submit; to die
- I had said I wasn't going to eat anything at the party, but when Ann held the tray of imported chocolates under my nose, I quickly *succumbed* and ate all of them.
- The Martians in *The War of the Worlds* survived every military weapon known to man but *succumbed* to the common cold.
- When Willard reached the age of 110, his family began to think that he would live forever, but he *succumbed* not long afterward.

SUFFICE (suh FYSE) *v* to be sufficient; to be enough
- At Thanksgiving dinner, Grandma said that she wasn't very hungry, and that a crust of bread and a few drops of water would *suffice*.
- Instruction in reading and writing alone will not *suffice* to prepare our children for the real world; they must also be given a solid grounding in mathematics, and a passing familiarity with the martial arts.

SUFFRAGE (SUF rij) *n* the right to vote

Women who advocated the extension of *suffrage* to women were known as *suffragettes* (suf ruh JETS).

- Amazing though it seems today, *suffrage* for women was a hotly contested issue at the beginning of the twentieth century. Many men—and many women, for that matter—seriously believed that choosing among political candidates would place too great a strain on women's supposedly feeble intellects, and women were not guaranteed the right to vote until 1920.

- Universal *suffrage* is the right of all people to vote, regardless of race, sex, ownership of property, and so forth.

QUICK QUIZ   #155

Match each word in the first column with its definition in the second column. Check your answers in the back of the book.

1. stratagem	a.	prove
2. stupendous	b.	stunned condition
3. stupor	c.	artifice
4. subside	d.	maneuver designed to outwit an enemy
5. subsidiary	e.	provide financial aid
6. subsidize	f.	remarkable
7. substantiate	g.	sink
8. subterfuge	h.	supplemental
9. suffice	i.	be sufficient
10. suffrage	j.	right to vote

SUFFUSE (suh FYOOZ) *v* to cover; to overspread; to saturate

- A crimson blush *suffused* the timid maiden's ivory cheeks as she realized that she had forgotten to put on clothes before leaving the house.

- The room that was once filled with dazzling sunbeams is now *suffused* with the ugly grayish light of a fluorescent lamp.

- *Suffusing* the meat with a marinade will add flavor, but it won't tenderize the meat.

The adjective is *suffuse* (suh FYOOS).

SUMPTUOUS (SUMP choo us) *adj* luxurious; splendid; lavish
- The walls were covered with *sumptuous* silk tapestries, the floors with the finest Eastern rugs, and I felt stupid standing there, because I was wearing cutoffs.
- A *sumptuous* feast awaited the travelers when they reached the great hall of the king's castle.

SUPERCILIOUS (soo pur SIL ee us) *adj* haughty; patronizing
- The *supercilious* Rolls-Royce salesman treated us like peasants until we opened our suitcase full of one-hundred-dollar bills.
- The newly famous author was so *supercilious* that he pretended not to recognize members of his own family, whom he now believed to be beneath him.

SUPERFICIAL (soo pur FISH ul) *adj* on the surface only; shallow; not thorough
- Tom had indeed been shot, but the wound was *superficial*; the bullet had merely creased the tip of his nose.
- The mechanic, who was in a hurry, gave my car what appeared to be a *superficial* tune-up. In fact, if he checked the oil, he did it without opening the hood.

A person who is *superficial* can be accused of *superficiality*.
- The *superficiality* of the editor's comments made us think that he hadn't really read the manuscript.

SUPERFLUOUS (soo PUR floo us) *adj* extra; unnecessary; redundant
- Andrew's attempt to repair the light bulb was *superfluous*, since the light bulb had already been repaired.
- Roughly 999 of the 1,000-page book's pages were *superfluous*.

The noun is *superfluity* (soo pur FLOO uh tee).

SUPERSEDE (soo pur SEED) *v* to take the place of; to supplant; to make (something) obsolete
- Every few minutes, someone introduces a new antiaging cream that allegedly *supersedes* all the existing antiaging creams on the market; it's a wonder we haven't all turned into babies.
- Your new address list *supersedes* the address list you were given last week, which *superseded* the list of the previous week, and will be *superseded* next week by an updated list to be distributed at that time.

SUPINE (soo PYNE) *adj* lying on one's back
- Shirley lay *supine* on her deck chair, soaking up the sunshine and, in the process, turning her complexion into leather.

- When you've got both broken legs in traction, you'd better stay *supine* or you'll be awfully uncomfortable.

Supine is sometimes used figuratively to describe a person who is inert or inactive. A Chinese legend speaks of a man so *supine* that he starved to death because he couldn't be bothered to turn around a necklace of biscuits his wife had placed around his neck. The opposite of *supine* is prone (prohn). To be prone is to be lying face down.

SUPPLICATION (sup luh KAY shun) *n* humble prayer; earnest entreaty
- It's almost frightening to walk through the streets of any city nowadays, there are so many people making *supplications* for food or spare change.
- The priest asked our prayers and *supplications* for the sick and dying of the parish.

To make a *supplication* is to *supplicate* (SUP luh kayt). A person who does so is a *supplicant* (SUP luh kunt).
- The king has set aside a part of every day to hear the petitions of his *supplicants*, some of whom have journeyed hundreds of miles in order to ask him favors.

SUPPRESS (suh PRES) *v* to overpower; to subdue; to squash
- Mom and Dad *suppressed* our brief show of rebellion by threatening to hold our hands in public if we didn't behave.
- Everyone had expected the Soviet army to *suppress* the uprisings against the coup, but for once the army was behind the populace. The soldiers' refusal to quash the demonstrators effectively ended the coup.

See our listing for repress.

SURFEIT (SUR fit) *n* excess; an excessive amount; excess or overindulgence in eating or drinking
- Thanksgiving meals are usually a *surfeit* for everyone involved.

SURMISE (sur MYZE) *v* to conjecture; to guess
- From the messages the eight-ball has been sending me, I *surmise* that someone's going to give me a present soon.
- Gazing at the group with a practiced eye, the tour guide *surmised* that 25 percent of the tourists would want to see famous people's houses, 25 percent would want to visit museums and cathedrals, and the remaining 50 percent would spend most of the tour wondering when they would have a chance to go to the bathroom.

This word can also be a noun, in which case it means guess or supposition. As Keats wrote, Cortez's men looked at each other "with a wild *surmise*" when they first saw the Pacific Ocean and realized that they had achieved their goal. Or, rather, they had achieved the goal of Balboa, who, as Keats either didn't know or didn't care, was actually the first European to see the Pacific from this spot. The noun is pronounced "SUR myze." Note carefully the pronunciation of these words.

SURREAL (suh REE ul) *adj* having an unreal, fantastic quality; hallucinatory; dreamlike
- Bob was so tired when he stepped off the train that his first view of India had a faintly *surreal* quality; the swarming crowds, the strange language, and, above all, the cows walking in the streets made him feel as though he'd stumbled into a dream.
- Alice's adventures in Wonderland were rather *surreal*, perhaps because it turned out (disappointingly) that they actually were part of a dream.

SURREPTITIOUS (sur up TISH us) *adj* sneaky; secret
- The dinner guest *surreptitiously* slipped a few silver spoons into his jacket as he was leaving the dining room.
- The babysitter made herself a *surreptitious* meal of lobster as soon as Mr. and Mrs. Robinson had driven away.

SURROGATE (SUR uh git) *adj* substitute
A *surrogate* mother is a woman who bears a child for someone else. This word is often a noun. A *surrogate* is a substitute.
- A kind parent offered to go to prison as a *surrogate* for his son, who had been convicted of extortion.

SUSCEPTIBLE (suh SEP tuh bul) *adj* capable of being influenced by something; vulnerable or receptive to
- In *The Wizard of Oz*, the emotionally *susceptible* Tin Man begins to cry every time a remotely sad thought passes through his hollow head.
- Ray's *susceptibility* (suh sep tuh BIL i tee) to new fads hasn't diminished in recent years; he now spends much of his time sitting on an aluminum foil mat in order to "metallicize" his joints and ligaments.

SWEEPING (SWEE ping) *adj* far-reaching; extensive; wide-ranging
- The new CEO's promise to bring *sweeping* change to the company basically amounts to him saying, "A lot of you had better be ready to get the ax."

- I wish Matthew wouldn't make such *sweeping* judgments; what gives him the right to decide that an entire continent is in bad taste?
- The principal's *sweeping* gaze made every kid in the lunchroom tremble.

SYCOPHANT (SIK uh funt) *n* one who sucks up to others
- The French class seemed to be full of *sycophants;* the students were always bringing apples to the teacher and telling her how nice she looked.

A *sycophant* is *sycophantic* (sik uh FAN tik).
- The exasperated boss finally fired his *sycophantic* secretary because he couldn't stand being around someone who never had anything nasty to say.

SYNTAX (SIN taks) *n* the patterns or rules governing the way grammatical sentences are formed in a given language
- Poor *syntax* is the same thing as bad grammar, ain't it?

SYSTEMIC (sys TEM ik) *adj* affecting the entire system, especially the entire body
- The consultant said that the problem was not isolated to one department, but was *systemic;* that is, it affected the entire company.
- "*Systemic* circulation" is another term for the circulatory system in vertebrates.

A *systemic* illness is one that affects the entire body. *Systemic* lupus erythematosus, for example, is an autoimmune disease in which the body essentially becomes allergic to itself. Don't confuse this word with *systematic* (sis tuh MAT ik), which means orderly or meticulous.

SYNTHESIS (SIN thuh sis) *n* the combining of parts to form a whole
- It seemed as though the meeting might end in acrimony and confusion until Raymond offered his brilliant *synthesis* of the two diverging points of view.
- A hot fudge sundae is the perfect *synthesis* of hot fudge and vanilla ice cream.

QUICK QUIZ #156

*Match each word in the first column with its definition in the
second column. Check your answers in the back of the book.*

1.	succumb	a.	haughty
2.	supercilious	b.	yield
3.	superficial	c.	flatterer
4.	superfluous	d.	substitute
5.	surfeit	e.	unnecessary
6.	surreptitious	f.	on the surface only
7.	surrogate	g.	sneaky
8.	sycophant	h.	excess
9.	synthesis	i.	combining of parts

QUICK QUIZ #157

*Match each word in the first column with its definition in the
second column. Check your answers in the back of the book.*

1.	suffuse	a.	humble prayer
2.	sumptuous	b.	overpower
3.	supersede	c.	lying on the back
4.	supine	d.	overspread
5.	supplication	e.	grammar
6.	suppress	f.	take the place of
7.	surmise	g.	far-reaching
8.	surreal	h.	luxurious
9.	susceptible	i.	hallucinatory
10.	sweeping	j.	affecting the entire system
11.	syntax	k.	conjecture
12.	systemic	l.	capable of being influenced

T

TACIT (TAS it) *adj* implied; not spoken
- Mrs. Rodgers never formally asked us to murder her husband, but we truly believed that we were acting with her *tacit* consent.

Tacit is related to *taciturn*.

TACITURN (TAS i turn) *adj* untalkative by nature
- The chairman was so *taciturn* that we often discovered that we had absolutely no idea what he was thinking.

- The *taciturn* physicist was sometimes thought to be brilliant simply because no one had ever heard him say anything that wasn't intelligent. Everyone misconstrued his *taciturnity*; he was actually quite dumb.

Taciturn is related to *tacit*.

TACTICAL (TAK ti kul) *adj* having to do with tactics, especially naval or military tactics; marked by clever tactics or deft maneuvering
- The admiral made a *tactical* error when he ordered his men to drag their ships across the desert as part of the surprise attack.

- "Tell me about that, Georgina," began Mr. Hopp—and then, realizing that the use of her first name so early in the evening had been a *tactical* blunder, he quickly added, "Miss Bringhurst, I mean."

TAINT (taynt) *n* contaminant; a trace of something spoiled, contaminated, off-flavor, or otherwise offensive
- The flavor of the rich, buttery sauce picked up a slight *taint* from the mouse that had fallen into the sauceboat and drowned.

- There's a *taint* of madness in that family; they're okay for a generation or two, and then suddenly one of them forsakes the comforts of the family house for the chicken coop.

This word can also be a verb.
- I'm sure my mother-in-law meant well, but as far as I'm concerned her peacemaking efforts are *tainted* by my knowledge that she tried to pay her daughter not to marry me.

TANGENTIAL (tan JEN shul) *adj* only superficially related to the matter at hand; not especially relevant; peripheral
- The vice president's speech bore only a *tangential* relationship to the topic that had been announced.

- Stuart's connection with our organization is *tangential;* he once made a phone call from the lobby of our building, but he never worked here.

When a writer or speaker "goes off on a *tangent,*" he or she is making a digression or straying from the original topic.

TANGIBLE (TAN juh bul) *adj* touchable; palpable
- A mountain of cigarette butts was the only *tangible* evidence that Luke had been in our house.
- There was no *tangible* reason I could point to, but I did have a sneaking suspicion that Ernest was a rodeo fan.

The opposite of *tangible* is *intangible.*

TANTAMOUNT (TAN tuh mownt) *adj* equivalent to
- Waving a banner for the visiting team at that football game would be *tantamount* to committing suicide; the home-team fans would tear you apart in a minute.
- Yvonne's method of soliciting donations from her employees was *tantamount* to extortion; she clearly implied that she would fire them if they didn't pitch in.

TAUTOLOGICAL (tawt uh LAH juh kul) *adj* redundant; circular
"When everyone has a camera, cameras will be universal" is a *tautological* statement, because "everyone having a camera" and "cameras being universal" mean the same thing.
- The testing company's definition of intelligence—"that which is measured by intelligence tests"—is *tautological.*

A *tautology* (taw TAHL uh jee) is a needless repetition of words, or saying the same thing using different words. For example:
- The trouble with bachelors is that they aren't married.

TEDIUM (TEE dee um) *n* dullness; monotony; boredom
- Oh, no, another evening at Gwen's house—always the same bland food, always the same people with nothing to say, always the same slide show of Gwen's tropical fish! I don't think I can stand the *tedium.*
- The initial excitement of summer vacation had gradually turned to *tedium,* and by the end of August, the children were ready to go back to school.
- Although some find the composer's work brilliant, others find it *tedious* (TEE dee us); for example, there is his seven-hour composition in which a single note is played over and over.

TEEM (teem) *v* to swarm; to be inundated; to overrun
- When the waiter brought Bob the cheese course, Bob gasped; the cheese was *teeming* with maggots.
- On a clear night high in the mountains, the sky *teems* with stars.
- We'd better hire some extra security for the concert; it's going to be *teeming* with hopped-up kids, and they'll be furious when they find out that the main act canceled last night.

TEMERITY (tuh MER uh tee) *n* boldness; recklessness; audacity
- Our waiter at the restaurant had the *temerity* to tell me he thought my table manners were atrocious.
- The mountain climber had more *temerity* than skill or sense. He tried to climb a mountain that was much too difficult and ended up in a heap at the bottom.

TEMPERATE (TEM pur it) *adj* mild; moderate; restrained
- Our climate is *temperate* during the spring and fall but nearly unbearable during the summer and winter.
- The teacher's *temperate* personality lent a feeling of calm and control to the kindergarten class.

The opposite of *temperate* is *intemperate,* which means not moderate.
- Becky's *intemperate* use of oregano ruined the chili.

To *temper* something is to make it milder.
- Anna laughed and shrieked so loudly at every joke that even the comedian wished she would *temper* her appreciation.

Temperance is moderation, especially with regard to alcoholic drinks.

TEMPORAL (TEM pur ul) *adj* pertaining to time; pertaining to life or earthly existence; noneternal; short-lived
- Jet lag is a kind of *temporal* disorientation; rapid travel across several time zones can throw off a traveler's sense of time.
- Why is it that *temporal* pleasures seem so much more fun than eternal ones? I'd rather eat a hot-fudge sundae than sit on a cloud playing a harp.
- As the rich old man approached ninety, he grew less concerned with *temporal* matters and devoted more and more energy to deciding which of his children should be left out of his will.

TEMPORIZE (TEM puh ryze) *v* to stall; to cause delay through indecision
- An important skill required of television newscasters is an ability to *temporize* during technical difficulties so that viewers don't become bored and switch channels.

- The co-op board was afraid to tell the actress flat out that they didn't want her to buy an apartment in their building, so they *temporized* by saying they had to look into some building restrictions first.
- "All right, all right, I'll open the safe for you," Clarence *temporized*, hoping that the police would arrive soon. "But in order to do it, I'll need lots of hot water and some birthday candles."

TENABLE (TEN uh bul) *adj* defensible, as in one's position in an argument; capable of being argued successfully; valid
- Members of the Flat Earth Society continue to argue that the Earth is flat, although even children dismiss their arguments as *untenable*.

Untenable means unable to be defended.

TENACIOUS (tuh NAY shus) *adj* persistent; stubborn; not letting go
- The foreign student's *tenacious* effort to learn English won him the admiration of all the teachers at our school.
- Louise's grasp of geometry was not *tenacious*. She could handle the simpler problems most of the time, but she fell apart on quizzes and tests.
- The ivy growing on the side of our house was so *tenacious* that we had to tear the house down to get rid of it.

To be *tenacious* is to have *tenacity* (tuh NAS us tee).

QUICK QUIZ #158

Match each word in the first column with its definition in the second column. Check your answers in the back of the book.

1.	tacit	a.	persistent
2.	taciturn	b.	naturally untalkative
3.	tangential	c.	boldness
4.	tangible	d.	equivalent to
5.	tantamount	e.	not deeply relevant
6.	tautological	f.	redundant
7.	temerity	g.	mild
8.	temperate	h.	defensible
9.	tenable	i.	implied
10.	tenacious	j.	touchable

TENET (TEN it) *n* a shared principle or belief
- The *tenets* of his religion prohibited him from dancing and going to movies.
- One of the most important *tenets* of our form of government is that people can be trusted to govern themselves.

TENTATIVE (TEN tuh tiv) *adj* experimental; temporary; uncertain
- George made a *tentative* effort to paint his house by himself; he slapped some paint on the front door and his clothes, tipped over the bucket, and called a professional.
- Our plans for the party are *tentative* at this point, but we are considering hiring a troupe of accordionists to play polkas while our guests are eating dessert.
- Hugo believed himself to be a great wit, but his big joke was rewarded by nothing more than a very *tentative* chuckle from his audience.

TENUOUS (TEN yoo us) *adj* flimsy; extremely thin
- The organization's financial situation has always been *tenuous*; the balance of the checking account is usually close to zero.

To *attenuate* is to make thin. *Extenuating* circumstances are those that lessen the magnitude of something, especially a crime.
- Cherrie admitted that she stole the Cracker Jacks, but claimed that there were *extenuating* circumstances: She had no money to buy food for her dog.

TEPID (TEP id) *adj* lukewarm; halfhearted
- Pizza is best when it's served piping-hot, while some salads taste better *tepid* or at room temperature.
- A baby's bathwater should be *tepid*, not hot; you can test it with your elbow before you put the baby in.
- The teacher's praise of Tina's painting was *tepid*, perhaps because Tina's painting was an unflattering caricature of the teacher.
- "Oh, I guess I'll go to the prom with you," Mona said *tepidly*, "but I reserve the right to change my mind if something better comes along."

TERSE (turs) *adj* using no unnecessary words; succinct
- The new recording secretary's minutes were so *terse* that they were occasionally cryptic.
- *Terseness* is not one of Rex's virtues; he would talk until the crack of dawn if someone didn't stop him.

THEOLOGY (thee AHL uh jee) *n* the study of God or religion
  • Ralph was a paradox: He was an atheist, yet he passionately studied *theology*.

THESIS (THEE sis) *n* a theory to be proven; a subject for a composition; a formal paper using original research on a subject
  • At the first Conference on Extraterrestrials, Caroline Riggs advanced her controversial *thesis* that aliens operate most of our nation's bowling alleys.

  • The *thesis* statement of a written composition is a sentence that states the theme of the composition.

  • Stu is writing his senior *thesis* on Anglo-Saxon building techniques, a topic he's fairly certain no one else in the senior class will be working on; the *thesis* of his *thesis* is that Anglo-Saxon building techniques were more sophisticated than modern scholars generally believe.

If you have more than one *thesis*, you have *theses* (THEE seez). *Antithesis* (an TITH uh sis) is a direct opposite, as in the *antithesis* of good is evil.

THORNY (THAWR nee) *adj* full of difficulties; tough; painful
A rosebush is literally *thorny*; a problem may be figuratively so.
  • Before we go any further, we'll have to resolve the *thorny* question of who's going to pay for the next round.

  • Whether to let children go out alone after dark is a *thorny* topic for the parents of urban teenagers. Is it more important to keep them safe at home or to allow them to develop a sense of independence?

THRESHOLD (THRESH ohld) *n* the sill of a doorway; a house's or building's entrance; any point of beginning or entering
  • No matter how many times I see home videos of a new groom dropping his bride when he tries to carry her over the *threshold*, I still laugh.

  • Ambrose hung a sheaf of grain over the *threshold* of his house to keep demons away; to keep burglars away, he put a leghold trap just inside the door.

  • The dean told the new graduates that they stood at the *threshold* of a great adventure; what he didn't say was that for many of them the adventure would be unemployment.

QUICK QUIZ #159

Match each word in the first column with its definition in the second column. Check your answers in the back of the book.

1. tactical	a. pertaining to time
2. taint	b. stall
3. tedium	c. having to do with tactics
4. teem	d. dullness
5. temporal	e. full of difficulties
6. temporize	f. sill of a doorway
7. tepid	g. swarm
8. thesis	h. contaminant
9. thorny	i. theory to be proven
10. threshold	j. lukewarm

THROTTLE (THRAH tul) *v* to choke; to strangle; to work a fuel lever or feed the flow of fuel to an engine

- "If that cat jumps onto the counter one more time, I'm going to *throttle* her," said Bryce, rising grimly to his feet.

- The pilot's frantic *throttling* was to no avail; the engine would not respond because the airplane was out of fuel.

This word can also be a noun. A car's *throttle* is its gas pedal. To make a car go faster, you step on the *throttle*. To run an engine at full *throttle* is to run it at full speed. To do anything else at full *throttle* is to do it rapidly and with single-mindedness.

- When Nicki has an idea for a poem, she runs to her desk and works at full *throttle* until the poem is finished; she doesn't even stop to answer the phone or go to the bathroom.

THWART (thwawrt) *v* to prevent from being accomplished; to frustrate; to hinder

- I wanted to do some work today, but it seemed as though fate *thwarted* me at every turn; first someone on the phone tried to sell me a magazine subscription, then my computer's printer broke down, then I discovered that my favorite movie was on TV.

- There's no *thwarting* Yogi Bear once he gets it into his mind that he wants a picnic basket; he will sleep till noon, but before it's dark, he'll have every picnic basket that's in Jellystone Park.

TIMOROUS (TIM ur us) *adj* fearful; easily frightened
- "Would you mind getting off my foot, sir?" the wizened old lady asked in a tiny, *timorous* voice.
- On Halloween night, the DeMados decorate their house with skeletons and bats, and *timorous* trick-or-treaters are afraid to approach their door.
- Hannah's *timorous* boyfriend broke up with her by asking her friend Tina to do it for him.

Timorous is related to the word timid.

TIRADE (TYE rayd) *n* a prolonged, bitter speech
- Preston launched into a *tirade* against imitation cheese on the school lunch menu.

TITILLATE (TIT uh layt) *v* to excite; to stimulate; to tease
- It's really cruel to *titillate* a friend's curiosity by starting to share a choice piece of gossip and then abruptly saying, "No, I really shouldn't spread this around."
- Appetizers are supposed to *titillate* people's appetites, not stuff them to the gills.

Titillation is the noun form of the word.
- Despite the *titillation* of the advertising, the movie itself was such a turkey that it failed after the first weekend.

TITULAR (TICH uh lur) *adj* in title or name only; nominal
- The *titular* head of the company is Lord Arden, but the person who's really in charge is his secretary; she tells him whom to hire, whom to fire, and whom to meet for lunch.
- The family's *titular* breadwinner is my father, but it's Mom's trust fund that actually puts food on the table.

Titular also means bearing the same name as the title.
- Flipper, the *titular* star of the TV show *Flipper*, was in reality a female dolphin named Suzy.

TOIL (TOY ul) *n* hard work; labor; drudgery; exhausting effort
- "Am I going to have to *toil* in the fields like this all day?" asked Celia plaintively after being asked by her mother to pick some chives from the garden.
- Meeting the manufacturing deadline required weeks of unremitting *toil* from the designers, some of whom worked past midnight nearly every night.

This word can also be a verb. To *toil* is to engage in hard labor.

- *Toiling* in the hot sun all morning had made Arnold tired and thirsty.

TORPOR (TOR pur) *n* sluggishness; inactivity; apathy

- After consuming the guinea pig, the boa constrictor fell into a state of contented *torpor* that lasted several days.

- The math teacher tried to reduce the *torpor* of his students by banging on his desk, but the students scarcely blinked.

To be in a state of *torpor* is to be *torpid*.

TORTUOUS (TOR choo wus) *adj* winding; twisting; serpentine; full of curves

Don't confuse this word with *torturous* (TOR chur us), which means torturing or excruciating. A movie with a *tortuous* plot is one that is hard for a viewer to follow; a movie with a *torturous* plot is one that is agonizing for a viewer to watch.

- On the *tortuous* path through the woods to the tent, one or two of the Cub Scouts always managed to get lost.

- Sybil had to use *tortuous* reasoning to persuade herself that it was really all right to shoplift, but after a bit of mental gymnastics she was able to accomplish the task.

TOUCHSTONE (TUCH stohn) *n* a standard; a test of authenticity or quality

- The size of a student's vocabulary is a useful *touchstone* for judging the quality of his or her education.

- A candidate's pronouncements about the economy provided a *touchstone* by which his or her fitness for office could be judged.

In its original usage, a *touchstone* was a dark stone against which gold and other precious metals were rubbed in order to test their purity. Now the word is used more loosely to describe a broad range of standards and tests.

TOUT (towt) *v* to praise highly; to brag publicly about

- Advertisements *touted* the chocolate-flavored toothpaste as getting rid of your sweet tooth while saving your teeth.

TOXIC (TAHK sik) *adj* poisonous

- After the storm, the beach was covered with spilled oil, spent nuclear fuel, contaminated medical supplies, and other *toxic* wastes.

- *Toxic* residues from pesticides can remain on or in fruits and vegetables even after they have been washed with soap.

- It is now clear that cigarettes are *toxic* not only to smokers but also to nonsmokers who breathe in exhaled smoke.

Something *toxic* is a *toxin* (TAHK sin).

- Some shellfish contain a *toxin* that can make diners violently ill.

TRANSCEND (tran SEND) *v* to go beyond or above; to surpass

- The man who claimed to have invented a perpetual motion machine believed that he had *transcended* the laws of physics.

- The basketball player was so skillful that she seemed to have *transcended* the sport altogether; she was so much better than her teammates that she seemed to be playing an entirely different game.

To be *transcendent* is to be surpassing or preeminent. Something *transcendent* is *transcendental* (tran sen DEN tul).

TRANSFIX (tranz FIKS) *v* to cause to stand motionless with awe, amazement, or some other strong emotion; to rivet

- The children stood *transfixed* at the astonishing sight of Mary Poppins rising into the air with her umbrella.

- The hunter aimed his flashlight at the eyes of the bullfrog, hoping to *transfix* his prey so that it would be easier to catch.

- The students were *transfixed* with disgust at the sight of their gym teacher setting up square dance equipment.

TRANSGRESS (trans GRES) *v* to violate (a law); to sin

- The other side had *transgressed* so many provisions of the treaty that we had no choice but to go to war.

- We tried as hard as we could not to *transgress* their elaborate rules, but they had so many prohibitions that we couldn't keep track of all of them.

An act of *transgressing* is a *transgression*.

- The bully's innumerable *transgressions* included breaking all the windows in the new gymnasium and pushing several first graders off the jungle gym.

TRANSIENT (TRAN shunt) *adj* not staying for a long time; temporary

- The *transient* breeze provided some relief from the summer heat, but we were soon perspiring again.

- The child's smile was *transient*; it disappeared as soon as the candy bar was gone.

- A hotel's inhabitants are *transient*; they come and go, and the population changes every night.

Transient can also be a noun. A *transient* person is sometimes called a *transient*. Hoboes, mendicants, and other homeless people are often called *transients*.

A very similar word is *transitory*, which means not lasting long. A *transient* breeze might provide *transitory* relief from the heat.

This word can also be pronounced "TRAN zee unt."

TRAUMA (TROW muh) *n* severe shock or distress; a violent wound; a wrenching experience
- Ella needs some spoiling right now to help her recover from the *trauma* of her parents' divorce.

In medical terms, a *trauma* is a serious wound or shock to the body.
- The gunshot victim was hurried to the hospital's new *trauma* center, which was staffed by physicians experienced in treating life-threatening wounds.

Anything that causes *trauma* is said to be *traumatic* (truh MAT ik).
- Having their carpets cleaned is a *traumatic* experience for people who believe that their carpets have suffered enough.

To induce *trauma* is to *traumatize* (TROW muh tyze).
- The fox *traumatized* the hens by sneaking into the henhouse and licking his lips.

QUICK QUIZ #160

Match each word in the first column with its definition in the second column. Check your answers in the back of the book.

1.	throttle	a.	severe shock
2.	thwart	b.	prevent from being accomplished
3.	timorous		
4.	titillate	c.	choke
5.	titular	d.	poisonous
6.	toil	e.	in name only
7.	tortuous	f.	excite
8.	toxic	g.	fearful
9.	transfix	h.	winding
10.	trauma	i.	cause to stand motionless
		j.	hard work

SAT POWER VOCAB

TRAVESTY (TRAV is tee) *n* a grotesque or shameful imitation; a mockery; a perversion
- The defense lawyer complained that the continual snickering of the judge had turned his client's trial into a *travesty*, and he demanded that the case be thrown out.
- Every year at homecoming, the college glee club puts on a *travesty* of a popular play or movie, and their show is always popular with alumni.

TRENCHANT (TREN chunt) *adj* concise; effective; caustic
- The reporter's *trenchant* questions about the national deficit unhinged the White House spokesman, and after stumbling through a halfhearted response, he declared the press conference over.
- Joellen's presentation was *trenchant* and well researched; that was not surprising since she had paid her clever new assistant to write it.
- As the landlord showed the couple around, Meave managed to sound most appreciative about the new apartment, but her *trenchant* asides to her husband made it clear that she thought the place was a dump.

TREPIDATION (trep uh DAY shun) *n* fear; apprehension; nervous trembling
- The nursery school students were filled with *trepidation* when they saw the other children in their class dressed in their Halloween costumes.
- The *trepidation* of the swimming team was readily apparent: Their knees were knocking as they lined up along the edge of the pool.

To be fearless is to be *intrepid*.
- The *intrepid* captain sailed his ship around the world with only a handkerchief for a sail.

TRIUMVIRATE (trye UM vuh rit) *n* a ruling coalition of three officials; any group of three working jointly
- The dying emperor appointed a *triumvirate* to succeed him because he wanted to make sure that no single person ever again held all the power in the realm.
- Mother Goose Land is ruled by a *triumvirate* consisting of the butcher, the baker, and the candlestick maker.
- Those three girls have been a *triumvirate* of best friends ever since the first day of nursery school, when all three of them had potty accidents at once.

TRYST (trist) *n* a secret meeting of lovers
- Jane and Greg were always arranging *trysts* that didn't work out; either it rained when they were going to meet under the stars or Greg's parents came home early when they were going to meet in his backyard swimming pool.
- "I'm perfectly happy for alley cats to have a little romance in their lives," groaned Barry, "but why do their *trysts* always have to be under my bedroom window?"
- In romance novels, the characters never have mere dates; they have *trysts*.

TUMULT (TOO mult) *n* violent, noisy commotion; uproar; outbreak
- In the *tumult* of the rock concert, Bernice was unable to find her dropped contact lens.
- Such a *tumult* breaks out when the end-of-school bell rings that the teachers have learned to jump onto their desks to avoid being trampled.

To be a *tumult* or like a *tumult* is to be *tumultuous* (tuh MUL choo wus).
- The fans' *tumultuous* celebration at the end of the football game left the field a muddy mess.

TURBID (TUR bid) *adj* murky; opaque; unclear
- The boys were reluctant to jump into the *turbid* water; mud stirred up by the flood had turned the water in their swimming hole the color of chocolate milk.
- The air was *turbid* with an oily black smoke that coated everything in soot and made noon look like midnight.

Turbid can also be used figuratively to mean confused or muddled.
- The professor was easily able to refute my *turbid* argument in favor of not having a final exam.

The noun is *turbidity* (tur BID uh tee).

TURMOIL (TUR moyl) *n* state of great confusion or commotion
- The president's sudden death threw his administration into *turmoil*, as his former deputies and assistants vied with one another for power.
- "Ever since the baby was born we've been in kind of a *turmoil*," Donna said cheerfully, kicking a pair of dirty socks under the table as she led her visitor on a tour of the house.

TURPITUDE (TUR puh tood) *n* shameful wickedness; depravity

- Paul was sacked by his boss because of a flagrant act of *turpitude:* He was caught stealing office supplies.

QUICK QUIZ #161

Match each word in the first column with its definition in the second column. Check your answers in the back of the book.

1.	tenet	a.	without unnecessary words
2.	tentative	b.	go beyond
3.	tenuous	c.	brag publicly about
4.	terse	d.	fearless
5.	torpor	e.	experimental
6.	theology	f.	not lasting long (2)
7.	tirade	g.	bitter speech
8.	touchstone	h.	shared principle
9.	tout	i.	wickedness
10.	transcend	j.	sluggishness
11.	transgress	k.	flimsy
12.	transient	l.	fear
13.	transitory	m.	study of religion
14.	trepidation	n.	standard
15.	intrepid	o.	violate
16.	turpitude		

QUICK QUIZ #162

Match each word in the first column with its definition in the second column. Check your answers in the back of the book.

1.	travesty	a.	secret meeting of lovers
2.	trenchant	b.	ruling coalition of three
3.	triumvirate	c.	murky
4.	tryst	d.	concise
5.	tumult	e.	violent, noisy commotion
6.	turbid	f.	grotesque imitation
7.	turmoil	g.	state of great confusion

U

UBIQUITOUS (yoo BIK wuh tus) *adj* being everywhere at the same time
- The new beer commercial was *ubiquitous*—it seemed to be on every television channel at once.
- Personal computers, once a rarity, have become *ubiquitous*.

To be *ubiquitous* is to be characterized by *ubiquity* (yoo BIK wuh tee). The *ubiquity* of fast-food restaurants is one of the more depressing features of American culture.

UNCANNY (un KAN ee) *adj* extraordinary; unimaginable; seemingly supernatural
- Jessica has an *uncanny* ability for sniffing out the most expensive item in a store.
- People often say that the similarity between Ted's and Fred's mannerisms is *uncanny*, but since the two men are identical twins who have lived together all their lives, it actually isn't all that unusual.

Uncanny is not the opposite of canny, which means artful, wily, or shrewd (and which, by the way, derives from the word can).

UNCONSCIONABLE (un KAHN shuh nuh bul) *adj* not controlled by conscience; unscrupulous
- Leaving a small child unattended all day long is an *unconscionable* act.
- Stealing money from every citizen of that town was *unconscionable*. Bert should be ashamed of himself for doing it.

Don't confuse this word with *unconscious*.

UNCTUOUS (UNGK choo us) *adj* oily, both literally and figuratively; insincere
Salad oil is literally *unctuous*. A used-car salesman might be figuratively *unctuous*—that is, oily in the sense of being slick, sleazy, and insincere.

UNDERLYING (un dur LYE ing) *adj* basic; fundamental; only noticeable under scrutiny
- The *underlying* cause of the cult's disintegration was not faithlessness but homesickness on the part of its members.
- Albert seems dopey at first, but there's a keen intelligence *underlying* those vacuous mannerisms of his.

UNDERMINE (UN dur myne) *v* to impair; to subvert; to weaken by excavating underneath

- The children's adamant refusal to learn French considerably *undermines* their teacher's efforts to teach it to them.
- The rushing waters of the flood had *undermined* the north end of the foundation, and the house was now leaning in that direction.

UNDERPINNING (UN dur pin ing) *n* a system of supports beneath; a foundation or basis

- The *underpinning* of Shing and Dyan's long-lasting marriage was a shared enthusiasm for bowling.
- The *underpinnings* of our friendship extend back to childhood, when I helped Kristie sew a purse for her mother.

UNDERSCORE (un dur SKAWR) *v* to underline; to emphasize

- Heidi was so nervous about the exam that she ended up *underscoring* her entire textbook in yellow marker.
- "I hate you!" Ryan shouted. To *underscore* his point, he added, "I think you stink!"
- Harold's terrible hunger *underscores* the importance of remembering to eat.

UNDERWRITE (un dur RYTE) *v* to sponsor; to subsidize; to insure

- There would be no such thing as public television in this country if rich American oil companies were not willing to *underwrite* the rebroadcast of expensive British television shows.
- The local bank agreed to *underwrite* the high school production of South Pacific, providing money for props, costumes, and the rental of a theater.

A person or company that *underwrites* something is called an *underwriter*.

UNIFORM (YOO nuh form) *adj* consistent; unchanging; the same for everyone

- Traffic laws are similar from one state to the next, but they aren't *uniform;* each state has its own variations.
- The school did not have a *uniform* grading policy; each teacher was free to mark students according to any system that he or she thought appropriate.

Something that is *uniform* has *uniformity* (yoo nuh FOR muh tee).

Uniforms are suits of clothing that are *uniform* in appearance from one person to the next.

UNILATERAL (yoo nuh LAT ur ul) *adj* involving one side only; done on behalf of one side only; one-sided; not mutual
- In my family, there was *unilateral* agreement on the subject of curfews; my parents agreed that I should be home by midnight, and I did not.

- *Unilateral* disarmament is the decision by one side in a conflict to lay down its arms.

In law, a *unilateral* contract is a contract in which only one of the signers bears any obligation. As might be expected, *bilateral* (bye LAT ur ul) means two-sided. In biology, a body whose left and right sides are mirror images of each other is said to exhibit bilateral symmetry. People's bodies are not bilaterally symmetrical—you have a spleen on only one side of your gut, for example—but worms' bodies are. Good for worms. As might further be expected, *multilateral* (mul tee LAT ur ul) means many-sided. In a *multilateral* treaty, many nations participate. And *lateral* (LAT ur ul) means of or pertaining to a side. A *lateral* move in a career is one in which you switch jobs without ascending or descending the corporate hierarchy.

UNREMITTING (un ri MIT ing) *adj* unceasing; unabated; relentless
- Superman waged an *unremitting* battle against evildoers everywhere.

UNWITTING (un WIT ing) *adj* unintentional; ignorant; not aware
- When Leo agreed to hold open the door of the bank, he became an *unwitting* accomplice to the bank robbery.

- My theft was *unwitting;* I hadn't meant to steal the car, but had absentmindedly driven it away from the automobile dealership and parked it in my garage.

- On the camping trip, Josephine *unwittingly* stepped into a bear trap and remained stuck in it for several days.

URBANE (ur BAYN) *adj* poised; sophisticated; refined
- The British count was witty and *urbane;* all the hosts and hostesses wanted to have him at their parties.

- The new magazine was far too *urbane* to appeal to a wide audience outside the big city.

Urbanity (ur BAN uh tee) is a quality more often acquired in an *urban* setting than in a rural one.

USURY (YOO zhur ee) *n* lending money at an extremely high rate of interest
 - My sister said she would lend me ten dollars if I would clean her room for a week, a bargain that I considered to be *usury*.

A *usurer* (YOO zhur ur) is someone who practices *usury*.
 - Eight-year-old Chuck is quite a little *usurer*; if a kid in his class borrows a dime for milk money, Chuck makes him pay back a quarter the next day.

The adjective is *usurious* (yoo ZHOOR ee us).

USURP (yoo SURP) *v* to seize wrongfully
 - The children believed that their mother's new boyfriend had *usurped* their father's rightful place in their family.
 - The founder's scheming young nephew *usurped* a position of power in the company.

The noun is *usurpation* (yoo sur PAY shun).

UTILITARIAN (yoo til uh TAR ee un) *adj* stressing usefulness or utility above all other qualities; pragmatic
 - Jason's interior-decorating philosophy was strictly *utilitarian*; if an object wasn't genuinely useful, he didn't want it in his home.

Utilitarian can also be a noun. Jason, just aforementioned, could be called a *utilitarian*.

UTOPIA (yoo TOH pee uh) *n* an ideal society
 - A country where nobody had to work would be Quentin's idea of *utopia*.
 - The little town wasn't just a nice place to live, as far as Ed was concerned; it was *utopia*.

A *utopian* is someone with unrealistic or impractical plans or expectations for society. Such plans or expectations are *utopian* plans or expectations.

The opposite of a *utopia* is a *dystopia*.

QUICK QUIZ   #163

Match each word in the first column with its definition in the second column. Check your answers in the back of the book.

1.	ubiquitous	a.	oily; slick
2.	unconscionable	b.	poised and sophisticated
3.	unctuous	c.	everywhere at once
4.	uniform	d.	pragmatic
5.	unremitting	e.	seize wrongfully
6.	unwitting	f.	unscrupulous
7.	urbane	g.	an ideal society
8.	usurp	h.	unintentional
9.	utilitarian	i.	consistent
10.	utopia	j.	unceasing

QUICK QUIZ   #164

Match each word in the first column with its definition in the second column. Check your answers in the back of the book.

1.	uncanny	a.	system of supports beneath
2.	underlying	b.	involving one side only
3.	undermine	c.	basic
4.	underpinning	d.	impair
5.	underscore	e.	sponsor
6.	underwrite	f.	extraordinary
7.	unilateral	g.	lending money at extremely high rates
8.	usury	h.	underline

V

VACILLATE (VAS uh layt) *v* to be indecisive; to waver
- We invited James to spend Thanksgiving with us, but he *vacillated* for so long that we finally became annoyed and disinvited him.

- Tyler *vacillated* about buying a new car. He couldn't decide whether to get one.

The act of *vacillating* is called *vacillation*.

VAPID (VAP id) *adj* without liveliness; dull; spiritless
An apathetic person just doesn't care about anything, and everything he does is *vapid*.
- The novelist's prose was so *vapid* that Mary couldn't get beyond the first page.

VACUOUS (VAK yoo wus) *adj* empty of content; lacking in ideas or intelligence
- I don't think that woman understands a word you're saying; her expression is as *vacuous* as a rabbit's.
- If Gail has to spend one more hour cooped up with Karen and her *vacuous* observations, she cannot answer for the consequences.

Vacuous and *vacant* (VAY kunt) both refer to emptiness, but not the same kind of emptiness. *Vacant* is generally used to mean literally empty; an apartment with no tenant is *vacant*, not *vacuous*. Similarly, a dull person's thoughts can be *vacuous*, even though his skull is not literally *vacant*. However, a *vacant* expression and a *vacuous* expression are the same thing.

VAGARY (VAY guh ree) *n* whim; unpredictable action; wild notion
- "This meal was a little *vagary* of your father's," said Mrs. Swain grimly as she sat the children down to plates of steak topped with whipped cream.
- Thanks to the *vagaries* of fashion, everyone is wearing tennis rackets instead of shoes this summer.
- The *vagaries* of Sean's boss are a little unsettling; one day he'll tell Sean that he is in line to become president of the company, and the next day he'll tell him to scrub the executive washroom.

This word often appears in the plural: *vagaries* (VAY guh reez).

VANQUISH (VANG kwish) *v* to conquer; to overpower
- Nancy finally *vanquished* her nail-biting habit by coating her nails with a distasteful chemical.
- "Nyah, nyah, we *vanquished* you!" the unsportsmanlike soldiers sang as their enemies retreated.

VEHEMENT (VEE uh munt) *adj* intense; forceful; violent
- Shaking his fist and stomping his foot, Gerry was *vehement* in his denial.

The noun is *vehemence*.

VENAL (VEEN ul) *adj* capable of being bribed; willing to do anything for money; corrupt
- The *venal* judge reversed his favorable ruling when the defendant refused to make good on his promised bribe.
- The young man's interest in helping the sick old woman was strictly *venal*; he figured that if he was kind to her, she would leave him a lot of money in her will.

A *venal* person is a person characterized by *venality* (vee NAL uh tee). Don't confuse this word with *venial* (VEE nee ul), which means trivial or pardonable. A peccadillo is a *venial*, harmless sin.

VENEER (vuh NEER) *n* facade; coating; outward appearance
- To a woodworker, a *veneer* is a thin sheet or strip of wood that has been sliced or peeled from a larger piece of wood; plywood, for example, is a sandwich of veneers.
- In general usage, a *veneer* is any thin outward surface.
- Under her *veneer* of sophistication—acquired, at great expense to her parents, at a Swiss finishing school—Holly is actually a shy, nervous hick.

VERDANT (VUR dunt) *adj* covered with green plants; leafy; inexperienced
Verdant is derived from the French word for green.
- In springtime, the *verdant* hills seem to whisper, "Skip school and come for a walk!"
- When the movie crew reached their destination, they were dismayed to find the landscape still *verdant*; they were supposed to be making a movie about skiing.

VENERATE (VEN uh rayt) *v* to revere; to treat as something holy, especially because of great age
- Lester *venerated* his grandfather; he worshiped the ground the old man limped on.
- The members of the curious religion *venerated* Elvis Presley and hoped that the pope would declare him a saint.

A person who is worthy of being *venerated* is said to be *venerable*.

VERACITY (vuh RAS uh tee) *n* truthfulness
- The *veracity* of young George Washington is apocryphal.

Veracious (vuh RAY shus) means truthful.

VERBOSE (vur BOHS) *adj* using too many words; not succinct; circumlocutory

Someone who is *verbose* uses too many words when fewer words would suffice.
- Lee handed in a 178-word final assignment; no one ever accused him of *verbosity* (vur BAHS uh tee).

VERGE (vurj) *n* border; brink; edge
- On the *verge* of the pond is a mushy spot where it's not safe to skate.
- Eleanor has been on the *verge* of tears ever since her mother told her that she would not be allowed to attend the prom.

This word can also be a verb.
- Nick's surly answer *verged* on rudeness, but his father decided not to punish him.

To *converge* (kun VURJ) is to come together or meet.
- The water is churning and frothy at the spot where the two rivers *converge*.

To *diverge* (di VURJ) is to separate.
- A fork in a road is a place where two roads *diverge*.

VERISIMILITUDE (ver uh si MIL uh tood) *n* similarity to reality; the appearance of truth; looking like the real thing
- They used pine cones and old truck tires to make statues of Hollywood celebrities that were remarkable for their *verisimilitude*.
- The *verisimilitude* of counterfeit eleven-dollar bills did not fool the eagle-eyed treasury officer, who recognized them immediately for what they were.

VERITY (VER uh tee) *n* the quality of being true; something true
- You could hardly doubt the *verity* of her story, especially when she had documents to prove her point.

Many truth-related words derive from the Latin root "verus" which means true. *Verisimilar* (ver i SIM uh lur) means having the appearance of truth, and *verisimilitude* (ver i si MIL uh tood) is the quality of being *verisimilar*.
- The plastics company had found a way to make fake leather of shocking *verisimilitude*.

Veracious (vur AY shus) means habitually truthful.

- It would be easier to trust Charlotte if she had a reputation for being *veracious*—but she doesn't. In fact, she's been called a liar many times before.

To *aver* (uh VUR) is to state with confidence, as though you know it to be the truth.

- "Yes, that's the man," Charlotte *averred*. "I recognize him for sure."

To *verify* (VER i fye) is to prove that something is true, to confirm it.

- The police were able to *verify* Olin's claim that he had been out of the country at the time of the crime, so they let him go.

VERNACULAR (vur NAK yuh lur) *n* everyday speech; slang; idiom

- Our teacher said that we should save our *vernacular* for the street; in the classroom we should use proper grammar.

VESTIGE (VES tij) *n* a remaining bit of something; a last trace

- The unhappy young man found *vestiges* of his fiancée in the rubble, but the explosion had effectively ended their romance.

- An old uniform and a tattered scrapbook were the only *vestiges* of the old man's career as a professional athlete.

Your appendix is a *vestige:* It used to have a function, but now this organ does nothing.

The adjective form of *vestige* is *vestigial* (vuh STIJ ee ul). The appendix is referred to as a *vestigial* organ. It is still in our bodies, although it no longer has a function. It is a mere *vestige* of some function our digestive systems no longer perform.

VEX (veks) *v* to annoy; to pester; to confuse

- Margaret *vexed* me by poking me with a long, sharp stick.

- Stuck at the bottom of a deep well, I found my situation extremely *vexing*.

The act of *vexing*, or the state of being *vexed*, is *vexation*. A *vexed* issue is one that is troubling or puzzling.

VIABLE (VYE uh bul) *adj* capable of living; workable

- When a doctor says that an organ is no longer *viable*, it means it can't be used as a transplant organ.

- A fetus is said to be *viable* when it has developed to the point when it is capable of surviving outside the womb.

- Lupe's plan for storing marshmallows in the dome of the Capitol just wasn't *viable*.

Something that is *viable* has *viability* (vye uh BIL uh tee).

VICARIOUS (vye KAR ee us) *adj* experienced, performed, or suffered through someone else; living through the experiences of another as though they were one's own experiences

To take *vicarious* pleasure in someone else's success is to enjoy that person's success as though it were your own.

- We all felt a *vicarious* thrill when the mayor's daughter won fourth prize in the regional kickboxing competition.

VICISSITUDE (vi SIS uh tood) *n* upheaval; natural change; change in fortune

- The *vicissitudes* of the stock market were too much for Karen; she decided to look for a job that would stay the same from one day to the next.

- The *vicissitudes* of the local political machine were such that one could never quite be certain whom one was supposed to bribe.

VIE (vye) *v* to compete; to contest; to struggle

- Sheryl *vied* with her best friend for a promotion.

- The two advertising agencies *vied* fiercely for the Lax-Me-Up account, which was worth $100 million a year in billings.

VIGILANT (VIJ uh lunt) *adj* constantly alert; watchful; wary

- Miss Grimble is *vigilant* against grammatical errors; when she spots a misplaced modifier, she pounces like a tiger.

- Dad *vigilantly* guarded the door of the living room to keep the children from seeing the Easter bunny at work.

To be *vigilant* is to exhibit *vigilance* (VIJ uh luns).

- Distracted by the loud noise in the hallway, the guard let his *vigilance* slip for a moment, and the prisoner quickly escaped.

Vigil is a related word that means a period of staying awake or peacefully protesting, as if *vigilantly* standing watch.

VIGNETTE (vin YET) *n* a small, decorative design or drawing; a short literary sketch; a brief but expressive scene in a play or movie

- Lauren decorated the top of each thank-you note with a tiny *vignette* of a dolphin leaping gracefully out of the water.

- The editor at the publishing company told Mrs. Proutie that the *vignettes* she had written about her garden would be unlikely to sell many more copies if published as a book.

- The boring movie was enlivened somewhat by half a dozen sexy *vignettes* sprinkled through it.

VILIFY (VIL uh fye) *v* to say vile things about; to defame

- The teacher was reprimanded for *vilifying* the slow student in front of the rest of the class.

- Our taxi driver paused briefly on the way to the airport to *vilify* the driver of the car that had nearly forced him off the road.

- The political debate was less a debate than a *vilification* contest. At first the candidates took turns saying nasty things about one another; then they stopped taking turns.

QUICK QUIZ   #165

Match each word in the first column with its definition in the second column. Check your answers in the back of the book.

1.	vacuous	a.	whim
2.	vagary	b.	border
3.	vanquish	c.	conquer
4.	veneer	d.	compete
5.	verdant	e.	covered with green plants
6.	verge	f.	facade
7.	verity	g.	empty of content
8.	vie	h.	quality of being true
9.	vigilant	i.	constantly alert
10.	vignette	j.	short literary sketch

QUICK QUIZ   #166

Match each word in the first column with its definition in the second column. Check your answers in the back of the book.

1.	vacillate	a.	annoy
2.	vapid	b.	be indecisive
3.	vehement	c.	defame
4.	venal	d.	capable of living
5.	venerate	e.	experienced through another
6.	veracity	f.	dull
7.	verbose	g.	upheaval
8.	verisimilitude	h.	revere
9.	vernacular	i.	last trace
10.	vestige	j.	similarity to reality
11.	vex	k.	truthfulness
12.	viable	l.	corrupt
13.	vicarious	m.	wordy
14.	vicissitude	n.	slang
15.	vilify	o.	intense

VINDICATE (VIN duh kayt) *v* to clear from all blame or suspicion; to justify
- George, having been accused of stealing money from the cash register, was *vindicated* when the store manager counted the money again and found that none was missing after all.
- Tom's claim of innocence appeared to be *vindicated* when several dozen inmates at the state mental hospital confessed to the crime of which he had been accused.

A person who has been *vindicated* is a person who has found *vindication*.

VINDICTIVE (vin DIK tiv) *adj* seeking revenge
- Jeremy apologized for denting the fender of my car, but I was feeling *vindictive*, so I made him buy me a new car.
- Samantha's *vindictive* ex drove all the way across the country just to put a stink bomb in her car.

To feel *vindictive* is to be filled with *vindictiveness*.

VIRTUOSO (vur choo WOH soh) *n* a masterful musician; a masterful practitioner in some other field
- The concert audience fell silent when the *virtuoso* stepped forward to play the sonata on his electric banjo.
- As an artist, he was a *virtuoso;* as a husband, he was a chump.

Virtuoso can also be an adjective. A *virtuoso* performance is a performance worthy of a *virtuoso.*

VIRULENT (VIR uh lunt) *adj* extremely poisonous; malignant; full of hate
- The *virulent* disease quickly swept through the community, leaving many people dead and many more people extremely ill.
- The snake was a member of a particularly *virulent* breed; its bite could kill an elephant.
- Jonathan is a *virulent* antifeminist; he says that all women should sit down and shut up.

To be *virulent* is to be characterized by *virulence. Virulent* is related to *virus,* not to *virile,* which means manly.

VISCOUS (VIS kus) *adj* thick; gluey; sticky
- I rapidly lost my thirst as I watched the water ooze from the tap in a *viscous,* brownish stream.
- That *viscous* sap dripping from the gash in the trunk of the pine tree may one day harden into amber.

To be *viscous* is to have *viscosity* (vis KAHS uh tee).
- Motor oils are rated according to their *viscosity;* less *viscous* oils are usually used in the winter because cold weather can cause more *viscous* grades to become excessively thick.

VISIONARY (VIZH uh ner ee) *n* a dreamer; someone with impractical goals or ideas about the future
- My uncle was a *visionary,* not a businessman; he spent too much time tinkering with his antigravity generator and not enough time working for his plumbing business.
- The candidate was a *visionary;* he had a lot of big ideas but no realistic plan for putting them into practice.

Visionary can also be an adjective. A *visionary* proposal is an idealistic and usually impractical proposal.

VITIATE (VISH ee ayt) *v* to make impure; to pollute
- For years a zealous group of individuals has campaigned against the use of fluoride in water, claiming that it has *vitiated* our bodies as well as our morals.

VITRIOLIC (vi tree AHL ik) *adj* caustic; full of bitterness
Vitriol is another name for sulfuric acid. To be *vitriolic* is to say or do something so nasty that your words or actions burn like acid.

- The review of the new book was so *vitriolic* that we all wondered whether the reviewer had some personal grudge against the author.

VIVACIOUS (vi VAY shus) *adj* lively; animated; full of pep

- The eighth-grade girls became bubbly and *vivacious* whenever a cute boy walked by, but as soon as he was out of sight they settled back into their usual grumpy lethargy.

To be *vivacious* is to have *vivacity* (vi VAS i tee).

- Beatrice's *vivacity* dimmed noticeably when she realized that the news she was waiting for would not be good.

VOCATION (voh KAY shun) *n* an occupation; a job
Your *vocation* is what you do for a living.

- If Stan could figure out how to make a *vocation* out of watching television and eating potato chips, he would be one of the most successful people in the world.

Vocational training is job training. Since your *vocation* is your job, your *avocation* is your hobby.

- The accountant's *vocation* bored her, but her *avocation* of mountain climbing did not.

VOCIFEROUS (voh SIF ur us) *adj* loud; noisy

- Randy often becomes *vociferous* during arguments. He doesn't know what he believes, but he states it loudly nevertheless.

VOGUE (vohg) *n* fashion; style

- Never throw away old clothes; outdated styles inevitably come back in *vogue*.

- *Vogue* is a famous magazine filled with fashion photographs, clothing advertisements, and articles about whatever is in *vogue* at the moment.

- The goldfish were sorry to learn that the campus *vogue* for swallowing live goldfish is back.

To be in *vogue*, or susceptible to *vogues*, is to be *voguish* (VOHG ish).

VOLATILE (VAHL uh tul) *adj* quick to evaporate; highly unstable; explosive

- A *volatile* liquid is one that evaporates readily. Gasoline is a *volatile* liquid. It evaporates readily, and then the vapor poses a great danger of explosion.

- A *volatile* crowd is one that seems to be in imminent danger of getting out of control or exploding.
- The situation in the Middle East was highly *volatile;* the smallest incident could have set off a war.

To be *volatile* is to be characterized by *volatility.*

VOLITION (voh LISH un) *n* will; conscious choice
- Insects, lacking *volition,* simply aren't as interesting to the aspiring anthropologist as humans are.
- The question the jury had to answer was whether the killing had been an accident or an act of *volition.*

VOLUMINOUS (vuh LOO muh nus) *adj* large; extensive; having great volume
- Kate frantically searched through her *voluminous* lecture notes for the phone number of the boy sitting next to her.
- Hidden in the folds of her *voluminous* skirts are a potted plant, a small child, an electric fan, three pairs of snowshoes, and a bag of breath mints.
- After Stacy's death, Henry burned their *voluminous* correspondence because he didn't want anyone to find out that he and Stacy had been exchanging letters for years.

VOLUPTUOUS (vuh LUP choo wus) *adj* pleasant to the senses; luxurious; pleasure-seeking; extra full and shapely
- The restaurant's most popular dessert is called Sinfully *Voluptuous* Chocolate Torte; each serving contains a pound each of chocolate and butter.
- Doreen's figure has passed the point of *voluptuous* and reached the point of fat.

A person addicted to *voluptuous* things is a *voluptuary* (vuh LUP choo ar ee).

VORACIOUS (vuh RAY shus) *adj* having a huge appetite; ravenously hungry
- Whenever he goes skiing, Reed comes home *voracious;* once he even ate an entire uncooked meat loaf that his mother had intended to prepare for dinner.
- The *voracious* lions circling outside her tent made Patty hesitant to step outside.
- Clay is a *voracious* reader; he always has his nose buried in a book.

QUICK QUIZ #167

Match each word in the first column with its definition in the second column. Check your answers in the back of the book.

1.	vindicate	a.	extremely poisonous
2.	vindictive	b.	masterful musician
3.	virtuoso	c.	dreamer
4.	virulent	d.	caustic
5.	visionary	e.	clear from suspicion
6.	vitiate	f.	will
7.	vitriolic	g.	quick to evaporate
8.	vocation	h.	seeking revenge
9.	vociferous	i.	occupation
10.	volatile	j.	make impure
11.	volition	k.	noisy

QUICK QUIZ #168

Match each word in the first column with its definition in the second column. Check your answers in the back of the book.

1.	viscous	a.	having a huge appetite
2.	vivacious	b.	pleasant to the senses
3.	vogue	c.	large
4.	voluminous	d.	fashion
5.	voluptuous	e.	lively
6.	voracious	f.	thick

W

WAFT (wahft) *v* to float; to drift; to blow
- First a gentle little breeze *wafted* through the window, then a typhoon blew the house down.
- Rick closed the kitchen door to keep the smell of popcorn from *wafting* upstairs because he didn't want his sister to know that he was making a snack.

WAIVE (wayv) *v* to relinquish (a right); to forgo; to put aside for the time being
- The murder suspect *waived* his right to have a lawyer present during his questioning, saying that he had nothing to hide.

An act or instance of *waiving* is a *waiver* (WAY vur).

WAKE (wayk) *n* an all-night vigil kept over a dead body before it is buried; the trail a boat leaves behind it in the water; a track or path left behind something
- Ryan's old friends turned his *wake* into a party on the assumption that if he had been present he would have been the first to break out the beer.
- Jonathan loves to stand at the back of the ferry so he can watch the churning, roiling *wake* behind the boat.
- What started out as an honest, pull-no-punches discussion left terribly hurt feelings in its *wake*, and the participants didn't speak to one another for many days afterward.

WANE (wayn) *v* to decrease in strength or intensity; to fade away; to decline in power
- Congressman Boote's political influence *waned* dramatically following his announcement that he had been kidnapped by creatures in a flying saucer.
- A trip to Greece did little to revive Barry's *waning* interest in Greek history; in fact, it strengthened his new conviction that Greece was boring.

The opposite of *wane* is *wax* (waks).
- As the moon grows full, it is said to *wax*; as it turns into a sliver, it is said to *wane*.

WANTON (WAHN tun) *adj* malicious; unjustifiable; unprovoked; egregious
- Terrorists commit *wanton* acts on a helpless populace to make their point.

Wanton also means intemperate.
- A hedonist lives a *wanton* life in the relentless, unremitting pursuit of pleasure; an ascetic does not.

WARRANT (WAWR unt) *v* to justify; to provide grounds for; to guarantee
- Mac's writing doesn't *warrant* a second glance; it's unreadable garbage.
- The employment agency *warrants* that its temporary secretaries can type 100 words per minute and that they don't mind making coffee.

When *warrant* is used as a noun, it means an authorization or official permit.
- It is illegal for the police to enter someone's home uninvited unless they have a search *warrant*.

A *warranty* (WAWR un tee) is a written guarantee.
- Did the store provide any kind of *warranty* with that vacuum cleaner? I hope so because it's already broken.

WARY (WAR ee) *adj* cautious; watchful; careful
- Billy Green is *wary* of new babysitters; he hides behind his father's legs and cries when it's time for his parents to go.
- The mouse cast a *wary* eye out of its hole and, seeing no cat, scampered into the living room.
- Ann is *wary* about picking up the telephone these days; she is afraid that a collection agency may be on the other end.

To be *wary* is to beware. So beware.

WILLFUL (WIL ful) *adj* deliberate; obstinate; insistent on having one's way
- The mother insisted that the killing committed by her son had not been *willful,* but the jury apparently believed that he had known what he was doing.
- When her mother told her she couldn't have a cookie, the *willful* little girl simply snatched the cookie jar and ran out of the room with it. She had stolen the cookies *willfully.*

WISTFUL (WIST ful) *adj* yearning; sadly longing
- I felt *wistful* when I saw Steve's fancy new car. I wished that I had enough money to buy one for myself.
- The boys who had been cut from the football team watched *wistfully* as the team put together an undefeated season and won the state championship.

WIZENED (WIZ und) *adj* shriveled; withered; shrunken
- The prince was horrified when he lifted his new bride's veil and found not the princess he had been expecting but a *wizened* old crone.
- A few *wizened* apples were all we found on the tree; all the nice ones had already been picked.
- Having only seen wizards in the movies, I expected Mervin to be bent and *wizened* with age, but actually he was young and quite attractive.

WOE (woh) *n* suffering; affliction; distress

- If I told you all the *woes* that have befallen Karl this year, you'd think I was making them up; no one could have that much bad luck.

- Jamie gazed up at his mother with a look of *woe*, pointing to the ant farm he had just dropped on the carpet.

- "Oh, *woe* is me," moaned Libby. "I'm turning forty tomorrow, and no one has planned a surprise party for me!"

The adjective is *woeful*.

WRATH (rath) *n* deep anger; fury

- Dawn's *wrath* knew no bounds when she realized that Ron had started the dishwasher during her shower.

- The *wrathful* vampire lurched toward Marlene and bared his pointy fangs.

- "Why are you treating me this way?" Catherine demanded *wrathfully*. "I'll bet I'm the only girl in the whole sixth grade who has to pay rent to live in her own house!"

Z

ZEALOUS (ZEL us) *adj* enthusiastically devoted to something; fervent

- The *zealous* young policeman made so many arrests that the city jail soon became overcrowded.

- The dictator's followers were so *zealous* that if he had asked them all to jump off a cliff, most of them would have done so.

To be *zealous* is to be full of zeal, or fervent enthusiasm. An overly *zealous* person is a *zealot*.

ZEITGEIST (ZYTE gyst) *n* the mood or spirit of the times
Zeitgeist is a German word that means, literally, time spirit.

- It's interesting to see how Americans always assume the *zeitgeist* changes automatically with the arrival of a new decade. The eighties were allegedly the decade of greed; then, on the first day of 1990, greed supposedly went out of style, and old-fashioned niceness became the order of the day. What did all those formerly greedy people do with their stuff?

ZENITH (ZEE nith) *n* highest point; peak; pinnacle

- The *zenith* of my career as a singer came when I was asked to give a recital in Carnegie Hall for the royal family, the president, Madonna, and a boy in high school whom I'd always had a crush on; since then, it's all sort of been downhill.

For antonyms to *zenith*, see our entries for apex and apogee at the beginning of this chapter.

QUICK QUIZ #169

Match each word in the first column with its definition in the second column. Check your answers in the back of the book.

1.	wanton	a.	fervent
2.	willful	b.	yearning
3.	wistful	c.	deliberate
4.	zealous	d.	malicious

QUICK QUIZ #170

Match each word in the first column with its definition in the second column. Check your answers in the back of the book.

1.	waft	a.	justify
2.	waive	b.	cautious
3.	wake	c.	deep anger
4.	wane	d.	float
5.	warrant	e.	suffering
6.	wary	f.	shriveled
7.	wizened	g.	spirit of the times
8.	woe	h.	highest point
9.	wrath	i.	all-night vigil
10.	zeitgeist	j.	decrease in strength
11.	zenith	k.	relinquish

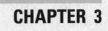

CHAPTER 3

THE
FINAL
EXAM

Final Exam Drill #1: COMPLETIONS

For each question below, choose the word that best completes the meaning of the sentence.

1. Because Stan had been preoccupied during his dynamite-juggling demonstration, the jury felt that he was not _____ for the destruction of the property.
   a. decorous
   b. decimated
   c. indiscreet
   d. culpable
   e. indiscrete

2. Sally was sad because Mr. Reeves, our English teacher, filled the margins of her term paper with _____ remarks about her spelling, grammar, and writing style.
   a. fatuous
   b. heretical
   c. ineffable
   d. prepossessing
   e. derogatory

3. The fans were _____ when the football team lost its fiftieth game in a row.
   a. irascible
   b. despondent
   c. rapacious
   d. stigmatized
   e. precipitous

4. Da-Shawn and Harry were given jobs on the stage crew because their _____ voices ruined the sound of the chorus.

   a. unremitting
   b. paternal
   c. wanton
   d. laconic
   e. dissonant

5. The baby kittens were so _____ that the nursery school children were able to pick them up, carry them around by the scruffs of their necks, and dress them up in doll clothes.

   a. abashed
   b. peripatetic
   c. docile
   d. agrarian
   e. nefarious

Final Exam Drill #2: SYNONYMS

For each question below, match the word on the left with the word most similar in meaning on the right.

1.	litigious	a.	ingenuous
2.	artless	b.	querulous
3.	taciturn	c.	auspicious
4.	refute	d.	perennial
5.	perjure	e.	avow
6.	allege	f.	reticent
7.	gauche	g.	delude
8.	officious	h.	rebut
9.	chronic	i.	inept
10.	propitious	j.	solicitous

Final Exam Drill #3: ODD MAN OUT

Each question below consists of four words. Three of them are related in meaning. Find the word that does not fit.

1. address	infer	construe	extrapolate
2. rigorous	punctilious	integral	painstaking
3. consecrate	revere	venerate	delineate
4. abstain	relegate	forbear	forgo
5. insubordinate	willful	didactic	intransigent
6. labyrinthine	profane	secular	atheistic
7. acrid	amoral	sardonic	virulent
8. analogous	perfunctory	cursory	desultory
9. decadent	degenerate	profligate	magnanimous
10. connoisseur	virtuoso	malleable	aesthete

Final Exam Drill #4: RELATIONSHIPS

For each question below, decide whether the pair of words are roughly similar (S) in meaning, roughly opposite (O) in meaning, or unrelated (U) to each other.

1.	sporadic	incessant
2.	beget	spawn
3.	malaise	subversion
4.	coerce	compel
5.	peccadillo	enormity
6.	charismatic	insipid
7.	countenance	condone
8.	usurp	appropriate
9.	espouse	extricate
10.	arbitrate	mediate

Final Exam Drill #5: COMPLETIONS

For each question below, choose the word that best completes the meaning of the sentence.

1. The applicant's credentials were _____, but I didn't like the color of his necktie so I didn't hire him.
   a. irreproachable
   b. aloof
   c. domestic
   d. vitriolic
   e. histrionic

2. Walter's skin took on a(n) _____ cast after his exposure to the pool of radioactive wastes.

   a. artful

   b. squalid

   c. luminous

   d. nebulous

   e. garrulous

3. The police spent seven months working on the crime case but were never able to determine the identity of the _____.

   a. demagogue

   b. dilettante

   c. egotist

   d. malefactor

   e. patriarch

4. The portions at the restaurant were so _____ that immediately after dessert we drove to another restaurant and ordered a second full meal.

   a. pertinent

   b. minuscule

   c. exhaustive

   d. futile

   e. misanthropic

5. Xavier thought that throwing some scraps to the bear would _____ it, but instead the beast tore apart our campsite in search of more to eat.

   a. accost

   b. mollify

   c. preclude

   d. efface

   e. tout

Final Exam Drill #6: RELATIONSHIPS

For each question below, decide whether the pair of words are roughly similar (S) in meaning, roughly opposite (O) in meaning, or unrelated (U) to each other.

1.	debacle	coup
2.	amenity	injunction
3.	cognizant	unwitting
4.	emigrate	expatriate
5.	concurrent	anachronistic
6.	blithe	morose
7.	disinterested	partial
8.	anachronism	archaism
9.	collusion	complicity
10.	insular	hermetic

Final Exam Drill #7: ODD MAN OUT

Each question below consists of four words. Three of them are related in meaning. Find the word that does not fit.

1.	sacrilege	renaissance	blasphemy	desecration
2.	ambiguous	equivocal	cryptic	requisite
3.	apprehensive	martial	contentious	belligerent
4.	arcane	esoteric	sacrosanct	recondite
5.	incense	replenish	foment	antagonize
6.	exacting	onerous	ponderous	arbitrary
7.	circumspect	eclectic	scrupulous	fastidious
8.	introverted	aloof	reclusive	elliptical
9.	allocate	relinquish	capitulate	succumb
10.	effusive	histrionic	avuncular	gesticulating

Final Exam Drill #8: RELATIONSHIPS

For each question below, decide whether the pair of words are roughly similar (S) in meaning, roughly opposite (O) in meaning, or unrelated (U) to each other.

1.	abyss	chasm
2.	substantive	ethereal
3.	loquacious	taciturn
4.	doctrinaire	dogmatic
5.	colloquial	pedantic
6.	encroach	transgress
7.	amorphous	nebulous
8.	domestic	endemic
9.	cogent	incisive
10.	lethargic	capricious

Final Exam Drill #9: COMPLETIONS

For each question below, choose the word or phrase that best completes the meaning of the sentence.

1. Mei _____ her daughter for putting the cat in the washing machine.
   a. expropriated
   b. disfranchised
   c. coerced
   d. broached
   e. chastised

2. David's salary was _____ his limited skills; he was paid nothing.
   a. as vapid as
   b. tenable despite
   c. vehement in view of
   d. commensurate with
   e. acerbic notwithstanding

3. After several decades of peace, the little country grew
_____ about defense and let its army slowly drift away.
   a. dissolute
   b. partisan
   c. catholic
   d. adamant
   e. complacent

4. None of us had enough money to undertake the project
alone, so we had to depend on the _____ of our parents.
   a. postulate
   b. vilification
   c. largess
   d. hedonism
   e. veracity

5. The court ruled that Ursula's covert discussions with the
Russian ambassador did not _____ treason.
   a. comprise
   b. abnegate
   c. libel
   d. broach
   e. constitute

Final Exam Drill #10: RELATIONSHIPS

For each question below, decide whether the pair of words are
roughly similar (S) in meaning, roughly opposite (O) in meaning,
or unrelated (U) to each other.

1.	bureaucracy	hierarchy
2.	extrapolate	infer
3.	mercurial	volatile
4.	impeccable	culpable
5.	corroborate	refute
6.	expedient	utilitarian
7.	censure	approbation
8.	propriety	decorum
9.	emulate	peruse
10.	mandate	touchstone

Final Exam Drill #11: RELATIONSHIPS

For each question below, decide whether the pair of words are roughly similar (S) in meaning, roughly opposite (O) in meaning, or unrelated (U) to each other.

1.	ameliorate	exacerbate
2.	candor	equivocation
3.	caricature	parody
4.	scrupulous	mendacious
5.	apartheid	mentor
6.	bane	panacea
7.	facile	arduous
8.	philistine	erudite
9.	absolute	commensurate
10.	kinetic	stagnant

Final Exam Drill #12: ODD MAN OUT

Each question below consists of four words. Three of them are related in meaning. Find the word that does not fit.

1.	awry	overt	salient	manifest
2.	duplicity	ascendancy	guile	chicanery
3.	contrition	remorse	cadence	penitence
4.	temperance	sobriety	celibacy	oblivion
5.	nominal	amiable	affable	congenial
6.	choleric	querulous	petulant	equitable
7.	dormant	latent	nostalgic	inert
8.	astute	bereft	sagacious	prudent
9.	copious	bourgeois	profuse	myriad
10.	ascetic	austere	frugal	pejorative

Final Exam Drill #13: RELATIONSHIPS

For each question below, decide whether the pair of words are roughly similar (S) in meaning, roughly opposite (O) in meaning, or unrelated (U) to each other.

1.	serendipitous	hapless
2.	lugubrious	facetious
3.	espouse	appease
4.	qualitative	pejorative
5.	exigency	periphery
6.	harbinger	precursor
7.	profound	desecrated
8.	despotic	autocratic
9.	engender	decimate
10.	pristine	unalloyed

Final Exam Drill #14: COMPLETIONS

For each question below, choose the word that best completes the meaning of the sentence.

1. Jarel was as clever as he was unscrupulous, and he knew what he could not obtain by legitimate means he could always obtain through _____.
   a. chicanery
   b. burlesque
   c. nihilism
   d. strife
   e. theology

2. The visiting professor was so _____ in his field that many of our faculty members became nervous in his presence.
   a. antithetical
   b. archetypal
   c. eminent
   d. plebeian
   e. pathological

3. The orator _____ a bizarre economic program whose central tenet was the abolition of all forms of money.
   a. scintillated
   b. espoused
   c. vacillated
   d. emulated
   e. inundated

4. "Kicking the bucket" is a humorous _____ for "dying."
   a. dictum
   b. stipulation
   c. incantation
   d. conjecture
   e. euphemism

5. The actor, pretending to be inebriated, made a(n) _____ attempt to open his umbrella in a telephone booth.
   a. viable
   b. enigmatic
   c. farcical
   d. cognitive
   e. aphoristic

Final Exam Drill #15: SYNONYMS

For each question below, match the word on the left with the word most similar in meaning on the right.

1. opaque	a. obscure
2. ostensible	b. secular
3. avaricious	c. mellifluous
4. mundane	d. prudent
5. judicious	e. venal
6. mercenary	f. specious
7. ramification	g. rapacious
8. saccharine	h. repercussion
9. archaic	i. dearth
10. paucity	j. anachronism

Final Exam Drill #16: RELATIONSHIPS

For each question below, decide whether the pair of words are roughly similar (S) in meaning, roughly opposite (O) in meaning, or unrelated (U) to each other.

1.	belie	aggregate
2.	legacy	bequest
3.	aptitude	propensity
4.	matriculate	purport
5.	fatalist	cynic
6.	fecund	desiccated
7.	exhort	admonish
8.	polarize	prevail
9.	condescension	adulation
10.	discreet	blatant

Final Exam Drill #17: ODD MAN OUT

Each question below consists of four words. Three of them are related in meaning. Find the word that does not fit.

1.	uniform	monolithic	existential	homogeneous
2.	flaunt	malign	slander	libel
3.	felicity	audacity	temerity	impetuosity
4.	meager	tenuous	pivotal	paltry
5.	indulgent	salutary	prodigal	profligate
6.	disparate	incongruous	heterogeneous	ubiquitous
7.	apprehensive	diffident	succinct	circumspect
8.	cogent	eminent	potent	robust
9.	farcical	affected	contrived	ostentatious
10.	ennui	satiety	languor	volition

Final Exam Drill #18: RELATIONSHIPS

For each question below, decide whether the pair of words are roughly similar (S) in meaning, roughly opposite (O) in meaning, or unrelated (U) to each other.

1.	zealous	catholic
2.	aloof	nefarious
3.	mitigate	assuage
4.	agnostic	atheist
5.	clique	consensus
6.	coalition	faction
7.	husbandry	itinerary
8.	coalesce	dissipate
9.	slavish	subservient
10.	flaunt	reproach

Final Exam Drill #19: COMPLETIONS

For each question below, choose the word that best completes the meaning of the sentence.

1. The Sandersons viewed the flaming image of the devil, which hovered above their house for thirteen days, as a(n) _____ of evil to come.

   a. stratum

   b. portent

   c. periphery

   d. infidelity

   e. aberration

2. There was nothing _____ about Herbert's scientific theories; in fact, they were quite shallow.

   a. sentient

   b. vociferous

   c. peremptory

   d. profound

   e. nepotistic

3. The _____ author turned out a new book every week of her adult life.
   a. prolific
   b. canine
   c. dialectical
   d. implicit
   e. contiguous

4. The _____ girls stubbornly refused to call off their rock fight, despite the pleadings of their mothers.
   a. recalcitrant
   b. pacific
   c. egalitarian
   d. exemplary
   e. fervent

5. Hal's disappointed wife _____ him for being a lazy, foul-smelling, obnoxious slob.
   a. instigated
   b. reproached
   c. flaunted
   d. desecrated
   e. belied

Final Exam Drill #20: RELATIONSHIPS

For each question below, decide whether the pair of words are roughly similar (S) in meaning, roughly opposite (O) in meaning, or unrelated (U) to each other.

1.	profess	espouse
2.	extrovert	introspective
3.	foible	hiatus
4.	caricature	touchstone
5.	debilitate	enervate
6.	placid	frenetic
7.	depravity	debauchery
8.	infinitesimal	grandiose
9.	grandiloquent	rhetorical
10.	malefactor	benefactor

Final Exam Drill #21: ODD MAN OUT

Each question below consists of four words. Three of them are
related in meaning. Find the word that does not fit.

1. avaricious	covetous	officious	parsimonious
2. reprove	scrutinize	censure	rebuke
3. reprehensible	transient	ephemeral	transitory
4. belittle	depreciate	disparage	founder
5. palpable	resolute	tenacious	steadfast
6. absolve	condone	qualify	exculpate
7. civil	culinary	aristocratic	genteel
8. stricture	reproach	admonishment	corollary
9. fidelity	proximity	steadfastness	resolution
10. circumlocutory	redundant	tautological	vicarious

Final Exam Drill #22: RELATIONSHIPS

For each question below, decide whether the pair of words are
roughly similar (S) in meaning, roughly opposite (O) in meaning,
or unrelated (U) to each other.

1. elude	circumvent
2. rustic	urbane
3. circuitous	oblique
4. beset	beleaguered
5. imperial	servile
6. pedestrian	prosaic
7. reprisal	reparation
8. daunt	stymie
9. apotheosis	epitome
10. inaugurate	abort

Final Exam Drill #23: COMPLETIONS

For each question on the next page, choose the word that best completes the meaning of the sentence.

1. Sally had already eaten all her cookies, so she _____ mine.
   a. permeated
   b. mortified
   c. protracted
   d. appropriated
   e. defamed

2. The country's _____ ruler required her citizens to receive official permission before changing channels on their television sets.
   a. definitive
   b. dubious
   c. indigenous
   d. autocratic
   e. redolent

3. I don't enjoy oysters myself, but I'm not _____ to letting others eat them.
   a. innate
   b. averse
   c. opaque
   d. adverse
   e. oblique

4. The president was so _____ by international crises that he found it difficult to watch an entire baseball game without being interrupted.
   a. beset
   b. belittled
   c. bereaved
   d. bequeathed
   e. bemused

5. The representative had _____ so many losing causes that he fainted dead away when his proposal was unanimously adopted by the legislature.

a. championed
b. caricatured
c. misappropriated
d. flouted
e. mediated

Final Exam Drill #24: RELATIONSHIPS

For each question below, decide whether the pair of words are roughly similar (S) in meaning, roughly opposite (O) in meaning, or unrelated (U) to each other.

1.	preempt	usurp
2.	turpitude	confluence
3.	incipient	culminating
4.	burgeon	arbitrate
5.	belittle	stymie
6.	dictum	paradigm
7.	luminous	incandescent
8.	mortified	chagrined
9.	precipitate	prudent
10.	inscrutable	obscure

Final Exam Drill #25: ODD MAN OUT

Each question below consists of four words. Three of them are related in meaning. Find the word that does not fit.

1.	intrinsic	innate	omnipotent	inherent
2.	fortuitous	gregarious	convivial	amicable
3.	cliché	verisimilitude	maxim	epigram
4.	belligerent	indignant	pertinent	contentious
5.	inane	hackneyed	platitudinous	conducive
6.	vitriolic	acrimonious	choleric	prolific
7.	gravity	austerity	vicissitude	sobriety
8.	noxious	obsequious	pernicious	deleterious
9.	finesse	competence	proficiency	euphemism
10.	incorrigible	recalcitrant	diffident	obdurate

Final Exam Drill #26: RELATIONSHIPS

For each question below, decide whether the pair of words are roughly similar (S) in meaning, roughly opposite (O) in meaning, or unrelated (U) to each other.

1.	catalyst	coherence
2.	concord	dissonance
3.	discord	consonant
4.	ingenuous	urbane
5.	infatuated	beguiled
6.	categorical	contingent
7.	novel	banal
8.	parsimony	munificence
9.	permeate	pervade
10.	tentative	definitive

Final Exam Drill #27: COMPLETIONS

For each question below, choose the word that best completes the meaning of the sentence.

1. The trees, vines, and other plants in the tropical forest were truly remarkable, but it was the exotic _____ that caught the zoologist's attention.

   a. accolade

   b. compendium

   c. acumen

   d. fauna

   e. surfeit

2. Ernesto hated to pay extra for a fancy name, but he had discovered that he greatly preferred expensive brand-name products to the cheaper _____ ones.

   a. generic

   b. hypothetical

   c. supercilious

   d. amorphous

   e. contentious

3. After several years of disappointing crops, the enormous harvest left the farmers confronting a(n) _____ of soybeans.
   a. alacrity
   b. blight
   c. glut
   d. chasm
   e. debacle

4. The previously undefeated team found it difficult to cope with the _____ of defeat.
   a. attrition
   b. ignominy
   c. prerequisite
   d. penchant
   e. neologism

5. The darkening sky indicated to all of us that a thunderstorm was _____.
   a. ambivalent
   b. imminent
   c. conciliatory
   d. inherent
   e. lugubrious

Final Exam Drill #28: RELATIONSHIPS

For each question below, decide whether the pair of words are roughly similar (S) in meaning, roughly opposite (O) in meaning, or unrelated (U) to each other.

1.	hegemony	heyday
2.	fortuitous	nominal
3.	deride	venerate
4.	deduce	infer
5.	supercilious	servile
6.	placid	nonchalant
7.	reverence	insolence
8.	extraneous	extrinsic
9.	levity	irony
10.	onerous	exacting

Final Exam Drill #29: ODD MAN OUT

Each question below consists of four words. Three of them are related in meaning. Find the word that does not fit.

1.	comprise	placate	appease	mollify
2.	beguile	bemuse	cajole	delude
3.	provident	egregious	flagrant	unconscionable
4.	adept	adroit	anecdotal	dexterous
5.	iconoclast	insurgent	maverick	prodigy
6.	cadence	incisiveness	acumen	acuity
7.	gratuitous	superfluous	soporific	inordinate
8.	incongruous	staunch	anomalous	eccentric
9.	vacillate	incense	foment	instigate
10.	aberration	vestige	anomaly	singularity

Final Exam Drill #30: RELATIONSHIPS

For each question below, decide whether the pair of words are roughly similar (S) in meaning, roughly opposite (O) in meaning, or unrelated (U) to each other.

1.	mandate	martyr
2.	laud	defame
3.	belabor	complement
4.	disdain	supercilious
5.	distinguish	distend
6.	eulogize	censure
7.	apocalypse	covenant
8.	segregate	sequester
9.	quixotic	utopian
10.	microcosm	magnate

Final Exam Drill #31: COMPLETIONS

For each question below, choose the word that best completes the meaning of the sentence.

1. The _____ salesperson bowed deeply and said, "Yes, sir, of course, sir," whenever I requested anything.
   a. verbose
   b. incumbent
   c. evanescent
   d. malingering
   e. obsequious

2. Because he had never lost a tennis match, Luther believed himself to be _____ on the court.

a. ascetic
b. deleterious
c. omnipotent
d. inane
e. amorous

3. Our teacher was so _____ in his interpretation of the novel that it was difficult to believe he had taken any pleasure in reading it.

a. pedantic
b. laudable
c. intrepid
d. inveterate
e. coherent

4. The prisoners were all _____ as they were led off to the firing squad, but they were shot all the same.

a. perfunctory
b. concise
c. virulent
d. prosaic
e. penitent

5. The divisive issue _____ the community; half the residents seemed to be strongly for it, and half strongly against.

a. circumscribed
b. polarized
c. assuaged
d. castigated
e. disseminated

Final Exam Drill #32: RELATIONSHIPS

For each question below, decide whether the pair of words are roughly similar (S) in meaning, roughly opposite (O) in meaning, or unrelated (U) to each other.

1.	reverence	disdain
2.	conjure	incant
3.	profound	superficial
4.	protract	curtail
5.	fauna	glut
6.	deprecate	lament
7.	abridge	augment
8.	eccentric	orthodox
9.	iconoclast	maverick
10.	idiosyncratic	conventional

Final Exam Drill #33: ODD MAN OUT

Each question below consists of four words. Three of them are related in meaning. Find the word that does not fit.

1.	infamous	abhorrence	innocuous	nefarious
2.	assimilate	abate	mitigate	alleviate
3.	laconic	unctuous	concise	terse
4.	relinquish	renounce	forsake	exult
5.	axiom	maxim	surrogate	precept
6.	virulent	tantamount	adverse	baneful
7.	catharsis	abhorrence	rancor	animosity
8.	idiosyncrasy	eccentricity	complacency	affectation
9.	antecedent	precursor	precedent	recrimination
10.	exonerate	patronize	exculpate	vindicate

Final Exam Drill #34: RELATIONSHIPS

For each question below, decide whether the pair of words are roughly similar (S) in meaning, roughly opposite (O) in meaning, or unrelated (U) to each other.

1.	slothful	assiduous
2.	affluent	opulent
3.	consummate	rudimentary
4.	chastisement	amnesty
5.	sycophant	cajoler
6.	implication	allusion
7.	quantitative	qualitative
8.	agenda	itinerary
9.	pragmatic	quixotic
10.	paradox	anomaly

Final Exam Drill #35: SYNONYMS

For each question below, match the word on the left with the word most similar in meaning on the right.

1.	torpid	a.	subservient
2.	sublime	b.	astuteness
3.	recapitulate	c.	ingenuous
4.	acuity	d.	subtlety
5.	replete	e.	provincial
6.	subordinate	f.	inert
7.	parochial	g.	transcendent
8.	credulous	h.	reiterate
9.	recant	i.	satiated
10.	nuance	j.	repudiate

Final Exam Drill #36: RELATIONSHIPS

For each question below, decide whether the pair of words are roughly similar (S) in meaning, roughly opposite (O) in meaning, or unrelated (U) to each other.

1.	colloquial	contiguous
2.	auspicious	portentous
3.	moribund	viable
4.	aristocratic	patrician
5.	perquisite	prerogative
6.	stagnation	metamorphosis
7.	ebullient	roguish
8.	turpitude	sordidness
9.	cosmopolitan	urbane
10.	denizen	lampoon

Final Exam Drill #37: COMPLETIONS

For each question below, choose the word that best completes the meaning of the sentence.

1. The _____ spring weather was a great relief to all of us who had struggled through the long, harsh winter.

   a. abortive
   b. volatile
   c. temperate
   d. pragmatic
   e. intrinsic

2. I made a(n) _____ effort to repair the leak, but my improvised patch didn't hold, and I soon realized that I would have to call a plumber.

   a. vindictive
   b. tentative
   c. pristine
   d. acrid
   e. caustic

3. The adoring members of the tribe _____ their old king even though he was blind and senile.
   a. squandered
   b. extrapolated
   c. beleaguered
   d. exacerbated
   e. venerated

4. The hikers were _____ by the billions of mosquitoes that descended upon them as soon as they hit the trail.
   a. extolled
   b. vitiated
   c. palliated
   d. vexed
   e. promulgated

5. Seeing the pictures of our old home made us feel _____ and nostalgic.
   a. adept
   b. fastidious
   c. wistful
   d. infamous
   e. impartial

Final Exam Drill #38: RELATIONSHIPS

For each question below, decide whether the pair of words are roughly similar (S) in meaning, roughly opposite (O) in meaning, or unrelated (U) to each other.

1.	ardent	indifferent
2.	adherent	forsaker
3.	poignant	redolent
4.	inundate	reconcile
5.	abject	exalted
6.	proselytize	implement
7.	latent	manifest
8.	burgeon	accost
9.	immutable	static
10.	perfidy	piety

Final Exam Drill #39: ODD MAN OUT

Each question below consists of four words. Three of them are related in meaning. Find the word that does not fit.

1. quixotic	scintillating	chimerical	visionary
2. antipathy	malfeasance	digression	malevolence
3. absolute	unqualified	categorical	wistful
4. static	cerebral	inert	immutable
5. destitute	insolvent	affable	indigent
6. altruist	benevolent	philanthropic	ideological
7. vexed	unequivocal	unalloyed	unmitigated
8. comprehensive	stringent	rigorous	exacting
9. abstract	abstruse	intangible	impervious
10. discernment	tirade	discrimination	sagacity

Final Exam Drill #40: RELATIONSHIPS

For each question below, decide whether the pair of words are roughly similar (S) in meaning, roughly opposite (O) in meaning, or unrelated (U) to each other.

1.	plethora	dearth
2.	autonomy	subjugation
3.	aggregate	augment
4.	vocation	avocation
5.	extraneous	intrinsic
6.	implicit	inferred
7.	invective	eulogy
8.	acerbic	caustic
9.	insinuation	hyperbole
10.	adulterated	unalloyed

Final Exam Drill #41: COMPLETIONS

For each question below, choose the word that best completes the meaning of the sentence.

1. An _____ current of dissatisfaction among the soldiers indicated to the ambassador that revolution was becoming a possibility.
   a. incipient
   b. inert
   c. impervious
   d. impeccable
   e. inept

2. The _____ baker had burnt an entire batch of chocolate chip cookies.
   a. bucolic
   b. ursine
   c. cosmopolitan
   d. infinitesimal
   e. incompetent

3. Irene's _____ cure for her husband's snoring was a paper bag tied snugly around his head.
   a. agnostic
   b. congenital
   c. extrinsic
   d. ingenious
   e. diffident

4. Myron looked harmless, but there was nothing _____ about his plan to enslave the human race.
   a. terse
   b. innocuous
   c. mendacious
   d. nominal
   e. preeminent

5. Attempting to bask in reflected glory, the candidate _____ the names of eleven past presidents in his speech to the convention of schoolteachers.

   a. absolved
   b. implied
   c. litigated
   d. invoked
   e. allocated

Final Exam Drill #42: RELATIONSHIPS

For each question below, decide whether the pair of words are roughly similar (S) in meaning, roughly opposite (O) in meaning, or unrelated (U) to each other.

1.	ambience	milieu
2.	literal	figurative
3.	hypothetical	empirical
4.	subjugate	enfranchise
5.	taciturn	integral
6.	congenital	innate
7.	enfetter	expedite
8.	peripheral	tangential
9.	usurp	abdicate
10.	consummate	abortive

Final Exam Drill #43: ODD MAN OUT

Each question below consists of four words. Three of them are related in meaning. Find the word that does not fit.

1.	cacophony	antagonism	rancor	antipathy
2.	discord	benefactor	contention	incongruity
3.	apathy	indifference	manifesto	languor
4.	amenable	tractable	docile	reciprocal
5.	clandestine	surreptitious	provisional	furtive
6.	intrepid	blithe	squalid	equanimity
7.	callow	apocryphal	dubious	spurious
8.	putative	overt	explicit	patent
9.	desultory	derisory	cursory	perfunctory
10.	conciliate	proscribe	appease	placate

Final Exam Drill #44: ANTONYMS

For each question below, match the word on the left with the word most nearly its **OPPOSITE** on the right.

1. deferential	a. irreverent
2. remonstrate	b. assiduous
3. tacit	c. amorous
4. clement	d. explicit
5. indolent	e. acquiesce
6. ambivalent	f. intemperate
7. aloof	g. aversion
8. lucid	h. antagonist
9. partisan	i. enigmatic
10. affinity	j. resolute

Final Exam Drill #45: RELATIONSHIPS

For each question below, decide whether the pair of words are roughly similar (S) in meaning, roughly opposite (O) in meaning, or unrelated (U) to each other.

1. artifice	machination
2. obtuse	myopic
3. respite	premise
4. exalt	laud
5. assimilate	appreciate
6. edify	obfuscate
7. pensive	ruminating
8. narcissist	egocentric
9. precipitate	stigmatize
10. polemical	contentious

Final Exam Drill #46: COMPLETIONS

For each question below, choose the word that best completes the meaning of the sentence.

1. The three-year-old was _____ in his refusal to taste the broccoli.
   a. recondite
   b. didactic
   c. fortuitous
   d. resolute
   e. genteel

2. We _____ the fine print in the document but were unable to find the clause the lawyer had mentioned.
   a. scrutinized
   b. reconciled
   c. exculpated
   d. cajoled
   e. accrued

3. A state in which one can see, hear, feel, smell, and taste little or nothing is known as _____ deprivation.
   a. aggregate
   b. subversive
   c. sensory
   d. sensual
   e. sensuous

4. The children tried to be _____ about the fact that their parents couldn't afford to give them Christmas presents, but you could tell that they were really quite depressed inside.
   a. tangential
   b. abysmal
   c. stoic
   d. disingenuous
   e. eclectic

5. We felt repeatedly _____ by the impersonal and inflexible bureaucracy in our attempt to win an exemption to the rule.

a. vindicated
b. deluged
c. stymied
d. reiterated
e. gesticulated

Final Exam Drill #47: RELATIONSHIPS

For each question below, decide whether the pair of words are roughly similar (S) in meaning, roughly opposite (O) in meaning, or unrelated (U) to each other.

1.	cliché	platitude
2.	malevolent	macroeconomic
3.	juxtaposed	contiguous
4.	defame	laud
5.	idyllic	bucolic
6.	inexorable	irrevocable
7.	despondent	sanguine
8.	lethargy	zeal
9.	dogma	tenet
10.	ebullient	stoic

Final Exam Drill #48: COMPLETIONS

For each question below, choose the word that best completes the meaning of the sentence.

1. The gasoline spill had so thoroughly _____ the town's main well that it was possible to run an automobile on tap water.

a. exulted
b. exalted
c. engendered
d. adulterated
e. preempted

2. Mr. Jones _____ the teenagers after they had driven the stolen car into his living room and put a dent in his new color TV.

    a. admonished
    b. usurped
    c. enervated
    d. alleged
    e. professed

3. Henry's legs were so severely injured in the roller-skating accident that he didn't become fully _____ again until more than a year later.

    a. decadent
    b. exemplified
    c. querulous
    d. portentous
    e. ambulatory

4. The kitchen in the new house had an electronic vegetable peeler, an automatic dish scraper, a computerized meat slicer, and dozens of other futuristic _____.

    a. proponents
    b. genres
    c. amenities
    d. mendicants
    e. protagonists

5. When Joe began collecting stamps, he had hoped that the value of his collection would _____ rapidly; instead, the collection has slowly become worthless.

    a. qualify
    b. appreciate
    c. polarize
    d. belabor
    e. rebuke

Final Exam Drill #49: DEFINITIONS

For each question below, match the word on the left with its definition on the right.

1.	suffrage	a.	arched passageway
2.	bauble	b.	difference
3.	enumerate	c.	gaudy trinket
4.	arcade	d.	greedy
5.	acquisitive	e.	right to vote
6.	clandestine	f.	secret
7.	shibboleth	g.	name one by one
8.	deign	h.	catchword
9.	discrepancy	i.	fashion
10.	vogue	j.	condescend

Final Exam Drill #50: ANTONYMS

For each question below, match the word on the left with the word most nearly its opposite on the right.

1.	denunciation	a.	dotage
2.	embroil	b.	ingratiate
3.	depose	c.	verdant
4.	cordial	d.	endearment
5.	conspicuous	e.	emancipate
6.	contumely	f.	champion
7.	alienate	g.	cloistered
8.	precocity	h.	abasement
9.	stark	i.	effrontery
10.	compunction	j.	brusque

Final Exam Drill #51: DEFINITIONS

For each question below, match the word on the left with its definition on the right.

1.	regimen	a.	perform without preparation
2.	toil	b.	regulated course
3.	supine	c.	lying on the back
4.	quell	d.	familiar
5.	prelude	e.	hard work
6.	tumult	f.	introduction
7.	impasse	g.	belligerent patriotism
8.	jingoism	h.	put an end to
9.	improvise	i.	violent, noisy commotion
10.	conversant	j.	deadlock

Final Exam Drill #52: ANTONYMS

For each question below, match the word on the left with the word most nearly its opposite on the right.

1.	explication	a.	depleted
2.	wizened	b.	anathema
3.	puritanical	c.	expunged
4.	appalling	d.	demise
5.	dismay	e.	estimable
6.	extant	f.	prurient
7.	resurrection	g.	corpulent
8.	benediction	h.	dissuade
9.	induce	i.	exuberance
10.	rife	j.	inquisition

Final Exam Drill #53: PRONUNCIATIONS

Pronounce each of the following words without looking at *column a* or *column b.* Then select the column that comes closer to your pronunciation.

1.	vacuity	a.	VAK yoo uh tee	b.	va KYOO uh tee
2.	draconian	a.	dra KOHN ee un	b.	dray KOH nee un
3.	tumult	a.	TUM ult	b.	TYOO mult
4.	explicable	a.	ek SPLIK uh bul	b.	EKS pli kuh bul
5.	patina	a.	puh TEE nuh	b.	PAT uh nuh
6.	presage	a.	pree SAYJ	b.	PRES ij
7.	grimace	a.	gri MAYS	b.	GRIM is
8.	licentious	a.	lye SEN shus	b.	lye SEN tee us
9.	cabal	a.	kuh BAL	b.	CAB ul
10.	auxiliary	a.	awg ZIL uh ree	b.	awg ZIL yuh ree

Final Exam Drill #54: ANTONYMS

For each question below, match the word on the left with the word most nearly its opposite on the right.

1.	fledgling	a.	influx
2.	advent	b.	defunct
3.	integral	c.	aftermath
4.	emanation	d.	auxiliary
5.	suppress	e.	affiliate
6.	aghast	f.	fuel
7.	secede	g.	flippant
8.	acquit	h.	forestall
9.	accede	i.	stupefy
10.	galvanize	j.	arraign

Final Exam Drill #55: DEFINITIONS

For each question below, match the word on the left with its definition on the right.

1.	antipodal	a.	make filthy
2.	partition	b.	division
3.	parallel	c.	tedious recounting
4.	implication	d.	sink
5.	subside	e.	harmful
6.	resplendent	f.	exactly opposite
7.	inimical	g.	abolish
8.	abrogate	h.	something suggested
9.	degrade	i.	similar
10.	litany	j.	brilliantly shining

Final Exam Drill #56: ODD ONE OUT

For each question below, choose the word that is least similar in meaning to the other two.

1.	a.	lobby	b.	abrogate	c.	nullify
2.	a.	pristine	b.	nebulous	c.	turbid
3.	a.	quell	b.	repress	c.	impending
4.	a.	apparition	b.	equestrian	c.	phantasm
5.	a.	obeisance	b.	supplication	c.	ascertain
6.	a.	predicament	b.	predominant	c.	preponderance
7.	a.	nonchalant	b.	nirvana	c.	tepid
8.	a.	karma	b.	augur	c.	herald
9.	a.	neophyte	b.	pundit	c.	fledgling
10.	a.	elegy	b.	dirge	c.	impasse

Final Exam Drill #57: ANTONYMS

For each question below, match the word on the left with the word most nearly its opposite on the right.

1. slake		a. emaciate
2. antedate		b. posturing
3. exodus		c. ensue
4. impassioned		d. nebulous
5. drollery		e. repugnant
6. insouciance		f. angst
7. distinct		g. confluence
8. redeeming		h. consternation
9. cohort		i. dispassionate
10. forthright		j. nemesis

Final Exam Drill #58: DEFINITIONS

For each question below, match the word on the left with its definition on the right.

1. deploy	a. cite
2. consign	b. line
3. olfactory	c. hand over
4. adduce	d. something that heals
5. mode	e. temporary encampment
6. balm	f. method of doing
7. bivouac	g. pertaining to the sense of smell
8. accouterments	h. trappings
9. queue	i. reduction
10. diminution	j. arrange strategically

Final Exam Drill #59: ANTONYMS

For each question below, match the word on the left with the word most nearly its opposite on the right.

1. fallacy	a. entity
2. insuperable	b. verity
3. doleful	c. pluralism
4. porous	d. superseded
5. chaste	e. dejected
6. cipher	f. sordid
7. gratis	g. exorbitant
8. jubilant	h. elated
9. bravado	i. impenetrable
10. solidarity	j. being demure

Final Exam Drill #60: PRONUNCIATIONS

Pronounce each of the following words without looking at *column a* or *column b*. Then select the column that comes closer to your pronunciation.

1.	diminution	a. di muh NOO shun	b. dim yoo NISH un
2.	insuperable	a. in SUP ur uh bul	b. in SOO pur uh bul
3.	hypertrophy	a. HYE pur troh fee	b. hye PUR truh fee
4.	triumvirate	a. trye UM vuh rit	b. trye um VYE rayt
5.	junta	a. HOON tuh	b. JOON tuh
6.	bivouac	a. BIV wak	b. BIV oo ak
7.	atrophy	a. A truh fee	b. ah TROH fee
8.	wizened	a. WYE zund	b. WIZ und
9.	adjunct	a. AD junkt	b. AJ unkt
10.	posthumous	a. pohst HUM us	b. PAHS chuh mus

Final Exam Drill #61: ANTONYMS

For each question below, match the word on the left with the word most similar in meaning on the right.

1.	capacious	a.	noisome
2.	expostulate	b.	propound
3.	allegory	c.	nomadic
4.	armistice	d.	voluminous
5.	citadel	e.	accord
6.	spurn	f.	arsenal
7.	curb	g.	bulwark
8.	armament	h.	rebuff
9.	errant	i.	avert
10.	odious	j.	parable

Final Exam Drill #62: DEFINITIONS

For each question below, match the word on the left with its definition on the right.

1.	annuity	a.	model of excellence
2.	paragon	b.	funeral song
3.	engaging	c.	ascribing human characteristics
4.	intervene	d.	far-reaching
5.	sanction	e.	annual allowance
6.	bilious	f.	charming
7.	anthropomorphic	g.	person skilled in a craft
8.	dirge	h.	come between opposing groups
9.	artisan	i.	official permission or approval
10.	sweeping	j.	ill-tempered

Final Exam Drill #63: ANTONYMS

For each question below, match the word on the left with the word most similar in meaning on the right.

1. zenith
2. facade
3. spate
4. purblind
5. ascribe
6. crux
7. sumptuous
8. ratiocinate
9. titillating
10. exemption

a. nescient
b. crescendo
c. surmise
d. epicurean
e. impunity
f. attribute
g. cascade
h. ribald
i. motif
j. facet

Final Exam Drill #64: ODD ONE OUT

For each question below, choose the word that is least similar in meaning to the other two.

1. a. emissary   b. incursion   c. liaison
2. a. generic   b. implication   c. corollary
3. a. dissident   b. posterity   c. refractory
4. a. propound   b. advocate   c. supersede
5. a. fickle   b. downcast   c. doleful
6. a. enumerate   b. litany   c. innuendo
7. a. repartee   b. banter   c. oxymoron
8. a. prurient   b. placebo   c. sordid
9. a. cull   b. scorn   c. spurn
10. a. foray   b. overture   c. menagerie

Final Exam Drill #65: DEFINITIONS

For each question below, match the word on the left with its definition on the right.

1. avant-garde
2. underlying
3. invoke
4. classic
5. exhume
6. evoke
7. mire
8. trenchant
9. placebo
10. inclination

a. fake medication
b. unbury
c. summon forth
d. vanguard
e. pray for
f. top-notch
g. marshy, mucky ground
h. basic
i. tendency
j. concise

Final Exam Drill #66: ANTONYMS

For each question below, match the word on the left with the word most similar in meaning on the right.

1. abeyance		a. rend
2. melee		b. replica
3. lout		c. cowering
4. fragment		d. cataclysm
5. clone		e. boor
6. craven		f. altercation
7. millennium		g. verge
8. threshold		h. moratorium
9. skirmish		i. disarray
10. conflagration		j. epoch

Final Exam Drill #67: PRONUNCIATIONS

Pronounce each of the following words without looking at *column a* or *column b*. Then select the column that comes closer to your pronunciation.

1. halcyon	a. HAL see un	b. HALK yun
2. hubris	a. HUB ris	b. HYOO bris
3. protégé	a. PROH tuh zhay	b. PROH teeg
4. inviolate	a. in VYE uh lit	b. in VYE oh layt
5. hypocrisy	a. hi PAHK ruh see	b. HYE poh kris ee
6. rhapsodic	a. RAP suh dik	b. rap SAHD ik
7. motif	a. MOH tif	b. moh TEEF
8. fiasco	a. fee AS koh	b. fye AS koh
9. rationale	a. RASH uh nul	b. rash uh NAL
10. fruition	a. froo ISH un	b. froo shun

Final Exam Drill #68: ANTONYMS

For each question below, match the word on the left with the word most similar in meaning on the right.

1. tryst		a. reactionary
2. concession		b. dilemma
3. dissidence		c. resignation
4. crux		d. divination
5. conservative		e. punctilious
6. augury		f. plight
7. decry		g. dissent
8. meticulous		h. abound
9. teem		i. deplore
10. affliction		j. liaison

Final Exam Drill #69: DEFINITIONS

For each question below, match the word on the left with its definition on the right.

1. amid	a. incitement
2. fiscal	b. system of names
3. delinquent	c. largely confined to sitting down
4. double entendre	d. word made up of initials
5. nomenclature	e. in the middle of
6. acronym	f. gray or white with age
7. provocation	g. monetary
8. concomitant	h. neglecting a duty
9. sedentary	i. following from
10. hoary	j. double meaning

Final Exam Drill #70: ANTONYMS

For each question below, match the word on the left with the word most similar in meaning on the right.

1. uncanny	a. elocution
2. deft	b. quaint
3. primal	c. gambit
4. articulation	d. forswear
5. peculiar	e. repartee
6. abjure	f. inexplicable
7. impassive	g. presume
8. retort	h. aboriginal
9. stratagem	i. canny
10. presuppose	j. objective

Final Exam Drill #71: DEFINITIONS

For each question below, match the word on the left with its definition on the right.

1. reprobate	a. rule or law
2. exposition	b. make an ugly face
3. rationale	c. greeting
4. canon	d. seemingly unending
5. interminable	e. depraved, wicked person
6. salutation	f. force of movement
7. ebb	g. explanation
8. momentum	h. diminish
9. materialistic	i. underlying reason
10. grimace	j. preoccupied with material things

Final Exam Drill #72: ODD ONE OUT

For each question below, choose the word that is least similar in meaning to the other two.

1. a. baroque   b. serene   c. halcyon
2. a. spectrum   b. gamut   c. interim
3. a. stolid   b. avid   c. phlegmatic
4. a. melancholy   b. crestfallen   c. solace
5. a. progeny   b. stratagem   c. gambit
6. a. conundrum   b. jingoism   c. quandary
7. a. harbinger   b. ominous   c. discursive
8. a. diatribe   b. epicure   c. fulminate
9. a. emanate   b. expiate   c. disperse
10. a. inculcate   b. dissent   c. perverse

Final Exam Drill #73: ANTONYMS

For each question below, match the word on the left with the word most similar in meaning on the right.

1. lobby   a. consolidate
2. muster   b. subsidiary
3. entrepreneurial   c. advocate
4. ennui   d. cull
5. serpentine   e. highest caste
6. elite   f. self-made
7. adjunct   g. commiseration
8. pathos   h. pristine
9. garner   i. tortuous
10. untainted   j. doldrums

Final Exam Drill #74: PRONUNCIATIONS

Pronounce each of the following words without looking at *column a* or *column b*. Then select the column that comes closer to your pronunciation.

1. bacchanal   a. BAK uh nul   b. Buh CHAN ul
2. schism   a. SIZ um   b. SKIZ um
3. reclamation   a. rek luh MAY shun   b. ree klam AY shun
4. punitive   a. PUN i tiv   b. PYOO nuh tiv
5. degradation   a. deg ruh DAY shun   b. duh gray DAY shun
6. integral   a. in TEG rul   b. IN tuh grul
7. ennui   a. AHN wee   b. EN wee
8. apostasy   a. AP oh stay see   b. uh PAHS tuh see
9. prescient   a. PREE see unt   b. PRESH unt
10. mores   a. mawrs   b. MAWR ayz

Final Exam Drill #75: ANTONYMS

For each question below, match the word on the left with the word most nearly its opposite on the right.

1.	singular	a.	tedious
2.	bracing	b.	serenity
3.	jaunty	c.	rarefied
4.	rampant	d.	hypertrophy
5.	festering	e.	anterior
6.	attest	f.	generic
7.	wane	g.	dismal
8.	bedlam	h.	query
9.	posterior	i.	wake
10.	harbinger	j.	remission

Final Exam Drill #76: DEFINITIONS

For each question below, match the word on the left with its definition on the right.

1.	careen	a.	shockingly horrible
2.	discursive	b.	classification
3.	apprise	c.	group of close associates
4.	sovereign	d.	crazed excitement
5.	ghastly	e.	supreme ruler
6.	denomination	f.	aimlessly rambling
7.	coterie	g.	swerve
8.	embargo	h.	display threateningly
9.	mania	i.	give notice to
10.	brandish	j.	government order suspending trade

Final Exam Drill #77: ANTONYMS

For each question below, match the word on the left with the word most similar in meaning on the right.

1.	lascivious	a.	reprimand
2.	inflammatory	b.	herald
3.	override	c.	occult
4.	revile	d.	eclipse
5.	perverse	e.	disposition
6.	demeanor	f.	prurient
7.	harp	g.	cavil
8.	mysticism	h.	incendiary
9.	apropos	i.	refractory
10.	presage	j.	apt

Final Exam Drill #78: DEFINITIONS

For each question below, match the word on the left with its definition on the right.

1.	apposite	a.	political meeting
2.	caucus	b.	direct
3.	channel	c.	biting irony
4.	impresario	d.	pertaining to a city or town
5.	commemorate	e.	distinctly suitable
6.	archipelago	f.	person who manages public entertainments
7.	municipal		
8.	sarcasm	g.	honor the memory of
9.	pastoral	h.	group of islands
10.	divulge	i.	rural
		j.	reveal

Final Exam Drill #79: ANTONYMS

For each question below, match the word on the left with the word most nearly its opposite on the right.

1.	confound	a.	averse
2.	genesis	b.	epilogue
3.	aver	c.	discourse
4.	prattle	d.	premeditated
5.	abet	e.	debunk
6.	enmity	f.	confederacy
7.	avid	g.	throttle
8.	inadvertent	h.	vigilant
9.	perpetuate	i.	envision
10.	impromptu	j.	thwart

Final Exam Drill #80: ODD ONE OUT

For each question below, choose the word that is least similar in meaning to the other two.

	a.	b.	c.
1.	abeyance	fiat	interlude
2.	pregnant	august	rife
3.	ennui	listless	ludicrous
4.	inviolate	licentious	ribald
5.	timorous	cower	demur
6.	alienate	mystic	estrange
7.	decry	deplore	depose
8.	duress	tortuous	convolution
9.	figment	pungent	trenchant
10.	harp	transfix	rivet

Final Exam Drill #81: PRONUNCIATIONS

Pronounce each of the following words without looking at *column a* or *column b*. Then select the column that comes closer to your pronunciation.

		a.	b.
1.	foray	a. FAWR ay	b. faw RAY
2.	bilious	a. BIL ee us	b. BIL yus
3.	dour	a. DOW ur	b. door
4.	deprivation	a. dep ruh VAY shun	b. duh prye VAY shun
5.	titular	a. TIT yoo lur	b. TICH uh lur
6.	insouciant	a. in SOO see unt	b. in SOO shee unt
7.	paroxysm	a. puh RAHK sum	b. PAR uk siz um
8.	retort	a. ri TAWRT	b. REE tawrt
9.	liaison	a. LEE uh zahn	b. lee AY zahn
10.	olfactory	a. ahl FAK tur ee	b. OHL fak tur ee

Final Exam Drill #82: ANTONYMS

For each question below, match the word on the left with the word most nearly its opposite on the right.

1.	mawkish	a.	convene
2.	corrugated	b.	explicable
3.	conundrumlike	c.	callous
4.	boon	d.	jocular
5.	dour	e.	adversity
6.	adjourn	f.	concerted
7.	embellish	g.	vivacity
8.	listlessness	h.	seamless
9.	quintessence	i.	dross
10.	unilateral	j.	dilapidate

Final Exam Drill #83: DEFINITIONS

For each question below, match the word on the left with its definition on the right.

1.	canvass	a.	shortage
2.	vagary	b.	free from injury
3.	inviolate	c.	disaster
4.	patrimony	d.	seek votes or opinions
5.	revamp	e.	inheritance
6.	calamity	f.	whim
7.	entreat	g.	revise
8.	balk	h.	diplomatic etiquette
9.	deficit	i.	ask earnestly
10.	protocol	j.	refuse abruptly

Final Exam Drill #84: ANTONYMS

For each question below, match the word on the left with the word most nearly its opposite on the right.

1.	paranoid	a.	ancillary
2.	halcyon	b.	harried
3.	timorous	c.	waive
4.	repose	d.	disquiet
5.	impending	e.	brazen
6.	assert	f.	stalwart
7.	exquisite	g.	botched
8.	apoplexy	h.	posthumous
9.	embryonic	i.	composure
10.	cardinal	j.	retrospective

Final Exam Drill #85: DEFINITIONS

For each question below, match the word on the left with its definition on the right.

1.	precarious	a.	a landing on the edge of the water
2.	duress	b.	float
3.	critique	c.	dangerous
4.	waft	d.	currently holding office
5.	brouhaha	e.	stridently loud
6.	muse	f.	reproduce
7.	propagate	g.	coercion
8.	quay	h.	ponder
9.	incumbent	i.	uproar
10.	raucous	j.	critical review

Final Exam Drill #86: ANTONYMS

For each question below, match the word on the left with the word most nearly its opposite on the right.

1.	foreclose	a.	infraction
2.	sophomoric	b.	opprobrium
3.	bland	c.	foster
4.	limpid	d.	august
5.	obeisance	e.	quiescence
6.	conviction	f.	hubris
7.	fawning	g.	pungent
8.	acclaim	h.	traumatize
9.	avail	i.	turbid
10.	paroxysm	j.	oscillation

Final Exam Drill #87: PRONUNCIATIONS

Pronounce each of the following words without looking at *column a* or *column b*. Then select the column that comes closer to your pronunciation.

1. satyr   a. SAY tur   b. SAT ur
2. quasi   a. KWAY zye   b. KWAH zee
3. exquisite   a. ek SWIZ it   b. EKS kwiz it
4. electoral   a. ee lek TAWR ul   b. i LEK tuh rul
5. emaciate   a. i MAY shee ayt   b. i MAY see ayt
6. remuneration a. ri myoo nuh RAY shun b. ree noom ur AY shun
7. crevasse   a. kruh VAS   b. KREV us
8. pathos   a. PAY thahs   b. PATH ohs
9. quay   a. kee   b. kway
10. trauma   a. TROW muh   b. TRAW muh

Final Exam Drill #88: ODD ONE OUT

For each question below, choose the word that is least similar in meaning to the other two.

1. a. veneer   b. facade   c. queue
2. a. baleful   b. vigilant   c. wary
3. a. enmity   b. exuberant   c. elation
4. a. quiescent   b. pastoral   c. lavish
5. a. apogee   b. aspersion   c. antipodal
6. a. prowess   b. atrophy   c. wizened
7. a. germane   b. converse   c. apposite
8. a. flippant   b. sarcasm   c. eulogy
9. a. embody   b. diffuse   c. propagate
10. a. oligarchy b. demography   c. triumvirate

Final Exam Drill #89: ANTONYMS

For each question below, match the word on the left with the word most nearly its opposite on the right.

1. impregnable   a. homage
2. affront   b. woe
3. allegiance   c. aspersion
4. replete   d. scant
5. copious   e. vacuous
6. bliss   f. empower
7. loathe   g. panegyric
8. eulogy   h. estrangement
9. diatribe   i. susceptible
10. nullify   j. rhapsodize

Final Exam Drill #90: DEFINITIONS

For each question below, match the word on the left with its definition on the right.

1.	arid	a.	loathing
2.	cloy	b.	out of proportion
3.	revulsion	c.	cause to feel too full
4.	equestrian	d.	very dry
5.	chaff	e.	displaying glowing, changing colors
6.	inimitable	f.	impair
7.	undermine	g.	worthless stuff
8.	disproportionate	h.	impossible to imitate
9.	devout	i.	having to do with horseback riding
10.	iridescent	j.	deeply religious

Final Exam Drill #91: ANTONYMS

For each question below, match the word on the left with the word most nearly its opposite on the right.

1.	wax	a.	atrophy
2.	discretionary	b.	imperative
3.	plausible	c.	perigee
4.	downplay	d.	insufferable
5.	captivate	e.	harass
6.	dissembling	f.	aggrandizement
7.	compatible	g.	ludicrous
8.	diminution	h.	disaffect
9.	coddle	i.	ballyhoo
10.	apex	j.	forthright

Final Exam Drill #92: DEFINITIONS

For each question below, match the word on the left with its definition on the right.

1.	elite	a.	most select group
2.	obviate	b.	remove by cutting
3.	corrosive	c.	make unnecessary
4.	stint	d.	restrict
5.	excise	e.	smuggled goods
6.	lyrical	f.	melodious
7.	contraband	g.	affecting the entire system
8.	demographics	h.	study of population characteristics
9.	ascertain	i.	determine with certainty
10.	systemic	j.	eating away

Final Exam Drill #93: ANTONYMS

For each question below, match the word on the left with the word most similar in meaning on the right.

1.	interlude	a.	famine
2.	toxic	b.	rhapsodic
3.	ineluctable	c.	interim
4.	elegiac	d.	carcinogenic
5.	privation	e.	jocose
6.	crevice	f.	booty
7.	cabal	g.	oxymoron
8.	antithesis	h.	cohort
9.	plunder	i.	ineradicable
10.	lyrical	j.	aperture

Final Exam Drill #94: PRONUNCIATIONS

Pronounce each of the following words without looking at *column a* or *column b*. Then select the column that comes closer to your pronunciation.

1.	psyche	a.	SYE kee	b.	syke
2.	harass	a.	HAR us	b.	ha RAS
3.	ascertain	a.	as SUR tun	b.	as ur TAYN
4.	antiquity	a.	AN tye kwit ee	b.	an TIK wuh tee
5.	calumny	a.	kuh LUM nee	b.	KAL um nee
6.	placebo	a.	PLAYS boh	b.	pluh SEE boh
7.	panegyric	a.	pan i JIR ik	b.	payn GYE rik
8.	balm	a.	bahlm	b.	bawm
9.	melee	a.	MAY lay	b.	MEE lee
10.	cordial	a.	KAWR jul	b.	KAWR dee ul

Final Exam Drill #95: ANTONYMS

For each question below, match the word on the left with the word most similar in meaning on the right.

1.	pallid	a.	derelict
2.	bestow	b.	melancholy
3.	ostracize	c.	infringe
4.	arrears	d.	blanched
5.	accentuate	e.	confer
6.	assess	f.	bandy
7.	banter	g.	aggrandize
8.	breach	h.	rebuff
9.	rueful	i.	assay
10.	amass	j.	underscore

Final Exam Drill #96: ODD ONE OUT

For each question below, choose the word that is least similar in meaning to the other two.

1. a. presentiment   b. forebode   c. evince
2. a. puritanical   b. moratorium   c. adjourn
3. a. doldrums   b. raucous   c. stupor
4. a. marginal   b. apex   c. zenith
5. a. chaste   b. reprobate   c. lascivious
6. a. diurnal   b. quotidian   c. singular
7. a. commodious   b. contumely   c. capacious
8. a. privation   b. odious   c. anathema
9. a. blanch   b. pallor   c. mire
10. a. chaff   b. wane   c. dross

Final Exam Drill #97: DEFINITIONS

For each question below, match the word on the left with its definition on the right.

1. inculcate   a. causing resentment
2. denote   b. mournful poem
3. suffice   c. be sufficient
4. ecosystem   d. instill
5. referendum   e. organisms and their environment
6. affidavit   f. harmful action
7. elegy   g. signify
8. titular   h. in name only
9. disservice   i. public vote
10. invidious   j. sworn written statement

Final Exam Drill #98: ANTONYMS

For each question below, match the word on the left with the word most similar in meaning on the right.

1. reassess   a. phlegmatic
2. defile   b. precocious
3. importune   c. meditate
4. rout   d. supplicate
5. vanquish   e. decree
6. stolid   f. fiasco
7. electorate   g. surmount
8. cogitate   h. constituency
9. shrewd   i. debase
10. ordinance   j. reappraise

Final Exam Drill #99: DEFINITIONS

For each question below, match the word on the left with its definition on the right.

1.	alchemy	a.	envy
2.	contretemps	b.	embarrassing occurrence
3.	forebode	c.	be an omen of
4.	apostasy	d.	with suspicion
5.	impoverish	e.	humorous misuse of a word
6.	punitive	f.	abandonment of faith
7.	askance	g.	reduce to poverty
8.	malapropism	h.	seemingly magical transformation
9.	habituate	i.	accustom to a situation
10.	begrudge	j.	inflicting a punishment

Final Exam Drill #100: ANTONYMS

For each question below, match the word on the left with the word most similar in meaning on the right.

1.	infrastructure	a.	savant
2.	baroque	b.	spectrum
3.	pundit	c.	underpinning
4.	entailment	d.	underwrite
5.	subsidize	e.	corollary
6.	shackle	f.	appellation
7.	gamut	g.	meander
8.	pseudonym	h.	convoluted
9.	peregrinate	i.	impetuous
10.	fickle	j.	impede

Final Exam Drill #101: DEFINITIONS

For each question below, match the word on the left with its definition on the right.

1.	obtrusive	a.	severe shock
2.	overture	b.	interfering
3.	trauma	c.	raw material
4.	fodder	d.	humorous
5.	concoct	e.	collection of animals
6.	aggrieve	f.	create by mixing ingredients
7.	menagerie	g.	opening move
8.	droll	h.	mistreat
9.	motley	i.	extremely varied
10.	congeal	j.	solidify

Final Exam Drill #102: PRONUNCIATIONS

Pronounce each of the following words without looking at *column a* or *column b*. Then select the column that comes closer to your pronunciation.

1.	importune	a. im PAWR toon	b. im pawr TOON
2.	ratiocination	a. rash ee oh suh NAY shun	b. ray shee oh sin ay shun
3.	bravado	a. bruh VAH doh	b. BRAY va doh
4.	savant	a. SAV unt	b. suh VAHNT
5.	sophomoric	a. sahf MAWR ik	b. sahf uh MAWR ik
6.	schematic	a. skuh MAT ik	b. skee MAT ik
7.	inculcate	a. IN kul kayt	b. in KUL kayt
8.	vivacity	a. vi VAS i tee	b. vye VAS uh tee
9.	stipend	a. STYE pund	b. STIP und
10.	byzantine	a. BYE zan teen	b. BIZ un teen

Final Exam Drill #103: ANTONYMS

For each question below, match the word on the left with the word most similar in meaning on the right.

1.	dolt	a.	phantom
2.	antiquity	b.	transfix
3.	rivet	c.	bemoaning
4.	odyssey	d.	rapture
5.	disgruntled	e.	delectable
6.	nirvana	f.	pilgrimage
7.	voluptuous	g.	quotidian
8.	diurnal	h.	posterity
9.	wraith	i.	lavish
10.	palatable	j.	buffoon

Final Exam Drill #104: ODD ONE OUT

For each question below, choose the word that is least similar in meaning to the other two.

1.	a. modulate	b. influx	c. teem
2.	a. cabal	b. junta	c. motley
3.	a. altercation	b. melee	c. bombast
4.	a. draconian	b. insouciant	c. astringent
5.	a. fiasco	b. excise	c. disarray
6.	a. conspicuous	b. meticulous	c. punctilious
7.	a. entreat	b. imbue	c. importune
8.	a. affront	b. attribute	c. ascribe
9.	a. incarnation	b. corporeal	c. vagary
10.	a. assail	b. barrage	c. cloister

Final Exam Drill #105: DEFINITIONS

For each question below, match the word on the left with its definition on the right.

1. deity   a. ignorant
2. figment   b. seat of government
3. zeitgeist   c. spacious
4. commodious   d. something made up
5. fulminate   e. god or goddess
6. benighted   f. insignificant
7. ad-lib   g. spirit of the times
8. marginal   h. denounce vigorously
9. capital   i. person with whom secrets are shared
10. confidant   j. improvise

Final Exam Drill #106: ANTONYMS

For each question below, match the word on the left with the word most similar in meaning on the right.

1. preponderant   a. incursion
2. mores   b. depredation
3. extortion   c. brusque
4. clout   d. dispirited
5. churl   e. ethics
6. foray   f. dominant
7. callous   g. curmudgeon
8. appurtenance   h. appendage
9. downcast   i. impecunious
10. impoverished   j. prowess

Final Exam Drill #107: DEFINITIONS

For each question below, match the word on the left with its definition on the right.

1. barrage	a. beginner
2. neophyte	b. accumulate
3. medium	c. highly significant
4. accrue	d. means by which something
5. cant	is conveyed
6. specious	e. false information purposely
7. guise	disseminated
8. wary	f. cautious
9. disinformation	g. deceptive
10. pregnant	h. outpouring of artillery fire
	i. appearance
	j. insincere speech

Final Exam Drill #108: ANTONYMS

For each question below, match the word on the left with the word most similar in meaning on the right.

1. annexation	a. cache
2. empathy	b. pontificating
3. allot	c. osmosis
4. dire	d. bromide
5. adage	e. disclaim
6. ratify	f. crest
7. asylum	g. apportion
8. sententious	h. solace
9. apogee	i. warrant
10. demur	j. grievous

Final Exam Drill #109: PRONUNCIATIONS

Pronounce each of the following words without looking at *column a* or *column b*. Then select the column that comes closer to your pronunciation.

1. forte
   a. for TAY
   b. fawrt
2. vagaries
   a. vuh GAR eez
   b. VAY guh reez
3. repartee
   a. rep ur TAY
   b. rep ur TEE
4. apostasy
   a. uh PAHS tuh see
   b. AP oh stay see
5. epochal
   a. EP uh kul
   b. uh PAHK ul
6. dolorous
   a. duh LAWR us
   b. DOH lur us
7. heinous
   a. HEE nis
   b. HAY nus
8. jocose
   a. JOH kohs
   b. joh KOHS
9. feign
   a. fee gun
   b. fayn
10. obeisance
    a. OHB i suns
    b. oh BAY suns

Final Exam Drill #110: ANTONYMS

For each question below, match the word on the left with the word most similar in meaning on the right.

1. fathom
2. proclaim
3. compliant
4. surreal
5. baleful
6. cavalier
7. assail
8. heinous
9. bristling
10. effectual

a. livid
b. underscore
c. pummel
d. ominous
e. arrant
f. pliable
g. paranormal
h. competent
i. nonchalant
j. delve

Final Exam Drill #111: DEFINITIONS

For each question below, match the word on the left with its definition on the right.

1. edifice
2. redress
3. circumnavigate
4. auspices
5. cleave
6. conservatory
7. efficacy
8. conjugal
9. genocide
10. correlation

a. sail all the way around
b. mutual relation
c. protection
d. cling
e. remedy
f. having to do with marriage
g. big, imposing building
h. extermination of a race or religion or people
i. effectiveness
j. greenhouse or music school

Final Exam Drill #112: ODD ONE OUT

For each question below, choose the word that is least similar in meaning to the other two.

1. a. derelict   b. depredate   c. delinquent
2. a. loath   b. aversion   c. rarefied
3. a. vivacious   b. objective   c. dispassionate
4. a. impecunious   b. arrears   c. vacuous
5. a. opprobrious   b. marginal   c. denounce
6. a. verdant   b. meander   c. peregrination
7. a. infrastructure b. expostulate   c. underpinning
8. a. subterfuge   b. pontificate   c. sententious
9. a. dissemble   b. ebb   c. feign
10. a. degrade   b. defile   c. devout

Final Exam Drill #113: ANTONYMS

For each question below, match the word on the left with the word most similar in meaning on the right.

1. suffuse   a. subterfuge
2. intrigue   b. disperse
3. contempt   c. gaffe
4. impeach   d. brink
5. discomfit   e. wrath
6. sally   f. disconcert
7. abomination   g. indict
8. threshold   h. scorn
9. folly   i. lax
10. cursory   j. reprisal

Final Exam Drill #114: DEFINITIONS

For each question below, match the word on the left with its definition on the right.

1. bona fide   a. demonstrate convincingly
2. underpinning   b. cause to spread out
3. evince   c. judge
4. emissary   d. human soul or mind
5. deem   e. eject
6. diffuse   f. thick and sticky
7. karma   g. good or bad emanations
8. viscous   h. sincere
9. psyche   i. system of supports beneath
10. oust   j. messenger or representative

Final Exam Drill #115: ANTONYMS

For each question below, match the word on the left with the word most similar in meaning on the right.

1. compilation		a. incarnate
2. astringent		b. edict
3. fiat		c. expiate
4. quandary		d. depict
5. specter		e. anthology
6. pandemic		f. draconian
7. corporeal		g. predicament
8. atone		h. veneer
9. patina		i. rampant
10. render		j. phantasm

Final Exam Drill #116: PRONUNCIATIONS

Pronounce each of the following words without looking at *column a* or *column b*. Then select the column that comes closer to your pronunciation.

1. reprobate	a. REP ruh bayt	b. ree PROH bayt
2. depredation	a. duh pray DAY shun	b. dep ruh DAY shun
3. prophesy	a. PRAHF uh sye	b. PRAHF uh see
4. cardinal	a. KAHR duh nul	b. KAHRD nul
5. deity	a. DAY uh tee	b. DEE uh tee
6. chutzpah	a. CHUTZ puh	b. HUT spuh
7. dissemble	a. di SEM bul	b. dis uh SEM bul
8. fiat	a. FEE ut	b. FYE ut
9. prelude	a. PREL yood	b. PRAY lood
10. tryst	a. trist	b. tryst

Final Exam Drill #117: ANTONYMS

For each question below, match the word on the left with the word most similar in meaning on the right.

1. oligarchy		a. dissemble
2. florid		b. triumvirate
3. feign		c. substantiate
4. document		d. intricate
5. usurious		e. implication
6. stipend		f. bacchanal
7. prescience		g. exorbitant
8. gastronomy		h. remuneration
9. licentious		i. presentiment
10. innuendo		j. cuisine

Final Exam Drill #118: DEFINITIONS

For each question below, match the word on the left with its definition on the right.

1. chortle		a.	short, literary sketch
2. cherub		b.	hint
3. vignette		c.	full of difficulties
4. access		d.	intruder
5. omniscient		e.	chuckle with glee
6. intimate		f.	accidental
7. interloper		g.	brazenness
8. chutzpah		h.	supercute child
9. adventitious		i.	right to approach
10. thorny		j.	all-knowing

Final Exam Drill #119: ANTONYMS

For each question below, match the word on the left with the word most similar in meaning on the right.

1. ostracism		a.	tactic
2. brawn		b.	intermittent
3. bluster		c.	bombast
4. idiom		d.	jargon
5. interspersed		e.	omnivorous
6. voracious		f.	infuse
7. imbue		g.	hypertrophy
8. schism		h.	dichotomy
9. embodiment		i.	effigy
10. connivance		j.	seclusion

Final Exam Drill #120: DEFINITIONS

For each question below, match the word on the left with its definition on the right.

1. epilogue		a.	pertaining to time
2. modulate		b.	afterword
3. temporal		c.	reduce or regulate
4. cartography		d.	command
5. behest		e.	having to do with the church
6. ecclesiastical		f.	highly changeable person
7. callous		g.	insensitive
8. bon vivant		h.	art of making maps
9. chameleon		i.	one who lives luxuriously
10. travesty		j.	grotesque imitation

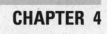

CHAPTER 4

THE
SAT HIT
PARADE

Despite all the talk about "reasoning ability," many of the hardest questions on the SAT are vocabulary-dependent. Some, such as sentence completions, mainly test vocabulary. Other questions are related to vocabulary in a more peripheral way; an erudite vocabulary helps you on the reading passages, grammar sections (especially those involving diction), and even the essay. If you learn every word on the main word list in this book, you'll have a big advantage on the SAT. The bigger your vocabulary, the better you'll do. But not every word on the main list is the sort of word that is tested on the SAT. If you're getting ready to take the SAT or a similar standardized test, you should focus your attention on the words in the following list, which we call the Hit Parade.

The Hit Parade is a list of the words tested most frequently on the SAT. We created the Hit Parade by using a computer to analyze released SATs. The Princeton Review students use the Hit Parade to get the maximum possible mileage out of their vocabularies and improve their Verbal SAT scores. Not all Hit Parade words appear on our main word list, but all of them have appeared on SATs.

We've included short definitions to make it easier for you to learn the words. These definitions aren't always exactly like the ones you'll find in the dictionary or the main word list of this book; they're the definitions of the words *as they are tested on the SAT.*

Keep in mind that these are not the *only* words you need to know for the SAT. They're just the words that have been tested most frequently in the past—the words that the Educational Testing Service's test writers tend to come back to over and over again. Also keep in mind that the words near the top of the list are more likely to turn up than the words near the bottom.

Some SATs are absolutely loaded with Hit Parade words; others don't contain as many. One of the most important things the Hit Parade will teach you is the *level* of the vocabulary on the test. Once you get a feel for this level, you'll be able to spot other possible SAT words in your reading.

soothe to calm; to ease pain; to relieve
vigor strength; liveliness
trivial unimportant; insignificant
vulnerable in danger; unprotected
qualify to state exceptions to a general statement
essential important; vital; absolutely necessary
detrimental harmful; working against
prosperous wealthy; well-off
somber gloomy; serious
terse brief; concise; to the point
opaque (opacity) dark; unclear; impossible to see through or understand
opposition disagreement; opinions against; people against; the other side
reprove to criticize mildly
uniform unchanging; the same everywhere
prolong to lengthen in extent or duration
viable workable; capable of living
enlighten to inform; to explain
inquisitive curious
solitary alone; isolated
modest shy; reserved; not extreme
progressive moving forward
plausible believable
spontaneous (spontaneity) happening without apparent cause; happening freely; free
distinguish to recognize something separately
serenity quiet; calm; peaceful
exotic foreign; uncommon; from a distant place; unusual
ruffle to disturb the smoothness of; to upset mildly
capricious (caprice) unpredictable; likely to change
transparent clear; easily seen; easily understood
theoretical not based on experience; in theory only; unproven
sympathy shared understanding or feeling

---

verify to prove or test the truth of

flourish to grow well; to grow strong; to grow abundantly

incidental occurring accidentally; by the side; of less importance

morose gloom; sullen; sad

rotund round

vital alive; of great importance; crucial

widespread occurring widely

expunge to erase; to strike out

repulse to send back; to reject

color to affect, especially to influence another's opinions or beliefs

prevaricate to lie

meticulous especially careful; paying close attention to detail

effectual effective

reserved self-restrained; modest; retiring; not showy

swindler a cheat; a con man

volunteer to offer freely; to join a cause

harmony pleasant agreement; friendship

inspire to encourage; to give hope to

glutton one who eats or consumes excessively

isolated alone; single; unconnected

integrity honesty; trustworthiness

responsive readily able to respond; friendly

wary cautious; unsure

deliberate to think over

barren unproductive; lacking; desolate

corrupt to make impure

rigidity stiffness; unwillingness to change or bend

tonic something that refreshes; a refreshing or invigorating drink

devotion loyalty

explicit to make clear and specific; stated

tragic disastrous

elegance refinement; grace

vivid clear and bright

weight importance

surfeit excess; excessive amount; overeating or overdrinking

void emptiness

revelation something revealed; insight; an understanding given by someone else

novice beginner

retaliation revenge

intensify to increase the strength, size, or force of; to make more severe

soporific sleep inducing; extremely boring
subjugate to subdue and dominate; to enslave
superfluous (superfluity) extra; unnecessary
remote far away; unfriendly
resourceful able to deal effectively with different situations
innate existing since birth; inborn
ratify to approve formally or officially
stalemate a stand-off; a situation where nobody wins
sporadic stopping and starting; scattered; occurring at irregular
    intervals
ominous threatening
vociferous loud; outspoken
monarch a single ruler; a king or queen
kindle to begin to burn
variable changing
trunk the main body of something
harsh severe; demanding; unfriendly
sanction formal or official approval; a legal penalty
tranquil quiet; calm; serene
synchronize to cause to act on the same schedule
swagger to strut
uproar noisy excitement or confusion
strut to walk with overconfidence
spurious false; fake
wayward going one's own way; erratic; unpredictable
optimism hope; a positive outlook
slight an insult
affectation (affected) artificial behavior, usually intended to
    impress
enhance to improve; to make better
extreme intense; remote; drastic; severe
malice ill will; a desire to harm
inhibit to hold back; to restrain
relieve to ease; to free from an unpleasant situation
stolid emotionless
severe harsh; demanding; painful; serious; without frills
weary tired; exhausted
endurance ability to last
thimble small protective cap that protects a fingertip
treachery betrayal of trust
troupe a company of actors, singers, or dancers
virtuous honest; moral; ethical

blueprint the plan of a building; a detailed plan
indifferent having no feeling about a matter; not really caring; unbiased
jovial happy; in good spirits; jolly
vestige (vestigial) the remains of something that no longer exists
soloist an individual performer
vent to give expression to; to release one's feelings
undermine to weaken the support of
replete (repletion) completely filled; stuffed; abounding
prudish (prude) overly concerned with being modest or proper
vindictive revengeful
trespass to invade another's property; to overstep; to commit an offense
bear to endure; to put up with
salutary beneficial; wholesome
renounce to resign; to disown; to give up formally; to reject
thrive to grow strong; to flourish
wince to shrink in pain
meager thin; of small quantity
flower to flourish; to mature well
turbulent stormy
erratic inconsistent; unpredictable; constantly changing; all over the place
spacious roomy; having a lot of space
determined firm of purpose; unwavering
hyperbole an exaggeration
hypocrisy (hypocrite) pretending to feelings or beliefs one does not have; insincere
uphold to maintain or fight for
swell to grow large
protrude to push outward
uncouth ill-mannered
warm friendly; kind
repress to hold back; to hold down; to restrain
irrational incoherent; illogical; without apparent reason
paradigm a good model or example
ponder to think over deeply
clarify to make clear
sinister evil; threatening
preposterous unbelievable; implausible
vertical upright; standing up; perpendicular to the ground.

table to remove from consideration
zany light-hearted; crazy
durable lasting
arrogant cocky; overconfident
tailor to shape or alter for a particular purpose
submissive giving in easily
mosaic a detailed pattern made from many different tiles or
  pieces
trite unoriginal; overused
vague unclear; lacking definite shape or substance
ethical moral; correct; honest
raucous harsh or rough-sounding
predicament a difficult situation, especially when a tough choice
  must be made
stupor mental confusion
reform to improve; to change for the better
scale to climb up
prose ordinary speech or writing (as opposed to poetry)
valid having legal force; sound
traditional as was done in the past; customary
tardy late
diminish to reduce; to make less
sullen sulky; in a bad mood
tirade a long, angry speech
wooden stiff; inflexible
rebuff to reject; to snub; to refuse abruptly
anonymous (anonymity) of unknown identity
sluggard a lazy person
theology the study of religion
surmise to guess
pompous (pomposity) arrogant; cocky; showy
profane (profanity) not having to do with religion; irreligious; un-
  holy; disrespectful
newfangled new; untested
intricate detailed; complex
well-founded based on solid evidence or good reasons
fertile productive; supporting plants
gill the breathing organ of a fish
unruly difficult to control; disobedient
stratagem a trick or deception
splinter a sharp, slender piece broken or split off from something;
  to split

lure an attraction

obstinate stubborn; unyielding

ascendancy dominance; being on top

sobriety (sober) seriousness

erroneous incorrect; false; mistaken

threadbare tattered

unsung unrecognized; uncelebrated

rectify to correct; to straighten; to make amends for

vulgarian a vulgar person

wake the track left when something leaves, especially a boat

anxiety (anxious) deep nervousness

gaunt thin and bony, especially from illness or lack of food

unilateral on one side only

embrace to hug; to accept; to adopt a cause; to include

check to stop; to hold back; to block

tangential (tangent) off to the side; secondary

trait a feature that characterizes someone

obliterate to wipe out; to destroy completely

extricate to free from difficulty; to remove something entangled; to untangle

tightfisted greedy

monotonous dull; boring; unchanging

superlative of the highest quality; superb; praiseworthy

utilize to use

fitful irregular; subject to sudden, violent outbursts

transcribe to write down

foolhardy overly brave; foolishly unaware of dangers

torso the body

variegated diversified; having great variety

humility being humble

whim a sudden idea; an impulse; a caprice

residual left over when something is gone

revive to bring back to life

oasis a fertile spot in a desert or barren place; an enjoyable place

motive a reason or justification to do something

vitality liveliness; energy

hindrance an obstruction; something that gets in the way

symbolism representation by signs or symbols

formal strictly following traditions or conventions; stiff; rigid

proliferate to spread rapidly

hasten to quicken; to speed up

summons an order to appear in court

heart courage; spirit

stymie to get in the way of; to hinder

stilts tall, slender supporting posts

effervescent bubbly

stratify (stratum) to make into layers

suppress to hold down; to hold back

tumor a local growth of abnormal tissue in the body

hangar storage facility for planes

subside to sink; to become less active

pushover a person easily influenced or exploited

condense to compress; to shorten

compromise to settle differences; to agree (rarely: to expose to suspicion or ridicule)

extensive widespread

paltry of a tiny or insignificant amount; meager; scant

ponderous heavy; difficult

turpitude shameful wickedness; evil

utter to say

shrine a holy site

surreptitious secret; sneaky

impose to establish on others by force or authority

accolade an award; an honor

impulsive tending to act thoughtlessly

material substantial; important

synopsis a brief statement or outline

seminary a school for religious training

placate to please; to soothe

proclaim to state publicly

savor to taste something delicious

distant unfriendly; uncommunicative

quandary a state of uncertainty

miser a greedy person

resplendent brilliant

provocative exciting; attracting attention

advocate to speak in favor of; to support

arrogant feeling superior to others; snooty

contempt reproachful disdain

skeptical doubting (opposite of gullible)

innovate to be creative; to introduce something new

profound deep; insightful (the opposite of superficial)

digress to go off the subject

---

tenacious tough; hard to defeat

nostalgia a sentimental longing for the past; homesickness

denounce to speak out against; to condemn

pragmatic practical; down-to-earth; based on experience rather than theory

rigorous strict; harsh; severe

inevitable unavoidable; bound to happen

superficial on the surface only; shallow; not thorough

aesthetic having to do with artistic beauty; artistic (not to be confused with ascetic, also on the Hit Parade)

disparage to belittle; to say uncomplimentary things about, usually in a somewhat indirect way

elaborate detailed; careful; thorough

ambivalent undecided; blowing hot and cold

esoteric hard to understand; understood by only a select few; peculiar

subtle not obvious; able to make fine distinctions; ingenious; crafty

indifferent not caring one way or the other; mediocre; lacking a preference; neutral

futile hopeless; without effect

resignation reluctant acceptance of a bad situation (secondary meaning)

negligence carelessness

contrite deeply apologetic; remorseful

objective without bias (as opposed to subjective)

disdain arrogant scorn; contempt

reticent restrained; uncommunicative

mitigate to lessen the severity of something

refute to disprove; to prove to be false

brevity briefness

benign gentle; not harmful; kind; mild

apathy lack of emotion or interest

revere to worship; to honor (think of a reverend)

enigma mystery

diverse varied

lucid clear; easy to understand

redundant repetitive; unnecessary; excessively wordy

alleviate to lessen; to relieve, usually temporarily or incompletely; to make bearable

ironic satiric; unexpected

belligerent combative; quarrelsome; waging war

neutral unbiased; not taking sides; objective

anecdote a brief, entertaining story

articulate speaking clearly and well

unprecedented happening for the first time; novel; never seen before

frivolous not serious; not solemn; with levity

indulgent lenient; yielding to desire

volatile quick to evaporate; highly unstable; explosive

stringent strict; restrictive

deference submission to another's will; respect; courtesy

congenial agreeably suitable; pleasant

benefactor a generous donor

amass to accumulate

authentic real

obscure unclear; clouded; partially hidden; hard to under stand

impartial unbiased; neutral

discriminate to differentiate; to make a clear distinction; to see the difference

relevant important; pertinent

candid honest; frank

discernment insight; ability to see things clearly

abstract theoretical; lacking substance (the opposite of concrete)

temperate moderate; restrained

eccentric not conventional; a little kooky; irregular

provincial limited in outlook to one's own small corner of the world; narrow

benevolent kind; good-hearted; generous

pious reverent or devout; outwardly (and sometimes falsely) reverent or devout

conciliatory making peace; attempting to solve a dispute through good will

resolute determined; firm; unwavering

servile submissive and subservient; like a servant

acute sharp; shrewd

anarchy absence of government or control; lawlessness; disorder

virulent extremely poisonous; malignant; full of hate

scrutinize to examine closely

discord disagreement (the opposite of concord)

repudiate to reject; to deny

diligent hardworking

prodigal extravagant; wasteful

augment to add to; to increase; to make bigger

---

complacent smug; self-satisfied; pleased with oneself; contented to a fault

guile cunning; duplicity

squander to waste

incessant unceasing; never-ending

laudable worthy of praise

deter to prevent; to stop; to keep from doing something

infamous shamefully wicked; having (and deserving) an extremely bad reputation; disgraceful

depravity moral corruption

gravity seriousness (secondary meaning)

banal unoriginal; ordinary

extol to praise

euphony pleasant sound (the opposite is cacophony)

deride to ridicule; to laugh at contemptuously

insipid dull; banal

austere unadorned; stern; forbidding; without much money

expedite to make faster or easier

heresy an opinion violently opposed to established beliefs

novel new; original

philanthropy love of mankind; donating to charity

tentative experimental; temporary; uncertain

vacillate to be indecisive; to waver back and forth

fervor passion

dispassionate without passion; objective; neutral

solemn serious; grave

conspicuous standing out; obvious

ascetic hermitlike; practicing self-denial

dogmatic arrogantly assertive of unproven ideas; arrogantly claiming that something (often a system of beliefs) is beyond dispute

condone to overlook; to permit to happen

dissent disagreement

volition will; conscious choice

voluntary willing; unforced

didactic instructive; intended to instruct

disparate different; incompatible

ephemeral short-lived; fleeting; not lasting

compliant yielding; submissive

prosaic dull; unimaginative; like prose

profuse flowing; extravagant

expedient providing an immediate advantage; serving one's immediate self-interest

fastidious meticulous; demanding

astute perceptive; intelligent

languish to become weak, listless, or depressed

censure to condemn severely for doing something bad

stagnation motionlessness; inactivity

reprehensible worthy of blame or censure

engender to create; to produce

exemplary outstanding; setting a great example

relegate to banish; to send away

anecdote a brief, entertaining story

scanty inadequate; minimal

fallacious false

acclaim praise; applause; admiration

uniform consistent; unchanging; the same for everyone

incoherent jumbled; chaotic; impossible to understand

repress to hold down

solicit to ask for; to seek

reproach to scold

condescend to stoop to someone else's level, usually in an offensive way; to patronize

orthodox conventional; adhering to established principles or doctrines, especially in religion; by the book

indolence laziness

preclude to prevent; to make impossible; to shut out

apprehensive worried; anxious

elaborate detailed; careful; thorough

elusive hard to pin down; evasive

efface to erase; to rub away the features of

taciturn untalkative by nature

ameliorate to make better or more tolerable

acquiesce to give in; to agree

atrophy to waste away from lack of use

dubious doubtful; uncertain

flagrant shocking; outstandingly bad

concise brief and to the point; succinct

immutable unchangeable; permanent

static stationary; not changing or moving (not radio fuzz)

credulous believing; gullible

blasphemy irreverence; an insult to something held sacred; profanity

coalesce to come together as one; to fuse; to unite

lax careless; not diligent; relaxed

cryptic mysterious; mystifying

levity lightness; frivolity; unseriousness

innate existing since birth; inborn; inherent

sycophant one who sucks up to others

amiable friendly

extraneous irrelevant; extra; unnecessary; unimportant

tedious boring

caustic like acid; corrosive

inadvertent lax; careless; without intention

exhaustive thorough; complete

incongruous not harmonious; not consistent; not appropriate

belittle to make to seem little

appease to soothe; to pacify by giving in to

instigate to provoke; to stir up

sage wise; possessing wisdom derived from experience or learning

predecessor someone or something that came before another

jeopardy danger

tangible touchable; palpable

remorse sadness; regret

pivotal crucial

scrupulous strict; careful; hesitant for ethical reasons

respite a rest; a period of relief

stoic indifferent (at least outwardly) to pleasure or pain, to joy or grief, to fortune or misfortune

peripheral unimportant

hedonistic pleasure-seeking; indulgent

idiom a peculiar expression

apocryphal of doubtful origin; false

virtuoso masterful musician; a masterful practitioner in some other field

slander to defame; to speak maliciously of someone

animosity resentment; hostility; ill will

deplete to use up; to reduce; to lessen

amity friendship

voluminous very large; spacious (this word has nothing to do with sound)

auspicious favorable; promising; pointing to a good result

fickle capricious; whimsical; unpredictable

lethargy sluggishness; laziness; drowsiness; indifference

hackneyed banal; overused; trite (a cliché is a hackneyed expression)

willful deliberate; obstinate; insistent on having one's way

bastion stronghold; fortress; fortified place
trepidation fear; apprehension; nervous trembling
desecrate to profane a holy place (the opposite is consecrate)
fortuitous accidental; occurring by chance
vehement urgent; passionate
assuage to soothe; to pacify; to ease the pain of; to relieve
prodigious extraordinary; enormous
torpor sluggishness; inactivity; apathy
furtive secretive
supercilious haughty; patronizing
prudent careful; having foresight
verbose wordy; overly talkative
pedestrian common; ordinary; banal (secondary meaning)
innocuous harmless; banal
fanatic one who is extremely devoted to a cause or idea
enhance to make better; to augment
retract to take back; to withdraw; to pull back
ambiguous unclear in meaning; confusing; capable of being
    interpreted in at least two similarly plausible ways
paucity scarcity
rescind to repeal; to take back formally
zealous fervent; enthusiastically devoted to something
compliant yielding; submissive
emulate to strive to equal or excel, usually through imitation
innumerable too many to number or count; many
meander to wander slowly, like a winding river
authoritarian like a dictator
brawn bulk; muscles
exemplify to serve as an example of
facilitate to make easier
hypothetical uncertain; unproven
recalcitrant stubbornly defiant of authority or control
ambulatory able to walk; walking
diffident timid; lacking in self-confidence
drone to talk on and on in a dull way
gullible overly trusting; willing to believe anything
marred damaged; bruised
nullify to make unimportant
parsimony stinginess
propriety properness; good manners
rejuvenate to make young and strong again
animated alive; moving

---

bias prejudice; tendency; tilt
blithe carefree; cheerful
dearth a lack of; scarcity
divert to change the direction of; to alter the course of; to amuse
enthrall to thrill
heed to listen to
hindrance an obstruction; an annoying interference or delay
irascible irritable
merger a joining or marriage
pretentious pompous; self-important
saccharine sweet; excessively or disgustingly sweet
stanza a section of a poem; verse

CHAPTER 5

WORD ROOTS YOU SHOULD KNOW

You Don't Have to Memorize These Roots—
You Already Know Them!

To show you how each root relates to words you already know, each list includes an easy word or two. For example, the root "spec" come from a Latin word meaning to look or see, as in the easy words *spectator* and *spectacles*. Recognizing that will help you memorize the definition of the less common words *specter and circumspect*, which are on the same list. And you thought you didn't know Latin!

You will notice that the same root can be spelled in different ways. We have included the most common spelling variations in the heading. Remember that roots tell us the common heritage of words thousands of years old. Over the centuries spelling variations are bound to occur.

A note to philologists (etymologically: "word lovers"): In keeping with our pragmatic philosophy, we have sometimes taken liberties in compiling this list.

A (without)	AB/ABS
amoral	(off, away from, apart, down)
atheist	abduct
atypical	abhor
anonymous	abolish
apathy	abstract
amorphous	abnormal
atrophy	abdicate
apartheid	abstinent
anomaly	absolution
agnostic	abstruse
	abrogate

abscond
abjure
abstemious
ablution
abominate
aberrant

AC/ACR (sharp, bitter)
acid
acute
acerbic
exacerbate
acrid
acrimonious
acumen

ACT/AG (to do, to drive, to force, to lead)
act
agent
agile
agitate
exacting
litigate
prodigal
prodigious
pedagogue
demagogue
synagogue

AD/AL (to, toward, near)
adapt
adjacent
addict
admire
address
adhere
administer
adore
advice
adjoin
adultery
advocate

allure
alloy

AL/ALI/ALTER (other, another)
alternative
alias
alibi
alien
alter ego
alienation
altruist
altercation
allegory

AM (love)
amateur
amatory
amorous
enamored
amity
paramour
inamorata
amiable
amicable

AMB (to go, to walk)
ambitious
amble
preamble
ambulance
ambulatory
perambulator
circumambulate

AMB/AMPH (around)
amphitheater
ambit
ambience
ambient

**AMB/AMPH
(both, more than one)**
ambiguous
amphibian
ambivalent
ambidextrous

ANIM (life, mind, soul, spirit)
unanimous
animosity
equanimity
magnanimous
pusillanimous

ANNU/ENNI (year)
annual
anniversary
biannual
biennial
centennial
annuity
perennial
annals
millennium

ANTE (before)
ante
anterior
antecedent
antedate
antebellum
antediluvian

ANTHRO/ANDR (man, human)
anthropology
android
misanthrope
philanthropy
anthropomorphic
philander
androgynous
anthropocentric

ANTI (against)
antidote
antiseptic
antipathy
antipodal

APO (away)
apology
apostle
apocalypse
apogee
apocryphal
apotheosis
apostasy
apoplexy

APT/EPT (skill, fitness, ability)
adapt
aptitude
apt
inept
adept

ARCH/ARCHI (chief, principal)
architect
archenemy
archetype
archipelago

ARCHY (ruler)
monarchy
matriarchy
patriarchy
anarchy
hierarchy
oligarchy

ART (skill, craft)
art
artificial
artifice
artisan

artifact
artful
artless

AUC/AUG/AUX (to increase)
auction
auxiliary
augment
august

AUTO (self)
automatic
autopsy
autocrat
autonomy

BE (to be, to have a certain quality)
belittle
belated
bemoan
befriend
bewilder
begrudge
bequeath
bespeak
belie
beguile
beset
bemuse
bereft

BEL/BELL (war)
rebel
belligerent
bellicose
antebellum

BEN/BON (good)
benefit
beneficiary
beneficent
benefactor
benign

benevolent
benediction
bonus
bon vivant
bona fide

BI (twice, doubly)
binoculars
biannual
biennial
bigamy
bilateral
bilingual
bipartisan

BRI/BREV (brief, short)
brief
abbreviate
abridge
brevity

CAD/CID (to fall, to happen by chance)
accident
coincidence
decadent
cascade
recidivism
cadence

CAND (to burn)
candle
incandescent
candor

CANT/CENT/CHANT (to sing)
chant
enchant
accent
recant
incantation
incentive

CAP/CIP/CAPIT/CIPIT
(head, headlong)
capital
cape
captain
disciple
principle
principal
precipice
precipitate
precipitous
capitulate
capitalism
precipitation
caption
recapitulate

CAP/CIP/CEPT (to take, to get)
capture
anticipate
intercept
susceptible
emancipate
recipient
incipient
percipient
precept

CARD/CORD/COUR (heart)
cardiac
courage
encourage
concord
discord
accord
concordance
cordial

CARN (flesh)
carnivorous
carnival
carnal
carnage

reincarnation
incarnation

CAST/CHAST (cut)
caste
castigate
chastise
chaste

CAUST (to burn)
caustic
holocaust

CED/CEED/CESS
(to go, to yield, to stop)
exceed
precede
recess
concede
cede
access
predecessor
precedent
antecedent
recede
abscess
cessation
incessant

CENTR (center)
central
concentrate
eccentric
concentric
centrifuge
egocentric

CERN/CERT/CRET/CRIM/CRIT
(to separate, to judge, to
distinguish, to decide)
concern
critic
secret
crime

discrete
ascertain
certitude
hypocrite
discriminate
criterion
discern
recrimination

CHRON (time)
synchronize
chronicle
chronology
chronic
chronological
anachronism
chronometer

CIRCU (around, on all sides)
circumference
circumstances
circuit
circumspect
circumvent
circumnavigate
circumambulate
circumlocution
circumscribe
circuitous

CIS (to cut)
scissors
precise
exorcise
excise
incision
incisive
concise

CIT (to set in motion)
excite
incite
solicit
solicitous

CLA/CLO/CLU (shut, close)
closet
enclose
conclude
claustrophobia
disclose
exclusive
recluse
preclude
seclude
cloister
foreclose
closure

CLAIM/CLAM (to shout, to cry out)
exclaim
proclaim
acclaim
clamor
disclaim
reclaim
declaim

CLI (to lean toward)
decline
recline
climax
proclivity
disinclination

CO/COL/COM/CON (with, together)
connect
confide
concede
coerce
cohesive
cohort
confederate
collaborate
compatible
coherent
comply

conjugal
connubial
congenial
convivial
coalesce
coalition
contrite
conciliate
conclave
commensurate

CRAT/CRACY (to govern)
bureaucracy
democracy
aristocracy
theocracy
plutocracy
autocracy

CRE/CRESC/CRET (to grow)
creation
increase
crescendo
increment
accretion
accrue

CRED (to believe, to trust)
incredible
credibility
credentials
credit
creed
credo
credence
credulity
incredulous

CRYP (hidden)
crypt
cryptic
apocryphal
cryptography

CUB/CUMB (to lie down)
cubicle
succumb
incubate
incumbent
recumbent

CULP (blame)
culprit
culpable
exculpate
inculpate
mea culpa

CUR/COUR (running, a course)
occur
recur
current
curriculum
courier
cursive
excursion
concur
concurrent
incur
incursion
discourse
discursive
precursor
recourse
cursory

DE (away, off, down, completely, reversal)
descend
detract
decipher
deface
defile
defraud
deplete
denounce
decry

defer
defame
delineate
deferential

DEM (people)
democracy
epidemic
endemic
demagogue
demographics
pandemic

DI/DIA (apart, through)
dialogue
diagnose
diameter
dilate
digress
dilatory
diaphanous
dichotomy
dialectic

DIC/DICT/DIT
(to say, to tell, to use words)
dictionary
dictate
predict
contradict
verdict
abdicate
edict
dictum
malediction
benediction
indict
indite
diction
interdict
obiter dictum

DIGN (worth)
dignity
dignitary
dignify
deign
indignant
condign
disdain
infra dig

DIS/DIF (away from, apart,
reversal, not)
disperse
disseminate
dissipate
dissuade
diffuse

DOC/DAC (to teach)
doctor
doctrine
indoctrinate
doctrinaire
docile
didactic

DOG/DOX (opinion)
orthodox
paradox
dogma
dogmatic

DOL (suffer, pain)
condolence
indolence
doleful
dolorous

DON/DOT/DOW (to give)
donate
donor
pardon
condone
antidote

anecdote
endow
dowry

DUB (doubt)
dubious
dubiety
indubitable

DUC/DUCT (to lead)
conduct
abduct
conducive
seduce
induct
induce
ductile

DUR (hard)
endure
durable
duress
dour
obdurate

DYS (faulty)
dysfunction
dystopia
dyspepsia
dyslexia

EPI (upon)
epidemic
epilogue
epidermis
epistle
epitome
epigram
epithet
epitaph

EQU (equal, even)
equation
adequate

equivalent
equilibrium
equable
equidistant
equity
iniquity
equanimity
equivocate
equivocal

ERR (to wander)
err
error
erratic
erroneous
errant
aberrant

ESCE (becoming)
adolescent
obsolescent
iridescent
luminescent
coalesce
quiescent
acquiescent
effervescent
incandescent
evanescent
convalescent
reminiscent

EU (good, well)
euphoria
euphemism
eulogy
eugenics
euthanasia
euphony

E/EF/EX (out, out of, from, former, completely)
evade
exclude

extricate
exonerate
extort
exhort
expire
exalt
exult
effervesce
extenuate
efface
effusion
egregious

EXTRA (outside of, beyond)
extraordinary
extrasensory
extraneous
extrapolate

FAB/FAM (speak)
fable
fabulous
affable
ineffable
fame
famous
defame
infamous

**FAC/FIC/FIG/FAIT/FEIT/FY
(to do, to make)**
factory
facsimile
benefactor
facile
faction
fiction
factitious
efficient
deficient
proficient
munificent
prolific

soporific
figure
figment
configuration
effigy
magnify
rarefy
ratify
ramification
counterfeit
feign
fait accompli
ex post facto

**FER (to bring, to carry,
to bear)**
offer
transfer
confer
referendum
infer
fertile
proffer
defer
proliferate
vociferous

**FERV (to boil, to bubble,
to burn)**
fervor
fervid
effervescent

FID (faith, trust)
confide
confident
confidant
affidavit
diffident
fidelity
infidelity
perfidy
fiduciary

infidel
semper fidelis
bona fide

FIN (end)
final
finale
confine
define
definitive
infinite
affinity
infinitesimal

FLAG/FLAM (to burn)
flame
flamboyant
flammable
inflammatory
flagrant
conflagration
in flagrante delicto

FLECT/FLEX (to bend)
deflect
flexible
inflect
reflect
genuflect

FLICT (to strike)
afflict
inflict
conflict
profligate

FLU, FLUX (to flow)
fluid
influence
fluent
affluent
fluctuation
influx
effluence

confluence
superfluous
mellifluous

FORE (before)
foresight
foreshadow
forestall
forgo
forbear

FORT (chance)
fortune
fortunate
fortuitous

**FRA/FRAC/FRAG/FRING
(to break)**
fracture
fraction
fragment
fragile
refraction
fractious
infraction
refractory
infringe

FRUIT/FRUG (fruit, produce)
fruitful
fruition
frugal

FUND/FOUND (bottom)
foundation
fundamental
founder
profound

FUS (to pour)
confuse
transfusion
profuse
effusive

diffuse
suffuse
infusion

GEN (birth, creation, race, kind)
generous
generate
genetics
photogenic
degenerate
homogeneous
genealogy
gender
genre
genesis
carcinogenic
genial
congenial
ingenuous
ingenue
indigenous
congenital
progeny
engender
miscegenation
sui generis

GN/GNO (know)
ignore
ignoramus
recognize
incognito
diagnose
prognosis
agnostic
cognitive
cognoscente
cognizant

GRAND (big)
grand
grandeur
grandiose

aggrandize
grandiloquent

GRAT (pleasing)
grateful
ingrate
ingratiate
gratuity
gratuitous

GRAV/GRIEV (heavy, serious)
grave
grief
aggrieve
gravity
grievous

GREG (herd)
congregation
segregation
aggregation
gregarious
egregious

GRESS/GRAD (to step)
progress
graduate
gradual
aggressive
regress
degrade
retrograde
transgress
digress
egress

HER/HES (to stick)
coherent
cohesive
adhesive
adherent
inherent

(H)ETERO (different)
heterosexual
heterogeneous
heterodox

(H)OM (same)
homogeneous
homonym
homosexual
anomaly
homeostasis

HYPER (over, excessive)
hyperactive
hyperbole

HYPO (under, beneath, less than)
hypodermic
hypochondriac
hypothesis
hypocritical

ID (one's own)
idiot
idiom
idiosyncrasy

IM/IN (not, without)
inactive
indifferent
innocuous
insipid
indolence
impartial
inept
indigent

IM/IN/EM/EN (in, into)
in
embrace
enclose
ingratiate
intrinsic

influx
incarnate
implicit
indigenous

INFRA (beneath)
infrastructure
infrared
infrasonic

INTER (between, among)
interstate
interim
interloper
interlude
intermittent
interplay
intersperse
intervene

INTRA (within)
intramural
intrastate
intravenous

JECT (to throw, to throw down)
inject
eject
project
trajectory
conjecture
dejected
abject

JOIN/JUNCT (to meet, to join)
junction
joint
adjoin
subjugate
juxtapose
injunction
rejoinder
conjugal
junta

JUR (to swear)
jury
perjury
abjure
adjure

LECT/LEG (to select, to choose)
collect
elect
select
electorate
predilection
eclectic
elegant

LEV (lift, light, rise)
elevator
relieve
lever
alleviate
levitate
relevant
levee
levity

LOC/LOG/LOQU (word, speech)
dialogue
eloquent
elocution
locution
interlocutor
prologue
epilogue
soliloquy
eulogy
colloquial
grandiloquent
philology
neologism
tautology
loquacious

LUC/LUM/LUS (light)
illustrate
illuminate
luminous
luminescent
illustrious
lackluster
translucent
lucid
elucidate

LUD/LUS (to play)
illusion
ludicrous
delude
elude
elusive
allude
collusion
prelude
interlude

LUT/LUG/LUV (to wash)
lavatory
dilute
pollute
deluge
antediluvian

MAG/MAJ/MAX (big)
magnify
magnitude
major
maximum
majestic
magnanimous
magnate
maxim
magniloquent

MAL/MALE (bad, ill, evil, wrong)
malfunction
malodorous

malicious
malcontent
malign
malignant
malaise
dismal
malapropism
maladroit
malevolent
malinger
malfeasance
malefactor
malediction

MAN (hand)
manual
manufacture
emancipate
manifest
mandate
mandatory

MATER/MATR (woman, mother)
matrimony
maternal
maternity
matriculate
matriarch

MIN (small)
minute
minutiae
diminution
miniature
diminish

MIN (to project, to hang over)
eminent
imminent
prominent
preeminent

MIS/MIT (to send)
transmit
manumit
emissary
missive
intermittent
remit
remission
demise

MISC (mixed)
miscellaneous
miscegenation
promiscuous

MON/MONIT (to warn)
monument
monitor
summons
admonish
remonstrate

MORPH (shape)
amorphous
metamorphosis
polymorphous
anthropomorphic

MORT (death)
immortal
morgue
morbid
moribund
mortify

MUT (change)
commute
mutation
mutant
immutable
transmutation
permutation

NAM/NOM/NOUN/NOWN/NYM (rule, order)

astronomy
economy
autonomy
antimony
gastronomy
taxonomy

NAT/NAS/NAI (to be born)

natural
native
naive
cognate
nascent
innate
renaissance

NEC/NIC/NOC/NOX (harm, death)

innocent
noxious
obnoxious
pernicious
internecine
innocuous
necromancy

NOM/NYM/NOUN/NOWN (name)

synonym
anonymous
nominate
pseudonym
misnomer
nomenclature
acronym
homonym
nominal
ignominy
denomination
noun
renown

nom de plume
nom de guerre

NOV/NEO/NOU (new)

novice
novel
novelty
renovate
innovate
neologism
neophyte
nouvelle cuisine
nouveau riche

NOUNC/NUNC (to announce)

announce
pronounce
denounce
renounce

OB/OC/OF/OP (toward, to, against, completely, over)

obese
object
obstruct
obstinate
obscure
obtrude
oblique
oblivious
obnoxious
obstreperous
obtuse
opprobrium
obsequious
obfuscate

OMNI (all)

omnipresent
omniscient
omnipotent

PAC/PEAC (peace)
peace
appease
pacify
pacifist
pacifier
pact

PAN (all, everywhere)
panorama
panacea
panegyric
pantheon
panoply
pandemic

PAR (equal)
par
parity
apartheid
disparity
disparate
disparage

PARA (next to, beside)
parallel
paraphrase
parasite
paradox
parody
paragon
parable
paradigm
paramilitary
paranoid
paranormal
parapsychology
paralegal

PAS/PAT/PATH (feeling, suffering, disease)
apathy
sympathy
empathy

antipathy
passionate
compassion
compatible
dispassionate
impassive
pathos
pathology
sociopath
psychopath

PATER/PATR (father, support)
patron
patronize
paternal
paternalism
expatriate
patrimony
patriarch
patrician

PAU/PO/POV/PU (few, little, poor)
poor
poverty
paucity
pauper
impoverish
puerile
pusillanimous

PED (child, education)
pedagogue
pediatrician
encyclopedia

PED/POD (foot)
pedal
pedestal
pedestrian
podiatrist
expedite
expedient
impede

impediment
podium
antipodes

PEN/PUN (to pay, to compensate)
penal
penalty
punitive
repent
penance
penitent
penitentiary
repine
impunity

PEND/PENS (to hang, to weigh, to pay)
depend
dispense
expend
stipend
spend
expenditure
suspense
compensate
propensity
pensive
indispensable
impending
pendulum
appendix
append
appendage
ponderous
pendant

PER (completely, wrong)
persistent
perforate
perplex
perspire
peruse
pervade

perjury
perturb
perfunctory
perspicacious
permeate
pernicious
perennial
peremptory
pertinacious

PERI (around)
perimeter
periscope
peripheral
peripatetic

PET/PIT (to go, to seek, to strive)
appetite
compete
petition
perpetual
impetuous
petulant
propitious

PHIL (love)
philosophy
philanthropy
philatelist
philology
bibliophile

PHONE (sound)
telephone
symphony
megaphone
euphony
cacophony

PLAC (to please)
placid
placebo
placate

implacable
complacent
complaisant

PLE (to fill)
complete
deplete
complement
supplement
implement
plethora
replete

PLEX/PLIC/PLY (to fold, to twist, to tangle, to bend)
complex
complexion
complicate
duplex
replica
ply
comply
implicit
implicate
explicit
duplicity
complicity
supplicate
accomplice
explicate

PON/POS/POUND (to put, to place)
component
compound
deposit
dispose
expose
exposition
expound
juxtapose
depose
proponent
repository

transpose
superimpose

PORT (to carry)
import
portable
porter
portfolio
deport
deportment
export
portmanteau
portly
purport
disport
importune

POST (after)
posthumous
posterior
posterity
ex post facto

PRE (before)
precarious
precocious
prelude
premeditate
premonition
presage
presentiment
presume
presuppose
precedent
precept
precipitous
preclude
predilection
preeminent
preempt
prepossess
prerequisite
prerogative

PREHEND/PRISE (to take, to get, to seize)
surprise
comprehend
enterprise
impregnable
reprehensible
apprehension
comprise
apprise
apprehend
comprehensive
reprisal

PRO (much, for, a lot)
prolific
profuse
propitious
prodigious
profligate
prodigal
protracted
proclivity
proliferate
propensity
prodigy
proselytize
propound
provident
prolix

PROB (to prove, to test)
probe
probation
approbation
probity
opprobrium
reprobate

PUG (to fight)
pugilism
pug
pugnacious

impugn
repugnant

PUNC/PUNG/POIGN/POINT (to point, to prick)
point
puncture
punctual
punctuate
pungent
poignant
compunction
expunge
punctilious

QUE/QUIS (to seek)
acquire
acquisition
exquisite
acquisitive
request
conquest
inquire
inquisitive
inquest
query
querulous
perquisite

QUI (quiet)
quiet
disquiet
tranquil
acquiesce
quiescent

RID/RIS (to laugh)
ridicule
derision
risible

ROG (to ask)
interrogate
arrogant

prerogative
abrogate
surrogate
derogatory
arrogate

SAL/SIL/SAULT/SULT (to leap, to jump)
insult
assault
somersault
salient
resilient
insolent
desultory
exult

SANCT/SACR/SECR (sacred)
sacred
sacrifice
sanctuary
sanctify
sanction
execrable
sacrament
sacrilege

SCI (to know)
science
conscious
conscience
unconscionable
omniscient
prescient
conscientious
nescient

SCRIBE/SCRIP (to write)
scribble
describe
script
postscript
prescribe
proscribe

ascribe
inscribe
conscription
scripture
transcript
circumscribe
manuscript
scribe

SE (apart)
select
separate
seduce
seclude
segregate
secede
sequester
sedition

SEC/SEQU (to follow)
second
prosecute
sequel
sequence
consequence
inconsequential
obsequious
non sequitur

SED/SESS/SID (to sit, to be still, to plan, to plot)
preside
resident
sediment
session
dissident
obsession
residual
sedate
subside
subsidy
subsidiary
sedentary

dissident
insidious
assiduous
sedulous

SENS/SENT (to feel, to be aware)
sense
sensual
sensory
sentiment
resent
consent
dissent
assent
consensus
sentinel
insensate
sentient
presentiment

SOL (to loosen, to free)
dissolve
soluble
solve
resolve
resolution
irresolute
solvent
dissolution
dissolute
absolution

SPEC/SPIC/SPIT (to look, to see)
perspective
aspect
spectator
specter
spectacles
speculation
suspicious
auspicious

spectrum
specimen
introspection
retrospective
perspective
perspicacious
circumspect
conspicuous
respite
specious

STA/STI (to stand, to be in a place)
static
stationary
destitute
obstinate
obstacle
stalwart
stagnant
steadfast
constitute
constant
stasis
status
status quo
homeostasis
apostasy

SUA (smooth)
suave
assuage
persuade
dissuade

SUB/SUP (below)
submissive
subsidiary
subjugate
subliminal
subdue
sublime
subtle
subversive

subterfuge
subordinate
suppress
supposition

SUPER/SUR (above)
surpass
supercilious
superstition
superfluous
superlative
supersede
superficial
surmount
surveillance
survey

TAC/TIC (to be silent)
reticent
tacit
taciturn

TAIN/TEN/TENT/TIN (to hold)
contain
detain
pertain
pertinacious
tenacious
abstention
sustain
tenure
pertinent
tenant
tenable
tenet
sustenance

TEND/TENS/TENT/TENU (to stretch, to thin)
tension
extend
tendency
tendon
tent

tentative
contend
contentious
tendentious
contention
contender
tenuous
distend
attenuate
extenuating

THEO (god)
atheist
apotheosis
theocracy
theology

TOM (to cut)
tome
microtome
epitome
dichotomy

TORT (to twist)
tort
extort
torture
tortuous

TRACT (to drag, to pull, to draw)
tractor
attract
contract
detract
tract
tractable
intractable
protract
abstract

TRANS (across)
transfer
transaction

transparent
transport
transition
transitory
transient
transgress
transcendent
intransigent
traduce
translucent

US/UT (to use)
abuse
usage
utensil
usurp
utility
utilitarian

VEN/VENT (to come, to move toward)
adventure
convene
convenient
event
venturesome
avenue
intervene
advent
contravene
circumvent

VER (truth)
verdict
verify
veracious
verisimilitude
aver
verity

VERS/VERT (to turn)
controversy
revert
subvert

invert
divert
diverse
aversion
extrovert
introvert
inadvertent
versatile
traverse
covert
overt
avert
advert

VI (life)
vivid
vicarious
convivial
viable
vivacity
joie de vivre
bon vivant

VID/VIS (to see)
evident
television
video
vision
provision
adviser
provident
survey
vista
visionary
visage

VOC/VOK (to call)
vocabulary
vocal
provocative
advocate
equivocate
equivocal
vocation

avocation
convoke
vociferous
irrevocable
evocative
revoke
convoke
invoke

VOL (to wish)
voluntary
volunteer
volition
malevolent
benevolent

CHAPTER 6

THE ANSWERS

Quick Quiz #1
1. j abash—embarrass
2. f abate—subside
3. a abdicate—step down from power
4. i aberration—deviation
5. g abhor—detest
6. b abject—hopeless
7. k abnegate—renounce
8. c abortive—unsuccessful
9. h abridge—shorten
10. e absolute—total
11. d absolve—forgive

Quick Quiz #2
1. h abase—humiliate
2. a abet—support
3. c abeyance—suspension
4. i abjure—repudiate
5. g abomination—something despised
6. b aboriginal—native
7. d abound—be very numerous
8. e abrogate—abolish
9. f accede—give in
10. j accentuate—emphasize

Quick Quiz #3
1. b abstinent—voluntarily avoiding
2. h abstract—theoretical
3. a abstruse—hard to understand
4. c abysmal—wretched
5. i accolade—award
6. j accost—approach
7. k acerbic—sour
8. e acquiesce—comply
9. f acrid—harsh
10. d acrimonious—bitter
11. g acumen—mental sharpness

Quick Quiz #4
1. h access—right to approach
2. c acclaim—praise publicly
3. d accord—agree
4. f accouterments—trappings
5. a accrue—accumulate
6. j acquisitive—greedy
7. e acquit—find not guilty
8. b acronym—word made up of initials
9. i adage—proverb
10. g adduce—cite

Quick Quiz #5
1. a acute—sharp
2. h adulation—wild admiration
3. g adamant—unyielding
4. e address—speak to
5. b adherent—follower
6. d admonish—scold gently
7. f adroit—skillful
8. f dexterous—skillful
9. c gauche—socially awkward

Quick Quiz #6
1. f adulterate—contaminate
2. h adverse—unfavorable
3. a averse—opposed to
4. e aesthetic—artistic
5. b affable—friendly
6. d affectation—unnatural behavior
7. g affinity—sympathy
8. c affluent—rich
9. i agenda—program

Quick Quiz #7
1. f adjourn—suspend
2. j adjunct—something added
3. i ad-lib—improvise
4. d advent—arrival
5. b adventitious—accidental
6. a advocate—person arguing for a position
7. g affidavit—sworn written statement
8. c affiliate—become closely associated
9. e affliction—misery
10. h afford—give

Quick Quiz #8
1. g aggregate—sum total
2. a congregate—get together
3. e segregate—keep apart
4. b integrate—unite
5. c agnostic—someone unconvinced about the existence of a god
6. k agrarian—relating to land
7. j alacrity—cheerful eagerness
8. i allege—assert
9. d alleviate—relieve
10. h allocate—distribute
11. f alloy—combination of metals

Quick Quiz #9
1. j affront—insult
2. a aftermath—consequence
3. i aggrandize—exaggerate
4. b aggrieve—mistreat
5. e aghast—terrified
6. f alchemy—seemingly magical transformation
7. c alienate—estrange
8. g allegiance—loyalty
9. h allegory—symbolic story
10. d allot—apportion

Quick Quiz #10
1. e allusion—indirect reference
2. b aloof—standoffish
3. d altruism—generosity
4. a ambience—atmosphere
5. c ambiguous—confusing
6. f ambivalent—undecided

Quick Quiz #11
1. f ameliorate—make better
2. c amenable—obedient
3. a amenity—pleasantness
4. j amiable—friendly
5. h amicable—politelyfriendly
6. i amnesty—official pardon
7. d amoral—without moral feeling
8. e amorous—feeling loving
9. g amorphous—shapeless
10. k anachronism—incongruity
11. b analogy—comparison

Quick Quiz #12
1. e altercation—heated fight
2. h amass—pile up
3. c amid—in the middle of
4. a anathema—something loathed
5. f ancillary—subordinate
6. i angst—anxiety
7. b annex—add
8. d annuity—annual allowance
9. j antedate—be older
10. g anterior—situated in front

Quick Quiz #13
1. i anarchy—lawlessness
2. h monarchy—government by king or queen
3. g anecdote—amusing account
4. f anguish—agonizing pain
5. a animosity—resentment
6. d anomaly—irregularity
7. e antecedent—what went before
8. c antipathy—firm dislike
9. j antithesis—direct opposite
10. b apartheid—racial oppression

Quick Quiz #14
1. i anthology—literary collection
2. e anthropomorphic—ascribing human characteristics
3. c antipodal—exactly opposite
4. h antiquity—ancientness
5. b aperture—opening
6. f apex—highest point
7. j apogee—most distant point of orbit
8. g apoplexy—stroke
9. d apostasy—abandonment of faith
10. a appalling—causing horror

Quick Quiz #15
1. d apathy—lack of interest
2. i aphorism—witty saying
3. f apocalypse—prophetic revelation
4. a apocryphal—of dubious authenticity
5. h apotheosis—the perfect example
6. e appease—soothe
7. c appreciate—increase in value
8. g depreciate—decrease in value
9. j apprehensive—worried
10. b misapprehension—misunderstanding

Quick Quiz 16

1. c apparition—ghost
2. g appellation—name
3. a appendage—something extra
4. e apportion—distribute proportionally
5. h appraise—estimate the value of
6. b apprise—give notice to
7. a appurtenance—something extra
8. f apropos—appropriate
9. i apposite—distinctly suitable
10. d apt—likely

Quick Quiz #17

1. f approbation—approval
2. c appropriate—take without permission
3: a misappropriate—misuse public money
4. h expropriate—take property officially
5. j aptitude—natural ability
6. i arbiter—judge
7. d arbitrate—weigh opposing views
8. g arbitrary—random
9. e arcane—mysterious
10. b archaic—extremely old

Quick Quiz #18

1. i arcade—arched passageway
2. f archipelago—group of islands
3. a archives—where documents are stored
4. g arid—very dry
5. c armament—implements of war
6. h armistice—truce
7. e arraign—accuse
8. b arrant—utter
9. d arrears—unpaid debts
10. j arsenal—supply of something useful

Quick Quiz #19

1. i archetype—original model
2. a ardent—passionate
3. e arduous—difficult
4. b aristocratic—of noble birth
5. h artful—crafty
6. f artifice—trickery
7. c ascendancy—supremacy
8. g ascetic—hermitlike
9. d assiduous—hardworking

Quick Quiz #20

1. f articulate—pronounce clearly
2. a artisan—person skilled in a craft
3. j ascertain—determine with certainty
4. c ascribe—credit to
5. g askance—with suspicion
6. b aspersion—slanderous remark
7. i assail—attack vigorously
8. d assert—claim strongly
9. h assess—evaluate
10. e astringent—harsh

Quick Quiz #21
1. g assimilate—absorb
2. e assuage—soothe
3. a astute—shrewd
4. i attrition—gradual wearing away
5. b audacity—boldness
6. d augment—make bigger
7. c auspicious—favorable
8. h austere—unadorned
9. f autocratic—extremely bossy

Quick Quiz #22
1. a asylum—refuge
2. e atone—make amends
3. h atrophy—wither away
4. c attest—give proof of
5. f attribute—credit to
6. n augur—serve as an omen
7. i august—inspiring awe
8. m auspices—protection
9. k auxiliary—secondary
10. g avail—help
11. j avant-garde—vanguard
12. b aversion—strong feeling of dislike
13. d avert—turn away
14. l avid—eager

Quick Quiz #23
1. d autonomous—acting independently
2. a avarice—greed
3. e avow—claim
4. b avuncular—like an uncle
5. f awry—off course
6. c axiom—self-evident truth

Quick Quiz #24
1. g bacchanal—party animal
2. b baleful—menacing
3. i balk—abruptly refuse
4. d ballyhoo—sensational advertising
5. j balm—something that heals
6. c bandy—toss back and forth
7. f banter—exchange of teasing remarks
8. a baroque—extravagantly ornate
9. e barrage—outpouring of artillery fire
10. h bauble—gaudy trinket

Quick Quiz #25
1. b banal—unoriginal
2. e bane—poison
3. d bastion—stronghold
4. h beget—give birth to
5. c belabor—go over repeatedly
6. g beleaguer—surround
7. f belie—give a false impression
8. a belittle—make to seem little

Quick Quiz #26
1. g belligerent—combative
2. e bemused—confused
3. b benefactor—donor
4. i beneficiary—one who receives benefits
5. f benevolent—generous
6. c benign—not harmful
7. d malignant—deadly
8. h malign—injure with lies
9. a malevolent—intending harm
10. j malefactor—evildoer

Quick Quiz #27
1. c bedlam—noisy uproar
2. f begrudge—envy
3. b behest—command
4. j bemoan—mourn about
5. a benediction—blessing
6. d benighted—ignorant
7. e bestow—present as a gift
8. g bilious—ill-tempered
9. i bivouac—temporary encampment
10. h blanch—turn pale

Quick Quiz #28
1. b bequest—something left in a will
2. e bequeath—leaving in a will
3. a bereaved—left desolate
4. c beset—harass
5. f blasphemy—irreverence
6. d blatant—offensively noisy

Quick Quiz #29
1. c bland—mild
2. e blandishment—flattery
3. g bliss—perfect contentment
4. i bluster—roar
5. a bombast—pompous speech
6. b bon vivant—luxurious liver
7. h bona fide—sincere
8. j boon—blessing
9. f boor—rude person
10. d booty—plunder

Quick Quiz #30
1. n blight—plant disease
2. c blithe—carefree
3. g bourgeois—middle class
4. e bovine—cowlike
5. m canine—doglike
6. d feline—catlike
7. h equine—horselike
8. l piscine—fishlike
9. j porcine—piglike
10. b ursine—bearlike
11. i brevity—briefness
12. o broach—open a subject
13. f bucolic—charmingly rural
14. k bureaucracy—inflexible administration
15. a burgeon—flourish
16. p burlesque—ludicrous imitation

Quick Quiz #31
1. f botch—bungle
2. c bracing—invigorating
3. i brandish—display threateningly
4. a bravado—ostentatious show of bravery
5. o brawn—big muscles
6. m brazen—impudent
7. j breach—violation
8. l brink—edge
9. b bristle—stiffen with anger
10. g bromide—dull saying
11. n brouhaha—uproar
12. k brusque—abrupt in manner
13. h buffoon—joker
14. d bulwark—defensive fortification
15. e byzantine—extremely intricate in structure

Quick Quiz #32
1. h cabal—group of conspirators
2. c cache—hiding place
3. j calamity—disaster
4. i callous—insensitive
5. a calumny—slander
6. b canon—rule or law
7. f cant—hypocritical speech
8. d canvass—seek votes or opinions
9. g capacious—roomy
10. e capital—seat of government

Quick Quiz #33
1. b cacophony—harsh mixture of sounds
2. l cadence—rhythm
3. j cajole—persuade deceptively
4. f callow—immature
5. a candor—truthfulness
6. g capitalism—free enterprise
7. c capitulate—surrender
8. i recapitulate—summarize
9. e capricious—unpredictable
10. d caricature—distorted portrait
11. k castigate—criticize severely
12. h catalyst—it makes things happen

Quick Quiz #34
1. e captivate—fascinate
2. j carcinogenic—causing cancer
3. g cardinal—most important
4. b careen—swerve
5. h cartography—art of making maps
6. d cascade—waterfall
7. a cataclysm—violent upheaval
8. c caucus—political meeting
9. i cavalier—arrogant
10. f cavil—quibble

Quick Quiz #35
1. a categorical—unconditional
2. b catharsis—relieving purification
3. i catholic—universal
4. g caustic—corrosive
5. c celibacy—abstinence from sex
6. h censure—condemn severely
7. d cerebral—brainy
8. e chagrin—humiliation
9. f charisma—magical attractiveness

Quick Quiz #36
1. h charlatan—fraud
2. i chasm—gaping hole
3. d chastise—punish
4. j chicanery—trickery
5. g chimera—illusion
6. c choleric—hot-tempered
7. b chronic—constant
8. a chronological—in order of occurrence
9. f chronology—a list in time order
10. e chronicle—an account of past times

Quick Quiz #37
1. a chaff—worthless stuff
2. b chameleon—highly changeable person
3. i champion—defend
4. g channel—direct
5. d chaste—pure and unadorned
6. f cherub—cute child
7. c chortle—chuckle with glee
8. j churl—rude person
9. h chutzpah—brazenness
10. e cipher—zero

Quick Quiz #38
1. e circuitous—roundabout
2. h circumlocution—indirect expression
3. b circumscribe—draw a line around
4. a circumspect—cautious
5. f circumvent—frustrate
6. d civil—polite
7. i clique—exclusive group
8. c clemency—mercy
9. j inclement—bad, as in weather
10. g cliché—overused saying

Quick Quiz #39
1. d circumnavigate—sail all the way around
2. g citadel—fortress defending a city
3. f clandestine—secret
4. i classic—top-notch
5. c cleave—cling
6. a climatic—having to do with the climate
7. e cloister—covered walk
8. h clone—exact duplicate
9. b clout—blow
10. j cloy—cause to feel too full

Quick Quiz #40
1. b coalesce—unite
2. g coalition—group with a purpose
3. d coerce—force someone to do something
4. h cogent—powerfully convincing
5. l cognitive—dealing with how we know our environment
6. a cognizant—perceptive
7. f coherent—making sense
8. c colloquial—conversational
9. k collusion—conspiracy
10. e commensurate—proportionate
11. j compelling—forceful
12. i compendium—summary

Quick Quiz #41
1. f coddle—baby
2. d cogitate—ponder
3. h cohort—group
4. b commemorate—honor the memory of
5. j commiserate—express sorrow for
6. a commodious—spacious
7. c compatible—harmonious
8. e competent—capable
9. g compile—gather together
10. i comply—act in accordance

Quick Quiz #42

1. h complacent—self-satisfied
2. b complement—complete
3. g complicity—participation in wrongdoing
4. a comprehensive—covering everything
5. c comprise—consist of
6. d compose—make up
7. d constitute—make up
8. f conciliatory —making peace
9. e concise—brief and to the point

Quick Quiz #43

1. h composed—calm
2. d compromise—settlement of differences
3. j compunction—remorse
4. g concave—curved inward
5. c concentric—having the same center
6. f concert—combined action
7. b concede—acknowledge as true
8. i concoct—create by mixing ingredients
9. e concomitant—following from
10. a confederate—ally

Quick Quiz #44

1. c concord—harmony
2. i discord—disharmony
3. h concurrent—happening at the same time
4. f condescend—stoop or patronize
5. g condone—overlook
6. e conducive—promoting
7. d confluence—flowing together
8. a congenial—agreeably suitable
9. b congenital—innate

Quick Quiz #45

1. h confer—exchange ideas
2. f confidant—person with whom secrets are shared
3. d configuration—arrangement
4. e conflagration—large fire
5. j confluence—flowing together
6. i confound—bewilder
7. a congeal—solidify
8. b conjugal—having to do with marriage
9. g connive—conspire
10. c conservatory—greenhouse

Quick Quiz #46

1. i congregate—get together
2. h conjecture—guess
3. e conjure—summon as if by magic
4. g connoisseur—artistic expert
5. c consecrate—make sacred
6. f desecrate—treat irreverently
7. d consensus—unanimity
8. b consonant—harmonious
9. a dissonant—incompatible

Quick Quiz #47

1. d consign—hand over
2. a consolidate—combine
3. j conspicuous—easily seen
4. h consternation—sudden confusion
5. e constituency—group of voters
6. g contempt—disdain
7. c continuum—continuous whole
8. f contraband—smuggled goods
9. b contretemps—embarrassing occurrence
10. i contumely—rudeness

Quick Quiz #48

1. b construe—interpret
2. c consummate—perfect
3. h contentious—argumentative
4. g contiguous—adjoining
5. e contingent—dependent
6. a contrite—admitting guilt
7. d contrived—labored
8. j conventional—common
9. i convivial—festive
10. f copious—abundant

Quick Quiz #49

1. b conundrum—puzzle
2. i convene—gather together
3. c conversant—familiar
4. h converse—opposite
5. e convey—transport
6. f conviction—strong belief
7. a convolution—twist or turn
8. j copious—abundant
9. g cordial—gracious
10. d corollary—natural consequence

Quick Quiz #50

1. g corollary—natural consequence
2. d corroborate—confirm
3. a cosmopolitan—worldly and sophisticated
4. b countenance—face
5. f coup—brilliant victory
6. e covenant—solemn agreement
7. h covert—secret
8. c covet—wish for enviously

Quick Quiz #51

1. e corporeal—tangible
2. c correlation—mutual relation
3. a corrosive—destructive
4. i corrugated—shaped with folds
5. h coterie—group of close associates
6. j cower—huddle in fear
7. g crass—extremely unrefined
8. b craven—cowardly
9. d crescendo—gradual increase in volume
10. f crestfallen—dejected

Quick Quiz #52

1. e credulous—eager to believe
2. b credible—believable
3. g incredible—unbelievable
4. f incredulous—unbelieving
5. c credence—believability
6. d creditable—worthy of praise
7. i criterion—standard
8. j cryptic—mysterious
9. a culinary—related to cooking
10. h culminate—climax

Quick Quiz #53

1. g crevice—narrow split
2. e cringe—shrink back with fear
3. c critique—critical review
4. f crux—central point
5. d cuisine—style of cooking
6. b cull—pick out from among many
7. a curb—restrain
8. i curmudgeon—difficult, bad-tempered person
9. h cursory—quick and unthorough

Quick Quiz #54

1. e culpable—guilty
2. a exculpate—free from guilt
3. d cursory—hasty
4. b curtail—shorten
5. c cynic—one who distrusts humanity

Quick Quiz #55

1. e daunt—make fearful
2. b dearth—lack
3. i debacle—violent breakdown
4. j debauchery—wild living
5. h debilitate—weaken
6. f decadent—decaying or decayed
7. c decimate—kill a large part of
8. g decorous—proper
9. a deduce—conclude from evidence
10. d defame—libel or slander

Quick Quiz #56

1. g debase—degrade
2. d debunk—expose the nonsense of
3. c decree—official order
4. j decry—denounce
5. a deem—judge
6. b deficit—shortage
7. f defile—make filthy
8. e deft—skillful
9. h defunct—no longer in effect
10. i degrade—lower in dignity

Quick Quiz #57

1. i deign—condescend
2. c deity—god or goddess
3. f dejected—depressed
4. a delectable—delightful
5. j delinquent—neglecting a duty
6. g delve—search intensively
7. h demeanor—behavior
8. b demise—death
9. e demography—study of population characteristics
10. d demur—take exception

Quick Quiz #58

1. i demure—shy
2. d denomination—classification
3. g denote—signify
4. b denounce—condemn
5. f depict—portray
6. a deplete—decrease the supply of
7. j deplore—lament
8. c deploy—arrange strategically
9. h depose—remove from office
10. e depredate—prey upon

Quick Quiz #59

1. d deference—respect
2. e definitive—conclusive
3. a degenerate—deteriorate
4. g deleterious—harmful
5. c delineate—describe accurately
6. i delude—deceive
7. j deluge—flood
8. l demagogue—rabble-rousing leader
9. h denizen—inhabitant
10. k depravity—extreme wickedness
11. f deprecate—express disapproval of
12. b deride—ridicule

Quick Quiz #60

1. h derogatory—disapproving
2. g desiccate—dry out
3. b despondent—extremely depressed
4. i despot—absolute ruler
5. e destitute—extremely poor
6. a desultory—without purpose
7. m dextrous—skillful
8. k dialectical—relating to discussions
9. l dictum—authoritative saying
10. j didactic—intended to reach
11. f diffident—timid
12. d digress—stray from the main subject
13. c dilettante—amateur

Quick Quiz #61

1. i derelict—neglectful
2. c desist—stop doing
3. f devout—deeply religious
4. j diatribe—bitter denunciation
5. a dichotomy—division into two parts
6. b diffuse—cause to spread out
7. h dilapidated—broken-down
8. g dilate—make larger
9. e dilemma—predicament
10. d diminution—reduction

Quick Quiz #62

1. j dire—disastrous
2. g dirge—funeral song
3. b disaffect—cause to lose affection
4. e disarray—disorder
5. a disclaim—renounce
6. d discomfit—frustrate
7. c disconcert—perturb
8. i discourse—conversation
9. f discrepancy—difference
10. h discursive—aimlessly rambling

Quick Quiz #63

1. a discern—have insight
2. f discreet—prudent
3. g discrete—unconnected
4. c indiscrete—not separated
5. h discriminate—differentiate
6. e disdain—arrogant scorn
7. d disinterested—not taking sides
8. b disparage—belittle

Quick Quiz #64
1. h disgruntle—make sulky
2. e disinformation—false information purposely disseminated
3. c dismal—dreary
4. i dismay—fill with dread
5. b dispassionate—impartial
6. a disperse—scatter
7. d dispirit—discourage
8. f disposition—characteristic attitude
9. g disproportionate—out of proportion
10. j disquiet—make uneasy

Quick Quiz #65
1. c dissemble—conceal the real nature of
2. a dissent—disagree
3. i disservice—harmful action
4. e dissident—person who disagrees
5. g dissuade—persuade not to
6. j distinct—separate
7. h diurnal—occurring every day
8. f divine—intuit
9. d divulge—reveal
10. b document—support with evidence

Quick Quiz #66
1. i disparate—incompatible
2. j disseminate—spread seeds
3. b dissipate—thin out
4. k dissolution— disintegration
5. g distend—swell
6. h distinguish—tell apart
7. e docile—easily taught
8. a doctrinaire—committed to a theory
9. f dogmatic—arrogantly assertive
10. d dogma—firmly held system of ideas
11. c domestic—of the household

Quick Quiz #67
1. c dormant—inactive
2. a dubiety—uncertainty
3. b duplicity—double-dealing

Quick Quiz #68
1. k doldrums—low spirits
2. j doleful—sorrowful
3. e dolt—stupid person
4. c dotage—senility
5. d double entendre— double meaning
6. a dour—forbidding
7. l downcast—dejected
8. i downplay—minimize
9. f draconian—harsh
10. b droll—humorous
11. g dross—worthless stuff
12. h duress—coercion

Quick Quiz #69
1. f ebullient—bubbling with excitement
2. d eccentric—not conventional
3. e eclectic—drawn from many sources
4. i edify—enlighten
5. g efface—erase
6. a effusion—pouring forth
7. j egalitarian—believing in social equality
8. h egocentric—selfish
9. b egotist—self-obsessed person
10. c egregious—extremely bad

Quick Quiz #70
1. i ebb—diminish
2. c ecclesiastical—having to do with the church
3. f eclipse—surpass
4. j ecosystem—organisms and their environment
5. a edict—official decree
6. d edifice—big, imposing building
7. g effectual—effective
8. h efficacy—effectiveness
9. e effigy—likeness of someone
10. b elation—feeling of great joy

Quick Quiz #71
1. b electorate—body of voters
2. f elegy—mournful poem
3. h elite—most select group
4. a elocution—art of public speaking
5. i emaciate—make extremely thin
6. j emanate—come forth
7. g emancipate—liberate
8. c embargo—government order suspending trade
9. d embellish—adorn
10. e embody—personify

Quick Quiz #72
1. b elicit—bring out
2. g elliptical—obscure
3. c elusive—hard to pin down
4. e emigrate—move from a country
5. f immigration—moving into a country
6. a eminent—well-known
7. d empirical—relying on experience

Quick Quiz #73
1. g emulate—strive to equal
2. j encroach—trespass
3. e endemic—native
4. d enervate—reduce the strength
5. f enfranchise—grant voting rights
6. c disfranchise—remove voting rights
7. a engender—cause to exist
8. b enigma—mystery
9. i enormity—extreme evil
10. h ephemeral—lasting a very short time

Quick Quiz #74

1. d embroil—involve in conflict
2. g embryonic—undeveloped
3. b emissary—messenger or representative
4. e empathy—identification with feelings
5. h empower—give authority
6. c endear—make dear
7. a engaging—charming
8. j enmity—deep hatred
9. f ennui—boredom
10. i ensue—follow immediately afterward

Quick Quiz #75

1. i entail—have as a necessary consequence
2. e entity—something that exists
3. g entreat—plead
4. c entrepreneur—independent businessperson
5. j enumerate—name one by one
6. d envision—imagine
7. f epicure—person with refined taste
8. h epilogue—afterword
9. b epoch—era
10. a equestrian—having to do with horseback riding

Quick Quiz #76

1. i epigram—brief, witty saying
2. e epigraph—apt quotation
3. g epitaph—inscription on a gravestone
4. j epithet—characterizing term
5. a epitome—brief summary
6. c equanimity—composure
7. b equitable—fair
8. d equivocal—intentionally confusing
9. f equivocate—say confusing things
10. h erudite—scholarly

Quick Quiz #77

1. a esoteric—peculiar
2. i espouse—advocate
3. h ethereal—heavenly
4. e euphemism—inoffensive substitute term
5. j evanescent—fleeting
6. b exacerbate—make worse
7. c exacting—extremely demanding
8. d exalt—raise high
9. g exasperate—annoy thoroughly
10. k exemplify—illustrate by example
11. l exhaustive—thorough
12. f exhort—urge strongly

Quick Quiz #78

1. j estimable—worthy of admiration
2. i estrange—make hostile
3. h ethics—moral standards
4. d eulogy—spoken or written tribute
5. g evince—demonstrate convincingly
6. a evoke—summon forth
7. b excise—remove by cutting
8. c exempt—excused
9. e exhume—unbury
10. f exodus—mass departure

Quick Quiz #79

1. m exigency—emergency
2. d existential—having to do with existence
3. a exonerate—free from blame
4. l expatriate—throw out of native land
5. i expedient—immediately advantageous
6. f expedite—speed up
7. b explicit—clearly expressed
8. c implicit—indirectly expressed
9. o extol—praise highly
10. j extraneous—unnecessary
11. g extrapolate—infer
12. h extricate—free from difficulty
13. e extrovert—outgoing person
14. k introvert—inwardly directed person
15. n exult—rejoice

Quick Quiz #80

1. a exorbitant—excessively costly
2. c expiate—make amends for
3. e explicate—make a detailed explanation of
4. g exposition—explanation
5. i expostulate—reason in order to dissuade
6. k expunge—erase
7. j exquisite—extraordinarily fine
8. h extant—still in existence
9. f extort—obtain through force
10. d extremity—outermost point
11. b exuberant—highly joyous

Quick Quiz #81

1. i fabrication—lie
2. e facetious—humorous
3. g facile—superficially skillful
4. h faction—group with a cause
5. c farcical—absurd
6. j fastidious—meticulous
7. d fatalist—one who believes in fate
8. k fatuous—foolish
9. f fauna—animals
10. a flora—plants
11. b fecund—fertile

Quick Quiz #82

1. e facade—front of a building
2. k facet—aspect
3. h fallacy—misconception
4. i fathom—penetrate the meaning of
5. l faux—false
6. b fawn—exhibit affection
7. d feign—make a false representation of
8. f fester—decay
9. a fetish—object of obsessive reverence
10. c fiasco—complete failure
11. g fiat—arbitrary decree
12. j fickle—likely to change for no good reason

Quick Quiz #83

1. j felicity—happiness
2. l fervor—zeal
3. c fetter—restrain
4. a fidelity—loyalty
5. g figurative—based on figures of speech
6. d literal—meaning exactly what it says
7. i finesse—skillful maneuvering
8. k flagrant—glaringly bad
9. f flaunt—show off
10. h flout—to disregard completely
11. e foible—minor character flaw
12. b foment—stir up

Quick Quiz #84

1. c figment—something made up
2. f fiscal—monetary
3. b fledgling—inexperienced
4. i flippant—frivolously disrespectful
5. g florid—flushed
6. d fodder—raw material
7. a folly—foolishness
8. e foray—quick raid
9. h forebode—be an omen of
10. j foreclose—shut out

Quick Quiz #85

1. a forensic—used in courts of law
2. d forestall—thwart
3. g forswear—retract
4. c forte—special talent
5. b forthright—outspoken
6. f foster—encourage
7. j fragmentary—incomplete
8. h fruitful—productive
9. e fuel—stimulate
10. i fulminate—denounce vigorously

Quick Quiz #86

1. e forbear—refrain from
2. b forebear—ancestor
3. d forgo—do without
4. i forsake—abandon
5. h fortuitous—accidental
6. f founder—sink
7. c flounder—move in confusion
8. j frenetic—frantic
9. a frugal—economical
10. g furtive—secretive

Quick Quiz #87
1. e gaffe—social blunder
2. c galvanize—startle into sudden activity
3. h gambit—scheme to gain an advantage
4. a gamut—full range
5. b garner—gather
6. d gastronomy—art of eating well
7. i generic—common
8. g genesis—origin
9. f genocide—extermination of a national, racial, or religious group
10. j germane—applicable

Quick Quiz #88
1. g futile—hopeless
2. a garrulous—chatty
3. m gauche—awkward
4. l genre—type of art
5. h genteel—refined
6. f gesticulate—make gestures
7. b glut—surplus
8. j grandiloquent—pompous
9. k grandiose—absurdly exaggerated
10. d gratuitous—unjustified
11. e gravity—seriousness
12. i gregarious—sociable
13. c guile—cunning

Quick Quiz #89
1. b ghastly—shockingly horrible
2. a gratis—free of charge
3. d grievous—tragic
4. c grimace—make an ugly face
5. e guise—appearance

Quick Quiz #90
1. i habituate—accustom to a situation
2. b halcyon—peaceful
3. f harass—attack repeatedly
4. k harbinger—precursor
5. h harp—repeat tediously
6. f harry—attack repeatedly
7. j heinous—shockingly evil
8. c herald—royal proclaimer
9. e hoary—gray or white with age
10. g homage—reverence
11. a hubris—arrogance
12. d hypocrisy—insincerity

Quick Quiz #91
1. f hackneyed—overused; trite
2. j hapless—unlucky
3. d harbinger—forerunner
4. p hedonism—lifelong pursuit of pleasure
5. a hegemony—leadership
6. q heresy—strongly contrary belief
7. c hermetic—airtight
8. h heyday—golden age
9. m hiatus—break
10. e hierarchy—pecking order
11. l histrionic—overly dramatic
12. n homily—sermon
13. b homogeneous—uniform
14. i heterogeneous—varied
15. o husbandry—thrifty management of resources
16. g hyperbole—exaggeration
17. k hypothetical—uncertain; unproven

Quick Quiz #92

1. c idiom—nonliteral expression
2. f imbue—inspire
3. i impasse—deadlock
4. a impeach—accuse
5. e impecunious—without money
6. d impede—obstruct
7. b impending—approaching
8. j impenetrable—impervious
9. h imperative—completely necessary
10. g impetuous—rash

Quick Quiz #93

1. e iconoclast—attacker of popular beliefs
2. h ideology—system of social ideas
3. a idiosyncrasy—peculiarity
4. b idyllic—naturally peaceful
5. j ignominy—deep disgrace
6. l illicit—illegal
7. f imminent—just about to happen
8. k immutable—unchangeable
9. g impartial—fair
10. d impeccable—flawless
11. c imperial—like an emperor
12. i imperious—bossy

Quick Quiz #94

1. d implication—something suggested
2. b importune—urge with annoying persistence
3. i impoverish—reduce to poverty
4. f impregnable—unconquerable
5. c impresario—person who manages public entertainments
6. g impromptu—done on the spur of the moment
7. j improvise—perform without preparation
8. e impunity—freedom from punishment
9. a inadvertent—unintentional
10. h inalienable—unassailable

Quick Quiz #95

1. d impervious—impenetrable
2. g impetuous—impulsive
3. b implement—carry out
4. c impotent—powerless
5. f impugn—attack the truth of
6. e inane—silly
7. a inaugurate—begin officially

Quick Quiz #96
1. j incandescent—brilliant
2. d incantation—chant
3. b incense—make very angry
4. i incessant—unceasing
5. c incipient—beginning
6. h incisive—cutting right to the heart
7. e incongruous—not harmonious
8. f incorrigible—incapable of being reformed
9. a increment—increase
10. g indifferent—not caring; mediocre

Quick Quiz #97
1. g incarnation—embodiment
2. c incendiary—used for setting property on fire
3. f inclination—tendency
4. b inculcate—instill
5. d incumbent—currently holding office
6. a incursion—hostile invasion
7. e indict—charge with a crime
8. h induce—persuade
9. j ineluctable—inescapable
10. i ineradicable—incapable of being removed

Quick Quiz #98
1. a indigenous—native
2. f indigent—poor
3. h indignant—angry
4. c indolent—lazy
5. j indulgent—lenient
6. k ineffable—inexpressible
7. i inept—clumsy
8. b inert—inactive
9. g inexorable—relentless
10. e infamous—shamefully wicked
11. d infatuated—foolish

Quick Quiz #99
1. c inflammatory—tending to arouse passion or anger
2. g influx—inflow
3. d infraction—violation
4. a infrastructure—basic framework of a system
5. b infringe—violate
6. i infuse—introduce into
7. h ingratiate—work to make yourself liked
8. f inimical—harmful
9. j inimitable—impossible to imitate
10. e innuendo—insinuation

Quick Quiz #100
1. f infer—conclude
2. c imply—hint at
3. i infinitesimal—infinitely small
4. d ingenuous—artless
5. b inherent—part of the nature of
6. j injunction—court order
7. e innate—inborn
8. h innocuous—harmless
9. g inordinate—excessive
10. a insatiable—hard or impossible to satisfy

Quick Quiz #101

1. h inquisition—ruthless questioning
2. a insouciant—nonchalant
3. b insufferable—unbearable
4. c insuperable—unable to overcome
5. d insurrection—act of open rebellion
6. i integral—essential
7. g interim—meantime
8. e interloper—intruder
9. j interlude—intervening episode
10. f interminable—seemingly unending

Quick Quiz #102

1. c insidious—treacherous
2. a insinuate—hint
3. h insipid—dull
4. j insolent—arrogant
5. e instigate—provoke
6. f insular—like an island
7. g insurgent—rebel
8. d integral—essential
9. k integrate—combine
10. b intractable—uncontrollable
11. i intransigent—uncompromising

Quick Quiz #103

1. g intermittent—occasional
2. i intersperse—place at intervals
3. f intervene—come between opposing groups
4. e intimate—hint
5. d intricate—complicated
6. a intrigue—secret scheme
7. h invidious—causing resentment
8. j inviolate—free from injury
9. c invoke—pray for
10. b iridescent—displaying glowing, changing colors

Quick Quiz #104

1. e intrinsic—inherent
2. f introspective—examining one's feelings
3. d inundate—flood
4. b invective—insulting speech
5. j inveterate—habitual
6. i irascible—irritable
7. g ironic—meaning other than what's said
8. a irrevocable—irreversible
9. h itinerant—moving from place to place
10. c itinerary—planned trip route

Quick Quiz #105

1. b jargon—specialized language
2. g jaunt—short pleasure trip
3. d jingoism—belligerent patriotism
4. a jocular—humorous
5. f jubilation—exultant joy
6. h junction—convergence
7. e junta—small ruling group
8. c karma—good or bad emanations

Quick Quiz #106

1. m judicious—exercising sound judgment
2. e juxtapose—place side by side
3. h kinetic—active
4. d labyrinth—maze
5. c laconic—using few words
6. k lament—mourn
7. j lampoon—satirize
8. i languish—become weak
9. f latent—present but not visible
10. l laud—praise
11. g legacy—bequest
12. a lethargy—sluggishness
13. b levity—lightness

Quick Quiz #107

1. b larceny—theft
2. f lascivious—lewd
3. e lavish—to spend freely
4. a lax—negligent
5. d layman—nonprofessional
6. c liaison—connection
7. f licentious—lewd
8. h limpid—transparent
9. i listless—sluggish
10. g litany—tedious recounting

Quick Quiz #108

1. e libel—written injurious falsehood
2. f slander—spoken injurious falsehood
3. b litigate—try in court
4. g loquacious—talking a lot
5. d lucid—easy to understand
6. c lugubrious—exaggeratedly mournful
7. a luminous—giving off light

Quick Quiz #109

1. c livid—black and blue
2. a loath—extremely unwilling
3. f lobby—urge legislative action
4. d lout—oaf
5. b ludicrous—ridiculous
6. e lyrical—melodious

Quick Quiz #110

1. e machination—scheming evil activity
2. a magnanimous—forgiving
3. n magnate—rich businessperson
4. c malaise—depression
5. p malevolent—wishing to do evil
6. k malfeasance—illegal act
7. o malignant—harmful
8. g malinger—pretend to be sick
9. b malleable—easy to shape
10. d mandate—command to do something
11. h manifest—visible
12. f manifesto—public declaration
13. j marshal—arrange in order
14. m martial—warlike
15. i martyr—one who dies for a cause
16. l matriculate—enroll

Quick Quiz #111

1. b malapropism—humorous misuse of a word
2. e mania—crazed excitement
3. g marginal—insignificant
4. d materialistic—preoccupied with material things
5. h mawkish—overly sentimental
6. a meander—travel along a winding route
7. c medium—the means by which something is conveyed
8. f melancholy—gloomy
9. j melee—brawl
10. i menagerie—collection of animals

Quick Quiz #112

1. i maudlin—overly sentimental
2. f maverick—nonconformist
3. b maxim—fundamental principle
4. d mediate—help settle differences
5. e mellifluous—sweetly flowing
6. c mendacious—lying
7. k mendicant—beggar
8. a mentor—teacher
9. j mercenary—hired soldier
10. g mercurial—emotionally unpredictable
11. h metamorphosis—magical change in form

Quick Quiz #113

1. m microcosm—world in miniature
2. j milieu—environment
3. h minuscule—very tiny
4. n misanthropic—hating mankind
5. b mitigate—moderate the effect of
6. f mollify—soften
7. c monolithic—massive and unyielding
8. l moribund—dying
9. i morose—gloomy
10. d mortify—humiliate
11. e mundane—ordinary
12. k munificent—very generous
13. g myopia—nearsightedness
14. a myriad—a huge number

Quick Quiz #114

1. g meticulous—precise and careful about details
2. e millennium—period of one thousand years
3. j mire—marshy, mucky ground
4. a mode—method of doing
5. b modulate—reduce or regulate
6. d momentum—force of movement
7. m moratorium—suspension of activity
8. i mores—customary moral standards
9. f motif—recurring theme
10. c motley—extremely varied
11. n municipal—pertaining to a city or town
12. l muse—ponder
13. k muster—assemble for battle
14. h mystic—otherworldy

Quick Quiz #115

1. a narcissism—excessive love of self
2. h nebulous—vague
3. e nefarious—evil
4. l neologism—new word
5. j nepotism—favoritism
6. k nihilism—belief in the absence of all values and morals
7. b nominal—in name only
8. i nostalgia—lónging for the past
9. g notorious—famous for something bad
10. d novel—original
11. c noxious—harmful
12. f nuance—subtle difference

Quick Quiz #116

1. b nebulous—vague
2. e nemesis—downfall
3. h neophyte—beginner
4. c nirvana—blissful, worry-free state
5. i noisome—offensive or disgusting
6. a nomadic—wandering from place to place
7. d nomenclature—system of names
8. g nonchalant—indifferent
9. f nullify—repeal

Quick Quiz #117

1. e obeisance—deep reverence
2. b objective—unbiased
3. g obtrusive—interfering
4. a obviate—make unnecessary
5. j occult—supernatural
6. i odious—hateful
7. h odyssey—long, difficult journey
8. c olfactory—pertaining to the sense of smell
9. f oligarchy—government by only a very few people
10. d ominous—threatening

Quick Quiz #118

1. c obdurate—stubborn
2. k obfuscate—confuse
3. g oblique—indirect
4. a oblivion—forgetfulness
5. b obscure—hard to understand
6. l obsequious—fawning
7. d obtuse—insensitive
8. n officious—annoyingly helpful
9. e onerous—burdensome
10. j opaque—impossible to see through
11. f opulent—luxurious
12. m orthodox—conventional
13. h ostensible—misleading apparent
14. i ostentatious—showing off

Quick Quiz #119
1. h omniscient—all-knowing
2. d opprobrious—damning
3. f ordinance—law
4. b oscillate—swing back and forth
5. e osmosis—gradual or subtle absorption
6. a ostracize—exclude from a group
7. c oust—eject
8. j override—prevail over
9. i overture—opening move
10. g oxymoron—figure of speech linking two contradictory words or phrases

Quick Quiz #120
1. g pacify—calm someone down
2. j painstaking—extremely careful
3. l palliate—alleviate
4. a palpable—obvious
5. i paltry—insignificant
6. h panacea—cure for everything
7. b paradigm—model
8. e paradox—contradictory truth
9. d parochial—narrow in point of view
10. k parody—satirical imitation
11. f parsimonious—stingy
12. c partisan—supporter of a cause

Quick Quiz #121
1. b palatable—pleasant to the taste
2. g pallor—paleness
3. d pandemic—prevalent throughout a large area
4. j panegyric—elaborate praise
5. e parable—morality tale
6. a paragon—model of excellence
7. i parallel—similar
8. h paranoia—unreasonable anxiety
9. c paranormal—supernatural
10. f paroxysm—sudden, violent outburst

Quick Quiz #122
1. i patent—obvious
2. l paternal—fatherly
3. f pathology—science of diseases
4. a patriarch—male head of a family
5. j patrician—aristocrat
6. g patronize—treat as an inferior
7. k paucity—scarcity
8. b peccadillo—minor offense
9. e pedantic—boringly scholarly
10. c pedestrian—unimaginative
11. h pejorative—negative
12. n penchant—strong liking
13. m penitent—sorry
14. d pensive—thoughtful and sad

Quick Quiz #123

1. b partition—division
2. c pastoral—rural
3. h pathos—that which makes people feel pity or sorry
4. f patina—surface discoloration
5. j patrimony—inheritance
6. i peculiar—unusual
7. g peregrination—wandering
8. d perpetrator—the one who committed the act
9. a perpetuate—keep from perishing
10. e perverse—stubborn

Quick Quiz #124

1. k peremptory—final
2. f perennial—continual
3. j perfidy—treachery
4. b perfunctory—unenthusiastic
5. l peripatetic—wandering
6. a periphery—outside edge of something
7. d perjury—lying under oath
8. c permeate—penetrate
9. n pernicious—deadly
10. e perquisite—job-related privilege
11. h prerequisite—necessity
12. m pertinent—relevant
13. g perturb—disturb greatly
14. i peruse—read carefully

Quick Quiz #125

1. i phantasm—apparition
2. e phlegmatic—calm or indifferent
3. d pilgrimage—religious journey
4. a placebo—fake medication
5. b platonic—nonsexual
6. g plausible—believable
7. f pliable—flexible
8. h plight—dangerous situation
9. j plunder—ransack
10. c pluralism—coexistence of distinct groups

Quick Quiz #126

1. b pervade—spread throughout
2. i petulant—rude
3. k philanthropy—love for mankind
4. d philistine—smugly ignorant person
5. g pious—reverent
6. j pivotal—crucial
7. c placate—pacify
8. f plaintive—expressing sadness
9. h platitude—trite remark
10. l plebeian—low class
11. e plethora —excess
12. a poignant—painfully emotional

Quick Quiz #127

1. g polarize—cause opposing positions
2. d polemic—powerful refutation
-3. a ponderous—massive and clumsy
4. j portent—omen
5. h portentous—ominous
6. k postulate—axiom
7. c pragmatic—practical
8. i precedent—earlier example
9. b precept—rule to live by
10. f precipitate—cause to happen abruptly
11. e precipitous—steep

Quick Quiz #128

1. g pontificate—speak pompously
2. d porous—filled with many tiny holes
3. b posterity—future generations
4. a posthumous—occurring after one's death
5. i posture—speak artificially
6. f prattle—chatter on and on
7. e precarious—dangerously insecure
8. c precocious—unusually mature
9. j predecessor—something that precedes in time
10. h predicament—dangerous situation

Quick Quiz #129

1. f predispose—make susceptible
2. c predominant—most important
3. h pregnant—highly significant
4. e prelude—introduction
5. g premeditated—planned beforehand
6. a preponderance—majority
7. b presage—portend
8. d presentiment—feeling that something is about to happen
9. j presumably—probably
10. i presuppose—assume beforehand

Quick Quiz #130

1. k preclude—prevent
2. j precursor—forerunner
3. f predilection—natural preference
4. a preeminent—outstanding
5. c preempt—seize by prior right
6. i premise—assumption
7. g prepossess—preoccupy
8. h prerogative—right or privilege
9. b prevail—triumph
10. e pristine—unspoiled
11. d prodigal—wastefully extravagant

Quick Quiz #131

1. f prodigious—extraordinary
2. e prodigy—extremely talented child
3. b profane—irreverent
4. a profess—declare
5. i proficient—thoroughly competent
6. j profligate—extravagantly wasteful
7. h profound—deep
8. d profuse—flowing
9. k proletariat—industrial working class
10. g proliferate—spread rapidly
11. c prolific—abundantly productive

Quick Quiz #132

1. c primal—original
2. h pristine—perfectly clean and untouched
3. e privation—lack of comforts
4. f proclaim—announce
5. j procure—obtain by special means
6. i progeny—offspring
7. a propagate—reproduce
8. b propound—set forth
9. d protégé—person under the care of someone
10. g protocol—diplomatic etiquette

Quick Quiz #133

1. l promulgate—proclaim
2. a propensity—natural inclination
3. j propitious—marked by favorable signs
4. c proponent—advocate
5. g proprietary—constituting property
6. b propriety—good manners
7. i prosaic—dull
8. d proscribe—prohibit
9. k proselytize—convert
10. f protagonist—leading character
11. e protract—prolong
12. h provident—frugal

Quick Quiz #134

1. c provincial—narrow in outlook
2. f provisional—conditional
3. b proximity—nearness
4. e prudent—careful
5. d purported—rumored
6. a putative—commonly accepted

Quick Quiz #135

1. d provocation—incitement
2. g prowess—exceptional skill or strength
3. b prurient—having lustful thoughts or desires
4. a pseudonym—false name
5. k psyche—human soul or mind
6. h pummel—pound with fists
7. j punctilious—meticulously attentive to detail
8. i pundit—learned person
9. l pungent—sharp-tasting
10. f punitive—inflicting a punishment
11. c purblind—dim-sighted
12. e puritanical—very severe about morals

Quick Quiz #136

1. d qualify—modify or restrict
2. e qualitative—having to do with quality
3. a quantitative—having to do with quantity
4. c querulous—complaining
5. b quixotic—foolishly romantic

Quick Quiz #137

1. a quaint—pleasantly old-fashioned
2. h quandary—state of perplexity
3. j quasi—almost
4. f quay—a landing on the edge of the water
5. e quell—put an end to
6. b query—question
7. k queue—line
8. c quiescent—motionless
9. d quintessential—being the most perfect example of
10. g quizzical—teasing
11. i quotidian—daily

Quick Quiz #138

1. e rampant—widespread
2. c rapture—ecstasy
3. g rarefied—esoteric
4. a ratify—confirm
5. b ratiocination—logical reasoning
6. h rationale—underlying reason
7. f raucous—stridently loud
8. d reactionary—ultra conservative
9. i rebuff—snub
10. j recidivism—act of repeating an offense

Quick Quiz #139
1. c ramification—consequence
2. f rancor—bitter resentment
3. j rapacious—greedy
4. b rebuke—criticize sharply
5. i rebut—contradict
6. g recalcitrant—stubbornly defiant
7. h recant—publicly deny
8. d reciprocal—mutual
9. e reclusive—hermitlike
10. a recondite—hard to understand

Quick Quiz #140
1. d reclaim—make fit for cultivation
2. h redeem—buy back
3. a redress—remedy
4. c referendum—public vote
5. b refractory—disobedient
6. j regime—governing power
7. f regimen—regulated course
8. e remission—disappearance of a disease
9. g remuneration—payment
10. i rend—rip

Quick Quiz #141
1. h recrimination—bitter counteraccusation
2. e redolent—fragrant
3. i redundant—unnecessarily repetitive
4. j refute—prove to be false
5. g reiterate—say again
6. f relegate—banish
7. a relinquish—surrender
8. d remonstrate—argue against
9. c renaissance—rebirth
10. b renounce—disown

Quick Quiz #142
1. f render—cause to be
2. c repartee—quick, witty reply
3. b replicate—reproduce exactly
4. j repose—tranquillity
5. h repress—hold back
6. a reprimand—stern reproof
7. e reprisal—retaliation
8. d reprobate—depraved, wicked person
9. g repugnant—repulsive
10. i resignation—passive submission

Quick Quiz #143
1. g reparation—paying back
2. d repercussion—consequence
3. j replenish—fill again
4. f replete—completely filled
5. c reprehensible—worthy of blame
6. a reprisal—act of revenge
7. e reproach—scold
8. i reprove—criticize mildly
9. k repudiate—reject
10. h requisite—necessary
11. b resolute—determined

Quick Quiz #144
1. g respite—period of rest
2. e reticent—restrained
3. i revere—honor
4. d rhetoric—formal writing or speaking
5. h rigorous—strict
6. c robust—vigorous
7. j rogue—scoundrel
8. a rudimentary—basic
9. b ruminate—contemplate
10. f rustic—rural

Quick Quiz #145

1. c resplendent—brilliantly shining
2. k resurrection—return to life
3. i retort—make a sharp reply
4. f retrospect—looking backward
5. e revamp—revise
6. a revel—enjoy thoroughly
7. b revile—scold abusively
8. n revulsion—loathing
9. m rhapsodize—speak extremely enthusiastically
10. l ribald—indecent
11. d rife—occurring frequently
12. g rivet—engross
13. j rout—put to flight
14. h rue—mourn

Quick Quiz #146

1. c saccharine—sweet
2. a sacrilege—blasphemy
3. h sacrosanct—sacred
4. j sagacious—discerning
5. b sage—wise
6. i salient—sticking out
7. e salutary—healthful
8. d sanctimonious—pretending to be devout
9. g sanguine—cheerful
10. f sardonic—mocking

Quick Quiz #147

1. c sally—sudden rushing attack
2. h salutation—greeting
3. g sanction—official permission or approval
4. a sarcasm—biting irony
5. b savant—scholar
6. j scant—limited
7. i schism—division
8. f scorn—disdain
9. e seamless—smooth
10. d secede—withdraw from an alliance

Quick Quiz #148

1. a scintillate—sparkle
2. f scrupulous—strict
3. h scrutinize—examine very carefully
4. b secular—having nothing to do with religion
5. c sedition—treason
6. k segregate—separate
7. d sensory—having to do with the senses
8. i sensual—devoted to pleasure
9. g sensuous—delighting the senses
10. j sentient—conscious
11. e sequester—set apart

Quick Quiz #149
1. i seclusion—aloneness
2. g sect—small religious subgroup
3. e sedentary—largely confined to sitting down
4. f self-made—having succeeded without help from others
5. c sententious—preachy
6. d serene—calm
7. b serpentine—snakelike
8. h shackle—manacle
9. j shibboleth—catchword
10. a shrewd—wily

Quick Quiz #150
1. a serendipity—accidental good fortune
2. e servile—submissive
3. j singular—unique
4. k sinister—wicked
5. i slavish—extremely subservient
6. g sloth—laziness
7. h sobriety—state of being sober
8. c solicitous—eager and attentive
9. d solvent—not bankrupt
10. f insolvent—broke
11. b soporific—sleep-inducing

Quick Quiz #151
1. e singular—exceptional
2. c skirmish—fight between small numbers of troops
3. g skittish—nervous
4. d slake—quench
5. a solace—consolation
6. h solidarity—sense of unity
7. f sophomoric—juvenile
8. j sordid—morally vile
9. i sovereign—supreme ruler
10. b spate—sudden outpouring

Quick Quiz #152
1. h sordid—vile
2. g spawn—bring forth
3. l specious—deceptively plausible
4. b sporadic—stopping and starting
5. m spurious—false
6. n squander—waste
7. d stagnation—inactivity
8. k static—stationary
9. i staunch—firmly committed
10. i steadfast—firmly committed
11. a stigmatize—disgrace
12. e stipulate—require
13. f stoic—indifferent to pain, pleasure
14. j stratum—layer
15. c stricture—restriction

Quick Quiz #153
1. h specious—deceptive
2. e specter—phantom
3. i spectrum—broad sequence
4. b spurn—reject
5. c stalwart—robust
6. f stark—desolate
7. d stint—restrict
8. j stipend—allowance
9. g stolid—not easily roused to emotion
10. a stout—stocky

Quick Quiz #154
1. k strife—bitter conflict
2. h stringent—strict
3. d stymie—thwart
4. e subjugate—subdue
5. b sublime—awesome
6. i subordinate—lower in importance
7. g insubordinate—not respectful of authority
8. j substantive—having substance
9. a subtle—not obvious
10. f subversive—corrupting
11. c succinct—brief and to the point

Quick Quiz #155
1. d stratagem—maneuver designed to outwit an enemy
2. f stupendous—remarkable
3. b stupor—stunned condition
4. g subside—sink
5. h subsidiary—supplemental
6. e subsidize—provide financial aid
7. a substantiate—prove
8. c subterfuge—artifice
9. i suffice—be sufficient
10. j suffrage—right to vote

Quick Quiz #156
1. b succumb—yield
2. a supercilious—haughty
3. f superficial—on the surface only
4. e superfluous—unnecessary
5. h surfeit—excess
6. g surreptitious—sneaky
7. d surrogate—substitute
8. c sycophant—flatterer
9. i synthesis—combining of parts

Quick Quiz #157
1. d suffuse—overspread
2. h sumptuous—luxurious
3. f supersede—take the place of
4. c supine—lying on the back
5. a supplication—humble prayer
6. b suppress—overpower
7. k surmise—conjecture
8. i surreal—hallucinatory
9. l susceptible—capable of being influenced
10. g sweeping—far-reaching
11. e syntax—grammar
12. j systemic—affecting the entire system

Quick Quiz #158
1. i tacit—implied
2. b taciturn—naturally untalkative
3. e tangential—not deeply relevant
4. j tangible—touchable
5. d tantamount—equivalent to
6. f tautological—redundant
7. c temerity—boldness
8. g temperate—mild
9. h tenable—defensible
10. a tenacious—persistent

Quick Quiz #159
1. c tactical—having to do with tactics
2. h taint—contaminant
3. d tedium—dullness
4. g teem—swarm
5. a temporal—pertaining to time
6. b temporize—stall
7. j tepid—lukewarm
8. i thesis—theory to be proven
9. e thorny—full of difficulties
10. f threshold—sill of a doorway

Quick Quiz #160
1. c throttle—choke
2. b thwart—prevent from being accomplished
3. g timorous—fearful
4. f titillate—excite
5. e titular—in name only
6. j toil—hard work
7. h tortuous—winding
8. d toxic—poisonous
9. i transfix—cause to stand motionless
10. a trauma—severe shock

Quick Quiz #161
1. h tenet—shared principle
2. e tentative—experimental
3. k tenuous—flimsy
4. a terse—without unnecessary words
5. j torpor—sluggishness
6. m theology—study of religion
7. g tirade—bitter speech
8. n touchstone—standard
9. c tout—brag publicly about
10. b transcend—go beyond
11. o transgress—violate
12. f transient—not lasting long
13. f transitory—not lasting long
14. l trepidation—fear
15. d intrepid—fearless
16. i turpitude—wickedness

Quick Quiz #162
1. f travesty—grotesque imitation
2. d trenchant—concise
3. b triumvirate—ruling coalition of three
4. a tryst—secret meeting of lovers
5. e tumult—violent, noisy commotion
6. c turbid—murky
7. g turmoil—state of great confusion

Quick Quiz #163

1. c ubiquitous—everywhere at once
2. f unconscionable—unscrupulous
3. a unctuous—oily; slick
4. i uniform—consistent
5. j unremitting—unceasing
6. h unwitting—unintentional
7. b urbane—poised and sophisticated
8. e usurp—seize wrongfully
9. d utilitarian—pragmatic
10. g utopia—an ideal society

Quick Quiz #164

1. f uncanny—extraordinary
2. c underlying—basic
3. d undermine—impair
4. a underpinning—system of supports beneath
5. h underscore—underline
6. e underwrite—sponsor
7. b unilateral—involving one side only
8. g usury—lending money at extremely high rates

Quick Quiz #165

1. g vacuous—empty of content
2. a vagary—whim
3. c vanquish—conquer
4. f veneer—facade
5. e verdant—covered with green plants
6. b verge—border
7. h verity—quality of being true
8. d vie—compete
9. i vigilant—constantly alert
10. j vignette—short literary sketch

Quick Quiz #166

1. b vacillate—be indecisive
2. f vapid—dull
3. o vehement—intense
4. l venal—corrupt
5. h venerate—revere
6. k veracity—truthfulness
7. m verbose—wordy
8. j verisimilitude—similarity to reality
9. n vernacular—slang
10. i vestige—last trace
11. a vex—annoy
12. d viable—capable of living
13. e vicarious—experienced through another
14. g vicissitude—upheaval
15. c vilify—defame

Quick Quiz #167

1. e vindicate—clear from suspicion
2. h vindictive—seeking revenge
3. b virtuoso—masterful musician
4. a virulent—extremely poisonous
5. c visionary—dreamer
6. j vitiate—make impure
7. d vitriolic—caustic
8. i vocation—occupation
9. k vociferous—noisy
10. g volatile—quick to evaporate
11. f volition—will

Quick Quiz #168
1. f viscous—thick
2. e vivacious—lively
3. d vogue—fashion
4. c voluminous—large
5. b voluptuous—pleasant to the senses
6. a voracious—having a huge appetite

Quick Quiz #169
1. d wanton—malicious
2. c willful—deliberate
3. b wistful—yearning
4. a zealous—fervent

Quick Quiz #170
1. d waft—float
2. k waive—relinquish
3. i wake—all-night vigil
4. j wane—decrease in strength
5. a warrant—justify
6. b wary—cautious
7. f wizened—shriveled
8. e woe—suffering
9. c wrath—deep anger
10. g zeitgeist—spirit of the times
11. h zenith—highest point

Final Exam Drill #1
1. d
2. e
3. b
4. e
5. c

Final Exam Drill #2
1. b
2. a
3. f
4. h
5. g
6. e
7. i
8. j
9. d
10. c

Final Exam Drill #3
1. address
2. integral
3. delineate
4. relegate
5. didactic
6. labyrinthine
7. amoral
8. analogous
9. magnanimous
10. malleable

Final Exam Drill #4
1. O
2. S
3. U
4. S
5. O
6. O
7. S
8. S
9. U
10. S

Final Exam Drill #5
1. a
2. c
3. d
4. b
5. b

Final Exam Drill #6
1. O
2. U
3. O
4. S
5. O
6. O
7. O
8. S
9. S
10. S

Final Exam Drill #7
1. renaissance
2. requisite
3. apprehensive
4. sacrosanct
5. replenish
6. arbitrary
7. eclectic
8. elliptical
9. allocate
10. avuncular

Final Exam Drill #8
1. S
2. O
3. O
4. S
5. O
6. S
7. S
8. U
9. S
10. U

Final Exam Drill #9
1. e
2. d
3. e
4. c
5. e

Final Exam Drill #10
1. U
2. S
3. S
4. O
5. O
6. S
7. O
8. S
9. U
10. U

Final Exam Drill #11
1. O
2. O
3. S
4. O
5. U
6. O
7. O
8. O
9. U
10. O

Final Exam Drill #12
1. awry
2. ascendancy
3. cadence
4. oblivion
5. nominal
6. equitable
7. nostalgic
8. bereft
9. bourgeois
10. pejorative

Final Exam Drill #13
1. O
2. O
3. U
4. U
5. U
6. S
7. U
8. S
9. O
10. S

Final Exam Drill #14
1. a
2. c
3. b
4. e
5. c

Final Exam Drill #15
1. a
2. f
3. g
4. b
5. d
6. e
7. h
8. c
9. j
10. i

Final Exam Drill #16
1. U
2. S
3. S
4. U
5. S
6. O
7. S
8. U
9. O
10. O

Final Exam Drill #17
1. existential
2. flaunt
3. felicity
4. pivotal
5. salutary
6. ubiquitous
7. succinct
8. eminent
9. farcical
10. volition

Final Exam Drill #18
1. U
2. U
3. S
4. S
5. U
6. S
7. U
8. O
9. S
10. U

Final Exam Drill #19
1. b
2. d
3. a
4. a
5. b

Final Exam Drill #20
1. S
2. O
3. U
4. U
5. S
6. O
7. S
8. O
9. S
10. O

Final Exam Drill #21
1. officious
2. scrutinize
3. reprehensible
4. founder
5. palpable
6. qualify
7. culinary
8. corollary
9. proximity
10. vicarious

Final Exam Drill #22
1. S
2. O
3. S
4. S
5. O
6. S
7. O
8. S
9. S
10. O

Final Exam Drill #23
1. d
2. d
3. b
4. a
5. a

Final Exam Drill #24
1. S
2. U
3. O
4. U
5. U
6. U
7. S
8. S
9. O
10. S

Final Exam Drill #25
1. omnipotent
2. fortuitous
3. verisimilitude
4. pertinent
5. conducive
6. prolific
7. vicissitude
8. obsequious
9. euphemism
10. diffident

Final Exam Drill #26
1. U
2. O
3. O
4. O
5. S
6. O
7. O
8. O
9. S
10. O

Final Exam Drill #27
1. d
2. a
3. c
4. b
5. b

Final Exam Drill #28
1. U
2. U
3. O
4. S
5. O
6. S
7. O
8. S
9. S
10. S

Final Exam Drill #29
1. comprise
2. bemuse
3. provident
4. anecdotal
5. prodigy
6. cadence
7. soporific
8. staunch
9. vacillate
10. vestige

Final Exam Drill #30
1. U
2. O
3. U
4. S
5. U
6. O
7. U
8. S
9. S
10. U

Final Exam Drill #31
1. e
2. c
3. a
4. e
5. b

Final Exam Drill #32
1. O
2. S
3. O
4. O
5. U
6. S
7. O
8. O
9. S
10. O

Final Exam Drill #33
1. innocuous
2. assimilate
3. unctuous
4. exult
5. surrogate
6. tantamount
7. catharsis
8. complacency
9. recrimination
10. patronize

Final Exam Drill #34
1. O
2. S
3. O
4. O
5. S
6. S
7. O
8. S
9. O
10. U

Final Exam Drill #35
1. f
2. g
3. h
4. b
5. i
6. a
7. e
8. c
9. j
10. d

Final Exam Drill #36
1. U
2. O
3. O
4. S
5. S
6. O
7. U
8. S
9. S
10. U

Final Exam Drill #37
1. c
2. b
3. e
4. d
5. c

Final Exam Drill #38
1. O
2. O
3. U
4. U
5. O
6. U
7. O
8. U
9. S
10. O

Final Exam Drill #39
1. scintillating
2. digression
3. wistful
4. cerebral
5. affable
6. ideological
7. vexed
8. comprehensive
9. impervious
10. tirade

Final Exam Drill #40
1. O
2. O
3. S
4. O
5. O
6. S
7. O
8. S
9. O
10. O

Final Exam Drill #41
1. a
2. e
3. d
4. b
5. d

Final Exam Drill #42
1. S
2. O
3. O
4. O
5. U
6. S
7. O
8. S
9. O
10. O

Final Exam Drill #43
1. cacophony
2. benefactor
3. manifesto
4. reciprocal
5. provisional
6. squalid
7. callow
8. putative
9. derisory
10. proscribe

Final Exam Drill #44
1. a
2. e
3. d
4. f
5. b
6. j
7. c
8. i
9. h
10. g

Final Exam Drill #45
1. S
2. S
3. U
4. S
5. U
6. O
7. S
8. S
9. U
10. S

Final Exam Drill #46
1. d
2. a
3. c
4. c
5. c

Final Exam Drill #47
1. S
2. U
3. S
4. O
5. S
6. S
7. O
8. O
9. S
10. O

Final Exam Drill #48
1. d
2. a
3. e
4. c
5. b

Final Exam Drill #49
1. e
2. c
3. g
4. a
5. d
6. f
7. h
8. j
9. b
10. i

Final Exam Drill #50
1. d
2. e
3. f
4. j
5. g
6. h
7. b
8. a
9. c
10. i

Final Exam Drill #51
1. b
2. e
3. c
4. h
5. f
6. i
7. j
8. g
9. a
10. d

Final Exam Drill #52
1. j
2. g
3. f
4. e
5. i
6. c
7. d
8. b
9. h
10. a

Final Exam Drill #53
1. b
2. b
3. b
4. b
5. b (a is also acceptable)
6. b
7. either is acceptable
8. a
9. a
10. b

Final Exam Drill #54
1. b
2. c
3. d
4. a
5. f
6. g
7. e
8. j
9. h
10. i

Final Exam Drill #55
1. f
2. b
3. i
4. h
5. d
6. j
7. e
8. g
9. a
10. c

Final Exam Drill #56
1. a
2. a
3. c
4. b
5. c
6. a
7. b
8. a
9. b
10. c

Final Exam Drill #57
1. a
2. c
3. g
4. i
5. f
6. h
7. d
8. e
9. j
10. b

Final Exam Drill #58
1. j
2. c
3. g
4. a
5. f
6. d
7. e
8. h
9. b
10. i

Final Exam Drill #59
1. b
2. d
3. h
4. i
5. f
6. a
7. g
8. e
9. j
10. c

Final Exam Drill #60
1. a
2. b
3. b
4. a
5. a (b is marginally acceptable)
6. a
7. a
8. b
9. b
10. b

Final Exam Drill #61
1. d
2. b
3. j
4. e
5. g
6. h
7. i
8. f
9. c
10. a

Final Exam Drill #62
1. e
2. a
3. f
4. h
5. i
6. j
7. c
8. b
9. g
10. d

Final Exam Drill #63
1. b
2. j
3. g
4. a
5. f
6. i
7. d
8. c
9. h
10. e

Final Exam Drill #64
1. b
2. a
3. b
4. c
5. a
6. c
7. c
8. b
9. a
10. c

Final Exam Drill #65
1. d
2. h
3. e
4. f
5. b
6. c
7. g
8. j
9. a
10. i

Final Exam Drill #66
1. h
2. i
3. e
4. a
5. b
6. c
7. j
8. g
9. f
10. d

Final Exam Drill #67
1. a
2. b
3. a
4. a
5. a
6. b
7. b
8. a
9. b
10. a

Final Exam Drill #68
1. j
2. c
3. g
4. b
5. a
6. d
7. i
8. e
9. h
10. f

Final Exam Drill #69
1. e
2. g
3. h
4. j
5. b
6. d
7. a
8. i
9. c
10. f

Final Exam Drill #70
1. f
2. i
3. h
4. a
5. b
6. d
7. j
8. e
9. c
10. g

Final Exam Drill #71
1. e
2. g
3. i
4. a
5. d
6. c
7. h
8. f
9. j
10. b

Final Exam Drill #72
1. a
2. c
3. b
4. c
5. a
6. b
7. c
8. b
9. b
10. a

Final Exam Drill #73
1. c
2. a
3. f
4. j
5. i
6. e
7. b
8. g
9. d
10. h

Final Exam Drill #74
1. a
2. a
3. a
4. b
5. a
6. b
7. a
8. b
9. b
10. b

Final Exam Drill #75
1. f
2. a
3. g
4. c
5. j
6. h
7. d
8. b
9. e
10. i

Final Exam Drill #76

1. g
2. f
3. i
4. e
5. a
6. b
7. c
8. j
9. d
10. h

Final Exam Drill #77

1. f
2. h
3. d
4. a
5. i
6. e
7. g
8. c
9. j
10. b

Final Exam Drill #78

1. e
2. a
3. b
4. f
5. g
6. h
7. d
8. c
9. i
10. j

Final Exam Drill #79

1. i
2. b
3. e
4. c
5. j
6. f
7. a
8. h
9. g
10. d

Final Exam Drill #80

1. b
2. b
3. c
4. a
5. c
6. b
7. c
8. a
9. a
10. a

Final Exam Drill #81

1. a
2. b
3. b
4. a
5. b
6. a
7. b
8. a
9. a (b is also acceptable)
10. a

Final Exam Drill #82

1. c
2. h
3. b
4. e
5. d
6. a
7. j
8. g
9. i
10. f

Final Exam Drill #83

1. d
2. f
3. b
4. e
5. g
6. c
7. i
8. j
9. a
10. h

Final Exam Drill #84

1. f
2. b
3. e
4. d
5. j
6. c
7. g
8. i
9. h
10. a

Final Exam Drill #85
1. c
2. g
3. j
4. b
5. i
6. h
7. f
8. a
9. d
10. e

Final Exam Drill #86
1. c
2. d
3. g
4. i
5. a
6. j
7. f
8. b
9. h
10. e

Final Exam Drill #87
1. a
2. a
3. b
4. b
5. a
6. a
7. a
8. a
9. a
10. a (b is marginally acceptable)

Final Exam Drill #88
1. c
2. a
3. a
4. c
5. b
6. a
7. b
8. c
9. a
10. b

Final Exam Drill #89
1. i
2. a
3. h
4. e
5. d
6. b
7. j
8. c
9. g
10. f

Final Exam Drill #90
1. d
2. c
3. a
4. i
5. g
6. h
7. f
8. b
9. j
10. e

Final Exam Drill #91
1. a
2. b
3. g
4. i
5. h
6. j
7. d
8. f
9. e
10. c

Final Exam Drill #92
1. a
2. c
3. j
4. d
5. b
6. f
7. e
8. h
9. i
10. g

Final Exam Drill #93
1. c
2. d
3. i
4. e
5. a
6. j
7. h
8. g
9. f
10. b

Final Exam Drill #94

1. a
2. a (b is marginally acceptable)
3. b
4. b
5. b
6. b
7. a
8. b
9. a
10. a

Final ExamDrill #95

1. d
2. e
3. h
4. a
5. j
6. i
7. f
8. c
9. b
10. g

Final Exam Drill #96

1. c
2. a
3. b
4. a
5. a
6. c
7. b
8. a
9. c
10. b

Final Exam Drill #97

1. d
2. g
3. c
4. e
5. i
6. j
7. b
8. h
9. f
10. a

Final Exam Drill #98

1. j
2. i
3. d
4. f
5. g
6. a
7. h
8. c
9. b
10. e

Final Exam Drill #99

1. h
2. b
3. c
4. f
5. g
6. j
7. d
8. e
9. i
10. a

Final Exam Drill #100

1. c
2. h
3. a
4. e
5. d
6. j
7. b
8. f
9. g
10. i

Final Exam Drill #101

1. b
2. g
3. a
4. c
5. f
6. h
7. e
8. d
9. i
10. j

Final Exam Drill #102

1. b
2. a
3. a
4. b
5. b
6. b
7. b (a is marginally acceptable)
8. a
9. a
10. b

Final Exam Drill #103

1. j
2. h
3. b
4. f
5. c
6. d
7. i
8. g
9. a
10. e

Final Exam Drill #104

1. a
2. c
3. c
4. b
5. b
6. a
7. b
8. a
9. c
10. c

Final Exam Drill #105

1. e
2. d
3. g
4. c
5. h
6. a
7. j
8. f
9. b
10. i

Final Exam Drill #106

1. f
2. e
3. b
4. j
5. g
6. a
7. c
8. h
9. d
10. i

Final Exam Drill #107

1. h
2. a
3. d
4. b
5. j
6. g
7. i
8. f
9. e
10. c

Final Exam Drill #108

1. c
2. h
3. g
4. j
5. d
6. i
7. a
8. b
9. f
10. e

Final Exam Drill #109

1. b
2. a
3. b
4. a
5. a
6. b
7. b
8. b
9. b
10. b

Final Exam Drill #110

1. j
2. b
3. f
4. g
5. d
6. i
7. c
8. e
9. a
10. h

Final Exam Drill #111

1. g
2. e
3. a
4. c
5. d
6. j
7. i
8. f
9. h
10. b

Final Exam Drill #112

1. b
2. c
3. a
4. c
5. b
6. a
7. b
8. a
9. b
10. c

Final Exam Drill #113

1. b
2. a
3. h
4. g
5. f
6. j
7. e
8. d
9. c
10. i

Final Exam Drill #114

1. h
2. i
3. a
4. j
5. c
6. b
7. g
8. f
9. d
10. e

Final Exam Drill #115

1. e
2. f
3. b
4. g
5. j
6. i
7. a
8. c
9. h
10. d

Final Exam Drill #116

1. a
2. b
3. a
4. b
5. b
6. b
7. a
8. b
9. a
10. a

Final Exam Drill #117

1. b
2. d
3. a
4. c
5. g
6. h
7. i
8. j
9. f
10. e

Final Exam Drill #118

1. e
2. h
3. a
4. i
5. j
6. b
7. d
8. g
9. f
10. c

Final Exam Drill #119

1. j
2. g
3. c
4. d
5. b
6. e
7. f
8. h
9. i
10. a

Final Exam Drill #120

1. b
2. c
3. a
4. h
5. d
6. e
7. g
8. i
9. f
10. j

NOTES

NOTES